ROUTLEDGE HANDBOOK OF SEABED MINING AND THE LAW OF THE SEA

For years, exploration of seabed natural resources has been ongoing while exploitation in deep marine areas remained unrealistic due to land-based mineral availability and costs. However, mounting pressures from the green transition, climate change, and long-lasting fears of terrestrial minerals scarcity now bring exploitation prospects closer to reality.

This has caused concern to a growing chorus of States, scientists, industries, NGOs, and parts of civil society due to the potential environmental and social impacts of these activities. As a result, the idea of a moratorium or 'precautionary pause' is gaining ground. Yet, an important number of interpretation and implementation issues of the United Nations Convention on the Law of the Sea (UNCLOS) and the 1994 Agreement remain to be answered as a means to move forward in accordance with international law.

This multidisciplinary book, designed to become the essential handbook on the matter, provides a global overview of the national, regional, and international regulatory frameworks applicable to the exploration and exploitation of seabed minerals on the continental shelf and the Area, as well as the related state of the science on the matter.

By presenting historical and geopolitical context crucial to understanding regulation evolution, the book equips readers with foundational legal and policy knowledge. It furthermore addresses contemporary and prospective issues and offers unique insights into regional and national practices, including non-Party States to UNCLOS.

Virginie Tassin Campanella is an internationally award-winning Attorney and Researcher. Avocat à la Cour (Paris, France and Zürich, Switzerland), and double Doctor in Law (Sorbonne, France and Melbourne, Australia), she is the Founder and Director of VTA Tassin, the first public international law firm dedicated to oceans and seas. With more than 15 years of experience in seabed management, her notable achievements include, amongst others, working at the Legal Office of the International Tribunal for the Law of the Sea on the 2011 *Seabed Disputes Chamber Advisory Opinion* and 2012 *Bangladesh/Myanmar* case.

ROUTLEDGE HANDBOOKS IN LAW

ABOUT THE SERIES

Routledge Handbooks in Law present state-of-the-art surveys of important and emerging topics in Law and Legal Studies, providing accessible yet thorough assessments of key fields, themes and recent developments in research.

All chapters for each volume are specially commissioned, and written by leading and emerging scholars in the field. Carefully edited and organized, Routledge Handbooks in Law provide indispensable reference tools for students and researchers seeking a comprehensive overview of new and exciting topics in the relevant subject areas. They are also valuable teaching resources as accompaniments to textbooks, anthologies, and research-orientated publications.

ROUTLEDGE HANDBOOK OF COMMERCIAL SPACE LAW
Edited by Lesley-Jane Smith, Ingo Baumann and Dr. Susan Wintermuth

ROUTLEDGE HANDBOOK OF SEABED MINING AND THE LAW OF THE SEA
Edited by Virginie Tassin Campanella

For more details, visit https://www.routledge.com/Routledge-Handbooks-in-Law/book-series/RHL

ROUTLEDGE HANDBOOK OF SEABED MINING AND THE LAW OF THE SEA

Edited by Virginie Tassin Campanella

Routledge
Taylor & Francis Group
LONDON AND NEW YORK

Cover credit: Getty Images

First published 2024
by Routledge
4 Park Square, Milton Park, Abingdon, Oxon OX14 4RN

and by Routledge
605 Third Avenue, New York, NY 10158

Routledge is an imprint of the Taylor & Francis Group, an informa business

British Library Cataloguing-in-Publication Data
A catalogue record for this book is available from the British Library

ISBN: 978-1-138-38761-4 (hbk)
ISBN: 978-1-032-61333-8 (pbk)
ISBN: 978-0-429-42616-2 (ebk)

DOI: 10.4324/9780429426162

Typeset in Times New Roman
by Deanta Global Publishing Services, Chennai, India

The Open Access version of In Memoriam of Robert Makgill and chapter VI.1.4 was funded by Research Institute for Sustainability, Ghent University and VTA Tassin.

The Open Access version of chapters I.3 and IV.1 was funded by Australian Research Council.

To my husband, Tommaso, my ray of sunshine and infinite love whose patience, endless encouragement and support have been so precious in making this book a reality.

CONTENTS

In Memoriam of Robert Makgill — *xi*
List of figures — *xiv*
Notes on contributors — *xv*
About the editor — *xxv*
List of abbreviations — *xxvii*

Introduction — 1
Virginie Tassin Campanella

PART I
Global perspectives — **9**

I.1 The scientific challenges of deep-sea mining — 11
Walter R. Roest, Malcolm R. Clark and Harald Brekke

I.2 The common heritage of mankind under international law: An overview — 33
Nilüfer Oral

I.3 Implementing the precautionary approach for seabed mining: A review of state practice — 48
Robert Makgill†, Aline Jaeckel, and Keith MacMaster

PART II
State Party rights, obligations and responsibilities — **79**

II.1 Rights and obligations of States on the continental shelf and the Area — 81
Virginie Tassin Campanella, Yacouba Cissé and Dire Tladi

II.2 State responsibility for deep seabed mining obligations 107
Cymie R. Payne

PART III
The continental shelf **125**

III.1 The extension of sovereign rights beyond 200 nautical miles 127
Øystein Jensen and Bjarni Már Magnússon

III.2 The article 82 conundrum: Implementing payment for the exploitation of the continental shelf beyond 200 nautical miles 141
Clive Schofield and Joanna Mossop

PART IV
The Area **155**

IV.1 The Area and the role of the International Seabed Authority 157
Aline Jaeckel

IV.2 The common heritage quandary: Devising a global payment regime for exploitation activities in the deep seabed Area 178
Joanna Dingwall

IV.3 Upcoming challenges for the International Seabed Authority 194
Frida M. Armas Pfirter

PART V
Dispute settlement **207**

V.1 Dispute settlement and seabed mining in the Area 209
Tullio Treves

V.2 Dispute settlement options and rights of participation in deep seabed mining disputes 224
James Harrison and Alberto Pecoraro

V.3 Mining the bottom of the sea: Potential future disputes and the role of the International Tribunal for the Law of the Sea 239
Monica Feria-Tinta and Maurice K. Kamga

PART VI
Regional and national practice **257**

VI.1 Regional practice 259

VI.1.1 Africa and seabed mining 261
Edwin Egede

VI.1.2 Antarctica and seabed mining 271
Leopoldo M. A. Godio

VI.1.3 The Arctic and seabed mining 280
Kristine Elfrida Dalaker and Hilde J. Woker

VI.1.4 The European Union and seabed mining 290
Pradeep A. Singh, Virginie Tassin Campanella and Frank Maes

VI.1.5 The Pacific Islands region and seabed mining 314
Cameron Diver

VI.1.6 South American region and seabed mining 324
Eduardo Jiménez Pineda

VI.1.7 Southeast Asia and seabed mining 333
Tara Davenport

VI.2 National practice 343

VI.2.1 Belgium and seabed mining 345
Klaas Willaert and Frank Maes

VI.2.2 Brazil and seabed mining 351
Carina Costa de Oliveira and Ana Flávia Barros-Platiau

VI.2.3 Colombia and seabed mining 358
Esteban Restrepo Uribe

VI.2.4 Côte d'Ivoire and seabed mining 365
Yacouba Cissé

VI.2.5 Germany and seabed mining 372
Nele Matz-Lück

VI.2.6 Guyana and seabed mining 379
Buba Bojang and Donnette Streete

VI.2.7 Iceland and seabed mining 386
Bjarni Már Magnússon

VI.2.8 India and seabed mining 391
Ipshita Chaturvedi Sadhale

VI.2.9 Korea and seabed mining 398
Hyun Jung Kim

VI.2.10 Mauritius and seabed mining 405
Edwin Egede

VI.2.11 Mozambique and seabed mining 414
Estevão Stefane Mahanjane

VI.2.12 New Zealand and seabed mining 419
Robert Makgill† and Elizabeth Macpherson

VI.2.13 Portugal and seabed mining 427
Mariana Neves and Pedro Madureira

VI.2.14 The United Kingdom and seabed mining 433
James Harrison

Index *441*

IN MEMORIAM OF ROBERT MAKGILL

Back in 2017, Robert's initial goal was to conceive the first book dedicated to seabed mining and the law of the sea and in doing so, to provide an original analysis of this topic which could be of use to a wider (and not necessarily academic) audience. The ambition of his vision obviously exceeded his availability, so Robert reached out to me to embark on this editorial adventure. Despite some obvious differences in our cultural backgrounds, we shared a passion for the law of the sea, an expertise in seabed mining and a unique experience from the 2011 advisory opinion of the Seabed Disputes Chamber of the International Tribunal for the Law of the Sea. We also shared the same profession and I would say, more importantly, we shared a profound respect, love and admiration for the ocean through our surfer souls.

Since then, a lot has happened: the Covid-19 pandemic, many professional and personal highlights and challenges, as well as a busy international agenda (the ongoing negotiations on biodiversity beyond national jurisdiction) that we wanted to take into consideration. Robert and I therefore decided to change our goal from publishing the first book dedicated to seabed mining and the law of the sea to rather concentrate on the quality and uniqueness of this book. With the passing of time, Robert unfortunately had to step down as being the main editor and co-editor of this book, leaving me the reins to do what was necessary to achieve our vision and goals. As a result, this book remains deeply marked by his touch and direct contributions.

Robert left us in December 2022, leaving us without enough words to express our shock and our pain.

All of us friends and colleagues admired Robert's energy and personality, his capacity to face challenges and engage with passion in everything he was doing. We admired his cultural curiosity, his sharp mind, intellect and his good humour. Wherever there was laughter and joy, Robert was there, in the middle of it, speaking with his loud voice.

We shared countless souvenirs from our time together in Europe, Australia and New Zealand, engaging in fascinating discussions about the rule of law, environmental protection, Māori rights, seabed mining, a lawyer's life, our commitments to pro bono activities, but also surfing, travelling and design.

Robert was truly passionate about the ocean, living his passion to the fullest. Surfing, for Robert, was a way of life, a way to communicate with the ocean and to express his respect towards it. Many magical waves and ocean sunsets blessed the life of Robert, whether on the New Zealand shores or on the Atlantic ones in Biarritz … a place that he deeply loved.

Robert was also a caring and kind friend and colleague, always generously offering his help … he was always there for the people and the communities he cared for. He even sponsored Zen Wallis at the 2018 World Surfing Games in Japan! Robert exemplified the collegiality that we are all supposed to display.

We also admired him as a colleague, for his commitment to live the law from the inside and for not shying away from taking controversial stances. Robert was an immensely knowledgeable and conscientious environmental law expert who was well known in Aotearoa New Zealand. He was a respected barrister with 25 years' experience in public, environmental, property and international law. Never far from the ocean, Robert drew on his lived experience and deep academic knowledge in the practise of domestic and international environmental law.

Robert's passion for surfing and for the cutting edge of environmental law combined with his innovative thinking led to his being legal advisor (as an Auckland University LLM student) in gaining consent for New Zealand's first intentional artificial surfing reef. He subsequently led the legal arguments that resulted in the legal protection of New Zealand's top surfing breaks. Established as perhaps New Zealand's leading coastal and marine planning legal expert, Robert represented local communities in overturning a government Minister's decision to decline a marine reserve application in Akaroa Harbour. As a direct consequence, a marine reserve was subsequently approved.

Robert was also a leading player for Māori tribes in partially successful court challenges to the decision to leave the wreckage of the Rena on a reef of particular significance to Māori. Although coastal and marine planning law was his forte, Robert also provided the successful legal arguments that resulted in local authorities being able to make rules in plans creating GMO-free areas.

Robert was furthermore a dedicated counsel for the International Union for the Conservation of Nature (IUCN) and the World Commission on Environmental Law (WCEL), which led him to act as counsel in the International Tribunal for the Law of the Sea (ITLOS)'s advisory opinion proceedings on deep sea mining in 2010. His expertise in law of the sea also led him to assist with advising a party to the ITLOS advisory opinion proceedings on illegal, unreported and unregulated fishing in 2015, advise foreign governments on numerous issues, chair the International Seabed Authority's legal working group on Environmental Management of Deep Sea Mining in 2011, and be involved in the 2012 *Pacific-ACP States Regional Environmental Management Framework for Deep Sea Minerals Exploration and Exploitation.* He also facilitated the ISA working group on Ecosystem-Based Management and Deep Sea Mining in 2016.

Robert regularly and confidently appeared on environmental law matters before a range of New Zealand government bodies, tribunals and courts from first instance to the appellate level. He had a leading role in some of New Zealand's most high-profile environmental law cases, including most recently the landmark 2021 Supreme Court seabed mining case *Trans-Tasman Resources v Taranaki-Whanganui Conservation Board.*[1]

In 2019, Robert completed his PhD on sustainable management, law of the sea and New Zealand State practice at Ghent University (Belgium),[2] giving his work a deep scholarly founda-

1 See the two chapters of Robert in this book: R. Makgill, A. Jaeckel and K. MacMaster, 'Implementing the precautionary approach for seabed mining: a review of State practice' in V. Tassin Campanella (ed) *Seabed mining and the law of the sea*, Routledge handbook collection, Routledge: London, 2023, chapter I.3 and R. Makgill and E. Macpherson, 'New Zealand and seabed mining' in V. Tassin Campanella (ed), *Seabed mining and the law of the sea*, idem, chapter VI.2.12.

2 R. Makgill, *Sustainable management of the sea: identifying a body of sustainable management jurisprudence composed of law of the sea doctrine and New Zealand state practice*, PhD Degree, Ghent University, 2019. Available online https://biblio.ugent.be/publication/8634229 (accessed February 2023).

tion. The hallmark of his research and academic studies was always its application to the protection of nature.

There have been few, if any, in New Zealand who had Robert's depth of theoretical and practical knowledge of the law of the sea. Profoundly fascinated, committed and engaged in legal research and theory, Robert was actually often saying that he was too much of an academic to be a barrister, and too much of a barrister to be an academic. To us, Robert was simply the best example of being able to be the two.

Robert also consistently gave back to the legal and scholarly community through board positions, teaching appointments, mentoring junior colleagues, presenting at academic and professional development conferences, and publishing in a range of scholarly and practice-focused outlets, including his leading role in developing the foundations for this book. He had valued connections and trusted relationships throughout New Zealand and the world, including with other practitioners, industry, government, academia and Māori.

Familiar to the authors of this book and his friends and colleagues beyond, we are sure that this is just a small subset of Robert's wide-ranging accomplishments. He was an active and engaged advisory board member of the project on Law and Policy for Ecosystem-Based Management in the New Zealand Sustainable Seas National Science Challenge.[3] He also chaired the Environment and Resource Management Law Committee of the Auckland District Law Society[4] and insisted on the obligation of all practising and academic lawyers to drive change and improvements in environmental law and policy for the benefit of present and future generations. At the time of his death, he was an advisor to a national research project on implementing ecosystem-based management in New Zealand law and a Research Fellow at Lincoln University's Land Environment and People Research Centre.

Robert was a great force for precaution in international law, and a very strong advocate for evidence-based decision-making. We have been honoured to know him, learn from him and work by his side.

Robert, we hope that this book can uphold your legacy and honour your work and values. You are already immensely missed.

From the bottom of our hearts, with our tight throats and wet eyes, we express our sincerest condolences to Robert's family and to all his friends and colleagues around the world.

Virginie Tassin Campanella together with friends and colleagues of Robert from this book and beyond

3 'Policy and Legislation for EBM', *Sustainable Seas National Science Challenge. Available online* <https://www.sustainableseaschallenge.co.nz/our-research/policy-and-legislation-for-ebm/> (accessed February 2023).

4 'Environment & Resource Management Law: ADLS' <https://adls.org.nz/EnvironmentandResourceCommittee> (accessed February 2023).

LIST OF FIGURES

I.1.1	(a) Global relief map based on GEBCO 2014 grid. The three white boxes highlight areas with different mineral occurrences. (b) Zoom on the area between the Clarion and Clipperton fracture zones in the east Pacific. The abyssal plain in this area is very flat and situated at depths around 5000 m, an ideal environment for polymetallic nodules. (c) Zoom on the Mid-Atlantic Ridge in the central north Atlantic. Hydrothermal vents and associated mineral deposits occur at several sites along the approximately north-south trending axis of the ridge. (d) Seamounts in the Western Pacific are targets for cobalt-rich manganese crust occurrences	13
I.1.2	Classification of mineral resources based on the general relationship between mineral exploration results assessment, mineral resources and mineral reserves	17
I.1.3	Assessment of biogeographic knowledge in selected deep-sea habitats	23
I.1.4	The linkages between ecosystem structure and function	26
I.1.5	Schematic diagram of the Adaptive Management Process	27
IV.1.1	The structure of the seabed mining regime	159
VI.1.1	Seven step implementation of strategic roadmap	269

NOTES ON CONTRIBUTORS

Frida M. Armas Pfirter has been judge for the International Tribunal of the Law of the Sea (ITLOS) since 2023. She is also Professor of Public International Law at the University of Buenos Aires and Austral University, Argentina. She has been Conciliator and Arbitrator of the dispute settlement system of the United Nations Convention on the Law of the Sea since 2009.

A member of the United Nations Ocean Decade Advisory Board, UNESCO-IOC, 2022–2023, she was also a Member of the Legal and Technical Commission (2001–2011) and of the Finance Committee (2012–2022) of the International Seabed Authority.

Ana Flávia Barros-Platiau is an associate professor at the International Relations Institute, University of Brasilia, Brazil. She is a researcher at the Superior Defence College, Brasilia, Brazil, and director of the Brasilia Research Centre from the Earth System Governance network (Utrecht University, the Netherlands). A researcher at the Centro de Estudos Globais at the International Relations Institute, University of Brasilia, her research topics include complexity thinking, global governance, United Nations, ocean and polar governance, Anthropocene, and planetary politics. She also works on Brazilian environmental laws and policies. With Professor Carina Oliveira, she organized the book *Conservation of Living Resources in Areas Beyond National Jurisdiction: BBNJ and Antarctica* in 2020. PhD degree in International Relations from the Université de Paris I (Panthéon-Sorbonne), 2000.

Buba Bojang is a legal officer in the Development Law Service of the FAO Legal Office and specialises in Fisheries law including providing technical assistance and advice to FAO Member Nations on national fisheries law development and related matters. He lectures at the ITLOS–Nippon Foundation capacity-building and training programme on dispute settlement under the United Nations Convention on the Law of the Sea (UNCLOS) at the International Tribunal for the Law of the Sea and the United Nations–Nippon Foundation (UNNF) Strategic Needs Fellowship at the United Nations Division for Ocean Affairs and Law of the Sea.

Before joining FAO, Buba was the Nippon Foundation Lecturer on Ocean Governance at the IMO International Maritime Law Institute, Malta (2016–2019). He was a State Counsel at the Attorney General Chamber and Ministry of Justice of the Gambia and Legal Officer and Registrar at the Gambia Maritime Administration (2007–2013). He served in the Gambia Armed Forces as legal officer. He holds a PhD in law from the University of Aberdeen, UK.

Harald Brekke is a project coordinator and senior geologist in the Norwegian Petroleum Directorate (NPD). He was project coordinator for the technical part of establishing the outer limits of the continental shelf of Norway. He was member of the Commission on the Limits of the Continental Shelf (CLCS) in New York from 1997 to 2012, including half a year as acting Chair. He was member of the Legal and Technical Commission (LTC) of the International Seabed Authority 2013–2022, holding the position as Chair of the LTC 2021–2022.

In 2022 he was re-elected as member of the CLCS for the period 2023–2028. In parallel with his work in the CLCS and the LTC, he has been the NPD coordinator for international Arctic research and is currently heavily involved in the NPD deep sea minerals programme.

Ipshita Chaturvedi Sadhale is a partner in Dentons Rodyk's Corporate practice group and co-heads the Environment and Natural Resources practice which includes carbon transactions, business and human rights, supply chain management, sustainable finance as well as the environment and social aspects in M&A transactions. Ipshita is also a visiting researcher at the Asia Pacific Center for environmental law at the National University of Singapore.

Ipshita has over 13 years of experience in practising environmental law and natural resources management. She has worked extensively with the private sector helping them transition to more sustainable processes, various governments and regulators (South Asia, ASEAN, European, and from the MENA region), as well as international organizations like the United Nations providing clients with a 360-degree understanding of Sustainable Development Goals (SDGs), Environmental, Social and Governance (ESG), and various issues around sustainability.

Prior to joining Dentons, Ipshita was the founding partner of an award-winning law firm offering end-to-end services exclusively on matters of sustainable development including environmental compliance and regulation, ESG strategy, scaling up clean-technology (venture-capital), waste management and Extended Producer Responsibility-related matters, carbon offsets and finance, as well as water law and oceans governance.

Yacouba Cissé is currently acting as Ambassador and Permanent Representative of the Ministry of Foreign Affairs of Côte d'Ivoire in Vienna, Austria. He is also Member of the International Law Commission of the United Nations and Professor of International Law at the University of Bouaké, Côte d'Ivoire. He holds an LLB and an LLM in Public International Law from the National University of Abidjan, Côte d'Ivoire. His degrees include a Master of Sciences in Marine Affairs from the University of Québec, Canada, and a PhD in Law from the University of Ottawa, Canada. Dr Cissé is an international law professor and a lawyer at the bar of Abidjan.

As a member of the International Law Commission, he is also a member of the Study Group on the issue of sea-level rise and its implications for international law. He is in charge of studying the African States Practice in connection to sea-level rise and its impacts on baselines and maritime boundaries delimitation of Coastal African States. He is widely published internationally on topics of maritime boundaries delimitation, fisheries law, the protection of coastal and marine environment, and more generally on issues concerning general international law, the international law of the sea, and private international maritime law, etc.

Dr Cissé is Ambassador and Permanent Representative of Côte d'Ivoire to Vienna in Austria.

Malcolm R. Clark is a principal scientist (Fisheries) at the National Institute of Water and Atmospheric Research (NIWA) in Wellington, New Zealand. Over a 40-year career he has led many deep-sea research programmes at NIWA on the biology and ecology of fish and benthic invertebrate communities associated with seamounts and other deep-sea habitats.

His work has an emphasis on evaluating environmental effects of human activities (especially commercial fishing and potential seabed mining) and development of ecological risk and impact assessments to help managers balance the impacts of exploitation with environmental sustainability and conservation. He has published widely, with over 150 journal papers and book chapters, and a similar number of technical reports and articles.

Carina Costa de Oliveira is Associate Professor of International and Environmental Law at the Law Faculty, University of Brasília, Brazil. She is also visiting Scholar at the C-EENRG, University of Cambridge, the University of Adelaide, Australia and the CERIC (Centre d'Études et de Recherches Internationales et Communautaires) at the University of Aix-Marseille (France). She has a PhD in International Law from Panthéon-Assas, France.

She is also the coordinator of the Research Group on Law, Natural Resources and Sustainability, and organizer of some books on marine environment and law on topics such as exploration and exploitation on the coastal zone, on the continental shelf, and on the deep seabed (2015 to 2021). Her research areas include public and private international law, environmental law, conservation, and sustainable use of marine resources.

Kristine Elfrida Dalaker, PhD (Law), JD, BA, is a lecturer at the Australian National Centre for Ocean Resources and Security (ANCORS) at the University of Wollongong in Australia, where she has presented, published, and taught on a wide range of law of the sea topics, including the conservation and sustainable use of marine biodiversity (BBNJ), deep seabed mining, the historical development of the law of the sea, and the preservation of the marine environment. She was previously a researcher at the Norwegian Centre for the Law of the Sea (NCLOS), UiT The Arctic University of Norway in Tromsø, Norway, and before that she was the Associate Director (Administration and Special Projects) at the Centre for International Law (CIL) at the National University of Singapore.

Her recent publications include a book that she co-wrote with the late Ambassador Satya N. Nandan entitled *Reflections on the Making of the Modern Law of the Sea.*

Tara Davenport is Deputy Director of the Asia-Pacific Centre for Environmental Law, an Assistant Professor at the Faculty of Law, National University of Singapore (NUS), and a Senior Research Fellow at the Centre for International Law (CIL) at NUS. She has an LLB from the London School of Economics, UK, an LLM in Maritime Law from NUS, and an LLM and JSD from Yale Law School, US.

She is a qualified advocate and solicitor in Singapore. Her current research interests are public international law, law of the sea and international dispute settlement. She has written on the South China Sea disputes, submarine cables, and deep seabed mining. She is a member of the Legal Working Group on Liability for Environmental Harm from Activities in the Area convened by the Centre for International Governance Innovation (CIGI), the Commonwealth Secretariat, and the Secretariat of the International Seabed Authority. She is also the Rapporteur for the International Law Association Study Committee on Submarine Cables and Pipelines.

Joanna Dingwall, PhD, University of Glasgow; LLM (International Legal Studies), New York University; DLP, Glasgow Graduate School of Law; LLB (First Class Honours), University of Glasgow, is a public international lawyer currently lecturing international law at the University of Glasgow, UK. She is also a lawyer to the Scottish Government concerning issues of law of the sea and marine environmental protection.

Cameron Diver is an experienced lawyer and senior leader with over 20 years' experience spanning international relations, public service and legal practice. Among other roles, he previously served as Deputy Director-General of the Pacific Community, the Pacific region's oldest and largest intergovernmental organization, and is currently Chief of Staff to Hon. Sonia Backes, President of the South Province (New Caledonia) and Secretary of State for Citizenship (Government of France).

Edwin Egede is a professor of International Law and International Relations. He is also an adjunct professor at the Department of Public Law, Nelson Mandela University, South Africa. Additionally, he is one of the editors of a six-volume book project on *The Law of the Sea – Contemporary Norms and Practice in Africa* and a member of the Advisory Board of the Brazilian Yearbook of Law of the Sea (BYLOS) and new member of the Legal and Technical Commission of the International Seabed Authority.

Prof. Egede, having a fine blend of experience in academia and practice, undertakes interdisciplinary teaching and research in the areas of Public International Law, Law of the Sea, International Relations, and International Organizations, especially as regards the United Nations. He has published widely in these areas and has also made academic and policy presentations at various international conferences. He has contributed to national and international law and policy development through his involvement in policy workshops and appointment as consultant to various entities, such as the United Nations (UN), International Seabed Authority (ISA), and African Union (AU).

Monica Feria-Tinta is a barrister at the Bar of England and Wales, practising from Twenty Essex, a leading barristers' Chambers in London, UK. She acts for sovereign States and private parties in cases before English courts, international courts, and arbitral tribunals. Her practice covers the full spectrum of public international law. Her scholarship has been cited by international courts in leading cases.

Prior to the Bar, Monica worked for international tribunals including at the International Court of Justice. She served as Assistant Legal Adviser to the United Kingdom Foreign and Commonwealth Office (2018–2019). Monica holds an LLM with merit from the LSE, was awarded the Diploma of the Hague Academy in International Law in 2000, and was Visiting Fellow at Jesus College, University of Cambridge (2021). In 2020, she was 'Barrister of the Year' Finalist in The Lawyer Awards and in 2007, the recipient of the Gruber Justice Prize.

Leopoldo M. A. Godio is a lawyer with a Master's in international relations and PhD in law from the University of Buenos Aires. His thesis was graded *Summa cum Laude* and recommended to 'Faculty Prize' by the Tribunal. He is Professor of Public International Law (since 2008) at Universidad de Buenos Aires (UBA), Universidad de San Isidro (USI), and Pontificia Universidad Católica Argentina (UCA); secretary of Institute of Public International Law, National Academy of Law and Social Sciences of Buenos Aires; Member of the Institute of International Law of the Argentine Council for the International Relations; Full Member of the Argentine Association of International Law; and Founding Member of the Latin American and Caribbean Society for the Law of the Sea. He is currently Director at Public International Law Institute of the San Isidro Lawyers' Bar Association.

He is the author and co-author of more than 200 papers in books, book chapters, and articles in his areas of expertise, principally on international law, law of the sea, international environmental law, and international trade, both in Argentina and abroad.

He has been part of the Argentine Delegation to meetings at international organizations.

James Harrison is Professor of Environmental Law at Edinburgh Law School, UK, where he has been a member of staff since 2007. James has broad interests across a wide range of environmental law issues, but with a particular focus on marine environmental protection and the law of the sea. He has written widely within this area, including on international and domestic fisheries law, global shipping regulation, and the legal framework for deep seabed mining. He also has a particular interest in environmental dispute settlement and the role of courts and tribunals in developing environmental rules. Alongside his academic work, he has acted as a legal adviser, consultant, or trainer for a number of governments, inter-governmental organizations and non-governmental organizations.

Aline Jaeckel is an associate professor at the Australian National Centre for Ocean Resources and Security (ANCORS) at the University of Wollongong. Her research focuses on law of the sea and international law with a particular focus on the regulation and governance of deep seabed mining. She has acted as an advisor and consultant and has authored numerous publications including a monograph on *The International Seabed Authority and the Precautionary Principle* (2017).

Øystein Jensen is a research professor at the Fridtjof Nansen Institute and a professor of law at Oslo Metropolitan University, Norway. He holds a PhD in international law from the University of Oslo. Jensen's substantive research foci include general issues of public international law, with a particular focus on law of the sea and international institutional law. He has published on various topics, such as the role of courts and tribunals in the law of the sea, the establishment of maritime limits and boundaries, the role of expert regimes in international law, and the Svalbard Treaty.

Eduardo Jiménez Pineda is Lecturer of Public International Law and European Union Law at the University of Córdoba, Spain. He studied the Bachelor of Laws at the University of Córdoba, with distinction (2016), and a LLM in European Union Law at the University of Sevilla (2017). He holds a PhD in International Law from the University of Córdoba, having been awarded the Extraordinary Doctorate Award (2021). He is a visiting professor at the Universidad Andina Simón Bolívar and at the Universidad Tecnológica Empresarial de Guayaquil, Ecuador. His main areas of research are the law of the sea and the international courts and tribunals, with a special focus on international arbitration.

Jiménez Pineda was a Nippon Foundation Fellow at the International Tribunal for the Law of the Sea (2017/2018), as well as a visiting researcher at the Max Planck Institute for Comparative Public Law and International Law (2017), at the King's College London (2019), at the Hague Academy of International Law and at the Peace Palace Library (2019, 2022), and at the Faculty of Law of the University of Buenos Aires (2022). He is a member of the Spanish Association of Professors of International Law and International Relations (AEPDIRI), being currently member of its board, and of the International Association of the Law of the Sea (AssIDMer).

Maurice K. Kamga, a Cameroonian diplomat (Minister Plenipotentiary) and scholar, is a judge of the International Tribunal for the Law of the Sea (ITLOS) since October 2020. He holds a PhD in International Relations (from the International Relations Institute of Cameroon), a PhD in International Law (from the Graduate Institute of International Studies, Geneva, Switzerland), and a HDR (*Habilitation à Diriger les Recherches*) from the University of Paris Nanterre, France.

Professor Kamga has been, *inter alia*, an assistant lecturer at the University of Yaoundé II (1993–1997), a legal officer at the International Criminal Tribunal for former Yugoslavia (1997–2001) and at ITLOS (2001–2003), the Legal Advisor of the Cameroonian Ministry of External Relations (2003–2008), and a legal secretary of the International Court of Justice (2008–2020). He has lectured in various African and European universities and has published several articles and books in International Law.

Hyun Jung Kim is an associate professor at the Department of Political Science and International Studies at Yonsei University (Republic of Korea). She holds a PhD in law (University of Paris I Panthéon-Sorbonne), LLMs (University of Paris I Panthéon-Sorbonne and Korea University), and LLB (Korea University). She was also a lecturer of the law of the sea at the United Nations Regional Course in International Law for Asia and the Pacific (2018).

Her main research fields are law of the sea, international institutions, and interrelations between international law and politics.

She has published legal articles in Korean, English, and French. Her recent journal publications are: 'An appraisal of Article 300 of the United Nations Convention on the Law of the Sea', *Ocean Development & International Law*, vol. 53, issue 2/3 (2022) (with Anne Thida Norodom), 'Third party fishing in an undelimited area under the Republic of Korea–Japan Fisheries Agreement', *Marine Policy*, vol. 125 (2021), 'What did the Republic of Korea and Japan mean by the term "joint development" in their 1974 agreement?', *Marine Policy*, vol. 117 (2020). Her multicultural research capacity is due to her academic background.

Keith MacMaster is the Purdy Crawford Fellow in Business Law and Assistant Professor at the Schulich School of Law, Dalhousie University, Canada. Keith concentrates on legal issues in environmental finance for banking and ocean-based industries. This research aims to enable an environmentally and socially sustainable mining industry for the post-pandemic, low-carbon world. He practised corporate and real estate law and is a licensed financial planner.

Elizabeth Macpherson is an associate professor in Natural Resources and Environmental Law at the University of Canterbury, New Zealand. She has published widely on comparative natural resource issues, constitutional law and Indigenous rights and leads international research projects on ecosystem-based marine management and environmental rights.

Pedro Madureira is an associate professor at the University of Évora, Portugal, where he got his PhD in igneous petrology and geochemistry. Currently, he is the Deputy Head at the Task Group for the Extension of the Portuguese Continental Shelf. He is the scientific and technical Coordinator of the Continental Shelf Project.

In his career, Dr Madureira served as a principal investigator of several oceanographic campaigns in the North Atlantic and from 2012 to 2022 as a member of the Legal and Technical Commission of the International Seabed Authority. His main academic interests include the evolution of volcanic islands, the formation and distribution of deep-sea mineral resources, marine environment and deep-seabed exploration.

Frank Maes is Professor Emeritus at the Faculty of Law and Criminology of Ghent University, Belgium. He is the former head of the Department of European, Public and International Law and director of the Maritime Institute. His research is focused on international environmental law, law of the sea and maritime spatial planning.

Estevão Stefane Mahanjane is a renowned international geoscientist with outstanding contributions to the petroleum industry and the continental shelf delineation since 2006. He is a member of the United Nations Commission on the Limits of the Continental Shelf (CLCS) since 2012 and co-authored Mozambique's submission. As a member of the CLCS, he serves as Chairman of the Subcommission on Nigeria, India, Côte d'Ivoire, Iceland, and Namibia submissions, as well as chairman of the confidentiality committee.

He has published more than thirty scientific works and holds a PhD in geosciences from the Institute of Geology at the Gottfried Wilhelm Leibniz Universität Hannover, Germany.

Robert Makgill† was a barrister who specialized in environmental and public law. He was legal counsel in the ITLOS' advisory Seabed Advisory Opinion and subsequent litigation concerning seabed mining proposals within New Zealand's EEZ. He was a member of the Ghent Maritime Institute, Ghent University, Belgium, with publications on the law of the sea, environmental law, sustainability, natural resource development and common property.

Bjarni Már Magnússon recently joined the Department of Law at Bifröst University, Iceland, after ten years at Reykjavik University, Iceland. His teaching and research focus has mainly been on international law, especially the law of the sea. He is the author of the monograph *The Continental Shelf beyond 200 Nautical Miles: Delineation, Delimitation and Dispute Settlement* (2015). Magnússon worked for Bangladesh in the dispute concerning delimitation of the maritime boundary between Bangladesh and Myanmar in the Bay of Bengal, the first maritime boundary case before the International Tribunal for the Law of the Sea.

He is a member of the working group of the Icelandic government on the preparation of submissions to the Commission on the Limits of the Continental Shelf and frequently advises various entities on law of the sea questions. Professor Magnússon holds a PhD from the University of Edinburgh (2013). He is a Chevening and Fulbright alumni.

Nele Matz-Lück, LLM, is Professor of Public Law with a focus on Public International Law including the Law of the Sea at Kiel University Law School and co-director of the Walther Schücking Institute for International Law at Kiel University, Germany. She is co-speaker of the Cluster of Excellency 'Future Ocean' and adjunct professor at Dalhousie University in Halifax, Canada.

Previous academic positions include one as adjunct professor at the K.G. Jebsen Centre on the Law of the Sea at the Arctic University of Norway (Tromsø) from 2013 until the end of 2018, one as senior research fellow at the Max Planck Institute for Comparative Public Law and International Law in Heidelberg, and one as a research fellow at the Federal Constitutional Court of Germany. Her main areas of research and publications include the law of the sea and international environmental law. As far as the law of the sea is concerned she publishes regularly on the sustainable use of marine resources, the protection of the marine environment, e.g. marine protected areas and ship emissions, as well as on rights over maritime zones.

Joanna Mossop, LLM (Colombia), LLB (Hons) BA (VUW), is a professor at Victoria University of Wellington, New Zealand. Her research interests include the continental shelf, marine biodiversity, dispute settlement, and resource management.

Joanna has been active in the Australia New Zealand Society of International Law including as a member of the ANZSIL Council and New Zealand Vice President. She is on the advisory board of several journals and has participated in a variety of international governmental and track two meetings on law of the sea including maritime security and governance of marine biodiversity in areas beyond national jurisdiction. Joanna's book, *The Continental Shelf Beyond 200 Nautical Miles: Rights and Responsibilities* (2016), was the joint winner of the JF Northey Memorial Book Award, presented by the New Zealand Legal Research Foundation for the best book by a New Zealand-based author published in 2016. In 2019 the New Zealand government nominated her to the list of arbitrators and conciliators under the United Nations Convention on the Law of the Sea.

New Zealand nominated her to the UNCLOS list of arbitrators and conciliators in 2019.

Mariana Neves is a legal advisor with a Master's degree in international law and international relations by the School of Law, University of Lisbon, Portugal. She has also completed the first phase of NOVA's School of Law PhD Programme.

Currently she is the legal adviser to the Task Group for the Extension of the Portuguese Continental Shelf. She has been working and studying in the field of law of the sea and public international law since 2008.

Nilüfer Oral is a member of the United Nations International Law Commission and co-chair of the Study Group on sea-level rise in relation to international law. She served as a legal advisor to the Turkish Foreign Ministry for law of the sea and as a climate change negotiator.

She is a Distinguished Fellow of the Law of the Sea Institute at Berkeley Law and has lectured at the Centre for International Law (NUS), the UN Regional Law Courses for International Law, and at the Rhodes Academy for the Law of the Sea.

Cymie R. Payne, Rutgers University, US, has appeared as counsel before the International Tribunal for the Law of the Sea in its deep seabed mining and fisheries advisory opinion cases and as a party-appointed expert on environmental reparations in the International Court of Justice case *Certain Activities (Costa Rica v. Nicaragua).*

She is legal advisor to the International Union for Conservation of Nature's delegation to the intergovernmental conference for a legally binding agreement on conservation and sustainable use of biological diversity in areas beyond national jurisdiction and Chair of the IUCN World Commission on Environmental Law – Ocean Law Specialist Group.

Alberto Pecoraro is Lecturer of Law at the University of Hull, UK, where he teaches public international law. He holds a PhD from the University of Antwerp, Belgium, and a LLM from the University of Edinburgh, UK. His research interests focus on investment protection and environmental regulation for deep seabed mining in the Area.

Esteban Restrepo Uribe is Attorney at Law, admitted in Colombia and specializing in public international law. Since 2008, he has acted as Adviser for the Ministry of Foreign Affairs of Colombia and since 2014, as Counsellor on the policy and legal issues of Maritime and Sea affairs – working mostly on the legal regime of maritime areas (including delimitation), marine environment, scientific research, multilateral and regional cooperation – and of Outer Space affairs to the Ministry.

Prior to these experiences, in addition to his professional practice, he held posts with the Office of the Vice President, the National Department of Planning, the Ministry of Trade and the National PECC Committee (Colpec), and has held academic positions with the Rosario University, the Externado University and the Pontifical Xaverian University of Bogotá, among others. He obtained his Law Degree from the Faculty of Jurisprudence of the Rosario University (JD (merit), 1989) and has taken further degrees specializing in the law of the sea, in government, and in international relations.

Walter R. Roest started his career as a geophysicist at the Geological Survey of Canada, first in Halifax, NS, and subsequently in Ottawa, ON. He is currently a senior marine geophysicist at Ifremer, the French institute for ocean research, where he was director of the Marine Geosciences department from 2003 to 2009, and subsequently in charge of marine geosciences and deep ecosystems within the Scientific Direction.

From 2003 to 2012 he led the French national programme for the determination of the outer limits of the continental shelf within the framework of UNCLOS. He was elected member and served as vice-chair of the Commission on the Limits of the Continental Shelf from 2012 to 2017.

His research interests include the geodynamic evolution of continental margins and adjacent ocean basins and their geological resources. He has (co-)authored over 80 peer-reviewed papers and a large number of technical reports.

Clive Schofield, PhD (Durham), LLM (UBC) is Professor and Head of Research at the WMU-Sasakawa Global Ocean Institute, World Maritime University and Professor with the Australian National Centre for Ocean Resources and Security (ANCORS), University of Wollongong, Australia. His research relates to international maritime boundary delimitation and geo-technical issues in the law of the sea.

Pradeep A. Singh is a Fellow at the Research Institute for Sustainability, Helmholtz-Centre Potsdam, Germany (RIFS, which is formerly known as the Institute for Advanced Sustainability Studies or IASS) where he works on topics related to ocean governance and deep seabed mining. He is also Deputy Chair of the Ocean Law Specialist Group of the World Commission on Environmental Law and Lead of the IUCN's Commission on Ecosystem Management Thematic Group on Deep Seabed Mining.

He holds an LLM from Harvard Law School and an LLM in Global Environment and Climate Change Law from the University of Edinburgh, UK, as well as an LLB (First Class Honours) from the University of Malaya in his home county, Malaysia. Pradeep regularly attends multilateral ocean meetings and negotiations, including the meetings of the International Seabed Authority as an observer delegate, and advises several State delegations on matters relating to deep seabed mining and marine biodiversity conservation in areas beyond national jurisdiction.

Donnette Streete is a Guyanese diplomat specialized in border issues and international maritime law. She holds a master's degree from the IMO International Maritime Law Institute in Malta and a Bachelor of Laws degree from the University of Guyana.

She is the current Director of the Frontiers Department of the Ministry of Foreign Affairs & International Cooperation, with responsibility for the management of Guyana's relation with the Bolivarian Republic of Venezuela and the Republic of Suriname and providing advice on the rights and obligations of Guyana under international law of the sea. Her professional experience covers various portfolios in the field of international maritime law and diplomacy including coordinator and negotiator for the government of Guyana in the UN process towards the negotiation of a treaty on the protection of biodiversity in areas beyond national jurisdiction (BBNJ) and membership of the Legal Sub-Commission of the Caribbean Sea Commission of the Association of Caribbean States.

Virginie Tassin Campanella is Avocat à la Cour (Paris Bar 2016), EU/EFTA Attorney-at-law (Zürich Bar 2020), and a double Doctor in Law in Melbourne and Sorbonne Universities (2010), Australia and France, respectively. An award-winning researcher in the law of the sea (INDEMER 2011, Monaco and ESDHC 2016, Brazil), Dr Tassin Campanella is currently acting as founder and managing director of VTA Tassin, a public international law firm dedicated to oceans and seas. She is also Vice President of the scientific council of the Institute of Economic Law of the Sea of Monaco (INDEMER), International Counsel of the Brazilian Law of the Sea Institute (IBDMAR), and member of the organizing Committee of the Kadir Has Law of the Sea Summer Academy, Turkey.

Previously Associate Legal Officer of the International Tribunal Law of the Sea, Dr Tassin Campanella was heavily involved in the 2011 Seabed Mining Advisory Opinion and the 2012 Bangladesh Myanmar case. With more than 15 years of experience in seabed mining, including a double-badged PhD on the extension of the continental shelf, Dr Tassin Campanella regularly conducts legal opinions and provides advice on seabed management, including mining, mapping and observation, as well as on the viability of advisory opinions.

Dire Tladi was elected Judge of the International Court of Justice in November 2023. At the time he was Professor and NRF/DST Chair in International Constitutional Law and Future Africa Chair in Global Equity in Africa.

He is former member and Chair of the United Nations International Law Commission and was its Special Rapporteur on Peeremptory Norms of General International Law. He is also a member of the Institut of Droit International.

He was previously Legal Advisor of the South African Mission in New York and Special Advisor to the South African Foreign Minister. In that capacity he served as lead lawyer on South Africa's continental shelf claim project team and was for many years South Africa's lead negotiator on all issues relating to the law of the sea.

Tullio Treves, born in 1942, is Emeritus Professor in the University of Milano Faculty of Law, Italy; Judge of the International Tribunal for the Law of the Sea (1996–2011); Legal Adviser to the Italian Mission to the UN in New York (1984–1992); and Member of the Institut de droit international since 1999. He is currently Senior Consultant of Curtis, Mallet-Prevost Colt & Mosle LLP, arbitrator and counsel in international cases.

Klaas Willaert works at the Maritime Institute, embedded within the Faculty of Law and Criminology of Ghent University. The law of the sea is his area of expertise and he has conducted research on the legal aspects of seabed mining over the last few years. Klaas has presented his research at various international conferences and has produced numerous academic publications and scientific reports. He has also provided legal consultancy services, is closely involved in the reform of the Belgian deep sea mining legislation and has participated in the annual sessions of the Council of the International Seabed Authority.

He is part of the editorial boards of the *Journal of International Maritime Law* and the *Journal for International Trade and Transport Law*, and holds memberships of the International Association for the Law of the Sea, the European Society of International Law, the Belgian Association of Maritime Law and the Royal Belgian Marine Academy.

Hilde J. Woker is Assistant Professor of Public International Law, affiliated with the Grotius Centre for International Legal Studies at Leiden University. Hilde holds a PhD degree in law from UiT – The Arctic University of Norway, an LLM degree in the law of the sea from UiT – The Arctic University of Norway, and an LLM degree in public international law from Leiden University.

Her research specialization is the law of the sea, with a particular focus on the law-science interface, the legal regime for marine scientific research and the legal regime for the continental shelf. Hilde teaches and coordinates various courses in public international law at Leiden University, and regularly provides (guest) lectures on the law of the sea or polar law. Hilde previously worked at the Norwegian Centre for the Law of the Sea (NCLOS) in Tromsø, Norway, where she also undertook her PhD research on the law-science interface within the law of the sea.

ABOUT THE EDITOR

Virginie Tassin Campanella is an Avocat à la Cour (Paris Bar 2016) and EU/EFTA Attorney-at-law (Zürich Bar 2020). She holds two PhDs in law (Melbourne and Sorbonne 2010). International award-winning researcher in the law of the sea (INDEMER, Monaco in 2011, and ESDHC, Brazil in 2016), she has a dual academic background in France and Australia in law, commerce, and leadership (2005 DEA International Economic Law, Sorbonne University; 2006 Grad Dip Commerce, Sydney University; 2009 Grad Cert Leadership and Advanced Learning, Melbourne University).

Since 2016, she has been acting as Founder and Managing Director of VTA Tassin, a Public International Law Firm dedicated to oceans and seas where she delivers advisory, representation, and capacity-building services to States, international and regional organizations, the private sector, NGOs, foundations, associations as well as investors. Mostly known for its avant-gardist services to the private sector and civil society, its experience in the Science-Business-Policy nexus, and for making international law accessible and of value to all actors (not only States), VTA Tassin works with a wide range of ocean sectors on topics such as deep sea mining and seabed management; ocean observation; fisheries cooperation; marine biodiversity use, access and management; marine spatial planning; carbon storage; blue finance; ocean trade; ocean governance as well as the creation and transformation of international organizations.

Dr Tassin Campanella regularly acts as a legal expert before international and regional organizations, including the European Union, the World Bank, the International Hydrographic Organization, the International Oceanographic Commission of UNESCO (including under the GEBCO Review Project), the IUCN French Committee (Overseas Group and Law Commission), and the IUCN World Commission on Environmental Law (Ocean Group).

Named in 2023 '*Avocat de l'océan*' by the French economic journal, *Les Echos*, Dr Tassin Campanella was in 2022 awarded with 'Outstanding Leadership' for her contributions to the rule of law through the work undertaken under the umbrella of VTA Tassin (Law 2.0 Conference). In April 2023, the World Law Alliance also awarded her with the 'Prominent Woman in International Law', representing Switzerland, for her exceptional performance in international law, her contributions to new laws, policies, and programs in the law of the sea, her pro bono work, and her engagement in continuous professional development.

Former Associate Legal Officer of the International Tribunal for the Law of the Sea (ITLOS), Dr Tassin Campanella worked on the 2011 *Seabed Advisory Opinion*, the 2012 *Bangladesh/ Myanmar* case, and the *M/V Louisa* and the *M/V Virginia G.* cases. She also previously worked for the World Health Organization on illicit tobacco trade products, the French Economic Mission in Ho Chi Minh City, Vietnam, as well as various international law firms, institutes, research centres, and think tanks in Australia, China, and Europe.

Dr Tassin Campanella has more than 15 years' experience on seabed mining issues, both as a researcher and a practitioner. Since her award-winning PhD on the extension of the continental shelf and her work experience at ITLOS, she has been involved in many deep sea mining public projects around the world, including the 2012 *Pacific-ACP States Regional Environmental Management Framework for Deep Sea Minerals Exploration and Exploitation*, the 2013 French Economic, Social and Environmental Counsel Advice on the Extension of the Continental Shelf, and the 2022 French Senate hearings on the exploration, protection, and exploitation of deep seabed where she acted as counsel for the French IUCN Committee. She regularly advises public and private entities on seabed mining and seabed management issues, including the feasibility of advisory opinions, legal proceedings, and pending legal questions before the International Seabed Authority.

Since 2021, Dr Tassin Campanella has been Vice President of the Scientific Council of the Economic Law of the Sea Institute (INDEMER) of Monaco making her the first Attorney being appointed by Royal Ordinance to this position. Since 2014, she has also been a registered researcher at the International Resources Law Group (ESDHC, Belo Horizonte, Brazil) and has been acting since 2016 as International Counsel to the Brazilian Law of the Sea Institute (IBDMAR). Often invited as a guest professor by leading institutions, universities as well as business schools around the world (including ITLOS, Sciences Po Paris, HEC Paris, Kadir Has Law of the Sea Summer Academy), she has a passion for transmitting her knowledge and practical experience to a wide audience and the younger generations.

She has published so far 30+ research articles, chronicles, and chapters, as well as two books on law of the sea issues in French and English (*Les défis de l'extension du plateau continental: consecration d'un nouveau rapport de l'Etat à son territoire*, 2013; *Guide to the Navigation of Marine Biological Diversity Beyond National Jurisdiction*, 2017, co-edited with André de Paiva Toledo). This book is a natural prolongation of her initial research interests and current practice.

LIST OF ABBREVIATIONS

ABNJ	Areas beyond national jurisdiction
ASEAN	Association of Southeast Asian Nations
AU	African Union
BBNJ	Biodiversity beyond national jurisdiction
CBD	Convention on Biological Diversity
CHM	Common heritage of mankind
CJEU	Court of Justice of the European Union
CLCS	Commission on the Limits of the Continental Shelf
CS	Continental shelf
DSM	Deep sea mining
EEZ	Exclusive economic zone
EIA	Environmental impact assessment
EU	European Union
FAO	United Nations Food and Agricultural Organization
GATT	General Agreement on Tariffs and Trade
HS	High Seas
ICJ	International Court of Justice
ICSID	International Centre for Settlement of Investment Disputes
ILC	International Law Commission
IOC-UNESCO	Intergovernmental Oceanographic Commission of UNESCO
ISA	International Seabed Authority
ITLOS	International Tribunal for the Law the Sea
LTC	Legal and Technical Commission of ISA
M	Nautical miles
MPA	Marine protected area
PCA	Permanent Court of Arbitration
PCIJ	Permanent Court of International Justice
SDC	Seabed Disputes Chamber
SDG	Sustainable development goals
UN	United Nations
UNC	United Nations Charter

UNCITRAL	United Nations Commission on International Trade Law
UNCLOS	United Nations Convention on the Law of the Sea
UNESCO	United Nations Educational, Scientific and Cultural Organization
UNFCC	United Nations Framework Convention on Climate Change
UNGA	United Nations General Assembly
UNITAR	United Nations Institute for Training and Research
WTO	World Trade Organization

INTRODUCTION

Virginie Tassin Campanella

Scientific discoveries and technological progress have driven profound recent changes in our society, allowing for the access and use of energy and metal resources that had for long been considered unreachable. These newfound resources have in turn facilitated the development of infrastructures and industries capable of fueling society's unrelenting drive for progress, enabling humanity not only to venture into outer space but also to explore the ocean's deepest depths.

Over the last 150 years, the marine environment has been the scene of an extraordinary expansion of activity. While this space has long served as a route of communication and trade, and as a vital reservoir of food for millennia, strategic interest towards this space, initially focused on its upper part, has more recently shifted to its depths. The nineteenth century marked a turning point with the discovery of promising non-living resources at sea. This was followed by an unprecedented interest in offshore oil and other seabed minerals in the aftermath of the Second World War to support reconstruction and development of the post-war society. These pressing and ongoing demands for supplies of commodities and raw materials have actually never dried up since.

Global acknowledgment of the depletion of resources and the concept of 'peak oil' however quickly came into play. As a result, the development of the exploitation of seabed resources has been subject to important forces of change. General worries associated with the improper use of science and technology against peoples and the environment during the Vietnam War, as well as the escalation of tensions during the Cold War, urged States to rethink the nexus between humans and nature. With the rise of newly independent States, international society was prompted to reshape its legal order, including the one of the oceans. It is in this context that the longest negotiations in the history of international law took place, the ones related to the *United Nations Convention on the Law of the Sea* (UNCLOS).

Interestingly, some of the most sensitive elements of these negotiations were related to the access and use of seabed resources. Indeed, scientific research in the 1970s confirmed the potential economic benefits of new mineral resources – polymetallic nodules. These exploitation prospects did not only offer States new alternatives to support their economic and industrial developments, but they also carried the promise that, due to their location in the deep sea, they could be acces-

DOI: 10.4324/9780429426162-1

sible and of benefit to both industrialised and developing countries if appropriate mechanisms and rules were elaborated at the international level. In the UNCLOS, this resulted in the creation of the concept of common heritage of mankind,[1] the creation of mechanisms for the transfer of technology, capacity development and the possibility of extending the continental shelf beyond 200 nautical miles (M).[2]

Despite the destabilising changes created by the *1994 Agreement relating to the Implementation of Part XI of the UNCLOS* (1994 Agreement)[3] to fit with new market realities of the 1990s and the related threats to multilateralism feared by some due to the United States not ratifying the UNCLOS, the Convention remains alive and is today considered a universal treaty which has gathered 168 State Party ratifications to the UNCLOS (as of 2023) and 151 State Party signatures to the 1994 Agreement. Further, even the few States who did not ratify the Convention because of disagreements on very specific provision(s) and/or due to internal political issues[4] remain subject to the many customary international law rules contained in the UNCLOS.[5] Some non-Party States to UNCLOS are further applying many provisions on a voluntary basis and sometimes even monitor the effective implementation of the UNCLOS, as in the case of the United States which commented some extension submissions considered by the Commission on the Limits of the Continental Shelf.

As a result, the UNCLOS not only managed to reconcile divergent interests in a highly complex and everchanging geopolitical and economic context, but it also created, in a single treaty, a framework able to regulate human activities at sea and to manage the marine space and its resources while ensuring its protection and preservation. It managed to do so despite scientific certainties about the structure of marine ecosystems and their functions. Moreover, the UNCLOS attests to the fact that persistent efforts (nine years of negotiations) deployed with the support of exceptional diplomatic and legal skills, can result in the making of a truly unique international legal framework ratified by an overwhelming majority of States.

Looking back today on what has evolved, especially in view of the fortieth anniversary of UNCLOS, it appears that seabed mining has always played an important role in the history of international law. The creation of the regime of the continental shelf by the *1958 Geneva Continental Shelf Convention* and its evolution through the UNCLOS attest to how law can provide stable and

1 See in this book N. Oral, 'The common heritage of mankind under international law: an overview', in V. Tassin Campanella (ed), *Routledge handbook of seabed mining and the law of the sea*, London: Routledge, 2023, chapter I.2.

2 See in this book Ø. Jensen and B. Már Magnússon, 'The extension of sovereign rights beyond 200 nautical miles', in V. Tassin Campanella (ed), *Routledge handbook of seabed mining and the law of the sea*, op. cit., chapter III.1.

3 For more information, see in this book A. Jaeckel, 'The Area and the role of the International Seabed Authority', in V. Tassin Campanella (ed), *Routledge handbook of seabed mining and the law of the sea*, op. cit., chapter IV.1.

4 For examples of non-State Parties to UNCLOS see in this book E. Restrepo Uribe, 'Colombia and seabed mining', in V. Tassin Campanella (ed), *Routledge handbook of seabed mining and the law of the sea*, op. cit., chapter VI.2.3. See also E. Jiménez Pineda, 'South American region and seabed mining', in V. Tassin Campanella (ed), idem, chapter VI.1.6 and L. Godio, 'Antarctica and seabed mining', in V. Tassin Campanella (ed), idem, chapter VI.1.2. See also C. Schofield and J. Mossop, 'The Article 82 conundrum: implementing payment for the exploitation of the continental shelf beyond 200 nautical miles', in V. Tassin Campanella (ed), idem, chapter III.2.

5 See in this book Jensen and Már Magnússon, op. cit., as well as Schofield and Mossop, op. cit. See also J. Dingwall, 'The common heritage quandary: devising a global payment regime for exploitation activities in the deep seabed Area', in V. Tassin Campanella (ed), *Routledge handbook of seabed mining and the law of the sea*, op. cit., chapter IV.2.

long-term solutions which balance societal, environmental and economic interests.[6] The overwhelming number of continental shelf extension submissions received by 2009 also revealed, quite unexpectedly,[7] that States have a high interest in securing vast areas of seabed for potential future exploration and exploitation, confirming the continued importance of the sovereign rights of exploration and exploitation in both current and future political agendas.

Economic pressures related to the access and use of minerals and metals have also continuously been driving the international agenda, especially when it comes to seabed mining. These pressures have however changed faces throughout time. Previously, economic pressures took the form of a need to support the reconstruction and development efforts of the post-war period. Today, economic pressures are still replying to the demands of industry but are adapting to the new paradigm of sustainable development and climate imperatives.[8] Unfortunately, some similarities remain. The spectre of resource depletion and arms race is still present, which will further impact commodity demands in the years to come if we stay on the same path.

In light of these demands, the seabed mining industry aims to exploit new mineral resources while promoting, in its own way, its key support for 'green' technologies (including batteries, computers, electrical cars and infrastructure components of renewable energies), its positive impact on global warming compared to terrestrial exploitation, and its contributions to the development of a circular metal economy which will support a transition to green energy.[9] Much like any new emerging industry, the few actors in the seabed mining industry are engrossed with technological developments and are concerned with the commercialisation and high return prospects of new seabed minerals. They are, without any doubt, driving innovation and investing heavily through exploration activities. They are consequently facing many uncertainties in the future exploitation and commercialisation phases of their activities and, as a result, are heavily exposing themselves to legal risks, financial risks and related responsibilities.[10]

6 See in this book V. Tassin Campanella, Y. Cissé and D. Tladi, 'State rights and obligations of States on the continental shelf and the Area', in V. Tassin Campanella (ed), *Routledge handbook of seabed mining and the law of the sea*, op. cit., chapter II.1.

7 See ibid.

8 See generally the regional and national sections of this book, and more specifically the European Union section mentioning the importance of commodities in relation to seabed mining. P. Singh, V. Tassin Campanella and F. Maes, 'The European Union and seabed mining', in V. Tassin Campanella (ed), *Routledge handbook of seabed mining and the law of the sea*, op. cit., chapter VI.1.4. For climate law, see the Paris Agreement adopted on 12 December 2015 and the subsequent declaration of the World Bank to stop financing upstream oil and gas after 2019. World Bank, *World Bank Group announcements at One Planet Summit, Press Release*, 12 December 2017. Available online <https://www.worldbank.org/en/news/press-release/2017/12/12/world-bank-group-announcements-at-one-planet-summit> (accessed January 2023). On the relationship between green transition and raw materials availability, see also the 2023 OECD Report, *Raw Materials Critical for the Green Transition: production, international trade and export restrictions*, OECD Trade Policy Paper 269, April 2023. This report highlights that supply of critical raw materials risks jeopardising the green transition. Available online <https://www.oecd.org/trade/topics/trade-in-raw-materials/> (accessed April 2023).

9 For more information, see The 2021 Metals Company Impact Report available at the following link: <https://metals.co/tmcs-inaugural-impact-report/> (accessed January 2023).

10 See in this book T. Treves, 'Dispute settlement and seabed mining in the Area', in V. Tassin Campanella (ed), *Routledge handbook of seabed mining and the law of the sea*, op. cit., chapter V.1. See also C. Payne, 'State responsibility for deep seabed mining obligations', in V. Tassin Campanella (ed), idem, chapter II.2, and J. Harrison and A. Pecoraro, 'Dispute settlement and rights of participation in deep seabed mining disputes', in V. Tassin Campanella (ed), idem, chapter V.2, as well as M. Feria-Tinta and M. Kamga, 'Mining the bottom of the sea: potential future disputes and the role of the International Tribunal for the Law of the Sea', in V. Tassin Campanella (ed), idem, chapter V.3.

In terms of risk evaluation, the main existing gaps actually concern what is often referred to as 'the social and environmental license to operate'. Indeed, despite the collection and processing of environmental data through exploration activities both *within* and *beyond* national jurisdictions, important knowledge gaps remain regarding resource estimation, the extent and timeframe of potential environmental and social damages due to exploitation (including damages which might affect local communities and indigenous peoples)[11] and the quantification and characterisation of these impacts as harmful or serious. This is due to the novelty of the technology and activities developed, the diversity of resources and related extraction methodologies, but also due to the simple fact that we are still discovering and making inventories rather than understanding the functions and structures of deep sea ecosystems.[12]

As a result, diverse opposing views are being expressed regarding the sustainability path of this new industry. The United Nations Environmental Programme and more specifically its 2022 Financial Initiative briefing paper, designed for investors and other financial institutions, expressed that, in light of the high levels of scientific uncertainty and the paucity of data to support a detailed understanding of future ecological impacts associated with deep sea mining, 'it could be argued that, at present, no robust precautionary approach exists to safeguard the ocean against the potential ecological impacts of deep sea mining'.[13] The briefing paper concluded that 'there is no foreseeable way in which the financing of deep sea mining activities can be viewed as consistent with the Sustainable Blue Economy Finance Principles, or compatible with the spirit and intent of the Sustainable Blue Economy'.[14]

On this note, it is worth noticing the current cacophony around the use of the concept of sustainable development and more specifically the various (sometimes conflicting or inconsistent) implementations of the concept despite the use of modern tools, such as Environmental Social and Governance reporting or low carbon funding, to support sustainable development arguments. While this book does not intend to focus on the relationship between seabed mining and sustainable development policies, nor conduct an overall assessment of the sustainability and related legal responsibilities of this nascent industry, many chapters and sections touch upon this subject. Some of them indeed analyse the concept of sustainable management of the marine environment and the implementation of the precautionary approach,[15] while others question the compatibility of seabed mining of minerals with sustainable developments goals and more specifically Goal 14 of Agenda 2030.[16]

11 See on this point the Arctic regional section of this book. K. Dalaker and H. Woker, 'The Arctic and seabed mining', in V. Tassin Campanella (ed), *Routledge handbook of seabed mining and the law of the sea*, op. cit., chapter VI.1.3.

12 See on this point the recommendations of W. Roest, M. Clark and H. Brekke, 'The scientific challenges of deep-sea mining', in V. Tassin Campanella (ed), *Routledge handbook of seabed mining and the law of the sea*, op. cit., chapter I.1.

13 On this point, see in this book R. Makgill, A. Jaeckel and K. MacMaster, 'Implementing the precautionary approach for seabed mining: a review of State practice', in V. Tassin Campanella (ed), op. cit., chapter I.3. See also the national chapter on New Zealand, R. Makgill and E. Macpherson, 'New Zealand and seabed mining', in V. Tassin Campanella (ed), idem, chapter VI.2.12.

14 United Nations Environment Programme Financial Initiative (UNEP-FI), *Harmful marine extractives: Understanding the risks and impacts of financing non-renewable extractive industries*, Geneva, 2022.

15 See Makgill, Jaeckel and MacMaster, op. cit.

16 See in this book N. Matz, 'Germany and seabed mining', in V. Tassin Campanella (ed), *Routledge handbook of seabed mining and the law of the sea*, op. cit., chapter VI.2.5 and B. Bojang and D. Streete, 'Guyana and seabed mining', in V. Tassin Campanella (ed), idem, chapter VI.2.6. For broader comments on sustainable development and seabed mining, see also C. Costa de Oliveira and A. Flávia Barros-Platiau, 'Brazil and seabed mining', in V. Tassin Campanella (ed), idem, chapter VI.2.2 and E. Stefane Mahanjane, 'Mozambique and seabed mining', in V. Tassin Campanella (ed), idem, chapter VI.2.11.

It is also worth noticing that a part of civil society's gathering of scientific experts,[17] the private sector,[18] associations,[19] non-governmental and other organisations[20] currently oppose the development of exploitation activities in the deep seabed due to potential harmful changes and effects to the marine environment. Some of them question the economic arguments put forth by the industry, especially its support of the 'green' transition and what environmental and social impacts the transition actually require, especially with regard to biodiversity conservation. Finally, at the State level, a wind of change has blown through in the last few years pushing twenty-two States at the time of writing to reconsider their positions regarding the short-term prospects of exploiting seabed minerals in the deep seabed which belongs to the common heritage of mankind (the Area).[21]

While most of these declarations are political in nature (calls for a moratorium of seabed mining of minerals) and concern exploitation the Area, some of them also concern the exploitation of the seabed of the continental shelf.[22] Important future developments thus now lie before us given that legal translations of these political declarations need to be made and a great number of legal questions remain to be addressed and solved at the national, regional and international levels.[23]

At the national and regional levels, States still have a long road ahead to fully and effectively implement their legal obligations under the UNCLOS. There generally remains many provisions and mechanisms to be explored, interpreted and implemented in both the UNCLOS and interna-

17 See for example D.J. Amon et al., 'Assessment of scientific gaps related to the effective environmental management of deep-seabed mining', *Marine Policy* 138, April 2022, 105006. The authors of this article mention that 'closing scientific gaps related to deep-seabed mining is a monumental task that is essential to fulfilling the overarching obligation to prevent serious harm and ensure effective protection, and will require clear direction, substantial resources, and robust coordination and collaboration'. They propose to establish a high-level road map of activities to close these gaps before exploitation starts.

18 Companies such as BMW, Breitling, Google, Patagonia, Philips, Samsung, Renault Group, Volkswagen and Volvo have committed to not using metals from deep sea mining and joined a call for the moratorium of the World Wild Foundation in 2022. See the full list and moratorium call at the following link <https://www.noseabedmining.org/> (accessed January 2023). Banks and financial institutions, such as ABN AMRO, Lloyds Banking Group, NatWest, BBVA Bank, Standard Chartered and The European Investment Bank but also Members of the Sustainable Blue Economy Finance Initiative Working Group (including BNP Paribas, Bank of China, Asian Development Bank, Palladium Impact Capital, China Industrial Bank and many other actors who are not necessarily part of the banking or financial worlds) have also expressed opposing views with regard to short-term deep sea mining and are calling for alternative strategies enabling the extraction of necessary rare earth and metals. These alternative strategies include the 1) reduction of the environmental footprint of terrestrial mining and 2) support of the transition towards a circular economy promoting the reuse of raw materials. For more information, see the full report of UNEP-FI, ibid.

19 See for exemple Systext, *Controverses minières: Exploration et exploitation minières en eaux profondes*, Tome 1, Volet 2, November 2022. This report highlights that exploitation of minerals in the deep seabed heavily relies on the use of fossil fuels. It also stresses the great differences between deep sea minerals and terrestrial ones (complex mineralogy, high porosity and water content) requiring time-consuming and energy-intensive processing. Available at the following link <https://www.systext.org/node/1931> (accessed January 2023). See also generally M. Simas, F. Aponte and K. Wiebe, *The future is circular: circular economy and critical minerals for the green transition*, SINTEF, 2022.

20 See for example the Deep Sea Conservation Coalition gathering today around 400 civil society organisations.

21 Number updated in October 2023. Please note the fast changes in the positioning of States towards seabed mining have prevented some regional and national chapters of this book to be updated accordingly.

22 See in this regard Singh, Tassin Campanella and Maes, op. cit.

23 See for example F. Armas-Pfirter, 'Upcoming challenges for the International Seabed Authority', in V. Tassin Campanella (ed), *Routledge handbook of seabed mining and the law of the sea*, op. cit., chapter IV.3. For regional perspectives, see also L. Godio, 'Antarctica and seabed mining', in V. Tassin Campanella (ed), idem, chapter VI.1.2, T. Davenport, 'Southeast Asia and seabed mining', in V. Tassin Campanella (ed), idem, chapter VI.1.7 and E. Egede, 'Africa and seabed mining' in V. Tassin Campanella (ed), idem, chapter VI.1.1.

tional law, especially with regard to marine scientific research, the implementation of the rights and obligations of States[24] and related responsibilities (including the responsibilities of private entities, State and international organisations).[25] With regard to the seabed mining of minerals both *within* and *beyond* national jurisdictions, the national and regional sections of this book generally attest to the delays and difficulties faced by most States and the European Union in the regulation of these activities, as well as in the creation of environmental policies and related governance mechanisms.[26] Even though a few States have already adapted their national legislations or are in the process of doing so[27] with some even currently moving forward with the potentially short-term exploitation of mineral resources on their continental shelf[28] and showing interest in doing the same in the Area,[29] the great majority of States lag too far behind with the national implementation of the UNCLOS to (seriously) consider any short-term exploitation prospects.

This multidisciplinary book intends to provide a global overview of the national, regional and international regulatory frameworks applicable to exploration and exploitation of seabed minerals on the continental shelf and the Area, as well as the related state of the science on the matter. While presenting the historical elements essential to the understanding of the context under which the law of the sea and international law was developed, this book also addresses thorny contemporary and

24 See in this book Tassin Campanella, Cissé and Tladi, op. cit. For a reference to capacity-building and the transfer of technology in relation to seabed mining, see Y. Cissé, 'Côte d'Ivoire and seabed mining', in V. Tassin Campanella (ed), *Routledge handbook of seabed mining and the law of the sea*, op. cit., chapter VI.2.4.

25 See in this book Payne, op. cit. as well as Harrison and Pecoraro, op. cit.

26 Various reasons can explain this. Some States have indeed legislations only applicable to oil and gas, as is the case for example for Brazil or the Ivory Coast. See in this book Costa de Oliveira and Flávia Barros-Platiau, op. cit., chapter VI.2.2 and Y. Cissé, op. cit., chapter VI.2.4. Others have not managed to adopt specific legislation for activities in the Area despite several attempts and current exploration contracts, as is the case for Korea. See H. Jung Kim, 'Korea and seabed mining', in V. Tassin Campanella (ed), idem, chapter VI.2.9. Some States are also facing challenges linked to maritime boundaries, slowing down any short- to medium-term exploration prospects on their continental shelves. See in this regard the Ivory Coast. It should also be noted that some States have also presently no interest in any exploration or exploitation activities, as is the case of Iceland. See B. Már Magnússon, 'Iceland and seabed mining', in V. Tassin Campanella (ed), idem, chapter VI.2.7. States which are not party to UNCLOS can also face challenges in contemplating exploration and exploitation activities in the Area. See for example the case of Colombia explained by Restrepo Uribe, op. cit., chapter VI.2.3. See also the issue of the over-regulation and clash of competence between ministries and legal frameworks applicable to seabed mining of minerals and the environment, I. Chaturvedi Sadhale, 'India and seabed mining', in V. Tassin Campanella (ed), idem, chapter VI.2.8, and the similar issue related to the division of responsibilities between mining and the environment in Mauritius, E. Egede, 'Mauritius and seabed mining', in V. Tassin Campanella (ed), idem, chapter VI.2.10, and in Portugal (together with potential conflict with the regional level, i.e. the European level), M. Neves and P. Madureira, 'Portugal and seabed mining', in V. Tassin Campanella (ed), idem, chapter VI.2.13.

27 See in this book C. Diver, 'The Pacific Islands region and seabed mining', in V. Tassin Campanella (ed), *Routledge handbook of seabed mining and the law of the sea*, op. cit., chapter VI.1.5. See also for example the case of the United Kingdom and potential issues related to compliance with the Exploration regulation of ISA. J. Harrison, 'The United Kingdom and seabed mining', in V. Tassin Campanella (ed), idem, chapter VI.2.14.

28 See for example Norway which discovered in January 2023 substantial amounts of metals and minerals on the seabed of its continental shelf and is planning exploitation in the near future. See also Japan planning to extract seabed minerals from its continental shelf in 2024 (off Minami-Torishima island) to reduce reliance on Chinese minerals. To do so, it established in 2022 eleven areas of specified critical materials under the Law for the Promotion of Economic Security. See S. Foster, 'Japan dives into rare earth mining under the sea', *Asia Times*, 10 January 2023. Available online <https://asiatimes.com/2023/01/japan-dives-into-rare-earth-mining-under-the-sea/> (accessed January 2023).

29 See the case of Nauru and the use of the two-year rule. For more on this, see P. Singh, 'The invocation of the "two-year rule" at the International Seabed Authority: legal consequences and implications', *The International Journal of Marine and Coastal Law* 37, 2022, 375–412.

prospective issues and provides unique insights into the complex regional and national practices attached to these activities *within* and *beyond* national jurisdiction, including the case of non-Party States to the UNCLOS.[30]

To further promote understanding, a balance has been struck in this book to ensure that equal attention is given to both the seabed mining of minerals on the continental shelf and the seabed mining of minerals in the Area. As a result, chapters have been designed to explain this duality, specific parts of the book have been created to present related challenges and each of this book's chapters clarifies the use of the term 'deep sea mining' and its specific geographical scope to provide further clarity.

This book also wants to highlight the complementarity of the contributions made by the various authors. While the various topics and research objectives of each chapter have been selected and organised by the editor of the book, together with Dr Robert Makgill, all authors have been invited to build on the work of others. Working in this way required more time than usual,[31] but it is hoped that this original approach will further add value to the field and promote the solid research work conducted by all under the umbrella of this book.

I am deeply grateful for all of the authors' commitment to this book, for their patience and their trust. I am also grateful to all the silent contributors, friends and colleagues who have provided insights, comments, attention and time to this project during the last five years. This journey has not been an easy one due to the many unique and heart-breaking events which have profoundly affected us and the difficult editorial choices that have had to be made from the start. I hope that this book will serve its original goals being, firstly, the promotion of an understanding and implementation of the rule of law at all levels, and secondly, the promotion of a diversity of analyses and practices regarding the regulation of the seabed mining of minerals throughout the world.

Bonne lecture à tous!

30 Colombia, the United States, Peru and Venezuela are studied in this book. For more information, see generally for Colombia, Restrepo Uribe, op. cit. For the United States see Schofield and Mossop, op. cit. For Peru and Venezuela see Jiménez Pineda, op. cit.

31 In this context, while some chapters have been diligently revised throughout 2023 to encompass the most recent developments, such as the BBNJ Agreement, others continue to reflect the state of law, policy, and practice, along with associated analyses, as of the year 2022.

PART I

Global perspectives

I.1
THE SCIENTIFIC CHALLENGES OF DEEP-SEA MINING

Walter R. Roest, Malcolm R. Clark and Harald Brekke

Introduction

The global demand for raw materials is increasing at a steady pace, notably because of demographic changes and the development of new technologies. The latter include green technologies that respond to concerns about climate change by reducing greenhouse gas emissions. Examples include the production of batteries or of high efficiency renewable energy equipment, such as latest generation wind turbines, and these need specific metals and minerals. At the same time, it is becoming increasingly more difficult to find good quality, accessible mineral reserves on land, and although recycling efforts are increasing, it is likely that new sources for key minerals need to be identified. To diversify and secure supply, several countries are undertaking the exploration of mineral resources from the seabed and subsoil. However, whether located on land, on the continental shelves surrounding the continents or in the deep sea, these resources formed over millions of years by geological processes and are by nature finite, so their extraction cannot be sustained over time. It is, therefore, essential to find responsible ways to extract these resources and sustainable ways to use them, while protecting the marine environment.

Despite on-going efforts of industry, scientific research institutes and recent international initiatives (e.g., Seabed 2030,[1] a programme that aims to have 100 per cent of the ocean floor mapped by 2030; Census of Marine Life,[2] a 10 year international effort undertaken from 2000 to 2010, to assess the diversity, distribution and abundance of marine life), our knowledge of the deep ocean floor remains poor. One of the main difficulties is that it takes an enormous amount of time to map accurately the ocean floor, as it requires acoustic measurements that can only be done from surface vessels and, more recently, from remotely operated or autonomous underwater vehicles (respectively ROV and AUV). Current estimates indicate that only between 15 and 20 per cent of the global ocean floor is mapped to modern standards, even at a resolution as low as 1 km.[3] Sampling

1 L. Mayer et al., 'The Nippon Foundation—GEBCO Seabed 2030 project: The quest to see the world's oceans completely mapped by 2030', *Geosciences* 8, 2018, 63.
2 A.D. McIntyre (ed.), *Life in the world's oceans: Diversity, distribution, and abundance*, Wiley Blackwell, Oxford, UK, 2010.
3 Ibid.

DOI: 10.4324/9780429426162-3

for the collection of biological specimens and information takes even more time, and at present only covers very small areas of the ocean. Biological investigations have occurred in less than 1 per cent of most deep-sea habitats.[4]

This chapter focusses on deep-sea mining, i.e., activities related to seabed and subsoil minerals located in water deeper than 200 m. There are many scientific challenges in common related to both shallow and deep-sea minerals. However, due to the current interest and focus on those in the deep sea, as well as the different environmental characteristics (e.g., extreme environments, low energy for biocommunities), we feel that the challenges related to mining in the deep sea are the most relevant to address in this chapter. Exploring and potentially exploiting deep-sea resources comes with many challenges, be they technological, economical or environmental. We will describe our current knowledge, or lack thereof, and how these challenges might be overcome, from a scientific and technical point of view. The major issues we address include technical complexities related to working in deep water, methods needed to locate specific mineral resources and assess their resource potential, technology to separate relevant minerals and handle contaminants and other waste products, as well as the science needed for robust assessment of environmental impacts and for adopting an ecosystem approach. Each of these topics could warrant a chapter in their own right, and so here we do not delve into extensive detail, but seek to highlight and briefly evaluate the principal challenges in order to provide scientific context for the other chapters in this book.

Mineral resources of the deep sea

Minerals of the deep sea essentially occur in three forms: polymetallic nodules, hydrothermal sulphides and cobalt-rich manganese crusts. Other mineral resources, such as phosphorites or placers (e.g., diamond), are also found offshore, but occur mainly in shallower areas and will be touched upon only briefly. We will not address energy resources, such as oil and gas, nor will we discuss the potential for exploitation of natural hydrogen associated with ultramafic-hosted hydrothermal vents.

Figure I.1.1a shows a bathymetric map using the global GEBCO 2014 data set[5] which has a grid cell size of approximately 1 km at the Equator. Despite their low resolution, these types of maps are a significant help in planning marine scientific cruises targeting specific geological formations, including the types of environments that are likely to host mineral occurrences. Figure I.1.1b–d shows examples of areas related to the main deep-sea mineral types (polymetallic nodules, hydrothermal sulphides and cobalt-rich manganese crusts) that are discussed in the text.

Nodules

Polymetallic nodules were first discovered at the end of the nineteenth century but interest in their economic potential, notably as a source for manganese, nickel, copper and cobalt, dates from the 1960s. Nodules are 5–10 cm-diameter 'balls', consisting of manganese and iron oxyhydroxides

4 E. Ramirez-Llodra et al., 'Deep, diverse and definitely different: Unique attributes of the world's largest ecosystem', *Biogeosciences* 7, 2010, 2851–99.

5 GEBCO 2014 Grid, December 2014. Available online <https://www.gebco.net/news_and_media/gebco_2014_grid.html> (accessed 15 May 2021).

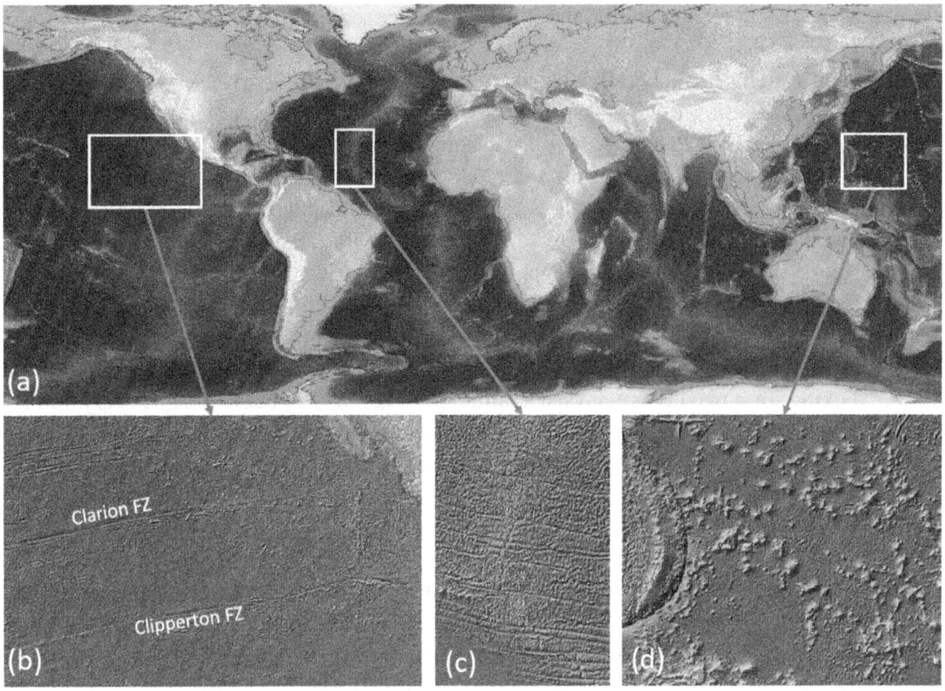

Figure I.1.1 (a) Global relief map based on GEBCO 2014 grid. The three white boxes highlight areas with different mineral occurrences. (b) Zoom on the area between the Clarion and Clipperton fracture zones in the east Pacific. The abyssal plain in this area is very flat and situated at depths around 5000 m, an ideal environment for polymetallic nodules. (c) Zoom on the Mid-Atlantic Ridge in the central north Atlantic. Hydrothermal vents and associated mineral deposits occur at several sites along the approximately north-south trending axis of the ridge. (d) Seamounts in the Western Pacific are targets for cobalt-rich manganese crust occurrences.

containing 40 per cent water. In addition, they contain copper, nickel, traces of molybdenum and rare earth elements (REE). They are formed at the seafloor, mainly at depths exceeding 4,000 metres in low sedimentation areas, i.e., away from continental sediment sources and at depths exceeding the carbonate compensation depth (CCD). The CCD represents the depth below which there is no net deposit of carbonate particles on the seafloor.

The process of nodule formation involves precipitation, around an initial core, of metal complexes dissolved in seawater or present in the surrounding sediments. Their growth rate is slow, only several millimetres per million years. It is thought that micro-organisms play a role in the formation of these nodules. The Clarion-Clipperton Zone (CCZ) in the North-East Pacific has one the richest deposits and it is no surprise that most of the exploration contracts with the International Seabed Authority (ISA) are located in that area (Figure I.1.1b).

Hydrothermal sulphides

Hydrothermal vent systems are the result of seawater circulating in the ocean crust under the influence of a heat source. Sulphide mineralisation has been found at depths of between 1,000 and

5,000 m on a variety of substrates (basalt, andesite, dacite, sediment and the ultramafic rocks of the mantle).

Hydrothermal systems are generally associated with volcanic activity. These systems are found on active seafloor spreading ridges, such as the Mid-Atlantic Ridge (Figure I.1.1c), the Southwest Indian Ridge, the East-Pacific Rise, on volcanic arcs related to subduction zones, in back-arc basins (e.g., southwest Pacific Ocean) and on volcanically active seamounts. The first active hydrothermal vent system was discovered in 1977 along the Galapagos Rift in the Pacific Ocean. One of the first Atlantic hydrothermal systems associated with hotspot activity was discovered south of the Azores, and its name is quite appropriate: Lucky Strike. A very well-known large seafloor massive sulphide deposit is located further south along the Mid-Atlantic Ridge and it is called TAG, named after the Trans-Atlantic Geotraverse project that identified the site in the 1970s. The total length of the mid-ocean ridge system is around 80,000 km, so looking for a hydrothermal vent is like looking for a needle in a haystack, although it is felt they occur at least every 100 km or so. As will be discussed later, it is more difficult still to locate sulphide deposits associated with inactive vents, i.e., vents that are no longer hydrothermally active.

Crusts

Cobalt-rich ferromanganese crusts are found in all oceans on hard, essentially volcanic, substrates in environments with low sedimentation rates. Like nodules, they are formed by the precipitation of metal complexes dissolved in seawater. They vary in thickness from a few millimetres to several tens of centimetres and they grow extremely slowly, from 1 to 6 millimetres over a million years. According to the ISA, one estimate shows that an area of 6.35 million km^2 of the ocean floor (or 1.7 per cent) is covered with crusts.[6] Cobalt- and platinum-rich deposits of economic interest are situated in the Pacific Ocean (Figure I.1.1d), at a depth of between 800 and 2,500 m, and consist of iron and manganese oxyhydroxides and a number of minor metals.

Phosphorite nodules and placers

The above mineral resource types are widely distributed in 'The Area' under the jurisdiction of the ISA, but also occur within national exclusive economic zones (EEZs) and continental shelfs. The latter is where a range of other mineral types and placer deposits occur on continental shelf and slope environments. For example, phosphorite nodules are found at shallower depths of 100 to 500 m, and in recent years have been subject to commercial exploration off Namibia, New Zealand and Mexico. Diamond placers are being exploited at depths of up to several hundreds of meters on the continental shelf, for example off South Africa.

Scientific and technical challenges

In this section, we address the considerable technical and scientific challenges presented by potential deep-sea mining, including the identification of resource location, potential impacts on ecosystems as well as technology challenges. These issues are discussed in the following four sections: exploration challenges, challenges in resource estimation, technical challenges and environmental challenges.

6 International Seabed Authority, March 2008. Available online <https://isa.org.jm/files/files/documents/eng9.pdf> (accessed 1 May 2021).

Exploration challenges

Polymetallic nodules occur in low sedimentation areas, mainly on the very deep abyssal plains in water depths exceeding 4000 m. Global bathymetry maps, including satellite-derived bathymetric maps allow for the identification of abyssal plains that potentially satisfy these criteria (e.g., Figure I.1.1a). Shipborne multi-beam echo sounder data, and especially backscatter data (measuring the reflectance of the seafloor) can assist in the interpretation of the seabed geology in target areas.[7] In particular, backscatter data can be used to distinguish hard substrates (rock outcrops), nodule fields and areas where no nodules are present. However, the presence, abundance and distribution of polymetallic nodules on the seafloor or within the superficial sediments can only be confirmed by visual means, seafloor photography and sampling (by grab, box core or dredge). Exploration for nodule occurrences on the seafloor does not seem to pose particular challenges, apart from the need to investigate extremely large areas. However, innovative methods may need to be developed to detect nodules that are buried under a thin layer of sediment.

Hydrothermal vent systems are generally not detectable with multi-beam echo sounders from the sea surface. However, strategies to explore for hydrothermal activity include searching for physical and chemical anomalies in the water column. Hydrothermal fluids are produced when seawater circulates within the oceanic crust, under the influence of a heat source. When the heated fluids rise from the seabed and mix with the cold seawater, a hydrothermal plume enriched in mineral particles and other elements is formed. Such plumes can rise several hundreds of meters above the seafloor and then spread laterally for several tens of kilometres, under the influence of ocean currents.

Fouquet and co-workers describe the strategy they used to detect active hydrothermal systems, using physical and chemical tracers.[8] During the first phase of exploration, water samples were taken with a CTD-Rosette, which also measured Conductivity, Temperature and Depth. The samples were then analysed on board the research vessel for methane and manganese concentrations. The multi-beam echo sounding system used at the same time can also detect physical anomalies in the water column associated with the rising plume. The second phase required the deployment of an AUV equipped with a multi-beam echo sounder and operating 70 m above the seafloor. This can map the seafloor at a resolution of 1 m and detect acoustic backscatter anomalies related to the rising hydrothermal plumes in the water column. Finally, the AUV was equipped with a magnetometer to measure the variations in the magnetic field caused by some mineral occurrences, including iron oxides and sulphides. One of the challenges is that the AUV data can only be retrieved, processed and analysed once the AUV has returned to the surface vessel.

In a final phase, a manned submersible was deployed to sample and study the hydrothermal fluids, the different types of mineralisation and associated ecosystems. This phase is now commonly performed using cameras and instruments fitted on a ROV.

This three-step approach provides a particularly efficient means to locate active vent systems. However, it is a very costly and labour-intensive process. In addition, there is a growing opinion that mining of hydrothermal deposits should only exploit inactive systems, as active vent systems are biodiversity hotspots that should be preserved.[9] Locating inactive systems is a challenge because

7 J. Parianos, L. Lipton and M. Nimmo, 'Aspects of estimation and reporting of mineral resources of seabed polymetallic nodules: A contemporaneous case study', *Minerals* 11, 2021, 200.

8 Y. Fouquet et al., 'Multi scales exploration strategy – example of research for hydrothermal mineralization in the French EEZ of Wallis and Futuna', *Offshore Technology Conference*, Houston, Texas, USA, 4–7 May 2015, OTC-25933-MS. Available online <https://doi.org/10.4043/25933-MS> (accessed 13 May 2021).

9 C.L. Van Dover et al., 'Scientific rationale and international obligations for protection of active hydrothermal vent ecosystems from deep-sea mining', *Marine Policy* 90, 2018, 20–28; C.L. Van Dover et al., 'Research is needed to

they are not associated with anomalies in the water column and are likely covered by sediments. Recent advances are the use of electric self-potential (SP) and controlled source electromagnetic (CSEM) surveys with AUV-fitted and/or AUV-towed instrumentation to locate anomalies related to hydrothermal sulphides.[10] These methods are being applied to locate sulphide deposits within sedimentary layers.[11] In order to obtain an accurate indication of the three-dimensional structure of a sulphide deposit, it is necessary to combine several methods, including bathymetric, electric and electromagnetic mapping, magnetics and gravity, seismic reflection methods, as well as drilling.

Unlike for active hydrothermal vents, there is no chemical signature in the water column, associated with ferromanganese crusts, although it seems that mineral growth is faster under low oxygen conditions. However, crusts form on hard substrates in low sedimentation areas. Therefore, volcanic edifices like seamounts and large igneous provinces relatively far away from continents and/or in environments swept by strong deep currents are good candidates for having extensive crusts. Many of these features can be detected using global bathymetric maps, based on characteristics of seamount geomorphology, depth, size and slope (e.g., Figure I.1.1d). Further investigations are then needed using research vessels to investigate crust thickness and composition. Recently, it was demonstrated that the use of a multi-beam echo sounder data combined with photos taken by a deep towed camera allows for the mapping of the spatial distribution of crusts on the summits and flanks of seamounts in the Western Pacific (Figure I.1.1d).[12] In particular, the use of acoustic backscatter and sea-bottom profiling seems promising in detecting ferromanganese crust occurrences.

Challenges in resource estimation

After discovery, a deep-sea mineral deposit will be subject to further studies to establish an estimate of its possible size. In order to have such an estimate officially recognised, it has to be reported in accordance with internationally accepted reporting standards. For this purpose, the ISA has adopted a reporting standard based on the standard of the Committee for Mineral Reserves International Reporting Standards (CRIRSCO).[13] According to this standard, a deposit may be defined as a 'mineral resource', i.e., a concentration or occurrence of solid material of economic interest in or on the Earth's crust in such form, grade or quality and quantity that there are reasonable prospects for eventual economic extraction.

Furthermore, the standard states that mineral resources are subdivided, in order of increasing geological confidence, into 'inferred', 'indicated' and 'measured' categories.

Hence, the ISA standard requires that the classification and reporting of a mineral deposit is to be based on the geological data available and associated scientific and technical studies (Figure I.1.2).

inform environmental management of hydrothermally inactive and extinct polymetallic sulfide (PMS) deposits', *Marine Policy* 121, 2020, 104183.

10 Y. Kawada and T. Kasaya, 'Marine self-potential survey for exploring seafloor hydrothermal ore deposits', *Scientific Reports* 17, 2017, 13552; S. Constable, P. Kowalczyk and S. Bloomer, 'Measuring marine self-potential using an autonomous underwater vehicle', *Geophysical Journal International* 215, 2018, 49–60; R. Gehrmann et al., 'Marine mineral exploration with controlled source electromagnetics at the TAG hydrothermal field, 26°N Mid-Atlantic Ridge', *Geophysical Research Letters* 46, 2019, 5808–16.

11 Z. Zhu et al., 'Self-potential tomography of a deep-sea polymetallic sulfide deposit on Southwest Indian Ridge', *Journal of Geophysical Research: Solid Earth* 125, 2020, e2020JB019738.

12 J. Jongmin et al., 'Seabed mapping using shipboard multibeam acoustic data for assessing the spatial distribution of ferromanganese crusts on seamounts in the Western Pacific', *Minerals* 10, 2020, 10, 155.

13 International Seabed Authority, Legal and Technical Commission, 4 August 2015, ISBA/21/LTC/15, Annex V.

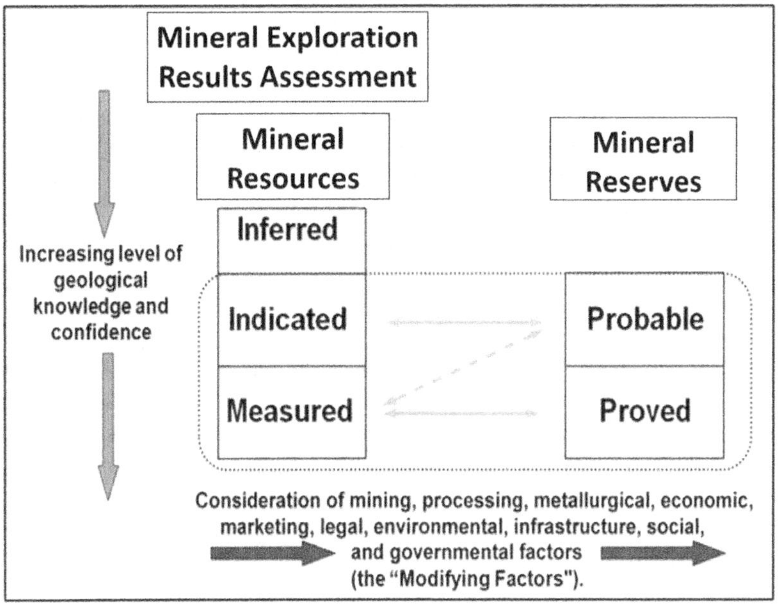

Figure I.1.2 Classification of mineral resources based on the general relationship between mineral exploration results assessment, mineral resources and mineral reserves. ISBA/21/LTC/15, Annex V, op. cit.

The scientific challenges involved here are the tasks of acquiring the necessary data, and processing and analysing the data systematically with the aim to establish a resource estimate that meets the standard. For all three types of deposits, the main parameters for a resource estimate are the area of the deposit, the volume, and data for characterisation of the ore (e.g., geological continuity, mineralogy, density, metal grades). In general, this information will have to be acquired by sampling, and by visual inspection of the deposit supplemented by bathymetric and geophysical data.

Nodule deposits form as blankets of nodules on the seafloor. Thus, calculating the quantity of nodules in the deposit is basically a two-dimensional problem; the area of a deposit is measured in square kilometres while the thickness is measured in centimetres (i.e., the diameter of the nodules). Estimating the resources in such a deposit requires knowledge of the total area, and reliable averages for spatial abundance (kg/m^2) and composition of the nodules. The spatial abundance of nodules may be established by box core sampling – which in number and distribution would give a representative average for the deposit as a whole – and visual inspection (from photo and video). However, a more practical and reliable multivariate statistical method for modelling nodule abundance based on conventional parameters of systematic areal coverage (including bathymetry, backscatter and oceanographic data) has recently been developed.[14] Establishing the average weight and composition would require a set of samples (e.g., by box corer).

Crust deposits form as thin blankets on bare rock surfaces on the seafloor. Like nodules, the area of a crust deposit is measured in square kilometres (km^2) while the thickness is measured in

14 T. Kuhn and C. Rühlemann, 'Exploration of polymetallic nodules and resource assessment: A case study from the German contract area in the Clarion-Clipperton Zone of the tropical northeast Pacific', *Minerals* 11, 2021, 618.

centimetres. The thickness varies to such a degree that it must be taken into account in calculating the resources of a crust deposit, thus making it a three-dimensional problem. Commonly recorded crust thicknesses are between 5 and 10 cm, in some cases up to 20–25 cm. The area of a crust deposit may be established by visual inspection (video) supplemented by high-resolution bathymetry, backscatter and sub-bottom profiler data. A representative set of samples for mineral characterisation may be acquired by drilling or cutting. However, the major problem is the lack of technology for efficiently producing representative thickness maps of the crusts. Currently, crust thickness is determined by drilling or cutting, methods that are not suitable for covering a large area. There is a need for technology that can measure the thickness from sensors moving above the crust surface, e.g., an adaption of seismic technology.

The sulphide deposits are formed by hydrothermal vent activity in the seafloor. Typically, they cover an area of 0.1–0.5 km^2, which may be established by high resolution bathymetry and side-scan data supplemented by visual inspection. Calculating the resources of these deposits is a three-dimensional problem, in which establishing the thickness (depth of mineralisation) is the major difficulty. Determining the thickness and ore characteristics of a deposit requires core drilling. Unfortunately, such core drilling has proven exceedingly difficult, probably because of the extensive brecciation of the subsurface host rock. The development of an efficient and low-cost core drilling technology is needed for 3-D modelling and resource estimation of these deposits.

Technical challenges in deep sea mining

Beyond the scientific and technical challenges of finding deep-sea minerals and assessing their resource potential, significant challenges are related to the operation of a deep-sea mine. Commercial deep-sea mining activities do not yet exist, but several pilot projects have been undertaken in the past, or are developing. Technological challenges are significant and relate to the operation at great depths in a 'hostile' environment. Taking the example of offshore oil and gas exploitation, it would seem that technical solutions will be found over time. However, these solutions will need to be cost-effective, and at the same time reduce as much as possible the impact on the environment, not only during routine operations but also in case of accidents.[15] Here, we briefly describe some of the technical challenges faced in relation to the exploitation of the three main mineral resource types.

During deep-sea mining, part of the operations will take place at the seafloor and another part at the sea surface. Conceptually, a deep-sea mine will have at least the following four components:

1. One or several engines that are capable to extract the minerals at the seafloor;
2. A lifting system that can bring (part of) the extracted materials to the sea surface, potentially several kilometres above;
3. A surface vessel to coordinate all operations and (pre-)treat the recovered materials; and
4. A system that will allow for the disposal of residual waste material on or near the seafloor.

Given the different mineral resources described before, the method of extraction will not be the same for each type, although engines for the extraction of hydrothermal sulphides could likely be similar to those needed to mine ferromanganese crusts. In all cases, heavy work-class ROVs are

15 L. Cuyvers et al., *Deep seabed mining: A rising environmental challenge*, Gland, Switzerland: IUCN and Gallifrey Foundation, 2020, p. 74.

operated from the surface platform. The technologies exist, but routinely operating them at great depths in a commercially and environmentally viable way is a significant challenge. For example, during a recent demonstration project by Global Sea Mineral Resources (GSR), a subsea polymetallic nodule collector prototype ('Patania II', a quarter-scale collector), suffered a cable problem resulting in a loss of contact with the engine, causing significant delays and requiring delicate recovery operations.

The 'Patania II' engine is a 12 × 4 × 5 m collection machine, which sucks in the nodules from the surrounding seabed. The collected nodules are then moved from the collection site to the edge of the site in preparation for a future step, which is transporting them to the sea surface by a riser device.[16] Scientists from 29 European institutions participate in a European research project 'MiningImpact' within the framework of the Joint Programming Initiative 'Oceans' to monitor independently these operations.[17]

Mining of manganese crusts and hydrothermal sulphides will require either drilling or crushing of hard rocks. This involves remote operation of multiple machines at the same time, extracting/grinding and tailing piles. This technology is significantly more complex than that used for mining of nodules. This may cause significant impact on the environment by creating plumes of fine-grained material that can potentially be dispersed over large areas. During the tests of the Solwara 1 project, Nautilus Minerals found it unworkable to provide hoods over the collectors to limit the spread of plumes, but this would seem an essential requirement to reduce environmental impact. However, other technical solutions for excavating that would avoid plumes are already proposed to be employed in the future, e.g., technologies involving vertical trench cutters.[18]

In 2017 and 2020, the Japan Oil, Gas and Metals National Corporation (JOGMEC) carried out the world's first pilot tests of excavating and ore lifting for seafloor polymetallic sulphides and manganese crusts, respectively. In the 2017 test, it was reported that there were issues with their riser pumps when testing their retrieval system, because friction of the grit wore out the seals very quickly. Technological challenges for the riser systems are indeed numerous, such as withstanding considerable differences in pressure and temperature in the water column, as well as coping with severe weather conditions many hundreds of kilometres offshore. Noise generated by the riser system can be a potential problem, in particular as the system traverses the depth of the SOFAR channel, a horizontal water layer in which low frequency sound travels for thousands of kilometres before dissipating. Technological innovations will be needed to restrict this noise and its environmental impact.

The next step is the processing of the mined materials on board the surface vessel, which involves drying, separating out the interesting minerals with mechanical and/or chemical methods and the subsequent disposal of waste. This step involves adaptation of land-based technologies to operation on a production support vessel. Significant space limitations are amongst the main challenges, taking into account environmental, safety and economic factors.

This leads to the last component of the mining system, the safe and environmentally acceptable disposal of residual waste. Waste remaining from the on-board processes is not only water but also

16 Anonymous, 19 April 2021. Available online <https://www.bairdmaritime.com/work-boat-world/offshore-world/column-deme-starts-subsea-mining-test-in-pacific-ocean-china-watches-closely-offshore-accounts/> (accessed 25 February 2022).

17 M. Haeckel (coord.), 'MiningImpact2', 2022. Available online <http://jpi-oceans.eu/miningimpact-2> (accessed 16 February 2022).

18 G. Spagnoli et al., 'Preliminary design of a trench cutter system for deep-sea mining applications under hyperbaric conditions', *IEEE Journal of Oceanographic Engineering* 41(4), 2016, 930–43.

contains fine particles and potentially toxic components. It is unlikely that all the residual waste can be safely deposited back to the seafloor, so storage capacity needs to be reserved on the vessel, and further on-land processing techniques developed to deal with this.[19] Part of the residual waste will be released on or near the seafloor, in an area restricted to the mining site. Technological challenges include dealing with the potential interference of this process with ongoing mining operations, limiting the plumes caused by waste dispersal, and environmental monitoring of the fate of the waste material over time. A portion of the waste may need to be treated and disposed of on land.

Environmental challenges

Previous sections have outlined the different physical conditions and geological settings in which each of the deep-sea mineral resources occur. These translate through to highly variable and differing biological communities associated with the resource types.

Biological communities of mineral resources

Manganese nodules fauna

Much of the biodiversity on the abyssal plains is composed of small animals living in the upper layers of the seafloor sediment (e.g., nematode and polychaete worms). Small single-celled foraminiferans dominate the nodules themselves, and large epifauna are diverse but not abundant.

There are several characteristics specific to nodule habitats that are important for evaluating potential impacts:[20] (a) Abyssal plains are physically stable relative to the more dynamic ridge and seamount environments, and their fauna are naturally poorly adapted to cope with disturbance; (b) Fauna differ between the nodules and soft sediment,[21] which is important for spatial management. Diversity can be high, but large numbers of rare species are thought to occur; and (c) Recolonisation rates of fauna appear low, and recovery from impacts is slow, taking at least several decades.[22]

Polymetallic sulphide fauna

The composition of faunal communities depends on whether the site is hydrothermally venting or inactive. Chemosynthetic species (e.g., tubeworms, mussels, barnacles, shrimps, and gastropods) dominate where venting occurs, whereas the benthic fauna associated with inactive deposit areas comprise typical fauna of hard substrates, such as corals, sponges, urchins and feather stars.

Particular biological characteristics relevant for this environment include (a) Many species may be endemic to the vent environment and its particular characteristics (depth, temperature, chemical composition). These species can be localised and hence vulnerable to small-scale mining activi-

19 W. Ma, D. Schott and G. Lodewijks, ‘A new procedure for deep sea mining tailings disposal’, *Minerals* 7, 2017, 47.

20 M.R. Clark and S. Smith, ‘Environmental management considerations’, in E. Baker and Y. Beaudoin (eds), *Deep sea minerals. Manganese nodules: A physical, biological, environmental, and technical review*, Secretariat of the Pacific Community, Norway, 2013, pp. 27–42.

21 E. Simon-Lledo et al., ‘Ecology of a polymetallic nodule occurrence gradient: Implications for deep-sea mining’, *Limnology and Oceanography* 64(5), 2019, 1883–94; T. Stratmann et al., ‘Polymetallic nodules are essential for food-web integrity of a prospective deep-seabed mining area in Pacific abyssal plains’, *Scientific Reports* 11, 2021, 12238.

22 D.O.B. Jones et al., ‘Biological responses to disturbance from simulated deep-sea polymetallic nodule mining’, *PLoS ONE* 12(2), 2017, e0171750.

ties; (b) Dispersal and colonisation potential of vent species is poorly known, but distance to other vent communities is important because of varying scales of dispersal and recolonisation;[23] and (c) The fauna of inactive or peripheral sites are often slow-growing and long-lived and recovery may take decades to centuries.[24]

Cobalt-rich crust fauna

Crusts on seamounts can host high densities of sessile benthic fauna such as corals and sponges, and a variety of crustacean, seastar and urchin species.

The following particular characteristics may affect potential impacts: (a) Seamounts may have varying levels of endemic species with localised distributions;[25] (b) The dominant benthic fauna on seamounts may include species with slow growth rates and high longevity making recovery very slow;[26] (c) It is uncertain whether cobalt-rich crust hosts different fauna from non-cobalt-rich crust.[27] This affects how spatial protection measures might be structured; and (d) Seamount ecosystems include significant interactions with pelagic communities,[28] and impacts throughout the water column must be considered.

Phosphorite nodules fauna

Faunal communities associated with such nodules are variable, but of particular note are sessile stony corals and sponges which can be common on the hard substrate the nodules provide. These share similar vulnerability to physical disturbance and clogging and burial effects from sediment plumes as for the previous resource fauna. Phosphorite particles can extend well into the sediment, and hence infauna (i.e., fauna living in the sediments below the seabed, such as nematodes, polychaetes) are also important to consider.

Environmental impacts of deep-sea mining

A number of impacts will affect all potential mining areas, irrespective of their resource and general type of faunal composition. There is a considerable literature on potential environmental impacts,[29] which highlight a number of key impacts:

23 A. Metaxas, 'Spatial patterns of larval abundance at hydrothermal vents on seamounts: Evidence for recruitment limitation', *Marine Ecology Progress Series* 437, 2011, 103–17; L.S. Mullineaux et al., 'Exploring the ecology of deep-sea hydrothermal vents in a metacommunity framework', *Frontiers in Marine Science* 5, 2018.

24 M.R. Clark et al., 'The impacts of deep-sea fisheries on benthic communities: A review', *ICES Journal of Marine Science* 73, 2016, supplement 1, i51–i69; S. Gollner et al., 'Resilience of benthic deep-sea fauna to mining activities', *Marine Environmental Research* 129, 2017, 76–101.

25 A.A. Rowden et al., 'Paradigms in seamount ecology: Fact, fiction and future', *Marine Ecology* 31, 2010, 226–41.

26 M.R. Clark et al., 'Little evidence of benthic community resilience to bottom trawling on seamounts after 15 years', *Frontiers in Marine Science* 6, 2019, 63; A.R. Baco, E.B. Roark and N.B. Morgan, 'Amid fields of rubble, scars, and lost gear, signs of recovery observed on seamounts on 30- to 40-year time scales', *Science Advances* 5(8), 2019.

27 T.A. Schlacher et al., 'Seamount benthos in a cobalt-rich crust region of the central Pacific: Conservation challenges for future seabed mining', *Diversity and Distributions* 20, 2014, 491–502; N.B. Morgan et al., 'Benthic megafaunal community structure of cobalt-rich manganese crusts on Necker Ridge', *Deep-Sea Research Part I: Oceanographic Research Papers* 104, 2014, 92–105.

28 J.C. Drazen et al., 'Report of the workshop: Evaluating the nature of midwater mining plumes and their potential effects on midwater ecosystems', *Research Ideas and Outcomes* 5, 2019, e33527.

29 Gollner et al., op. cit.; K.A. Miller et al., 'An overview of seabed mining including the current state of development, environmental impacts, and knowledge gaps', *Frontiers in Marine Science* 4, 2018, 418; P.P.E. Weaver

- *Surface* effects include vessel activities and potential pollution and collisions; changes in primary production through shading or nutrient levels in surface discharges; and effects on behaviour of surface marine mammals, fish and birds through water composition or clarity and lighting/noise from vessel activity.
- *Water column* impacts comprise sediment plumes through the water column from riser pipe leaks or post-processing discharge, changing oxygen levels, nutrient and trace metal levels, water temperature and chemistry; effects on deep-diving marine mammals and fish behaviour, from the plume and noise; toxic effects and bioaccumulation through the food chain to higher predators; and plankton/mesopelagic fish mortality and behavioural avoidance of contaminants.
- *Seafloor* impacts include benthic organism mortality from direct physical impact of mining gear; smothering/burying of animals by deposited or resuspended sediment; clogging of animals' feeding structures by suspended sediment; change in seafloor sediment characteristics (important for burrowing animals); toxic effects with metal and contaminant release through the food chain; and effects from light and noise generated by the mining machines.

An understanding of these impacts, and their effects on the structure and function of ecosystems, is a critical determinant of the environmental knowledge that is required to support robust environmental assessment and management. This starts with understanding natural variability through collection of extensive baseline data, and then adding the predicted impacts from deep-seabed mining to evaluate future changes. Subsequently it requires implementing monitoring programmes to ensure that environmental sustainability is not compromised whenever/however deep-seabed mining may develop.

Key environmental challenges

This wide range of environmental impacts needs to be confronted in the development of scientific research that will support environmental risk assessments, impact assessments and management and monitoring plans required prior to exploitation.[30] There is a large number of scientific gaps[31] that could be considered here, but in this section we focus on elements of three key groups of scientific challenges that we believe are among the most essential to resolve to ensure sustainability of the environment and ecosystems:

1) Limited scientific data and knowledge
2) The need for an ecosystem approach
3) Dealing with uncertainty

and D. Billett, 'Environmental impacts of nodule, crust and sulphide mining: An overview', in R. Sharma (ed.), *Environmental issues of deep-sea mining: Impacts, consequences and policy perspectives*, Springer, Switzerland, 2019, pp. 27–62; D.O.B. Jones, D.J. Amon and A.S.A. Chapman, 'Deep-sea mining: Processes and impacts', in M.C. Baker et al. (eds), *Natural capital and exploitation of the deep ocean*, Oxford University Press, Oxford, UK, 2020, pp. 91–110.

30 ISA, *Draft regulations on exploitation of mineral resources in the Area*, 2019, ISBA/25/C/WP.1.

31 D.J. Amon et al., 'Assessment of scientific gaps related to the effective environmental management of deep-seabed mining', *Marine Policy* 138, 2022.

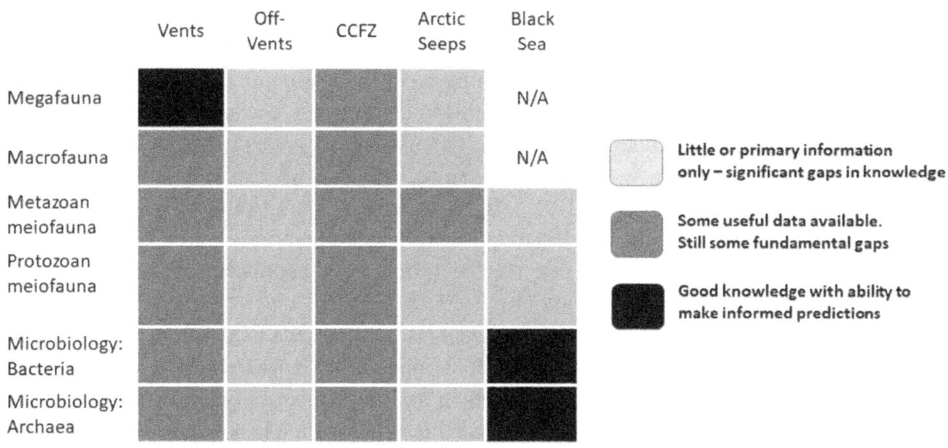

Figure I.1.3 Assessment of biogeographic knowledge in selected deep-sea habitats (modified from Paterson et al., op. cit.).

While we expand on each of these below, within the scope of this book, we do not intend nor are we able to be exhaustive. Bibliographic references point the reader to an extensive literature associated with a wide range of environmental issues.

Limited scientific data and knowledge

Exploration efforts to collect baseline environmental data for areas of interest for deep-sea mining have greatly increased scientific knowledge. However, even in what are arguably the best studied areas related to deep-sea mineral resources, hydrothermal vent sites for polymetallic sulphides and the Clarion-Clipperton Zone in the central-eastern Pacific Ocean for polymetallic nodules, current baseline knowledge remains incomplete (Figure I.1.3).[32]

The elements of environmental baseline data are specified in detail in recommendations from the International Seabed Authority[33] covering a range of scientific aspects across physical, oceanographic and biological disciplines. Efforts have also been made in the scientific literature to improve the quality of baseline data, and especially the consistency and standardisation of data sampling, processing, analysis, storage and presentation,[34] although this is still 'work in progress'.[35] These data needs also intersect other marine uses, as well as societal and cultural issues.[36]

32 G.L.J. Paterson et al., 'Biogeography and connectivity in deep seabed habitats with mineral resource potential-gap analysis', *MIDAS deliverable 4.2*, 2014; A.D. Thaler and D. Amon, '262 voyages beneath the sea: A global assessment of macro- and megafaunal biodiversity and research effort at deep-sea hydrothermal vents', *PeerJ* 7, 2019, e7397.

33 ISBA/25/C/WP.1, op. cit.; ISA, *Recommendations for the guidance of contractors for the assessment of the possible environmental impacts arising from exploration for marine minerals in the Area*, 2013, ISBA/19/LTC/8.

34 M.R. Clark, M. Consalvey and A.A. Rowden (eds), *Biological sampling in the deep sea*, Wiley Blackwell, Oxford, UK, 2016; L.C. Woodall et al., 'A multidisciplinary approach for generating globally consistent data on mesophotic, deep-pelagic, and bathyal biological communities', *Oceanography* 31, 2018, 76–89; A.G. Glover et al., 'An end-to-end DNA taxonomy methodology for benthic biodiversity survey in the Clarion-Clipperton Zone, central Pacific abyss', *Journal of Marine Science and Engineering* 4, 2017, 34.

35 K.L. Howell et al., 'A blueprint for an inclusive, global deep-sea Ocean Decade field programme', *Frontiers in Marine Science* 7, 2020, 584861.

36 Clark and Smith, op. cit.

There are recognised gaps in major aspects such as biodiversity knowledge,[37] the role of species,[38] species connectivity,[39] ecological characteristics/traits[40] and ecological services.[41] For many habitats, science is still at the stage of describing ecosystem structure rather than understanding function,[42] and unable to estimate ecological thresholds for use in decision-making.[43]

There are also major gaps in understanding the specific nature and extent of potential mining impacts.[44] The deep sea is an open system, and while direct physical impacts can be well predicted, secondary effects involving the dispersal of sediment and/or contaminants are poorly known.[45] Exploration, by definition, does not involve major disturbance operations, and until larger-scale component-testing or test-mining takes place there will be limited confidence in models and predictions of these wider, and potentially cumulative, effects.

This 'double-whammy' of limited basic ecological information and incomplete understanding of the effects of seabed mining means it is difficult at present for environmental science to quantify what level of impact constitutes a 'harmful effect' or 'serious harm' under either the United Nations Convention on the Law of the Sea or national legislation, and hence develop meaningful thresholds of impact.[46] Deep-seabed mining will, by definition, cause some environmental damage, and sufficient data are needed to predict the nature and extent of these impacts, and the spatial scale over which they will occur. This enables an evaluation of whether a mining operation is likely to affect ecological structure and function, and whether those effects will operate at species, community or ecosystem level.

It is unrealistic in the deep sea to expect detailed knowledge of biodiversity and all the ecological factors one might wish to understand in an ideal world. There are good reasons for trying to collect as much data as possible at a species level, to try and determine true species richness and whether rare species are localised and vulnerable, or widespread but in low densities. The importance of this varies between habitat types. It is well recognised with hydrothermal vents,[47] but the amount of research effort and sampling to do this can be huge, as evidenced with nodule fauna in the CCZ.[48] Hence, it is critical that sampling and data collection are based on an early and robust

37 C.R. Smith et al., 'Deep-sea misconceptions cause underestimation of seabed-mining impacts', *Trends in Ecology & Evolution* 35(10), 2020, 853–57.

38 A.S.A. Chapman, V. Tunnicliffe and A.E. Bates, 'Both rare and common species make unique contributions to functional diversity in an ecosystem unaffected by human activities', *Diversity and Distributions* 24(5), 2018, 568–78.

39 Mullineaux et al., op. cit.

40 R.E. Boschen-Rose et al., 'Assessing the ecological risk to deep-sea megafaunal assemblages from seafloor massive sulphide mining using a functional traits sensitivity approach', *Ocean & Coastal Management* 210, 2021, 105656.

41 K.J. Thornborough et al., 'Towards an ecosystem approach to environmental impact assessment for deep-sea mining', in R. Sharma (ed.), *Environmental issues of deep-sea mining: Impacts, consequences and policy perspectives*, Springer, Switzerland, 2019, pp. 63–94.

42 M.R. Clark et al., 'Science priorities for seamounts: Research links to conservation and management', *PLoS ONE 7(1)*, 2012; Smith et al., 2020, op. cit.

43 L.A. Levin et al., 'Defining "serious harm" to the marine environment in the context of deep-seabed mining', *Marine Policy* 74, 2016, 245–59.

44 Ibid.; Weaver and Billett, op. cit.

45 C. Hauton et al., 'Identifying toxic impacts of metals potentially released during deep-sea mining—a synthesis of the challenges to quantifying risk', *Frontiers in Marine Science* 4, 2017, 368; J. Spearman et al., 'Measurement and modelling of deep sea sediment plumes and implications for deep sea mining', *Scientific Reports* 10(1), 2020.

46 Levin et al., op. cit.

47 Van Dover et al., 2018, op. cit.

48 C.R. Smith et al., 'Editorial: Biodiversity, connectivity and ecosystem function across the Clarion-Clipperton Zone: A regional synthesis for an area targeted for nodule mining', *Frontiers in Marine Science* 8, 2021, 5–7.

environmental risk assessment, to highlight areas of greatest risk from certain activities on environmental components. Data collection can then be focussed more on these priority interactions or aspects of greatest uncertainty to ensure relevant and targeted information is maximised to support the environmental impacts assessment process.[49]

Recovery dynamics also needs to be considered if restoration was to become a management objective. Most studies on recovery from natural or anthropogenic disturbance in the deep sea suggest it is variable between faunal types, but in general very slow relative to inshore/shallow waters. The feasibility and cost of restoration is questionable,[50] but a combination of mitigation and restoration measures could be considered.[51] For more information on this topic see also the MERCES website.[52]

The need for an ecosystem approach

Differences between the environments associated with each resource mean 'one size fits all' does not apply to the science required. Despite issues associated with limited scientific data, this highlights the need to adopt an ecosystem approach that is tailored for the particular mineral habitat and its environmental setting. While contractors collect large amounts of data on various components of the ecosystem throughout the exploration process, there is a critical need to focus on the key components and relationships that may drive the system, and/or are at risk from mining operations.

Knowledge of species-level biodiversity is important to inventory baseline communities, recognise rare species and endemic species, and evaluate risk of localised extinctions.[53] However, arguably more important is ensuring that general elements of ecosystem structure and function are not disrupted. The starting point for many ecosystem structure approaches are complex food web diagrams[54] to show linkages between the main functional groups in the system, and this can enable more holistic thinking that moves on from not knowing all the species that comprise those groups. Equally important is the need to consider the ecosystem services that are provided and contribute to human well-being: supporting, regulating, provisioning and cultural.[55] In developing an ecosystem approach, the linkages between faunal components (ecosystem structure) and the supporting services (ecosystem functions) are the starting point, as they then lead into the assessment of provisioning, regulating and cultural services (Figure I.1.4). This higher-level perspective can help focus baseline assessments and environmental impact assessments, selecting appropriate indicators for monitoring programmes, and inform proposed mitigation measures.

49 M.R. Clark, J.M. Durden and S. Christiansen, 'Environmental impact assessments for deep-sea mining: can we improve their future effectiveness?', *Marine Policy* 114, 2020, 103363.

50 C.L. Van Dover et al., 'Ecological restoration in the deep sea: Desiderata', *Marine Policy* 44, 2014, 98–106.

51 D. Cuvelier et al., 'Potential mitigation and restoration actions in ecosystems impacted by seabed mining', *Frontiers in Marine Science* 5, 2018, 467; D. Billett, D.O.B. Jones and P. Weaver, 'Improving environmental management practices in deep-sea mining', in R. Sharma (ed.), *Environmental issues of deep-sea mining: Impacts, consequences and policy perspectives*, Springer, Switzerland, 2019, pp. 403–46.

52 Marine Ecosystem Restoration in Changing European Seas. Available online <www.merces-project.eu>.

53 H.J. Niner et al., 'Deep-sea mining with no net loss of biodiversity—an impossible aim', *Frontiers in Marine Science* 5, 2018, 53.

54 B.T. Fulton, T. Morato and T.J. Pitcher, 'Modelling seamount ecosystems and their fisheries', in T.J. Pitcher et al. (eds), *Seamounts: Ecology, fisheries & conservation*, Blackwell Publishing, Oxford, UK, 2007, pp. 296–332.

55 J.T. Le, L.A. Levin and R.T. Carson, 'Incorporating ecosystem services into environmental management of deep-seabed mining', *Deep-Sea Research Part II: Topical Studies in Oceanography* 137, 2017, 486–503; Thornborough et al., op. cit.

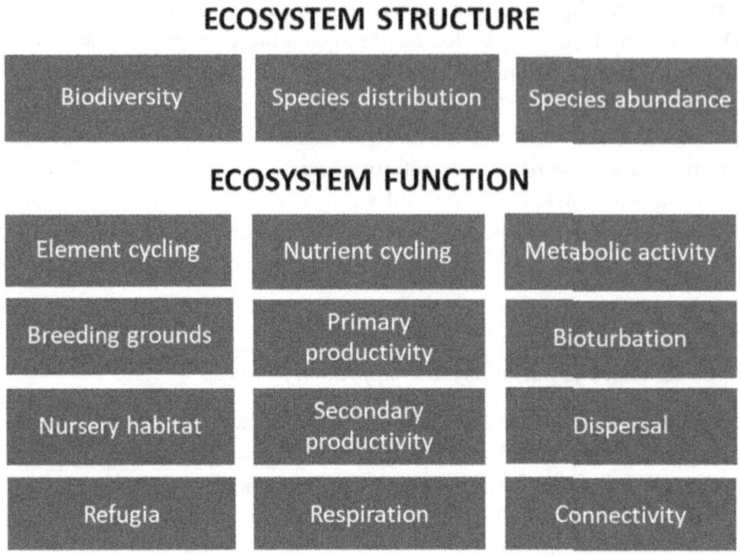

Figure I.1.4 The linkages between ecosystem structure and function (adapted from Le et al., op. cit.).

The ecosystem approach also needs to extend to management, in that environmental and societal objectives and commercial expectations need to be balanced. This can involve a management framework with step-wise but iterative steps of research,[56] incorporate mitigation hierarchy stages[57] and combine operational, spatial and temporal measures[58] that can cover individual mining areas as well as larger-scale regional management. There are many ways to progress an ecosystem approach, and it needs to be evaluated on a case-by-case basis depending on the particular mining situation, and the type and quantity of available information.

Dealing with uncertainty

Even with improved data and ecosystem-level assessments, there will remain considerable scientific uncertainty about the environment and the extent of impact resulting from mining operations. Uncertainty is a key constraint for completing robust environmental impact assessments,[59] which affects how precautionary any development can be.[60] The precautionary approach is an essential

56 J.M. Durden et al., 'A procedural framework for robust environmental management of deep-sea mining projects using a conceptual model', *Marine Policy* 84, 2017, 193–201; J.I. Ellis et al., 'Environmental management frameworks for offshore mining: The New Zealand approach', *Marine Policy* 84, 2017, 178–92; D.O.B. Jones et al., 'Existing environmental management approaches relevant to deep-sea mining', *Marine Policy* 103, 2019, 172–81.

57 Billett et al., op. cit.

58 R. Cormier, 'Ecosystem approach for the management of deep-sea mining activities', in R. Sharma (ed.), *Environmental issues of deep-sea mining: Impacts, consequences and policy perspectives*, Springer, Switzerland, 2019, pp. 381–402.

59 Clark, Durden and Christiansen, op. cit.

60 See in this book analysis related to the precautionary approach and sustainable management of resources, R. Makgill, A. Jaeckel and K. MacMaster, 'Implementing the precautionary approach for seabed mining: A review of state practice', in V. Tassin Campanella (ed.) *Routledge handbook of seabed mining and the law of the sea*, Routledge, London, 2023, Chapter I.3.

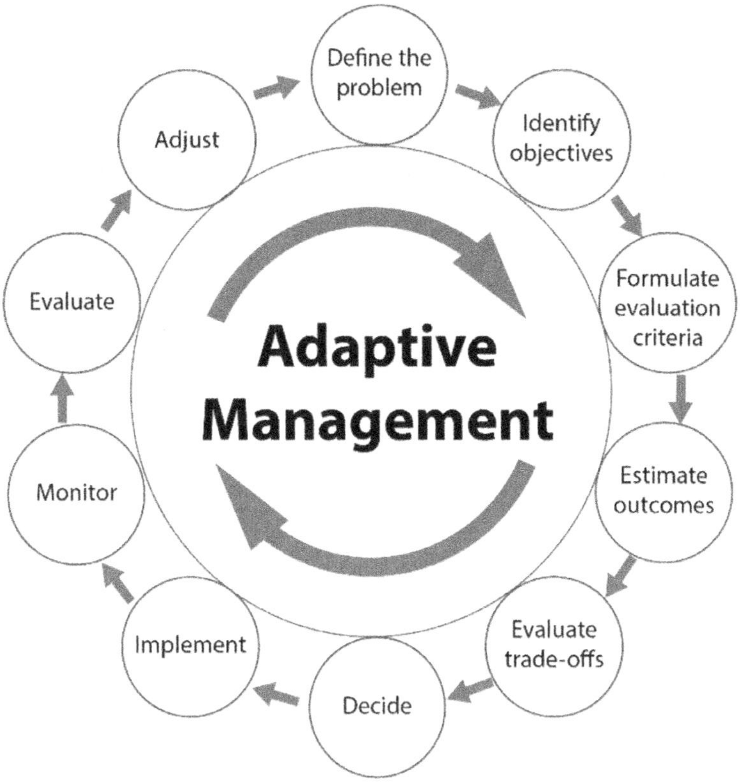

Figure I.1.5 Schematic diagram of the Adaptive Management Process (from M. Clark et al., 'Preparing environmental impact assessments: General guidelines for offshore mining and drilling with particular reference to New Zealand', *NIWA Science and Technology Series* 81, 2017, 106.).

part of any mining development under ISA jurisdiction, which applies also to how uncertainty in science is measured and conveyed. This includes gaps in knowledge, unpredictability of random events, structural uncertainty (e.g., model assumptions), value (where data are inaccurate) and uncertain interpretations. Uncertainty needs to be managed through identifying its sources, reducing it where possible and acknowledging and managing the residuals. This is important for managing scientific risk[61] and ensuring adequate transparency and communication with decision-makers.[62]

Adaptive management (Figure I.1.5) is a promising approach to manage uncertainty about environmental impacts while allowing initial exploitation to proceed.[63] However, it must not be

61 R. Cormier, M. Elliott and J. Rice, 'Putting on a bow-tie to sort out who does what and why in the complex arena of marine policy and management', *Science of the Total Environment* 648, 2019, 293–305.

62 A. Tenney, J. Kvaerner and K.I. Gjerstad, 'Uncertainty in environmental impact assessment predictions: The need for better communication and more transparency', *Impact Assessment and Project Appraisal* 24, 2006, 45–56.

63 ISA, 'Environmental assessment and management for exploitation of minerals in the Area', *ISA Technical Study* 16, 2017, 66; Jones et al., 2019, op. cit.; N. Craik, 'Implementing adaptive management in deep seabed mining: Legal and institutional challenges', *Marine Policy* 114, 2020.

viewed as a 'trial and error' method, but as a structured process that works from a known state and integrates information, learning and management responses to support flexible decision-making.[64] Adaptive management enables operations to be adjusted as scientific data or results accumulate, or stopped if unacceptable harm is likely. The criteria under which adaptive management can be successful need to be carefully evaluated, the significant scientific requirements considered and clear decision-points established.[65] A systematic adaptive management approach proposed for seabed mining[66] combines environmental and social elements through stakeholder engagement in the modelling process that informs each decision step. This participatory method ensures all stakeholder views and opinions can be considered in the development of a plan that is as widely acceptable as possible. It is subject to continual updating as new information is gathered on system responses to the operations. Adaptive management is a challenging, but likely essential, undertaking to manage the levels of uncertainty caused by the absence of comprehensive data on the ecosystem and environmental impacts that could prevent mining from proceeding.

Discussion

This chapter has highlighted numerous challenges to seabed mining. Many are technological, especially those associated with resource estimation and extraction. The environmental challenges are somewhat different, and more about scientific data and methodology. However, all these challenges relate to developing an industry that meets societal expectations and legal obligations for both resource use and environmental sustainability. Hence, there is a clear need for integration of technology and science across stakeholders (e.g., governments, contractors, non-governmental organisations [NGOs], academic institutes, managers) as well as across disciplines (geology, oceanography, biology, engineering, etc.) and between science, management and governance to reduce cumulative uncertainties.[67] So we stress considering the challenges raised here as a package, and not as discrete issues to be tackled independently.

Carver and co-workers[68] highlight that deep-sea mining is an interdisciplinary issue. It is underpinned by a multitude of social, cultural and political dimensions, and the confines of disciplinary norms must therefore be exceeded to facilitate a deeper understanding of both the practices of deep-sea mining and their consequences.[69]

Communication and transparency are additional challenges. The publication record and amount of environmental science associated with deep-sea mining exploration in recent years is very impressive. In most papers there is discussion about what the ISA or national environmental managers should do, and how, to improve management. However, this communication often happens only through the scientific literature. From the outset, science needs to consider better its applica-

64 B.K. Williams, R.C. Szaro and C.D. Shapiro, *Adaptive management: The US Department of the Interior technical guide*, Washington, DC, US Department of the Interior, 2009.

65 M.R. Clark, R. Johnson and J. Hyman, 'Adaptive management as a tool for effective environmental management of deep-sea mining', in R. Sharma (ed.), *Perspectives on deep-sea mining*, Springer, Switzerland, 2022, 339–71.

66 J. Hyman, R.A. Stewart and O. Sahin, 'Adaptive management of deep-seabed mining projects: A systems approach', *Integrated Environmental Assessment and Management*, 2021.

67 A. Kung et al., 'Governing deep sea mining in the face of uncertainty', *Journal of Environmental Management* 279, 2020, 111593.

68 R. Carver et al., 'A critical social perspective on deep sea mining: Lessons from the emergent industry in Japan', *Ocean and Coastal Management* 193, 2020, 105242.

69 Ibid.

tion and uptake, which should not be an after-thought in the concluding paragraph of a paper's discussion section. It also needs to be delivered in a way that is neutral, and can be readily understood by the wide range of stakeholders in the ISA and national Ministries and Departments – scientists, NGOs, policy, management, diplomats, and the public.

Conclusion

Ongoing research efforts will undoubtedly improve knowledge, although the complexity of natural systems and the limited scientific data available imply that we will probably not understand enough to reduce all risks before exploitation might start. Therefore, to reduce such risks as much as possible, scientific efforts must be targeted at the main elements of environmental uncertainty, and shift away from detailed inventory-type descriptions to focus on core elements of ecosystem structure and function. Scientific cooperation must increase between disciplines, and also develop further between industry, scientists and managers to ensure that synergies between research programmes are maximised, and that they are producing the results and information that industry and managers need to balance the demands of exploitation of required resources on the one hand, and sustainability and conservation of the environment on the other.

References

Alfaro L.J.M. et al., 'High environmental stress and productivity increase functional diversity along a deep-sea hydrothermal vent gradient', *Ecology* 101(11), 2020, e03144.

Amon D.J. et al., 'Assessment of scientific gaps related to the effective environmental management of deep-seabed mining', *Marine Policy* 138, 2022, 105006.

Anonymous, 19 April 2021. Available online <https://www.bairdmaritime.com/work-boat-world/off-shore-world/column-deme-starts-subsea-mining-test-in-pacific-ocean-china-watches-closely-offshore-accounts/> (accessed 25 February 2022).

Baco A.R., Roark E.B. and Morgan N.B., 'Amid fields of rubble, scars, and lost gear, signs of recovery observed on seamounts on 30- to 40-year time scales', *Science Advances* 5(8), 2019, eaaw4513.

Billett D., Jones D.O.B. and Weaver P., 'Improving environmental management practices in deep-sea mining', in R. Sharma (ed.), *Environmental issues of deep-sea mining: Impacts, consequences and policy perspectives*, Switzerland: Springer, 2019, 403–446.

Boschen-Rose R.E. et al., 'Assessing the ecological risk to deep-sea megafaunal assemblages from seafloor massive sulphide mining using a functional traits sensitivity approach', *Ocean & Coastal Management* 210, 2021, 105656.

Carver R. et al., 'A critical social perspective on deep sea mining: Lessons from the emergent industry in Japan', *Ocean and Coastal Management* 193, 2020, 105242.

Chapman A.S.A., Tunnicliffe V. and Bates A.E., 'Both rare and common species make unique contributions to functional diversity in an ecosystem unaffected by human activities', *Diversity and Distributions* 24(5), 2018, 568–578.

Clark M.R. et al., 'Science priorities for seamounts: Research links to conservation and management', *PLoS One* 7(1), 2012, e29232.

Clark M.R. et al., 'The impacts of deep-sea fisheries on benthic communities: A review', *ICES Journal of Marine Science* 73, 2016, supplement 1, i51–i69.

Clark M.R. et al., 'Preparing environmental impact assessments: General guidelines for offshore mining and drilling with particular reference to New Zealand', *NIWA Science and Technology Series* 81, 2017, 106.

Clark M.R. et al., 'Little evidence of benthic community resilience to bottom trawling on seamounts after 15 years', *Frontiers in Marine Science* 6, 2019, 63.

Clark M.R. and Smith S., 'Environmental management considerations', in E. Baker and Y. Beaudoin (eds.), *Deep sea minerals. Manganese nodules: A physical, biological, environmental, and technical review*, Secretariat of the Pacific Community, Norway, 2013, 27–42.

Clark M.R., Consalvey M. and Rowden A.A. (eds.) *Biological sampling in the deep sea*, Oxford: Wiley Blackwell, 2016.

Clark M.R., Durden J.M. and Christiansen S., 'Environmental impact assessments for deep-sea mining: Can we improve their future effectiveness?', *Marine Policy* 114, 2020, 103363.

Clark M.R., Johnson R. and Hyman J., 'Adaptive management as a tool for effective environmental management of deep-sea mining', in R. Sharma (ed.), *Perspectives on deep-sea mining*, Switzerland: Springer, 2022, 339–371.

Constable S., Kowalczyk P. and Bloomer S., 'Measuring marine self-potential using an autonomous underwater vehicle', *Geophysical Journal International* 215, 2018, 49–60.

Cormier R., 'Ecosystem approach for the management of deep-sea mining activities', in R. Sharma (ed.), *Environmental issues of deep-sea mining: Impacts, consequences and policy perspectives*, Switzerland: Springer, 2019, 381–402.

Cormier R., Elliott M. and Rice J., 'Putting on a bow-tie to sort out who does what and why in the complex arena of marine policy and management', *Science of The Total Environment* 648, 2019, 293–305.

Craik N., 'Implementing adaptive management in deep seabed mining: Legal and institutional challenges', *Marine Policy* 114, 2020, 103256.

Cuvelier D. et al., 'Potential mitigation and restoration actions in ecosystems impacted by seabed mining', *Frontiers in Marine Science* 5, 2018, 467.

Cuyvers L. et al., *Deep seabed mining: A rising environmental challenge*, Gland: IUCN and Gallifrey Foundation, 2020, p. 74.

Drazen J.C. et al., 'Report of the workshop: Evaluating the nature of midwater mining plumes and their potential effects on midwater ecosystems', *Research Ideas and Outcomes* 5, 2019, e33527.

Durden J.M. et al., 'A procedural framework for robust environmental management of deep-sea mining projects using a conceptual model', *Marine Policy* 84, 2017, 193–201.

Ellis J.I. et al., 'Environmental management frameworks for offshore mining: The New Zealand approach', *Marine Policy* 84, 2017, 178–192.

Fouquet Y. et al., 'Multi scales exploration strategy - Example of research for hydrothermal mineralization in the French EEZ of Wallis and Futuna', *Offshore Technology Conference*, Houston, Texas, USA, 4–7 May 2015, OTC-25933-MS. Available online <https://doi.org/10.4043/25933-MS> (accessed 13 May 2021).

Fulton B.T., Morato T. and Pitcher T.J., 'Modelling seamount ecosystems and their fisheries', in T.J. Pitcher et al. (eds.), *Seamounts: Ecology, fisheries & conservation*, Oxford: Blackwell Publishing, 2007, 296–332.

GEBCO 2014 Grid, December 2014. Available online <https://www.gebco.net/news_and_media/gebco_2014_grid.html> (accessed 15 May 2021).

Gehrmann R. et al., 'Marine mineral exploration with controlled source electromagnetics at the TAG hydrothermal field, 26°N Mid-Atlantic Ridge', *Geophysical Research Letters* 46, 2019, 5808–5816.

Girard F. et al., 'Currents and topography drive assemblage distribution on an active hydrothermal edifice', *Progress in Oceanography* 187, 2020, 102397.

Glover A.G. et al., 'An end-to-end DNA taxonomy methodology for benthic biodiversity survey in the Clarion-Clipperton Zone, central Pacific abyss', *Journal of Marine Science and Engineering* 4, 2017, 34.

Gollner S. et al., 'Resilience of benthic deep-sea fauna to mining activities', *Marine Environmental Research* 129, 2017, 76–101.

Haeckel M. (coord.), 2022, 'MiningImpact2'. Available online <http://jpi-oceans.eu/miningimpact-2> (accessed 16 February 2022).

Hauton C. et al., 'Identifying toxic impacts of metals potentially released during deep-sea mining—A synthesis of the challenges to quantifying risk', *Frontiers in Marine Science* 4, 2017, 368.

Howell K.L. et al., 'A blueprint for an inclusive, global deep-sea ocean decade field programme', *Frontiers in Marine Science* 7, 2020, 584861.

Hyman J., Stewart R.A. and Sahin O., 'Adaptive management of deep-seabed mining projects: A systems approach', *Integrated Environmental Assessment and Management* 18, 2021, 674–681.

International Seabed Authority, March 2008. Available online <https://isa.org.jm/files/files/documents/eng9.pdf> (accessed 1 May 2021).

International Seabed Authority, *Recommendations for the guidance of contractors for the assessment of the possible environmental impacts arising from exploration for marine minerals in the Area*, 2013, ISBA/19/LTC/8.

International Seabed Authority, Legal and Technical Commission, 4 August 2015, ISBA/21/LTC/15, Annex V.

International Seabed Authority, 'Environmental assessment and management for exploitation of minerals in the Area', *ISA Technical Study* 16, 2017, 66.

International Seabed Authority, *Draft regulations on exploitation of mineral resources in the Area*, 2019, ISBA/25/C/WP.1.

Jones D.O.B. et al., 'Biological responses to disturbance from simulated deep-sea polymetallic nodule mining', *PLoS One* 12(2), 2017, e0171750.

Jones D.O.B. et al., 'Existing environmental management approaches relevant to deep-sea mining', *Marine Policy* 103, 2019, 172–181.

Jones D.O.B., Amon D.J. and Chapman A.S.A., 'Deep-sea mining: Processes and impacts', in M.C. Baker et al. (eds.), *Natural capital and exploitation of the deep ocean*, Oxford: Oxford University Press, 2020, 91–110.

Jongmin J. et al., 'Seabed mapping using shipboard multibeam acoustic data for assessing the spatial distribution of ferromanganese crusts on seamounts in the Western Pacific', *Minerals* 10, 2020, 155.

Kawada Y. and Kasaya T., 'Marine self-potential survey for exploring seafloor hydrothermal ore deposits', *Scientific Reports* 17, 2017, 13552.

Kuhn T. and Rühlemann C., 'Exploration of polymetallic nodules and resource assessment: A case study from the German contract area in the clarion-Clipperton zone of the Tropical Northeast Pacific', *Minerals* 11, 2021, 618.

Kung A. et al., 'Governing deep sea mining in the face of uncertainty', *Journal of Environmental Management* 279, 2020, 111593.

Le J.T., Levin L.A. and Carson R.T., 'Incorporating ecosystem services into environmental management of deep-seabed mining', *Deep-Sea Research Part II-Topical Studies in Oceanography* 137, 2017, 486–503.

Levin L.A. et al., 'Defining "serious harm" to the marine environment in the context of deep-seabed mining', *Marine Policy* 74, 2016, 245–259.

Ma W., Schott D. and Lodewijks G., 'A new procedure for deep sea mining tailings disposal', *Minerals* 7, 2017, 47.

Makgill R., Jaeckel A. and MacMaster K., 'Implementing the precautionary approach for seabed mining: A review of state practice', in V. Tassin Campanella (ed.), *Routledge handbook of seabed mining and the law of the sea*, London: Routledge, 2023, chapter I.3.

Marine Ecosystem Restoration in Changing European Seas. Available online <www.merces-project.eu> (accessed July 2022).

Marticorena J. et al., 'Recovery of hydrothermal vent communities in response to an induced disturbance at the Lucky Strike vent field (Mid-Atlantic Ridge)', *Marine Environmental Research* 169, 2021, 105316.

Mayer L. et al., 'The Nippon Foundation—GEBCO Seabed 2030 project: The quest to see the world's oceans completely mapped by 2030', *Geosciences* 8, 2018, 63.

McIntyre A.D. (ed.) *Life in the world's oceans: Diversity, distribution, and abundance*, Oxford: Wiley Blackwell, 2010.

Metaxas A., 'Spatial patterns of larval abundance at hydrothermal vents on seamounts: Evidence for recruitment limitation', *Marine Ecology Progress Series* 437, 2011, 103–117.

Miller K.A. et al., 'An overview of seabed mining including the current state of development, environmental impacts, and knowledge gaps', *Frontiers in Marine Science* 4, 2018, 418.

Morgan N.B. et al., 'Benthic megafaunal community structure of cobalt-rich manganese crusts on Necker Ridge', *Deep-Sea Research Part I-Oceanographic Research Papers* 104, 2014, 92–105.

Mullineaux L.S. et al., 'Exploring the ecology of deep-sea hydrothermal vents in a metacommunity framework', *Frontiers in Marine Science* 5, 2018, 00049.

Niner H.J. et al., 'Deep-sea mining with no net loss of biodiversity-an impossible aim', *Frontiers in Marine Science* 5, 2018, 53.

Parianos J., Lipton I. and Nimmo N., 'Aspects of estimation and reporting of mineral resources of seabed polymetallic nodules: A contemporaneous case study', *Minerals* 11, 2021, 200.

Paterson G.L.J. et al., 'Biogeography and connectivity in deep seabed habitats with mineral resource potential-gap analysis', *MIDAS deliverable 4.2*, 2014, 45 pp.

Ramirez-Llodra E. et al., 'Deep, diverse and definitely different: Unique attributes of the world's largest ecosystem', *Biogeosciences* 7, 2010, 2851–2899.

Rowden A.A. et al., 'Paradigms in seamount ecology: Fact, fiction and future', *Marine Ecology* 31, 2010, 226–241.

Schlacher T.A. et al., 'Seamount benthos in a cobalt-rich crust region of the central Pacific: Conservation challenges for future seabed mining', *Diversity and Distributions* 20, 2014, 491–502.

Sharma R., 'Deep-sea mining: Economic, technical, technological, and environmental considerations for sustainable development', *Marine Technology Society Journal* 45, 2011, 28–41.

Simon-Lledo E. et al., 'Ecology of a polymetallic nodule occurrence gradient: Implications for deep-sea mining', *Limnology and Oceanography* 64(5), 2019, 1883–1894.
Smith C.R. et al., 'Deep-sea misconceptions cause underestimation of seabed-mining impacts', *Trends in Ecology & Evolution* 35(10), 2020, 853–857.
Smith C.R. et al., 'Editorial: Biodiversity, connectivity and ecosystem function across the Clarion-Clipperton zone: A regional synthesis for an area targeted for nodule mining', *Frontiers in Marine Science* 8, 2021, 5–7.
Spagnoli G. et al., 'Preliminary design of a trench cutter system for deep-sea mining applications under hyperbaric conditions', *IEEE Journal of Oceanographic Engineering* 41(4), 2016, 930–943.
Spearman J. et al., 'Measurement and modelling of deep sea sediment plumes and implications for deep sea mining', *Scientific Reports* 10(1), 2020, 5075.
Stratmann T. et al., 'Polymetallic nodules are essential for food-web integrity of a prospective deep-seabed mining area in Pacific abyssal plains', *Scientific Reports* 11, 2021, 12238.
Tenney A., Kvaerner J. and Gjerstad K.I., 'Uncertainty in environmental impact assessment predictions: The need for better communication and more transparency', *Impact Assessment and Project Appraisal* 24, 2006, 45–56.
Thaler A.D. and Amon D., '262 Voyages beneath the Sea: A global assessment of macro- and megafaunal biodiversity and research effort at deep-sea hydrothermal vents', *PeerJ* 7, 2019, e7397.
Thornboroug K.J. et al., 'Towards an ecosystem approach to environmental impact assessment for deep-sea mining', in R. Sharma (ed.), *Environmental issues of deep-sea mining: Impacts, consequences and policy perspectives*, Switzerland: Springer, 2019, 63–94.
Van Dover C.L. et al., 'Ecological restoration in the deep sea: Desiderata', *Marine Policy* 44, 2014, 98–106.
Van Dover C.L. et al., 'Scientific rationale and international obligations for protection of active hydrothermal vent ecosystems from deep-sea mining', *Marine Policy* 90, 2018, 20–28.
Van Dover C.L. et al., 'Research is needed to inform environmental management of hydrothermally inactive and extinct polymetallic sulfide (PMS) deposits', *Marine Policy* 121, 2020, 104183.
Weaver P.P.E. and Billett D., 'Environmental impacts of nodule, crust and sulphide mining: An overview', in R. Sharma (ed.), *Environmental issues of deep-sea mining: Impacts, consequences and policy perspectives*, Springer, 2019, 27–62.
Williams B.K., Szaro R.C. and Shapiro C.D., *Adaptive management: The US department of the interior technical guide*, Washington, DC: US Department of the Interior, 2009.
Woodall L.C. et al., 'A multidisciplinary approach for generating globally consistent data on mesophotic, deep-pelagic, and bathyal biological communities', *Oceanography* 31, 2018, 76–89.
Wölfl A.-C. et al., 'Seafloor mapping – The challenge of a truly global ocean bathymetry', *Frontiers in Marine Science* 6, 2019, 283.
Zhu Z. et al., 'Self-potential tomography of a deep-sea polymetallic sulfide deposit on Southwest Indian Ridge', *Journal of Geophysical Research: Solid Earth* 125, 2020, e2020JB019738.

I.2

THE COMMON HERITAGE OF MANKIND UNDER INTERNATIONAL LAW

An overview

Nilüfer Oral

Introduction

This chapter seeks to provide a broad overview of the common heritage of mankind (CHM) principle in *res communes*. First, by examining the origin of the CHM principle, this chapter reveals how the CHM principle had two competing conceptions. Second, this chapter analyses the CHM principle in the *United Nations Convention on the Law of the Sea* (UNCLOS) regime, with particular focus given to the Area and the marine genetic resources. Third, this chapter proceeds to examine applications of the CHM principle in other contexts, such as outer space, world heritage, and plant genetic resources.

The emergence of the principle of the common heritage of mankind

The regime of the CHM developed in relation to the governance of certain global commons and their resources. In general, global commons are considered to be areas that lie beyond the national jurisdiction and control of any State.[1] They are open spaces that belong to no State, a *res communes* – a common space, where no State can claim or exercise sovereignty or sovereign rights. Examples of *res communes* include the deep seabed, the high seas, the atmosphere, the Moon and outer space, and according to some, Antarctica. However, they are not subject to the same legal regime. While the high seas have been governed by the open access regime of the freedom of the high seas, a new understanding for the governance of the global commons and its resources emerged with the CHM principle. While today the CHM is closely identified with the deep seabed and its mineral resources of Part XI of UNCLOS, the CHM principle was also developed in relation to outer space, and the Moon, as will be explained. The principle of CHM was, however,

1 V. Nanda and G. Pring, *International environmental law and policy for the 21st century*, 2nd edition, Brill, 2013, p. 37; H. Xue, J. Crawford and J. Bell, *Transboundary damage in international law*, Cambridge University Press, 2003, p. 191. According to the authors, there is no agreed definition or understanding on the scope of the concept of 'global commons' other than a collective reference to regions that are beyond national jurisdiction and control.

DOI: 10.4324/9780429426162-4

transformed into a concrete regime for the Area, under Part XI of UNCLOS. It was a radical shift from the open access regime of the high seas.

Key issues concerning the governance of the global commons concern the rules of access and exploitation of the resources found therein. Back in the days of Hugo Grotius, when he wrote his famous treatise *Mare Liberum* (Freedom of the Seas) published in 1609, he based his views on the notion that the high seas were a global common with open and unfettered access for all – a *res communes*. His notion of *res communes* applied both to access to the navigational routes as well as to the resources of the open sea. According to Grotius, the sea was a common property, in that it was common to all with limitless and inexhaustible resources, and thus could not be under the possession of anyone.[2] As eloquently summarized by Schrijver,

> according to Grotius, common property consists of those things which either cannot be reduced to possession or are in infinite supply and thus suffice for the common use of all persons. It appears that for Grotius it is not so much the inexhaustibility of things that is of defining character, but their susceptibility to universal use. Common property cannot be occupied 'either by nature or on grounds of public utility'.[3]

The open access regime of freedom of the high seas is codified in the 1958 Geneva Convention on the High Seas[4] and UNCLOS.[5] The legal regime that governs the high seas as a global commons is not one for the common benefit of all humankind, but is based on the first-come first-served open access notion of freedom of the high seas. It rejects the notion of any State to claim sovereignty over the high seas, thereby creating a vast ocean space without limits on exploitation.

The CHM principle has become closely associated with the famous and historic speech made by Ambassador Arvid Pardo before the United Nations General Assembly (UNGA) in 1967 that initiated the Third United Nations Conference of the Law of the Sea, which in turn led to the adoption of the CHM regime for the Area, marking an entirely new regime for the law of the sea, one diametrically opposed to the Grotian view. His speech centred on the valuable minerals in the deep seabed. By the time of the 1960s, development of modern technology meant that exploitation of these minerals seemed plausible. Additionally, the period of the 1960s was the transitional period from colonial rule to independence for many countries. In this decolonization context, Pardo raised the concern that many newly independent States, which lacked the capacity and resources of the developed world, would be left behind economically, technologically, and socially. It is within this context that he called for the CHM to apply to the deep seabed and its mineral resources.

However, he was not the first to contemplate the notion of a common heritage.[6] The CHM principle had been raised years earlier by José Leon Suarez, a member of the League of Nations Committee of Experts for the Codification of International Law, in 1927.[7] In his report to the Committee entitled '*Rapport sur l'exploitation de la richesse de la mer*', José Leon Suarez detailed

2 V. Prislan and N. Schrijver, 'From mare liberum to the global commons: Building on the grotian heritage', *Grotiana* 30, 2009, 168.

3 Ibid., 172–173.

4 *Convention on the High Seas*, 29 April 1958, 450 UNTS, article 2.

5 *United Nations Convention on the Law of the Sea*, 10 December 1982, 450 *UNTS* 11, article 87 (UNCLOS, article 87).

6 S. Ranganathan, 'Global commons', *European Journal of International Law* 27 (2016) 693–717.

7 Société des Nations, *Questionnaire no. 7: Richesse de la mer: rapport du sous-comité chargé d'étudier la question de procédure par le Rapporteur M. Jose Leon Suarez*, Genève: Société des Nations (1927) 123.

his concerns that natural living resources faced the threat of extinction and the lack of international legal regulations governing natural living resources, particularly for cetaceans and whales. He described the richness of the sea and the immense area of the Antarctic to be the heritage of humanity: '*Les richesses de la mer, en particulier les richesses immenses de la région antarctique, constituent un patrimoine de l'humanité*'.[8]

There is, however, a distinct difference between the underlying concerns of Pardo and Suarez. Pardo was concerned about the economic development of the newly independent States in the period of decolonization. He feared that the developed States with advanced technology would obtain an economic advantage over developing States in the then unexplored and unexploited virgin area of valuable resources. Consequently, the CHM concept is intrinsically linked to the exploitation and sharing of economic benefits. By contrast, Suarez conceived the common heritage as a legal framework for conserving marine life in the high seas, which was lacking an international legal framework and thus threatened with extinction. His view proved remarkably prescient nearly a century later as States embark on negotiation of a new agreement for the conservation and sustainable use of biodiversity in areas beyond national jurisdiction under the UNCLOS.[9]

The United Nations Convention on the Law of the Sea and the common heritage of mankind regime

The common heritage of mankind regime of the Area

The CHM regime was eventually adopted in Part XI of UNCLOS. Part XI of UNCLOS was different from the laissez-faire regime of the high seas because it subjected the global commons of the Area to international rules and an international administration. Per UNCLOS article 1(1), the 'Area' is defined as 'the seabed and ocean floor and subsoil thereof, beyond the limits of national jurisdiction'. The water column above remained unaltered in its legal status. Article 136 established that the Area and its resources are the CHM. This means that the seabed is subject to the CHM whereas the high seas water column is subject to the open access regime of the high seas. These are two very opposite approaches to governance of the global commons.

The core components of the CHM in Part XI include the prohibition against any State claiming or exercising sovereignty or sovereign rights over any part of the Area or its resources, which is parallel to the high seas regime. However, this prohibition goes further and it is here that a stark difference emerges from the open access and exploitation regime of the high seas.[10] There is no private ownership because all rights in the resources of the Area are vested in mankind as a whole[11] and on whose behalf the International Seabed Authority (ISA) acts. Article 137 expressly prohibits the alienation of the resources of the Area, stating that the 'minerals recovered from the Area (...) may only be alienated in accordance with this Part and the rules, regulations and procedures of the Authority' and further that no State, natural or juridical person shall claim, acquire or exercise any rights.[12] All State Parties are *ipso facto* members of the ISA. The ISA is the only mechanism under the UNCLOS where State Parties have a continuous role in the implementation of UNCLOS

8 Ibid., p. 4; T. Scovazzi, 'The seabed beyond the limits of national jurisdiction: General and institutional aspects', in A.G Oude Elferink and E.J. Molenaar (eds), *The international legal regime of areas beyond national jurisdiction*, Brill, 2010, footnote 2.

9 UNGA Resolution 72/249, 24 December 2017.

10 Article 137(1), UNCLOS.

11 Article 137(2), ibid.

12 Ibid.

in relation to Part XI, which is arguably akin to the role of Conference of the Parties under certain multilateral environmental agreements. The ISA is composed of different organs, namely, the Assembly (composed of one representative of each member of the ISA), a Council (composed of 36 elected members of the ISA in accordance with the conditions set forth in article 161), and a Secretariat.

An important principle for the Area is that it shall be open to use exclusively for peaceful purposes by all States and the conduct of marine scientific research is also to be carried out exclusively for peaceful purposes and for the benefit of mankind as a whole.[13]

A defining aspect of the CHM regime under Part XI is that it transferred all management and decision-making authority from individual States to the ISA. Although the ISA remains under the control of State Parties, it acts as a collective body[14] and is to act only on behalf of mankind.[15] It provides for the management component of the CHM principle, transferred from the traditional sovereign State acting in its own interests to that of a collective body acting in the interest of all humanity.

The ISA is also a legal institutionalization of the CHM principle. This is because the State Parties act collectively through the ISA, and it is through the ISA that they organize and control activities in the Area, in particular the administration of the resources in the Area. Part XI further establishes the creation of the Enterprise, which is the organ of the ISA responsible for carrying out the activities in the Area.[16] The CHM regime in the Area includes a benefit-sharing system that is implemented through a mechanism for the sharing of the net proceeds of mining activities undertaken in the Area.[17] However, the issue of the criteria used to distribute the benefits derived from deep seabed mining is another challenge facing the ISA in implementing the CHM principle.

The equitable sharing of the benefits from the exploitation of the natural resources of the Area is core to the CHM regime under Part XI. The net proceeds from mining activities in the Area for mineral resources, as defined under article 133, are to be equitably shared among both coastal and landlocked State Parties, and other economic benefits derived from mining activities are also to be equitably shared.[18] However, in order to meet the concerns of the industrialized States regarding the role of the Enterprise, mandatory technological transfer, the provisions on financial terms, decision-making, and costs to the State Parties, the CHM regime under Part XI was subsequently modified by the Agreement to the Implementation of Part XI adopted in 1994 (the 1994 Agreement).[19] The language of the provisions on revenue sharing and technology transfer between developed and developing States was changed from mandatory to exhortative.[20] Specifically, the 1994 Agreement Annex section 5, paragraph 2 renders the mandatory technology transfer provisions in UNCLOS Annex III article 5 inapplicable. Moreover, annex section 5(1)(b) introduces the requirement that any cooperation to facilitate the acquisition of deep seabed mining technology must be 'consistent with the effective protection of intellectual property rights'. Given that

13 Article 143(1), ibid.
14 Article 156(2), ibid.
15 Article 137(2), ibid.
16 Article 170, ibid.
17 Article 13, Annex III, UNCLOS.
18 Article 140(2), ibid.
19 *Agreement relating to the Implementation of Part XI of the United Nations Convention on the Law of the Sea of 10 December 1982*, adopted by Resolution 48/263, on 28 July 1994, by the General Assembly of the United Nations.
20 R.R. Churchill and A.V. Lowe, *The law of the sea*, Juris Pub, 1999, p. 244. Other changes made included the system of financing of the activities of the Enterprise. Under the Implementing Agreement, States are no longer required to finance mine sites or any activities of the Enterprise.

contractors are no longer obligated to 'make available to the Enterprise on fair and reasonable commercial terms and conditions' the technology they used to carry out activities in the Area, the 1994 Agreement creates barriers for developing States to directly participate in, access, and benefit from deep seabed mining activities. Although the key aspects of the CHM such as the limitations on access to and the exploitation of the mineral resources of the seabed and subsoil as well as the equitable sharing of the economic benefits remain intact, developing States without the necessary technology ultimately depend on the benefit-sharing arrangement to benefit from the Area as a CHM. Accordingly, the degree to which the eventual benefit-sharing arrangement is equitable will determine the extent to which the legal regime governing the Area realizes its CHM principle.

The competence to adopt such regulations belongs to the ISA. A comprehensive deep sea mining code, which would include environmental provisions, is being developed by the ISA.[21] The ISA to date has issued Regulations on Prospecting and Exploration for Polymetallic Nodules in the Area, Regulations on Prospecting and Exploration for Polymetallic Sulphides in the Area, and Regulations on Prospecting and Exploration for Cobalt-Rich Crusts.

Currently, the Draft Exploitation Regulations[22] are under consideration by the Council and stakeholder comments are ongoing for the draft standards and guidelines to support the implementation of the Draft Regulations for Exploitation of mineral resources in the Area.[23] The mining code, which defines the details of benefit-sharing, is under development and has been delegated to an Open-Ended Ad Hoc Working Group of the Council.[24] A payment mechanism, whereby payments are made to the ISA for deep seabed mining activities, is an important implementation of CHM principle under Part XI because it is 'a means to ensure that all humankind, including future generations, enjoys the benefits of its shared stewardship of the Area'.[25] Apart from equitable sharing of financial benefits among States, the fees paid to the ISA 'could be used for exploration, protecting mineral resources, subsidizing the immature mining industry, and protecting the environment'.[26] Environmental protection is essential to ensuring that future generations enjoy the benefits of the Area. However, challenges facing the payment mechanism include the purposes for which the payments should be used, as well as the criteria used to determine how the payments should be equitably and proportionately distributed.

Part XI also includes provisions for the protection and preservation of the marine environment.[27] This addresses the notion that the CHM for the Area is principally of an economic dimension. Whereas, the conservation of marine life was part of the heritage of humanity. Part XI, by

21 See the website of the International Seabed Authority at 'The Mining Code | International Seabed Authority'. Available online <https://www.isa.org.jm/miningcode#targetText=The%20%22Mining%20Code%22%20refers%20to> (accessed 19 November 2021). 'The "Mining Code" refers to the whole of the comprehensive set of rules, regulations and procedures issued by ISA to regulate prospecting, exploration and exploitation of marine minerals in the international seabed Area'.

22 ISA, *Draft Regulations on Exploitation of Mineral Resources in the Area*, ISBA/25/C/WP.1, 28 March 2019.

23 Draft Exploitation Regulations | International Seabed Authority. Available online <https://www.isa.org.jm/mining-code/ongoing-development-regulations-exploitation-mineral-resources-area>/ (accessed 19 November 2021). 'In accordance with UNCLOS and the 1994 Agreement, since 2014, ISA has undertaken work to develop regulations for exploitation of mineral resources in the Area'.

24 T. Thiele, H.P. Damian and P. Singh, *A comprehensive approach to the payment mechanism for deep seabed mining*, Institute for Advanced Sustainability Studies, Potsdam, 2021, p. 3.

25 Ibid., p. 3.

26 K. Van Nijen, S. Van Passel, C. G. Brown, M. W. Lodge, K. Segerson and D. Squires, 'The development of a payment regime for deep sea mining activities in the Area through stakeholder participation', *The International Journal of Marine and Coastal Law* 34, 2019, 583.

27 Article 145, UNCLOS.

including important environmental protection requirements in article 145, cements the notion that environmental protection, including for future generations, is part of the CHM principle. However, as concerns over the environmental impact of deep seabed mining have grown over the years, this has drawn attention to the need for a robust set of conservation regulations.[28] Indeed, in 2021 the IUCN Members Assembly responded to these concerns with a resolution for a seabed mining moratorium.[29]

The environmental protection aspect of the CHM principle gives rise to the obligations of due diligence and cooperation, which become even more critical to legal regimes governing global commons. Since no State can claim sovereignty or sovereign rights in the Area, which means that no State can or will take enforcement measures to protect the environment in the Area, the Area is thus vulnerable to resource overexploitation and environmental degradation.[30] Accordingly, procedural obligations of conduct, in particular the obligation of due diligence and cooperation, provide a practical way to address the collective action problems facing protection of the environment of a global commons. Indeed, the Part XI Seabed Disputes Chambers (Chambers), which is an institutional mechanism that settles contentious legal disputes relating to disputes arising from Part XI, and provides advisory opinions, has affirmed the legal status of the obligation of due diligence and cooperation in its first and only advisory opinion.

The responsibilities and obligations of States sponsoring persons and entities with respect to activities in the Area[31] was ground-breaking in many ways, including its clarification of the due diligence obligations of sponsoring States for activities carried out in the Area. Focusing on article 139 and the obligations of State Parties to ensure that activities in the Area are carried out in conformity with Part XI, the Chambers defined the obligation as one of due diligence. Citing the *Pulp Mills* decision of the International Court of Justice, the Chambers defined the due diligence obligation as

> an obligation which entails not only the adoption of appropriate rules and measures, but also a certain level of vigilance in their enforcement and the exercise of administrative control applicable to public and private operators, such as the monitoring of activities undertaken by such operators.[32]

In addition, the advisory opinion clarified that the sponsoring State is under a due diligence obligation to ensure that the sponsored contractor complies with the obligation to conduct an environmental impact assessment (EIA) as required under section 1(7) of the annex to the 1994

28 On the concerns over the adverse impact of deep seabed mining on biodiversity and sensitive deep sea ecosystems, see International Union for Conservation of Nature, *Deep sea mining threatens unique marine life, experts warn*, International Union for Conservation of Nature, 2017. Available online <https://www.iucn.org/news/secretariat/201706/deep-sea-mining-threatens-unique-marine-life-experts-warn> (accessed 10 September 2021).

29 IUCN, *069 – Protection of Deep-Ocean Ecosystems and Biodiversity through a Moratorium on Seabed Mining*, IUCN World Conservation Congress, 2020. Available online <https://www.iucncongress2020.org/motion/069> (accessed 10 September 2021).

30 For a more in-depth analysis of the rights and obligations of States in the Area, see V. Tassin Campanella, Y. Cissé and D. Tladi, 'Rights and obligations of States on the continental shelf and the Area', in V. Tassin Campanella (ed.), *Routledge handbook of seabed mining and the law of the sea*, Routledge, 2023, chapter II.1.

31 *Responsibilities and obligations of States with respect to activities in the Area, Advisory Opinion, ITLOS Reports 2011*, p. 10.

32 Ibid., para. 115.

Agreement.[33] Importantly, referring to article 206, the Chambers stressed 'that the obligation to conduct an environmental impact assessment is a direct obligation under the Convention and a general obligation under customary international law'.[34]

Marine genetic resources and the conservation and sustainable use of biological diversity in areas beyond national jurisdiction

In 2015, the UN General Assembly adopted Resolution 69/292 for the establishment of a Preparatory Committee to develop an implementing agreement under the UNCLOS on the conservation and sustainable use of marine biological diversity of areas beyond national jurisdiction (BBNJ Agreement). This was later followed with a decision by the General Assembly in 2017 to convene an Intergovernmental Conference to negotiate a BBNJ Agreement under UNCLOS based on the recommendation of the Preparatory Committee.[35] Included among the issues is whether access and benefit-sharing of marine genetic resources under the new agreement will be governed by the CHM regime under Part XI or the freedom of the high seas regime.[36] Developed States seek to maintain the open access[37] of the high seas for marine genetic resources. By contrast, developing States take the position that the CHM regime under Part XI of UNCLOS should be extended to include marine genetic resources in areas beyond national jurisdiction.[38] The legal issue is whether the CHM regime for access and benefit-sharing under Part XI is restricted to mineral resources

33 Ibid., para. 141.
34 Ibid., para. 145.
35 UN Resolution 72/249 (24 December 2017).
36 S.J. Park, 'Changes in the law of marine genetic resources in the ABNJ under UNCLOS', in H.N. Scheiber, N. Oral and M. Kwon (eds), *Ocean law debates: The 50-year legacy and emerging issues for the years ahead*, Brill, 2018, pp. 419–444; M. Essam, *Equity and benefit sharing from marine genetic resources in areas beyond national jurisdiction*, International Institute for Environment and Development, 2018; N.Y. Morris-Sharma, 'Marine genetic resources in areas beyond national jurisdiction: Issues with, in and outside of UNCLOS', *Max Planck Yearbook of United Nations Law* 20, 2017, 71–97; A. Broggiato, 'Exploration and exploitation of marine genetic resources in areas beyond national jurisdiction and environmental impact assessment', *European Journal of Risk Regulation* 4, 2013, 247–251; D. Tladi, 'The common heritage of mankind and the proposed treaty on biodiversity in areas beyond national jurisdiction: The choice between pragmatism and sustainability', *Yearbook of International Environmental Law* 25, 2015, 113–132; D. Tladi, 'Genetic resources, benefit sharing and the law of the sea: The need for slarity', *Journal of International Maritime Law* 13, 2007, 183–193; D. Tladi, 'Conservation and sustainable use of marine biodiversity in areas beyond national jurisdiction: Towards an implementing agreement' in R. Rayfuse (ed.), *Research handbook on international marine environmental law*, Edward Elgar Publishing, 2015, pp. 259–271.
37 The European Union adopts a practical position towards the question of the legal status of marine genetic resources in areas beyond national jurisdiction. Access should be free based on the provisions related to scientific research under UNCLOS and benefit-sharing should focus on non-monetary benefits. See European Union, 'Development of an international legally-binding instrument under UNCLOS on the conservation and sustainable use of marine biological diversity of areas beyond national jurisdiction (BBNJ Process), written submission of the EU and its member states: Marine genetic resources, including questions on the sharing of benefits', 22 February 2017. Available online: <https://www.un.org/depts/los/biodiversity/prepcom_files/rolling_comp/EU_Written_Submission_on_Marine_Genetic_Resources.pdf> (accessed 13 September 2021). See also P.A. Singh, V. Tassin Campanella and F. Maes, 'The European Union and seabed mining' in V. Tassin Campanella (ed.), *Routledge handbook of seabed mining and the law of the sea*, op. cit., chapter VI.1.4.
38 E.M. Mattar, 'Interventions on behalf of the Group of 77 and China on agenda item 7: Marine genetic resources, including questions on the sharing of benefits, at the first session of the intergovernmental conference on an international legally binding instrument under the United Nations convention on the law of the sea on the conservation and sustainable use of marine biological diversity of areas beyond national jurisdiction', 13 September 2018. Available online: <http://www.g77.org/statement/getstatement.php?id=180913> (accessed 10 September 2021).

as defined to be 'all solid, liquid or gaseous mineral resources *in situ* in the *Area* at or beneath the seabed, including polymetallic nodules'[39] or broadly to the Area in its entirety.[40]

Other applications of the common heritage of mankind

Outer space and the Moon

The application of the CHM principle in outer space also deserves attention, especially in light of how outer space rules have been informed and discussed in relation to the law of the sea.[41] The same year that Arvid Pardo made his historic speech on the deep seabed as a CHM, States adopted the *Treaty on Principles Governing the Activities of States in the Exploration and Use of Outer Space, including the Moon and Other Celestial Bodies* (Outer Space Treaty),[42] which recognized the common interest of all mankind in the progress of the exploration and use of outer space for peaceful purposes. The notion of the CHM was formulated differently but shared the same spirit.

The Outer Space Treaty establishes that the Moon and other celestial bodies are not *res nullius* and cannot be subject to national appropriation by claims of sovereignty.[43] Moreover, the Outer Space Treaty further provides that the exploration and use of outer space, including the Moon and other celestial bodies, shall be carried out for the benefit and in the interests of all countries, irrespective of their degree of economic or scientific development, and shall be the province of all mankind. However, unlike the regime of CHM for the Area, the Outer Space Treaty supports open access, that is, the free exploration and use by all States based on equal rights to all areas of the celestial bodies, subject to international law.[44] The Treaty recognizes freedom of scientific investigation and requires States to facilitate and encourage international cooperation in such investigation.[45] It also includes the principle that the Moon and other celestial bodies must only be used for peaceful purposes.

The Outer Space Treaty was followed by the *Agreement Governing the Activities of States on the Moon and Other Celestial Bodies* (the Moon Treaty), which was adopted in 1979, three years before UNCLOS, and entered into force in 1984.[46] In its preamble, the Moon Treaty highlighted the collective determination to promote on the basis of equality the further development of cooperation among States in the exploration and use of the Moon and other celestial bodies. It also provided that the principle of the common heritage governs the exploration and use of the Moon. Article 11 expressly states that the Moon and its natural resources are the common heritage of mankind.

The non-appropriation principle features prominently in the Moon Treaty, which means that no State can appropriate any part of the Moon by any claim of sovereignty,[47] nor can any part of the Moon become the property of any State, international intergovernmental or non-govern-

39 Article 31(a), UNCLOS.

40 Article 36, ibid.

41 F. von der Dunk, 'International space law', in von der Dunk and Tronchetti (eds), *Handbook of space law*, Edward Elgar Publishing, 2015, p. 74.

42 *The Treaty on Principles Governing the Activities of States in the Exploration and Use of Outer Space, including the Moon and other Celestial Bodies*, 1967, 610 UNTS 204.

43 Article 2, ibid.

44 Article 1, ibid.

45 Ibid.

46 *Agreement Governing the Activities of States on the Moon and Other Celestial Bodies* 1979, 1363 UNTS 3.

47 Ibid., article 11(2).

mental organization, national organization or non-governmental entity or of any natural person.[48] However, article 6, paragraph 1, which mandates the right of freedom of scientific research for all States and without discrimination of any kind, goes on to recognize the rights of State Parties in conducting scientific research to appropriate, namely, to 'collect and remove' from the Moon samples of minerals and other substance. However, State Parties are to have regard to the desirability of making a portion of such samples available to other interested State Parties and the international scientific community for scientific investigation.[49] In this regard, the Moon Treaty does not provide for a benefit-sharing regime even though reference is made in its preamble to the benefits which may be derived from the exploitation of the natural resources of the Moon and other celestial bodies. While State Parties also undertake a commitment to establish an international regime, including appropriate procedures, to govern the exploitation of the natural resources of the Moon as such exploitation is about to become feasible, this has not yet materialized. The sharing of scientific information, which is a benefit, however, is not strictly mandated but couched in the vague language 'to the greatest extent feasible and practicable'.[50]

The Moon Treaty also provides for an open access regime providing that State Parties have the right to explore and use the Moon without discrimination and on the basis of equality and in accordance with international law.[51] Unlike the regime governing the Area, there is no international authority from which an exploration licence or permit must be obtained. At most, the Moon Treaty provides for an obligation to provide information, in that State Parties are required to inform the United Nations Secretary-General, the public, and the international scientific community of their activities concerned with the exploration and use of the Moon to the greatest extent feasible and practicable. Such information includes sharing the results of each mission, including scientific results.[52]

Regarding environmental protection, the Moon Treaty includes provisions requiring State Parties to take measures to prevent the 'disruption of the existing environmental balance of the Moon', as well as to protect the Earth's environment against the harmful effects from the introduction of extraterrestrial matter.[53] Additionally, State Parties are to notify the United Nations Secretary General of measures taken.[54]

Antarctica

The Antarctic is governed by a special treaty regime collectively referred to as the *Antarctic Treaty System* (ATS),[55] which includes the 1959 Antarctic Treaty.[56] While there is no express reference

48 Ibid., article 11(3).
49 Ibid., article 6(2).
50 Ibid., article 5; The Outer Space Treaty, op. cit., article 11.
51 The Moon Treaty, op. cit., article 11 (4).
52 Ibid., article 5(1).
53 Ibid., article 7(1).
54 The Moon Treaty, op. cit., articles 7(1) and (2).
55 The Antarctic Treaty System (ATS) is composed of the Antarctic Treaty, 1959, 402 UNTS 71; *Agreed Measures for the Conservation of Antarctic Fauna and Flora*, 1964; *Convention for the Conservation of Antarctic Seal*, 1972, 1080 UNTS 175; *Convention on the Conservation of Antarctic Marine Living Resources*, 20 May 1980; and *Protocol on Environmental Protection to the Antarctic Treaty*, 4 October 1991, 2941 UNTS 3. See G. Triggs (ed.), *The Antarctic treaty regime: Law, environment and resources*, Cambridge University Press, 1987; C.C. Joyner and S.K. Chopra (eds), *The Antarctic legal regime*, Martinus Nijhoff, 1988, pp. 51–182.
56 Antarctic Treaty, 1959, 402 UNTS 71.

to the CHM principle,[57] the preamble of the Antarctic Treaty sets out that 'in the interests of all mankind that Antarctica shall continue forever to be used exclusively for peaceful purposes and shall not become the scene or object of international discord'. However, distinct from other global commons, the Antarctic is unique, in that its regime has evolved from territorial claims made by a group of States into a complex regime that is increasingly internationalized. While the Antarctic Treaty expressly preserves the territorial claims asserted by the Contracting Parties, it prohibits any of the State Parties to assert any new or expanded sovereignty claims over any part of the area covered during the period the Treaty remains in force.[58] Moreover, such claims are not recognized by all States, especially developing States that see such claims as vestiges from the colonial period.[59] Nonetheless, in 1959, against the backdrop of the Cold War, States made a historic decision to recognize the common interest of humankind over the individual national interests – at least so long as the Treaty remains in force. The ATS includes a mining ban under the 1991 *Protocol on Environmental Protection to the Antarctic Treaty* (Madrid Protocol), which recognizes the importance of developing a comprehensive regime for the protection of Antarctica as being 'in the interest of mankind as a whole'.[60] Several UNGA resolutions have affirmed that 'mankind as a whole has a common interest in the Antarctic'.[61] During the 1980s, there was also a strong push to have the Antarctic recognized as a CHM, similar to the deep seabed and outer space. Indeed, in 1985, the Organization of African Unity adopted a resolution declaring Antarctica 'to be [the] common heritage of mankind'.[62]

Over time environmental concerns and scientific research have overshadowed the mineral exploitation aspects of the evolving governance of the ATS. In 1964, Antarctica was designated as a Special Conservation Area where the international community reached a common agreement that there is to be no exploitation of its natural resources.[63] In 2016, the Parties took a bold step in establishing the world's largest marine protected area in the Ross Sea, measuring some 1.57 million square kilometres (600,000 square miles), which includes a no-take zone for fishing activities.[64] As Oxman observed, the Antarctic Treaty provides a framework for cooperation in the common interest of States.[65]

In one sense, the unarticulated CHM approach in the Antarctic has evolved into a conservation regime and not an exploitation regime. In contrast, the CHM regime of the Area retains its focus on the exploitation of mineral resources.

Similar to Part XI of UNCLOS and the Moon Treaty, the ATS recognizes the freedom of scientific research and scientific cooperation,[66] the requirement for the exchange of scientific obser-

57 Efforts were made within the United Nations by some States for the express recognition of Antarctica as a common heritage of mankind. See Herber, op. cit., 396.

58 Antarctic Treaty, op. cit., article IV (2); M. Haward, 'Contemporary challenges to the Antarctic Treaty and Antarctic Treaty system: Australian interests, interplay and the evolution of a regime complex', *Australian Journal of Maritime & Ocean Affairs* 9, 2016, 21–24.

59 M. Hayashi, 'The Antarctica question in the United Nations', *Cornell International Law Journal* 19, 1986, 280.

60 *Protocol on Environmental Protection to the Antarctic Treaty*, op. cit., article 7.

61 K. Scott, 'Institutional developments within the Antarctic treaty system', *The International and Comparative Law Quarterly* 52, 2003, 476.

62 Hayashi, op. cit., 287

63 *Agreed Measures for the Conservation of Antarctic Fauna and Flora*, 1964.

64 CCAMLR, Conservation Measure 91-05, Ross Sea region marine protected area, 28 October 2016.

65 B.H. Oxman, 'Evaluating the Antarctic minerals convention: The decision-making system', *University of Miami Inter-American Law Review* 21, 1989, 17.

66 Antarctic Treaty, op. cit., article II.

vations and results which are to be made freely available,[67] the exclusive use of the Antarctic for peaceful purposes, and protection of its environment.[68] There is a legitimate question as to whether the Antarctic is evolving into a full global commons governed by its own rules of common heritage.

Plant genetic resources

In 1981, at the biennial meeting of the United Nations Food and Agricultural Organization (FAO), a request was made to the Director General for a draft international convention on plant genetic resources.[69] However, because of concerns raised by developed countries the non-binding *International Undertaking on Plant Genetic Resources* (International Undertaking) was adopted instead of a binding convention.[70] The preamble recognizes plant genetic resource as the 'heritage of mankind to be preserved (…) to be freely available for use, for the benefit of present and future generations'.[71] Article 1 describes the International Undertaking to be 'based on the universally accepted principle that plant genetic resources are a heritage of mankind and consequently should be available without restriction'. Notably, the reference to 'common' was omitted and what was meant by 'heritage of mankind' was never explained. Bordwin opines it was likely based on the 'common heritage principle' developed by the Law of the Sea Conference for deep seabed mineral resources, which had been adopted in 1982.[72] Bordwin makes an interesting analysis of the applicability of the CHM principle as developed for the law of the sea to plant genetic resources, explaining those elements that can be carried over and those that cannot.[73] While the developing States were seeking access without restrictions to all plant genetic resources, the developed countries sought to restrict access to modified and new plant variant genetic resources on grounds of intellectual property rights.[74] By contrast, in the case of the mineral resources in the Area, access is strictly regulated by the ISA equally for all State Parties and persons.

Eight developed States (Canada, France, Germany, Japan, New Zealand, Switzerland, the United Kingdom, and the United States) did not agree to the International Undertaking and registered their reservations. This led to a series of agreed interpretations to bridge the gap. It was

67 Emphasis by the author. Ibid., article III.

68 Ibid., article I.

69 Report of the Conference FAO, *Twenty First Session of the Conference, FAO Resolution 6/81 On Plant Genetic Resources*, Rome, 1981 (adopted 25 November 1981); H.J. Bordwin, 'The legal and political implications of the international undertaking on plant genetic resources', *Ecology Law Quarterly* 12, 1985, 1053–1069.

70 Report of the Conference FAO, *Twenty Second Session of the Conference FAO Resolution 8/83 International Undertaking on Plant Genetic Resources*, Rome, 1983 (adopted 23 November 1983). See also Commission on Genetic Resources for Food and Agriculture, Food and Agriculture Organization of the United Nations, *Second Report of the State of the World's Plant Genetic Resources for Food and Agriculture*, Rome, 2010; E. Tabaro, 'Food security and access to plant genetic resources: An analysis of the multilateral system of access and benefit sharing', 15 *eLaw Journal* 15, 2008, 212–229; Bordwin, op. cit., 1068: both States and the Director General had two concerns: 'First, a convention would take too long to implement. Second, the binding nature of the convention could inhibit it from achieving the broadest possible support'.

71 Report of the Conference FAO, *Twenty Second Session of the Conference FAO Resolution 8/83 International Undertaking on Plant Genetic Resources*, Rome, 1983 (adopted 23 November 1983).

72 Bordwin, op. cit., 1063–1068.

73 Ibid. In distilling four elements of the CHM for the deep seabed resources, Bordwin notes, 'Only some of these elements can guide the application of the common heritage principle to plant genetic resources'.

74 D. Cooper, 'The international undertaking on plant genetic resources', *Review of European Community and International Environmental Law* 2, 1993, 161–162.

only in the 1989 Interpretation Resolution that the term 'common heritage of mankind' appeared in relation to the draft resolution for farmers' rights, which became an annex to the International Undertaking.[75] This remains as the sole reference ever made to the CHM in relation to plant genetic resources. In addition to intellectual property issues, sovereignty was another barrier to acceptance of the 'heritage of mankind' notion, thereby leading to the adoption of Resolution 3 in 1991, which expressly recognized that 'the common heritage principle was subject to the sovereignty of States over their plant genetic resources'.[76]

The International Undertaking was eventually followed up with the negotiation of a treaty, namely, the International Treaty on Plant Genetic Resources.[77] Its objective includes the conservation and sustainable use of plant genetic resources for food and agriculture and the fair and equitable sharing of the benefits. Modelled on the Convention on Biological Diversity (CBD),[78] the Treaty abandoned any notion of CHM or heritage of mankind in favour of the notion of 'common concern of humankind', which is found in the preamble of the CBD. It develops a framework for access and benefit-sharing under the multilateral system (Multilateral System).[79] Fair and equitable sharing of plant genetic resources under the treaty applies to the use, 'including commercial plant genetic resources for food and agriculture under the Multilateral System, the exchange of information, access to and transfer of technology, capacity-building, and the sharing of the benefits arising from commercialization.'[80] Under the Treaty, Parties are required to develop a global information system to facilitate the exchange of information,[81] which was established in 2015.[82] The institutional make-up of the Treaty includes a Governing Body composed of all the Contracting Parties with the authority to adopt decisions for the implementation of the Treaty.[83]

World Heritage Convention

The notion of cultural and natural heritage as a common heritage was recognized in the 1972 *Convention Concerning the Protection of the World Cultural and Natural Heritage* (World Heritage Convention).[84] As is the case for the International Undertaking for plant genetic resources, the reference is made to the 'heritage of mankind' and not 'common heritage'. The World Heritage Convention creates obligations for States to inventory, recognize, and protect unique and irreplaceable properties both cultural and natural of universal value.[85] States recognized that there were portions of cultural and natural heritage that were of outstanding interests, and ought to be

75 Ibid., 161. A series of interpretations were adopted to respond to the concerns of eight states with reservations to the International Undertaking. See K. ten Kate and C.L. Diaz, 'The undertaking revisited: A commentary on the revision of the international undertaking on plant genetic resources for food and agriculture', *Review of European Community and International Environmental Law* 6, 1997, 284–292.

76 Ibid., 285.

77 *International Treaty on Plant Genetic Resources*, adopted on 3 November 2001, 2400 UNTS 303, article 1.1.

78 Convention on Biological Diversity, adopted on 5 June 1992, 1760 UNTS 69.

79 Tabaro, op. cit., 217–19.

80 *International Treaty on Plant Genetic Resources*, op. cit., article 13.2.

81 Ibid., article 17.

82 At its sixth session on 9 October 2015, the governing body adopted the vision and the first programme of work on the global information system as contained in Resolution 3/2015.

83 *International Treaty on Plant Genetic Resources*, op. cit., article 19.

84 *Convention for the Protection of the World Cultural and Natural Heritage*, 16 November 1972, 1037 UNTS 151.

85 F. Pfeifle, 'The 1972 world heritage convention. Commentary by Francesco Franconi, Frederico Lenzerini', *Archiv des Völkerrechts* 47, 2009, 138–142.

protected and preserved as part of the world heritage of humankind.[86] At the same time, since the World Heritage Convention recognizes the territorial sovereignty of the State where the natural or cultural heritage is found, it creates a duty of the international community to protect the heritage of humankind as a whole through cooperation.[87] Thus, it is the value of the cultural or natural heritage that is the heritage of mankind.

Conclusion

The CHM principle does not have a common understanding or application. Its first articulation by Suarez in 1927 focused on the need to protect living resources of the high seas and especially the Antarctic. In contrast, Pardo had focused on the CHM for the right of all States to equal access and right to the benefits of the minerals in the deep seabed. There has been no application of the CHM principle since the adoption of the UNCLOS. Subsequent instruments, such as world heritage and plant genetic resources have avoided making direct reference to the language of common heritage and instead they refer to the 'heritage of mankind'. Moreover, with the exception of Part XI of UNCLOS and its highly detailed regime for access and benefit-sharing of resources of the Area, including institutional structures, the Moon Treaty has not yet developed a similar CHM regime even though it adopted the CHM as a legal principle. The CHM principle has reappeared in the current negotiations for the BBNJ Agreement in relation to marine genetic resources. However, as the negotiations are on-going, the outcome remains to be determined. Nonetheless, developed States take the view that the CHM regime of Part XI applies only to mineral resources as defined in article 131 or broadly to the Area itself.

Acknowledgement

The author thanks Zhifeng Jiang (Yale-NUS Law School '22) for his valuable assistance.

References

Bordwin H.J., 'The legal and political implications of the international undertaking on plant genetic resources', *Ecology Law Quarterly* 12, 1985, 1053–1069.

Bourrel M., Thiele T. and Currie D., 'The common heritage of mankind as a means to assess and advance equity in deep sea mining', *Marine Policy* 95, 2018, 311–316.

Broggiato A., 'Exploration and exploitation of marine genetic resources in areas beyond national jurisdiction and environmental impact assessment', *European Journal of Risk Regulation* 4, 2013, 247–251.

Churchill R.R. and Lowe A.V., *The law of the sea*, Manchester: Juris Pub, 1999.

Commission On Genetic Resources for Food and Agriculture Food and Agriculture Organization of the United Nations, *Second report of the state of the world's plant genetic resources for food and agriculture*, Rome, 2010.

Cooper D., 'The international undertaking on plant genetic resources', *Review of European Community and International Environmental Law* 2, 1993, 158–166.

Essam M., *Equity and benefit sharing from marine genetic resources in areas beyond national jurisdiction*, International Institute for Environment and Development, 2018.

Haward M., 'Contemporary challenges to the Antarctic treaty and Antarctic treaty system: Australian interests, interplay and the evolution of a regime complex', *Australian Journal of Maritime & Ocean Affairs* 9, 2016, 21–24.

86 J. Mulvaney, 'A question of values: Museums and cultural property', in I. McBryde (ed.) *Who owns the past?* Melbourne: Papers from the annual symposium of the Australian Academy of the Humanities, 1985, pp. 86–98.

87 World Heritage Convention, op. cit., article 6(1).

Hayashi M., 'The Antarctica question in the United Nations', *Cornell International Law Journal* 19, 1986, 275–290.

Herber B.P., 'The common heritage principle: Antarctica and the developed nations', *American Journal of Economics and Sociology* 50, 1991, 391–406.

Iavicoli V., 'The legal regime of outer space in light of the law of the sea', in S. Aricò (ed.), *Ocean sustainability in the 21st century*, Cambridge University Press, 2015, 249–274.

International Union for Conservation of Nature, *Deep sea mining threatens unique marine life, experts warn*, International Union for Conservation of Nature, 2017. Online. Available HTTP: <https://www.iucn.org /news/secretariat/201706/deep-sea-mining-threatens-unique-marine-life-experts-warn> (accessed 10 September 2021).

Joyner C.C. and Chopra S.K. (eds.) *The Antarctic legal regime*, The Hague: Martinus Nijhoff, 1988.

Kate K.T. and Diaz C.L., 'The undertaking revisited: A commentary on the revision of the international undertaking on plant genetic resources for food and agriculture', *Review of European Community and International Environmental Law* 6, 1997, 284–292.

Lord T., 'The Antarctic treaty system and the peaceful governance of Antarctica: The role of the ATS in promoting peace at the margins of the world', *The Polar Journal* 10, 2020, 3–21.

Morris-Sharma N.Y., 'Marine genetic resources in areas beyond national jurisdiction: Issues with, in and outside of UNCLOS', *Max Planck Yearbook of United Nations Law* 20, 2017, 71–97.

Mulvaney J., 'A question of values: Museums and cultural property', in I. McBryde (ed.), *Who owns the past?*, Melbourne: Papers from the annual symposium of the Australian Academy of the Humanities, 1985, 86–98.

Nanda V.P. and Pring G.W., *International environmental law and policy for the 21st century (2nd volume)*, Leiden: Brill, 2013.

Oxman B.H., 'Evaluating the Antarctic minerals convention: The decision-making system', *University of Miami Inter-American Law Review* 21, 1989, 17–80.

Park S.J., 'Changes in the law of marine genetic resources in the ABNJ under UNCLOS', in H.N. Scheiber, N. Oral and M. Kwon (eds.), *Ocean law debates: The 50-year legacy and emerging issues for the years ahead*, Brill, 2018, 419–444.

Pfeifle F., 'The 1972 world heritage convention. Commentary by Francesco Franconi, Frederico Lenzerini', *Archiv des Völkerrechts* 47, 2009, 138–142.

Prislan V. and Schrijver N., 'From mare liberum to the global commons: Building on the grotian heritage', *Grotiana* 30, 2009, 168–206.

Ranganathan S., 'Global commons', *European Journal of International Law* 27, 2016, 693–717.

Scott K., 'Institutional developments within the Antarctic treaty system', *The International and Comparative Law Quarterly* 52, 2003, 473–487.

Scovazzi T., 'The seabed beyond the limits of national jurisdiction: General and institutional aspects', in G.O. Elferink and E.J. Molenaar (eds.), *The international legal regime of areas beyond national jurisdiction*, Brill, 2010, 41–60.

Singh P., Tassin Campanella V. and Maes F., 'The European Union and seabed mining', in V. Tassin Campanella (ed.), *Routledge handbook of seabed mining and the law of the sea*, London: Routledge, 2023, chapter VI.1.4.

Société des Nations, *Questionnaire no. 7: Richesse de la mer: rapport du sous-comité chargé d'étudier la question de procédure par le Rapporteur M. Jose Leon Suarez*, Genève: Société des Nations, 1927.

Tabaro E., 'Food security and access to plant genetic resources: An analysis of the multilateral system of access and benefit sharing', *eLaw Journal* 15, 2008, 212–229.

Tassin Campanella V., Cissé Y. and Tladi D., 'Rights and obligations of States on the continental shelf and the Area', in V. Tassin Campanella (ed.), *Routledge handbook of seabed mining and the law of the sea*, London: Routledge, 2023, chapter II.1.

Thiele T., Damian H.P. and Singh P., *A comprehensive approach to the payment mechanism for deep seabed mining*, Potsdam: Institute for Advanced Sustainability Studies, 2021.

Tladi D., 'Conservation and sustainable use of marine biodiversity in areas beyond national jurisdiction: Towards an implementing agreement', in R. Rayfuse (ed.), *Research handbook on international marine environmental law*, Cheltenham: Edward Elgar Publishing, 2015, 259–271.

Tladi D., 'Genetic resources, benefit sharing and the law of the sea: The need for clarity', *Journal of International Maritime Law* 13, 2007, 183–193.

Tladi D., 'The common heritage of mankind and the proposed treaty on biodiversity in areas beyond national jurisdiction: The choice between pragmatism and sustainability', *Yearbook of International Environmental Law* 25, 2015, 113–132.
Triggs G.D. (ed.) *The Antarctic treaty regime: Law, environment and resources*, Cambridge: Cambridge University Press, 1987.
Van Nijen K., Van Passel S., Brown C.G., Lodge M.W., Segersone K. and Squires D., 'The development of a payment regime for deep sea mining activities in the Area through stakeholder participation', *The International Journal of Marine and Coastal Law* 34, 2019, 571–601.
Von der Dunk F., 'International space law', in F. von der Dunk and F. Tronchetti (eds.), *Handbook of space law*, Edward Elgar Publishing, 2015, 29–126.
Wolfrum R., 'The principle of the common heritage of mankind', *Zeitschrift für ausländisches öffentliches Recht und Völkerrecht* 43, 1983, 312–337.
Xue H., Crawford J. and Bell J., *Transboundary damage in international law*, Cambridge: Cambridge University Press, 2003.

I.3

IMPLEMENTING THE PRECAUTIONARY APPROACH FOR SEABED MINING: A REVIEW OF STATE PRACTICE

Robert Makgill†, Aline Jaeckel, and Keith MacMaster

Robert had a sharp intellect and an unwavering passion for the ocean and international and environmental law. He conceived of and led this chapter. The idea for this chapter arose from his involvement in judicial proceedings on the matter of the precautionary approach. He was passionate about demonstrating that the practical obligations arising from the precautionary approach are indeed better understood by courts than some might believe.
When Robert invited us to co-write the chapter with him, his passion for the subject matter was evident from the outset. He was an excellent team player, and we learned a great deal from him during the research and writing of this chapter. We enjoyed frank, rigorous, and insightful discussions during online meetings.

We profoundly appreciate that it was possible to capture Robert's insights and extensive legal experience in this chapter, in honour of his legacy.

Robert will be deeply missed.

Introduction

Much was written on precaution during the 1990s and 2000s, including criticisms that the principle is too vague.[1] This chapter contends that contemporary administrative approaches, international law, and State practice indicate that the obligations arising from the precautionary approach are reasonably well understood. There is little room for debate concerning its requirement for action to be taken to prevent environmental degradation. Incomplete information and scientific uncertainty cannot justify a failure to act to prevent damage. Perhaps, more fundamentally, incomplete information and uncertainty are often invoked as grounds for preventing development from taking place. Precaution is particularly apposite to seabed mining because of the paucity of scientific information presently available on the relevant marine environments and the consequential difficulty in assessing the risk of harm.

1 P. Sandin et al., 'Five charges against the precautionary principle', *Journal of Risk Research* 5, 2002, 287–99; A. Arcuri, 'Reconstructing precaution, deconstructing misconceptions', *Ethics & International Affairs* 21, 2007, 359–79.

DOI: 10.4324/9780429426162-5

The precautionary approach is not expressly provided for in the United Nations Convention on the Law of the Sea 1982 (UNCLOS).[2] However, it is found in the International Seabed Authority's (ISA) Exploration Regulations[3] and Draft Exploitation Regulations,[4] and discussed in the Seabed Advisory Opinion.[5] This chapter reviews the ISA's approach to precaution against selected State practice concerning implementation of the precautionary approach. The first part of the chapter provides an overview of the precautionary principle within different administrative contexts including regulation, impact assessment, and seabed mining operations. Next, the chapter discusses how international courts and tribunals have developed the precautionary approach from a soft law principle to one that stands on the cusp of attaining customary law status.

The chapter then considers the role of State practice in clarifying the interpretation and implementation of the precautionary approach in relation to four Commonwealth State Parties to the UNCLOS: New Zealand, Australia, Canada, and the United Kingdom (UK). The authors acknowledge, from the outset, that these States have been selected based on their familiarity with Commonwealth jurisdictions and for ease of comparison. Each State's precautionary practices vary in their direct relevance to seabed mining. New Zealand sits at one end of the spectrum with legislative provisions and judicial decisions concerning the precautionary approach and seabed mining. Australia, Canada, and the UK, on the other hand, exhibit differing levels of preparedness concerning precaution and its implementation in relation to seabed mining. The chapter concludes with a discussion of how the State practice identified might assist the ISA to satisfy its precautionary obligation in respect of the Area. This includes implementing measures for prerequisite information on the receiving environment, environmental impact assessment (EIA), the burden of proof, and where an adaptive management approach might be consistent with precaution.

Precaution in an administrative context

The precautionary approach administratively and judicially applies to all stages of seabed mining.[6] First, it applies to States and the ISA when determining the rules and regulations for seabed mining, including the types of precautionary measures that should be imposed. Second, applicants must implement precaution when undertaking preliminary work in support of an application for exploration or exploitation, including establishing environmental baseline information and preparing environmental impact assessments of the proposal's potential environmental effects. Third, States, the ISA, and private applicants (including contractors within the Area) must apply a precautionary approach when managing or overseeing mining operations. Lastly, precaution informs judicial consideration of the legal and evidential questions that might arise concerning the first three stages of seabed mining. In an administrative context, the precautionary approach requires actors to take *early* measures to protect the environment, even if scientific uncertainties remain.[7]

2 *United Nations Convention on the Law of the Sea*, 10 December 1982, 1833 UNTS 3. Hereinafter 'UNCLOS'.

3 ISA, *Regulations on Prospecting and Exploration for Polymetallic Nodules in the Area*, 22 July 2013, ISBA/19/C/17, regulations 2(2), 5(1), 31. Hereinafter 'ISA, Regulations on Prospecting and Exploration'.

4 ISA, *Draft Regulations on Exploitation of Mineral Resources in the Area*, 22 March 2019, ISBA/25/C/WP.1, regulation 2(e)(ii). Hereinafter 'ISA, Draft Regulations on Exploitation'.

5 *Responsibilities and Obligations of States Sponsoring Persons and Entities with Respect to Activities in the Area, Advisory Opinion, ITLOS Reports 2011, case no 17.* Hereinafter 'Seabed Advisory Opinion'.

6 See e.g., Seabed Advisory Opinion, op. cit. note 5; and ISA, Regulations on Prospecting and Exploration, op. cit. note 3, regulations 2(2), 5(1), 31(2), 31(5), Annex IV, section 5.1.

7 Rio Declaration on Environment and Development, 14 June 1992, 31 ILM 874, Principle 15; N. de Sadeleer, 'The precautionary principle and climate change', in M. Faure (ed.), *Elgar encyclopedia of environmental law*, Edward

This mirrors the pro-active rationale of precaution, which contrasts with the outdated notion of waiting for substantial evidence before taking action to prevent environmental harm.[8]

Deciding which precautionary measures are appropriate for seabed mining requires an assessment of the potentially harmful effects and the risks posed by incomplete information and uncertainty. This can be problematic within all UNCLOS' jurisdictional zones due to the paucity of scientific knowledge presently held concerning the biophysical characteristics of the seabed and associated water column together with the costs of obtaining adequate information at a suitable scale. Scientific research, nevertheless, indicates that seabed mining activities may have significant adverse effects on the marine environment and ecosystems.[9] The paucity of available quantitative and qualitative environmental data means that a high degree of uncertainty remains concerning potential adverse impacts, and their spatial and temporal dimensions. While a short-term localised adverse effect may cause an inappropriate level of harm, a long-term adverse effect could result in an irreversible ecosystem-wide level of harm. The precautionary approach is intended to be applied to seabed mining until science closes information gaps concerning the receiving environment, the range of potential adverse effects, and the measures necessary to address those effects.

The precautionary approach seeks to enable decision-making despite the existence of uncertainty and incomplete information. The degree of risk that we allow ultimately depends on the relative values we assign to the exploitation of seabed minerals versus protection and preservation of the marine environment and its ecosystem-wide services and integrity. This raises important questions concerning the level of environmental harm deemed acceptable[10] and the degree of harm we are prepared to risk in the pursuit of seabed minerals. Science can readily identify what is known and the extent of our knowledge, but value judgments determine 'how safe do we want to play'.[11] These value judgments are normally expressed through environmental goals and objectives that must be achieved when making risk-based decisions. They should include a clear framework of effects-based thresholds and precautionary measures to ameliorate the risk that those thresholds might be exceeded. Precautionary measures[12] should be *effective* in achieving environmental goals and objectives. They should also be *proportionate* to the goals and objectives so that they are no more restrictive than is necessary.[13]

Elgar, 2016, 20–31, pp. 25–29; E. Morgera, 'The ecosystem approach and the precautionary principle', in M. Faure (ed.) *Elgar encyclopedia of environmental law*, Edward Elgar, 2017, 70–80.

8 A. Trouwborst, 'The precautionary principle in general international law: Combating the Babylonian confusion', *Review of European Community & International Environmental Law* 16, 2007, 185–95; A.L. Jaeckel, *The international seabed authority and the precautionary principle*, Brill Nijhoff, 2017.

9 W. Roest, H. Brekke and M. Clark, 'The scientific challenges of deep-sea mining', in V. Tassin Campanella (ed.), *Routledge handbook of seabed mining and the law of the sea*, Routledge, 2023, Chapter I.1; K. Miller et al., 'An overview of seabed mining including the current state of development, environmental impacts, and knowledge gaps', *Frontiers in Marine Science* 4(418), 2018. Available online <http://dx.doi.org/10.3389/fmars.2017.00418.> (accessed 15 December 2021).

10 M. Stanley and T. Arin, *Precautionary management of deep sea minerals – Pacific Possible Background Paper No 2*, The World Bank, 2017, p. 41.

11 Jaeckel, op. cit. note 8, p. 49.

12 For an overview of potential protective measures for deep seabed mining, see Stanley and Arin, op. cit. note 10, pp. 48–49; and Jaeckel, op. cit. note 8, p. 311.

13 S. Marr, *The precautionary principle in the law of the sea: Modern decision-making in international law*, Martinus Nijhoff, 2003, pp. 35–37; and R. Harding and E. Fisher, 'Introducing the precautionary principle', in R. Harding and E. Fisher (eds.), *Perspectives on the precautionary principle*, Federation Press, 1999, 2–25, p. 12.

The State Parties discussed in this chapter have cultivated a reasonable level of jurisprudence and technical expertise concerning the implementation of precautionary measures to achieve different environmental goals. The ISA, on the other hand, has yet to provide clear regulatory guidance on how to implement the key environmental obligations that apply to seabed mining within the Area. The ISA and States are required 'to ensure effective protection for the marine environment from harmful effects that may arise from [seabed mining] activities' and 'the prevention of damage to the flora and fauna of the marine environment' (article 145, UNCLOS). While the Mining Code restates the 'effective prevention' obligation,[14] it does not provide any measurable direction (e.g., objectives or targets) on how this obligation should be achieved.[15] Further, the ISA has yet to promulgate environmental thresholds beyond which the adverse impacts of seabed mining would be determined unacceptable.[16]

This means that the 30 scientists and lawyers who comprise the Legal and Technical Commission (LTC) are tasked with interpreting the meaning of 'effective prevention' and how the precautionary approach should be implemented to achieve that goal.[17] While the LTC has an important role to play, it does not represent the diverse range of State, inter-governmental organisation (IGO), or stakeholder views concerning environmental goals and objectives, let alone how the precautionary approach should be implemented to achieve them.

It may be that the ISA has been slow to develop environmental goals due to debate concerning whether UNCLOS prioritises seabed mining or protection of the marine environment. Some commentators, presently, appear to consider that the decision to permit seabed mining took place at the time parties agreed to the Convention. On this view, seabed mining activities are a *fait accompli*, and the regulatory goal should be minimising harm to the marine environment. Lodge, who is presently the ISA Secretary-General, and Verlaan contend, in this respect, that:

> It must be stressed (…) that it is useless and counter-productive to argue that an a priori condition for deep-sea mining is an existential debate about whether it should be permitted to go ahead or not. The international community passed that point already many years ago. This is because the one factor that distinguishes deep seabed mining from any other extractive activity, or indeed any other ocean use, is the nature of the underlying legal regime established by the Law of the Sea Convention.[18]

It is unlikely that Lodge or Verlaan intended the above commentary to mean that seabed mining should be permitted in all cases. Framing the question of whether seabed mining should be permitted (or not) as existential, in every case, would clearly risk breaching international obligations to protect and preserve the marine environment. The Seabed Advisory Opinion identified, in this

14 See e.g., ISA, Regulations on Prospecting and Exploration, op. cit. note 3, regulation 21(4)(b); ISA, Draft Regulations on Exploitation, op. cit. note 4, regulation 13(4)(c).

15 V. Tunnicliffe et al., 'Strategic environmental goals and objectives: Setting the basis for environmental regulation of deep seabed mining', *Marine Policy* 114, 2020, 103347.

16 A. Jaeckel, *The implementation of the precautionary approach by the international seabed authority*, ISA Discussion Paper No. 5, 2017. Available online <https://www.isa.org.jm/files/documents/EN/Pubs/DPs/DP5.pdf> (accessed 25 August 2021), p. 3.

17 Ibid., p. 8.

18 M. Lodge and P. Verlaan, 'Deep-sea mining: International regulatory challenges and responses', *Elements* 14(5), 2018, 331–36, p. 336.

respect, numerous *a priori* obligations[19] and measures[20] that must be satisfied before seabed mining activities can be permitted.

In any event, it appears that there is some tension within the ISA as to the circumstances under which seabed mining should take place. Some State Parties contend that the benefit of (hu)mankind principle has a broad application that goes beyond the equitable sharing of economic benefits from seabed mining (article 140, UNCLOS). Those States assert that they will only support deep-sea mining in the Area 'if it is demonstrably beneficial to mankind'.[21] It would be pragmatic, if nothing else, to engage States and their governing agencies (as well as IGOs and stakeholders) in the preparation of further regulations for the Area, as their regulatory, judicial, and technical experiences could provide valuable sources of scientific information and decision-making expertise.

Precaution in international law

The precautionary approach is a central and well-established principle under international environmental law.[22] At its core, it aims to prevent environmental harm by taking *early* action, even if scientific uncertainty about the risks remains. It is applicable to seabed mining within the Area principally because States, the ISA, and contractors are expressly required to apply a precautionary approach under the ISA's Mining Code.[23] It applies more generally to seabed mining within that Area and areas under national jurisdiction because it is a means of achieving the protection and preservation obligations under Part XII of UNCLOS. The South China Sea Arbitration underlined the broad jurisdiction of Part XII, in this respect, stating that its obligations 'apply to all States with respect to the marine environment in all maritime areas, both inside the national jurisdiction of States and beyond it'.[24]

The precautionary approach prevents scientific uncertainty from being used as a reason for failing to take steps to prevent environmental damage where there is a risk of harm. The definition most frequently referred to is found in Principle 15 of the Rio Declaration.[25] Normally, science, by way of an EIA, provides relatively comprehensive information on the adverse impacts of a proposed activity. This enables decision-making powers to be exercised with a degree of certainty as to whether a proposal satisfies regulatory goals. However, the paucity of scientific information

19 R. Makgill and A.P. Linhares, 'Deep seabed mining – Key obligations in the emerging regulation of exploration and development in the Pacific', in R. Warner and S. Kaye (eds.) *Routledge handbook of maritime regulation and enforcement*, Routledge, 2016, 231–61, pp. 234–36; Seabed Advisory Opinion, op. cit. note 5, see obligation to ensure and due diligence paras. 107–20, and direct obligations paras. 121–40, and environmental impact assessment paras. 141–50.

20 Ibid., pp. 237–38; and Seabed Advisory Opinion, op. cit. note 5, see due diligence and necessary measures paras. 117–20, and laws and regulations and administrative measures paras. 218–22.

21 African Group, *Request for Consideration by the Council of the African Group's Proposal on the Economic Model/Payment Regime and Other Financial Matters in the Draft Exploitation Regulations under Review*, 9 July 2018. Available online <https://www.isa.org.jm/files/files/documents/nv.pdf> (accessed 25 August 2021).

22 G. Warwick, 'The contribution of the precautionary principle to marine environmental protection', in R. Barnes and S. Kaye (eds.) *Frontiers in international environmental law: Oceans and climate challenges*, Brill Nijhoff, 2021, pp. 368–406.

23 ISA, Regulations on Prospecting and Exploration, op. cit. note 3, regulation 31; ISA, Draft Regulations on Exploitation, op. cit. note 4, regulations 2(e)(ii), 44(a).

24 *Re. Arbitration Between the Republic of the Philippines and the People's Republic of China, Award, 12 July 2016, PCA Case No. 2013–19*, para. 940. Hereinafter 'South China Sea Arbitration'.

25 C. Foster, 'Adjudication, arbitration and the turn to public law "Standards of Review": Putting the precautionary principle in the crucible', *Journal of International Dispute Settlement*, 2012, 525–58, p. 531.

on marine ecosystems, and seabed mining impacts, means that decision-makers are often faced with incomplete information against which to assess the achievement of environmental goals.[26] UNCLOS does not make express provision for the precautionary approach, as it predates the rise of the principle in international law. Nonetheless, it has been argued by judges and scholars alike that the precautionary approach can be implied into the Convention.[27] It is relevant, in this respect, that various international courts and tribunals have jurisdiction over the 'interpretation and application' of UNCLOS (articles 287(1) and 288). Tribunals considering questions of interpretation may 'take in account … any relevant rules' of international law pursuant to article 31, paragraph 3 (c) of the Vienna Convention.[28] This includes the use of international jurisprudence as an interpretive aid.

The due diligence doctrine has been used in this manner to interpret the relationship between the obligation to protect the marine environment under Part XII of UNCLOS and the requirement for a precautionary approach to risk. Resort to due diligence originated from an examination of the words 'to ensure' under the Convention. State Parties are required 'to ensure' effective control of activities within the Area, 'protection of the marine environment from harmful effects', and that 'activities do not cause damage by pollution' (articles 139(1), 145, and 194(2)). The Seabed Advisory Opinion observed that the words 'to ensure' concern conduct and may be characterised as an obligation of due diligence.[29] The South China Sea Arbitration, more recently, concurred that the obligation 'to ensure' requires 'due diligence' in the sense that a State should not only adopt appropriate rules and measures but also a certain level of vigilance in their administration and enforcement.[30]

The Seabed Advisory Opinion determined that the precautionary approach is an integral part of the due diligence obligation.[31] This is because due diligence requires States to take 'appropriate measures to prevent damage' and applies 'where scientific evidence concerning the scope and potential negative impact of the activity is insufficient but where there are plausible indications of potential risks'.[32] There is an implicit link between due diligence and precaution where there is scientific uncertainty,[33] and States who disregard the risk of negative impacts do not satisfy the due diligence obligation or comply with the precautionary approach.[34] The Chamber concluded by observing that the incorporation of the precautionary approach into a growing number of international treaties, and other instruments, reflecting the formulation of Principle 15 'has initiated a trend towards making this approach part of customary international law'.[35] It might be argued

26 ISA, 'Biodiversity, species ranges, and gene flow in the abyssal Pacific nodule province: Predicting and managing the impacts of deep seabed mining', Jamaica: ISA Technical Study No. 3, 2008, pp. 4–6; J. Halfar and R. Fujita, 'Precautionary management of deep-sea mining', *Marine Policy* 26, 2002, 103–6, p. 105.

27 For a summary of the discussion, see Jaeckel, op. cit. note 8, Ch. 4.4.

28 *Vienna Convention on the Law of Treaties*, 23 May 1969, 1155 UNTS 331.

29 Seabed Advisory Opinion, op. cit. note 5, para. 110.

30 South China Sea Arbitration, op. cit. note 24, para. 944. See also *Request for Advisory Opinion submitted by the Sub-Regional Fisheries Commission (SRFC), Advisory Opinion, 2 April 2015*, paras. 130–32. Hereinafter 'Fisheries Advisory Opinion'; Seabed Advisory Opinion, op. cit. note 5, para. 117; *Pulp Mills on the River Uruguay (Argentina v. Uruguay) Merits, Judgment, I.C.J. Reports 2010*, paras. 101 and 197. Hereinafter '*Pulp Mills*'.

31 Seabed Advisory Opinion, op. cit. note 5, para. 131.

32 Ibid.

33 Ibid., para. 132. See also *Southern Bluefin Tuna (New Zealand v. Japan; Australia v. Japan), Provisional Measures, Order of 27 August 1999, ITLOS Reports 1999*, paras. 77, 79–80.

34 Seabed Advisory Opinion, op. cit. note 5, para. 131.

35 Ibid., para. 135.

that the precautionary approach applies (as a rule of law) to seabed mining activities in all maritime areas under UNCLOS, irrespective of whether the principle remains an emerging rule or has attained customary status. This is because precaution might be said to be held aloft through its intrinsic relationship with the customary law of due diligence.

State practice: fleshing out the meaning of precaution

Introduction

The chapter turns to a descriptive review of the precautionary practices of four Commonwealth State Parties to UNCLOS: New Zealand, Australia, Canada, and the UK. The UK and New Zealand are governed by traditional Westminster-styled parliamentary democracies;[36] Australia and Canada differ slightly from the UK and New Zealand insofar as they are governed by constitutional democracies with federal and State levels of government. Despite the differences between these States, their Commonwealth heritage provides a shared foundation for their respective policy, legislation, and judicial decisions.[37] This means that the environmental law of one State is often familiar to another. It is not unusual, in this respect, for doctrine established in one jurisdiction to be found (or at least reiterated) in the common law of the others.

With the ISA's mandate being restricted to seabed minerals, its experience in managing marine activities and applying a precautionary approach is limited. The State Parties discussed, in contrast, have built up varying levels of expertise and experience in the application of the precautionary principle. Their administrative and judicial branches of government are regularly required to consider terrestrial and marine development proposals that are characterised by incomplete information, scientific uncertainty, and the risk of environmental damage. They have variously enacted legislation to govern resource development (including seabed mining) within their territorial sea (TS), exclusive economic zone (EEZ), continental shelf, and the Area.

New Zealand

New Zealand's reliance on natural resources means that their management is a principal focus of environmental policy (irrespective of government).[38] Environmental law in New Zealand is largely a branch of public law, comprising a comprehensive set of statutes that codify environmental rights and duties. New Zealand's environmental common law comprises its own judicial decisions and other common law decisions where relevant (especially those of Australia, Canada, and the UK).[39] The precautionary approach as a principle of New Zealand public law is concerned with managing risk in the face of uncertain science concerning complex ecosystems. Adaptive management facilitates risk management by enabling an activity to be reviewed, refined, amended, or stopped as information comes to hand.[40]

36 Makgill, 'New Zealand', in R. Martella & B. Grosko (eds.), *International environmental law: The practitioner's guide to the laws of the planet*, American Bar Association, 2014, 909–32, p. 909.

37 Ibid. J. Taberner, 'Australia', 885–908, pp. 885–6; and G. Taylor, 'Canada', 329–48, pp. 330–31.

38 Makgill, 'New Zealand', op. cit. note 36, p. 909.

39 Ibid., p. 910.

40 R. Somerville, 'Policy adjudication, adaptive management and the environment court', *Resource Management Theory and Practice* 9, 2013, 1–28, p. 12.

The Resource Management Act 1991[41] (RMA) is the principal statute for managing natural and physical resources on land and sea.[42] It has jurisdiction over land (including seabed and foreshore), air, and water out to the TS's 12 nautical mile (M) boundary. The purpose of the RMA (i.e., goal) is deliberately expressed as sustainable management[43] rather than sustainable development. The Act does not seek to redistribute wealth or equitably allocate rights to development.[44] Sustainable management is essentially a science-based statutory goal. It relies on applicants avoiding, remedying, or mitigating the effects of proposed activities rather than strictly prescribing how and where development should occur.[45] The TS (including the seabed) is part of the public domain, and there is a presumption against its use and development.[46] This means that the proponents of a development activity must apply for consent and provide a supporting EIA.[47]

The Exclusive Economic Zone and Continental Shelf (Environmental Effects) Act 2012[48] (EEZ Act) establishes an effects-based regime to manage activities within New Zealand's EEZ and Continental Shelf. It was enacted to fill the gaps in New Zealand's existing environmental management regime beyond the 12 M territorial sea boundary and give effect to New Zealand's obligations under UNCLOS to manage and protect natural resources within those jurisdictional areas.[49] The EEZ Act continues or enables the implementation of New Zealand's obligations under various international conventions, including UNCLOS.[50] The EEZ Act's two purposes (i.e., goals) are to (a) promote the sustainable management of natural resources; and (b) protect the environment from pollution.[51] The sustainable management purpose enables integrated decision-making where resource development proposals have cross-boundary effects between the TS, EEZ, and Continental Shelf.[52] There is a presumption against the use and development of natural resources unless the activity in question is permitted by regulations under the EEZ Act.[53]

Decision-makers considering applications for marine consents and discharge consents must apply the EEZ Act's information principles to achieve the purposes of the Act.[54] The information principles require decision-makers to 'take into account any uncertainty or inadequacy in the information available'.[55] If 'the information available is uncertain or inadequate' the decision-maker 'must favour caution and environmental protection'.[56] 'If favouring caution and environmental protection means that an activity is likely to be refused' the decision-maker 'must first consider

41 Resource Management Act 1991 No. 69 (RMA).
42 Makgill, 'New Zealand', op. cit. note 36, p. 910.
43 RMA, section 5.
44 Makgill, 'New Zealand', op. cit. note 36, pp. 910–11.
45 Ibid., p. 911.
46 R. Makgill and H. Rennie, 'A model for integrated coastal management legislation: A principled analysis of New Zealand's resource management act 1991', *The International Journal of Marine and Coastal Law* 27, 2012, 135–65, p. 151; Makgill, 'New Zealand', op. cit. note 36, p. 917.
47 RMA, sections 12, 88(2).
48 Exclusive Economic Zone and Continental Shelf (Environmental Effects) Act 2012 No. 72. Hereinafter 'EEZ Act'.
49 R. Makgill, K. Dawson, and N. de Wit, 'The exclusive economic zone and continental shelf (environmental effects) bill', *Resource Management Journal*, April 2012, p. 1.
50 EEZ Act, section 11.
51 Ibid., section 10(1)(a)–(b).
52 Makgill, 'New Zealand', op. cit. note 36, pp. 917–18.
53 EEZ Act, section 35.
54 Ibid., sections 10(3)(b), and 61.
55 Ibid., section 61(1)(c).
56 Ibid., section 61(2).

whether taking an adaptive management approach would allow the activity to be undertaken'.[57] An adaptive management approach is prohibited where the application is for a marine discharge consent (i.e., pollution).[58] This is likely because allowing adaptive management of pollution would be inconsistent with the Act's goal of protecting the environment from pollution. In simple terms, once pollution occurs it cannot be undone (i.e., the effects are irreversible).

In *Sustain Our Sounds Inc v New Zealand King Salmon Company Ltd*,[59] the New Zealand Supreme Court considered whether adaptive management was consistent with a requirement for a precautionary approach under the RMA and, if so, whether the requirements of adaptive management were satisfied.[60] The Court considered international commentary and New Zealand, Australian, and Canadian case law. It observed that the IUCN guidelines on the application of the precautionary principle[61] included a guideline on adaptive management.[62] The Court noted that the IUCN guidelines recognise that the precautionary principle may require the prohibition of activities. This may be the case where the potential damage is likely to be irreversible or vulnerable species or ecosystems are at risk.[63]

The Supreme Court observed that an applicant should not be placed in a position of anticipating and researching all hypotheses before making an application for development. However, an applicant must establish a sufficient case to persuade a decision-maker to grant approval based on an adaptive management plan.[64] It is important that baseline knowledge is collected, upon which adaptive management plans can build an ongoing and cycling process. Furthermore, plans should have certain and enforceable objectives and establish a process for evaluating monitoring results that enables the review and refinement of hypotheses.[65]

The Court found that the question of whether an adaptive management approach can be considered a part of a precautionary approach is contingent on whether there is an adequate evidential foundation that adaptive management will sufficiently reduce uncertainty and manage any remaining risk for the purpose of achieving the statutory goal. The Supreme Court concluded that whether risk and uncertainty will be sufficiently diminished, for an adaptive management approach to be consistent with the precautionary approach, ultimately depends on the extent of risk and uncertainty and the gravity of the consequences. For example, a small risk of annihilation of an endangered species may mean an adaptive management approach is unavailable. A larger risk of consequences of less gravity may leave room for adaptive management.[66]

There have been several proposals to undertake seabed mining within New Zealand's EEZ and Continental Shelf under the EEZ Act.[67] Trans-Tasman Resources Ltd's (TTR) proposal to

57 Ibid., section 61(3).

58 Ibid., section 61(4)(a)(ii).

59 *Sustain Our Sounds Inc v New Zealand King Salmon Company Ltd* (2014) NZSC 40, 17 ELRNZ 520 *(Sustain Our Sounds Inc)*.

60 Ibid., para. 95.

61 International Union for Conservation of Nature, *Guidelines for applying the precautionary principle to biodiversity conservation and natural resource management*, as approved by the 67th meeting of the IUCN Council, 14–16 May 2007. Hereinafter 'IUCN, *Guidelines for applying the precautionary principle*'.

62 Ibid., guideline 12.

63 *Sustain Our Sounds Inc*, op. cit. note 59, para. 111.

64 Ibid., para. 114.

65 Ibid., para. 115.

66 Ibid., para. 139.

67 In addition to the *TTR decisions* discussed below, see *Decision on Marine Consent Application by Chatham Rock Phosphate Limited, Environmental Protection Authority, 10 February 2015.*

mine large quantities of iron sand within New Zealand's EEZ and Continental Shelf has been the most lengthy and litigious (by far). TTR's first seabed mining proposal was declined by the Environmental Protection Authority (EPA) in 2014 due to inadequate information. The EPA found that the application was premature, and more time should have been taken to understand the proposed operation, its effects on the receiving environment, and existing interests. For those reasons, the application did not meet the sustainable management purpose of the EEZ Act.[68]

TTR's second seabed mining proposal, while reduced in scope, still sought approval to mine up to 50 million tonnes (per annum) of seabed material for a term of 35 years.[69] The proposal was not supported by any substantive new information on the receiving environment or potential adverse effects. In addition, legislative changes intended to satisfy international law meant that the proposal's sediment plume was now treated as pollution under the EEZ Act and ineligible for an adaptive management approach. The most fundamental change between the first and second proposals was that the second proposal was supported by a more sophisticated predictive model. TTR sought to withhold the predictive model information and certain data on sediment plume effects from public notification on the basis that the information was commercially sensitive.

The Environment Court ruled, on an application for procedural directions, that the 'public's right to information enabling its effective participation' overrode 'trade secrecy and commercial prejudice considerations'.[70] Ultimately, the crucial nature of the predictive model in informing the conclusions in the impact assessment, combined with the public's right to participate effectively in the consent process, outweighed any trade secret or business prejudice to TTR by a considerable margin.[71]

The EPA ultimately granted TTR's second application[72] despite the finding that the resulting sediment plume would have significant adverse effects on benthos and other marine life (including within the territorial sea). As the EPA lacked sufficient baseline information to formulate environmental conditions, it imposed conditions requiring TTR to undertake two further years of pre-commencement monitoring to obtain the baseline information necessary to formulate clear effects-based thresholds. The pre-commencement monitoring conditions were, in turn, supplemented by management plan conditions establishing broadly stated goals to be defined as hard thresholds after the pre-commencement baseline information had been collated (i.e., following the two years of pre-commencement monitoring).[73]

A wide range of sectoral stakeholders appealed the majority decision to approve the seabed mining proposal to the High Court. The joint parties claimed that the majority decision failed to observe the Act's requirement for the decision-maker to 'favour caution and environmental protection' where 'the information available is uncertain or inadequate'.[74] The High Court allowed the stakeholder appeals finding the EPA had erred by using adaptive management to manage pollution

68 *Trans-Tasman Resources Ltd Marine Consent Decision, Environmental Protection Authority, 17 June 2014 (TTR decision 2014)*; Makgill and Linhares, 'Deep seabed mining', op. cit. note 19, p. 251.

69 *Trans-Tasman Resources Ltd Marine Consents and Marine Discharge Consents Decision, Environmental Protection Authority, 3 August 2017*, pp. xi and xvi. Hereinafter '*TTR decision 2017*'.

70 *Kiwis Against Seabed Mining Inc. v Environmental Protection Authority* (2016) NZEnvC 217, para. 62. Hereinafter '*Kiwis Against Seabed Mining Inc*'.

71 Ibid., para. 68.

72 *TTR decision 2017*, op. cit. note 69, p. xi, para. 2.

73 R. Makgill, J. Gardiner-Hopkins, and N. Coates, 'Current legal developments: New Zealand', *The International Journal of Marine and Coastal Law* 35, 2020, p. 837.

74 Ibid., p. 838.

effects (i.e., sediment plume) which is prohibited under the EEZ Act.[75] It is noteworthy, in light of the following judgments, that the High Court went on to observe that it was doubtful that an adaptive management approach would have been available, in any event, 'because one of the prerequisites for using an adaptive management approach is to have sufficient baseline information so that appropriate conditions can be drafted. There must be real doubt that this is the case here'.[76] TTR appealed the High Court's decision to the New Zealand Court of Appeal.

The Court of Appeal set the scene for its judgment, describing it as an inquiry that 'must be informed by the principles of international law to which the EEZ Act is intended to give effect'.[77] The Court observed that the EEZ Act provides a clear direction to decision-makers to 'favour caution and environmental protection' where the available information is 'uncertain or inadequate' (i.e., the information principles).[78] The Court was clear that these information principles are how New Zealand has sought to implement its international obligations, including under the 'precautionary approach' or 'precautionary principle' contemplated by Principle 15 of the Rio Declaration.[79] The Court did not agree that the EPA had erred by imposing an 'adaptive management approach' in contravention of the prohibition under the EEZ Act. Rather, the error was more fundamental. The EPA had failed to make the connection between favouring caution and the protection purpose of the Act (i.e., protecting the environment from pollution).[80] The 'high degree' of uncertainty about the effects of the proposal could not be cured by 'post-decision information gathering and monitoring of effects'. This uncertainty, moreover, was not solved by 'overly broad' conditions that employed vague requirements to avoid adverse effects on certain environments which, in turn, were 'to be fleshed out through subsequent management plans'.[81] TTR was granted leave to appeal to the Supreme Court.

The Supreme Court's judgment[82] was delivered in four parts reflecting some differences in reasoning. Nevertheless, the judges largely agreed on most matters before them, including New Zealand's obligations under international law. It determined that UNCLOS and the Convention on Biological Diversity 1992[83] directly applied to TTR's application.[84] Most of the Court's discussion went on to focus on UNCLOS, commencing with the simple observation that UNCLOS applies to activities within the EEZ. Part XII of UNCLOS, as set out in article 192, is identified as establishing the fundamental obligation of all State Parties to 'protect and preserve the marine environment'.[85]

Article 194 of UNCLOS is referenced as establishing obligations to take measures to prevent, reduce, and control pollution of the marine environment. Article 194, paragraph 3 is specifically

75 *Taranaki-Whanganui Conservation Board v. Environmental Protection Authority* (2018) NZHC 2217, (2019) NZRMA 64, para. 404.

76 Ibid., para. 405.

77 *Trans-Tasman Resources Limited v. The Taranaki-Whanganui Conservation Board & Ors* (2020) NZCA 86, (2020) 21 ELRNZ 700, para. 3. Hereinafter '*TTR Court of Appeal*'.

78 Ibid., para. 114; EEZ Act, section 61.

79 Ibid., paras. 114, 127.

80 Ibid., paras. 129–31.

81 Ibid., para. 227.

82 *Trans-Tasman Resources v. Taranaki-Whanganui Conservation Board* [2021] NZSC 127 (*TTR Supreme Court*). For a discussion, see E. Macpherson et al., 'Case analysis: A new "high-water mark" for seabed mining', *New Zealand Journal of Environmental Law* 25, 2021, 277–91.

83 *Convention on Biological Diversity*, 5 June 1992, 1760 UNTS 79.

84 *TTR Supreme Court*, per Young and France JJ, op. cit. note 82, para. 87.

85 Ibid., para. 88.

identified as requiring that the obligation to take measures includes, amongst other things, 'those designed to minimise to the fullest possible extent' pollution from various sources, including pollution from seabed activities subject to national jurisdiction. The judgment notes, referencing one commentator, that the objective of article 194, paragraph 3 'is not to eliminate pollution as such but to reduce it, thus minimising it to the greatest extent possible'. That is seen as a 'realistic approach, as otherwise most kinds of ocean uses would have to be banned'.[86]

It is evident, the Court reasoned, that environmental protection has priority over economic development because article 193 'provides that States can exploit resources "in accordance with" their duty to protect and preserve the environment'.[87] Moreover, UNCLOS and the Convention on Biological Diversity support the proposition that the protection purpose of the EEZ Act[88] imposes a heightened threshold in favour of environmental protection.[89] The EPA's key legal error was its failure to achieve the environmental bottom line imposed under the protection purpose of the EEZ Act.[90] Protection is a separate and additional consideration to whether the sustainable management goal is achieved.[91] The environmental bottom line requires that a proposed discharge (i.e., pollution) must be refused where the environment cannot be protected from material harm.

The Supreme Court also considered whether the EEZ Act's requirement to favour caution and environmental protection is a statutory implementation of the 'precautionary principle' under international environmental law. The Court acknowledged that counsel, while observing the Seabed Advisory Opinion had identified 'a trend towards making' the precautionary 'approach part of customary international law',[92] did not contend that precaution had attained that status.[93] Referencing international commentary, the Court found that: '[a]t its most basic, environmental precaution involves the idea that it is better to be safe than sorry when the effects of activities are uncertain'. The concern underlying the reference to the need to favour caution in the EEZ Act clearly reflects that idea,[94] and the language under the Act's information principles[95] could 'be taken to embody' the precautionary principle.[96]

The Supreme Court unanimously found that the principal error in the decision granting approval to TTR's proposal was the failure to favour caution and environmental protection. The judgment states, in a finding reminiscent of the earlier Environment Court decision,[97] that the EPA's attempt to rectify the information deficits by pre-commencement monitoring inappropriately deprived the public of the right to be heard on a fundamental aspect of TTR's proposal.[98] The Supreme Court, ultimately, agreed with the Court of Appeal that there was insufficient information for the decision-maker to be satisfied it had taken the required cautious approach under the Act.[99]

86 Ibid., paras. 89–91.
87 Ibid., para. 93.
88 EEZ Act, section 10(1)(b).
89 *TTR Supreme Court*, op. cit. note 82, per Young and France JJ, para. 101.
90 Ibid., para. 3; per Glazebrook J, paras. 250 and 267; per Williams J, para. 294; per Winkelmann CJ, paras. 305, 320.
91 *TTR Supreme Court*, op. cit. note 82, per Glazebrook J, para. 245.
92 Seabed Advisory Opinion, op. cit. note 5, para. 135.
93 *TTR Supreme Court*, op. cit. note 82, per Young and France JJ, fn. 290.
94 Ibid., para. 108.
95 EEZ Act, section 61 (and repealed s. 87E).
96 *TTR Supreme Court*, op. cit. note 82, per Young and France JJ, para. 110.
97 *Kiwis Against Seabed Mining Inc*, op. cit. note 70.
98 *TTR Supreme Court*, op. cit. note 82, para. 11.
99 Ibid., per Young and France JJ, para. 205; per Glazebrook J, para. 271.

New Zealand State practice shows evidence and belief that the precautionary principle is an obligation under UNCLOS and international environmental law. It is sufficient, here, to signal some of the key themes evident from New Zealand's application of the precautionary principle to seabed mining. First, it does not matter whether legislation expressly refers to the precautionary principle, the precautionary approach, caution, or some other language. It is all one principle where the objective is to prevent environmental harm in the face of uncertain science or incomplete information. Second, the precautionary approach may require that a seabed mining proposal be declined because inadequate information and uncertainty mean that the risk of harm cannot be sufficiently diminished. Third, an adaptive management approach may be consistent with precaution, provided it can be proven that the proposed form of adaptive management will sufficiently diminish the risk of harm. Fourth, the precautionary approach requires adequate baseline information concerning the receiving environment and the proposal's potential impacts to determine whether a risk will be sufficiently diminished. Fifth, adequate baseline information is a prerequisite of adaptive management as the alternative is prohibition until any deficiencies in baseline information are remedied. Sixth, seeking to withhold information concerning risk for commercial or trade competition reasons is inconsistent with the precautionary obligation to base decisions on the best available information.

Australia

Australian precautionary practice, as compared to New Zealand, is not as clearly established in terms of its application to seabed mining. Its precautionary policy, legalisation, and judicial decisions may be discerned from the principle's general implementation in marine and terrestrial environment decision-making. We do not provide an exhaustive review of Australia's precautionary practice. Rather, it seeks to draw on examples of practice that are relevant to the precautionary principle's application to seabed mining. The precautionary principle, likely, first found expression under the Great Barrier Reef Marine Park Act 1975[100] (GBMP Act). The Act's objective is the 'ecologically sustainable use' of the Great Barrier Reef and its natural resources. The precautionary principle is listed as one of the subsidiary principles of that statutory goal.[101] Of more direct relevance, Australia's Northern Territory declared a moratorium on seabed mining in 2012 pending a review of the likely impacts of seabed mining on the environment and other resources (including commercial and recreational fishing).[102] In July 2021, the Minister for the Environment invoked precautionary language to declare a ban on seabed mining, stating that it 'poses real risks of significant impacts (…) and due to the risks and uncertainty (…) seabed mining is unable to be adequately assessed and appropriately regulated'.[103]

The Environment Protection and Biodiversity Conservation Act 1999[104] (EPBC Act) is relevant because it provides that proposed activities (including seabed mining) must not have a significant

100 Great Barrier Reef Marine Park Act 1975 No. 85 (GBMP Act).

101 GBMP Act, sections 3AA–3AB.

102 *Moratorium on exploration and mining in coastal waters of Northern Territory until 2015*, Northern Territory Government (2012). Available online <https://ntepa.nt.gov.au/__data/assets/pdf_file/0003/504255/seabed_mining_moratorium.pdf> (accessed 2 September 2021), para. 5b(ii).

103 *Declaration of Prohibition Action: Subsea Mining, Environmental Protection Act 2019*, 30 July 2021. Available online <https://depws.nt.gov.au/__data/assets/pdf_file/0012/1032150/declaration-prohibited-action-subsea-mining.pdf> (accessed 16 September 2021), paras. 2, 7(b).

104 Environment Protection and Biodiversity Conservation Act 1999 No. 91. Hereinafter 'EPBC Act'.

impact on the marine areas within the Territorial Sea (beyond 3 M), EEZ, and Continental Shelf.[105] The EPBC Act's objectives include promoting 'ecologically sustainable development through the conservation and ecologically sustainable use of natural resources'.[106] The precautionary principle, as with the GBMP Act, is listed as a subsidiary principle of the Act's 'ecologically sustainable development' object (i.e., goal).[107] The precautionary principle must be taken into account when making decisions in relation to such things as EIA and approval.[108] The onus is on a proponent of an activity to identify whether an EIA is required under the EPBC Act.[109]

Australia's principal judicial decisions on the precautionary approach concern its terrestrial environment. These decisions, despite their terrestrial focus, confirm several precautionary practices of general application. In *Telstra Corp Ltd v Hornsby Shire Council*[110] the New South Wales (NSW) Land and Environment Court considered a decision declining an application to develop a mobile telephone tower. Members of the community had raised concerns that the development would potentially have adverse radiofrequency and electromagnetic energy effects on public health. The Court observed that the case raised questions about 'fear, rationality and the law', and the application of the precautionary principle when 'thinking about public health, safety, and the environment'.[111] It found that precautionary jurisprudence created a two-part test for the application of the precautionary principle: (a) a threat of serious or irreversible environmental damage; and (b) scientific uncertainty as to the environmental damage.[112] Both parts need to be satisfied for a precautionary approach to be applied to an anticipated threat of environmental damage. Scientific uncertainty must be grounded in reasonable scientific plausibility.[113] The burden then shifts to the proponent of the activity to demonstrate that the threat does not exist or is negligible.[114] It is not necessary that serious or irreversible environmental damage has occurred. It is sufficient that there is a threat of such damage, and the environmental damage threatened reaches the threshold of being serious or irreversible.[115] If there is no threat of serious or irreversible environmental damage, the precautionary principle is not triggered.[116] The Court held that the requirement of serious or irreversible environmental damage was not met in this case.[117]

In *Environment East Gippsland Inc. v VicForests*,[118] the Victorian Supreme Court stated that the precautionary principle does not require the avoidance of all risks.[119] The degree of precaution will depend upon the combined effect of the seriousness of the threat and the degree of uncertainty.[120] The test for the application of the precautionary principle raised the following fundamental issues: (a) is there a real threat of serious or irreversible damage; (b) is it attended by a lack of full scien-

105 EPBC Act, sections 23(1)–(2), 24.
106 Ibid., section 3(1)(b).
107 Ibid., section 3A(b).
108 Ibid., section 391.
109 Ibid., section 68.
110 *Telstra Corp Ltd v Hornsby Shire Council* (2006) 67 NSWLR 256. Hereinafter '*Telstra Corp Ltd*'.
111 Ibid., para. 9.
112 Ibid., para. 128.
113 Ibid., paras. 133–134.
114 Ibid., para. 148.
115 Ibid., para. 149.
116 Ibid., paras. 137–138.
117 Ibid., para. 185.
118 *Environment East Gippsland Inc. v VicForests* (2010) VSC 335. Hereinafter '*East Gippsland Inc*'.
119 Ibid., para. 203.
120 Ibid., para. 204.

tific certainty; (c) if yes to (a) and (b), has the proponent demonstrated the threat is negligible; (d) is the threat able to be addressed through adaptive management; and (e) is the measure allegedly required proportionate to the threat in issue.[121] The Court observed that measures should not go beyond what is appropriate and necessary to achieve the objective in question.[122] Uncertainty may, in some circumstances, be adequately managed through an adaptive management approach.[123]

In *Telstra Corp Ltd*, the Court observed, regarding the margin of error to implement a step-wise or adaptive management approach, that the more significant and uncertain the threat the greater the degree of precaution required.[124] Prudence would suggest some margin of error is retained.[125] One means of managing the potential for error is through an adaptive management approach, whereby the scale of the development increases as the extent of the uncertainty is reduced.[126] In *Newcastle v Upper Hunter Shire Council*,[127] the NSW Land and Environment Court described adaptive management as:

> a concept which is frequently invoked but less often implemented in practice. Adaptive management is not a 'suck it and see', trial and error approach to management, but it is an iterative approach involving explicit testing of the achievement of defined goals. Through feedback to the management process, the management procedures are changed in steps until monitoring shows that the desired outcome is obtained. The monitoring program has to be designed so that there is statistical confidence in the outcome. In adaptive management the goal to be achieved is set, so there is no uncertainty as to the outcome and conditions requiring adaptive management do not lack certainty, but rather they establish a regime which would permit changes, within defined parameters, to the way the outcome is achieved.[128]

Australian State practice demonstrates evidence and belief that the precautionary principle is an obligation. The discussion of Australia's application of the precautionary approach illustrates some further themes of precautionary practice. First, the precautionary principle has been invoked to declare a ban on seabed mining in the Northern Territory on the grounds that seabed mining poses real risks of significant impacts and is unable to be adequately assessed and appropriately regulated at present. Second, the precautionary approach obligation is not invoked merely because there is a perceived risk of harm. The threat of damage arising from harm must be scientifically plausible. The burden of proof then shifts to the proponent to demonstrate that either there is no threat or that any threat is negligible. Third, precautionary measures should be proportionate to the objective in question. Fourth, adaptive management may be used to manage risk in some circumstances. It is not a 'suck it and see' approach based on trial and error. It requires an iterative approach where monitoring is undertaken against clear triggers designed to achieve specific outcomes.

121 Ibid., para. 212.
122 Ibid., para. 207.
123 Ibid., para. 205.
124 *Telstra Corp Ltd*, op. cit. note 110, para. 161.
125 Ibid., para. 162.
126 Ibid., para. 163.
127 *Newcastle & Hunter Valley Speleological Society Inc. v Upper Hunter Shire Council* (2010) NSWLEC 48. Hereinafter '*Newcastle & Hunter Valley Speleological Society Inc*'.
128 Ibid., 320, para. 184.

Canada

Canada, as with Australia, has not established clear precautionary measures for the regulation of seabed mining. The federal government has not enacted seabed mining legislation and has been slow to adopt legislation and regulations concerning the precautionary approach.[129] Precaution, on the other hand, is incorporated into many provincial statutes, regulations, and policies for the purpose of protecting the environment.[130] The Oceans Act sets out Canada's federal responsibilities for ocean governance within its TS, EEZ, and Continental Shelf.[131] The Act's preamble states: 'Canada promotes the wide application of the precautionary approach to the conservation, management and exploitation of marine resources in order to protect these resources and preserve the marine environment'.

The Oceans Act requires that strategies and plans for the marine environment are based on sustainable development, integrated management, and the precautionary approach.[132] The Act calls on the Minister to lead and facilitate the development of a national oceans strategy that guides the management of Canada's estuarine, coastal, and marine ecosystems. These principles are to be applied through the preparation and implementation of integrated management plans.[133] The principles guiding integrated management under the Act include ecosystem-based management, sustainable development, the precautionary approach, conservation, shared responsibility, flexibility, and inclusiveness. These principles apply to all activities or measures in (or affecting) estuaries, coastal waters, and marine waters that form part of Canada or in which Canada has sovereign rights under international law.[134]

Although the Oceans Act would appear to set out a regime for implementing precaution to seabed mining, the authors have not been able to unearth any significant policy or judicial decisions that might help inform a description of State practice. On the other hand, decision-making under the Fisheries Act 1985[135] has been the subject of significant litigation and is a source of legal precedent concerning Canadian precautionary practice. The Fisheries Act's purpose (i.e., goal) is to provide a framework for the management, control, conservation, and protection of Canada's fisheries.[136] The responsible Minister, when making a decision under the Act, may consider the application of a precautionary approach, an ecosystem approach, and the sustainability of fisheries.[137] In addition,

129 D. VanderZwaag, S. Fuller, and R. Myers, 'Canada and the precautionary principle/approach in ocean and coastal management: Wading and wandering in tricky currents', *Ottawa Law Review* 34-1, 2002, 117–58, p. 125.

130 For example, see the Canadian Environmental Protection Act, Fisheries Act, and Impact Assessment Act.

131 Oceans Act, SC 1996, Ch. 31, sections. 4, 7, 8(1), 10, 13(1), 14, 15(1), 17(1), 18, 19(1). These provisions set out the Act's jurisdiction over Canada's TS, EEZ, and Continental Shelf.

132 Ibid., sections 29, 30.

133 A. Chircop and L. Hildebrand, 'Beyond the buzzwords: A perspective on integrated coastal and ocean management in Canada', in D. Rothwell and D. VanderZwaag (eds.), *Towards principled oceans governance: Australian and Canadian approaches and challenges*, Routledge, 2006, pp. 19–71. For an overview of the principle of 'integrated management' see Makgill and Rennie, 'A model for integrated coastal management', op. cit. note 46, 138–43.

134 Canada, *Policy and Operational Framework for Integrated Management of Estuarine, Coastal and Marine Environments in Canada* (last updated 17 August 2016). Available online <https://www.dfo-mpo.gc.ca/oceans/publications/cosframework-cadresoc/page01-eng.html> (accessed 23 September 2021); Fisheries and Oceans Canada, *Canada's Oceans Strategy* (2002). Available online <https://waves-vagues.dfo-mpo.gc.ca/Library/264678.pdf> (accessed 23 September 2021), p. 6.

135 Fisheries Act 1985, R.S.C., Ch. F-14.

136 Ibid., section 2.1.

137 Ibid., section 2.5.

the Act empowers the Minister to create policies and guidelines for (amongst other things) conservation, management, scientific study, and protection of the ocean.[138]

The Supreme Court of Canada in *Castonguay Blasting v Ontario*,[139] recognising its foundation in international law, stated that the precautionary principle as an 'emerging international law principle recognises that since there are inherent limits in being able to determine and predict environmental impacts with scientific certainty, environmental policies must anticipate and prevent environmental degradation'.[140] The Federal Court of Canada in *Morton v Canada (2015)*[141] considered the application of precaution to a ministerial decision authorising the transfer of diseased salmon from their hatchery to a fish farm in territorial waters under the Fisheries Act 1985 (and subsidiary regulations).[142] The Court commenced its decision by stating that the 'precautionary principle is, at a minimum, an established aspect of statutory interpretation, and arguably, has crystallised into a norm of customary international law and substantive domestic law'.[143]

The Court overturned the Minister's decision authorising the transfer. It made it clear, in doing so, that it was not arbitrating the science. Rather, clear evidence that there was a risk that the diseased salmon could be harmful was inconsistent with the legislative requirements to protect fish.[144] The Court found that a purposive, contextual, and plain meaning analysis of the words 'may be harmful' suggested that any disease or disease agent that might be harmful to the 'protection and conservation' of fish required a precautionary approach to decision-making.[145] The Minister, on the evidence, had not erred on the side of caution.[146] The phrase 'may be harmful' did not require scientific certainty that harm would be a likely consequence of the transfer.[147] It was sufficient that the proposed transfer risked harming fish for it to be contrary to the goal of protection.

In *Morton v Canada (2019)*,[148] the Federal Court of Canada held that a subsequent ministerial transfer policy had disregarded *Morton (2015)* by allowing transfer licences to be issued without testing fish for disease. The Court found that the policy appeared to allow a threshold or 'level' of potential harm that permitted transfer of diseased fish unless the transfer placed genetic diversity, species, or conservation units of fish at risk. This approach was not consistent with the requirement for conservation because it risked severe potential impact and serious or irreversible harm on a localised scale.[149] The Court observed that:

> the Minister's Interpretation (sic) permits harm to genetic diversity, species or ecosystem of a stock or conservation unit to the point where a stock or conservation unit "cannot" sustain

138 Ibid., section 10(1).
139 *Castonguay Blasting Ltd v Ontario (Environment)*, (2013) 3 SCR 323, 2013 SCC 52. Hereinafter '*Castonguay Blasting Ltd*'.
140 Ibid., para. 20.
141 *Morton v Canada (Fisheries and Oceans)* (2015) FC 575. Hereinafter '*Morton v Canada*'.
142 Ibid., para. 3. *Fishery (General) Regulations*, 1993, SOR/93-53.
143 Ibid., para. 43.
144 Ibid., para. 47.
145 Ibid., paras. 56–57.
146 Ibid., paras. 63, 65.
147 Ibid., para. 97.
148 *Morton v Canada (Minister of Fisheries and Oceans)* (2019) FCJ No 178. Varied on other grounds by the Federal Court of Appeal in *Namgis First Nation v. Canada (Minister of Fisheries, Oceans and Canadian Coast Guard)* (2020) FCJ No. 778.
149 *Morton v. Canada* (2019), op. cit. note 141, para. 140.

biodiversity and the continuation of evolutionary and natural production. It is difficult to see how this is consistent with the precautionary principle. And, in my view, it is not.[150]

Canadian State practice demonstrates both evidence and belief that the precautionary principle is an obligation under international and domestic law. Key themes evident from the Canadian State practice include, first, in terms of legislation, a precautionary approach is necessary for achieving other environmental goals and principles (e.g., integrated management, ecosystem-based management, and sustainability). Second, judicial acknowledgement that the precautionary approach is an accepted norm of international law. Third, the precautionary approach will require a proposal to be declined where the risk of harm is not sufficiently diminished to achieve the goal of environmental protection. Fourth, the risk of a severe adverse impact on a local marine environment cannot be justified on the basis that it does not pose a more existential threat to wider marine environments or ecosystems.

United Kingdom

Although the United Kingdom (UK) makes legislative provisions for seabed mining and the precautionary principle, its judicial decisions concerning precaution, like Australia and Canada, have not directly grappled with any seabed mining proposals. Its case law does, however, agree with and add to the Commonwealth jurisprudence on precaution that is generally applicable to seabed mining. In terms of legislation, the Marine and Coastal Access Act 2010 (MCAA)[151] regulates a range of activities within the UK's marine area, including its TS, EEZ, and Continental Shelf.[152] The MCAA requires activities within the marine area to be managed with the objective (i.e., goal) 'of making a contribution to the achievement of sustainable development (…) taking account of all relevant facts and matters'.[153] Seabed mining proposals are regulated under the MCAA's general licencing framework.[154] A decision-maker considering an application for a seabed mining licence must have regard to requirements to protect the environment and prevent interference with other legitimate uses of the sea.[155] A seabed mining proponent must prepare an EIA if the activity is likely to have a significant effect due to its size, nature, or location.[156]

The Deep Sea Mining Act 1981 (DSMA) regulates seabed mining activities under UK jurisdiction within the Area.[157] A decision-maker considering an exploration or exploitation licence must 'have regard to the need to protect (as far as reasonably practicable) marine creatures, plants and other organisms and their habitat from any harmful effects' that might arise from authorising a licence.[158] It is UK government policy that decisions made under the DSMA need to take account of the Seabed Advisory Opinion's findings on environmental obligations, including EIA and the precautionary approach.[159]

150 Ibid., para. 170.
151 Marine and Coastal Access Act 2010 (c. 23) (MCAA).
152 Ibid., section 42.
153 Ibid., section 2(1)(a)–(b).
154 MCAA, Part IV, Ch. 1, section 66.
155 MCAA, section 69(1)(a) and (c).
156 The Marine Works (Environmental Impact Assessment) Regulations 2007, No. 1518, regulations 2(F3), 2(F28)(b), 8.
157 Deep Sea Mining Act 1981 (c. 53), and Deep Sea Mining Act 2014 (c. 15) (DSMA).
158 DSMA, section 5(1).
159 J. Harrisson, 'The United Kingdom and seabed mining', in V. Tassin Campanella (ed.), *Routledge Handbook of seabed mining and the law of the sea*, op.cit., chapter VI.2.14.

The precautionary approach has general application under UK environmental law. The role of the precautionary approach appears to have been first outlined in government policy during the early 1990s.[160] *This common inheritance* stated that the government should take precautionary action to limit the use of potentially dangerous materials or the spread of potentially dangerous pollutants, where scientific knowledge was inconclusive as to whether likely costs outweighed the benefits.[161] More recently, the UK, as part of the Brexit Trade and Cooperation Agreement,[162] committed to respecting European Union (EU) environmental law principles, including the principles of precaution and prevention.[163] The Environment Bill is intended to give effect to the UK's commitment to the EU's environmental law principles in its domestic decision-making.[164] The Bill calls for long-term targets and environmental improvement plans to be established for the natural environment (including marine, terrestrial, and water environments).[165] This is intended to enable the promulgation of regulations to achieve the Bill's principles within the UK's TS, EEZ, and Continental Shelf.[166]

In *Bova v Highland Council*,[167] the Inner Court of Scotland was asked to consider whether amendments to the Scottish Planning Policy's (Policy) requirement for a precautionary approach to flood management were material.[168] The old Policy had obliged the Council to 'err on the side of caution where flood risk is an issue', whereas the new Policy directed developers and planning authorities to take a 'precautionary approach' to decision-making where flood risk is an issue.[169] The Court approvingly cites Jans and Vedder's comment in *European environmental law*[170] that:

> the precautionary principle is all about 'risk management,' which does not mean that all risks must be reduced to zero. Judging what is an acceptable level of risk for society is a political responsibility. Where the action is deemed necessary, measures based on the precautionary principle should be proportional to the chosen level of protection.[171]

The Court found, on this basis, that adopting a precautionary approach rather than erring on the side of caution means the same thing.[172] The Court emphasised there may be multiple types of precautionary approaches, as the language used in the Policy refers to 'a' rather than 'the' precau-

160 J. Zander, *The application of the precautionary principle in practice: Comparative dimensions*, Cambridge University Press, 2010, p. 215.

161 Great Britain, Department of the Environment, *This common inheritance: Britain's environmental strategy*, HMSO Publications 1990.

162 *Trade and Cooperation Agreement between the European Union and the European Atomic Energy Community, of the one part, and the United Kingdom of Great Britain and Northern Ireland, of the other part*, 30 April 2021.

163 Ibid., Part Two, Heading One, Title XI, Ch. 7, article 7.4.

164 The Environment Bill, *26 May 2021*, HL Bill 16, clause 16(5)(d).

165 UK Government, *Explanatory Notes to Bill 16, 2021*, sections 65, 110, 370. Hereinafter 'Explanatory Notes to Bill'.

166 Ibid., para. 564.

167 *Bova v Highland Council*, 2013, CSIH 41, 2013 SC 510.

168 Scotland, *Scottish Planning Policy*, June 2014. Available online <https://www.gov.scot/publications/scottish-planning-policy/pages/7/> (accessed 23 September 2021), sections 204, 255. Local Government and Housing Directorate.

169 Ibid., para. 36.

170 Ibid., para. 42. See J. Jans and H. Vedder, *European environmental law*, Europa Law Publishing, 2008, p. 38.

171 Ibid., para. 43.

172 Ibid., paras. 30, 36, 40, 52.

tionary approach.[173] The intention and effect of the amendment did not substantively change the Policy's precautionary approach to assessing flood risk. The alteration in the language used was no more than textual or cosmetic. The amendment expressed the precautionary nature of the existing policy more emphatically and did not introduce a new and different policy approach.[174] The Court found, on this basis, that adopting a precautionary approach rather than erring on the side of caution means the same thing.[175]

In *BASF Agro BV and ECPA and ESA,* the Court of Justice of the European Union (CJEU) was asked to consider the precautionary principle in relation to UK law and decision-making.[176] The CJEU commenced by observing that the precautionary principle is a general principle under EU law. It requires decision-makers to take appropriate measures to prevent specific potential risks to (amongst other things) the environment by giving precedence to the requirements related to protecting that interest over economic interests.[177] It enables protective measures to be taken where there is scientific uncertainty as to the existence or extent of risks, without waiting until the reality and seriousness of those risks become fully apparent or materialise.[178] The Court identified three stages to precaution, including: (a) identification of the potentially adverse effects arising from a phenomenon; (b) assessment of the risks to the environment related to that phenomenon; and (c) when the potential risks identified exceed the acceptable threshold for risk management by adopting appropriate protective measures.[179]

The CJEU observed that scientific risk assessment is not required to provide conclusive scientific evidence of the reality of the risk or the seriousness of the potential adverse effects. Adopting preventive measures or withdrawing them cannot be made subject to proof of the lack of risk, as proof is generally impossible to give in scientific terms. Zero risk does not exist.[180] Scientific risk assessment should be based on the best scientific data available and should be undertaken in an independent, objective, and transparent manner.[181] It may prove impossible to carry out a full scientific risk assessment because of the inadequate nature of the available scientific data. That does not stop a decision-maker from taking preventive measures in accordance with the precautionary principle.[182] Preventive measures may be taken if the risk, while not 'fully' demonstrated by conclusive scientific evidence, appears to be adequately backed up by the scientific data available at the time.[183]

The CJEU found that responsibility for determining the level of risk deemed unacceptable lies, provided that the applicable rules are observed, with the institutions responsible for the political choice of determining an appropriate level of protection. It is for those decision-makers to determine the critical thresholds for adverse effects. They must then exercise their judgment in deciding the point at which such adverse effects are no longer acceptable for society.[184] Their decision-making powers, and exercise of judgment, are subject to the obligation to ensure a high level of

173 Ibid., para. 49.
174 Ibid., para. 53.
175 *Bova v Highland Council*, op. cit. note 167, para 49.
176 *BASF Agro BV and ECPA and ESA*, Case T-584/13, ECLI:EU:T:2018:279. *Hereinafter 'BASF Agro BV'*.
177 Ibid., para. 58.
178 Ibid., para. 59.
179 Ibid., para. 60.
180 Ibid., para. 65.
181 Ibid., para. 66.
182 Ibid., para. 67.
183 Ibid., para. 69.
184 Ibid., para. 71.

protection is afforded to the environment, but that does not have to be the highest that is technically possible.[185] The precautionary principle requires the withdrawal or amendment of approval where new data invalidates an earlier conclusion that the approval criteria have been satisfied.[186]

UK State practice demonstrates evidence and belief that the precautionary principle is domestically applicable through UNCLOS, international environmental law, EU law, and UK law. Key themes evident from the UK include, first, recognition that the Seabed Advisory Opinion's environmental obligations, including the precautionary approach, must be satisfied when considering seabed mining proposals. Second, as in the case of New Zealand, different legislative expressions of precaution normally recognise the precautionary principle unless the language is clearly inconsistent with the international obligation. Third, it requires decision-makers to take appropriate measures to prevent potential risks to protect the environment and give precedence to protection over economic interests. Fourth, preventive measures may be taken if the risk is adequately backed up by the scientific data available at the time. Fifth, the precautionary principle requires that an application for a proposed development is declined where the risk of harm jeopardises achieving a high level of environmental protection.

Precautionary lessons from State practice

International law

It is reasonable to contend that the precautionary principle has evolved from a soft statement of international law into a hard obligation. It is evident from the four States discussed that they acknowledge the precautionary principle as an international law obligation through legislation, policy, and judicial decisions. By way of example, the EEZ Act expressly enables the implementation of New Zealand's obligations under UNCLOS. New Zealand Courts have, in turn, found that decisions under the EEZ Act must be informed by international law obligations, including the precautionary approach.[187] Australia incorporates the language of the precautionary principle directly into the GBMP Act. In *Morton v Canada (2015)* the Court held that the precautionary principle is an established aspect of statutory interpretation and, arguably, a crystallised norm of customary international and domestic law.[188] Likewise, seabed mining decisions under the UK's DSMA need to take account of the Mining Advisory Opinion's findings on international law obligations (i.e., including the precautionary principle).

Meaning of precaution

The language of precaution differs slightly between each of the four States. New Zealand has elected under the EEZ Act to require decision-makers to 'favour caution and environmental protection'.[189] Elsewhere New Zealand, Australia, Canada, and the UK have variously incorporated Principle 15 of the Rio Declaration, the precautionary approach, or precautionary language into their legislation, policy, and judicial decisions. The States described appear to concur that it

185 Ibid., para. 72.

186 Ibid., para. 91.

187 *TTR Supreme Court*, op. cit. note 82, per Young and France JJ, paras. 108 and 110; *TTR Court of Appeal*, op. cit. note 77, paras. 114, 127; Makgill et al., 'Current legal developments: New Zealand', op. cit. note 73, p. 841.

188 *Morton v. Canada (2015)*, op. cit. note 141, para. 43.

189 EEZ Act, section 61(2).

is the intent of precautionary language that is important rather than textual or cosmetic differences in expression.[190] It seems agreed that policy or legislative language adheres to the precautionary principle where it calls for caution or prudence where there is a risk of harm accompanied by incomplete information and/or scientific uncertainty (e.g., due diligence is required).

A precautionary approach is required where there is a risk of serious or irreversible damage and a lack of full scientific certainty.[191] It commonly requires the following measures: (a) obtaining adequate baseline information on the receiving environment; (b) assessing the potential impacts of a proposed activity on that receiving environment through EIA; (c) establishing whether there is a risk of serious or irreversible harm; (d) discerning whether the risk of harm can be sufficiently diminished; and (e) preventing approval of any element of a proposal where the contingent risk cannot be diminished.[192]

The precautionary principle may enable the approval of an activity where the risk of harm can be appropriately managed or require refusal where there is insufficient information to establish that risk can be sufficiently diminished. The ISA, at the time of writing, is still to promulgate regulations for commercial-scale mining operations. The ISA might, in the meantime, promulgate policies or guidance on the meaning of precaution and its common requirements. This would provide contractors with some preliminary indication of the measures they will need to take to satisfy information requirements and diminish risk.

UNCLOS requires the ISA to take an active role in assessing the environmental implications of seabed mining in the area (articles 165(2)(d), UNCLOS), while the LTC is to consider such assessments when drafting rules, regulations, and procedures. In practice, the ISA's Mining Code places the burden of conducting EIAs on contractors.[193] ISA contractors are required to collect baseline information during their exploration work.[194] This is intended to provide the foundation for a contractor's assessment of the effects of exploration[195] and future mineral exploitation. Four EIAs were submitted to the ISA between 2018 and 2021. All focus on small-scale testing of a nodule collector pre-prototype or prototype mineral exploration work.[196] It is unlikely that these EIAs provide sufficient information against which to assess the potential implications of exploitation let alone inform rules, regulations, or procedures for exploitation. It is difficult to make a definitive statement, in this respect, however, as the contractors' annual reports are treated as confidential. The ISA might consider, as a step towards promulgating exploitation regulations, making existing and future baseline and EIA information publicly available. State Parties (and key stakeholders) could be provided with an opportunity to scientifically review that data for information gaps, adverse effects, and alternative approaches to minimising harm. Scientific transparency would be

190 *TTR Court of Appeal*, op. cit. note 77, para. 114; *Bova v. Highland Council*, op. cit. note 167, paras. 49, 53.

191 *Sustain Our Sounds Inc*, op. cit. note 59, para. 111; *Telstra Corp Ltd*, op. cit. note 110, para. 128; *BASF Agro BV*, op. cit. note 176, para. 59.

192 Ibid., para. 129; *East Gippsland Inc.*, op. cit. note 118, para. 212; *BASF Agro BV*, ibid., para. 60.

193 Jaeckel, op. cit. note 8, p. 231.

194 ISA, Regulations on Prospecting and Exploration, op. cit. note 3, regulation 32; ISA, *Recommendations for the Guidance of Contractors for the Assessment of the Possible Environmental Impacts Arising from Exploration for Marine Minerals in the Area*, 30 March 2020, ISBA/25/LTC/6/Rev.1, paras. 32–33.

195 ISA, Regulations on Prospecting and Exploration, op. cit. note 3, regulation 32.

196 The environmental impact assessments for Belgium and Germany are available online <https://www.isa.org.jm/minerals/environmental-impact-assessments> (accessed 25 September 2021); the Environmental Impact Statement for Nauru is available online <https://www.eisconsultationnauruun.org/> (accessed 12 November 2021), and a summary of the Environmental Impact Statement for India is contained in ISA, *Review of the environmental impact statement submitted by the Ministry of Earth Sciences of the Government of India*, 18 June 2020, ISBA/26/LTC/5.

consistent with the interest that all State Parties have in the Area. Moreover, it would offer the ISA another avenue through which data and analysis could be collated to assess the implications of seabed mining and discern the regulatory steps required to implement precaution within the Area.

The regulatory goal of precaution

It is evident from the State practice described that there are a range of statutory goals that the precautionary principle might serve. The statutory goal invariably informs the outcome that the precautionary principle is intended to achieve, including the threshold of harm which might be appropriate in any case. New Zealand's judiciary has ruled that 'sustainable management' and 'protection' establish two different environmental goals that must be satisfied under the Act. The protection purpose is cumulative to the sustainable management purpose.[197] It may be consistent with sustainable management for a seabed mining activity to cause adverse effects on the environment provided such effects can be appropriately remedied or mitigated under the sustainable management purpose. However, protecting the environment from pollution means keeping it safe from harm caused by the discharge of harmful substances. Protection from pollution can only be achieved by ensuring the proposed seabed mining activity avoids pollution causing material harm to the environment or by prohibiting the discharge.[198] Whatever goal precaution is intended to achieve, it is evident from State practice that the precautionary approach would oblige a decision-maker to decline approval of a seabed mining proposal where the risk of harm means that the environmental goal cannot be achieved.[199]

The ISA faces a similar interpretative exercise to the one addressed under New Zealand law. On the one hand, the ISA is tasked with ensuring 'the development of the resources of the Area'.[200] On the other hand, the ISA must 'adopt rules, regulations, and procedures' for 'prevention, reduction and control of pollution'[201] and 'prevention of damage to the flora and fauna of the marine environment'.[202] New Zealand practice illustrates that the precautionary principle can affect the interpretation of express instruments, by requiring decision-makers to err on the side of caution and in cases requiring 'environmental protection' to minimise environmental harm. The ISA's mandate, namely to 'organize and control' mining activities in the Area,[203] affords the ISA some scope to determine its policy direction and apply the precautionary principle. However, the ISA's discretion is subject to Part XII of UNCLOS, including the general obligation to protect and preserve the marine environment (i.e., goal).

State practice seems to acknowledge the difficulties of mitigating or remediating marine pollution once it has occurred. Pollution from sediment plumes is one of the key potential adverse effects to arise from seabed mining within the Area. The ISA will need to determine how the risk of pollution satisfies the due diligence obligations to control activities within the Area and protect

197 *TTR Supreme Court*, op. cit. note 82, per Glazebrook J, para. 245.

198 *TTR Court of Appeal*, op. cit. note 77, para. 86; Makgill et al., 'Current legal developments: New Zealand', op. cit. note 73, p. 840.

199 *TTR Supreme Court*, op. cit. note 82, para. 3; per Glazebrook J, paras. 250 and 267; per Williams J, para. 294; per Winkelmann CJ, paras. 305 and 320; *TTR Court of Appeal*, op. cit. note 77, para. 86; *Morton v. Canada (2015)*, op. cit. note 141, para. 47, 140; *BASF Agro BV*, op. cit. note 176, para. 91.

200 UNCLOS, article 150(a).

201 Ibid., article 145(a).

202 Ibid., article 145(b).

203 Ibid., article 157(1).

the marine environment from harmful effects (articles 139, paragraph 1, and 145). State practice indicates that harm includes such things as the significance of the impact, scale, and duration. Harm cannot be minimised simply on the basis that its impacts are localised as opposed to having ecosystem-wide significance.[204] The ISA requires contractors to prevent, reduce, and control pollution,[205] while working towards a regime that enables seabed mining in the medium-term future. The ISA will need to reconcile aspirations for development with the requirement for protection before it commences assessing applications for mineral exploitation.

Baseline information and assessment of potential impacts

It is a basic premise of the State precautionary practice described that incomplete information and/or scientific uncertainty cannot be used as a reason for postponing action to prevent degradation of the environment. The flip side of this premise is a requirement for adequate baseline information and EIA. It is for the proponent of a seabed mining activity to prove that the potential adverse effects of the proposal on the environment can be adequately avoided, remedied, or mitigated.[206] If the information provided in support of a proposal is so incomplete and uncertain that potential effects and/or risks of harm are unable to be adequately assessed, the proposal cannot be approved. State practice suggests that, in these circumstances, the ISA should consider preparing regulatory provisions that include express directions on the need for adequate baseline information and EIA. These regulations should make it clear that paucity of baseline information and inadequate impact assessment will trigger the requirement for a precautionary approach with greater emphasis on caution and environmental protection depending on the nature of the information deficit.

Threshold of potential harm

As a rule of thumb, the more significant and uncertain the threat, the greater the degree of precaution required.[207] The risk of a severe adverse impact on a local marine environment cannot be justified on the basis that it does not pose a more existential threat to wider marine environments or ecosystems.[208] The precautionary principle does not require the avoidance of all risks, and the degree of precaution will depend upon the seriousness of the threat and the degree of uncertainty.[209] The question of whether a proposal is consistent with the precautionary approach ultimately rests on whether the extent of risk and uncertainty and the gravity of the consequences can be sufficiently diminished. A small risk of annihilation of an endangered species may mean a proposal is inconsistent with the precautionary approach, while a greater risk of an impact with less gravity may be consistent.[210] This suggests that the ISA should identify express environmental goals, objectives, thresholds, and indicators. ISA regulatory measures presently lack this level of clarity.[211] Important questions include whether the impacts of deep seabed mining can be

204 *TTR Court of Appeal*, op. cit. note 77, paras. 12(a) and 111; Makgill et al., 'Current legal developments: New Zealand', op. cit. note 73, pp. 839–40.
205 ISA, Regulations on Prospecting and Exploration, op. cit. note 3, regulation 31(5); ISA, Draft Regulations on Exploitation, op. cit. note 4, regulation 49.
206 *Sustain Our Sounds Inc*, op. cit. note 59, para. 114.
207 *Telstra Corp Ltd*, op. cit. note 110, para. 161.
208 *Morton v. Canada (2019)*, op. cit. note 141, para. 170.
209 *East Gippsland Inc.*, op. cit. note 118, paras. 203–4.
210 *Sustain Our Sounds Inc*, op. cit. note 59, para. 139.
211 Tunnicliffe et al., op. cit. note 15.

reduced sufficiently to avoid biodiversity loss.[212] If a seabed mining activity results in biodiversity loss, it will contravene the Convention on Biological Diversity and its express provision for the precautionary principle.[213] If ISA regulations for exploitation do not provide thresholds for environmental impacts, they will need to set out clear pathways through which decision-makers can identify those thresholds on a case-by-case basis, in order to satisfy environmental obligations within the Area.

Burden of proof

It is a basic principle of resource development that it is for the proponent of an activity to prove their case through a supporting EIA. This should include adequate information on the receiving environment and the potential effects of the proposal on that environment. The States described have developed several salient principles around where the burden of proof lies in terms of risk identification. The mere perception of risk is not sufficient to require a proponent to adduce evidence that there is no risk. Rather, an allegation of scientific uncertainty, where such uncertainty has not been identified in the proponent's EIA or where it is not clear on the face of the EIA, must be grounded in reasonable scientific plausibility.[214] Equally, scientific risk assessment does not require conclusive evidence of the risk or the seriousness of the potential adverse effects. This is because the existence or absence of risk, by its very nature, is the subject of scientific uncertainty (e.g., zero risk does not exist).[215] Scientific risk assessment should be based on the best available data.[216] Preventative measures may be taken if the risk appears to be demonstrated by the scientific information available at the time.[217] It would be judicious for the ISA to make it clear that mineral exploitation can only occur where the risks have been reduced to an acceptable level. In this context, it may be recalled that the draft regulations developed by the ISA's Preparatory Commission in 1990 provided that '[a]ctivities in the Area shall only take place if they do not cause serious harm to the marine environment'.[218]

Adaptive management

It is evident from the State practice discussed that adaptive management is the principal tool for enabling an application to proceed in the face of incomplete information or scientific uncertainty. The core elements of adaptive management include: (a) monitoring of impacts on agreed indicators; (b) promoting research to reduce uncertainty; (c) ensuring evaluation of outcomes to review and adjust measures adopted; and (d) establishing efficient and effective compliance.[219] Adaptive management should not be available where the precautionary principle requires the prohibition of activities (e.g., the potential damage is likely to be irreversible or vulnerable species or ecosystems

212 H. Niner et al., 'Deep-sea mining with no net loss of biodiversity—An impossible aim', *Frontiers in Marine Science* 5, 2018, 53; C.L. Van Dover et al., 'Biodiversity loss from deep-sea mining', *Nature Geoscience*, 10, 2017, 464–65.

213 *Convention on Biological Diversity*, preamble.

214 *Telstra Corp Ltd*, op. cit. note 110, paras. 133–34.

215 *BASF Agro BV*, op. cit. note 176, para. 65.

216 EEZ Act, section 61(1)(b); *Kiwis Against Seabed Mining Inc*, op. cit. note 70, para. 64; *BASF Agro BV*, op. cit. note 176, para. 66.

217 EEZ Act, section 62(2); *BASF Agro BV*, op. cit. note 176, para. 67.

218 *Preparatory Commission for the ISA and ITLOS*, 8 February 1990, LOS/PCN/SCN.3/WP.6/Add.5, article 105.

219 IUCN, *Guidelines for applying the precautionary principle*, op. cit. note 61, guideline 12.

are at risk).[220] Adaptive management may include such things as commencing on a small scale for a short period so that effects can be monitored, or allowing an activity to be undertaken so that its effects can be assessed and continued or discontinued on the basis of those effects.[221] In the case that an activity is continued or discontinued based on its effects, it is important to have adequate baseline information and ongoing monitoring in order to enable evaluation of targets and refinement of hypothesis.[222]

Adaptive management is not a 'suck it and see' approach.[223] It does not allow a development to proceed based on trial and error. Rather, it requires explicit testing against defined goals. The goal to be achieved is established with certainty as to the outcome. Adaptive management conditions only permit changes within defined parameters to ensure that established outcomes are achieved.[224] In simple terms, adaptive management must be calibrated against clear thresholds that can be monitored to determine whether an activity should be adjusted or stopped all together. It is respectfully suggested that the ISA should seek to ensure through regulation that any adaptive management machinery employed within the Area is based on scientifically verifiable thresholds that are designed to prevent harmful impacts.

Conclusion

The scientific uncertainties surrounding the potential environmental impacts of seabed mining present significant challenges for this nascent industry and trigger an obligation to apply the precautionary principle. Commonwealth States and domestic courts have developed considerable experience in applying the precautionary principle, both in marine and terrestrial contexts. It is clear from a cursory review of each State that there is a fair degree of consensus on the principle's meaning and the kinds of measures necessary to ensure its implementation. Although legislative wording may differ in its expression of the precautionary approach, State practice exhibits many similarities when it comes to determining what the obligation means and requires. This includes such things as the requirement for sound baseline information on the receiving environment and avoidance of irreversible environmental damage. The principle requires regulators to minimise harm and, where necessary, prevent an activity, or, at minimum, postpone it until adequate environmental baseline data exists and EIA is possible.

The ISA's broad mandate to 'organize and control' mining activities in the Area is subject to the precautionary principle. State practice provides some salient ideas on the kinds of measures the ISA might consider when giving expression to precaution in future regulations. First, the meaning of precaution should be defined to include commonly accepted precautionary measures ranging from requirements for sufficient baseline information and EIA through to demonstrating the risk of harm can be satisfactorily diminished. Second, the goal of precaution should be expressly identified (e.g., protection, sustainability, etc.). Third, it should be clear that insufficient baseline information and inadequate EIA will trigger a greater emphasis on caution and environmental protection. Fourth, the regulations should incorporate environmental thresholds, or a decision-making pathway for determining thresholds, that the adverse effects of a proposal may not exceed. Fifth, it should be plain that the onus of satisfying information and EIA requirements rests with the propo-

220 *Sustain Our Sounds Inc*, op. cit. note 59, para. 111.

221 EEZ Act, section 64(2).

222 *Sustain Our Sounds Inc*, op. cit. note 59, para. 114.

223 Ibid., para. 125; *Newcastle & Hunter Valley Speleological Society Inc*, op. cit. note 127, para. 184.

224 *Newcastle & Hunter Valley Speleological Society Inc*, op. cit. note 127, para. 184.

nent of an activity. Proponents should not, however, be placed in a position of having to disprove an allegation of risk in the absence of evidence as to the existence of a risk. Sixth, the precautionary approach does not always enable an adaptive management approach. Adaptive management should only be employed where clearly calibrated parameters can be monitored in a manner that enables a mining operator to avert environmental harm before it occurs.

Acknowledgement

This chapter is current as of February 2022. The authors gratefully acknowledge the research assistance provided by Alessandra Guida and Ayla Do Vale Alves. Aline Jaeckel received funding from the Australian Research Council's DECRA scheme (grant number: DE190101081).

References

Policy Documents & Regulatory Instruments

ISA Documents

ISA, *Biodiversity, Species Ranges, and Gene Flow in the Abyssal Pacific Nodule Province: Predicting and Managing the Impacts of Deep Seabed Mining*, Jamaica: ISA Technical Study No. 3, 2008
——— *Draft Regulations on Exploitation of Mineral Resources in the Area*, 22 March 2019, ISBA/25/C/WP.1
——— *Preparatory Commission for the ISA and ITLOS*, 8 February 1990, LOS/PCN/SCN.3/WP.6/Add.5
——— *Recommendations for the Guidance of Contractors for the Assessment of the Possible Environmental Impacts Arising from Exploration for Marine Minerals in the Area*, 30 March 2020, ISBA/25/LTC/6/Rev.1
——— *Regulations on Prospecting and Exploration for Polymetallic Nodules in the Area*, 22 July 2013, ISBA/19/C/17
——— *Review of the Environmental Impact Statement Submitted by the Ministry of Earth Sciences of the Government of India*, 18 June 2020, ISBA/26/LTC/5

Statutes and Cases

African Group, *Request for Consideration by the Council of the African Group's Proposal on the Economic Model/Payment Regime and Other Financial Matters in the Draft Exploitation Regulations Under Review*, 9 July 2018. Available online <https://www.isa.org.jm/files/files/documents/nv.pdf> (accessed 25 August 2021).
BASF Agro BV and ECPA and ESA, Case T-584/13, ECLI:EU:T:2018:279.
Bova v Highland Council (2013) CSIH 41, 2013 SC 510.
Canada, *Policy and Operational Framework for Integrated Management of Estuarine, Coastal and Marine Environments in Canada* (last updated 17 August 2016). Available online <https://www.dfo-mpo.gc.ca/oceans/publications/cosframework-cadresoc/page01-eng.html> (accessed 23 September 2021).
Castonguay Blasting Ltd v Ontario (Environment) (2013) 3 SCR 323, 2013 SCC 52.
Convention on Biological Diversity, 5 June 1992, 1760 UNTS 79.
Decision on Marine Consent Application by Chatham Rock Phosphate Limited, Environmental Protection Authority, 10 February 2015.
Declaration of Prohibition Action: Subsea Mining, Environmental Protection Act 2019, 30 July 2021. Available online <https://depws.nt.gov.au/__data/assets/pdf_file/0012/1032150/declaration-prohibited-action-subsea-mining.pdf> (accessed 16 September 2021)
Deep Sea Mining Act 1981.
Deep Sea Mining Act 2014.
Environment East Gippsland Inc. v VicForests (2010) VSC 335.
Environment Protection and Biodiversity Conservation Act 1999 No. 91.

Exclusive Economic Zone and Continental Shelf (Environmental Effects) Act 2012 No. 72.
Fisheries Act 1985, R.S.C.
Fisheries and Oceans Canada, *Canada's Oceans Strategy* (2002). Available online <https://waves-vagues.dfo-mpo.gc.ca/Library/264678.pdf> (accessed 23 September 2021).
Fishery (General) Regulations, 1993, SOR/93-53.
Great Barrier Reef Marine Park Act 1975 No. 85.
International Union for Conservation of Nature, *Guidelines for Applying the Precautionary Principle to Biodiversity Conservation and Natural Resource Management, as Approved by the 67th Meeting of the IUCN Council*, 14–16 May 2007.
Kiwis Against Seabed Mining Inc. v Environmental Protection Authority (2016) NZEnvC 217.
Marine and Coastal Access Act 2010.
Moratorium on Exploration and Mining in Coastal Waters of Northern Territory Until 2015, Northern Territory Government (2012). Available online <https://ntepa.nt.gov.au/__data/assets/pdf_file/0003/504255/seabed_mining_moratorium.pdf> (accessed 2 September 2021).
Morton v Canada (Fisheries and Oceans) (2015) FC 575.
Morton v Canada (Minister of Fisheries and Oceans) (2019) FCJ No 178.
Namgis First Nation v. Canada (Minister of Fisheries, Oceans and Canadian Coast Guard) (2020) F.C.J. No. 778.
Newcastle & Hunter Valley Speleological Society Inc. v Upper Hunter Shire Council (2010) NSWLEC 48.
Oceans Act, SC 1996.
Pulp Mills on the River Uruguay (Argentina v. Uruguay) Merits, Judgment, I.C.J. Reports 2010.
Re. Arbitration Between the Republic of the Philippines and the People's Republic of China, Award, 12 July 2016, PCA Case No. 2013-19.
Request for Advisory Opinion submitted by the Sub-Regional Fisheries Commission (SRFC), Advisory Opinion, 2 April 2015.
Resource Management Act 1991 No. 69 (RMA).
Responsibilities and Obligations of States Sponsoring Persons and Entities with Respect to Activities in the Area, Advisory Opinion, ITLOS Reports 2011, Case No. 17.
Rio Declaration on Environment and Development, 14 June 1992, 31 ILM 874.
Scotland, *Scottish Planning Policy* (June 2014). Available online <https://www.gov.scot/publications/scottish-planning-policy/pages/7/> (accessed 23 September 2021).
Southern Bluefin Tuna (New Zealand v. Japan; Australia v. Japan), Provisional Measures, Order of 27 August 1999, ITLOS Reports 1999.
Sustain Our Sounds Inc v New Zealand King Salmon Company Ltd (2014) NZSC 40, 17 ELRNZ 520.
Taranaki-Whanganui Conservation Board v. Environmental Protection Authority (2018) NZHC 2217, (2019) NZRMA 64.
Telstra Corp Ltd v Hornsby Shire Council (2006) 67 NSWLR 256.
The Case of SS "Lotus" (France v Turkey), Judgment, PCIJ (1927).
The Environment Bill, 26 May 2021, HL Bill 16.
The Marine Works (Environmental Impact Assessment) Regulations 2007, No. 1518.
Trade and Cooperation Agreement Between the European Union and the European Atomic Energy Community, of the One Part, and the United Kingdom of Great Britain and Northern Ireland, of the Other Part, 30 April 2021. Available online <https://ec.europa.eu/info/strategy/relations-non-eu-countries/relations-united-kingdom/eu-uk-trade-and-cooperation-agreement_en> (accessed 7 September 2021).
Trans-Tasman Resources Limited v. The Taranaki-Whanganui Conservation Board & Ors (2020) NZCA 86, (2020) 21 ELRNZ 700.
Trans-Tasman Resources Ltd Marine Consent Decision, Environmental Protection Authority, 17 June 2014.
Trans-Tasman Resources Ltd Marine Consents and Marine Discharge Consents Decision, Environmental Protection Authority, 3 August 2017.
Trans-Tasman Resources v Taranaki-Whanganui Conservation Board (2021) NZSC 127.
UK Government, *Explanatory Notes to Bill 16, 2021*. Available online <https://bills.parliament.uk/publications/41685/documents/327> (accessed 23 September 2021).
United Nations Convention on the Law of the Sea, 10 December 1982, No. 31363, p. 397.
Vienna Convention on the Law of Treaties, 23 May 1969, 1155 UNTS 331.

Articles, books, and reports

Arcuri A., 'Reconstructing precaution, deconstructing misconceptions', *Ethics & International Affairs* 21, 2007, 359–379.

Chircop A. and Hildebrand L., 'Beyond the buzzwords: A perspective on integrated coastal and ocean management in Canada', in D. Rothwell and D. VanderZwaag (eds.), *Towards principled oceans governance: Australian and Canadian approaches and challenges*, London and New York: Routledge, 2006, 19–71.

Commission of the European Communities, *Communication from the commission on the precautionary principle*, COM(2000) 1 final, 2 February 2000.

de Sadeleer N., 'The precautionary principle and climate change', in M. Faure (ed.), *Elgar Encyclopedia of Environmental Law*, Edward Elgar, 2016, 20–31.

Durden J.M. et al., 'A procedural framework for robust environmental management of deep-sea mining projects using a conceptual model', *Marine Policy* 84, 2017, 193–201.

Foster C., 'Adjudication, arbitration and the turn to public law "Standards of Review": Putting the precautionary principle in the crucible', *Journal of International Dispute Settlement* 3(1), 2012, 525–558.

Great Britain, Department of the Environment, *This common inheritance: Britain's environmental strategy*, London: HMSO Publications, 1990.

Halfar J. and Fujita R., 'Precautionary management of deep-sea mining', *Marine Policy* 26, 2002, 103–106.

Harding R. and Fisher E., 'Introducing the Precautionary Principle', in R. Harding and E. Fisher (eds.), *Perspectives on the precautionary principle*, Federation Press, 1999, 2–25.

Harrison J., 'The United Kingdom and seabed mining', in V. Tassin Campanella (ed.), *Routledge handbook of seabed mining and the law of the sea*, London: Routledge, 2023, chapter VI.2.14.

Jaeckel A., *The implementation of the precautionary approach by the international seabed authority*, ISA Discussion Paper No. 5, 2017. Available online <https://www.isa.org.jm/files/documents/EN/Pubs/DPs/DP5.pdf> (accessed 25 August 2021).

——— *The international seabed authority and the precautionary principle*, Leiden: Brill/Nijhoff, 2017.

Jans J. and Vedder H., *European environmental law*, Groningen: Europa Law Publishing, 2008.

Lodge M. and Verlaan P., 'Deep-sea mining: International regulatory challenges and responses', *Elements* 14(5), 2018, 331–336.

Lu M., 'Critical thinking about the precautionary principle in china's food safety law', *Frontiers of Law in China* 11(4), 2016, 692–717.

Macpherson E. et al., 'Case analysis: A new 'high-water mark' for seabed mining', *New Zealand Journal of Environmental Law*, forthcoming.

Makgill R., 'New Zealand', in R. Martella and B. Grosko (eds.), *International environmental law: The practitioner's guide to the laws of the planet*, Chicago: American Bar Association, 2014, 909–932.

——— Dawson K., and de Wit N., 'The exclusive economic zone and continental shelf (environmental effects) bill', *Resource Management Journal* April, 2012.

——— and Rennie H., 'A model for integrated coastal management legislation: A principled analysis of New Zealand's Resource Management Act 1991', *The International Journal of Marine and Coastal Law* 27, 2012, 135–165.

——— and Linhares A.P., 'Deep seabed mining – Key obligations in the emerging regulation of exploration and development in the PACIFIC', in R. Warner and S. Kaye (eds.), *Routledge handbook of maritime regulation and enforcement*, London and New York: Routledge, 2016, 231–261.

——— Gardiner-Hopkins J. and Coates N., 'Current legal developments: New Zealand', *The International Journal of Marine and Coastal Law* 35, 2020, 835–845.

Marr S., *The precautionary principle in the law of the sea: Modern decision-making in international law*, The Hague: Martinus Nijhoff, 2003.

Miller K. et al., 'An overview of seabed mining including the current state of development, environmental impacts, and knowledge gaps', *Frontiers in Marine Science* 4(418), 2018. Available online <http://dx.doi.org/10.3389/fmars.2017.00418>.

Morgera E., 'The ecosystem approach and the precautionary principle', in M. Faure (ed.), *Elgar Encyclopedia of environmental law*, Edward Elgar, 2017, 70–80.

Niner H. et al., 'Deep-sea mining with no net loss of biodiversity—An impossible aim', *Frontiers in Marine Science* 5, 2018, 1–12.

Roest W., Brekke H. and Clark M., 'The scientific challenges of deep-sea mining', in V. Tassin Campanella (ed.), *Routledge handbook of seabed mining and the law of the sea*, London: Routledge, 2023, chapter I.1.

Sandin P. et al., 'Five charges against the precautionary principle', *Journal of Risk Research* 5, 2002, 287–299.

Somerville R., 'Policy adjudication, adaptive management and the environment court', *Resource Management Theory and Practice* 9, 2013, 1–28.

Stanley M. and Arin T., *Precautionary management of deep sea minerals – Pacific Possible Background Paper No 2*, The World Bank, 2017.

Taberner J., 'Australia', in R. Martella & B. Grosko (eds.), *International environmental law: The practitioner's guide to the laws of the planet*, Chicago: American Bar Association, 2014, 885–908.

Taylor G., 'Canada', in R. Martella & B. Grosko (eds.), *International environmental law: The practitioner's guide to the laws of the planet*, Chicago: American Bar Association, 2014, 329–348.

Trouwborst A., 'The precautionary principle in general international law: Combating the Babylonian confusion', *Review of European Community & International Environmental Law* 16, 2007, 185–195.

Tunnicliffe V. et al., 'Strategic environmental goals and objectives: Setting the basis for environmental regulation of deep seabed mining', *Marine Policy* 114, 2020, 103347.

Van Dover C.L. et al., 'Biodiversity loss from deep-sea mining', *Nature Geoscience* 10, 2017, 464–465.

VanderZwaag D., Fuller S. and Myers R., 'Canada and the precautionary principle/approach in ocean and coastal management: Wading and wandering in tricky currents', *Ottawa Law Review* 34, 2002, 117–158.

Warwick G., 'The contribution of the precautionary principle to marine environmental protection', in R. Barnes and S. Kaye (eds.), *Frontiers in international environmental law: Oceans and climate challenges*, Leiden: Brill | Nijhoff, 2021, 368–406.

Zander J., *The application of the precautionary principle in practice: Comparative dimensions*, Cambridge: Cambridge University Press, 2010.

PART II

State Party rights, obligations and responsibilities

II.1

RIGHTS AND OBLIGATIONS OF STATES ON THE CONTINENTAL SHELF AND THE AREA

Virginie Tassin Campanella, Yacouba Cissé and Dire Tladi

Introduction

Exploration and exploitation of seabed resources continue to be at the heart of major geopolitical and geostrategic interests over ocean spaces. Thanks to modern and sophisticated marine technologies, these activities are not only being undertaken at greater depths, in the 'ultra deep', their number is also increasing, and the resources they target are being diversified. First focused on oil and gas resources, exploration is currently being conducted on new solid minerals such as polymetallic nodules, sulfurs and ferromanganese crusts.[1] While the prospects of exploitation of these resources – both within and beyond national jurisdiction – is currently debated in many countries, and at the International Seabed Authority, there is a general misunderstanding around the commonalities and differences between exploration and exploitation activities on the continental shelf, and those conducted in the Area, which, *in fine*, affects the identification and mitigation of risks of these activities. Furthermore, despite the existence of a solid international legal framework defining and describing coastal States' rights and obligations, tensions and conflicts over seabed resources are rising between States, and in between States and the civil society.

The right and obligations of States in respect of any activity in the ocean depends, in the first place, on the maritime zone in which the activity is taking place. This is because, as is now well-known, the *United Nations Convention on the Law of the Sea* adopts a zonal approach to regulation and governance. But the nature of the activity also impacts on the rights and obligations of States. Thus, whether the activity is taking place in the territorial waters, exclusive economic zone, continental shelf, High Seas or in the Area, will influence the nature and scope of the rights and obligation of States. At the same time, whether the activity in question concerns fishing, exploration and exploitation for mineral resources, laying of cables, research activities or mining, will affect the rights and obligations of States.

This chapter intends to bring clarity into the various basic rights and obligations of States when conducting exploration and exploitation activities on the seabed within and beyond national juris-

1 W.R. Roest, H. Brekke and M.R. Clark, 'The scientific challenges of deep-sea mining', in V. Tassin Campanella (ed.) *Routledge handbook of seabed mining and the law of the sea*, London: Routledge, 2023, Chapter I.1.

DOI: 10.4324/9780429426162-7

diction, so either on the continental shelf within and beyond 200 nautical miles or in the Area. By doing so, it also intends, in a non-exhaustive way, to highlight the history and challenges surrounding basic provisions applicable to these activities.

Rights and obligations of States when mining the continental shelf

The concept of continental shelf and the work of the International Law Commission

References to the seabed and subsoil outside territorial waters can be traced back to the 1942 *Treaty of Paria* between the United Kingdom and Venezuela. The seabed was then described as 'submarine areas'.[2] Shortly after, and following the end of the Second World War, President Harry Truman (United States) declared in 1945 the jurisdiction and control of the State on the natural resources of the American continental shelf.[3] While highlighting conservation and prudent utilization of these resources, this proclamation clarified the intentions of the United States to exploit – in the near future – 'new sources of petroleum and other mineral', and protect the resources and the coasts.[4] Together with the specific economic and geopolitical context of the after-war, this declaration triggered a cascade of unilateral claims in Latin America,[5] which encouraged the International Law Commission (ILC) to study, as soon as 1950, the question of the continental shelf.[6]

The task of the ILC was delicate. The ILC had to find a way to justify and regulate these claims on new ocean spaces, in view of the economic 'necessity' to exploit these new resources.[7] The question of the continental shelf was thus integrated into the 'codification' task related to the High Seas. This codification exercise undoubtedly contributed to the development of international law on the matter. Indeed, the choice of the ILC to disregard the concept of *res nullius* and *res communis*[8] and retain an *ipso jure* status for the continental shelf posed the foundations of the legal regime of the continental shelf to be later created under the Geneva Convention on the Continental Shelf of 1958.

2 *Treaty between his Majesty in respect of the United Kingdom and the President of the United States of Venezuela relating to the submarine areas of the Gulf of Paria*, Signed at Caracas, 26 February 1942, Société des Nations, Recueil des Traités, 1944, N° 4829, pp. 122–130.

3 Policy of the United States with respect to the natural resources of the subsoil and seabed of the continental shelf, Proclamation 2667 of 28 September 1945, 10 Federal Reg. 12, 305, 1945.

4 'since self-protection compels the coastal national to keep close watch over activities off its shores which are of the nature necessary for utilization of these resources'. Ibid.

5 Presidential declaration of Mexico, 29 October 1945; Decree of Panama N° 449, 17 December 1946; Decree of Argentina n° 14.708; 11 October 1946; Decree of Peru N° 781, 1 August 1947, Decree-law of Costa Rica N° 803, 2 November 1949; Law of Guatemala on oil, 30 August 1949, Decree of Honduras N° 25, 17 January 1951.

6 For a full study on the work of the International Law Commission on the continental shelf, see V.J.M. Tassin, *Les défis de l'extension du plateau continental: la consécration d'un nouveau rapport de l'Etat à son territoire*, Pedone, 2013, pp. 207–219.

7 As highlighted by ILC Rapporteur J.P.A. François in 1951. See *Deuxième rapport sur la haute mer*, Annuaire de la Commission du droit international, Vol. II, 10 avril 1951, Doc A/CN.4/42, para. 155, p. 101.

8 This option was refused as efficient exploitation would have been prevented. 'One member of the Commission expressed the view that the exploitation of the products of the continental shelf might be entrusted to the international community; the other members considered that there were insurmountable difficulties in the way of such internationalization'. Quote by J.P.A. Francois from the second session of the ILC, 'Summary records', *Yearbook of the International Law Commission* 1, 117th Meeting, 4 July 1951, paragraph 98, p. 301. G. Amado also stated earlier in the same meeting that 'the Commission would be taking a very serious and dangerous step if it decided to grant the right of control and jurisdiction to all countries'. Ibid., paragraph 44, p. 297.

The Geneva Convention on the Continental Shelf of 1958

The 1958 *Geneva Convention on the Continental Shelf* (the CS Geneva Convention) introduces the concept of 'sovereign rights for the purpose of exploring it and exploiting its natural resources',[9] which is a new type of rights created to reflect the monopoly of the coastal State over the sole activities of exploration and exploitation.[10] These rights are exclusive[11] in the sense that their exercise by third parties, either foreign States or foreign offshore oil and gas companies, requires the explicit consent of the coastal State. They also do not depend on occupation or express proclamation. As a result, the coastal State can decide to not exercise activities on its continental shelf without fearing to lose its grip and control of it. These rights are however limited in their scope since they only concern the *exploration* and *exploitation* of the natural resources of the continental shelf.

The 'natural resources' of the continental shelf include, in addition to sedentary species,[12] the 'mineral and other non-living resources of the seabed and subsoil',[13] which cover a diversity of resources such as diamonds, oil and gas, sand but also nodules, sulphurs and other potential resources to be discovered in the future. The sovereign rights of exploration and exploitation on these natural resources are therefore the same, whether they concern nodules or diamonds.

Since these rights are limited in their scope, other activities could be conducted on the continental shelf. As a result, the continental shelf is, *a priori*, a shared space in which coexists various activities exercised under different legal regimes. The main articulation existing at the time of the CS Geneva Convention is with the regime of the High Seas,[14] and more specifically activities conducted under the freedom of the High Seas: navigation, fishing, laying of submarine cables and pipelines. [15]

Interestingly, fundamental oceanographic or other scientific research activities on the continental shelf are not included in the freedom of the High Seas, but in the continental shelf regime

9 Article 2 para. 1 of the *Convention on the Continental Shelf*, 29 April 1958, in *United Nations Treaty Series* 1964, No. 7302.

10 As mentioned by the ILC, 'The legal consequence of the operating monopoly conferred on the coastal State would be the exercise of effective sovereignty and this sovereignty would exist although the word was not pronounced (…) In view of the fact that it is therefore a question of sovereignty subject to limitations of a very special character, the Commission persists in believing that one should avoid speaking of sovereignty pure and simple, but it has no objection to indicating the rights of the State referred to as sovereign rights of control and jurisdiction' (translated by the authors). ILC, *Yearbook of the International Law Commission* II, Chapitre IV, 'Projet d'articles révisés relatifs au plateau continental et aux sujets voisins', para. 7, p. 47.

11 Ibid., Article 2 para. 2.

12 These species of high commercial value after the Second World War include, for example, sponges, pearl-shell, anemones, starfish or some worms which are immobile or unable to move except in constant physical contact with the seabed and subsoil. It therefore excludes bottom fish. This inclusion was, however, not obvious due to the impli cations of inserting fisheries law into a mining regime. Before the continental shelf concept, debates on sedentary species access were often assimilating these species as 'fructus of the seabed, to be harvested rather than hunted like swimming fish', connecting these harvesting rights to property rights of the seabed. See R. Young, 'Sedentary fisheries and the Convention on the Continental Shelf', *American Journal of International Law* 55, 1961, at 361. The ILC on its side considered in 1951 distinguishing the continental shelf regime from the sedentary species access (the continental shelf regime being confined to mineral resources), before reconsidering its position in 1953. ILC, 1953 Report 14, UN Doc A/2456, *American Journal of International Law* 48, Supp. 32, 1954. As highlighted by R. Young, 'in nature, there is no simple line of demarcation between sedentary and other fish, but only a long series of gradations from the unquestionably fixed at one extreme to the unquestionably free at the other'. Ibid., at 365.

13 Article 2 para. 4, CS Geneva Convention.

14 *Geneva Convention on the High Seas*, 29 April 1958, in *United Nations Treaty Series* 450, N° 6465, 1963, p. 11.

15 And the freedom to fly over the High Seas.

of the CS Geneva Convention.[16] While the continental shelf regime requires the coastal State, in the conduct of exploration and exploitation activities, to not interfere in a non-justifiable way with navigation, fishing or the conservation of living resources at seas,[17] or impede the laying or maintenance of submarine cables or pipelines,[18] the same is required for these research activities vis-à-vis to the sovereign rights of the coastal State. As a result, these research activities are subject to the State's consent in case of research concerning the continental shelf.[19] In principle, this consent should not be refused if the request is submitted by a qualified institution involved in a 'purely scientific research into the physical or biological characteristics of the continental shelf'.[20] For that purpose, the coastal State could seek to participate or be represented in the research, and the results of the research have to be published.[21]

In sum, the two concepts of 'sovereign rights' and 'exclusive rights' over the continental shelf are very specific to ocean space and boundaries law. They derived from the assertion that the continental shelf constitutes 'the natural prolongation of the land territory into and under the sea'.[22] The International Court of Justice (ICJ) made clear in 1969[23] that 'there is no jurisdiction over the super jacent waters, and over the seabed only for purposes of exploration and exploitation'.[24] On this basis, the ICJ concluded that the rights on the continental shelf are rights that need to be 'declared' not to be 'constituted',[25] meaning that there is no need for the coastal State to follow a particular legal process or to take any legal act to claim its rights over the continental shelf.[26] The sovereign rights exist *ipso facto* and *ab initio*, they are exclusive and inherent.[27]

In terms of geographical scope, the CS Geneva Convention defines the limits of the continental shelf with regard to adjacency, depth and exploitability. Article 1 states that the continental shelf consists of the seabed and the subsoil of the submarine regions adjacent to the coast. It is located outside the territorial sea and up to a depth of 200 meters.[28] This depth limit can nevertheless be circumvented when exploration and exploitation activities on natural resources can be carried out beyond. The islands can also have a continental shelf if the latter is adjacent to the coasts of the islands.

The CS Geneva Convention however failed to gather universal support, and State practice proved that the appetite of States[29] regarding mineral resources went much beyond the geographical scope of the continental shelf as defined by the CS Geneva Convention. More specifically, and in the light of the decolonization economic and political context, the exploitability criterion of the continental shelf definition has been claimed by many to be discriminatory, and in favour of

16 Marine scientific research activities were later moved out of the continental shelf regime into a specific regime under UNCLOS.
17 Article 5, CS Geneva Convention.
18 Article 4, ibid.
19 Article 5, para. 8, ibid.
20 Ibid.
21 Ibid.
22 *North Sea Continental Shelf, Judgment ICJ Report 1969*, para. 19, p. 22.
23 Ibid.
24 Ibid., para. 59, p. 37.
25 Ibid., para. 19, p. 22.
26 Article 2, para. 3, CS Geneva Convention.
27 *North Sea Continental Shelf*, op. cit., para. 19, p. 22.
28 We note that the limit of the 200-meter depth remains nowadays as a criterion to describe ultra deep activities or what is often described as 'deep sea mining' activities.
29 G. Scelle, 'Obsession du territoire: Essai d'étude réaliste de droit international', *Symbolae Verzijl*, Martinus Nijhoff, 1958, p. 360.

developed States who were the only ones able, thanks to their technological advances, to exploit at certain depth. This convention however remains in force and is still applicable to certain States who did not ratify the *United Nations Convention on the Law of the Sea.*[30]

The continental shelf regime of the United Nations Convention on the Law of the Sea

To a large extent, the exploration and exploitation sovereign rights and related obligations on the continental shelf contained in the CS Geneva Convention were largely reproduced in the *United Nations Convention on the Law of the Sea* (the UNCLOS). These rights were not even questioned, nor debated during the negotiations of the UNCLOS despite the presence of newly independent States at the table of negotiations.[31] They are the backbone of the continental shelf regime and are, without a doubt, part of international customary law.

In view of the articulation between the *Implementing Agreement of UNCLOS on the conservation and sustainable use of marine biological diversity of areas beyond national jurisdiction* (BBNJ Agreement) and the UNCLOS continental shelf regime, and in the case of the establishment of a marine protected area or other area-based management tools, these sovereign rights refrain the extension of the protected area located in the High seas on the continental shelf situated below.[32] In the case of a proposal regarding the establishment of an area-based management tool, the BBNJ Agreement also plans the consultation of the adjacent coastal State – as well as other States[33] – to ensure that they will be notified and invited to provide input on the related proposal. This consultation includes but is not limited to the following elements, to be provided before the decision-making: (1) views on the potential implications of the proposal for areas within national jurisdiction, as well as (2) information regarding any existing measures or activities in adjacent or related areas within national jurisdiction and beyond national jurisdiction.

With regard to the term 'activities of exploration and exploitation', in the same way as the CS Geneva Convention,[34] the UNCLOS does not provide any specific definition or list of these activities. It however includes into the regime of the continental shelf related activities such as artificial

30 See for example the case of Colombia in this book. E. Restrepo Uribe, 'Colombia and seabed mining', in V. Tassin Campanella (ed.), *Routledge handbook of seabed mining and the law of the sea*, op. cit., chapter VI.2.3. For cases on Non-Party States to UNCLOS and UNCLOS Parties, see the series of ICJ cases between Nicaragua and Colombia.

31 'What gave the Conference its importance and urgency, was the dramatic revelation of the wealth which lay on and beneath the seabed. Oil was the best-known example (…) the maintenance of existing right to explore and exploit the resources of the continental shelf, and the security of its installations from damage and destruction, accidental or intentional, were thus vital. Its need was shared by the majority of countries as oil exploration and production was now being undertaken off the coasts of almost two thirds of the countries represented at the Conference (…) the mineral wealth to be gained from manganese nodules on the deep seabed might prove to be even more important than oil'. Mr. Ennals (UK), second session, *Summary Records of Plenary Meetings: Third United Nations Conference on the Law of the Sea*, 29th Meeting, Thursday 4 July 1974, A/CONF.62/SR.29, paras. 20–21.

32 See Article 18, 'the establishment of area-based management tools shall not include any areas within national jurisdiction, and shall not be relied upon as a basis for asserting or denying any claims to sovereignty, sovereign rights, or jurisdiction'. *Agreement under the United Nations Convention on the Law of the Sea on the conservation and sustainable use of marine biological diversity of areas beyond national jurisdiction*, June 2023. Hereinafter 'BBNJ Agreement'.

33 Article 21, para. 2, BBNJ Agreement. Please note that the consultation mechanism is not limited to States or coastal States since it includes 'all relevant stakeholders'. See article 21, para. 1, id.

34 The CS Geneva Convention mentions installations and other devices necessary for the exploration and exploitation of the natural resources. See article 5.

islands, installations and structures,[35] tunnelling[36] and a new activity added into the UNCLOS: drilling, which was meant to reflect fast technological progress and the interests of States towards oil and gas resources. The lack of precise definition of exploration and exploitation activities should be understood as a way to ensure adaptability and relevance of the UNCLOS through time. Techniques of exploration and exploitation evolve quickly (compared to the lifetime of an international treaty) and reply to the uniqueness of the resources they explore and exploit. It would be therefore impossible to list these activities into the UNCLOS, except perhaps through the mechanism of a non-exhaustive list in an Annex to be adapted through time, an option which was not contemplated at the time of the negotiations.

The construction, operation and use of artificial islands, installations and structures,[37] and drilling activities are all exclusive rights of the coastal States on the continental shelf, which is not the case of tunnelling rights. These rights have been inserted into the continental shelf regime as a way to reflect different method of exploitation of the seabed and subsoil. They appear related to the sovereign rights of exploration and exploitation of the natural resources of the continental shelf but are not subject to them. Indeed, the exclusive rights of construction and use of artificial islands and installations could be used under the sovereign rights of exploration and exploitation,[38] but also for 'other economic purposes'.[39] Drilling is furthermore allowed on the continental shelf for 'all purposes'.[40] As a result, both of these exclusive rights could be used for activities not concerning the exploration and exploitation of the natural resources of the continental shelf, such as carbon dioxide storage in the seabed. In view of this rather new activity, questions remain as to the interpretation(s) which could be given to the expression 'other economic purpose' of article 60, paragraph 1 b), especially in light of the blue economy concept and climate change mitigation mechanisms. But there seems to be no doubt as to the suitability of the drilling exclusive right of the coastal State to the case of carbon dioxide storage since it is permitted for 'all purposes'.

Apart from these various activities, the continental shelf regime of the UNCLOS is most known for the new definition of the continental shelf it provides, distinguishing the process of delineation of the continental shelf below and beyond 200 nautical miles. The delineation below 200 nautical miles is measured by a distance criterion, the one beyond 200 nautical miles is measured by combined criteria mixing the distance as well as geological and geomorphological characteristics.[41] As a result, the continental shelf within 200 nautical miles can exist as a legal fiction, even though there is no continental shelf *stricto sensu* (with the view to give to all coastal States the benefits

35 The CS Geneva Convention mentions installations and other devices necessary for the exploration and exploitation of the natural resources. See article 5.

36 See the reference in article 7 of the CS Geneva Convention.

37 For an in-depth study of the implementation of this provision to the case of offshore platforms, see P. Gautier and V.J.M. Tassin, 'Les plates-formes en mer et le droit international', *Annuaire français de droit international* LIX, CNRS Edition, 2013, 185–220.

38 Article 60, para. 1 b), UNCLOS mentions that these rights can be used for the purpose provided for in article 56 (so under the EEZ sovereign rights). While UNCLOS does not specifically mention that these rights can also be used for the purpose provided for in article 77 (sovereign rights on the continental shelf), it is reasonable to believe that such interpretation could be possible considering the insertion of article 80 into the regime of the continental shelf.

39 Article 60, para. 1 b), UNCLOS.

40 Article 81, ibid.

41 For more on this point, see in this book Ø. Jensen and B. Már Magnússon, 'The extension of sovereign rights beyond 200 nautical miles', in V. Tassin Campanella (ed.), *Routledge handbook of seabed mining and the law of the sea*, op. cit., chapter III.1.

of the sovereign rights),[42] while the natural existence of the continental shelf beyond 200 nautical miles shall be demonstrated through a specific scientific procedure placed under the Commission on the Limits of the Continental Shelf.[43] As a result, the sovereign rights and exclusive rights on the continental shelf are the same whether they are conducted below or beyond 200 nautical miles. For this reason, the International Tribunal for the Law of the Sea recognized in the *Bangladesh/Myanmar case* the concept of 'single continental shelf'.[44]

Another key obligation attached to these sovereign rights is the one requiring the coastal State to make payments or contributions in kind in case of exploitation of non-living resources of the continental shelf beyond 200 nautical miles, annually after the first five years of production of a site.[45] Since there is currently no exploitation of natural resources on the extended continental shelf, the contour and related implementation of this obligation remain blurry. Some countries such as Canada as well as the International Seabed Authority, in charge of the receipt and distribution of these payments to the UNCLOS State Parties, are currently working on clarifying and developing implementation mechanisms.[46]

Relationship between the continental shelf and the exclusive economic zone regimes

The legal regime of the exclusive economic zone (EEZ) is a fairly young legal regime compared to the one of the continental shelf. The notion of EEZ was indeed first presented by Kenya in 1972 during the Seabed Committee, before being integrated as one of the legal regimes of the UNCLOS due to the will of States to create a new fishery zone.[47]

Despite these great historical differences, the regime of the EEZ seems to be often confused with the one of the continental shelf. There are indeed many unfortunate examples at the policy level where the term 'EEZ' appears instead of the one of 'continental shelf'. While some tolerance should be paid towards non legal documents, there are general issues related to the confusion between these two marine spaces which should be clarified.

Under the EEZ legal regime, the rights of coastal States are qualified as 'sovereign rights' for the purpose of exploring and exploiting, conserving and managing the natural resources, whether

42 See J.M. Van Dyke, 'Sharing ocean resources – in a time of scarcity and selfishness', in H.N. Scheiber (ed.), *Law of the sea: the common heritage and emerging challenges*, The Hague: Kluwer Law International 2000, pp. 3–26.

43 For a study on the tension between sovereign rights and the definition/delineation of the extended continental shelf in the case of Non UNCLOS Party States, see V.J.M. Tassin, 'Territorial and maritime dispute (Nicaragua v. Colombia)', in P. Wojcikiewicz and J-M Sorel (eds.), *Latin America and the International Court of Justice: contributions to international law*, London and New York: Routledge, 2017, 2001, pp. 225–236.

44 *Dispute concerning the delimitation of the maritime boundary between Bangladesh and Myanmar in the Bay of Bengal (Bangladesh/Myanmar), Judgment, 14 March 2012*, Case 16, para. 361. See also the *Arbitration between Barbados and Trinidad and Tobago, Decision of 11 April 2006, RIAA, Vol. XXVII*, p. 147, para. 213. See as well *Bay of Bengal Maritime Boundary Arbitration between Bangladesh and India, Award, 7 July 2014*, para. 77, p. 21.

45 Article 82, UNCLOS. For more information, see in this book C. Schofield and J. Mossop, 'The article 82 conundrum: implementing payment for the exploitation of the continental shelf beyond 200 nautical miles', in V. Tassin Campanella (ed.), *Routledge handbook of seabed mining and the law of the sea*, op. cit., chapter III.2.

46 See International Seabed Authority, *A study of key terms in article 82 of the United Nations Convention on the Law of the Sea*, ISA Technical Study No 15, 2016. See also A. Chircop, 'Implementation of Article 82 of the United Nations Convention on the Law of the Sea, the challenge for Canada', in C. Banet (ed.), *The law of the seabed: access, uses and protection of seabed resources*. Leiden and Boston: Brill/Nijhoff, 2000, pp. 371–394.

47 For an exhaustive study on the EEZ legal regime, see B. Kunoy, 'La zone économique exclusive', in M. Forteau and J-M. Thouvenin (eds.), *Traité de droit international de la mer*, Paris: Pedone, 2017, pp. 384–399.

living or non-living, of the waters superjacent to the seabed and of the seabed and its subsoil.[48] The sovereign rights on the continental shelf are, on their side, for the purpose of exploring it and exploiting its natural resources. At first sight, the sovereign rights on the EEZ thus seem to embrace a broader scope of application than the ones on the continental shelf which are (only) restricted to exploration and exploitation of natural resources. These rights also appear to overlap on the seabed, since both the EEZ and continental shelf regimes apply on the seabed and subsoil beyond the territorial sea. Does it therefore mean that the regime of the continental shelf has been absorbed by the EEZ regime due to this overlap? This question was actually addressed by the *Barbados vs. Trinidad and Tobago Arbitration* within the context of the delimitation of the continental shelf. The arbitral tribunal clearly answered with the following, 'the continental shelf and the EEZ coexist as separate institutions, as the latter has not absorbed the former (…) and as the former does not displace the latter'.[49]

With regard to the rights of the coastal State, both legal regimes use the same terminology of 'sovereign rights', but their scope varies in significant ways. Under the continental shelf regime, the sovereign rights are *ipso facto*, *ab initio*, exclusive and inherent rights which do not depend on occupation nor any express proclamation. They only concern the natural resources of the continental shelf, i.e. non-living resources and living resources, but which for the latter are limited to sedentary species. On the contrary, the natural resources covered by the EEZ legal regime have a broader scope. They not only include the non-living resources of the seabed and subsoil – in the same way as the continental shelf regime. They also cover biological resources which are not limited to sedentary species, and not limited to the seabed and subsoil.

Interestingly, not all States have made an explicit declaration of an EEZ. The Mediterranean Sea offers an interesting example of the reluctancy of States to declare EEZs[50] due to important overlaps and tensions related to the access of biological and minerals resources, and the potential (and lengthy) prospects of delimitation disputes.[51] It should however be noted that despite these specific (semi) enclosed seas cases, a widespread number of States around the world (130 States) have declared EEZs and the 'institution of the EEZ' is recognized as part of customary law.[52]

Even though the scope of the sovereign rights differs, the synergies between the two legal regimes are strong. The case of construction, operation and use of artificial islands, installations and structures for the exploration and exploitation of the natural resources of the continental shelf illustrates this synergy. While the continental shelf regime refers to exclusive rights of the coastal State to construct, operate and use these islands, installations and structures '*on* the continental shelf',[53] many of these islands, installations and structures are actually located in the water above

48 Article 56, para. 1, UNCLOS.

49 *Arbitration between Barbados and Trinidad and Tobago, Decision of 11 April 2006*, op. cit., para. 234. See also in the same way *Continental Shelf (Lybia Arab Jamahiriya/Malta), ICJ Reports 1985*, p. 33, para. 33.

50 This attitude is sometimes referred to as 'EEZ phobia'. See F. Schneider, 'Le régime de la zone économique exclusive et la pratique des Etats méditerranéens', *Annuaire du droit de la mer XVIII*, 2013, 13–46, and T. Scovazzi, 'The Mediterranean sea maritime boundaries', in D.A. Colson and R.W. Smith (eds.), *International maritime boundaries*, Volume 5, Leiden and Boston: Brill/Martinus Nijhoff, 2005, at 3483.

51 See for example the reactions of Greece, Cyprus and Egypt following the Turkey-Libyan Memorandum of Understanding for the delimitation of the respective EEZs. See also the case of Israel which declared an EEZ while not ratifying UNCLOS.

52 See *Alleged violations of sovereign rights and maritime spaces in the Caribbean Sea (Nicaragua v. Colombia), Judgment, 21 April 2022*, para. 56. See also *Continental Shelf (Lybia Arab Jamahiriya/Malta), Judgement, ICJ Reports 1985*, p. 33, para. 34.

53 Highlighted by the authors. Article 80, UNCLOS.

(subject to the EEZ regime, if declared).[54] Thanks to a mechanism of *renvoi* between article 80, to article 60, and for the case of installations and structures,[55] to another *renvoi* to article 56 of the UNCLOS, the two legal regimes are deeply intertwined.

The synergy between the continental shelf and EEZ regimes goes beyond the direct articulation between these two maritime zones. Indeed, in the absence of a declared EEZ and in the case of construction of artificial islands and other installations in the waters above the continental shelf below 200 nautical miles, the regime of the High Seas. According to the High Seas regime, the *construction* of these islands and 'other installations' is part of the 'freedom of the High Seas',[56] which only restricts this activity to what is permitted under international law, subject to Part VI of the UNCLOS (so the regime of the continental shelf). As a result, the regime of the High Seas operates a *renvoi* including to article 80 of the regime of the continental shelf (applicable to artificial islands, installations and structure *on* the continental shelf – **which covers the case of fixed and floating offshore platforms used for exploration and exploitation of natural resources**), which makes another *renvoi* to article 60 (applicable to the construction, authorization and regulation of construction, operation and use of artificial islands, installations and structures) and article 56 of the UNCLOS, both part of the EEZ regime. It seems that all roads lead to the EEZ regime!

Other rights and obligations of the coastal State in exploring and exploiting the natural resources of the continental shelf

The articulation of the continental shelf regime with other legal regimes is further demonstrated by other emblematic obligations. One of them is to refrain from doing anything that may affect the legal regime of the superjacent waters or of the airspace above those waters over which apply the freedom of air space[57] and the freedom of navigation[58] under the regime of the High Seas. These obligations could be explained by the fact that a coastal State, for the purpose of exploring and exploiting natural resources of the continental shelf, could construct artificial islands, installations and structures on the waters above the continental shelf, as well as use the airspace above, which if not properly planned, could be located in maritime or air routes.

Another set of obligations corresponds to the articulation between the exercise of the sovereign rights of the continental shelf and the freedom of the High Seas, and more specifically the laying of submarine cables and pipelines, and conduct of marine scientific research on the continental shelf. With regard to the latter, it is interesting to notice that the conduct of marine scientific research on the continental shelf has always been the subject of great sensitivity for the coastal State. Indeed, under normal circumstances, the coastal State should grant its consent for these scientific projects. But

54 Under article 56, the coastal State can set up and use artificial islands, installations and works for economic purposes, in particular, the right to produce energy from the winds and ocean currents. Such facilities and other works may include turbines, wind turbines, tidal power plants, pipelines, submarine cables and pipelines for the exploration, exploitation and transportation of oil, gas and other minerals of the continental shelf.

55 'installations and structures for the purposes provided for in article 56 and *other economic purposes*'. Article 60, para. 1 b). Note that article 56 uses a different concept '*other activities for the economic exploitation and exploration of the zone,* such as the production of energy from the water, currents and winds'. Article 56, para. 1 a). Highlighted by the authors. For comments on the concepts of 'other economic purposes', see V.J.M. Tassin, 'L'exploration et l'exploitation des ressources naturelles du plateau continental à l'heure de l'extension du plateau continental au-delà des 200 milles marins', *Annuaire du droit de la mer XV*, 2010, at 98–99.

56 Article 87 of UNCLOS only mentions the freedom to construct and does not mention anything specific regarding the operation and use of these islands and 'other installations', as is the case in article 60 of UNCLOS.

57 Article 78, para. 1, ibid.

58 Article 78, para. 2, ibid.

the coastal State, in its discretion, may withhold its consent if the marine scientific project directly impacts its sovereign rights of exploration and exploitation, and its exclusive rights of drilling and construction, operation and use of artificial islands, installations and structures.[59] Therefore, the freedom to conduct marine scientific research ends where the sovereign rights of exploration and exploitation begin.

Typically, a marine scientific research project, aiming at collecting data and information on natural resources on the continental shelf, or on the geological features of the continental shelf, will most likely not receive the consent of the coastal State. Other activities of ocean observation cause issues in the collection of data and information related to the natural resources of the continental shelf. Certain observations can indeed be conducted through the use of telecommunication cables equipped with fiber optics. Since the general use of these cables is not regulated under the UNCLOS, and their use does not necessarily correspond to marine scientific research activities,[60] there is currently uncertainties regarding the legal regime and related limitations applicable to these observation activities. Indeed, article 79 of the UNCLOS gives to the coastal State the power to establish 'conditions' for cables (and pipelines) entering its jurisdiction when these pipelines are constructed or used in connection with the exploration and exploitation of its continental shelf, or exploitation of its resources, or the operations of artificial islands, installations and structures under its jurisdiction.[61] This article could thus allow the coastal State to restrict the collection of sensitive ocean data and information related to the natural resources of its continental shelf – but only for cables and pipelines *constructed or used in connection with* exploration and exploitation activities. Other types of cables located on the continental shelf, such as those used for telecommunication, or pipelines used for carbon dioxide storage, will fall outside the scope of the UNCLOS, raising important regulatory issues which could negatively impact the risks surrounding the investments made in relation to these activities, but also the conduct of these activities and related responsibilities of actors.

Finally, the conduct of marine scientific research on the extended continental shelf is regulated by specific rules. In the event of such project proposal, the coastal State cannot withhold its consent, but can publicly designate, at any time, 'specific areas' in which it can conduct 'exploitation or detailed exploratory operations' within a 'reasonable period of time'.[62] This right given to the coastal State could be used 'as a trick to preserve [its] (remaining) discretionary rights',[63] and therefore block marine scientific research on the extended continental shelf.

Rights and obligations related to the delineation and delimitation of the continental shelf

The delineation of the continental shelf is a singular procedure due to the existence of a unique institution, created by the UNCLOS, the Commission on the Limits of the Continental Shelf ('the Commission' or 'CLCS').[64]

59 Article 246, para. 5, ibid. This list is not exhaustive, see also article 246, para. 5 d).

60 See the general principles for the conduct of marine scientific research at article 240 of UNCLOS.

61 Article 79, para. 4, ibid.

62 More generally on this question, see V.J.M. Tassin 'Between freedom and control: the regulation of marine scientific research on the continental shelf', in INDEMER (ed.), *Knowing the oceans for achieving sustainable development*, Pedone, 2018, pp. 77–94.

63 Ibid., at 85.

64 The functions of the CLCS are limited to the interpretation of data and materials for the issuance of a recommendation and to the scientific and technical advising. Article 3, Annex II, UNCLOS. For a detailed study of the delineation procedure and the role of the CLCS, see S. Suarez, 'The Commission on the limits of the continental shelf and

At first sight, the obligations of the coastal States are rather straightforward when it comes to the delineation of the continental shelf. The coastal State establishes the outer edge and delineates the outer limits of the extended continental shelf according to the rules set in article 76 of the UNCLOS.[65] To do so, it files an extension submission to the CLCS to demonstrate that the extension beyond 200 nautical miles replies to the scientific criteria set out in article 76, paragraphs 2 to 7.[66] This submission is then examined and, during this process, the CLCS might engage in a dialogue with the coastal State in order to understand and analyze its submission, and potentially ask for further information. Following the Commission's recommendation, the coastal State may decide either to publish the outer limits of its continental shelf on the basis of the Commission's recommendation, or, in the event of disagreement,[67] to submit to the Commission a 'revised submission'[68] or a 'new submission' in order to provide new data and information, update the submission according to the feedback given by the CLCS, or hope to obtain a more favourable or new recommendation.[69]

While it is clear that the CLCS procedure and related recommendation was originally designed for the coastal State submitting the request, the practice has revealed that third States, Parties to UNCLOS and non-Party States to the UNCLOS, have used the extension procedure to voice their disagreements on the extension submissions filed. The procedure has therefore become, unexpectedly, a procedure revealing potential disputes. Unexpectedly because the workload under which the CLCS is, is a workload that corresponds to the 'worst case scenario', as mentioned by the CLCS Chairman at the 17th session.[70] It should be also highlighted that in the absence of any legal power to interpret the criteria of article 76 of the UNCLOS, the Commission can anyhow *only* formulate scientific and technical recommendations to the coastal State. Furthermore, the mechanism of revision of the submission, similar to a game of ping-pong between the CLCS and the coastal State, reveals the weak authority of the CLCS's recommendations and the central role and responsibilities of the coastal State in the extension procedure, consolidating doubts as to the interpretation to be given to the expression 'final and binding' stated in article 76, paragraph 8.[71]

---

its function to provide scientific and technical advice', *Chinese Journal of International Law* 12, 2013, 339–345. See also in this book Jensen and Már Magnússon, op. cit.

65 See generally A.G. Oude Elferink, 'Article 76 of the LOSC on the definition of the continental shelf: questions concerning its interpretation from a legal perspective', *The International Journal of Marine and Coastal Law* 21-3, 2006, 269–285.

66 See in this regard *Territorial and maritime dispute (Nicaragua v. Colombia), Judgment, I.C.J. Reports 2012*, p. 624.

67 See for example the submission of Barbados which, following a disagreement regarding the CLCS recommendation of 2010 (due to the location of the slope and a fixed point), submitted a revised request to the CLCS in 2011.

68 See for example the Russian revised submission dated 14 February 2023, which follows two other revised submissions dated 28 February 2013 and 3 August 2015. Brazil also filed throughout the years an important number of revised submissions (three in total).

69 Article 52, para. 2, CLCS Rules. See also generally T.L. MacDorman, 'The role of the Commission on the limits of the continental shelf: a technical body in a political world', *The International Journal of Marine and Coastal Law* 17-3, 2002, 301–324.

70 CLCS, Statement by the Chair on the progress in the work of the Commission, CLCS/50, 10 May 2006, p. 14. For an analysis of this point, see V.J.M. Tassin, 'La Commission des limites du plateau continental: clef de voûte fragile de la procédure d'extension', *Les défis de l'extension du plateau continental: consécration d'un nouveau rapport de l'Etat à son territoire*, op. cit., pp. 313–382, at 322.

71 Questions are raised as to whether recommendations of the CLCS are final and binding, or if the the limits of the shelf established by the coastal State, on the basis of the recommendation, are final and binding. A. Oude Elferink highlights that 'the State is to act on the basis of the recommendations of the CLCS is clear, not so much the exact implications of that requirement'. A.G. Oude Elferink, 'Commission on the limits of the continental shelf', in R. Wolfrum (ed.), *The Max Planck encyclopaedia of public international law*, Oxford: Oxford University Press,

In reality, it is only when the coastal State (which submitted the extension file) deposits charts and 'relevant information' permanently indicating the outer limit of the continental shelf with the Secretary-General of the United Nations – and the Secretary General of the International Seabed Authority ('ISA' or the 'Authority') for the case of the outer limits of the extended continental shelf[72] – that due publicity is given. This filing and the subsequent publication of these maps and information are essential. They are a unilateral State declaration of the new limits of its jurisdiction, which allow it to be exposed to the dispute settlement mechanism of Part XV of the UNCLOS in case of overlapping claims. This is also only at this time that other States (adjacent, opposite, but others as well) will be able to potentially notice whether the coastal State has defined its continental shelf 'on the basis of the recommendations' of the CLCS or has made an excessive claim, and therefore decide to accept it or not.[73]

Despite the importance of this publicity, very few States have nowadays implemented their obligations according to article 76, paragraph 9, and article 84 of the UNCLOS.[74] Such lack of implementation does not seem at the moment to impact States with overlapping claims, since most of them are solving their disputes either through provisional arrangements[75] – as is the case for the Mauritius Seychelles Joint Management Area[76] – or through Part XV of the UNCLOS. It however impacts the management and protection of the Area, as deplored by the Secretary General of ISA.[77] Indeed, the inner limits of the Area depend on the outer limits of the continental shelf.[78] Since there are no 'overlapping claims' possible between the coastal State and the International Seabed Authority,[79] article 83 of the UNCLOS does not apply. There are actually no specific mechanisms in the UNCLOS applicable to a dispute between ISA and the coastal State, allowing ISA to defend the geographical scope of the Area.[80] When facing this issue, the arbitral tribunal working on the *St*

2011. On this issue, see generally V.J.M. Tassin, 'La crédibilité de l'institution subordonnée au pouvoir de l'Etat côtier', *Les défis de l'extension du plateau continental: consécration d'un nouveau rapport de l'Etat à son territoire*, op. cit., at pp. 360–378 and M.S.-t Gau, 'The Commission on the limits of the continental shelf as a mechanism to prevent enchroachment upon the Area', *Chinese Journal of International Law* 10-3, 2011.

72 Article 84, para. 2, UNCLOS.

73 See Jensen and Már Magnússon, op. cit. See also G. Eriksson, 'The case of disagreement between a coastal state and the Commission on the limits of the continental shelf', in M.H Nordquist et al. (eds.), *Legal and scientific aspects of continental shelf limits*, Martinus Nijhoff, 2004, pp. 251–258.

74 At the time of writing this article, 93 States submitted an extension file, 36 recommendations were issued by the CLCS, and only 12 States have implemented their obligations of publicity according to article 76, paragraph 9.

75 Article 83, para. 3, UNCLOS.

76 *Treaty concerning the joint exercise of sovereign rights over the continental shelf in the Mascarene Plateau region between the Government of the Republic of Seychelles and the Government of the Republic of Mauritius, Vacoas, 13 March 2012*, and *Treaty concerning the joint management of the continental shelf in the Mascarene Plateau region between the Government of the Republic of Seychelles and the Government of the Republic of Mauritius, Vacoas, 13 March 2012*, United Nations Treaty Series 2847, Nos. 49782 and 4983, pp. 277 and 307.

77 ISA, 'ISA at the Commission on the Limits of the Continental Shelf Open Meeting', Press Release, 10 March 2017.

78 See article 1, para. 1 (1) as well as article 134, para. 4 of UNCLOS.

79 ISA does not have entitlements on the seabed of the Area. See *Agreement relating to the implementation of Part XI of UNCLOS*, Annex, Section 1, para. 1.

80 The obligation to settle disputes by peaceful means applies to States Parties only (Article 279, UNCLOS), however the Preamble of UNCLOS, stressing the importance of the promotion of the peaceful uses of the seas and oceans is applicable to actors subject to UNCLOS, including ISA. As a result, as explained by Jensen and Már Magnússon in this book, a potential window of opportunity through the Seabed Dispute Chamber (Area legal regime) could be contemplated, but does not have the most chances compared to a classical State-to-State dispute settlement. Jensen and Már Magnússon, op. cit. See as well on this point the International Law Association Committee on Legal Issues

Pierre Miquelon delimitation case[81] refused to operate a delimitation on the extended continental shelf due to the lack of representation of a party which was not before the tribunal.[82] While such analysis has now been disregarded by more recent judgements and awards, potentially due to the detrimental effect that such interpretation could have on the dispute settlement mechanism in the case of a delimitation, it is worth noting that the specific relationship between the outer limits of the continental shelf and the inner limits of the Area is far from being fully addressed under the UNCLOS, and in the practice. Such disregard of the interest of humankind in the geographical scope of the Area is generally in favour of the coastal State which gains access and control of significant natural resources due to the extension mechanism introduced into the UNCLOS.[83]

Considerable delays in the publicity of the outer limits of the continental shelf, together with a lack of adoption of relevant environmental policy[84] could, in the event of damage to the marine environment, expose the coastal State to potential issues related to its responsibility according to Part XII of the UNCLOS (environmental obligations).[85] A hypothetical scenario would be the case in which a coastal State received a CLCS recommendation, did not yet publish the limits, but is already conducting exploration activities[86] which, for some reason, create a pollution to the marine environment of the continental shelf,[87] spreading in the High Seas and the Area, and thus affecting fisheries resources and the general health of the marine environment in both maritime zones.

While the recommendation of the CLCS gives 'a green light' to the coastal State to delineate the outer limits of its extended continental shelf in a certain way, this scientific recommendation does not have the legal value of a State declaration. The International Tribunal for the Law of the Sea ('ITLOS' or 'the Tribunal'), in the 2012 *Bangladesh Myanmar case*, recognized that entitlement to a continental shelf beyond 200 nautical miles should be determined by reference to the outer edge, and 'to interpret it otherwise is warranted neither by the text of article 76 nor by its object

---

of the Outer Limits of the Continental Shelf, First Report, in *International Law Association Report of the Seventy First Conference*, Berlin 2004, p. 783.

81 *Case concerning the delimitation of maritime areas between Canada and France, Reports of international arbitral awards XXI, Decision 10 June 1992*, pp. 265–341. On this delimitation case, E. Jarmache expresses that 'we are entitled to be surprised, or to wonder, about the quasi-absence of the ISA in a process of transfer of territories and resources from humanity to States without being associated with it'. E. Jarmache, 'La pratique de la Commission des limites du plateau continental', *Annuaire français du droit international* 54, 2008, at 441 (translated by the authors).

82 'Any decision by which the tribunal recognizes the parties' rights to the continental shelf beyond 200 nautical miles or rejects such rights would constitute a decision involving a delimitation not "between the parties", but between each of them and the international community represented by the organs responsible for the administration and the protection of the international seabed area (…) which has been declared the common heritage of mankind'. Ibid., para. 78 (translated by the authors). See also the recent judgment of ITLOS stating that 'Application of the standard of significant uncertainty affords similar protection to the interests of the international community in the Area and the common heritage of mankind (…) the exercise of caution is called for in the circumstances of the present case, where there may be a risk of prejudice to the interests of the international community in the Area and the common heritage of mankind principle'. *Dispute concerning delimitation of the maritime boundary between Mauritius and Maldives in the Indian Ocean (Mauritius/Maldives)*, Judgment, 28 April 2023, paragraphs 452–453.

83 See M. Bennouna, 'La limite extérieure du plateau continental et la gestion des ressources pour l'humanité', in R-J. Dupuy (ed.), *La gestion des ressources pour l'humanité: le droit de la mer*, The Hague and Boston: Martinus Nijhoff, 1982, at 116.

84 Article 193, UNCLOS.

85 See generally in this book C.R Payne, 'State responsibility for deep seabed mining obligations', in V. Tassin Campanella (ed.), *Routledge handbook of seabed mining and the law of the sea*, op. cit., chapter II.2.

86 According to A. Chircop, 'the LOSC does not require a coastal Sate to refrain from activities on the extended continental shelf until the process of definition of the outer limits pursuant to Article 76 has been completed', op. cit, online edition.

87 Article 194, para. 3, c) and article 208, UNCLOS.

and purpose'.[88] When facing the issue of determining the existence of a natural prolongation, in the absence of a CLCS recommendation either for Bangladesh or Myanmar, the Tribunal noted that both Parties, in their respective submissions, included data indicating that their entitlements to the continental margin extend beyond 200 nautical miles.[89]

Therefore, in the case of a CLCS recommendation, if an *a contrario* reasoning is applied, although the coastal State did not publish the outer limits according to article 76 paragraph 9, it is reasonable to believe that the entitlement beyond 200 nautical miles would be considered as proven since the CLCS recommendation has been formulated. Furthermore, in view of the *ipso facto* and *ab initio* sovereign rights, the regime of the continental shelf would apply to the extended continental shelf, pending the publication of its outer limits. The CLCS recommendation will thus only confirm the exact geographical extent of these rights (and not the entitlements).[90]

As a result, a State conducting High Seas fisheries in the waters above the extended continental shelf could potentially engage the responsibility, under Part XII,[91] of the coastal State conducting exploration activities, if these activities are harming the fisheries, even pending the publication of the outer limits of its continental shelf.[92] The ISA on its side would not be able to do the same since the UNCLOS does not allow ISA to engage into dispute settlement outside of the Area legal regime.[93]

Other limitations exist in the relationship between the ISA and the coastal State. In the case of resource deposits in the Area lying across the limits of national jurisdiction, activities in the Area shall be conducted with due regard to the rights and legitimate interests of any coastal State across whose jurisdiction such deposits lie.[94] Interestingly, no such provision exists in the regime

88 *Dispute concerning the delimitation of the maritime boundary between Bangladesh and Myanmar in the Bay of Bengal (Bangladesh/Myanmar)*, op. cit., para. 437. See also *Maritime delimitation in the Indian Ocean (Somalia v. Kenya), Judgment, ICJ Reports 2021*, p. 206 at para. 189. Recalling the Bangladesh/Myanmar case, the ICJ states that 'the lack of delineation of the outer limit of the continental shelf is not, in and of itself, an impediment to its delimitation between two States with adjacent coasts'.

89 The Tribunal also noted the 'uncontested scientific evidence regarding the unique nature of the Bay of Bengal and information submitted during the proceedings', paragraph 446. Under a different scenario (case of a submission of preliminary information only), the International Court of Justice concluded that insufficient data provided by Nicaragua through a preliminary information filed at the CLCS was not sufficient to prove the location of the outer limits of the continental shelf. See *Territorial and maritime dispute (Nicaragua v. Colombia)*, op. cit., para. 129, p. 669. On an analysis of this case, see Tassin 'Territorial and maritime dispute (Nicaragua v. Colombia) 2001', op. cit.

90 See the declaration of Judge Heidar in the 2023 Mauritius v. Maldives case of ITLOS, 'the fact that a party has made a submission to the CLCS does not *per se* constitute proof of its entitlement to a continental shelf beyond 200 nm'. Declaration of Judge Heidar, para. 18 in *Dispute concerning delimitation of the maritime boundary between Mauritius and Maldives in the Indian Ocean (Mauritius/Maldives)*, op. cit.

91 Through articles 193, 194 paragraph 3, but also articles 206 and 208 of UNCLOS, and potentially failure to apply the precautionary approach. See in this book cases from New Zealand and related analysis (even though these cases apply to EEZ and continental shelf areas, the reasoning could be extended to the case of the extended continental shelf). R. Makgill, A. Jaeckel and K. MacMaster, 'Implementing the precautionary approach for seabed mining: a review of State Practice', in V. Tassin Campanella (ed.), *Routledge handbook of seabed mining and the law of the sea*, op. cit., chapter I.3, and R. Makgill and E. Macpherson, 'New Zealand and seabed mining', id., chapter VII.2.13.

92 See in this regard and later in the chapter the obligation of coastal State to conduct environmental impact assessment if the activity conducted *within* national jurisdiction may cause substantial pollution of or significant and harmful changes to the marine environment *beyond* national jurisdiction. Article 28, para. 2, BBNJ Agreement.

93 See Payne, op. cit. See also T. Treves, 'Dispute settlement and deep-sea mining', in V. Tassin Campanella (ed.), *Routledge handbook of seabed mining and the law of the sea*, op. cit., chapter V.1.

94 Article 142, UNCLOS.

of the continental shelf, requiring the coastal State to conduct exploration and exploitation activities with due regard to the legitimate interests of the common heritage of mankind. Furthermore, since article 83 of the UNCLOS does not apply, no requirements of provisional arrangements[95] nor any dispute settlement are applicable to this type of transboundary resources management.[96] Theoretically, a joint development zone could be established between the coastal State and the ISA,[97] but realistically speaking, it is very unlikely that the coastal State would agree to reach a compromise on the access and benefit of its natural resources to take into account the legitimate interests of the common heritage of mankind. As a matter of fact, the reason behind the creation of the continental shelf regime, and article 82 of the UNCLOS, was to allow easy and exclusive access to resources,[98] while already making a compromise on the benefits issued from the exploitation.[99]

Despite these shortcomings of the legal regime of the continental shelf, it should be noted that the obligation to negotiate and cooperate between States remains a key obligation in the sharing of natural resources, which is inherent to the delimitation of the continental shelf.[100] In exercising its sovereign rights over the continental shelf, the coastal State is obliged, in return, to take into account the rights claimed by other States, and do so in a manner compatible with the provisions of the UNCLOS, in particular to respect the freedoms recognized to other States, nor to hinder the exercise of these freedoms in an unjustifiable manner.[101]

The obligation to negotiate is an obligation of conduct that requires States to refrain from undertaking any unilateral exploitation of common mineral resources found on the continental shelf. This obligation comes under general international law and is based on the rules and principles defined and codified by the UNCLOS and subsequently crystallized by international jurisprudence on this particular matter.

Obligations of the coastal State in relation to the protection and preservation of the marine environment.

In addition to this obligation of conduct with respect to the natural resources of the continental shelf, the coastal State is also obliged to protect and preserve the marine environment[102] and

95 As it is the case in article 83, ibid.

96 The Preamble of UNCLOS however applies to ISA and the coastal State, which requires the maintenance of peace, justice and progress for all peoples of the world, as well as the promotion of the peaceful uses of the seas and oceans and the equitable and efficient utilization of marine resources.

97 See Chircop, op. cit.

98 See Tassin, *Les défis de l'extension du plateau continental: consécration d'un nouveau rapport de l'Etat à son territoire*, op. cit.

99 See Schofield and Mossop, op. cit.

100 The relationship between delineation and delimitation is not addressed in this chapter. See cases *the Barbados v. Trinidad Tobago case*, op. cit.; *Territorial and Maritime dispute between Nicaragua and Honduras in the Caribbean Sea (Nicaragua v. Honduras), Judgment, ICJ Reports 2007*, p. 659; The *Bangladesh/Myanmar case*, op. cit.; *Maritime boundary arbitration between Bangladesh and India, Award*, 7 July 2014; *Question of the delimitation of the continental shelf between Nicaragua and Colombia beyond 200 nautical miles from the Nicaraguan Coast (Nicaragua v. Colombia), (Preliminary objections)*, 17 March 2016; *Maritime delimitation in the Indian Ocean*, op. cit. See also generally G. Vega-Barbosa, 'The admissibility of outer continental shelf delimitation claims before the ICJ absent a recommendation by the CLCS', *Ocean Development and International Law* 49-2, 2018, 103–117.

101 Article 78, para. 2, UNCLOS.

102 Article 192, UNCLOS.

more specifically against pollution resulting from the exploration and exploitation activities on the continental shelf.[103] These activities are diverse and might include the use of many different installations and devices (including unmanned autonomous vehicles) which can create potential environmental issues due to the challenges faced in deep water areas (for example due to visibility, pressure and transmission issues with the home vehicle).[104] To prevent pollution from these installations and devices, the coastal State has the obligation to take measures for preventing accidents and dealing with emergencies, ensuring the safety of operations at sea, and regulating the design, construction, equipment, operation and manning of such installations and devices.[105] The taking of these measures cannot however justify interfering with activities carried out by other States.[106]

In addition, the UNCLOS specifies that coastal States shall adopt laws and regulations to prevent, reduce and control pollution of the marine environment arising from or in connection with seabed activities subject to their jurisdiction and from artificial islands, installations and structures under their jurisdiction pursuant to articles 60 and 80 of UNCLOS.[107] The implementation of such an obligation is carried out in particular by the adoption of relevant legislative and regulatory measures.[108] Thus, the obligation to legislate at the national level may have a wider scope since coastal States at the regional level 'shall endeavor to harmonize their policies'[109] in this respect. At the multilateral level, coastal States shall establish global and regional rules, standards and recommended practices and procedures to prevent, reduce and control pollution of the marine environment arising from seabed activities subject to national jurisdiction.[110] In practice, the development of such harmonization at the regional level has appeared to be difficult in many regions of the world. This is due to either the lack of regional integration allowing such harmonization,[111] or to the lack of ratification of regional instruments dedicated to seabed activities, as is the case of the Offshore Protocol of the Barcelona Convention.[112]

Generally speaking, it should be noted that the legal regime of the continental shelf does not contain any specific obligations dedicated to environmental protection and preservation, in contrast to the legal regimes of the EEZ in Part V and of the Area in Part XI. There is similarly no obligation with regard to the conservation and management of natural resources in Part VI. The environmental obligations of the coastal State are therefore only expressed in Part XII of the UNCLOS. This could come as a surprise since exploration and exploitation of natural resources, especially new mineral resources, generally carry important risks for the marine environment due their impact on the water column, and the fact that these activities are gradually moving towards

103 Article 194, ibid.

104 An incident occurred in 2021 with an unmanned autonomous vehicle which became uncoupled, during a exploration deep dive in the Area, from a cable connecting it to the surface vessel. Similar incidents could happen when conducting similar activities on the continental shelf.

105 Article 194, para. 3, c), UNCLOS.

106 Article 194, para. 4, ibid.

107 Article 208, para. 1, ibid.

108 Article 214, ibid. See for example the case of the Barcelona Convention and the Offshore Protocol. For an analysis of this Protocol with European law, see P.A. Singh, V. Tassin Campanella and F. Maes, 'The European Union and seabed mining', in V. Tassin Campanella (ed.), *Routledge handbook of seabed mining and the law of the sea*, op. cit., chapter VI.1.4.

109 Article 208, para. 4, ibid. See also Singh, Tassin Campanella and Maes, ibid.

110 Article 208, para. 5, ibid.

111 See for example T. Davenport, 'Southeast Asia and seabed mining', in V. Tassin Campanella (ed.), *Routledge handbook of seabed mining and the law of the sea*, op. cit., chapter VII.I.7. See also E. Jiménez Pineda, 'South American region and seabed mining', id., chapter VII.1.6.

112 See on this point Singh, Tassin Campanella and Maes, op. cit.

new depths and with new technologies. These activities are also conducted in areas closer to the coasts, particularly rich in biodiversity, including fisheries, thus increasing risks of pollution, disturbances and competing uses of the marine space. Furthermore, since the access to natural resources of the continental shelf is easier and of higher interest than the access to natural resources located in the Area (resources are closer to the shores, the financial return is more interesting under the continental shelf regime, and the licensing is easier than in the Area with less international obligations in place), exploitation below 200 nautical miles is well developed, and it is expected that exploitation on the extended continental shelf will follow this trend.

In 1950, Scelle highlighted that 'the purpose of the true conception of the continental shelf was to permit States to exploit the marine subsoil', which, according to Tassin, resulted in an evident inclusion of mineral resources into the legal regime, and an evident exclusion of these resources from any mechanism of protection and preservation.[113] Different hypotheses could be formulated to explain the lack of environmental considerations into the legal regime of the continental shelf. The first one is maybe the most obvious. By not including any specific environmental obligations into the regime of the continental shelf, the UNCLOS reflects the will of States to have a facilitated access to natural resources by logically, in return, giving the power to the State to establish its own environmental policy. The inclusion of environmental considerations into the regime of the continental shelf was therefore not forgotten, but excluded on purpose as a way to counterbalance the more restricted and regulated access of these minerals in the Area.[114] Another hypothesis has been formulated by Friedheim and Bowen explaining that 'it may be advantageous for the world that not much attention was lavished upon them because examination of the facts of the situation would indicate that such issues contain foreseeable problems of public policy'.[115]

As an extension to this reflection, it is interesting to notice that the BBNJ Agreement, although *only* applying to areas beyond national jurisdiction, imposes an obligation to conduct environmental impact assessment (EIA) to its future States Parties for activities conducted *within* national jurisdiction. This obligation applies to the case of an activity which may cause substantial pollution or significant and harmful changes to the marine environment beyond national jurisdiction. As a result, the BBNJ Agreement takes into consideration the event of an activity conducted on the continental shelf and or/the EEZ, impacting either the High Seas and/or the Area marine environment(s). Under this scenario, the coastal State conducting this activity, for example exploration and exploitation of natural resources on the continental shelf, has the obligation to ensure that the EIA is conducted either in compliance with the BBNJ Agreement or through its national process. If the national process is chosen by the coastal State, mandatory elements will then need to be considered, namely (1) making the relevant information available through the clearing-house mechanism in a timely manner during the national process, (2) ensuring that the activity is monitored in a manner consistent with the requirements of its national process, (3) ensuring that the EIA reports and any relevant monitoring reports are made available through the clearing-house mechanism.[116] This new obligation is first and foremost an implementation of the ecosystem approach,

113 Tassin, *Les défis de l'extension du plateau continental: consécration d'un nouveau rapport de l'État à son territoire*, op. cit., at 112.

114 Ibid., pp. 112–139.

115 R.L. Friedheim and R.E Bowen, 'Neglected issues at the Third United Nations Law of the Sea Conference', *Law of the sea: Neglected issues, Proceedings of the twelfth annual conference of the Law of the Sea Institute*, The Hague, Netherlands, 23–26 October 1978, University of Hawai'i, p. 3.

116 See Article 28, BBNJ Agreement.

which finally modernizes UNCLOS and reduces the detrimental effects of maritime zoning and related artificial boundaries.

Rights and obligations of States when conducting activities in the Area

This part of the chapter is concerned with the rights and obligations of States when engaging in mining activities in the Area. These rights and obligations are provided for in the Convention, particularly in Part XI of the UNCLOS on the Area. There are, however, other parts of the UNCLOS that are of relevance. Since in general, the waters super-adjacent to the Area will be High Seas, there may be provisions of Part VII of the UNCLOS that are relevant to the assessment of the rights and obligations of States. Part XII, which concerns the protection of the marine environment in general, applies to all the maritime zones and would therefore be applicable in the determination of the rights and obligations of States. In a similar vein, Part XIII of the UNCLOS, which concerns marine scientific research in the different zones, is generally applicable and would thus apply also to activities in the Area. Moreover, it has to be recalled that the ocean is a single ecosystem which does not recognize the artificial boundaries created by man-made law. This means that while the UNCLOS adopts a zonal approach, an analysis of the rights and obligations in respect of one maritime zone has to be assessed by taking into account the context of other maritime zones. In the framework of the UNCLOS, the latter principle is reflected in the due regard principle, which is reflected in different parts of the UNCLOS.

However, the rights and obligations of States are not only to be found in the UNCLOS. The rights and obligations of States are also to be found in customary international law, decisions of international courts and tribunals and rules adopted by relevant international organizations with the competence to bind States. This part of the chapter will rely on all of these to create a mosaic that describes, as best as possible, the rights and obligations of States when engaging in mining activities in the Area.

Rights and obligations of States in relation to the resources of the Area

The UNCLOS defines the Area as the 'seabed and ocean floor and subsoil thereof beyond the limits of national jurisdiction.'[117] The Area is, together with the High Seas, part of what is commonly referred to as 'areas beyond national jurisdiction', which is to say it forms part of areas outside the jurisdiction of any individual. These areas beyond national jurisdiction are subject to two principles which pull in different directions. While the High Seas is governed, generally, by freedom of the High Seas, the Area is governed by the common heritage of mankind.[118] It is from these broad principles that the rights and duties of States in areas beyond national jurisdiction are established.

The basic principle governing the Area and from which the rights and duties of States are derived is to be found in article 136,[119] which provides that the 'Area and its resources are the

117 Article 1, para. 1, UNCLOS.

118 See in this book N. Oral, 'The common heritage of mankind under international law: an overview', in V. Tassin Campanella (ed.) *Routledge handbook of seabed mining and the law of the sea*, op. cit., chapter I.2.

119 For a brief and accessible history of the evolution of the legal framework for the Area, see J. Dingwall 'Commercial mining activities in the deep seabed beyond national jurisdiction: The international legal framework', in C. Banet (ed.) *The law of the seabed: Access, uses and protection of the seabed resources*, op. cit., at 141 et seq. See also A. Jaeckel, 'The Area and the role of the International Seabed Authority', in V. Tassin Campanella (ed.) *Routledge handbook of seabed mining and the law of the sea*, op. cit., chapter IV.1.

common heritage of mankind'.[120] From the perspective of the rights and obligations of States, this basic principle implies that the resources in the Area are communally owned – the resources are owned by mankind as a whole.[121] Article 137, paragraph 1, also states that '[n]o State shall claim or exercise sovereignty or sovereign rights over any Part of the Area or its resources, nor shall any State or natural or juridical person appropriate any part of thereof'.[122]

The essence of these provisions is that there is an obligation on States to ensure that they and other entities under their control do not freely access the mineral resources of the Area outside of the governance framework established under Part XI. The UNCLOS establishes in Part XI a complex system for the exploration for and exploitation of resources in the Area. It is only in accordance with this complex system established in Part XI that a State, and persons and entities within their jurisdiction, can explore for and exploit resources in the Area.

The International Seabed Authority, which is considered in more detail elsewhere in this volume,[123] is the entity established to organize and control the activities in the Area.[124] The Seabed Authority acts for and on behalf of humanity.[125] It is composed of a number of organs, the most of important of which are the Assembly and the Council.[126] The rights of States, described below, are to be enjoyed in accordance with the policy and regulations established by the Seabed Authority. The Assembly has, for more than a decade, been working on a set of instruments, in the form of regulations and recommendations, that govern the exploration for and exploitation of mineral resources.[127] These instruments provide detailed provision that apply to the exploration for and exploitation of mineral resources in the Area and therefore bind any State (and an entity with a license) that engages in activities in the Area.

120 This provision, in particular the phrase '*[t]he Area and* its resources', has given rise to long-standing debate on whether resources not provided for in the definition of resources for the purposes of Part XI, are also the common heritage of mankind. This debate falls outside the scope of this chapter, for literature on it see F. Millicay, 'A legal regime for the biodiversity of the Area', in M. Nordquist, T. Heidar and J.N. Moore (eds.), *Law, science and ocean management*, Leiden: Brill/Martinus Nijhoff, 2007; D. Tladi 'Genetic resources, benefit sharing and the law of the sea: the need for clarity', *Journal of International Maritime Law* 13, 200, 183; P. Drankier et al., 'Marine genetic resources in areas beyond national jurisdiction: access and benefit sharing', *International Journal of Marine and Coastal Law* 27, 2012, 375.

121 See article 137, para. 2 of UNCLOS which states that '[a]ll right in the resources of the Area are vested in mankind as a whole'.

122 See also article 137, para. 3 of UNCLOS, 'No State or natural or juridical person shall claim, acquire or exercise rights with respect to the minerals recovered in the Area'.

123 See Jaeckel, op. cit.

124 See article 156, UNCLOS, under which the Seabed Authority is established. See also article 157, id.

125 See article 137, ibid.

126 The voting system of these organs has been significantly changed by the 1994 Agreement. For more on this, see generally on the 1994 Agreement T. Meyer 'Elisabeth Mann Borgese and the law of the sea', *Studies in the history of international law* 59-23, Leiden and Boston: Brill Nijhoff, 2022.

127 See Draft Regulations (adopted by the Legal and Technical Commission, but yet to be approved by the Council) on Exploitation of Mineral Resources in the Area, 2019, ISBA/25/C/WP.1. This text is based on previous work of the Authority: Regulations on Prospecting and Exploration for Polymetallic Nodules in the Area, 2013, ISBA/19/C/17; Regulations on Prospecting and Exploration for Polymetallic Sulphides in the Area, 2010, ISBA/16/A/12/Rev.1; Regulations on Prospecting and Exploration for Polymetallic Sulphides in the Area, 2012, ISBA/16/A/12/Rev.1; Regulations on Prospecting and Exploration for Cobalt-rich Ferromanganese Crusts in the Area, 2012, ISBA/18/A/11; Procedures and criteria for the extension of an approved plan of work for exploration pursuant to section 1, paragraph 9, of the annex to the Agreement relating to the Implementation of Part XI of the United Nations Convention on the Law of the Sea of 10 December 1982; 2015, ISBA/21/C/19.

In terms of rights, all States Parties have the right to apply for licenses to explore for or exploit mineral resources in the Area.[128] In addition, States may sponsor other entities to carry out mining activities in the Area.[129] A State can sponsor an entity that either 'possesses the nationality of State Parties or are effectively' controlled by such States Parties or their nationals.[130] Article 4 of annex III requires, in the case of applicants that are sponsored by States, the applicant to be 'sponsored by the State Party of which it is a national'. The effect of the sponsorship is to make the obligations under the UNCLOS, which are binding on States Parties, also binding, albeit indirectly, on the non-State entities that may be the recipient of the contract.[131] In this connection, a State Party that sponsors a person or entity is under a duty to ensure that such person or entity complies with the UNCLOS.[132]

It should be emphasized that it is States Parties to the UNCLOS that have the right to apply for rights to engage in activities in the Area, and if successful, to explore for and exploit mineral resources in the Area. It is also only States Parties that can sponsor non-State entities to apply for mining contracts in the Area. The effect of this is that States that are not party to the UNCLOS are not entitled to explore for and exploit mineral resources in the Area.[133] A significant caveat is necessary here: an entity from a non-Party State can be involved in activities in the Area through subsidiaries registered in States Parties, just as a national of a non-Party State can register an entity in a State Party which could engage in activities in the Area.

While it is the case that as a treaty regime, Part XI is, as such, only applicable to States Parties which would mean, for non-Party States, freedom of the seas continues to apply, it is generally accepted that the regime established in Part XI applies as a matter of customary international law.[134] Quite apart from the large number of States that have ratified the UNCLOS, even States that are not party to the UNCLOS have not openly objected to the regime established in Part XI, nor has there been any attempt to engage in mining activities in the Area outside the confines of Part

128 See article 153, UNCLOS. See also article 3 of annex III (Basic Conditions of Prospecting, Exploration and Exploitation) to the Convention ('The Enterprise, States Parties and other entities ... may apply for approval of plans of work in the Area').

129 See article 153, para. 2 (b), UNCLOS.

130 Ibid.

131 See para. 75 of the *Responsibilities and Obligations of States Sponsoring Persons and Entities with Respect to Activities in the Area,* Advisory Opinion of the International Tribunal for the Law of the Sea, 1 February 2021. Hereinafter 'Seabed Advisory Opinion'.

132 See article 139 of UNCLOS.

133 See Dingwall, op. cit., at 152 et seq. Although, it should be said that Dingwall's assessment is rather equivocal about the legal position. Dingwall's assessment is based as much on the law as it is on practical realities. She notes that an 'entity conducting mining operations in the Area without ISA authorization – and absent the right of exclusivity and security of tenure that an ISA contract affords – would expose itself to tremendous risk' (at 153). Thus, from this perspective, the exclusion of actors from non-Party States is not, or at least not necessarily, because of the position in law but due to the economic risk versus reward assessment that any entity would make.

134 See M. Koskenniemi and M. Lehto, 'The privilege of universality, economic ideology and seabed resources', *Nordic Journal of International Law* 65, 1996, 533, at 551, making the case notwithstanding the adoption of the 1994 Implementing Agreement to the Convention, designed to undermine the economic ideology of the seabed regime established by Part XI, the essence of the regime remains intact (in part because the technical aspects of the legalese in the Agreement will remain obscure) and '[u]nilateral mining outside the Convention will be illegal'. See also E. Holmila, 'The common heritage of mankind in the law of the sea', *Acta Societatis Martensis* 1, 2005, 187, especially at 202, where she makes the argument that, at least in relation to the law of the sea, the common heritage of mankind principle is firmly established. See also E. Egede, *Africa and the deep seabed regime: politics and international law of the common heritage of mankind*, Heidelberg: Springer, 2011, at 69.

XI.[135] Moreover, General Assembly Resolution 2749 (XXV), which declared the Area the common heritage of mankind was adopted without a single vote against.

Perhaps the most important right is the right of States Parties, collectively, to share in the benefits from the exploitation of resources of the Area.[136] This includes States Parties that are themselves not engaged in activities in the Area. In this connection, the UNCLOS provides 'for the equitable sharing of financial and other economic benefits derived from the activities in the Area'.[137] The formula for equitable sharing is to be determined by the Council and approved by the Assembly.[138] To date the Finance Committee – a Committee under the Council – remains engaged in the discussion of the formula.[139]

Rights and obligations of States in relation to the protection of the environment during mining operations in the Area

The general obligation relating to the protection of the environment contained in Part XII applies also to activities in the Area. This includes the duty in article 194 to 'protect and preserve the marine environment'. Similarly, the duty to 'take, individually or jointly, all measures consistent with [the] Convention that are necessary to prevent, reduce and control pollution from any source'.[140] These duties apply to 'all sources', including harmful effects from mining. Part XII also identifies particular rules for pollution from activities in different maritime zones. For the Area, it requires States 'to adopt laws and regulations' for the purposes preventing, reducing and controlling 'pollution of the marine environment from activities in the Area', which rules and regulations should meet standards of international law.[141]

Part XI itself contains a number of provisions relevant to the protection of the environment. The most important of these is article 145, which provides as follows:

> Necessary measures shall be taken in accordance with the Convention with respect to activities in the Area to ensure effective protection for the marine environment from harmful effects which may arise from such activities.

Yet, these rules lack the necessary specificity to establish standards against which to hold operators in the Area, or the States sponsoring them. Thus, the UNCLOS makes provision for more detailed rules for the effective protection of the marine environment. Article 209 provides that '[i]nternational rules, regulations and procedures shall be established (…) to prevent, reduce, and control pollution of the marine environment from activities in the Area'. This provision echoes

135 For the case of non-Party States to UNCLOS and related questions with regard to seabed mining in the Area, see in this book the case of Colombia. Restrepo Uribe, op. cit.

136 See article 140, para. 1, UNCLOS.

137 Article 140, para. 2, UNCLOS.

138 See article 160, para. 2(f), ibid.

139 See Report of the Secretary-General of ISA, *Rules, regulations and procedures on the equitable sharing of financial and other economic benefits derived from activities in the Area*, 2018, ISBA/24/FC/4. See also Report of the Finance Committee, *Development of rules, regulations and procedures on the equitable sharing of financial and other economic benefits derived from activities in the Area pursuant to section 9, paragraph 7 (f), of the annex to the Agreement relating to the Implementation of Part XI of the United Nations Convention on the Law of the Sea of 10 December 1982*, ISBA/26/A/24–ISBA/26/C/39, 2021.

140 See article 194, para. 1, UNCLOS.

141 See article 209, para. 2, ibid.

Article 145 which requires that the Authority adopts appropriate 'rules, regulations and procedures' for the protection of the marine environment from harm that might arise from activities in the Area.

These 'rules, regulations and procedures' are to be found in the (yet to be finally adopted) Mining Code.[142] The Code includes a number of rules designed to ensure the protection of the marine environment. Regulation 44, as currently drafted for example, provides that activities for exploitation of mineral resources in the Area are to be carried out in accordance with 'the precautionary approach, as reflected in principle 15 of the Rio Declaration on Environment and Development',[143] and are to apply 'Best Available Techniques and Best Environmental Practices' in carrying out such precautionary assessments. The Regulations then proceed to describe the relevant best practices.[144] The Regulations further detail environmental impact assessments to be carried out for activities in the Area, detailing the content of impact statements as well as the environmental management plan for addressing identified impacts.[145] Also contained in the Regulations is the duty to take measures to control the extent of pollution from mining activities.[146]

These duties described in the Regulations are mainly on the contractors and are incorporated into any contracts concluded with the contractor. Yet, the implications of the sponsorship described above is that, through the sponsorship arrangement, the sponsoring State assumes the duty of due diligence to ensure that any contract sponsored by it complies with the duty. To this end article 139 of the UNCLOS states the following:

> States Parties shall have the responsibility to ensure that activities in the Area, whether carried out by States Parties, or state enterprises or natural or juridical persons which possess the nationality of States Parties or are effectively controlled by them or their nationals, shall be carried out in accordance with this Part.

The International Tribunal for the Law of the Sea explained that the duty of States, emanating from due sponsorship is a duty of care, requires the adoption of 'reasonably appropriate' under the circumstances.[147] The standard of what is 'reasonably appropriate' will shift depending on factors such as the risk of the activity.[148]

In addition to the obligations of due diligence owed by States on the basis of the sponsorship relationship with contractors, States owe obligations directly flowing from the UNCLOS provisions. These include the obligation to take measures to prevent harm to the environment under article 145 and article 192.[149] Since much of the responsibility for the management and administration of the Area is done by the Authority on behalf of States, the most important of these obligations

142 See Draft Regulations on the Exploitation of Minerals (above note 544).

143 For more information about the implementation of the precautionary approach within and outside national jurisdiction, see Makgill, Jaeckel and MacMaster, op. cit. See also generally the chapter on potential future disputes and the role of ITLOS, M. Feria Tinta and M. Kamga, 'Mining the bottom of the sea: Potential future disputes and the role of the International Tribunal for the Law of the Sea', in V. Tassin Campanella (ed.) *Routledge handbook of seabed mining and the law of the sea*, op. cit., chapter V.3.

144 Draft Regulations on the Exploitation of Minerals, Regulation 45.

145 Ibid., Regulations 47 and 48.

146 Ibid., Regulations 49 and 50.

147 Seabed Advisory Opinion, op. cit., at para. 120.

148 Ibid., paras. 117–120.

149 For the characterization of these obligations by ITLOS, see Seabed Advisory Opinion, op. cit., at paras. 121 et seq.

is to cooperate with the Authority, and assist the Authority in carrying out its functions, including through the provision of necessary information.

Generally speaking, since the Area is located below the High Seas, challenges remain as to ensure effective protection of the marine environment throughout ecosystems. Indeed, activities conducted in the Area affect the water column of the High Seas and can have potential impacts in the High Seas but also in areas within national jurisdiction.

The Biodiversity Beyond National Jurisdiction Agreement (BBNJ Agreement), the third Implementing Agreement of UNCLOS, was developed with this in mind. At the heart of this BBNJ Agreement lies the obligation of cooperation which aims at not only strengthening and enhancing cooperation, but also promoting cooperation among relevant legal instruments and frameworks and relevant global, regional, subregional and sectoral bodies in the achievement of conservation and sustainable use of marine biological diversity.[150] The existing obligation of cooperation of States towards ISA is therefore strengthened by a new obligation to cooperate to achieve the goals of the BBNJ Agreement. This obligation requires State to promote, as appropriate, the objectives of the BBNJ Agreement when participating in decision-making under other relevant frameworks and bodies, therefore including ISA.

While this BBNJ Agreement has not yet entered into force at the time of writing, some provisions and mechanisms are of interest for future developments. The BBNJ Agreement, for example, much like the Mining Code, includes an obligation to conduct environmental impact assessment.[151] However, the thresholds and factors to conduct EIA differ between the BBNJ Agreement on the one hand, and the exploration regulations and recommendation, and current draft of the exploitation regulations developed by the ISA on the other hand. Such difference of thresholds is acknowledged by the BBNJ Agreement, which actually only requires compliance with the regulations or standards of relevant legal instruments, frameworks and bodies to prevent, mitigate and manage potential impacts, even if these ones are below than those of the BBNJ Agreement (Article 29, paragraph 4 b) ii)). If these differences persist at the time of adoption of the exploitation regulations, some complications might occur in practice since States could be subject to different legal frameworks and/or standards during the conduct of their activities in the Area. The case of European Member States is of interest. These States might be subject to future EIA European rules applicable in areas beyond national jurisdiction, which thresholds applicable within national jurisdiction are already higher than those of the Mining Code. Therefore, it is likely that if and when the EU will ratify the BBNJ Agreement,[152] it will align – at least – its thresholds of the EIA in areas beyond national jurisdiction with the ones of the BBNJ Agreement.[153] As a result, European Member States might apply higher thresholds during the same activities than other non-European Member States, who will (only) comply with the potential lower thresholds of the Mining Code. While this scenario will be in compliance with the BBNJ Agreement, questions could be raised as to whether the effective protection and preservation of the marine environment can be compatible with this multi-gear system, which might encourage certain entities conducting activities in the Area to consider what is called 'forum shopping' in order to choose the best sponsors, with the least obligations. The implementation mechanisms of the BBNJ Agreement as well as the ISA will, with no doubt, be able to clarify these issues that remain at the time being only prospective.

150 Article 2 and article 8, BBNJ Agreement.

151 Article 27, ibid.

152 At the time of writing, the EU and its Member States have yet to find an agreement on the split of competences related to the implementation of the BBNJ Agreement (and related transposition into national laws). This concerns the EIA, but also other matters such as the proposal related to the establishment of marine protected areas.

153 For more information on this scenario, see in this book Singh, Tassin Campanella and Maes, op. cit.

References

Armas F., 'The future role of the International Seabed Authority', in V. Tassin Campanella (ed.), *Routledge handbook of seabed mining and the law of the sea*, London: Routledge, 2023, chapter IV.3.

Bennouna M., 'La limite extérieure du plateau continental et la gestion des ressources pour l'humanité', in R.-J. Dupuy (ed.), *La gestion des ressources pour l'humanité : le droit de la mer*, The Hague and Boston: Martinus Nijhoff, 1982, 116.

Chircop A., 'Implementation of article 82 of the United Nations Convention on the law of the sea, the challenge for Canada', in C. Banet (ed.), *The law of the seabed: Access, uses and protection of seabed resources*, Leiden and Boston: Brill/Nijhoff, 2000, 371–394.

Davenport T., 'Southeast Asia and seabed mining', in V. Tassin Campanella (ed.), *Routledge handbook of seabed mining and the law of the sea*, London: Routledge, 2023, chapter VI.1.7.

Dingwall J., 'Commercial mining activities in the deep seabed beyond national jurisdiction: The international legal framework', in C. Banet (ed.), *The law of the seabed: Access, uses and protection of the seabed resources*, Leiden and Boston: Brill Martinus Nijhoff, 2020, at 141 et seq.

Drankier P. et al., 'Marine genetic resources in areas beyond national jurisdiction: Access and benefit sharing', *International Journal of Marine and Coastal Law* 27, 2012, 375.

Egede E., *Africa and the deep seabed regime: Politics and international law of the common heritage of mankind*, Heidelberg: Springer, 2011.

Eriksson G., 'The case of disagreement between a coastal state and the Commission on the Limits of the Continental Shef', in M.H. Nordquist et al. (eds.), *Legal and scientific aspects of continental shelf limits*, Leiden, Boston: Martinus Nijhoff, 2004, 251–258.

Feria Tinta M. and Kamga M., 'Mining the bottom of the sea: Potential future disputes and the role of the International Tribunal for the Law of the Sea', in V. Tassin Campanella (ed.), *Routledge handbook of seabed mining and the law of the sea*, London: Routledge, 2023, chapter V.3.

Friedheim R.L. and Bowen R.E., 'Neglected issues at the Third United Nations Law of the sea conference', *Law of the sea: Neglected issues, Proceedings of the twelfth annual conference of the Law of the Sea Institute*, The Hague, 23–26 October 1978, Honolulu: University of Hawai'i.

Gau M.S.-T., 'The commission on the limits of the continental shelf as a mechanism to prevent enchroachment upon the Area', *Chinese Journal of International Law* 10–3, 2011.

Gautier P. and Tassin V.J.M., 'Les plates-formes en mer et le droit international', *Annuaire français de droit international* LIX, CNRS Edition, 2013, 185–220.

Holmila E., 'The common heritage of mankind in the law of the sea', *Acta Societatis Martensis* 1, 2005.

Jarmache E., 'La pratique de la Commission des limites du plateau continental', *Annuaire français du droit international* 54, 2008, 429–441.

Jaeckel A., 'The Area and the role of the international seabed authority', in V. Tassin Campanella (ed.), *Routledge handbook of seabed mining and the law of the sea*, London: Routledge, 2023, chapter IV.1.

Jensen Ø., *The Commission on the limits of the continental shelf: Law and legitimacy*, Brill/Nijhoff, 2014.

Jensen Ø. and Már Magnússon B., 'The extension of sovereign rights beyond 200 nautical miles', in V. Tassin Campanella (ed.), *Routledge handbook of seabed mining and the law of the sea*, London: Routledge, 2023, chapter III.1.

Jiménez Pineda E., 'South American region and seabed mining', in V. Tassin Campanella (ed.), *Routledge handbook of seabed mining and the law of the sea*, London: Routledge, 2023, chapter VI.1.6.

Koskenniemi M. and Lehto M., 'The privilege of universality, economic ideology and seabed resources', *Nordic Journal of International Law* 65, 1996, 533.

Kunoy B., 'La zone économique exclusive', in M. Forteau and J.-M. Thouvenin (eds.), *Traité de droit international de la mer*, Paris: Pedone, 2017, 384–399.

MacDorman T.L., 'The role of the Commission on the limits of the continental shelf: A technical body in a political world', *The International Journal of Marine and Coastal Law* 17–3, 2002, 301–324.

Makgill R., Jaeckel A. and MacMaster K., 'The precautionary approach: Cautionary progressions and future directions', in V. Tassin Campanella (ed.), *Routledge handbook of seabed mining and the law of the sea*, London: Routledge, 2023, Chapter I.3.

Már Magnússon B., *The continental shelf beyond 200 nautical miles*, Brill/Nijhoff, 2015.

Meyer T., *Elisabeth Mann Borgese and the law of the sea*, Studies in the history of international law 59–23, Leiden and Boston: Brill/Nijhoff, 2022.

Millicay F., 'A legal regime for the biodiversity of the Area', in M. Nordquist, T. Heidar and J.N. Moore (eds.), *Law, science and ocean management*, 739–850, Leiden: Brill Martinus Nijhoff, 2007.

Mossop J., *The continental shelf beyond 200 nautical miles: Rights and responsibilities*, New York: Oxford University Press, 2017.

Oral N., 'The common heritage of mankind under international law', in V. Tassin Campanella (ed.), *Routledge handbook of seabed mining and the law of the sea*, London: Routledge, 2023, chapter I.2.

Oude Elferink A.O., 'Article 76 of the LOSC on the definition of the continental shelf: Questions concerning its interpretation from a legal perspective', *The International Journal of Marine and Coastal Law* 21–3, 2006, 269–285.

Oude Elferink A.O., 'Commission on the limits of the continental shelf', in R. Wolfrum (ed.), *The Max Planck encyclopaedia of Public International Law*, Oxford University Press, 2011.

Oxman B.H., 'The 1994 agreement and the convention', *The American Journal of International Law* 88–4, 1994, 687–696.

Payne C.R., 'State responsibility for deep seabed mining obligations', in V. Tassin Campanella (ed.), *Routledge handbook of seabed mining and the law of the sea*, London: Routledge, 2023, chapter II.2.

Restrepo Uribe E., 'Colombia and seabed mining', in V. Tassin Campanella (ed.), *Routledge handbook of seabed mining and the law of the sea*, London: Routledge, 2023, chapter VI.2.3.

Roest W.R., Brekke H. and Clark M.R., 'The scientific challenges of deep-sea mining', in V. Tassin Campanella (ed.), *Routledge handbook of seabed mining and the law of the sea*, London: Routledge, 2023, chapter I.1.

Scelle G., 'Obsession du territoire: Essai d'étude réaliste de droit international', *Symbolae Verzijl*, The Hague: Martinus Nijhoff, 1958, 360.

Schneider F., 'Le régime de la zone économique exclusive et la pratique des Etats méditerranéens', *Annuaire du droit de la mer* XVIII, 2013, 13–46.

Schofield C. and Mossop J., 'The article 82 conundrum: Implementing payment for the exploitation of the continental shelf beyond 200 nautical miles', in V. Tassin Campanella (ed.), *Routledge handbook of seabed mining and the law of the sea*, London: Routledge, 2023, chapter III.2.

Scovazzi T., 'The Mediterranean and Black Sea maritime boundaries', in D.A. Colson and R.W. Smith (eds.), *International maritime boundaries*, Volume 5, Leiden and Boston: Brill Martinus Nijhoff, 2005, 3477–3483.

Singh P.A., Tassin Campanella V. and Maes F., 'The European Union and seabed mining', in V. Tassin Campanella (ed.), *Routledge handbook of seabed mining and the law of the sea*, London: Routledge, 2023, chapter VI.1.4.

Sohn L.B., 'International law implications of the 1994 Agreement', *The American Journal of International Law* 88–4, 1994, 696–705.

Suarez S.V., *The outer limits of the continental shelf*, Springer, 2008.

Suarez S.V., 'The Commission on the limits of the continental shelf and its function to provide scientific and technical advice', *Chinese Journal of International Law* 12, 2013, 339–345.

Tassin V.J.M., *Les défis de l'extension du plateau continental: consécration d'un nouveau rapport de l'Etat à son territoire*, Paris: Pedone, 2013.

Tassin V.J.M., 'Territorial and maritime dispute (Nicaragua v. Colombia)', in P. Wojcikiewicz and J.-M. Sorel (eds.), *Latin America and the international court of justice: Contributions to international law*, London and New York: Routledge, 2017, 2001, 225–236.

Tassin V.J.M., 'L'exploration et l'exploitation des ressources naturelles du plateau continental à l'heure de l'extension du plateau continental au-delà des 200 milles marins', *Annuaire du droit de la mer* XV, 2010, 98–99.

Tassin V.J.M., 'Between freedom and control: The regulation of marine scientific research on the continental shelf', in INDEMER (ed.), *Knowing the oceans for achieving sustainable development*, Paris: Pedone, 2018, 77–94.

Tladi D., 'Genetic resources, benefit sharing and the law of the sea: The need for clarity', *Journal of International Maritime Law* 13, 2007, 183.

Treves T., 'Dispute settlement and deep-sea mining', in V. Tassin Campanella (ed.), *Routledge handbook of seabed mining and the law of the sea*, London: Routledge, 2023, chapter.V.1.

Van Dyke J.M., 'Sharing ocean resources – In a time of scarcity and selfishness', in H.N. Schieber (ed.), *Law of the sea: The common heritage and emerging challenges*, The Hague: Kluwer Law International, 2000, 3–26.

Vega-Barbosa G., 'The Admissibility of outer continental shelf delimitation claims before the ICJ absent a recommendation by the CLCS', *Ocean Development and International Law* 49-2, 2018.

Young R., 'Sedentary fisheries and the convention on the continental shelf', *American Journal of International Law* 55, 1961, 361.

International courts and tribunals

Alleged Violations of Sovereign Rights and Maritime Spaces in the Caribbean Sea (Nicaragua v. Colombia), Judgment, 21 April 2022.

Arbitration Between Barbados and Trinidad and Tobago, Decision of 11 April 2006, RIAA, Vol. XXVII, p. 147, para 213.

Bay of Bengal Maritime Boundary Arbitration Between Bangladesh and India, Award, 7 July 2014, p. 21, para 77.

Case Concerning the Delimitation of Maritime Areas Between Canada and France, Reports of International Arbitral Awards XXI, Decision, 10 June 1992, pp. 265–341.

Continental Shelf (Lybia Arab Jamahiriya/Malta), Judgement, ICJ Reports 1985, p. 33, para 34.

Dispute Concerning Delimitation of the Maritime Boundary Between Mauritius and Maldives in the Indian Ocean (Mauritius/Maldives), Judgment, 28 April 2023.

Dispute Concerning the Delimitation of the Maritime Boundary Between Bangladesh and Myanmar in the Bay of Bengal (Bangladesh/Myanmar), Judgment, 14 March 2012, Case 16, para 361.

Maritime Delimitation in the Indian Ocean (Somalia v. Kenya), Judgement, ICJ Reports 2021, p. 206.

Maritime Delimitation in the Indian Ocean (Somalia v. Kenya), (Preliminary Objections), 2 February 2017.

North Sea Continental Shelf, Judgment, ICJ Report 1969, p. 3.

Question of the Delimitation of the Continental Shelf Between Nicaragua and Colombia Beyond 200 Nautical Miles from the Nicaraguan Coast (Nicaragua v. Colombia), (Preliminary Objections), 17 March 2016.

Responsibilities and Obligations of States Sponsoring Persons and Entities with Respect to Activities in the Area, Advisory Opinion of the International Tribunal for the Law of the Sea, 1 February 2021.

Territorial and Maritime Dispute Between Nicaragua and Honduras in the Caribbean Sea (Nicaragua v. Honduras), Judgment, ICJ Reports 2007, p. 659.

II.2

STATE RESPONSIBILITY FOR DEEP SEABED MINING OBLIGATIONS

Cymie R. Payne

Introduction

Deep seabed mining has the potential to cause harms that include damage to the marine environment, to biological diversity, to natural ocean carbon sequestration, and to human life.[1] Operators may also infringe or impede activities of other sectors of human activity, including navigation, fishing, laying and maintaining submarine cables, marine scientific research, and eventually, carbon sequestration. State sponsors of mining operators could fail to observe their due diligence obligation to provide effective legal oversight to ensure compliance with the measures intended to prevent these harms. Revenues from seabed mining in areas beyond national jurisdiction (ABNJ) could be mishandled by the answerable international organization, or the organization could fail to provide adequate oversight of miners and their activities.

International agreements, customary international law, and general principles of law are intended to avoid these unfortunate outcomes. When a State or international organization breaches an obligation established by international law, it is responsible for consequences. This concept of State responsibility is fundamental to international law; but in the context of the physically dynamic and connected global ocean, its meaning becomes ambiguous to the point of dilution and potential dissolution. The dominant roles of transnational corporations and international organizations in the world ocean test the adequacy of the legal doctrine of State responsibility. This is especially true where the home or host State has weak legal capacity.

The consequences to the marine environment of a failure to satisfy legal responsibility are dire. States, international organizations, and private actors have duties to each other and to the international community that are only meaningful when breach has consequences. Responsibility can be strengthened, and the rule of law can be sustained if States view their duties and rights in terms of Earth systems, looking to long-term existential interests. Adjustments to the inter-state system are needed to impose responsibility on these and other actors involved in deep sea mining when there are weaknesses and gaps in the present legal system.

1 L.A. Levin et al., 'Defining "serious harm" to the marine environment in the context of deep-seabed mining,' *Marine Policy* 74, 2016, 245–59.

DOI: 10.4324/9780429426162-8

State responsibility applies to relations between States and entities with international legal personality. According to the International Law Commission's Articles on State Responsibility (ASR), 'for particular conduct to be characterized as an internationally wrongful act, it must first be attributable to the State.'[2] When a State fails to fulfill its international obligations, its responsibility is engaged and it is liable for the consequences. An international obligation is a duty to act or refrain from acting that one State (or other international actor) owes another; an injured State may be said to have had its rights infringed. The United Nations Convention on the Law of the Sea (UNCLOS, the Convention) and the Agreement relating to the Implementation of Part XI of UNCLOS (1994 Agreement) are the primary sources of legal obligations related to deep seabed mining for States Parties to those treaties,[3] along with customary international law, treaties and other sources of international law that also apply to States that are not parties to UNCLOS or the 1994 Agreement. Assessment of how these principles and rules apply to deep seabed mining remains the province of jurists, as no international court has ruled on these questions in a contentious case as yet. However, the Seabed Disputes Chamber (SDC) of the International Tribunal for the Law of the Sea (ITLOS) has issued an advisory opinion interpreting State responsibility and liability of States sponsoring deep seabed mining in 'the Area,' that is, in the seabed of areas beyond national jurisdiction (ABNJ), under UNCLOS.[4]

A first step in determining international legal responsibility in relation to deep seabed mining is identifying where the deep seabed is and what legal measures—rights and duties—pertain to it. The seabed is simply the ocean floor and has no legal definition in UNCLOS;[5] it is located both within and beyond national jurisdiction. Thus, seabed minerals that are sought for exploration and exploitation are found within and beyond national jurisdiction. States' obligations and their consequent international responsibility encompass seabed mining activities in both zones.

Coastal State rights and duties with respect to the seabed and subsoil of submarine areas are defined in UNCLOS to apply from a State's landward baseline as far as 200 nautical miles (the Exclusive Economic Zone (EEZ)),[6] and throughout 'the natural prolongation of its land territory to the outer edge of the continental margin' up to a specified limit (the continental shelf).[7] These

2 International Law Commission, *Draft Articles on Responsibility of States for Internationally Wrongful Acts, with Commentaries*, 2001, 35 (comment on article 2, para. 5), (hereinafter 'ASR').

3 *United Nations Convention on the Law of the Sea*, 10 December 1982, 1833 UNTS 396; *Agreement relating to the Implementation of Part XI of the UNCLOS*, 28 July 1994. A number of States that ratified UNCLOS before the 1994 Agreement was adopted did not join the new implementing agreement. Subsequently, a State becoming party to UNCLOS was automatically party to the 1994 Agreement. 1994 Agreement, article 4. As at 13 October 2021, 167 States and the EU were party to UNCLOS; 150 States and the EU were party to the 1994 Agreement.

4 *Responsibilities and obligations of States with respect to activities in the Area, Advisory Opinion, 1 February 2011, ITLOS Reports 2011*, p. 10 (hereinafter 'Advisory Opinion' or 'Case No. 17').

5 Compare 'prospecting means any activity undertaken for the purpose of identifying sea-bed or subsoil likely to contain mineral deposits or occurrences' in New Zealand Exclusive Economic Zone and Continental Shelf (Environmental Effects—Discharge and Dumping) Regulations 2015, New Zealand, 28 September 2015, Article 3; and United States 30 USC § 1403 (4), the term 'deep seabed' means 'the seabed, and the subsoil thereof to a depth of ten meters, lying seaward of and outside— (A) the continental shelf of any nation; and (B) any area of national resource jurisdiction of any foreign nation, if such area extends beyond the Continental Shelf of such nation and such jurisdiction is recognized by the United States.'

6 Many States have not declared an EEZ, or have only declared an EEZ for a portion of their coasts.

7 UNCLOS, article 76. The average width of states' continental shelves is about 65 km, or 40 miles. The Editors of *Encyclopedia Britannica*, 'continental shelf,' *Britannica*. Available online <https://www.britannica.com/science/continental-shelf> (accessed July 2022). For further explanation of how the legal continental shelf is delineated see L. Bernard and C. Schofield, 'Disputes concerning the delimitation of the continental shelf beyond 200 nautical

zones may be modified where States' claims overlap.[8] Within the EEZ, a coastal State has sovereign rights over living and non-living resources on the seabed, subsoil and superjacent waters; and other economic activities related to the economic exploitation and exploration of the EEZ; and duties vis-à-vis other States.[9] Coastal State rights and duties are replaced by the High Seas legal regime in the water column and air space above the portion of the continental shelf beyond the EEZ (referred to informally as the extended continental shelf). On the extended continental shelf, the coastal State has sovereign rights to extract natural resources but limited by the obligation that in doing so it may not infringe the rights of other States in the water column and air space above.[10] This may remind some of Portia's judgment, 'This bond doth give thee here no jot of blood. The words expressly are "a pound of flesh",' but not a drop of blood.[11] Minerals may be extracted from the seabed by the coastal State, but not to the detriment of others' interest in the water column. Coastal States specifically have the duty to 'adopt laws and regulations to prevent, reduce and control pollution of the marine environment' from seabed activities in the EEZ and extended continental shelf under UNCLOS, article 208.

Where the deep seabed of a State's EEZ or continental shelf contains minerals worth exploiting, the question of coastal State responsibility arises, along with potential liability for harm. About three quarters of sovereign States have deep ocean within their EEZ and for 80 per cent of small island developing States the deep ocean occupies more than 90 per cent of their national waters.[12] This means that most sovereign States have deep seabed within waters subject to their jurisdiction, conferring coastal State rights (for example, to extract seabed minerals) and duties (for example, to prevent transboundary pollution) on them vis-à-vis adjacent coastal States and the international community.

Landlocked States, though lacking direct access to the sea, benefit from many rights under UNCLOS, including the right to register ships and to sponsor seabed mining in the Area. When a landlocked State takes one of these roles, it assumes the obligations of a flag State or sponsoring State under UNCLOS and other relevant international law. Landlocked States may also benefit from 'payments or contributions in kind in respect of the exploitation of the non-living resources' of the extended continental shelf[13] and the Area.[14]

In the High Seas, a State's rights and duties are most often tied to its status as the State of registration for a vessel, the flag State. Flag States have a duty to ensure effective enforcement of a legal regime to prevent, reduce and control pollution.[15] The State that registers a vessel involved in mining is therefore potentially responsible when it fails to provide appropriate oversight and legal enforcement. ITLOS's Seabed Disputes Chamber concluded that 'the general provisions concern-

miles,' in T. Heidar (ed.) *New knowledge and changing circumstances in the law of the sea*, Leiden/Boston: Brill Nijhoff, 2020, 157–82.

8 For example, *Delimitation of the maritime boundary in the Bay of Bengal (Bangladesh/Myanmar), Judgment, ITLOS Reports 2012*, p. 4.

9 UNCLOS, article 56.

10 UNCLOS, articles 77, 78. See also generally in this book Ø. Jensen and B. Mar Magnussen, 'The extension of sovereign rights beyond 200 nautical miles,' in V. Tassin Campanella (ed.), *Routledge handbook of seabed mining and the law of the sea*, London: Routledge, 2023, chapter III.1.

11 William Shakespeare, *The Merchant of Venice*, Act 4, Scene 1.

12 D.J. Amon et al., 'My deep sea, my backyard: a pilot study to build capacity for global deep-ocean exploration and research,' *Phil. Trans. R. Soc.* B 377: 20210121, 2022.

13 UNCLOS, article 82 (4).

14 UNCLOS, article 140.

15 UNCLOS, article 217.

ing the responsibilities and liability of the sponsoring State apply equally to all sponsoring States, whether developing or developed.'[16]

All States have High Seas rights of navigation, overflight, submarine cable and pipeline installation, artificial island and other installations, fishing, and scientific research, subject to the obligation of due regard for the interests of other States.[17] In conflicts between the mining industry and other sectors seeking to use the same geographic spaces, rights that are given equal weight in the Convention face off against each other.[18]

The international community, also expressed as mankind (henceforth rendered here as 'humankind') as a whole in the Convention, is a rights-bearer under UNCLOS, with a heightened role in the EEZ and ABNJ where some individual State rights become community rights.[19] The common heritage of humankind includes 'the sea-bed and the ocean floor, and the subsoil thereof, beyond the limits of national jurisdiction.'[20] This special status raises unique concerns: shared rights to a healthy ocean are difficult to enforce and defend in the traditional bilateral system of international law.[21] UNCLOS, article 59, recognizes that the international community's interests must be taken into account in the resolution of conflicts regarding the attribution of rights and jurisdiction in the EEZ.

Sponsoring States are the likeliest stakeholders to incur responsibility for wrongful acts associated with mining in the Area. Any State party to UNCLOS and the 1994 Agreement, including landlocked States, may sponsor 'States Parties, or state enterprises or natural or juridical persons which possess the nationality of States Parties or are effectively controlled by them or their nationals' or a group of these to mine in the Area.[22] While they have the right to benefit financially as sponsoring States, States have liability if they fail to provide adequate legal control over mining operators and harm results.[23]

Transnational corporations were the first entities to prospect and explore the deep seabed for potential mineral extraction, and logically they should be subject to international responsibility through one or more States. The legal assumption (and the requirement of the Convention for activities in the Area) is that each of these non-State entities has the nationality of a State, and as such is subject to the State's laws, or is effectively controlled by a State or its nationals.[24] The home State has an international obligation to provide a legal regime sufficient to compel its nationals, including corporations, to comply with international obligations the State has taken on. All UNCLOS States Parties—home, host and sponsoring States alike—are responsible 'to ensure that activities under their jurisdiction or control are so conducted as not to cause damage by pollution

16 ITLOS, Case No. 17, para. 158.

17 UNCLOS, article 87, Part XI.

18 See ISA, 'Submarine cables and deep seabed mining: advancing common interests and addressing common interests and addressing UNCLOS "Due Regard" obligations,' *Technical Study No. 14*, 2015.

19 See N. Oral, 'The common heritage of mankind under international law: An overview,' in V. Tassin Campanella (ed.), *Routledge handbook of seabed mining and the law of the sea*, op. cit., chapter I.2.

20 UNCLOS, article 136, UNGA res. 25/2749 (XXV) (1970); see also UNCLOS, articles 125, 140 ('mankind as a whole').

21 C.R. Payne, 'Responsibility to the international community for marine biodiversity beyond national jurisdiction,' *Cambridge International Law Journal* 11-1, 24–50, 2022; J. R. Crawford, 'Responsibility to the international community as a whole,' *Indiana Journal of Global Legal Studies* 8-2, 2001, 303–22.

22 UNCLOS, article 153.

23 UNCLOS, article 139; International Tribunal for the Law of the Sea, *Responsibilities and Obligations of States Sponsoring Persons and Entities with Respect to Activities in the Area, Advisory Opinion*, 2011.

24 See UNCLOS, article 139 (1).

to other States and their environment.'[25] Whether all States have the desire or ability to exercise sufficient authority over non-State entities has been questioned by other States, civil society, and scholars.

The International Seabed Authority (ISA), constituted by UNCLOS to administer deep seabed mining in ABNJ, is yet another entity that joins coastal States, flag States, the international community, and sponsoring States as a possible right- or duty-holder and as a potential bearer of responsibility. It has the duty, *inter alia*, to carry out activities in the Area subject to the social, economic and environmental policies listed in UNCLOS, article 150.

This chapter addresses State responsibility and liability for failure to comply with the obligations established in respect of deep-seabed mining under UNCLOS.[26] It takes as its jumping-off point the Seabed Dispute Chamber's interpretation of the Convention and the 1994 Agreement. First it considers what might constitute a breach of State party obligations under UNCLOS, the 1994 Agreement, and other sources of international law. It then discusses the liability and remedies that are the consequences of a breach of an international obligation that engages a State's responsibility. Finally, it considers three special cases of responsibility for non-State entities: the responsibility of international organizations, notably the ISA; the responsibility of corporate entities; and the role of the international community to which responsibility may be owed.

Breach of international law obligations

Source and nature of States' obligations

A State's responsibility is engaged by its primary obligations under treaties that it is party to and relevant customary international law. Seabed mining rights and duties are, for States Parties to UNCLOS, determined in the first instance by UNCLOS and the 1994 Agreement. Some of these are highlighted in the preceding chapter.[27] Specific rights and duties are set out in other treaties including the 1958 Conventions, sectoral agreements, and environmental treaties. General rules regarding duties of environmental protection and rights to pursue traditional activities in the ocean apply to non-parties as a matter of customary international law. States' obligations with regard to seabed mining vary to some extent depending on where the mining takes place and the treaty status of the State.[28]

All UNCLOS States Parties have the general obligation under article 192 'to protect and preserve the marine environment' and other specific obligations to protect and preserve the marine environment agreed in Part XII which apply to their marine activities wherever they occur. Article 194 requires that they 'prevent, reduce and control pollution of the marine environment from any source' and ensure that activities under their jurisdiction or control do not pollute areas beyond 'areas where they exercise sovereign rights.' This is accompanied by several specific implement

25 UNCLOS, article 194 (2); article 145.

26 For a complementary analysis of potential future disputes and the role of the International Tribunal for the Law of the Sea, see in this book M. Feria Tinta and M. Kamga, 'Mining the bottom of the sea: Potential future disputes and the role of the international tribunal for the law of the sea,' in V. Tassin Campanella (ed.), *Routledge handbook of seabed mining and the law of the sea*, op. cit., chapter V.3.

27 V. Tassin Campanella, Y. Cissé and D. Tladi, 'Rights and obligations of States on the continental shelf and the Area,' in V. Tassin Campanella (ed.), *Routledge handbook of seabed mining and the law of the sea*, ibid., chapter II.1.

28 For more information on regional and national practice, see chapters VI of this book, including specific challenges raised by the EU. P. Singh, V. Tassin Campanella and F. Maes, 'The European Union and seabed mining,' in V. Tassin Campanella (ed.), *Routledge handbook of seabed mining and the law of the sea*, ibid., chapter VI.1.4.

ing obligations relevant to seabed mining, including environmental assessment and pollution control for seabed mining within and beyond national jurisdiction, and dumping.[29] States that extract natural resources from the seabed of their continental shelf have a financial obligation to pay royalties or contributions in kind through the ISA to other States parties to UNCLOS.

UNCLOS and the 1994 Agreement function together to create an administrative system for overseeing mining in the Area, including prospecting, exploration, exploitation, and sharing financial benefits. States that sponsor commercial entities or their own State-owned enterprises have the obligation to establish a legal regime that can ensure sponsored contractors comply with their contracts, ISA regulations, and the Convention. The ISA is the organization through which States Parties administer the mineral resources of the Area.[30]

Breach

Given the many different aspects of deep seabed mining that give rise to international obligations, an incident or practice may breach more than one obligation. The nature of each obligation will determine 'the substance of the conduct required, the standard to be observed, the result to be achieved, etc.'[31] An example would be an event that gives rise to significant pollution of the marine environment.[32] If a State sponsoring a mining operator had failed to provide or enforce laws to prevent this kind of pollution, the State would likely have breached general and specific obligations under UNCLOS, the ISA regulations, and the fundamental customary rule prohibiting harm to another State or shared spaces.

A breach of an obligation only occurs if the rule is in force for that State at the time of the conduct in question. For example, a State that becomes a party to UNCLOS after the act or omission causing a breach might not be subject to the ISA regulations, which apply only to UNCLOS parties. However, the background customary international law of environmental protection that is codified in UNCLOS would be relevant at all times. In the previous example, the State's failure to conform its national legal regime to satisfy its international obligations could be a continuing breach.[33] The existence of this or another kind of continuing breach could influence the remedy.[34]

Deep seabed mining can take place within and beyond national jurisdiction and the obligations of care are owed to the international community as a whole, as well as to other States Parties to a relevant treaty or to individual States that are specially affected.[35]

29 Articles 204-206, 208–11, UNCLOS.

30 UNCLOS, article 157.

31 International Law Commission, ASR, 123.

32 For a description of various harms, see MIDAS (Managing Impacts of Deep Sea Resource Exploitation), 'Toxic Impacts of Deep-Sea Mining,' 2016; A. Vanreusel et al., 'Threatened by mining, polymetallic nodules are required to preserve abyssal epifauna,' *Nature: Scientific Reports* 6:26808, 2016; *Kiwis Against Seabed Mining, Inc., et al. v. Trans-Tasman Resources* (Wellington, Environment Court, Decision No. [2016] NZEnvC 217). It has been suggested that the responsibility of a State sponsoring marine scientific research could be engaged if the research activities were to excessively burden a contractor's mineral extraction. V.J.M. Tassin, 'La zone et l'autorité internationale des fond marins,' *Annuaire du Droit de la Mer*, Vol. XXI, 2016, 429.

33 International Law Commission, ASR, 139.

34 UN Reports of International Arbitral Awards (UNRIAA), *Rainbow Warrior (New Zealand/France)*, Vol. XX, 1990, 217, 264, para. 101.

35 International Law Commission, ASR, article 33 ('The obligations of the responsible State set out in this Part may be owed to another State, to several States, or to the international community as a whole').

Attribution

When a State sponsors a private mining company or a State-owned enterprise under the rules promulgated for mining in the Area, the question arises of whether mining activities will be attributable to the State, as they must be for responsibility to be incurred. Some of the questions that cloud attribution in other contexts are excluded here by the legal context, at least as to States Parties to UNCLOS and the 1994 Agreement, but others remain.

A State is responsible for its own direct conduct and for its failure provide an adequate legal regime to regulate conduct within its jurisdiction or control. A State acts directly either through its own personnel and State bodies or by directing others. The SDC identified States' direct obligations as including: (a) to assist the Authority; (b) to apply a precautionary approach; (c) to apply the 'best environmental practices'; (d) to adopt measures to ensure the provision of guarantees in the event of an emergency order by the Authority for protection of the marine environment; and (e) to provide recourse for compensation.[36]

It is expected that mining operations will be conducted by either private companies or State-owned enterprises. Since in these circumstances sovereign States are not likely acting directly, whether and when conduct can be attributed to them is a threshold matter. It is likely that multiple States might be responsible, given that there are already co-sponsors of mining contractors for sites in the Area.[37]

Tribunals and academic authors have taken the position that, in general, the conduct of private persons is not attributable to the State, and the State therefore does not bear responsibility for it.[38] To the lay perception, this approach seems peculiar, since the result appears to be the impossibility of holding accountable some of the most influential, and polluting, industrial sectors, including mining. However, this is not the end of the story.

The State's obligation to take necessary measures to implement its international commitments is the link between these State engagements and the activities of private actors over which the State exercises jurisdiction or control. This is described by the SDC as the obligation of due diligence; 'it is an obligation to deploy adequate means, to exercise best possible efforts, to do the utmost,' to obtain compliance.[39]

Attribution of breach to a State rather than to the enterprise that had direct control of the breach is likely necessary. Most international fora lack the flexibility of the Iran-U.S. Claims Tribunal, which analyzed some claims against State-owned and State-controlled entities according to private law, distinguishing them from claims against the State itself.[40] Seabed mining governance in ABNJ, like other areas of environmental governance, is a matter of public law, so a private law

36 ITLOS, Case No. 17, para. 242.

37 UNCLOS, Article 139 (2), states 'States Parties or international organizations acting together shall bear joint and several liability.' See also, *Certain Phosphate Lands in Nauru (Nauru v. Australia), Preliminary Objections, I.C.J. Reports 1992*, 240, para. 48 (The claim could be brought against Australia alone, and the question of whether its liability was joint and several was reserved for the merits).

38 D.D. Caron, 'The basis of responsibility: attribution and other transubstantive rules of state responsibility,' in D.J. Bederman, R.B. Lillich and D.B. Magraw, (eds.), *The Iran United States Claims Tribunal: Its contribution to the law of State responsibility*, 1998, 109–84, 115.

39 ITLOS, Case No. 17, paras. 110, 172; see also UNCLOS, annex III, article 4, para. 4 ('A sponsoring State shall not, however, be liable for damage caused by any failure of a contractor sponsored by it to comply with its obligations if that State Party has adopted laws and regulations and taken administrative measures which are, within the framework of its legal system, reasonably appropriate for securing compliance by persons under its jurisdiction.').

40 D.D. Caron, op. cit., n. 38, 112–14.

approach to the liability of companies engaged in seabed mining is not tenable at first glance; however, there may be avenues for litigation in national courts.

If a State-owned enterprise can be shown to not be truly independent of the State, the 'corporate veil' can be 'lifted' and the State can be treated as directly responsible.[41] A sponsoring State might be found directly responsible for the conduct of a mining enterprise if it directs, controls, or authorizes the enterprise's activities, resulting in a breach of international obligations.[42] The SDC stated that 'the liability regime established in Annex III to the Convention and related instruments does not provide for the attribution of activities of sponsored contractors to sponsoring States' but it is an open question of whether the SDC would distinguish this argument in light of specific facts.[43]

The limit on attribution that only holds States responsible for a due diligence obligation of conduct results in the probability of orphan liability—that is, harm to the environment for which no responsible party can be held liable. This outcome is troubling, given that humankind now lives in a 'full world' and damage that is neither avoided nor repaired by humans will likely not be repaired by the normal function of Earth systems as it would have been in the days of the 'empty world,' or in less fragile environments.[44]

Defenses

The factual context of deep seabed mining in the Area does not appear to permit use of some defenses to responsibility–consent, self-defense, and countermeasures. However, *force majeure*, distress, or necessity may be invoked as a defense; the question then would be whether a State remains responsible, either because of the inherently hazardous nature of mining, because the State has assumed the risk of harm, or because it has contributed to the circumstances of necessity.

Consequences of breach: liability

A State at fault must first bring its conduct into compliance—that is, cease the harmful act or take the required action and, where appropriate, provide assurances and guarantees that it will not be repeated (or if an affirmative action is required, that it will be performed)—and then address the consequences of its wrongful conduct.[45] In this context, cessation could mean that a State would halt mining operations that exceed prescribed water quality or seafloor integrity indicators; withdraw from a protected area that has been infringed; install and maintain protective measures; enact laws; or rectify financial payments.

Bilateral agreements between adjacent coastal States may provide alternative consequences for problems arising from deep seabed mining within national jurisdiction. Such agreements could constitute *lex specialis* as between those States. While adjacent and opposite coastal States are the most likely to be affected by activities nearby, other States are also likely to be injured by pollution or serious injuries to living resources, considering the ocean's continuous, connected nature. Thus it is unlikely that a State can fully control its legal liability through bilateral arrangements.

41 *Barcelona Traction, Light and Power Company, Limited, Judgment, I.C.J Reports 1970*, para. 56.

42 The Commentary on article 8 lists several arbitral decisions on this point. ILC, ASR, 104, footnote 161.

43 ITLOS, Case No. 17, para. 182.

44 See H.E. Daly, 'Economics in a full world,' *Scientific American*, 2005, 100–7; I. Plakokefalos, 'The limits of responsibility: Liability for damage in the deep seabed?,' in P. Pazartzis and P. Merkouris (eds.) *Permutations of responsibility in international law*, Leiden/Boston: Brill/Martinus Nijhoff, 2019.

45 International Law Commission, ASR, article 30.

Treaties can define what constitutes breach and specific results when a party contravenes a treaty term. UNCLOS, article 139 paragraph 2 establishes that a breach by multiple States or international organizations acting together will result in joint and several liability, if it actually causes damage; the Seabed Disputes Chamber noted that this differs from the customary rule stated in the ASR, article 2, that liability may be incurred without material damage.[46] Where seabed mining results in harm involving non-UNCLOS parties or the mining takes place on a State's continental shelf, liability will be incurred without the harm requirement of UNCLOS, article 139 paragraph 2. Further, UNCLOS, article 304, states that 'The provisions of this Convention regarding responsibility and liability for damage are without prejudice to the application of existing rules and the development of further rules regarding responsibility and liability under international law.'

Consequences of breach: remedies

Where reparations are owed, international law remedies are categorized by the ASR as restitution, satisfaction, and compensation. Negative consequences of mining operations might include: spills or intentional releases of pollutants on the seabed and in the water column that damage populations of living inhabitants including commercially fished species, protected species and, more generally, biodiversity and ecosystem function; mining operations in areas where they are not permitted; injuries to vessels, submarine cables, or people; intrusion into sovereign waters or seabed; or interference with other activities. This discussion focuses on remedies for environmental damage because wrongful acts that involve many of the other types of injury are both better known and are likely to be less catastrophic than environmental impacts of deep seabed mining.

Scientists currently believe that active remediation of damage to ecosystems is infeasible and that natural recovery, if possible, will take hundreds and even millions of years;[47] 'no-mining areas can be expected to feature as an important mechanism to avoid and minimize some biodiversity loss' but 'cannot be expected *prima facie* to avert all biodiversity losses associated with mining.'[48] Different remedies are appropriate depending on the circumstances, but clearly prevention is preferred to reparation for activities affecting the deep seabed.

The basic rule of reparation applies in all circumstances:

> The essential principle contained in the actual notion of an illegal act (…) is that reparation must, as far as possible, wipe-out all the consequences of the illegal act and re-establish the situation which would, in all probability, have existed if that act had not been committed. Restitution in kind, or, if this is not possible, payment of a sum corresponding to the value which a restitution in kind would bear; the award, if need be, of damages for loss sustained which would not be covered by restitution in kind or payment in place of it (…)[49]

46 ITLOS, Case No. 17, para. 178, which also refers to *Rainbow Warrior Arbitration (Case concerning the difference between New Zealand and France concerning the interpretation or application of two agreements, concluded on 9 July 1986 between the two States and which related to the problems arising from the Rainbow Warrior Affair)*, UNRIAA, 1990, Vol. XX, p. 215, at para. 110.

47 H.J. Niner et al., 'Deep-sea mining with no net loss of biodiversity—an impossible aim,' *Frontiers in Marine Science*, 2018. Available at https://doi.org/10.3389/fmars.2018.00053.

48 Ibid.

49 'Case concerning the factory at Chorzów' (*Germany v Poland*, Series A, No. 17, *Publications of the Permanent Court of International Justice 1927*), para. 125.

The baseline situation 'which would, in all probability, have existed' would generally be considered to be the pre-mining condition of the seabed. A chief difficulty in implementing environmental reparations is that the incremental harm from the wrongful act must be calculated by adequate information about the original and current condition of the environment, information which may not be available. Environmental baseline conditions are notoriously difficult to describe because of the limited scientific knowledge that we have relative to the complexity of ecosystems even when they are terrestrial. In the deep seabed this problem is multiplied because of the difficulty and expense for scientists to study it. Nonetheless, national and international decisions do grapple successfully with this challenge.

Establishing and reinforcing legal and social norms, particularly treaty norms, is a valuable function of international law and in this sense, avowal of wrongful conduct by responsible States and enterprises should be included in every reparations package. Satisfaction is the remedy for a non-material injury or where the alternatives of restitution and compensation are not available. It is sometimes characterized as the remedy for an 'affront' to the injured State. It can be used in combination with other reparations. However, it is not by itself a complete remedy for environmental damage.

The International Court of Justice (ICJ) declared, in the *Certain Activities* case, that 'it is consistent with the principles of international law governing the consequences of internationally wrongful acts, including the principle of full reparation, to hold that compensation is due for damage caused to the environment, in and of itself, in addition to expenses incurred by an injured State as a consequence of such damage.'[50] Further, the court stated that this included 'the consequent impairment or loss of the ability of the environment to provide goods and services.'[51] In the *Certain Activities* case, Costa Rica successfully argued for reparations covering damage and destruction of trees and other elements of its wetland, including market (for example, timber) and non-market (for example, carbon sequestration and biodiversity) ecosystem services.[52] Identifying ecosystem services can aid in describing all the aspects of an ecosystem that should be included in an award of reparations.

Restitution is the preferred remedy as a general matter in international law and in national environmental law. State practice of restitution includes the return of persons, property or territory–for example, redrawing a border, repatriating artworks and returning prisoners of war.[53] Restoring the damaged environment can be considered another form of restitution.

Compensation is generally understood to mean financial compensation. It has been a default remedy for transnational environmental damage,[54] notably when a country that has suffered harm from its neighbour will not invite that State to perform remediation on its territory. Financial compensation for environmental damage has gradually become accepted in international and national courts, and techniques for valuing non-market elements of the environment have become more sophisticated. The ICJ *Certain Activities* judgment further developed the ASR position that compensation may be sought for 'any financially assessable damage'; a principle that excludes

50 *Certain Activities Carried Out by Nicaragua in the Border Area (Costa Rica v. Nicaragua), Compensation, Judgment, I.C.J. Reports 2018*, para. 41. See also, United Nations Compensation Commission, *Report and recommendations made by the Panel of Commissioners concerning the fifth installment of 'F4' claims* (S/AC.26/2005/10), para. 58 (UNCC F4 Fifth Installment).

51 Para. 42, ibid.

52 International Court of Justice, *Certain Activities*, para. 55.

53 International Law Commission, ASR, 96.

54 C.R. Payne, 'Valuation of climate change loss and damage' in M. Doelle and S. Seck (eds.) *Research handbook on climate change law and loss & damage*, Cheltenham, UK: Edward Elgar, 2021, 190.

so-called moral damage (which is addressed by the remedy of satisfaction), but includes non-economic environmental damage.[55]

The approach adopted by some legal systems considers financial compensation alone an inadequate remedy for environmental harm, requiring instead that the damaged environment be repaired. The European Union Environmental Liability Directive prioritizes 'actions that provide natural resources and/or services of the same type, quality and quantity as those damaged.'[56] Under United States law restoration is the preferred remedy and any financial compensation must be used for restoration.[57] The United Nations Compensation Commission applied the same rule in an international environmental liability context, creating a 'Follow-up Programme' to ensure that compensation awards would be used to restore the damaged environment.[58] These strategies focus on restoring ecological integrity.

A conundrum is thus posed by the limitations of compensation as a remedy and the fact that significant damage to the environment might not be reversible to restore conditions that would have existed before the harm, and in particular not in the conditions of the deep seabed.[59] The argument made by some that a value for financial compensation unaccompanied by restoration could be calculated—apparently taking the view that it is better to get something than nothing—is barren. Biodiversity is an essential Earth system and as a practical matter it cannot be converted to money awarded to a claimant.

If the damage cannot be repaired, neither restitution nor compensation can serve the purpose that they are meant to in international law, of restoring the conditions *ex ante*. International law publicists urge that reparations should not be punitive. Prevention of harm is the better alternative, making the precautionary principle an important approach.[60] State responsibility can contribute to observance of precautionary measures. Sufficiently high costs of reparations could provide a disincentive for rational noncompliance—that is, a 'rational actor's' noncompliance where the economic cost of compensation is outweighed by the benefits to be gained. It has been argued that extremely costly remediation should not be ordered where it exceeds the market value of the damaged environment. However, providing a strong disincentive for those who might harm the deep seabed environment is a supplementary rationale for valuing reparations by the measure of environmental damage, not the market value of the resource that has been injured. If a State or enterprise cannot afford the cost of the harm that it might do, and it expects that it will be required to pay full reparations, it may be deterred from taking the risk.

While in the past, when UNCLOS and the 1994 Agreement were adopted, it seemed that the environment could absorb the damage from seabed mining, it is clear that is not true. Because

55 International Law Commission, ASR, article 36 (2).

56 Directive 2004/35/CE of the European Parliament and of the Council of 21 April 2004 on Environmental Liability with Regard to the Prevention and Remedying of Environmental Damage [2004] OJ L143/56 annex II, 1.2.2.

57 *Comprehensive Environmental Response, Compensation, and Liability Act of 1980*, 42 USC § 9601 et seq. (1980); *Oil Pollution Act of 1990*, 33 USC § 2701 et seq. (1990); *Consumer Price Index Adjustments of Oil Pollution Act of 1990 Limits of Liability – Vessels, Deepwater Ports and Onshore Facilities*, 33 CFR § 138 (2015). (*U.S. Oil Pollution Act* is intended to deter incidents and breaches of law under the 'polluter pays' principle.)

58 C.R. Payne, 'Oversight of environmental awards and regional environmental cooperation,' in C.R. Payne and P.H. Sand (eds.), *Gulf war reparations and the UN Compensation Commission: Environmental liability*, New York: Oxford University Press, 2011, 105–38.

59 Niner et al., op. cit., 53.

60 For a detailed analysis of the implementation of the precautionary approach, see generally in this book R. Makgill, A. Jaeckel and K. MacMaster, 'Implementing the precautionary approach for seabed mining: A review of State practice,' in V. Tassin Campanella (ed.), *Routledge handbook of seabed mining and the law of the sea*, op. cit., chapter I.3.

States' obligations are limited to due diligence, a liability gap results. To address this, in its advisory opinion the SDC recommended use of a fund in case of damage from deep seabed mining:[61]

> Taking into account that (…) situations may arise where a contractor does not meet its liability in full while the sponsoring State is not liable under article 139, paragraph 2, of the Convention, the Authority may wish to consider the establishment of a trust fund to compensate for the damage not covered. The Chamber draws attention to article 235, paragraph 3, of the Convention which refers to such possibility.

UNCLOS, article 235 paragraph 2, states that, as part of the regime for protection and preservation of the marine environment, 'States shall cooperate in … development of criteria and procedures for payment of adequate compensation, such as (…) compensation funds.'[62] In such cases, a fund might be used to provide emergency response, mitigate, remediate, repair, restore, or off-set the damage. Where the responsible party cannot be identified, the fund functions as a practical response (although it loses its normative influence on behaviour).

Non-State actors and responsibility

International organization responsibility

An international organization can incur international responsibility for conduct that is a breach of its obligations.[63] The conduct of its agents or its organs is considered the conduct of the organization.[64] The ILC's Draft Articles on Responsibility of International Organizations (ARIO), article 2(c) defines 'Agent' to include 'officials and other persons or entities through whom the organization acts.'[65]

The International Seabed Authority could incur international responsibility under the rules identified in the ARIO.[66] It is an international organization with legal personality[67] that functions as the administrative agency for mineral extraction in the Area. It has four principal organs, the

61 ITLOS, *Responsibilities and Obligations of States Sponsoring Persons and Entities with Respect to Activities in the Area, Advisory Opinion*, 2011, para. 205.

62 UNCLOS. See also, Principle 13, *Rio Declaration*, stating: 'States shall develop national law regarding liability and compensation for the victims of pollution and other environmental damage. States shall also cooperate in an expeditious and more determined manner to develop further international law regarding liability and compensation for adverse effects of environmental damage caused by activities within their jurisdiction or control to areas beyond their jurisdiction.' Principle 22, *Stockholm Declaration* states: 'States shall cooperate to develop further the international law regarding liability and compensation for the victims of pollution and other environmental damage caused by activities within the jurisdiction or control of such States to areas beyond their jurisdiction.'

63 International Law Commission, *Draft Articles on Responsibility of International Organizations*, A/64/10, article 4. Hereinafter 'ARIO.'

64 International Law Commission, ARIO, article 5.

65 See also, *Reparation for Injuries Suffered in the Service of the United Nations, Advisory Opinion: I.C.J. Reports 1949*, 177. ('The Court understands the word "agent" in the most liberal sense, that is to say, any person who, whether a paid official or not, and whether permanently employed or not, has been charged by an organ of the organization with carrying out, or helping to carry out, one of its functions – in short, any person through whom it acts.')

66 For a useful overview, see P.A. Singh, 'International organizations and the protection of the marine environment,' in M.C. Ribeiro, F.L. Bastos, and T. Henriksen (eds.), *Global challenges and the law of the sea*, Cham: Springer International Publishing, 2020, pp. 37–58.

67 Article 176, UNCLOS. The ISA fits the definition of 'international organization' for the purposes of the ILC Draft Articles on Responsibility of International Organizations, as it has states and other entities (the European Community/Union) for members, and it is established by a treaty. UNCLOS, Article 2. See A. Jaeckel, 'The Area and the role of the International Seabed Authority,' in V. Tassin Campanella (ed.), *Routledge handbook of seabed mining and*

Assembly and the Council, whose members are UNCLOS States Parties; the Legal and Technical Commission, whose members are experts appointed in their individual capacity; and a secretariat with a Secretary-General and other employees through whom the ISA acts.[68] The ISA performs the central (and sole) regulatory role for deep seabed mining in the Area:[69] it drafts and adopts the regulations that implement the rules and safeguards required by UNCLOS and the 1994 Agreement, licenses mining operators, oversees compliance, and issues sanctions. The ISA also manages its own finances. Failure to carry out these responsibilities in conformity with UNCLOS, the 1994 Agreement, and other rules of international law could breach international obligations.[70] UNCLOS confirms that 'the Authority shall have responsibility or liability for any damage arising out of wrongful acts in the exercise of its powers and functions.'[71]

The ISA's supreme organ is the Assembly. It establishes general policies and gives final approval of rules, regulations and procedures for prospecting, exploration and exploitation that are referred to it by the Council.[72] The Council is the ISA's executive body.[73] It adopts and provisionally applies mining regulations, pending approval by the Assembly.[74] It has decision making authority for approval of exploration and exploitation plans of work based on recommendations of the Legal and Technical Commission.[75] And the Council can institute proceedings before the ITLOS SDC in cases of non-compliance.[76] The Legal and Technical Commission's oversight of contractors has been questioned as possibly ineffective and definitely not transparent.[77] This is just one malfunction of an institution that lacks the checks and balances of a well-designed administrative body.[78]

The Secretary-General is the ISA's chief administrative officer. The Secretary-General's authority and responsibility includes management of the budget and secretariat staff; the incumbent also has significant ability to set the agenda of the ISA bodies and to develop the information that they consider in setting regulations, approving plans of work, and other activities of the Authority.[79] The functions of the ISA secretariat are not specified in UNCLOS or the 1994

the law of the sea, op. cit., chapter IV.1; and F. Armas, 'The future role of the International Seabed Authority,' in V. Tassin Campanella (ed.), *Routledge handbook of seabed mining and the law of the sea*, id., chapter IV.3.

68 Article 158, UNCLOS.

69 Article 157, UNCLOS; 1994 Agreement, annex, section 1, para. 1. Non-parties to UNCLOS can participate as observers in meetings of ISA organs, but they have no decision-making role. Although some argue that nationals of non-party states can ignore the ISA regulatory regime, no mining operation has taken the risk of operating outside it.

70 International Law Commission, ARIO, article 9.

71 Article 22, Annex III, UNCLOS.

72 Article 160, UNCLOS.

73 Article 162, ibid.

74 Article 162 (2) (o) (ii), UNCLOS (which also provides that regulations for mining 'any resource other than polymetallic nodules shall be adopted within three years from the date of a request to the Authority by any of its members').

75 Section 1, paras. 5–6, and section 3, para. 11, Annex, 1994 Agreement. In reviewing plans, the ISA has the obligation to evaluate whether a sponsoring state or states might acquire a dominant position in deep seabed mining and to prevent that from occurring; however, there are difficulties in implanting this obligation. Article 6, Annex III, 1994 Agreement; see also, V.J.M. Tassin, 'La zone et l'autorité internationale des fond marins,' *Annuaire du Droit de la Mer*, 2014, Vol. XIX, 524–27; V.J.M. Tassin, op. cit., 2016, 432–33. Other obligations of the ISA that could give rise to liability include its role in balancing the interests of marine scientists and mining contractors; and the responsibilities allocated to the Enterprise under the 1994 Agreement. Ibid., 429.

76 Article 162, UNCLOS.

77 H. Lilly and S.E. Roady, 'Regulating the common heritage of mankind: Challenges in developing a mining code for the Area,' in M.C. Ribeiro, F.L. Bastos, and T. Henriksen (eds.), *Global challenges and the law of the sea*, Cham: Springer International Publishing, 2020, 337–38.

78 Ibid.

79 For example, ISA, 'Rules of Procedure of the Legal and Technical Commission,' Rule 7.

Agreement.[80] According to the ILC approach, conduct of the secretariat (or one of its employees) in the performance of its functions is attributable to the ISA,[81] so the vagueness about the nature and scope of secretariat functions creates ambiguity.

The ISA will benefit financially from the mining operations that it regulates, which results in a conflict of interest. Its operating budget initially derives from assessed contributions, but its future existence and potential for expansion will depend on royalties paid by miners when minerals are being commercially extracted from the deep seabed.[82] Thus, the ISA has a financial and institutional interest in encouraging exploitation of seabed minerals. Subsequent to UNCLOS's adoption, scientists have discovered that the Earth's greatest biodiversity appears to exist in the seabed, that the life forms that can survive the extreme conditions there are slow-growing and consequently fragile, and that some of these life forms are essential elements of Earth's biophysical systems. The ISA's interest in revenues from mining could affect its judgment when it is acting as a regulator, potentially neglecting its international legal obligations to act with precaution and to protect the marine environment.

For example, international organization responsibility might be invoked if the ISA were to issue mining licenses that failed to adequately consider its international legal obligations to protect the marine environment and human life, to act on behalf of humankind as a whole, to ensure equitable sharing of economic benefits, give due regard to the rights and interests of coastal States whose mineral deposits are associated with those in the Area, or to preserve or dispose of archeological and historical objects for the benefit of humankind as a whole.[83] The permanent and serious harm that could result would provide a powerful argument for preventive provisional measures. The ARIO Commentary understands the relationship of international organizations such that '[a]n international obligation may be owed by an international organization to the international community as a whole, one or several States, whether members or non-members, another international organization or other international organizations and any other subject of international law.'[84] This view is relevant to the responsibility of an administrative body regulating conduct in a location that is beyond the territorial jurisdiction of the treaty parties, and where the harm could affect common concerns of the international community including biodiversity and the atmosphere.

The drafters of UNCLOS attempted to constrain the ability of injured parties to pursue legal recourse against the ISA. UNCLOS, article 187(b)(ii), provides SDC jurisdiction for acts of the ISA alleged by a State party 'to be in excess of jurisdiction or a misuse of power.'[85] Article 189 states that the SDC does not have jurisdiction for the Authority's exercise of it discretionary powers; 'in no case shall it substitute its discretion for that of the Authority;' and that the SDC cannot consider whether the ISA's rules, regulations, and procedures are consistent with UNCLOS. Under UNCLOS, article 187, the SDC can consider the interpretation and application of Part XI of UNCLOS as between States Parties; disputes between States Parties and the ISA over violations of Part XI or ISA rules, regulations, and procedures; and some disputes over contracts. This apparent contradiction between States Parties rights to dispute acts of the ISA and the limitations on the SDC's jurisdiction remains to be resolved.

80 Articles 166–69, UNCLOS.
81 International Law Commission, ARIO, article 5.
82 Articles 171, 173, UNCLOS; Section 1, para. 14, Annex, 1994 Agreement.
83 Articles 137, 139–42, 145–47, 149, UNCLOS.
84 International Law Commission, ARIO, 79; cf. ARIO, articles 42, 48.
85 Article 187 (b) (ii), UNCLOS.

States that are not parties to UNCLOS would, in any case, not be bound by such restrictions. If the ISA, through action or inaction in its administration of the deep seabed mining regime, causes serious harm to the marine environment it is difficult to argue that it does not bear responsibility to the international community that is at least equivalent to that borne by States.

Responsibility of sponsored entities

Ships, mining equipment, and personnel that will be deployed to mine the seabed will belong either to private or State-owned enterprises.[86] Within the EEZ and on the extended continental shelf of a coastal State, they will be subject to the law of the coastal State. In the Area, they will be subject to the national law of their State sponsors and the terms of their contracts with the ISA, consistent with the SDC Advisory Opinion and applicable international law. This sounds very straightforward. In practice, it is likely to be anything but that.

Where the mining company is private, it may involve multiple entities as investors, operators of equipment, personnel and vessels. They may have different nationalities, which raises complicated legal issues of which State's laws apply, and therefore which State has responsibility and liability.[87] In principle, it would be the State that is registered with the ISA as sponsor. In practice, the sponsor might be a small, impoverished developing nation[88]—the equivalent of an asset-less corporate subsidiary set up to provide cover for a polluting industry—and the corporate structure might be as convoluted as that constructed by the responsible parties in many notorious mass pollution incidents. Where the mining company is a State-owned enterprise, there is an inherent conflict of interest between the State roles as regulator and regulated entity.

National law is unable to control the power and complex structures of corporations and international law does not address them directly. The concept of 'corporate responsibility' is commonly used to refer to voluntary actions taken by an individual enterprise or by an industrial sector. It is not a parallel concept to the doctrine of State responsibility discussed here.[89]

The suggestion that corporations could be subject to a form of direct international responsibility is still novel but it arises in a legal context where these entities have gained rights to access international courts and arbitral tribunals. Foreign investment treaties grant private enterprises the right to challenge States hosting their investments in arbitral tribunals. Even more relevant, UNCLOS, article 187, provides access to the SDC for contractors, be they State enterprises or natural or

86 For example, Nauru Ocean Resources Inc., a wholly owned subsidiary of The Metals Company, itself a merger of DeepGreen Metals, Inc. and the Sustainable Opportunities Acquisition Corporation (NYSE: SOAC), is sponsored by the Republic of Nauru, one of the smallest states on Earth; China established China Ocean Mineral Resources Research and Development Association (COMRA) as a state enterprise for deep seabed mining. Both have exploration contracts with the ISA.

87 The *Draft Norms on the Responsibilities of Transnational Corporations and Other Business Enterprises with regard to Human Rights* provides a useful definition of 'transnational corporation' as 'an economic entity operating in more than one country or a cluster of economic entities operating in two or more countries – whatever their legal form, whether in their home country or country of activity, and whether taken individually or collectively'; and of 'other business enterprise' as 'any business entity, regardless of the international or domestic nature of its activities, including a transnational corporation; the corporate, partnership, or other legal form used to establish the business entity; and the nature of the ownership of the entity.' UN Doc. E/CN.4/Sub.2/2002/13, 15 August 2002, Annex, paras. 19 and 20.

88 ISA, *Proposal to seek an advisory opinion from the Seabed Disputes Chamber of the International Tribunal for the Law of the Sea on matters regarding sponsoring State responsibility and liability*, ISBA/16/C/6 (2010) para. 1.

89 For a discussion of why corporations appear to escape both spheres of law, see A. Nollkaemper, 'Responsibility of transnational corporations in international environmental law: Three perspectives,' in G. Winter (ed.), *Multilevel governance of global environmental change*, Cambridge: Cambridge University Press, 2006.

juridical persons. The ILC struggled with this problem, recognizing that applying the polluter pays principle would place responsibility on the operator of a hazardous activity that resulted in transboundary harm; yet in its draft principles on the topic it defaulted to State responsibility.[90] The current state of international law reflects a lopsided bargain where corporations have rights to use international courts directly, but are shielded from being sued in them.

Obligations to the international community

Respect for State sovereignty leads to the position that an injured State may choose an alternative form of reparation, in particular, it may choose financial compensation in place of restitution.[91] However, it would be unjust if one or more States were to successfully pursue legal claims and choose to receive financial compensation for an injury to a global commons such as a healthy ocean or marine biodiversity, in which all States have an interest.

Reparations pose additional novel concerns in ABNJ, specifically the question of to whom the obligation is owed, and who is capable of enforcing it. Injured States have the right to reparations. In the High Seas, it may seem that all States are injured or no States are.

The complexities of this situation include admissibility and standing, and have been invoked by two ICJ judges, Hanqin Xue and James Crawford, in the ICJ case, *Legal Consequences of the Separation of the Chagos Archipelago from Mauritius in 1965* (Request for Advisory Opinion).

The ILC took the position, in the ASR, that 'the focus obligations to the international community as a whole is essentially on the legal interest of all States in compliance—i.e., in terms of the present Articles, in being entitled to invoke the responsibility of any State in breach.'[92] This framing suggests that 'the international community' refers to the collectivity of sovereign States.

Conclusion

The anemic link of State control over natural and juridical persons may lead some to shrug their shoulders and say 'international law is weak.' A more assertive approach will demand that States exercise real authority over these entities by using their national jurisdiction to prevent shell companies and offshore operations. It may require firmer rules and greater clarity in international law itself to root out flags of convenience and sponsors of convenience.

Acknowledgements

The author thanks Kristina Gjerde for insightful comments and Kyra Bostic for her assistance. All errors are my own.

References

Bernard L. and Schofield C., 'Disputes concerning the delimitation of the continental shelf beyond 200 nautical miles', in T. Heidar (ed.), *New knowledge and changing circumstances in the law of the sea*, Leiden/Boston: Brill Nijhoff, 2020, 157–182.

90 International Law Commission, *Draft Articles on Prevention of Transboundary Harm from Hazardous Activities, Report of the ILC on the work of its fifty-third session*, A/56/10; *Draft Principles on the Allocation of Loss Arising out of Hazardous Activities*, A/CN.4/L.686 and Corr.1, 2006.

91 International Law Commission, ASR, article 43.

92 Ibid., 281.

Caron D.D., 'The basis of responsibility: Attribution and other transubstantive rules of state responsibility', in R.B. Lillich, D.B. Magraw and D.J. Bederman (eds.), *The Iran United States claims tribunal: Its contribution to the law of state responsibility*, Irvington-on-Hydson, NY: Transnational Publishers, 1998, 109–184.

Crawford J.R., 'Responsibility to the international community as a whole', *Indiana Journal of Global Legal Studies* 8–2, 2001, 303–322.

Daly H.E., 'Economics in a full world', *Scientific American*, 2005, 100–107.

Editors of Encyclopedia Britannica, 'Continental shelf', *Britannica*. Available at: https://www.britannica.com/science/continental-shelf.

Feria Tinta M. and Kamga M., 'Mining the bottom of the sea: Potential future disputes and the role of the international tribunal for the law of the sea', in V. Tassin Campanella (ed.), *Routledge handbook of seabed mining and the law of the sea,* London: Routledge, 2023, chapter V.3.

Jensen Ø. and Mar Magnussen B., 'The extension of sovereign rights beyond 200 nautical miles', in V. Tassin Campanella (ed.), *Routledge handbook of seabed mining and the law of the sea,* London: Routledge, 2023, chapter III.1.

Levin L.A., 'Defining "serious harm" to the marine environment in the context of deep-seabed mining', *Marine Policy* 74, 2016, 245–259.

Lily H. and Roady S.E., 'Regulating the common heritage of mankind: Challenges in developing a mining code for the Area', in M.C. Ribeiro, F.L. Bastos and T. Henriksen (eds.), *Global challenges and the law of the sea*, Cham: Springer International Publishing, 2020, 333–349.

Makgill R., Jaeckel A. and MacMaster K., 'Implementing the precautionary approach for seabed mining: A review of state practice', in V. Tassin Campanella (ed.), *Routledge handbook of seabed mining and the law of the sea*, London: Routledge, 2023, chapter II.3.

Niner H.J. et al., 'Deep-sea mining with no net loss of biodiversity—An impossible aim', *Frontiers in Marine Science*, 2018. Available at: https://doi.org/10.3389/fmars.2018.00053.

Nollkaemper A., 'Responsibility of transnational corporations in international environmental law: Three perspectives', in G. Winter (ed.), *Multilevel governance of global environmental change*, Cambridge: Cambridge University Press, 2006, 179–199.

Oral N., 'The common heritage of mankind under international law: An overview', in V. Tassin Campanella (ed.), *Routledge handbook of seabed mining and the law of the sea*, London: Routledge, 2023, chapter I.2.

Payne C.R., 'Oversight of environmental awards and regional environmental cooperation', in C.R. Payne and P.H. Sand (eds.), *Gulf war reparations and the UN compensation commission: Environmental liability*, New York: Oxford University Press, 2011, 105–138.

Payne C.R., 'Valuation of climate change loss and damage', in M. Doelle and S. Seck (eds.), *Research handbook on climate change law and loss & damage*, Edward Elgar, 2021, 184–200.

Plakokefalos I., 'The limits of responsibility: Liability for damage in the deep seabed?' in F. Pazartzis and P. Merkouris (eds.), *Future challenges to state responsibility*, Leiden/Boston: Brill/Martinus Nijhoff; Forthcoming; 'Amsterdam Law School Research Paper No. 2013-36', *Amsterdam Center for International Law*, No. 2013-11. Available at SSRN: http://ssrn.com/abstract=2289751.

Payne, C.R., 'Responsibility to the international community for marine biodiversity beyond national jurisdiction', *Cambridge International Law Journal* 11–1, 24–50, 2022.

Shakespeare W., *The merchant of venice*, Act 4, Scene 1.

Singh P.A., 'International organizations and the protection of the marine environment', in M.C. Ribeiro, F.L. Bastos and T. Henriksen (eds.), *Global challenges and the law of the sea*, Cham: Springer International Publishing, 2020, 37–58.

Singh P., Tassin Campanella V. and Maes F., 'The European Union and seabed mining' in V. Tassin Campanella (ed.), *Routledge handbook of seabed mining and the law of the sea*, London: Routledge, 2023, chapter VI.1.4.

Tassin Campanella V., Cissé Y. and Tladi D., 'Rights and obligations of States on the continental shelf and the Area', in V. Tassin Campanella (ed.), *Routledge handbook of seabed mining and the law of the sea*, London: Routledge, 2023, chapter II.1.

Tassin V.J.M., 'La Zone et l'Autorité Internationale des Fond Marins', *Annuaire du Droit de la Mer* XIX, 2014, 524–527.

Tassin V.J.M., 'La Zone et l'Autorité Internationale des Fond Marins', *Annuaire du Droit de la Mer* XXI, 429, 2016, 432–433.

Vanreusel A. et al., 'Threatened by mining, polymetallic nodules are required to preserve abyssal epifauna', *Nature: Scientific Reports* 6, 2016, 26808.

Permanent Court of International Justice and International Court of Justice

Barcelona Traction, Light and Power Company, Limited, Judgment, I.C.J Reports 1970, p. 3.

Case Concerning the Factory at Chorzów ' (*Germany v Poland, Series A, No. 17, Publications of the Permanent Court of International Justice 1927*), para 125.

Certain Activities Carried Out by Nicaragua in the Border Area (*Costa Rica v. Nicaragua*); *Compensation, Judgment, I.C.J. Reports 2018*, p. 15.

Certain Phosphate Lands in Nauru (Nauru v. Australia), Preliminary Objections, Judgment I.C.J. Reports 1992, p. 240.

Reparation for Injuries Suffered in the Service of the United Nations, Advisory Opinion: I.C.J. Reports 1949, p. 174.

United Nations

Agreement Relating to the Implementation of Part XI of the UNCLOS, 28 July 1994.

Delimitation of the Maritime Boundary in the Bay of Bengal (*Bangladesh/Myanmar*), *Judgment, ITLOS Reports 2012*, p. 4.

Draft Norms on the Responsibilities of Transnational Corporations and Other Business Enterprises with regard to Human Rights, U.N. Doc. E/CN.4/Sub.2/2002/13, 15 August 2002, Annex.

International Law Commission, *Draft Articles on Responsibility of States for Internationally Wrongful Acts, with Commentaries*, 2001.

International Seabed Authority, 'Submarine Cables and Deep Seabed Mining: Advancing Common Interests and Addressing Common Interests and Addressing UNCLOS "Due Regard" Obligations', *Technical Study No. 14*, 2015.

International Seabed Authority, *Rules of Procedure of the Legal and Technical Commission*, 1994.

Responsibilities and Obligations of States with Respect to Activities in the Area, Advisory Opinion, 1 February 2011, ITLOS Reports 2011, p. 10.

United Nations Compensation Commission, *Report and Recommendations Made by the Panel of Commissioners Concerning the Fifth Installment of 'F4' claims* (S/AC.26/2005/10).

United Nations Convention on the Law of the Sea, 10 December 1982, 1833 UNTS 396.

United Nations Reports of International Arbitral Awards (UNRIAA), *Rainbow Warrior (New Zealand/ France)*, vol XX, 1990, 217, 264, para. 101.

Various instruments and decisions

Comprehensive Environmental Response, Compensation, and Liability Act of 1980, 42 USC § 9601 et seq. (1980).

Consumer Price Index Adjustments of Oil Pollution Act of 1990 Limits of Liability—Vessels, Deepwater Ports and Onshore Facilities, 33 CFR § 138 (2015).

Directive 2004/35/CE of the European Parliament and of the Council of 21 April 2004 on Environmental Liability with Regards to the Prevention and Remedying of Environmental Damage [2004] OJ L143/56 annex II, 1.2.2.

Kiwis Against Seabed Mining, Inc., et al. v. Trans-Tasman Resources (Wellington, Environment Court, Decision No. [2016] NZEnvC, 217).

New Zealand Exclusive Economic Zone and Continental Shelf (Environmental Effects—Discharge and Dumping) Regulations 2015, New Zealand, 28 September 2015.

Oil Pollution Act of 1990, 33 USC § 2701 et seq. (1990).

Others

MIDAS (Managing Impacts of Deep Sea Resource Exploitation), 'Toxic Impacts of Deep-Sea Mining', 2016.

PART III

The continental shelf

III.1

THE EXTENSION OF SOVEREIGN RIGHTS BEYOND 200 NAUTICAL MILES

Øystein Jensen and Bjarni Már Magnússon

Introduction

This chapter examines legal aspects related to the extension of coastal states' sovereign rights beyond 200 nautical miles (M), focusing on the legal framework of the *1982 United Nations Convention on the Law of the Sea* (UNCLOS or the Convention).[1] The first part of the chapter will present a brief chronology of the development of the legal regime of the outer limits of the continental shelf (CS). Focus is on the Third United Nations Conference on the Law of the Sea and those parts of the negotiations relating specifically to the outer limits of the CS, as well as the independent institutional mechanism set up to oversee the application of the legal framework – the Commission on the Limits of the Continental Shelf (CLCS or the Commission).

The second part of the chapter will emphasize two main issues: first, the ambiguous criteria for delineating the CS contained in article 76 of the Convention. Second, focus will be placed on the procedures for establishing CS limits beyond 200 M, including the role and significance of the work of the CLCS. A brief overview of the CLCS' most recent state practice and work is also provided.

The last part of the chapter reflects on the junction between the regime for establishing the CS beyond 200 M and the adjacent International Seabed Area (the Area). As mineral extractions from deeper CS areas and the deep seabed are gaining momentum, we examine some important legal questions relating to who can protect the territorial scope of the Area against states that establish their outer limits of its CS beyond 200 M in a manner that cannot be justified with references to article 76 of UNCLOS.

Legal developments during 1945 and 1982

The first real attempt to create an international legal regime for the CS came with US President Truman's proclamation in 1945.[2] Prompted by the US initiative, several other coastal states put

1 1833 UNTS 397.

2 Reprinted in M. M. Whiteman (ed.), *Digest of international law*, Washington, D.C.: U.S. Government Printing Office, 1965, pp. 756–757. A second proclamation was issued by Truman on the same day: 'Policy of the United States with

DOI: 10.4324/9780429426162-10

forward their claims to the CS. Irregular in content, they created confusion as to the legal status of the seabed beyond the territorial sea. International regulation was needed, and the International Law Commission (ILC) was tasked with drawing up draft rules for the definition of the CS.[3]

The First United Nations Conference on the Law of the Sea adopted the Convention on the Continental Shelf in 1958.[4] However, it became clear that this treaty was unable to balance considerations arising from international politics over the course of the 1960s. The main problem of the 1958 Convention was that its provisions did not adequately take into account nor envisage the technological developments already underway at that time. Its article 1 reads as follows:

> For the purpose of these articles, the term 'continental shelf' is used as referring (a) to the seabed and subsoil of the submarine areas adjacent to the coast but outside the area of the territorial sea, to a depth of 200 metres or, beyond that limit, to where the depth of the superjacent waters admits of the exploitation of the natural resources of the said areas; (b) to the seabed and subsoil of similar submarine areas adjacent to the coasts of islands.

Thus, it defines the outer limits of the CS by a vague criterion, entailing the risk of coastal states 'grabbing' seabed areas.[5] The language of this provision is open to several possible interpretations, of which the most extreme – resting solely on the exploitability criterion – would ultimately permit all submarine areas to be claimed by coastal states.

Calls to redefine the criteria for determining the outer limits of the CS were made in the second half of the 1960s. However, states' views were divided. Some coastal states in favourable geographical positions and with technological possibilities pushed for an extensive outer limit, whereas states that lacked these advantages argued for the opposite. The latter group of states were increasingly concerned that the dual criterion under article 1 of the Convention on the Continental Shelf was insufficiently precise to serve as a rule for setting the outer limits of the CS under international law. They argued that a new definition of the CS was needed to stop the gradual extension of individual national rights over ever-larger parts of submarine areas.

In 1967, the issue again received global attention when Ambassador Arvid Pardo of Malta spoke before the United Nations General Assembly (UNGA). Pardo turned to the world community in calling for a new legal order for the oceans that would define the limits of national jurisdiction in a more satisfactory manner while recognizing that the seabed beyond should be designated as the common heritage of all mankind.[6] This Maltese initiative spurred the United Nations (UN) to establish a provisional *ad hoc* committee to deal with the subsea question and the definition of

---

Respect to Coastal Fisheries in Certain Areas of the High Seas'. That proclamation concerned, in essence, the establishment of conservation zones in those areas of the high seas contiguous to US coasts where fishing activities had been or might be developed and maintained on a substantial scale (ibid.).

3 For the evolution of rights and obligations on the seabed and related challenges, see generally in this book V. Tassin Campanella, Y. Cisse and D. Tladi, 'Rights and obligations of States on the continental shelf and the Area', in V. Tassin Campanella (ed.), *Routledge handbook of seabed mining and the law of the sea*, London: Routledge, 2023, chapter II.1.

4 499 UNTS 311.

5 L. Henkin, *Law for the sea's mineral resources*, New York: Institute for the Study of Science in Human Affairs Columbia University, 1968, 18–19.

6 *United Nations General Assembly, Twenty-Second Session, First Committee, 1515th Meeting, Official Records*, UN Doc. A/C.1/PV.1515, 1 November 1967. See in this book N. Oral, 'The common heritage of mankind under international law: an overview', in V. Tassin Campanella (ed.), *Routledge handbook of seabed mining and the law of the sea*, op. cit., chapter I.2.

the CS. The committee was later made permanent, and in 1970, its mandate extended: the UN Sea-Bed Committee would begin work on a new global conference on the law of the sea.

The Third United Nations Conferences on the Law of the Sea commenced in 1973. On the negotiation table with respect to the outer limits of the CS were drafts of treaty provisions from the UN Sea-Bed Committee, the definition in article 1 from the *Convention on the Continental Shelf*, the increasing and widespread perception that coastal states had the right to some kind of 'economic jurisdiction' out to 200 M from their coasts, and the judgment from the International Court of Justice (ICJ) in the *North Sea Continental Shelf* cases from 1969. In these cases, the Court had determined that the CS legally comprised the natural extension of a coastal state's territory.[7]

The Third United Nations Conferences on the Law of the Sea involved at least two opposing constellations. On one side were states that wanted CS rights to the end of the continental margin: the margineers. On the other were geographically disadvantaged states, land-locked states and most of the African states. Briefly put, this latter group wanted to limit the sovereign rights of the coastal states to 200 M.

It soon became clear that a compromise would have to be sought, and here the rules of coastal state entitlement to an exclusive economic zone (EEZ) would be crucial. The rules on 200 M fishery zones had evolved into customary law around the mid-1970s.[8] This was a good negotiation card for the margineers, who claimed that rights to the CS should extend that far in any case. However, it also was a negotiation card for those who wanted to limit the CS to 200 M, in the sense that this limit should apply to the seabed as well. It was not necessary to negotiate separate rules for the CS, they argued, since the rules on the EEZ 'consumed' the claims to the seabed.[9]

However, the margineers were determined to see rights extended to the CS *beyond* 200 M. To this end, they drew on the definition in article 1 of the Convention on the Continental Shelf and the judgment of the ICJ in the *North Sea Continental Shelf* cases. An essential element in this picture during the Third United Nations Conferences on the Law of the Sea was also the willingness shown by both the USA and the Soviet Union to accept broad CS rights for coastal states.

The ultimate compromise between the margineers and the states wanting a more geographically restricted CS produced a two-way split. First, there had to be a provision for sharing the revenue arising from gains enjoyed by coastal states in the exercise of their exclusive rights between 200 M and the outer edge of the continental margin. This became article 82 of UNCLOS, under which coastal states commit to pay a tax on economic activities beyond 200 M.[10]

Second, the outer limit of the CS had to be established with the greatest possible degree of precision. Landlocked states, developing countries and geographically disadvantaged states would not accept imprecise regulation that did not entail any real outer limit of the CS. Therefore, article 76 of UNCLOS contains detailed rules on the extent of the CS, enabling a more sophisticated and clearly defined determination of outer limits than those under article 1 of the Convention on the Continental Shelf. The physical extension of coastal state jurisdiction to the seabed is no longer indefinite, although the outer limits of the CS may be established in a very seaward position.

7 *North Sea Continental Shelf* cases (Federal Republic of Germany/Denmark/The Netherlands), ICJ Reports 1969, 3.

8 See A. Hollick, 'The origins of 200-mile offshore zones', *American Journal of International Law* 71, 1977, 494–500.

9 C. A. Fleischer, 'The continental shelf beyond 200 nautical miles – A crucial element in the "package deal": Historic background and implications for today', in D. Vidas (ed.) *Law, technology and science for oceans in globalisation*, Leiden/Boston: Martinus Nijhoff Publishers, 2010, 429–448.

10 For a detailed analysis of article 82 of UNCLOS, see in this book C. Schofield and J. Mossop, 'The Article 82 conundrum: Implementing payment for the exploitation of the continental shelf beyond 200 nautical miles', in V. Tassin Campanella (ed.), *Routledge handbook of seabed mining and the law of the sea*, op. cit., chapter III.2.

In addition, an essential component of this last part of the compromise was the creation of the CLCS – a 21-person expert body to facilitate implementation of UNCLOS by making recommendations to coastal states on matters related to the establishment of the outer limits of the CS beyond 200 M from the territorial sea baselines.[11] The creation of an independent entity under the Convention to be involved in the process of establishing the outer limits of the CS is one of the most notable innovations of the whole UNCLOS.

Criteria for delineating the outer continental shelf

Article 76 defines the CS in a new way compared to article 1 of the Convention on the Continental Shelf. The provision consists of ten paragraphs, most of them (paragraphs 2 to 8) relating exclusively to the limits of the CS where it extends beyond 200 M from the baseline.

The first paragraph of article 76 establishes the principal rule that the CS comprises the natural extension of the land to the outer edge of the continental margin. The definition combines two distinct criteria: a distance criterion and a geomorphological criterion. The first is a simple criterion of 200 M, independent of the geological conditions at the seabed and in line with the coastal state's rights to an EEZ under articles 56 and 57 of UNCLOS. This criterion therefore has independent importance only in cases in which the coastal state has not proclaimed an EEZ or the continental margin does not extend out to 200 M. The second criterion – 'edge of the continental margin' – is inspired by the ICJ's judgment concerning the CS in the *North Sea Continental Shelf* cases, in which the Court described the CS in the legal sense as being the *natural prolongation* of the continental territory.

Limitations to the extent of the CS is then contained in paragraphs 2–6 of article 76. Paragraph 2 refers to the limitations specified in paragraphs 4 to 6. Paragraph 3 provides for a geomorphological definition of the continental margin including the 'shelf', the 'slope' and the 'rise'. Excluded is the deep ocean floor with its oceanic ridges or the subsoil thereof.

There are certain technical rules for how the coastal state shall establish the outer edge of the continental margin when it extends beyond 200 M. The coastal state must choose one of two options in paragraph 4 (a)(i) or paragraph 4 (a)(ii). Both require determination of the 'foot of the slope', which is defined in *litra* (b); it is up to states to choose which option to use. The coastal state is free to choose the alternative that offers the most favourable.

Pursuant to the option in article 76, paragraph 4 (a)(i), the outermost points of the outer limit of the continental margin shall be determined by reference to the thickness of the sedimentary rocks of the continental rise. The continental margin may extend to the area where the sediment thickness at fixed points on the continental rise is at least 1 per cent of the shortest distance from each fixed point to the foot of the continental slope. For example, if the sediment thickness is 1 kilometre in an area of the continental rise, the outer limit of the CS can be established 100 kilometres from the nearest site of 'the foot of the slope'. Application of this formula thus requires sediment measurements on the floor of the vast ocean deep.

The option in article 76, paragraph 4 (a)(ii) provides that the outer limit may be a maximum of 60 M from the foot of the slope: a pure distance criterion. However, for this method, the location of the foot of the slope must also be determined. In the absence of evidence to the contrary, the foot of the slope shall, according to paragraph 4 (b), be set at the point where the change of fall-off is

11 T. L. McDorman, 'The continental shelf regime in the law of the sea convention: A reflection on the first thirty years', *The International Journal of Marine and Coastal Law* 27, 2012, 743–745.

steepest. The rule seems difficult to apply in practice, as local topographical differences may make it difficult to locate the 'correct' measure.

Paragraph 5 sets maximum limits. The maximum outer limits of the CS shall be either 350 M from the baselines or a maximum of 100 M from the 2,500 metres isobath. The coastal state may choose the more favourable option.

A special rule for submarine ridges is contained in paragraph 6. The outer limit of the CS on ridges can be located no further than 350 M from the baselines. Thus, the 100 M + 2,500 metre isobath rule in paragraph 5 does not apply to ridges. This limitation does not, however, apply to subsea elevations that are part of the natural extensions of the continental margin. Therefore, in many situations, the coastal state would prefer formations at the bottom of the sea to be considered submarine elevations rather than submarine ridges.[12]

Taking into consideration the two maximum constraint lines for the outer limits of the CS in article 76, paragraph 5, it follows from paragraphs 1 to 6 that there are four possible outer limits to the CS, in principle: (1) 200 M from the baselines from which the breadth of the territorial sea is measured; (2) the outer edge of the continental margin; (3) 350 M from the baselines from which the breadth of the territorial sea is measured; or (4) 100 M from the 2,500 metre isobath.

Ultimately, article 76, paragraphs 7 to 9 give rules on how the coastal state shall establish the outer limits of CS. First, the coastal state delineates its outer limits. The coastal state shall then submit information on these limits to the CLCS. The Commission follows the procedures set out in annex II and makes recommendations to the coastal state. The coastal state shall then establish the limits and deposit marine charts and relevant information with the Secretary General of UN in conjunction with article 1, paragraph 1 and article 134, paragraph 3 of UNCLOS – the outer limits of the CS established by a coastal state determine at the same time the extent of the seabed beyond national jurisdiction, and the Area.

Procedure – the role of the Commission on the Limits of the Continental Shelf

If a coastal state decides to claim a shelf of 200 M, article 76 is easy to apply. However, if a state makes a claim beyond that distance, certain peculiarities come into play. First – as noted above – article 76 allows a coastal state to claim all parts of the ocean floor extending 'beyond its territorial sea throughout the natural prolongation of its land territory to the outer edge of the continental margin' as its CS.[13] This definition creates certain difficulties in the application of article 76, as does the application of the maximum constraint lines for determining the seaward extent of the CS provided for.[14] Notably, article 76 does not operate with the standard definitions scientists use for

12 See, for instance, the message of 7 October 1994 from the president of the USA to the US Senate, where it is argued that the Chukchi plateau north of Alaska and the Bering Strait is an elevation, not a ridge: 'The United States understands that features such as the Chukchi plateau and its component elevations, situated to the north of Alaska, are covered by this exemption, and thus not subject to the 350 mile limitation set forth in paragraph 6. Because of the potential for significant oil and gas reserves in the Chukchi plateau, it is important to recall the U.S. statement made to this effect on 3 April 1980 during a Plenary session of [The Third United Nations Conferences on the Law of the Sea], which has never given rise to any contrary interpretation. In the statement, the United States representative expressed support for the provision now set forth in article 76(6) on the understanding that it is recognized that features such as the Chukchi plateau situated to the north of Alaska and its component elevations cannot be considered a ridge and are covered by the last sentence of paragraph 6'. *US Department of State Dispatch*, Vol. 6, 1995, 32. Published by the *Office of Public Communication, Bureau of Public Affairs*.

13 UNCLOS, article 76, para. 1.

14 See UNCLOS article 76, paragraphs 5 and 6, according to which the maximum extent of the CS is 350 M from the baselines from which the territorial sea is measured, or 100 M from a depth of 2,500 metres.

establishing the outer edge of the continental margin: states cannot rely on pre-existing scientific understandings of the ocean floor when they delineate their outer limits but must gather and interpret fresh data according to article 76.[15]

The second peculiarity relates to the *procedures* by which the outer limits of the CS beyond 200 M are to be established. To support its claim to a CS extending beyond 200 M, a coastal state must present a submission to the specialized treaty body set up to oversee the application of article 76 (the CLCS) within a determined deadline.[16]

Article 3 of Annex II to the UNCLOS specifies that the Commission has two separate functions. First, it shall consider data and other material submitted by a coastal state to substantiate its claim to a CS beyond 200 M, and, whenever requested, provide scientific and technical advice during the preparation of such data and material. Second, it shall make recommendations concerning the claim submitted by the coastal state 'in accordance with article 76'. Accordingly, the CLCS becomes involved when a coastal state (1) is a party to UNCLOS; (2) intends to establish the outer limits of its CS beyond 200 M from the baselines from which the breadth of the territorial sea is measured; and (3) submits to the Commission the particulars of outer limits with such an extent, along with supporting scientific and technical data.

The procedures under UNCLOS for establishing the outer limits of the CS *beyond* 200 M can be summarized briefly as follows. After the coastal state has provisionally delineated the outer limits on the basis of the provisions of UNCLOS, it shall submit information on these limits to the Commission. The Commission follows the procedure provided for in Annex II to UNCLOS and makes recommendations to the coastal state on matters related to the establishment of the outer limits. The CLCS then submits the recommendations to the coastal state. Outer CS limits subsequently established by a coastal state on the basis of the CLCS' recommendations are legally final and binding, according to article 76, paragraph 8.

The CLCS is to consist of individuals who are to be experts in the fields of geology, geophysics or hydrography.[17] Thus, in terms of its composition, the Commission is indeed a technical or scientific institution comparable to certain other scientific international bodies established to give advice relating to the implementation of treaty provisions. The CLCS itself emphasizes its role as a technical review body charged with ensuring that states follow the technical and scientific requirements of article 76, such as properly identifying the foot of the slope and using sound scientific methods for measuring sedimentary thickness.[18] In the *Bay of Bengal* case, the

15 A. Cavnar, 'Accountability and the Commission on the Limits of the Continental Shelf: Deciding who owns the ocean floor', *Cornell International Law Journal* 42, 2009, 398–399.

16 UNCLOS, article 4 of annex II. The deadline was modified in 2001 by a decision of the Meeting of the States Parties as 'having commenced on 13 May 1999' for states for which UNCLOS had entered into force before that date (*Decision regarding the date of commencement of the ten-year period for making submissions to the Commission on the Limits of the Continental Shelf set out in article 4 of Annex II to the United Nations Convention on the Law of the Sea*, UN doc. SPLOS/72, 29 May 2001). In 2008, the Meeting further decided that the 2009 deadline could consist only in the submission of 'preliminary information' and description of the status of preparation and intended date for making a full submission (*Report of the Eighteenth Meeting of States Parties*, UN doc. SPLOS/184, 21 July 2008). Thus, the State Parties to UNCLOS have decided that a state's deadline can be met by the provision of preliminary information signalling the state's intent to make a full submission later. Under the Commission's Rules of Procedure, a submission relating to only one portion of a state's continental shelf – a 'partial' submission – also can satisfy the prescribed deadline (Rule 3 of annex I to the Rules of Procedure of the Commission. *Rules of Procedure of the Commission on the Limits of the Continental Shelf*, Doc. CLCS/40/Rev. 1, 17 April 2008).

17 UNCLOS, annex II, art. 2, para. 1.

18 N. Francis, 'The continental shelf Commission', in M. H. Nordquist and J. N. Moore (eds.), *Oceans policy: New institutions, challenges and opportunities*, The Hague: Martinus Nijhoff Publishers, 1999, 141–142.

International Tribunal for the Law of the Sea stated that the Commission was 'a scientific and technical body'.[19]

This is, nonetheless, merely a starting point for considering what kind of institution the Commission is. In assessing coastal state claims, the CLCS must analyze scientific concepts through the lens of treaty interpretation. The Commission cannot simply review a coastal state's shelf submission against a technical checklist.[20] Instead, the CLCS must take a position on complicated treaty wording and on how to resolve conflicts of norms.[21] Therefore, the Commission's function does not differ from how any given treaty interpreter must construe and seek out the meaning of the language in article 76 in one important respect. If actions similar to those performed by the Commission were performed by a domestic state agency, most lawyers would probably label the Commission's activity as a type of public administration involving judicial-like tasks.

The Commission's decisions – its 'recommendations' – also carry important legal effects. While they are not binding *strictu sensu* on coastal states, only outer limits established based on the Commission's recommendations are, according to article 76, paragraph 8, 'final and binding'. Coastal states will therefore seek to establish their outer limits based on the CLCS' recommendations, as noncompliance with them may result in certain legal disadvantages.

Another factor that attaches legal consequences to the Commission's recommendations is related to the significance of the recommendations as a means of interpretation under the general rules of treaty interpretation in international law. The Commission's recommendations cannot be seen as an expression of the parties' practice and thus relevant as a means of interpretation under article 31, paragraph 3(b) of the *Vienna Convention on the Law of Treaties*,[22] that is, as subsequent practice establishing an agreement of the parties regarding the interpretation of UNCLOS. However, since UNCLOS has been established to make recommendations in accordance with article 76 of UNCLOS, considerations of object and purpose under article 31, paragraph 1 of the Vienna Convention mean that this role should be underpinned. Obviously, the best way to do that is by emphasizing the Commission's recommendations in the interpretation of article 76, or, put differently, what would be the point of having the Commission issue recommendations if coastal states do not take them into consideration when interpreting article 76? The Commission was not created to provide vague indications as to how to apply the definition of the CS under UNCLOS. According to article 3 of annex II to UNCLOS, the function of the Commission is to inform coastal states exactly where, in the view of the Commission, the outer limits beyond 200 M lie in each individual case. Considerations of purpose strongly indicate that this role should be supported. Otherwise, the role of the CLCS under UNCLOS will be undermined and, thus, also the intention of the parties.[23] Giving weight to the Commission's recommendations as interpretive factors in assessing the meaning of article 76 of UNCLOS follows the path taken by the ICJ in, for instance, the *Wall*[24] and *Diallo* cases.[25]

19 *Delimitation of the maritime boundary in the Bay of Bengal (Bangladesh/Myanmar)*, Judgment, ITLOS Reports 2012, p. 4, para. 411.

20 Cavnar, op. cit., 400.

21 A. Serdy, 'The Commission on the Limits of the Continental Shelf and its disturbing propensity to legislate', *International Journal of Marine and Coastal Law* 26, 2011, 355–383.

22 1155 UNTS 331.

23 Ø. Jensen, 'Maritime boundary delimitation beyond 200 nautical miles: The International Judiciary and the Commission on the Limits of the Continental Shelf', *Nordic Journal of International Law* 84, 2015, 595–598.

24 *Legal Consequences of the Construction of a Wall in the Occupied Palestinian Territory*, Advisory Opinion, ICJ Reports 2004, 136.

25 *Ahmadou Sadio Diallo (Republic of Guinea v. Democratic Republic of the Congo)*, Merits, ICJ Reports 2010, 639.

State practice

When UNCLOS was negotiated in the 1970s and early 1980s, it was anticipated that approximately 40–50 states had an *extended* CS. State practice since the Convention came into force in 1994 indicates that many more states potentially have rightful claims to a CS beyond 200 M. As of 1 October 2021, the CLCS has received 88 submissions.

The very first submission was lodged by the Russian Federation on 20 December 2001.[26] It concerned seabed areas beyond 200 M in the Pacific Ocean and the Arctic Ocean.[27] In 2002, the Commission recommended that Russia made 'a revised submission [...] based on the findings contained in the recommendations'.[28] On 28 February 2013 and in August 2015, Russia made new and revised submissions to the CLCS regarding the limits of its CS beyond 200 M in the Pacific Ocean and Arctic Ocean, respectively.[29] It must also be noted that on 31 March 2021, Russia submitted two Addenda to the 2015 partial revised submission in respect of the Arctic Ocean. According to these addenda, Russia now claims to have found scientific evidence to prove that also the last piece of the Area – the Gakkel Ridge – is legally CS under article 76 of UNCLOS. If Russia is correct, this means that the entire Arctic Ocean seabed may become subject to coastal state jurisdiction and that there is no international seabed area left in the Arctic Ocean after all.

The last original submission was that of Indonesia, on 28 December 2020. Submissions are examined in the order in which they are received, but it will take many years until the Commission makes recommendations to Indonesia. The last recommendations to be adopted were on 4 March 2020, to France regarding La Réunion Island and Saint-Paul and Amsterdam Islands.[30] France made its submission on 8 May 2009.

The CLCS is thus struggling with a heavy backlog, which has given rise to some debate. Notably, state representatives have voiced concerns because the workload of the CLCS has 'increased beyond imaginable and expected levels'.[31] In order to clear the backlog, one suggestion has been that states should investigate the possibility of funding the Commission members to stay full-time at UN Headquarters in New York.[32]

When the CLCS adopted its Scientific and Technical Guidelines in 1999,[33] it became clear that developing states in particular would have great difficulty meeting those standards because of low capacity and the short time remaining for many of them in the 10-year period prescribed

26 CLCS, *Statement by the Chairman of the Commission on the Limits of the Continental Shelf on the progress of work in the Commission*, Doc. CLCS/32, 12 April 2002.

27 On continental shelf submission relating to the Arctic Ocean, see in this book K. Dalaker Kraabel and H. Woker, 'Arctic and seabed mining', in V. Tassin Campanella (ed.), *Routledge handbook of seabed mining and the law of the sea*, op. cit., chapter VI.1.3.

28 UN General Assembly, *Oceans and the law of the sea*, Report of the Secretary-General, Addendum, UN Doc. A/57/57/Add.1, 8 October 2002, para 41.

29 CLCS, *Progress of work in the Commission on the Limits of the Continental Shelf, Statement by the Chair*, Doc. CLCS/80, 24 September 2013; CLCS, *Progress of work in the Commission on the Limits of the Continental Shelf, Statement by the Chair*, Doc. CLCS/93, 18 April 2016.

30 CLCS, *Progress of work in the Commission on the Limits of the Continental Shelf, Statement by the Chair*, Doc. CLCS/52/2, 25 March 2020.

31 Meeting of States Parties of UNCLOS, *Report of the Twenty-Second Meeting of States Parties*, UN Doc. SPLOS/251, 11 July 2002.

32 Ibid.

33 CLCS, *Scientific and Technical Guidelines of the Commission on the Limits of the Continental Shelf*, Doc. CLCS/11, 13 May 1999.

by annex II to UNCLOS.[34] With the aim of providing capacity building and technical and scientific support, GRID-Arendal's Shelf Programme was established in 2004, with support from the Norwegian Ministry of Foreign Affairs, to assist developing states and small island developing states with CLCS-submissions to secure rights to the full extent of their marine jurisdiction. Since inception of the Shelf Programme, varying levels of assistance have been provided to a great many states with potential for extended CS areas.[35] In addition to providing data and technical training to states, the Shelf Programme has assisted in the production of final submissions for several developing states, including Papua New Guinea, Palau, Federated States of Micronesia, Solomon Islands, Cook Islands, Vanuatu, Tuvalu, Kiribati, seven West African states and Somalia.[36] Initiatives such as the Shelf Programme are important to keep alive, despite there being few (if any) developing states that still have to complete their CS submissions. As noted by one prominent former member of the CLCS, Harald Brekke, when the submissions of African and Pacific states are to be examined by the Commission, those states will need further technical assistance to communicate and interact with the CLCS during the examination of their submissions.[37]

Some states still have not ratified UNCLOS. Notably, one of the original architects of UNCLOS – the USA – remains off the list of the 168 State Parties to the Convention. However, customary international law also confers rights and obligations related to the CS of coastal states. The ICJ has declared article 76, paragraph 1, to have the status of customary international law.[38] The USA have also stated that they consider the substantive elements of article 76 (paragraphs 2 to 7) to reflect customary international law and that they intend to delineate the seaward limits of their extended CS in conformity with article 76, which they have in a few instances.[39] This is supported by the state practice of about forty different States[40] which shows that a large number of States view these provisions to reflect customary international law.

Who can protect the territorial scope of the Area?

The establishment of the outer limits of the CS beyond 200 M does not only fix the maximum scope of a coastal state's CS but also establishes the demarcation line between the CS and the Area. The guiding principle for the Area is the common heritage of mankind as mentioned

34 K. Thygesen and E. Baker, *The shelf programme: A decade of successfully helping to secure the maritime rights of developing coastal states*, GRID Arendal, 2015, preface. Available online <https://cld.bz/bookdata/PlptVho/basic-html/page-1.html> (accessed 1 September 2021).

35 Ibid., 11.

36 Ibid., 21.

37 Ibid., preface.

38 *Territorial and Maritime Dispute (Nicaragua v. Colombia)*, Judgment, ICJ Reports 2012, 624. See also R. Churchill and A.V. Lowe, *The Law of the Sea*, Manchester: Manchester University Press, 1999, 150, stating that it 'would be difficult to argue that any continental shelf claim consistent with the article 76 formula was not compatible with customary international law'. For more information on the case of Colombia, see in this book E. Restrepo Uribe, 'Colombia and Seabed Mining', in V. Tassin Campanella (ed.), *Routledge handbook of seabed mining and the law of the sea*, op. cit., chapter VI.2.3.

39 See the 'United States policy governing the continental shelf of the United States of America', issued 17 November 1987, reprinted in J. A. Roach and R. W. Smith, *U.S. responses to excessive maritime claims*, The Hague: Martinus Nijhoff Publishers, 1996, 201–202. See also K. Baumert, 'The outer limits of the continental shelf under customary international law', *American Journal of International Law* 111, 2017, 827–872.

40 Ibid., 849–857.

above. The main components of the principle have been described as the 'non-appropriation of the seabed by states or private entities; internationalised management via the International Seabed Authority (...) the sharing of benefits for the common good of mankind; and peaceful use'.[41] Part XI creates a complicated administrative structure which includes a few organs, most notably 'the Authority', which acts on the behalf of mankind as a whole, in whom the resources of the Area are vested, as discussed in the chapter about the International Seabed Authority.[42]

If a state establishes the outer limits of its CS beyond 200 M in a manner that cannot be justified with references to article 76 of UNCLOS (as treaty law or customary law), it limits the territorial scope of the Area and consequently limits the rights of other states. In these circumstances, the question arises who can invoke responsibility for internationally wrongful acts to shield the territorial scope of the Area. Although the CLCS plays a pivotal role in curtailing the territorial temptations of broad margin states with its recommendations, it has no power to enforce them. The Authority has no role in the establishment of the outer CS,[43] except for the limited task of depositing charts and coordinates which states have submitted to show the outer limit lines of their CS. The only way for the Authority to act against states that establish their CS beyond 200 M in inconformity with article 76 is through a very narrow window before the Seabed Disputes Chamber. The possibility exists that the Seabed Disputes Chamber could indirectly consider the delineation of the outer limits of the extended CS if a coastal state purported to exercise its CS rights in an area the Authority considered to be part of the Area. If a coastal state attempted to explore or exploit minerals in part of the Area, this would constitute a violation of article 137 and would bring the matter within the jurisdiction of the Chamber under article 187, as it concerns 'activities in the Area'. Consequently, the Authority could challenge the coastal state under article 187(b)(i), which states that the Seabed Disputes Chamber has jurisdiction in disputes concerning activities in the Area, under part XI and the related Annexes, specifically, 'between a State Party and the Authority concerning (...) acts or omissions (...) of a State Party alleged to be in violation of this Part or the Annexes relating thereto or of rules, regulations and procedures of the Authority adopted in accordance therewith'.[44] In short, the Authority has very little scope to react in the situation of a state that is exceeding the territorial scope of the Area when establishing the outer limits of the CS.

It seems that the most straightforward international actors to react to the illegal determination of the outer limits of a coastal states CS are other states. A specially affected state may invoke the responsibility of a coastal state, in line with article 42 of the ILC Draft Articles on the Responsibility of States for Internationally Wrongful Acts (ILC Draft Articles on States Responsibility),[45] for establishing outer limits in violation of the substantive or procedural requirements of UNCLOS whether or not the outer limits were allegedly based upon a recommendation of the Commission

41 D. R. Rothwell and T. Stephens, *The international law of the sea*, Oxford: Hart Publishing, 2010, 120.

42 UNCLOS Article 137, para. 2. See generally in this book A. Jaeckel, 'The Area and the role of the International Seabed Authority', in V. Tassin Campanella, *Routledge handbook of seabed mining and the law of the sea*, op. cit, chapter IV.I. See also F. Armas Pfirter, 'The future role of the International Seabed Authority', id., chapter IV.3.

43 See articles 134, para. 4, and 84, para. 2, of UNCLOS, read in conjunction with para. 1 of section 1 of the 1994 Agreement relating to the implementation of Part XI of UNCLOS, 28 July 1994, 1836 UNTS 3.

44 See B. M. Magnússon, *The continental shelf beyond 200 nautical miles*, Leiden: Brill Nijhoff, 2015, 238–239.

45 *Draft Articles on the Responsibility of States for Internationally Wrongful Acts*, 2001, ILC Yearbook, vol. II, Part II, 26–30.

or not.[46] The International Law Association's Committee on Legal Issues of the Outer Limits of the Continental Shelf noted in its 2004 report:

> [T]he Area and its resources are the common heritage of mankind as a whole, on whose behalf the (…) Authority (…) shall act, States individually have an interest in the exploration for and exploitation of the resources of the Area (…) States can exercise certain high seas freedoms in the sea-bed and subsoil beyond the limits of national jurisdiction as specified in article 87 of the Convention. The existence of these high seas freedoms gives individual States a legal interest in the definition of these limits. A State may consider that these limits have not been established in accordance with the substantive or procedural requirements of article 76. This would constitute a dispute for the purposes of article 279 of the Convention.[47]

An interesting question is whether a State whose legal rights have not been specially affected by an unlawfully established outer CS limit, can defend the collective interest or international community as a whole and invoke article 48 of ILC's Draft Articles on the Responsibility of States for International Wrongful Acts.[48] Paragraph 1 of article 48 identifies the circumstances necessary to invoke responsibility for an internationally wrongful act:

> Any State other than an injured State is entitled to invoke the responsibility of another State in accordance with paragraph 2 if:
>
> (a) the obligation breached is owed to a group of States including that State, and is established for the protection of a collective interest of the group; or
> (b) the obligation breached is owed to the international community as a whole.

According to article 48, paragraph 2, to which paragraph 1 of the article refers, the claimant state may claim cessation of the wrongful conduct and reparation 'in the interest of the injured State or of the beneficiaries of the obligation breached'. Rüdiger Wolfrum believes that draft article 48 is applicable for states other than a specially affected state in a case regarding the delineation of the outer limits of the extended CS. He has argued that '[l]imiting the scope of the Area inevitably means limiting the potential economic use by States. Thus, States defending the scope of the Area in the interest of the international community, may also act in their own interest'.[49] Although it seems possible that third parties can invoke responsibility, the likelihood that a state would challenge the outer limits of the outer CS of another state without having significant direct political or economic interests for doing so is slight.[50]

46 J. Noyes, 'Judicial and arbitral proceedings and the outer limits of the continental shelf', *Vanderbilt Journal of Transnational Law* 42, 2009, 1246.

47 *Legal Issues of the Outer Limits of the Continental Shelf.* Report of the International Law Association's Committee on the Outer Continental Shelf, 2004, 8.

48 Text adopted by the International Law Commission at its fifty-third session, in 2001, and submitted to the General Assembly as a part of the Commission's report covering the work of that session. The report, which also contains commentaries on the draft articles, appears in *Yearbook of the International Law Commission*, 2001, vol. II (Part Two). Text reproduced as it appears in the annex to General Assembly resolution 56/83 of 12 December 2001, and corrected by document A/56/49(Vol. I)/Corr.4.

49 R. Wolfrum, 'The role of international dispute settlement institutions in the delimitation of the outer continental shelf' in R. Lagoni and D. Vignes (eds.) *Maritime delimitation*, Leiden: Martinus Nijhoff Publishers, 2006, 30 and 31.

50 See Magnússon, op. cit., footnote 44, 235–246.

Final remarks

Coastal states' expansive CS claims in the first decades after World War II were, admittedly, in line with international law, as prescribed by the 1958 Geneva Convention on the Continental Shelf. The problem, however, was that the 1958 Convention in reality did not entail any outer limit. Thus, the exploitation criteria of the Geneva Convention favoured industrialized coastal states. Arvid Pardo's speech to the UN General Assembly in 1967 drew an immediate response from the international community and was an important milestone in the process of making new treaty law. And the UN Convention on the Law of the Sea – adopted in 1982 and entered into force in 1994 – brought significant change. The new convention applied regulations with a more precise definition of the CS, more effectively halting the gradual extension of coastal states' sovereign rights to the seabed, albeit still at a very seaward position.

Forty years after the adoption of the 1982 Convention, the work of demarcating the outer limits of the CS is busier than ever. Notably, the peculiar procedures entailed by article 76 of the Convention – under which coastal states shall involve the experts of the Commission on the Limits of the Continental Shelf – show that 88 states now have claimed CS areas beyond 200 M. That is many more than was expected when the Convention was negotiated in the 1970s and early 1980s. The Commission's processing of shelf submissions has been ongoing since 2001. Since the late 2000s, however, it has struggled with a heavy backlog and the average processing time is currently several years. Thus, it will take many years for the Commission to adopt recommendations on the last shelf submissions. In addition, practice shows that when coastal states obtain new scientific evidence related to the properties of their adjacent seabed areas, that information is also put before the Commission, slowing down its productivity. For instance, Russia recently submitted new information to the Commission regarding their CS claim in the Arctic Ocean. According to those addenda, Russia will now claim the Gakkel Ridge as CS, an area previously considered by all coastal states to be international seabed area and part of our common heritage.

This development also prompts discussion of what legal role other states can play in establishing the outer limits of the CS. The Authority and the CLCS play a very limited supporting role. The CLCS has no role in enforcing its recommendations and the Authority has only a very narrow window before the Seabed Disputes Chamber to act against unlawful infringements of the territorial scope of the Area.[51] It seems clear that States were not eager to share competence with other entities in this context.

References

Armas Pfirter F., 'The future role of the International Seabed Authority', in V. Tassin Campanella (ed.), *Routledge handbook of seabed mining and the law of the sea*, London: Routledge, 2023, chapter IV.3.

Baumert K., 'The Outer Limits of the continental shelf under customary international law', *American Journal of International Law* 111, 2017, 827–872.

Cavnar A., 'Accountability and the commission on the limits of the continental shelf: Deciding who owns the ocean floor', *Cornell International Law Journal* 42, 2009, 387–440.

Churchill R. and Lowe A.V., *The law of the sea*, Manchester: Manchester University Press, 1999.

Dalaker Kraabel K. and Woker H., 'Arctic and seabed mining', in V. Tassin Campanella (ed.), *Routledge handbook of seabed mining and the law of the sea*, London: Routledge, 2023, chapter VI.1.3.

51 For more information on the jurisdiction of the Seabed Disputes Chamber, see in this book T. Treves, 'Dispute settlement and seabed mining in the Area', in V. Tassin Campanella (ed.), *Routledge handbook of seabed mining and the law of the sea*, op. cit., chapter V.1.

Fleischer C.A., 'The continental shelf beyond 200 nautical miles – A crucial element in the 'package deal': Historic background and implications for today', in D. Vidas (ed.), *Law, technology and science for oceans in globalisation*, Leiden/Boston: Martinus Nijhoff Publishers, 2010, 429–448.

Francis N., 'The continental shelf commission', in M.H. Nordquist and J.N. Moore (eds.), *Oceans policy: New institutions, challenges and opportunities*, The Hague: Martinus Nijhoff Publishers, 1999, 141–146.

Henkin L., *Law for the sea's mineral resources*, New York: Institute for the Study of Science in Human Affairs Columbia University, 1968.

Hollick A., 'The origins of 200-mile offshore zones', *American Journal of International Law* 71, 1977, 494–500.

Jaeckel A., 'The Area and the role of the international seabed authority', in V. Tassin Campanella (ed.), *Routledge handbook of seabed mining and the law of the sea*, London: Routledge, 2023, chapter IV.1.

Jensen Ø., 'Maritime boundary delimitation beyond 200 nautical miles: The international judiciary and the commission on the limits of the continental shelf', *Nordic Journal of International Law* 84, 2015, 580–604.

Magnússon B.M., *The continental shelf beyond 200 nautical miles*, Leiden: Brill Nijhoff, 2015.

McDorman T.L., 'The continental shelf regime in the law of the sea convention: A reflection on the first thirty years', *The International Journal of Marine and Coastal Law* 27, 2012, 743–775.

Noyes J., 'Judicial and arbitral proceedings and the outer limits of the continental shelf', *Vanderbilt Journal of Transnational Law* 42, 2009, 1211–1264.

Oral N., 'The common heritage of mankind', in V. Tassin Campanella (ed.), *Routledge handbook of seabed mining and the law of the sea*, London: Routledge, 2023, chapter II.2.

Restrepo Uribe E., 'Colombia and seabed mining', in V. Tassin Campanella (ed.), *Routledge handbook of seabed mining and the law of the sea*, London: Routledge, 2023, chapter VI.2.3.

Roach J.A. and Smith R.W., *U.S. responses to excessive maritime claims*, The Hague: Martinus Nijhoff Publishers, 1996.

Rothwell D.R. and Stephens T., *The international law of the sea*, Oxford: Hart Publishing, 2010.

Schofield C. and Mossop J., 'The article 82 Conundrum: Implementing payment for the exploitation of the continental shelf beyond 200 nautical miles', in V. Tassin Campanella (ed.), *Routledge handbook of seabed mining and the law of the sea*, London: Routledge, 2023, chapter IV.2.

Serdy A., 'The Commission on the Limits of the Continental Shelf and its disturbing propensity to legislate', *International Journal of Marine and Coastal Law* 26, 2011, 355–383.

Tassin Campanella V., Cissé Y. and Tladi D., 'Rights and obligations of States on the continental shelf and the Area', in V. Tassin Campanella (ed.), *Routledge handbook of seabed mining and the law of the sea*, London: Routledge, 2023, chapter II.1.

Thygesen K. and Baker E., *The shelf programme: A decade of successfully helping to secure the maritime rights of developing coastal states*, Grid Arendal, 2015. Available online <https://cld.bz/bookdata/PlptVho/basic-html/page-1.html> (accessed 1 September 2021).

Treves T., 'Dispute settlement and seabed mining in the Area', in V. Tassin Campanella (ed.), *Routledge handbook of seabed mining and the law of the sea*, London: Routledge, 2023, chapter V.1.

Whiteman M.M. (ed.) *Digest of international law*, Washington, DC: U.S. Government Printing Office, 1965.

Wolfrum R., 'The role of international dispute settlement institutions in the delimitation of the outer continental shelf', in R. Lagoni and D. Vignes (eds.), *Maritime delimitation*, Leiden: Martinus Nijhoff Publishers, 2006, 19–31.

Policy documents and regulatory instruments

Agreement Relating to the Implementation of Part XI of the United Nations Convention on the Law of the Sea of 10 December 1982, 28 July 1994. Published in 1836 *United Nations Treaty Series* 3.

CLCS, *Progress of Work in the Commission on the Limits of the Continental Shelf, Statement by the Chair*, Doc. CLCS/80, 24 September 2013.

CLCS, *Progress of Work in the Commission on the Limits of the Continental Shelf, Statement by the Chair*, Doc. CLCS/93, 18 April 2016.

CLCS, *Progress of Work in the Commission on the Limits of the Continental Shelf, Statement by the Chair*, Doc. CLCS/52/2, 25 March 2020.

CLCS, *Rules of Procedure of the Commission on the Limits of the Continental Shelf*, Doc. CLCS/40/Rev. 1, 17 April 2008.

CLCS, *Scientific and Technical Guidelines of the Commission on the Limits of the Continental Shelf*, Doc. CLCS/11, 13 May 1999.

CLCS, *Statement by the Chairman of the Commission on the Limits of the Continental Shelf on the Progress of Work in the Commission*, Doc. CLCS/32, 12 April 2002.

Convention on the Continental Shelf. Adopted in Geneva 29 April 1858; Entered into Force 10 June 1964. Published in 499 *United Nations Treaty Series* 311.

Decision Regarding the Date of Commencement of the Ten-Year Period for Making Submissions to the Commission on the Limits of the Continental Sehlf Set Out in Article 4 of Annex II to the United Nations Convention on the Law of the Sea, UN Doc SPLOS/72, 29 May 2011.

Meeting of States Parties of UNCLOS, *Report of the Twenty-Second Meeting of States Parties,* UN Doc. SPLOS/251, 11 July 2002.

Meeting of States Parties of UNCLOS, *Report of the Eighteenth Meeting of States Parties*, UN Doc. SPLOS/184, 21 July 2008.

Responsibility of States for Internationally Wrongful Acts. Published in *Yearbook of the International Law Commission*, 2001, vol. II (Part Two).

UN General Assembly, *Oceans and the Law of the Sea, Report of the Secretary-General, Addendum*, UN Doc. A/57/57/Add.1, 8 October 2002, para. 41.

United Nations Convention on the Law of the Sea. Adopted at Montego Bay 10 December 1982; Entered into Force 14 November 1994. Published in 1833 *United Nations Treaty Series* 397.

Vienna Convention on the Law of Treaties. Adopted in Vienna 23 May 1969; Entered into Force 27 January 1980. Published in 1155 *United Nations Treaty Series* 311.

III.2

THE ARTICLE 82 CONUNDRUM

Implementing payment for the exploitation of the continental shelf beyond 200 nautical miles

Clive Schofield and Joanna Mossop

Introduction

The United Nations Convention on the Law of the Sea (UNCLOS)[1] provides, through article 82, a benefit-sharing arrangement with respect to the development of the mineral resources of continental shelf areas located seawards of 200 nautical miles (M) from baselines along the coast. The payments or contributions in kind involved are to be made through the International Seabed Authority (ISA) and distributed by the Authority to States Parties to the Convention on the basis of equitable sharing criteria with particular reference to the needs of developing States, especially least developed and land-locked States. This provision has been dormant in the absence of such resource exploitation commencing in such 'outer' or 'extended' continental shelf areas.[2] There are, however, indications that this is set to change in the foreseeable future, as indicated by growing exploration efforts in areas seawards of 200 M limits.

This chapter explores the article 82 'conundrum', as alluded to in the title, a term employed because of the significant ambiguities and uncertainties contained in the provisions of the article which are likely to impact on its practical implementation. These challenges to the interpretation and implementation of article 82 are identified and explored. A discussion of emerging State practice concerning resource exploration efforts in continental shelf areas seawards of 200 M limits follows. The status of article 82 as customary international law is then discussed, and emerging State practice is explored before concluding observations are offered.

1 *United Nations Convention on the Law of the Sea*, 10 December 1982, 1833 UNTS 3 (entered into force 16 November 1994). Hereinafter, UNCLOS or the Convention.

2 It can be noted that both of these terms are problematic. In particular, the former term suggests that there are distinct 'inner' and 'outer' portions of the continental shelf when legally this is not the case. Further, referring to the 'extended' continental shelf arguably gives a somewhat misleading impression that coastal States are somehow advancing claims to 'additional' areas of continental shelf when, in fact, continental shelf rights are inherent and 'do not depend on occupation, effective or notional, or on any express proclamation' in accordance with UNCLOS, article 77(3).

DOI: 10.4324/9780429426162-11

The drafting and aims of article 82

Article 82 of the UNCLOS obliges coastal States undertaking the exploitation of non-living resources in areas of continental shelf beyond 200 M from baselines along the coast to make payments or contributions in kind for the benefit of developing States, especially least developed and land-locked States.

Article 82 is designed to provide for revenue sharing between broad shelf coastal States and the international community with payments or contributions in kind channelled through the ISA, which must distribute them equitably with priority given to least developed and land-locked States. As such, article 82 represents a negotiated compromise between the sovereign rights of coastal States within their continental shelf areas seawards of 200 M limits from baselines along the coast and the common heritage of mankind.[3] These revenue-sharing arrangements have been characterised as a form of 'royalty' payment.[4]

During the negotiation of the UNCLOS, States with broad continental margins (known as the 'margineers') were keen to exercise control over the resources of their entire shelves, including that portion located beyond 200 M from baselines. Other States were convinced that the regime applying the common heritage of mankind to the deep seabed should apply to continental shelves beyond 200 M.[5] Some argued that coastal States could share a part of the revenue resulting from all areas under national jurisdiction.[6] Article 82 provides a means of reconciling these conflicting positions through a benefit-sharing arrangement, originally proposed by the United States, applicable to the exploitation of non-living resources beyond 200 M.[7]

The sliding scale of payments contained in article 82 provides for 1 per cent of value or volume of production from a particular site in the sixth year of operation increasing by a further 1 per cent per year through to a maximum of 7 per cent from the 12th year of production until production ceases at that site. The initial five-year 'grace period' on payments and their gradually escalating nature was drafted in recognition of the high costs likely to be associated with such developments inevitably located far from shore, especially during early phases of operation. Additionally, such production is specified as not including resources that are utilised in the course of exploitation.

Tuerk, who was a delegate on behalf of Austria during the Third United Nations Conference on the Law of the Sea and who suggested the figure of 7 per cent as a compromise value between competing proposals during discussions on this provision, has reflected that this five-year grace period which was deemed to be reasonable for cost recovery by the operator was 'probably somewhat too short given the enormous financial outlay required for deep-sea mining at great depths'.[8] Here it can be noted that while the costs associated with deep and ultra-deepwater drilling are

3 On the evolution of rights and obligations of States on the seabed, see generally in this book V. Tassin Campanella, Y. Cissé and D. Tladi, 'Rights and obligations of States' in V. Tassin Campanella (ed), *Routledge handbook of seabed mining and the law of the sea*, London: Routledge, 2023, chapter II.1.

4 M.W. Lodge, 'Enclosure of the oceans versus the common heritage of mankind: The Inherent Tension between the Continental Shelf Beyond 100 Nautical Miles and the Area', *International Legal Studies* 97, 2021, 803–832, at p. 827.

5 See generally in this book Ø. Jensen and B.M. Magnússon, 'The extension of sovereign rights beyond 200 nautical miles' in V. Tassin Campanella (ed), *Routledge handbook of seabed mining and the law of the sea*, op. cit., chapter III.1.

6 Ibid., at p. 828.

7 A. Chircop, 'Article 82' in A. Proelss (ed), *United Nations Convention on the Law of the Sea: A commentary*, London: Bloomsbury, 2017, pp. 639–651, at pp. 643–644.

8 H. Tuerk, 'Questions relating to the continental shelf beyond 200 nautical miles: Delimitation, delineation, and revenue sharing', *International Legal Studies* 97, 2021, 232–258, at p. 253.

indeed extremely and potentially prohibitively high, some parts of the outer continental shelf are, in fact, relatively shallow.[9]

For example, it has been observed that over 7 million km^2 of the Arctic Ocean's continental shelf is less than 500m deep.[10] Moreover these broad areas of continental shelf, including extensive outer continental shelf areas, have been characterised as perhaps constituting the 'geographically largest prospective area for petroleum remaining on Earth'.[11] More specifically, the Chukchi Plateau, located north of Alaska, includes approximately 51,000 km^2 of continental shelf area seawards of 200 M limits from baselines along the coast, yet in less than 500 m depths of water. Around 212,000 km^2 of continental shelf area on this feature is located beyond 200 M from baselines along the coast and in less than 2,500 m depth of water.[12] As noted above, such depths of water appear to be well within the scope of current drilling technology.

It has been suggested that the benefit-sharing arrangement in article 82 represents a residual element of the common heritage of mankind concept embedded within, and to an extent diminishing, the sovereign rights of the coastal States within its areas of outer continental shelf. For example, the International Law Association (ILA)'s Committee on the Outer Continental Shelf in its useful Report on article 82 states that article 82 'provides for the common heritage of mankind (CHM) principle within the OCS [outer continental shelf], even though the OCS is within the coastal State's maritime jurisdiction'.[13] The ILA Report goes on to quote Oda's view that article 82 was 'instituted in such a manner that the concept of the common heritage of mankind plays a role in controlling over-expansion of the exclusive interests of coastal States in their continental shelves'.[14]

An alternative view is that the common heritage of mankind principle does not apply to the outer continental shelf.[15] Rather, article 82 has been perhaps better characterised as a form of compensation to developing and land-locked States for the reduction in the spatial extent of the Area as a result of outer continental shelf limits exceeding 200 M from baselines along the coast.[16]

9 While there is no commonly accepted definition of deep and ultra-deepwater drilling, one industry source suggests that deepwater drilling is that taking place in water depths deeper than 4–5,000 feet (1,219–1,524 m) whilst ultra-deepwater drilling can be taken to be that taking place in waters deeper than 7,000 feet (2,133 m). It should, however, be noted that these definitions can be expected to change as drilling technology advances. See J. Lavis, 'Shallow, mid to ultra-deepwater definitions', Drillers.com, 6 April 2018.

10 K.J. Bird et al., 'Circum-polar resource appraisal: Estimates of undiscovered oil and gas north of the arctic circle', USGS *Fact Sheet* 2008-3049. Available online at <http://pubs.usgs.gov/fs/2008/3049/fs2008-3049.pdf> (accessed 24 May 2021).

11 Ibid.

12 The authors thank Mr Robert van de Poll (Global Director, Law of the Sea, Fugro) for providing this calculation which is based on a 2020 General Bathymetric Chart of the World (GEBCO) gridded bathymetric dataset, which provides a global terrain model for ocean and land at 15 arc-second intervals, coupled with calculations made through CARIS LOTS (Law of the Sea) geographical information systems (GIS) software. It should be noted that the western limit for these calculations was taken to be the 168° 58' 37" W. meridian consistent with Article 1 of the *Agreement between the United States of America and The Union of the Soviet Socialist Republics on the Maritime Boundary* of 1 June 1990.

13 International Law Association (ILA), Committee on the Outer Continental Shelf, 'Report on Article 82 and the 1982 UN Convention on the Law of the Sea', 2008, para. 1.3. See also Joanna Mossop, *The continental shelf beyond 200 nautical miles: Rights and responsibilities*, Oxford: Oxford University Press, 2016, at p. 128.

14 ILA Report, op. cit., quoting S. Oda, *International control of sea resources*, Dordrecht: Martinus Nijhoff, 1989, xxxii. See also B. Kwiatkowska, *The 200 mile exclusive economic zone in the new law of the sea*, Dordrecht: Martinus Nijhoff, 1989, at p. 18.

15 See Mossop, op. cit., pp. 128–130.

16 Ibid. See also S.C. Vasciannie, *Land-locked and geographically disadvantaged states in the international law of the sea*, Oxford: Clarendon Press, 1990, p. 127.

Accordingly, the outer continental shelf areas subject to article 82 remain part of the continental shelf of the coastal States themselves and are distinct from those parts of the seabed and subsoil, in the Area, constituting the common heritage of mankind.

A further aspect of article 82 that should be mentioned is that developing States that are net importers of a mineral resource produced from their continental shelf are exempt from making payments in respect of that resource. This may have seemed uncontroversial at the time, but some developing States, such as Brazil, are now net exporters of some resources.[17]

Ambiguities and uncertainties in article 82

Article 82 is replete with undefined terms that are capable of varied interpretation. These include 'payments', 'contributions in kind', 'resource', 'all production', 'value', 'volume', 'site', and 'annually'. Indeed, the ISA, in one of its Technical Studies, has itself observed that article 82 includes significant 'textual ambiguities and process gaps'.[18] In the absence of commonly understood definitions of these terms there is significant scope for varied interpretation and disagreement.

While it is clear that coastal States have a choice over whether to make monetary payments or contributions in kind, there is uncertainty over whether these options might be combined or whether the coastal State may vary these modes of payment over time.[19] If monetary payments are to be made, the question then occurs as to what currency such payments are to be provided in. Further, article 82 is silent as to what resources may form 'contributions in kind'. The article does not explicitly indicate that contributions in kind should be directly derived from the resource development on the outer continental shelf or whether other resources of equivalent value might instead be used. In practical terms, monetary payments would surely be far easier to deal with from the perspective of the ISA.[20] If contributions in kind in the form of, for example, quantities of oil or other minerals, were instead delivered to the ISA, this would place a considerable burden on the Authority in terms of their storage and sale or distribution.[21]

It is also unclear who is obliged to either pay or make contributions in kind – whether it is the coastal State concerned or the contractor undertaking the exploitation of non-living resources of the continental shelf. While the Secretary General of the International Seabed Authority has indicated that the ISA only enters into agreements with Governments, suggesting that contractors such as international oil companies are not directly responsible for such payments or contributions, nonetheless coastal States may nonetheless potentially impose obligations through contractual terms with the entities that they license (see below).

The role of the ISA has also been subject to debate. In particular, it is unclear how active or passive the ISA's role should be. Payments or contributions in kind are, in accordance with article 82, to be made 'through the Authority', not, as Tuerk notes, 'to the Authority' as was proposed in earlier drafts of the provision, meaning that the Authority can be considered the 'trustee' in relation

17 See, for example, A. Pereira da Silva, 'Dealing with Articles 76 and 82 of the United Nations Convention on the Law of the Sea: Legal and political challenges for Brazil', *Ocean Yearbook* 28, 2014, 145–172.

18 International Seabed Authority, *Implementation of Article 82 of the United Nations Convention on the Law of the Sea*, ISA Technical Study No. 12, 2013, p. 20.

19 Mossop, op. cit., p. 131.

20 M.W. Lodge, 'The International Seabed Authority and Article 82 of the UN Convention on the Law of the Sea', *International Journal of Marine and Coastal Law* 21, 2001, 323–333, p. 326.

21 'Outcomes of the international workshop on further consideration of the implementation of Article 82 of the United Nations Convention on the Law of the Sea', Report of the Secretary General, ISBA/19/A/46 May 2013, para. 4(a).

to these payments or contributions in kind.[22] Article 82 does not assign any particular mandate or powers to the ISA in terms of monitoring or compliance in the implementation of article 82 obligations on the part of the coastal States involved. States are, however, required to 'fulfil in good faith' the obligations assumed under the Convention.[23]

The Secretary-General of the ISA has acknowledged the view that the Authority lacks a role in respect of 'the process of determining the value and volume of the resources' or concerning how any payments and contributions arising from them were derived 'but simply to proceed to make a distribution of them' in keeping with article 82 paragraph 4.[24] However, he has observed that this is 'not a reasonable position to take', since 'at the very least, there needs to be consultation and agreement with the ISA so that it can discharge its fiduciary duty to mankind as a whole'.[25] On this 'unresolved question' Tuerk has commented that transparency is needed and that consultation and agreement between coastal States and the ISA is 'indispensable' in this context, as well as in respect of the exemption provision for developing States.[26]

What is clearer is that the ISA is tasked with distributing such payments or contributions in kind to developing States on the basis of equitable sharing with particular mention made of least developed and land-locked States.[27] In particular, the ISA has to develop equitable sharing criteria for the distribution of any payments or contributions in kind for the benefit of developing States and particularly least developed and land-locked States under article 82(4). Once developed, it is for the ISA Council to recommend to the Assembly the necessary rules, regulations, and procedures on equitable sharing.[28]

Commentators have suggested that the above-mentioned uncertainties and ambiguities were left open by the drafters of the Convention at Third United Nations Conference on the law of the sea and so as to avoid complicating the negotiating process.[29] Negotiators were arguably mindful that this provision was unlikely to be implemented in the near term. Thus, key terms within the article were considered to be best left for future elaboration such that article 82 was intentionally left as 'unfinished business'.

As article 82 remains dormant four decades on from the Convention opening for signature, it seems that the drafters of the Convention have proved to be sagacious in their approach to this provision. In the absence of substantive State practice on the issue, the ISA has played an important role as a forum for discussion on issues relating to the interpretation and implementation of article 82 of the UNCLOS. To this end the ISA has convened a series of workshops,[30] leading to the publication of a series of Technical Studies on issues related to the implementation of article 82.[31] The

22 See Tuerk, op. cit., p. 255.
23 Article 300, UNCLOS.
24 Lodge (2021), op. cit., p. 829. See also ILA Report on Article 82, op. cit., Conclusions 6 and 7.
25 Lodge (2021), ibid.
26 Tuerk, op. cit. p. 256.
27 Article 82(3), UNCLOS.
28 Article 162(2)(o)(i), ibid.
29 Tuerk, op. cit., p. 253.
30 The Authority convened a workshop on issues arising from Article 82 in conjunction with the Royal Institute of International Affairs (Chatham House) in London in 2009, leading to the publication of ISA Technical Studies 4 and 5. A further workshop, which the first author of this chapter participated in, took place in Beijing in 2012, leading to the publication of ISA Technical Study 12 (op. cit.).
31 See ISA, *Issues Associated with the Implementation of Article 82 of the United Nations Convention on the Law of the Sea*, ISA Technical Study No. 4, 2015; ISA, *Non-Living Resources of the Continental Shelf Beyond 200 Nautical Miles: Speculations on the Implementation of Article 82 of the United Nations Convention on the Law of the Sea*,

Authority also commissioned a comparative study of how certain terms used in article 82 are used, especially in the context of seabed hydrocarbon resources, across nine selected jurisdictions.[32]

Emerging State practice

Developments in exploration efforts on extended continental shelf areas

There are clear indications of exploration interest in seabed hydrocarbon developments on parts of the outer continental shelf. As of the time of writing, a total of 21 coastal States had designated oil and gas exploration blocks seawards of 200 M exclusive economic zone (EEZ) limits. Of these 21 coastal States, 12 had issued exploration permits relating to a total of 119 such blocks across the world. Additionally, blocks located partially or wholly seawards of 200 M EEZ limits remained either open (89), subject to current bid rounds (7), or had been designated broad areas subject to future bid rounds (30) (see Table III.2.1).[33]

With respect to the exploration blocks located wholly or partially beyond 200 M EEZ limits set out in Table III.2.1, a number of caveats can be noted. An overarching caveat is that while every effort has been made to ensure that these calculations are as accurate as possible, mismatches can occur between datasets.[34] It can also be observed that on occasion it appears that coastal States have designated rectilinear exploration blocks that, while they broadly approximate 200 M arcs delineating EEZ limits, appear to marginally stray beyond these limits into areas of outer continental shelf.

It is therefore somewhat uncertain in some cases whether all of the blocks listed in Table III.2.1 were actually intended to extend into areas of the outer continental shelf.[35] In contrast, certain States, such as the US, have designated blocks which extend well beyond 200 M limits, apparently foreshadowing future US assertions over its outer continental shelf.

It can also be noted that the 49 blocks designated by Mauritius and the Seychelles are located on the Mascarene Plateau area of the outer continental shelf which was subject to a joint submission by these States to the CLCS[36] and is subject to 2012 agreements concerning the joint exercise of sovereign rights[37] and joint management of this 396,000 km^2 area of continental shelf between them.[38] Should seabed resources be developed in this area, the obligations under article 82 of the

ISA Technical Study No. 5, 2015; ISA Technical Study No. 12, op. cit.; W. Spicer and E. McIsaac, *A Study of Key Terms in Article 82 of the United Nations Convention on the Law of the Sea*, ISA Technical Study No. 15, 2016.

32 The nine jurisdictions covered in the study include royalty regimes, namely the United States, Brazil, Canada (Alberta), Australia, Nigeria, Canada (Newfoundland and Labrador), and tax regimes, namely the Russian Federation, United Kingdom, Norway. See Spicer and McIsaac, op. cit.

33 Ibid.

34 For example, between the block limits provided through Drilling info and the 200 M limits calculated using CARIS LOTS.

35 Examples include blocks designated by Denmark on behalf of Greenland and the Faroes as well as some of Namibia's blocks.

36 Mauritius and the Seychelles made their joint partial submission relating to the Mascarene Plateau region to the CLCS on 1 December 2008. The Commission adopted its recommendations on this joint submission on 30 March 2011. See generally the Africa regional section of this book. E. Egede, 'Africa and seabed mining' in V. Tassin Campanella (ed), *Routledge handbook of seabed mining and the law of the sea*, op. cit., chapter VI.1.1.

37 See *Treaty concerning the Joint Exercise of Sovereign Rights over the Continental Shelf in the Mascarene Plateau Region between the Government of the Republic of Mauritius and the Republic of Seychelles* (entry into force 18 June 2012), *Law of the Sea Bulletin* 79: 25–40.

38 *Treaty concerning the Joint Management of the Continental Shelf in the Mascarene Plateau Region between Government of the Republic of Mauritius and the Government of the Republic of Seychelles* (entry into force 18 June 2012), *Law of the Sea Bulletin* 79: 41–52.

Table III.2.1 Exploration blocks located partially or wholly seawards of 200 M EEZ limits[1]

State	*Blocks Issued*	*Blocks Open*	*Current Bid Round*	*Future Bid Round*
Angola	—	1	—	—
Argentina	5	—	—	—
Australia	1	—	—	—
Bangladesh	—	4	—	—
Brazil	—	—	3	—
Canada	29	—	—	3
China	1	—	—	—
Colombia	—	—	3	—
Denmark	—	—	2[2]	12[3]
Guinea-Bissau	1	1	—	—
Malaysia	3	1	1	—
Mozambique	—	6	—	—
Myanmar	—	1	—	—
Namibia	2	9	—	—
Norway	3	—	—	—
Seychelles/ Mauritius	—	49	—	—
Somalia	—	1	—	—
South Africa	1	15	—	—
Suriname	1	—	—	—
USA	68	—	—	15[4]
Vietnam	3	1	—	—
Total	**119**	**89**	**7**	**30**

[1] The information contained in Table III.2.1 was provided by Mr Robert van de Poll, through personal correspondence with the first author, May 2021. Analysis is based on information on exploration blocks and current and future bid rounds derived from Enverus Drilling info datasets (April 2021 edition) coupled with 200 M limits calculated using CARIS LOTS software integrated in the Fugro Global Law of the Sea database.
[2] On behalf of Greenland.
[3] On behalf of the Faroe Islands.
[4] It can be noted that future bid rounds for the United States cover broad areas divided into numerous open blocks involving five in the Arctic region (comprising 22,691 blocks), five in the Pacific (10,861 blocks), three in the Atlantic (9,354 blocks), and two in the Gulf of Mexico (920 blocks).

Convention would be shared equally by Mauritius and the Seychelles in keeping with the equal sharing of revenue established under the latter treaty.[39]

Further, with respect to Colombia's designated blocks included in Table III.2.1, these are located seawards of the EEZ of Nicaragua established through the International Court of Justice's (ICJ) 2012 judgment. They thus encompass areas of what Nicaragua considers to be part of its outer continental shelf in keeping with its submission to the CLCS.[40] These blocks also partially extend beyond 200 M limits from Colombia. These areas are subject to a further case before the ICJ between the parties which, at the time of writing, was ongoing.[41]

39 Article 5(a), ibid.

40 Republic of Nicaragua, 'Submission to the Commission on the Limits of the Continental Shelf pursuant to Article 76', paragraph 8 of the United Nations Convention on the Law of the Sea, 1982, June 2013.

41 See *Question of the Delimitation of the Continental Shelf between Nicaragua and Colombia beyond 200 Nautical Miles from the Nicaraguan Coast (Nicaragua v. Colombia)*, ICJ. See also generally in this book the regional section

Even more contentiously, the exploration blocks established by China, the Philippines, and Vietnam that are included in Table III.2.1 are all located in the central South China Sea. However, such areas of outer continental shelf underlying a high seas pocket in the central part of the South China Sea only exist if the disputed islands in the South China Sea are legally 'rocks' in keeping with article 121 paragraph 3 of the Convention. This was one of the findings of the Arbitral Tribunal in the case between China and the Philippines.[42] It was clear prior to this case that a number of the South China Sea littoral States took this view, as evidenced by their full or preliminary submissions to the CLCS.[43] However, it is also abundantly clear both from its protests concerning these submissions[44] and rejection of the Tribunal's Award[45] that China takes an opposing view. China would therefore not view these blocks as being part of the outer continental shelf and subject to article 82. Indeed, the block that China has designated and issued is located in the Rifleman Bank area of the south-western South China Sea, straddling the 200 M limit of Vietnam and part of the area covered by the Malaysia-Vietnam joint submission to the CLCS.[46]

A Canadian precedent?

At the time of writing no mineral exploitation is taking place seawards of 200 M EEZ limits that would trigger article 82. However, as noted above, there is clearly exploration interest in parts of the outer continental shelf.

In particular, from 2013 discoveries of potentially commercially viable deepwater hydrocarbon deposits have been made as part of the Bay du Nord project in the Flemish Pass Basin.[47] Further,

on South America, E. Jimenez Pineda, 'South American region and seabed mining' in V. Tassin Campanella (ed), *Routledge handbook of seabed mining and the law of the sea*, op. cit., chapter VI.1.6.

42 *South China Sea Arbitration, Philippines v China, Award*, PCA Case No 2013-19, ICGJ 495 (PCA 2016), 12 July 2016, Permanent Court of Arbitration, paras 626 and 646. Available online https://pca-cpa.org, at https://pcacases.com/web/view/7 (accessed 24 May 2021). See also C.H. Schofield, 'The Regime of Islands reframed: Developments in the definition of islands and their role in the delimitation of maritime boundaries under the international law of the sea', *Brill Research Perspectives in the Law of the Sea*, 3(1-2), 2021, 1–126, at 58–62.

43 Malaysia and Vietnam made a joint submission to the CLCS in 2009 as well as individual submissions in 2009 (Vietnam) and 2019 (Malaysia) with respect to areas of outer continental shelf in the central South China Sea. Brunei also made a submission of preliminary information to the Commission in 2009. China and the Philippines have also made partial submissions to the CLCS but relating to outer continental shelf limits outside the South China Sea. See Schofield, ibid., at 100–101.

44 See, for example, Communications Received with regard to the Joint Submission made by Malaysia and Vietnam to the CLCS, China, 7 May 2009 and 14 April 2011.

45 China did not participate directly in the case and stated that it 'neither accepts nor recognizes' the Award and solemnly declaring it to be 'null and void' and of 'no binding force'. See, for example, 'Statement of the Ministry of Foreign Affairs of the People's Republic of China on the Award of 12 July 2016 of the Arbitral Tribunal in the South China Sea Arbitration Established at the Request of the Republic of the Philippines'. See also Schofield, op. cit., at 75.

46 Malaysia-Vietnam, 'Joint Submission by Malaysia and Socialist Republic of Viet Nam', Executive Summary (6 May 2009). For a detailed analysis of Southeast Asia and seabed mining, see in this book T. Davenport, 'Southeast Asia and seabed mining' in V. Tassin Campanella (ed), *Routledge handbook of seabed mining and the law of the sea*, op. cit., chapter VI.1.7.

47 The operator of the Bay du Nord Project, Equinor, indicates that three light oil fields have been discovered, namely, the Bay du Nord field in 2013, the Bay du Verde field in 2015 and the Baccalieu field in 2016 with overall recoverable reserves estimated at approximately 300 million barrels of oil. An investment decision on the project is anticipated in 2021 which if positive would see potential first oil in 2025. See Equinor, 'The Bay du Nord Project'. Available online at <https://www.equinor.com/en/where-we-are/canada-bay-du-nord.html> (accessed 1 May 2021).

a framework agreement between Equinor and the government of Newfoundland and Labrador for the development of the Bay du Nord project was announced in July 2018.[48] These discoveries have been made approximately 500 km (270 M) east of St. John's, Newfoundland in 1,200 m of water.[49] They are therefore located seawards of Canada's 200 M EEZ limit but well within its submitted continental shelf limits in the Atlantic Ocean.[50] If developed, this would represent the first non-living resource development on the outer continental shelf thus raising the prospect that Canada would be the first coastal State faced with implementing article 82 in practice.

Significant domestic complications exist for Canada in this context. While there is little doubt that the revenue-sharing obligations contained in article 82 of the UNCLOS fall to the coastal State and thus Canada's Federal Government, the reality is that it is the Provincial rather than Federal authorities that benefit from any offshore oil and gas activities offshore Newfoundland and Labrador. This is in keeping with resource revenue arrangements between Ottawa and these Provinces under the *Atlantic Accord of 2005*.[51] In this regard McDorman has observed, with admirable understatement, any attempt to 'revisit, or even hint at the possibility of revisiting' such arrangements 'has long been perceived as politically problematic'.[52] This situation has led to debate within Canada as to whether the payments or contributions in kind arising from article 82 should be met by the Federal Government in Ottawa or the Provinces.[53] An indication of Canada's intentions should non-living resource developments go ahead on parts of its outer continental shelf can perhaps be gleaned from the 'Bid information' included with calls for bids in respect of Canadian Blocks which, with respect to blocks entirely or partially beyond Canada's 200 M limits states that 'in order to meet obligations arising pursuant to article 82 of the United Nations Convention on the Law of the Sea, additional terms and conditions may be applied through legislation, regulations, amendments to licences or otherwise'.

This leaves it opaque as to precisely where the revenue-sharing burden falls, but would appear to open the way for Canada to shift the burden from the State or Provinces to the contractor. Such a move would, however, likely serve as a major disincentive to investment, potentially rendering the development of the seabed hydrocarbon resources unattractive commercially. While both Norway and the United States appear to adopt a similar approach, requiring payments to cover article 82 costs from the licence holder, it is clear that these costs would be deducted from taxation or royal-

48 See Newfoundland and Labrador Natural Resources Executive Council, 'Premier ball marks first step into new frontier for oil and gas industry', News Release, 26 July 2018. Available online <https://www.gov.nl.ca/releases/2018/exec/0726n01/> (accessed 20 May 2021).

49 Ibid.

50 See Partial Submission by Canada to the Commission on the Limits of the Continental Shelf regarding its Continental Shelf in the Atlantic Ocean, Executive Summary, 6 December 2013.

51 The Atlantic Accord provides that 'Newfoundland and Labrador already receives and will continue to receive 100 per cent of offshore revenues as if these resources were on land'. See Arrangement between the Government of Canada and the Government of Newfoundland and Labrador on Offshore Revenues ('Atlantic Accord 2005'), 14 February 2005, Article 2.

52 T. McDorman, 'An ISA side issue: LOS Convention, Article 82 and revenue sharing', Presentation April 2020, to be included in a forthcoming ISA Report.

53 See W. Spicer, 'Canada, the Law of the Sea Treaty and international payments: Where will the money come from?', University of Calgary, School of Public Policy, *SPP Research Papers* 8-31, September 2015, at 18–20. See also R.J. Harrison, 'Article 82 of UNCLOS: The day of reckoning approaches', *Journal of World Energy Law and Business* 10, 2017, 488–504; R.J. Harrison, 'Offshore oil development in uncharted legal waters: Will the proposed Bay du Nord project precipitate another federal-provincial conflict?', *Energy Regulation Quarterly* 6-4, December 2018; A. Chircop, 'Implementation of Article 82 of the United Nations Convention on the Law of the Sea: The challenge for Canada' in C. Banet (ed), *The law of the seabed*, Leiden: Brill, 2020, pp. 371–394.

ties to be paid to the governments of the States concerned.[54] In contrast, New Zealand's legislation clearly specifies that 'The Crown shall make all payments and contributions in kind required to be made to the Authority from time to time under the terms of article 82 of the Convention' and that 'New Zealand's rights and obligations under article 82 of the Convention' should be taken into account in setting the rate of royalties payable in relation to the resource development.[55] In any case, such developments will not take place for the foreseeable future in New Zealand's case, as a moratorium on new offshore oil and gas exploration has been in place since 2018.[56]

Status of article 82 in customary international law

At least one State that is not a party to the UNCLOS (the United States), may, in the near future, begin exploitation of resources on its shelf beyond national jurisdiction. As already discussed, the United States is actively soliciting expressions of interest in exploring these resources. As the United States is not a party to the UNCLOS, a key question becomes whether the US is nonetheless bound to observe the provisions of article 82 as a part of customary international law.[57]

Here it is worth observing that it is possible for a treaty provision to also be part of customary international law. In the *North Sea Continental Shelf* cases, the ICJ established conditions for the recognition of a treaty provision as customary law. In particular, the provision must be of a norm-creating character that could be regarded as forming the basis of a general rule of international law.[58] State practice should be extensive, virtually uniform, and include specially affected States.[59]

In the past a number of international courts and tribunals have considered aspects of the Convention to be customary international law. Although some provisions of UNCLOS reflected custom at the time the negotiations concluded, others have subsequently been found to have developed into custom.

In relation to the continental shelf, one of the most frequently considered questions is whether article 76, which establishes the circumstances in which a continental shelf may extend beyond 200 M, has become a rule of customary international law. Some scholars (and States) have suggested that article 1 of the 1958 Geneva Convention on the Continental Shelf,[60] which stated that one determinant of the outer limit of the shelf was 'where the depth of the superjacent waters admits of the exploitation of the natural resources of the said areas', allows States to claim rights to the shelf beyond 200 M.[61] Article 1 of the Continental Shelf Convention was

54 See R.J. Harrison, 'Offshore oil development in uncharted legal waters: Will the proposed Bay du Nord project precipitate another federal-provincial conflict?', *Energy Regulation Quarterly* 6(4), 2018. See also Tuerk, op. cit., p. 254.

55 New Zealand, Continental Shelf Act 1964, section 5A. See also Tuerk, at 254.

56 New Zealand, Crown Minerals (Petroleum) Amendment Bill, 2018.

57 For a more in-depth discussion of the customary international law status of Part VI of UNCLOS, see Mossop, op. cit., pp. 82–91.

58 *North Sea Continental Shelf (Federal Republic of Germany/Denmark; Federal Republic of Germany/Netherlands)* ICJ Reports 1969, p. 3 [*North Sea Continental Shelf Cases*], at paras 70–74.

59 Aara. 74, ibid.

60 Convention on the Continental Shelf (opened for signature 29 April 1958, entered into force 10 June 1964), 499 UNTS 312.

61 See D. Attard, *The Exclusive Economic Zone in international law*, Oxford: Clarendon Press, 1987, p. 134; K.A. Baumert, 'The outer limits of the continental shelf under customary international law', *American Journal of International Law* 111, 201, 827 at 834. See also Letter of Submittal, Treaty between the United States and Mexico on the Delimitation of the Continental Shelf in the Western Gulf of Mexico beyond 200 Nautical Miles as cited in *Digest of United States Practice in International Law*, 2000, p. 699. Available online https://www.state.gov/wp-content/uploads/2020/02/US_Mexico_2000_withExtension.pdf (accessed 24 May 2021).

considered by the ICJ to be part of customary international law in the North Sea Continental Shelf cases.[62]

The next question is whether all of article 76 of the UNCLOS is customary international law. International courts have only expressed a view that paragraph 1 is customary international law,[63] and there appears to be sufficient evidence that the extension of coastal state rights to the continental shelf extends to the continental margin under customary international law.[64] However, the official position of the United States is that paragraphs 1 to 7 of article 76 are customary international law.[65] Baumert details evidence that 40 coastal States have relied on paragraphs 2 to 7, either prior to entry into force of the Convention, or as non-parties.[66]

The reason that the customary status of article 76 is relevant here, is that articles 76 and 82 were inextricably linked in the minds of many delegates. In return for allowing broad-margin states to delineate continental shelf limits beyond 200 nautical miles from baselines along the coast, these States agreed to both the constraints or 'cut off' lines included in article 76[67] and the revenue sharing regime in article 82 of the UNCLOS.[68] This balance was reflected in statements by Tommy Koh in his closing statement to the Conference on the Law of the Sea in 1982. Ambassador Koh identified the package deal in the UNCLOS meant that 'it is not possible for a State to pick what it likes and disregard what it does not like'.[69] In 1985 Caminos and Molitor argued that the deliberate reliance on a package deal approach 'has created some profound juridical implications for the traditional treaty-custom rules' although they admitted being unsure exactly what they were.[70] However, the authors suggested that third States may begin to acquire rights from the UNCLOS, but that 'such a process represents a two-edged sword in that it may make equally applicable to third states the innovative obligations in the Convention'.[71]

In contrast to article 76, it is very difficult to find State practice or opinion juris that supports article 82 being customary international law. Roach and Smith state that it is 'widely accepted' that the broad principles in articles 76–81 were established as customary international law, omitting reference to article 82.[72] The absence of public statements or exploitation on extended continental shelves and thus implementation of article 82 in practice, makes this much more difficult to argue than with respect to article 76.

62 *North Sea Continental Shelf Cases*, op. cit., para. 63.

63 See *Territorial and Maritime Dispute* op. cit., p. 624, paras 117–118. Columbia's position was that paragraphs 4 to 9 of article 76 were not part of customary international law, but the ICJ decided it did not need to consider the status of other paragraphs.

64 See generally Baumert, op. cit., p. 845.

65 Memorandum from Assistant Secretary John D. Negroponte to Deputy Legal Adviser Elizabeth Verville, 17 November 1987, State Department File No P89 0140-428, II *Cumulative Digest* p. 1878, cited in J. Ashley Roach and R.W. Smith, *Excessive maritime claims*, 3rd ed, Leiden: Martinus Nijhoff, 2012, p. 188. See also Baumert, op. cit.

66 Baumert, op. cit., p. 853.

67 Namely, 350 M from baselines along the coast or 100 M seaward of the 2,500 metre isobath or depth contour in keeping with article 76(5) of the UNCLOS.

68 See, for example, R.R. Churchill and A.V. Lowe, *The law of the sea*, 3rd ed, Manchester: Manchester University Press, 1999, p. 157.

69 *Official Records* Vol XVII, 193rd Meeting, 19 December 1982, pp. 132–136, para. 47.

70 H. Caminos and M. Molitor, 'Progressive development of international law and the package deal', *American Journal of International Law* 79, 1985, 871–890, at 884.

71 Ibid., 888. See also William T. Burke, 'Customary law as reflected in the LOS Convention: A slippery formula' in John P. Craven, Jan Schneider and Carol Stimson (eds) *The international implications of extended maritime jurisdiction in the pacific,* Honolulu: Law of the Sea Institute, 1987, pp. 402–409, at p. 404, arguing that article 82 and 76 were interlinked and so if article 82 was not custom, article 76 could not be.

72 Roach and Smith, op. cit., p. 193.

> The US has frequently commented on its perception of the status of the [UNCLOS] as customary international law. In 1987 an Interagency Group on the Law of the Sea and Ocean Policy affirmed its belief that the provisions of Article 76 reflect customary international law. A commentary prepared for the US Senate did not take a position on Article 82's status in customary international law, but did state that the revenue-sharing arrangements relating to continental shelf areas seaward of 200 M from the coast 'is part of a package that establishes with clarity and legal certainty the control of coastal States over the full extent of their geological continental margins' and that '[o]n balance' the package contained in the Convention, 'including revenue sharing at the modest rate set forth in article 82, clearly serves United States interests'.[73]

However, The United States Minerals Management Service has advised potential leaseholders that additional royalty payments may apply if the US 'becomes a party to the 1982 Law of the Sea Convention (…) prior to or during the life of a lease' issued by the US concerning a block or portion of a block located beyond the US EEZ'[74] indicating that additional royalty payments become relevant only when the US ratifies the UNCLOS.

The only coherent argument to be made in favour of article 82's customary status is based on the idea that the status of article 82 is tied to the customary international law of article 76. This would reflect an argument similar to that used in *Nicaragua v Colombia* by the ICJ, such that the paragraphs of article 121 were an 'indivisible regime' so that the customary status of the first two paragraphs implied the same status for the third.[75] This is supported by the views expressed by Caminos and Molitar that the package deal has significant implications for the formation of customary law. However, unlike the paragraphs of article 121, there is no explicit link in the text between articles 76 and 82.[76] A further problem is that article 82 refers to the ISA which is a creation of the UNCLOS, perhaps indicating that the article is not of a 'norm-creating nature' as per the *Continental Shelf* cases.

Of course, for a non-party to the UNCLOS to rely on (even implicitly) article 76 to determine the outer limits of the continental shelf beyond 200 nautical miles but simultaneously deny the customary status of article 82 would seem to stretch the boundaries of good faith. It would therefore be appropriate for States in that position to carefully consider applying Article 82 as a matter of policy.[77]

Conclusion

Article 82 was drafted as a compromise between the opposing view of broad shelf States and those that were keen to restrain coastal State jurisdiction over both water column and continental shelf

73 Commentary – The 1982 United Nations Convention on the Law of the Sea and the Agreement on Implementation of Part XI, Senate Treaty Doc. 103–139, cited in Roach and Smith, op. cit., p. 192.

74 See, for example, MMS, Department of the Interior, Lease Stipulations, Western Planning Area, Oil and Gas Lease Sale 207, Final Notice of Sale, Stipulation 4; and Gulf of Mexico OCS Oil and Gas Lease Sale 2012, Central Planning Area Lease Sale 216/222. BOEM 2012-058.

75 *Nicaragua v Colombia* para. 139. For a detailed analysis of the position of Colombia with regard to seabed mining of minerals, see in this book E. Restrepo Uribe, 'Colombia and seabed mining' in V. Tassin Campanella (ed), *Routledge handbook of seabed mining and the law of the sea*, op. cit., chapter VI.2.3.

76 See further, Mossop, op. cit., p. 89.

77 Ibid., 91.

rights to 200 M from baselines along the coast. While the broad shelf States were successful in retaining their claimed rights over continental shelf areas, there was, however, a twofold 'price' to pay. First was acceptance of the constraints concerning the outer limits to the continental shelf seawards of 200 M limits contained in article 76 of the UNCLOS. The second was acceptance of the revenue-sharing provisions provided under article 82 of the Convention.

It is well established that article 82 is replete with terms that are undefined and capable of varied interpretation. It appears that this definitional uncertainty was deliberate on the part of the drafters of the Convention. Clarity regarding the uncertainties inherent in article 82 has remained elusive, despite valuable work by the ILA and ISA as well as the law of the sea community.

A key reason for continuing uncertainty is also the absence of State practice implementing article 82. It is, however, clear that there is considerable seabed resource exploration interest in parts of the outer continental shelf, notably from the oil industry with over 100 exploration blocks located wholly or partially beyond 200 M limits. Further, discoveries have been made around 270 M offshore Newfoundland, raising the prospect that Canada may be the first coastal State to implement this heretofore dormant provision of the Convention.

That said, it remains to be seen whether these discoveries are commercially viable. Moreover, against the context of the present climate crisis, it would surely be wiser to leave hydrocarbon resources in the shelf. This would be consistent with the practice of some broad margin States such as New Zealand which has imposed a moratorium on new offshore oil and gas developments as well as the International Energy Agency's call for no new fossil fuel developments to be initiated.[78] If this path is followed, then article 82 will become a redundant provision of the Convention and this contribution will be similarly irrelevant!

References

Attard D., *The exclusive economic zone in international law*, Oxford: Clarendon Press, 1987.

Baumert K.A., 'The outer limits of the continental shelf under customary international law', *American Journal of International Law* 111, 2017, 827–872.

Bird K.J. et al., 'Circum-polar resource appraisal: Estimates of undiscovered oil and gas north of the arctic circle', USGS *Fact Sheet* 2008-3049. Available online <http://pubs.usgs.gov/fs/2008/3049/fs2008-3049.pdf> (accessed 18 May 2021).

Caminos H. and Molitor M., 'Progressive development of international law and the package deal', *American Journal of International Law* 79, 1985, 871–189.

Chircop A., 'Article 82', in A. Proelss (ed.), *United Nations Convention on the Law of the Sea: A commentary*, London: Bloomsbury, 2017, 639–651.

Chircop A., 'Implementation of Article 82 of the United Nations convention on the law of the sea: The challenge for Canada', in C. Banet (ed.), *The law of the seabed*, Leiden: Brill, 2020, 371–394

Churchill R.R. and Lowe A.V., *The law of the sea*, 3rd ed., Manchester: Manchester University Press, 1999.

Davenport T., 'Southeast Asia and seabed mining', in V. Tassin Campanella (ed.), *Routledge handbook of seabed mining and the law of the sea*, London: Routledge, 2023, chapter VI.1.7.

Egede E., 'Africa and seabed mining', in V. Tassin Campanella (ed.), *Routledge handbook of seabed mining and the law of the sea*, London: Routledge, 2023, chapter VI.1.1.

Harrison R.J., 'Article 82 of UNCLOS: The day of reckoning approaches', *Journal of World Energy Law and Business* 10, 2017, 488–504.

Harrison R.J., 'Offshore oil development in uncharted legal waters: Will the proposed Bay du Nord project precipitate another federal-provincial conflict?', *Energy Regulation Quarterly* 6(4), December 2018. Online. Available at <https://energyregulationquarterly.ca/articles/offshore-oil-development-in-uncharted

78 See International Energy Agency (IEA), *Net Zero by 2050: A Roadmap for the Global Energy Sector*, at pp. 20–21. Paris: IEA, May 2021.

-legal-waters-will-the-proposed-bay-du-nord-project-precipitate-another-federal-provincial-conflict #sthash.fT6SGqsz.dpbs> (accessed 24 May 2021).

Jensen Ø. and Magnússon B.M., 'The extension of sovereign rights beyond 200 nautical miles', in V. Tassin Campanella (ed.), *Routledge handbook of seabed mining and the law of the sea*, London: Routledge, 2023, chapter III.1.

Jimenez Pineda E., 'South American region and seabed mining', in V. Tassin Campanella (ed.), *Routledge handbook of seabed mining and the law of the sea*, London: Routledge, chapter VI.1.6.

Kwiatkowska B., *The 200 mile exclusive economic zone in the new law of the sea*, Dordrecht: Martinus Nijhoff, 1989.

Lavis J., 'Shallow, mid to ultra-deepwater definitions', *Drillers.com*, 6 April 2018. Available online at <https://drillers.com/shallow-mid-to-ultra-deepwater-definitions/#:~:text=%E2%80%A6,at%20the%20time%20of%20writing.> (accessed 24 May 2021).

Lodge M.W., 'The international seabed authority and Article 82 of the UN Convention on the law of the sea', *International Journal of Marine and Coastal Law* 21, 2001, 323–333.

Lodge M.W., 'Enclosure of the oceans versus the common heritage of mankind: The inherent tension between the continental shelf beyond 100 nautical miles and the Area', *International Legal Studies* 97, 2021, 803–883.

Mossop J., *The continental shelf beyond 200 nautical miles: Rights and responsibilities*, Oxford: Oxford University Press, 2016.

Restrepo Uribe E., 'Colombia and seabed mining', in V. Tassin Campanella (ed.), *Routledge handbook of seabed mining and the law of the sea*, London: Routledge, 2023, chapter VI.2.3.

Roach A.J. and Smith R.W., *Excessive maritime claims*, 3rd ed., Leiden: Martinus Nijhoff, 2012.

Schofield C.H., 'The regime of islands reframed: Developments in the definition of islands and their role in the delimitation of maritime boundaries under the international law of the sea', *Brill Research Perspectives in the Law of the Sea* 3(1–2), 2021, 1–126.

da Silva A.P., 'Dealing with Articles 76 and 82 of the United Nations convention on the law of the sea: Legal and political challenges for Brazil', *Ocean Yearbook* 28, 2014, 145–172.

Spicer W., 'Canada, the law of the sea treaty and international payments: Where will the money come from?', University of Calgary, School of Public Policy, *SPP Research Papers* 8-31, September 2015, at 18–20. Available online at https://papers.ssrn.com/sol3/papers.cfm?abstract_id=2658802 (accessed 24 May 2021).

Spicer W. and McIsaac E., *A study of key terms in Article 82 of the United Nations Convention on the Law of the Sea*, ISA Technical Study No. 15, 2016.

Tassin Campanella V., Cissé Y. and Tladi D., 'Rights and obligations of States', in V. Tassin Campanella (ed.), *Routledge handbook of seabed mining and the law of the sea*, London: Routledge, 2023, chapter II.1.

Tuerk H., 'Questions relating to the continental shelf beyond 200 nautical miles: Delimitation, delineation, and revenue sharing', *International Legal Studies* 97, 2021, 232–258.

Vasciannie S.C., *Land-locked and geographically disadvantaged states in the international law of the sea*, Oxford: Clarendon Press, 1990.

Policy documents

International Energy Agency (IEA), Newt Zero by 2050: A Roadmap for the Global Energy Sector. Paris: IEA, May 2021. Online. Available at https://www.iea.org/reports/net-zero-by-2050.

International Law Association (ILA), Committee on the Outer Continental Shelf, 'Report on Article 82 and the 1982 UN Convention on the Law of the Sea', 2008.

International Seabed Authority, *Implementation of Article 82 of the United Nations Convention on the Law of the Sea*, ISA Technical Study No. 12, 2015.

International Seabed Authority, *Issues Associated with the Implementation of Article 82 of the United Nations Convention on the Law of the Sea*, ISA Technical Study No. 4, 2015.

International Seabed Authority, *Non-Living Resources of the Continental Shelf Beyond 200 Nautical Miles: Speculations on the Implementation of Article 82 of the United Nations Convention on the Law of the Sea*, ISA Technical Study No. 5, 2015.

PART IV

The Area

IV.1

THE AREA AND THE ROLE OF THE INTERNATIONAL SEABED AUTHORITY

Aline Jaeckel

Introduction

In Arvid Pardo's well-known speech to the United Nations (UN) in 1967, he not only outlined his and Elisabeth Mann Borgese's vision of the international seabed becoming the common heritage of (hu)mankind but also envisaged an entity to give practical effect to this status. He imagined an 'agency with adequate powers to administer in the interests of mankind the oceans and the ocean floor beyond national jurisdiction'.[1] The entity established under the *United Nations Convention on the Law of the Sea* (UNCLOS) to fulfil this role is the International Seabed Authority (hereinafter ISA or Authority).[2] Its jurisdiction covers the entire seabed beyond national jurisdiction, otherwise known as 'the Area'.[3] In other words, the ISA is the institutional manifestation of the Area's legal status as the common heritage of humankind.[4] Details on the concept of the common heritage of (hu)mankind are provided in Chapter I.2 of this book.

Instead of offering a description of the ISA's mandate under UNCLOS, as is already available in the literature,[5] this chapter critically examines the ISA's role and mandate in light of current developments. In doing so, it discusses the extent to which the ISA has given effect to the common heritage principle to date, including through the Enterprise, site-banking system, and a benefit sharing regime.

The underlying reason for declaring the Area to be the common heritage of humankind was to ensure that all states, no matter their economic status, would share the benefits of the mineral resources that lie beyond national jurisdiction. This would prevent a small number of technologically advanced states from reaping all the benefits at the expense of the international community.[6]

1 UNGA, 1 November 1967, UN Doc A/C.1./PV.1516, paras. 8–9 (UNGA, A/C.1./PV.1516).

2 *United Nations Convention on the Law of the Sea*, 10 December 1982, 1833 UNTS 3. Hereinafter 'UNCLOS'.

3 Article 1(1)(1), UNCLOS.

4 Article 136, UNCLOS.

5 M.W. Lodge, 'The deep seabed', in D. Rothwell et al. (eds), *The Oxford handbook of the law of the sea*, Oxford University Press, 2015, 226–53; A.L. Jaeckel, *The International Seabed Authority and the precautionary principle*, Brill Nijhoff, 2017, Chs 3, 4.

6 R. Churchill and A.V. Lowe, *The law of the sea*, Manchester University Press, 1999, p. 224.

DOI: 10.4324/9780429426162-13

In line with this aim, Part XI of UNCLOS as well as the 1994 Agreement[7] set out a framework regime for the Area. Central to this regime is the ISA, which was created in 1994 and is headquartered in Kingston, Jamaica. It is mandated to organise, carry out, and control 'activities in the Area',[8] a term of art that encompasses all activities relating to exploration for and exploitation of mineral resources in the Area.[9] This mandate is underpinned by far-reaching competencies which include regulatory, enforcement, inspection, and oversight powers.[10]

While UNCLOS and the 1994 Agreement set out the broad legal framework for the activities in the Area, the ISA is tasked with filling the gaps and developing detailed and binding regulations that determine who can access minerals in the Area and under what conditions. Indeed, the ISA is currently in the process of developing the first international regulations for the commercial-scale exploitation of minerals in the Area. These extensive powers to regulate access to and management of minerals in the Area distinguish the ISA from other international organisations and make it 'an unprecedented experiment in international law-making'.[11]

The next section introduces the actors of the seabed mining regime and offers reflections on the challenges created by the ISA's contractual system. Following that, the chapter discusses the ISA's mandate against the background of current discussions regarding the implementation of the common heritage concept. The discussion is structured in sub-sections on regulating seabed mining, controlling access to minerals, the participation of developing states, the sharing of benefits, and compliance and enforcement. The final section offers concluding remarks.

Actors and the contractual system of the deep seabed mining regime

Before examining the mandate and role of the ISA, this section provides a brief introduction to the actors involved in the seabed mining regime. While the ISA is the central regulator and administrator of the regime, the mining activities are carried out by so-called contractors. As illustrated in Figure IV.1.1, these can be the Enterprise (as discussed below), states parties, state enterprises, or natural or juridical persons which possess the nationality of states parties or are effectively controlled by them or their nationals.[12] Thus, both public and private actors can be involved in mining operations although they have to be sponsored by a state party.[13]

The sponsoring state has an oversight role and a due diligence obligation to ensure that the contractor complies with all legal obligations.[14] The sponsoring state can be held liable if environmental harm is caused by the contractor and the state did not meet its due diligence obligation.[15] However, the precise parameters of the role of the sponsoring state remain unclear.

7 *Agreement Relating to the Implementation of Part XI of the United Nations Convention on the Law of the Sea*, 28 July 1994, 1836 UNTS 3. Hereinafter '1994 Agreement'.

8 Articles 153(1), 157(1), UNCLOS.

9 Article 1(1)(3), UNCLOS.

10 See e.g. Articles 137(2), 145, 153, 157, 160(2), 162(2), UNCLOS.

11 J. Harrison, *Making the law of the sea: A study in the development of international law*, Cambridge University Press, 2011, pp. 151–2.

12 Article 153(2), UNCLOS.

13 Article 153(2)(b), ibid., and article 4, Annex III, UNCLOS.

14 *Responsibilities and Obligations of States Sponsoring Persons and Entities with Respect to Activities in the Area, Advisory Opinion, ITLOS Reports 2011, case no 17*. Hereinafter 'ITLOS, *Responsibilities and Obligations of States*'.

15 Ibid.

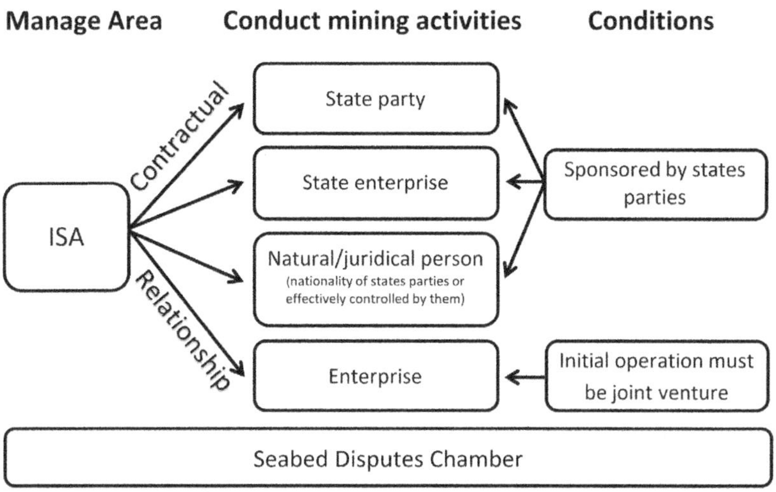

Figure IV.1.1 The structure of the seabed mining regime.
Source: Aline Jaeckel, *The International Seabed Authority and the Precautionary Principle* (Brill, 2017).

Finally, the Seabed Disputes Chamber offers judicial oversight of the seabed mining regime.[16] Originally intended to be an organ of the ISA,[17] the Seabed Disputes Chamber is based within the International Tribunal for the Law of the Sea (ITLOS) in Hamburg. As discussed in detail by Treves, Harrison, and Pecoraro in Chapters V.1 and V.2,[18] the Chamber has compulsory jurisdiction in respect of most disputes concerning activities in the Area[19] as well as jurisdiction to give advisory opinions at the request of the ISA Assembly or Council.[20]

Instead of the mining operators working under a license from the regulator, as is often the case for resource extraction under domestic governance, the Area regime involves a contractual system. Exploration and exploitation work in the Area can only be conducted under a contract issued by the ISA, which grants exclusive but temporary rights to the contractor.[21] This ensures a high degree of legal certainty for the contractor, as the conditions under which the contractor operates can, largely, not be changed unilaterally by the ISA.

However, the contractual system poses at least two challenges. First, it constrains the ISA's regulatory power and ability to impose new conditions on mining operators if new circumstances arise.[22] For example, if states were to agree on a new treaty with stringent measures to protect

16 Articles 186–191, Annex VI, articles 35–40, UNCLOS.

17 Judge Dolliver Nelson, 'The International Tribunal for the Law of the Sea', Presentation given at the Sensitization Seminar on the Work of the International Seabed Authority, 28–30 March 2011. Available online <www.isa.org.jm/files/documents/EN/Seminars/2011/ITLOS-DNelson.pdf> (accessed 18 August 2021).

18 T. Treves, 'Dispute settlement and seabed mining in the Area', in V. Tassin Campanella (ed), *Routledge handbook of seabed mining and the law of the sea*, Routledge, 2023, chapter V.1; and J. Harrison and A. Pecoraro, 'Dispute settlement options and rights of participation in deep seabed mining disputes', in V. Tassin Campanella (ed), op. cit., chapter V.2.

19 Article 187, UNCLOS.

20 Article 191, ibid.

21 Articles 3, 16, Annex III, UNCLOS.

22 For a detailed discussion, see A. Jaeckel, 'Deep seabed mining and adaptive management: the procedural challenges for the International Seabed Authority', *Marine Policy* 70, 2016, 205–11.

marine biodiversity, the ISA would have very limited ability to require current contractors to alter their operations to give effect to the new treaty. Instead, contractors would need to agree to the change, as their interests are protected through the contract. Indeed, the same applies to amendments of the ISA's regulations. In 2013, the Nodules Exploration Regulations were formally amended largely to increase environmental standards and obligations. The ISA Council did not ask for existing contracts to be renegotiated.[23] Thus, we can assume[24] that those operators that concluded their nodules exploration contracts prior to July 2013 continue to be subject to the lower environmental standards under the previous version of the Nodules Exploration Regulations.[25]

In light of the contractual system, designing flexibility into the contracts and the ISA's rules, regulations, and procedures becomes all the more important. Given that exploration contracts have a 15-year lifespan and exploitation contracts could be valid for 30 years, good regulatory design will be crucial to ensure that the ISA can regulate and manage deep seabed mining flexibly and reflect policy and legal changes that will inevitably occur over the coming decades as scientific knowledge about the effects of deep seabed mining increases.

Second, the contractual system poses challenges for transparency. Exploration contracts have been largely treated as confidential. While the standard contract clauses are publically available,[26] the actual contract and any subsequent modifications agreed between the parties remain confidential with only a few exceptions.[27] This prevents member states of the Authority from exercising oversight. Indeed, it is reflective of a culture of confidentiality at the ISA that has been widely criticised, especially in light of the ISA's mandate to act on behalf of humankind as a whole.[28] The current (2019) draft exploitation regulations might deliver some improvement in this regard as they foresee publication of exploitation contracts.[29]

Mandate of the International Seabed Authority

The core mandate of the ISA is to act on behalf of humankind in administering the Area and its mineral resources.[30] This involves ensuring that activities in the Area are benefitting humankind

23 ISA, *Regulations on Prospecting and Exploration for Polymetallic Nodules in the Area*, ISBA/19/C/17, 22 July 2013, para. 3. Hereinafter 'ISA, *Regulations on Prospecting and Exploration for Polymetallic Nodules in the Area*'.

24 Because the exploration contracts between the ISA and the contractors are confidential, it is difficult to know whether any amendments were negotiated and what these entail.

25 The Seabed Disputes Chamber aimed to address this gap in environmental standards by finding e.g. that the obligation to apply best environmental practices, which was only incorporated in later sets of exploration regulations, forms part of a sponsoring state's due diligence obligation, and thus applies beyond the scope of the exploration regulations. See ITLOS, *Responsibilities and Obligations of States*, op. cit., note 14, para. 136.

26 They are annexed to the relevant exploration regulations. See e.g. ISA, *Regulations on Prospecting and Exploration for Polymetallic Nodules in the Area*, op. cit., note 23, Annex IV.

27 See e.g. the information published by one of the ISA contractors, UK Seabed Resources Ltd. Available online <https://www.lockheedmartin.com/en-gb/products/uk-seabed-resources/uk-seabed-resources-documents.html> (accessed 18 August 2021).

28 J.A. Ardron et al., 'Incorporating transparency into the governance of deep-seabed mining in the Area beyond national jurisdiction', *Marine Policy* 89, 2018, 58–66; K. Willaert, 'Public participation in the context of deep sea mining: luxury or legal obligation?', *Ocean and Coastal Management* 198, 2020, 105368; K. Komaki and D. Fluharty, 'Options to improve transparency of environmental monitoring governance for polymetallic nodule mining in the Area', *Frontiers in Marine Science* 7, 2020, 247.

29 ISA, *Draft Regulations on Exploitation of Mineral Resources in the Area*, ISBA/25/C/WP.1, draft regulation 17(3), 22 March 2019. Hereinafter 'ISA, *Draft Regulations on Exploitation of Mineral Resources*'.

30 Articles 153(1), 157(1), UNCLOS.

as a whole and that the benefits are shared equitably amongst states.[31] Discussions are underway as to which benefits humankind can best derive from the Area and how those might be shared. UNCLOS provides some guidance by providing for preferential treatment of developing states, including through the site-banking system and the Enterprise, as discussed below.

The ISA is to use its conferred powers to organise, control, and carry out activities in the Area, particularly with a view to administering the mineral resources of the Area.[32] This requires the ISA to develop the legal framework by adopting detailed rules, regulations, and procedures for prospecting, exploration, and exploitation of minerals in the Area.

Simultaneously, the ISA has an environmental mandate, requiring it to take 'necessary measures [...] to ensure effective protection for the marine environment from harmful effects which may arise' from seabed mining.[33] This umbrella provision in UNCLOS, supported by a number of more specific provisions,[34] grants the ISA a broad capacity to enact environmentally protective measures as it deems necessary.[35] Striking a balance between mining and environmental protection is one of the core challenges for the ISA.

In line with its common heritage mandate, the constituency of the ISA reaches beyond its member states and encompasses humankind as a whole. Nonetheless, decision-making power at the ISA rests with its 167 member states, which are represented in the ISA Assembly.[36] In practice though, decisions are largely taken by a small sub-set of states, namely the 36 member states on the ISA Council.[37] This is unusual amongst international organisations. While many organisations have a small council or board that assists the plenary body, that organ ordinarily has a narrow task.[38] In contrast, the Council is the ISA's primary decision-making organ with an extensive mandate to establish specific policies on *any matter* within the competencies of the ISA, including developing and adopting the Mining Code,[39] granting access to minerals,[40] and 'exercis[ing] control over the activities in the Area'.[41] In other words, despite the fact that the ISA has the unique mandate to govern our common heritage of humankind, its institutional structure is unusually restrictive, conferring governing responsibilities to a small group of 36 states.[42] It is perhaps questionable whether

31 Article 140, ibid.

32 Articles 153(1), 157(1), ibid.

33 Article 145, ibid.

34 For a detailed discussion of the ISA's environmental mandate, see Jaeckel, op. cit., note 5, Ch. 4.

35 F.M. Armas-Pfirter, 'The International Seabed Authority and the protection of biodiversity', in A. de Paiva Toledo and V.J.M. Tassin (eds), *Guide to the navigation of marine biodiversity beyond national jurisdiction*, Editora D'Placido, 2017, 223–48.

36 As of May 2020, the ISA has 168 members (167 states plus the EU). See ISA, *Report of the Secretary-General of the International Seabed Authority under article 166, paragraph 4, of the United Nations Convention on the Law of the Sea*, ISBA/26/A/2, 6 July 2020, para. 4.

37 For a detailed discussion on the ISA Council, see Jaeckel, 2017, op. cit., note 5, Ch. 3.4.2.

38 H.G. Schermers and N.M. Blokker, *International institutional law*, 6th ed, Brill, 2018, pp. 316–29.

39 Article 162(2)(o), UNCLOS; Sections 1(15)–(16), Annex, 1994 Agreement.

40 Section 3(11), Annex, 1994 Agreement.

41 Articles 153(4), 162(2)(l), UNCLOS.

42 Reflecting the importance of the ISA Council, its membership rotates and follows a complex formula of five interest groups: (a) consumers and importers of relevant minerals, (b) investors in seabed mining activities, (c) net exporters of relevant minerals, (d) developing states representing special interests such as island states, and (e) members representing equitable geographic distribution. See section 3(15), Annex, 1994 Agreement; for a table of the current membership of the Council see the list available online <https://www.isa.org.jm/authority/council-members> (accessed 18 August 2021).

decisions that are meant to reflect the interests of humankind as a whole[43] are best taken by a small group of states. The shifting of power from the ISA's plenary organ to the small Council occurred as part of renegotiating the Area regime in the early 1990s, culminating in the 1994 Agreement. The changes introduced by the Implementing Agreement jeopardised the operationalisation of the common heritage principle, while maintaining the label.[44]

As the ISA's focus is limited to mineral resources, unrelated seabed activities, such as deep sea fishing[45] or laying submarine cables and pipelines,[46] fall outside of its mandate. Furthermore, the ISA's jurisdiction is spatially limited to the international seabed, ocean floor, and subsoil thereof and does not include the waters superjacent to the Area.[47] One exception is the ISA's environmental mandate. Indeed, the obligation to protect the marine environment extends to the water column and coastal areas.[48] Thus, the ISA must protect all marine flora and fauna, regardless of where they occur in the ocean, though only from the effects of seabed mining.[49]

The magnitude of the ISA's task should not be underestimated. Despite only having a small Secretariat and its main organs only meeting twice a year, the ISA must administer and regulate a frontier industry which carries serious environmental risks[50] and which is riddled with uncertainties regarding the economic profitability,[51] technological feasibility,[52] and environmental sustainability of mining,[53] all while acting on behalf of humankind as a whole, and ensuring that benefits are shared equitably. In recognition of these factors, the mandate of the ISA is broad and extensive, comprising the following:

(1) regulatory powers to adopt the Mining Code and balance environmental protection with mineral development;
(2) gate-keeping functions to control access to minerals in the Area through the aforementioned contractual system;
(3) obligation to enable effective participation of developing states, including through the site-banking system and the Enterprise;
(4) obligation to share the benefits of activities in the Area; and
(5) far-reaching competencies to ensure compliance.

Each of these functions is discussed in turn in the following sections.

43 Article 140, UNCLOS.
44 See e.g. B.H. Oxman, 'The 1994 Agreement and the Convention', *The American Journal of International Law* 88, 1994, 687–96.
45 Articles 87(1), 116, UNCLOS.
46 Article 112, ibid.
47 Article 135, ibid.
48 Article 145, ibid.; S.N. Nandan et al., *United Nations Convention on the Law of the Sea, 1982: A commentary, volume VI*, Martinus Nijhoff Publishers, 2002, p. 196.
49 A. Jaeckel, 'An environmental management strategy for the international seabed authority? The legal basis', *The International Journal of Marine and Coastal Law* 30, 2015, 93–119, pp. 100–1.
50 D.O.B. Jones et al., 'Mining deep-ocean mineral deposits: what are the ecological risks?', *Elements* 14, 2018, 325–30.
51 M.V. Folkersen et al., 'Depths of uncertainty for deep-sea policy and legislation', *Global Environmental Change* 54, 2019, 1–5.
52 Midas Consortium, 'Managing impacts of deep sea resource exploitation: research highlights', 2016. Available online <https://www.eu-midas.net/sites/default/files/downloads/MIDAS_research_highlights_low_res.pdf> (accessed 18 August 2021), p. 24.
53 H.J. Niner et al., 'Deep-sea mining with no net loss of biodiversity—an impossible aim', *Frontiers in Marine Science* 5, 2018, 53, 1–12.

Regulating deep seabed mining

From the inception of the Area regime, Arvid Pardo stressed the need for the common heritage to be administered by an entity that has 'the power effectively to regulate the commercial exploitation of the ocean floor'.[54] This was realised through the ISA's regulatory powers.

UNCLOS requires the ISA to adopt rules, regulations, and procedures for all aspects of activities in the Area.[55] These include environmental protection,[56] financial management and internal administration of the ISA,[57] and equitable sharing of the financial and other economic benefits from seabed mining.[58] Importantly, the Mining Code must build upon, and add detail to, the general obligations contained in UNCLOS. As such, the Mining Code is considered 'subsidiary and supplementary to the Convention'.[59]

The Mining Code includes legally binding regulations as well as non-binding recommendations. It is envisaged that the future exploitation regulations will be supplemented by legally binding standards as well as guidelines.[60]

What is particularly significant is the ISA's power to adopt regulations that are *legally binding* on *all* member states, as well as contractors. This is highly unusual for an international organisation.[61] Amongst the few international organisations with the power to take binding decisions on matters beyond internal issues, most allow their member states to opt out of decisions. In contrast, ISA regulations are binding on all members without them needing to give individual consent and, more importantly, without the possibility to opt out.

These exceptionally far-reaching regulatory powers must be understood in light of the ISA's mandate to act on behalf of humankind as a whole. There are no precedents for this. The ISA is the only 'international resource management' organisation.[62] It acts as what Pardo called the 'trustee'[63] of the mineral wealth in areas beyond national jurisdiction. In doing so, the ISA must determine which rules apply to anyone seeking to access and mine the minerals. If a state could opt out, the integrity of the entire system would be compromised.

Using its regulatory powers, the ISA has adopted three sets of regulations for prospecting and exploration of polymetallic nodules,[64] polymetallic sulphides,[65] and ferromanganese crusts[66]

54 UNGA, A/C.1./PV.1516, op. cit., note 1, paras. 8–9.

55 Articles 137(2), 160(2)(f)(ii) 162(2)(o)(ii), 209, UNCLOS, and article 17(1), Annex III, UNCLOS.

56 Article 145, UNCLOS.

57 Articles 160(2)(f)(ii), 162(2)(o)(ii), ibid.

58 Articles 82, 160(2)(f)(i), 162(2)(o)(i), ibid.

59 Preparatory Commission for the ISA and ITLOS, LOS/PCN/SCN.3/WP.1, 8 March 1984, para. 2.

60 ISA, *Draft Regulations on Exploitation of Mineral Resources in the Area*, op. cit., draft regulations 94, 95.

61 For a detailed discussion of the ISA's regulatory powers, see Harrison, op. cit., note 11; Jaeckel, op. cit., note 5, Ch. 5.2.

62 A.E. Boyle, 'Saving the world – implementation and enforcement of international environmental law through international institutions', *Journal of Environmental Law* 3(2), 1991, 229–45, p. 240.

63 UNGA, A/C.1./PV.1516, op. cit., note 1, para. 8.

64 ISA, *Regulations on Prospecting and Exploration for Polymetallic Nodules in the Area*, op. cit., note 23.

65 ISA, *Regulations on Prospecting and Exploration for Polymetallic Sulphides in the Area*, ISBA/16/A/12/Rev.1, 7 May 2010. Hereinafter 'ISA, *Regulations on Prospecting and Exploration for Polymetallic Sulphides in the Area*'.

66 ISA, *Regulations on Prospecting and Exploration for Cobalt-rich Ferromanganese Crusts in the Area*, ISBA/18/A/11, 22 October 2012. Hereinafter 'ISA, *Regulations on Prospecting and Exploration for Cobalt-rich Ferromanganese Crusts in the Area*'.

as well as a range of supplementary recommendations.[67] Regulations for the commercial-scale exploitation of minerals are currently being developed.

In an effort to broaden input into its regulatory work, the ISA has conducted a series of stakeholder consultations on various aspects of the draft exploitation regulations in recent years. This has allowed states without a seat on the ISA Council, as well as civil society organisations and others, to communicate their views on the evolving draft regulations. However, the extent to which their suggestions have been considered is unclear.

Controlling access to minerals in the Area

The ISA controls access to minerals in the Area. Deciding who receives an exploration or, in the future, exploitation contract, is one of its core mandates.

Assessing applications for so-called plans of work involves the ISA Council and its subsidiary body, the Legal and Technical Commission (LTC).[68] The LTC assesses applications and recommends approval or rejection to the Council which has the final decision-making power with respect to granting mining contracts.[69] A number of challenges exist with respect to the granting of mining contracts.

First, the decision-making process based on UNCLOS is biased in favour of approving an application. Where the LTC recommends approval of an application, the Council 'is essentially required to approve it',[70] except in very unlikely circumstances. If the LTC recommends disapproval or refrains from making any recommendation, the Council can still approve the application.[71] This is problematic as Council members do not have access to the actual application documents but merely to a brief summary of the application provided by the LTC.[72] Thus, the Council is unable to assess an application on its merits. Interestingly, the ISA's plenary organ, the Assembly, is not involved in the approval of exploration or exploitation contracts.

Given this procedural framework, it is perhaps unsurprising that the ISA has never rejected an application to date. Over 30 applications for exploration contracts have been approved.[73] The procedural bias towards approving applications can arguably limit the ISA's ability to implement an ecosystem-based approach,[74] which could involve minimising cumulative environmental impact by limiting the number of parallel mining operations within a region at any one time.

The limited powers of the Council in the approval process can be partially explained by industrialised states, during the negotiations of UNCLOS, seeking to ensure that the ISA would not restrict access to minerals, including on political grounds.[75] Thus, the LTC must approve an appli-

67 A list of ISA Recommendations is available online at <https://www.isa.org.jm/mining-code/recommendations> (accessed 18 August 2021).

68 For details on the process of assessing an application, see Jaeckel, op. cit., note 5, Ch. 3.5.2.

69 Article 165(2)(b), UNCLOS; Annex 3(11), 1994 Agreement.

70 Jaeckel, op. cit., note 5, p. 104; Annex 3(11), 1994 Agreement.

71 Sections 3(5), 3(11), Annex, 1994 Agreement.

72 See e.g. ISA, *Regulations on Prospecting and Exploration for Polymetallic Nodules in the Area*, op. cit., note 2, annex, regulation 36(3); UNCLOS, article 163(8).

73 A list of current contracts is available online at <https://www.isa.org.jm/exploration-contracts> (accessed 18 August 2021).

74 Ecosystem-based management is increasingly incorporated into ISA instruments. See M. Guilhon et al., 'Recognition of ecosystem-based management principles in key documents of the seabed mining regime: implications and further recommendations', *ICES Journal of Marine Science* 78(3), 2021, 884–99.

75 S.N. Nandan et al., *The development of the regime for deep seabed mining*, Kluwer Law International, 2002, p. 40; E.D. Brown, *Sea-bed energy and minerals: the international legal regime, volume 2: sea-bed mining*, Martinus Nijhoff Publishers, 2001, 113–16.

cation if it meets the 'objective and non-discriminatory criteria' set out in article 4 of Annex III to UNCLOS.[76] These criteria are discussed in the following paragraph. As noted by the then UN Secretary General: 'This procedure should ensure that access would not be denied to applicants who are found by the Legal and Technical Commission to be qualified under the rules and regulations of the Authority'.[77] However, as the following paragraphs argue, these criteria are not entirely objective and certainly involve a degree of discretion on the part of the LTC.

Second, there is a lack of transparency around the approval process. Application documents are only accessible to the LTC and are assessed in closed session.[78] The LTC has no guidance for how to determine whether an application complies with all requirements. As part of its assessment, the LTC must determine for example whether an applicant has 'the financial and technical capability to carry out the proposed plan of work' and whether the latter provides for 'effective protection of human health and safety' as well as 'effective protection and preservation of the marine environment' including its biodiversity.[79]

These assessments are difficult to make for a frontier activity that has never been undertaken before, for which no agreed environmental objectives exist, and that is characterised by significant uncertainties as to the environmental impacts, technological feasibility, and financial viability and requirements. Most importantly, the LTC is unable to independently verify the data and information provided by applicants.[80] Given these challenges and the role of acting on behalf of humankind as a whole, transparency would appear to be particularly important.

The lack of transparency may be partially explained by the fact that the legal framework for the Area regime was negotiated more than four decades ago, when international organisations operated predominantly on the assumption that 'information should be kept secret and public access should be an exception'.[81] Since then, transparency has become a widespread normative administrative standard for international organisations.[82] The ISA has lagged behind this trend, although some improvements in transparency have been registered in recent years.[83] This lack of transparency is particularly concerning in light of the ISA's mandate to govern the common heritage of humankind.

Participation of developing states through the Enterprise and the site-banking system

A core aim of negotiating Part XI of UNCLOS was to prevent the Area from only being accessible to a handful of technologically advanced states to the detriment of the rest of humankind. Indeed,

76 'Information note concerning the Secretary-General's informal consultation on outstanding issues relating to the deep sea-bed mining provisions of the UN Convention on the Law of the Sea, New York, 16 and 17 June 1992', reprinted in ISA, *Secretary-General's Informal Consultations on Outstanding Issues Relating to the Deep Seabed Mining Provisions of the United Nations Convention on the Law of the Sea: Collected Documents*, ISA, 2002, 79–84, para. 18.

77 Ibid.

78 Articles 153(3), 165(2)(b), UNCLOS.

79 Articles 4(6), 6, Annex III, UNCLOS; ISA, *Regulations on Prospecting and Exploration for Polymetallic Nodules in the Area*, op. cit., note 23, Annex, Regulation 21.

80 Jaeckel, op. cit., note 5, p. 103.

81 J. Tallberg, 'Transparency', in J. Katz Cogan et al. (eds), *The Oxford handbook of international organizations*, Oxford University Press, 2017, 1170–92, p. 1184.

82 M. Donaldson and B. Kingsbury, 'The adoption of transparency policies in global governance institutions: justifications, effects, and implications', *Annual Review of Law and Social Science* 9, 2013, 119–47.

83 Ardron et al., op. cit., note 28; J.A. Ardron, 'Transparency in the operations of the International Seabed Authority: an initial assessment', *Marine Policy* 95, 2018, 324–31.

ensuring participation of developing states is a key feature of Part IX[84] and was to be achieved primarily through two mechanisms: the Enterprise and the site-banking system. In practice, however, both of these mechanisms have so far failed to meet their intended aims, as the following paragraphs discuss.

The Enterprise

The Enterprise was planned to be the commercial arm of the ISA that would conduct mining operations on par with private or state-owned commercial mining companies. The profits generated by the Enterprise would be shared amongst ISA member states. The Enterprise was supposed to be a body that enables developing states to directly participate in mining the Area.[85] To allow the Enterprise to compete with other mining operators, it would receive funding from member states of the ISA, as well as technology transfer and training programmes to ensure the Enterprise has qualified staff.[86]

These measures were substantially altered by the 1994 Agreement,[87] which removed not only any obligation of states to finance the Enterprise,[88] but also the obligatory technology transfers, requiring instead for such transfers to be consistent with the protection of intellectual property rights.[89] The training programmes were maintained although with a focus on training scientific and technical experts from developing states generally rather than staff of the Enterprise.[90] While the vision of the Enterprise itself survived the 1994 amendments, its operational potential was significantly altered as a result of withdrawing funding and guaranteed access to technology.

Moreover, the 1994 Agreement delayed the independent functioning of the Enterprise and made it conditional upon approval by the ISA Council and adherence to commercial principles.[91] Specifically, the Implementing Agreement provides:

> Upon the approval of a plan of work for exploitation for an entity other than the Enterprise, or upon receipt by the Council of an application for a joint-venture operation with the Enterprise, the Council shall take up the issue of the functioning of the Enterprise independently of the Secretariat of the Authority. If joint-venture operations with the Enterprise accord with sound commercial principles, the Council shall issue a directive pursuant to article 170, paragraph 2, of the Convention providing for such independent functioning.[92]

84 Article 148, UNCLOS.

85 E. Egede et al., *A study on issues related to the operationalization of the Enterprise* (ISA, 2019). Available online <https://www.isa.org.jm/node/19575> (accessed 18 August 2021).

86 Final Act of the Third United Nations Conference on the Law of the Sea, Resolution II 'Governing Preparatory Investment in Pioneer Activities Relating to Polymetallic Nodules', para. 12(a)(ii).

87 ISA, *Legislative History of the Enterprise*, 2002. Available online <https://isa.org.jm/files/files/documents/enterprise-ae.pdf> (accessed 18 August 2021).

88 *1994 Agreement*, annex, section 2(3).

89 *1994 Agreement*, annex, section 5(1)(b). The original obligation for transferring technology was laid out in article 5, Annex III, UNCLOS.

90 ISA, *Recommendations for the Guidance of Contractors and Sponsoring States Relating to Training Programmes under Plans of Work for Exploration Issued by the Legal and Technical Commission,* 12 July 2013, ISBA/19/LTC/14; article 143(3), 144, UNCLOS and article 15, Annex III, UNCLOS.

91 Section 2(2), Annex, 1994 Agreement.

92 Ibid.

Despite the fact that expressions of interests for a joint-venture with the Enterprise have been received in 2012[93] and 2018,[94] discussions about establishing an independent Enterprise have been slow. Developing states have repeatedly voiced frustrations at the lack of momentum in creating the Enterprise.[95] For instance, in 2018 the African Group noted the following:

> [T]he African Group is concerned that principles and mechanisms designed to render the Area a level playing field, and which are the cornerstones of the Convention, are at risk of being eroded. The African Group does not wish to see an exploitation regime that facilitates the loss of common heritage resources in return for minimal or no benefit to the population of African countries, and other developing States.[96]

The African Group's call to establish an independently functioning Enterprise[97] 'received cross-regional support'.[98] However, progress remains slow. In March 2020, the LTC finally recommended appointing an interim director general of the Enterprise from within the ISA Secretariat.[99] Prior to that, an independent Special Representative for the Enterprise had been appointed on a temporary basis to participate in the negotiations for the draft exploitation regulations and liaise with Poland on a possible joint-venture arrangement.[100] No outcome has yet been achieved on the latter.[101]

The Commission, on the basis of what was stated in paragraphs 37 to 40 above, recommended that the Council consider requesting the Assembly, subject to the availability of the requisite funds, to establish the position of interim director general within the Secretariat and for the Secretary General to appoint a person to the position to oversee the specified functions listed in section 2(1) of the Annex to the 1994 Agreement.

The dismay of developing states is understandable, given that until recently, the ISA had neglected its functions and responsibilities regarding the Enterprise. Until the Enterprise functions independently, its rather modest initial functions, such as monitoring world metal markets and assessing approaches to joint-venture operations, are to be performed by the ISA Secretariat,[102] though this has not been the case since 2012, due to concerns over conflicts of interest.[103] Similarly,

93 ISA, *Proposal for a joint venture operation with the Enterprise*, ISBA/19/C/4, 20 March 2013.

94 ISA, *Considerations Relating to a Proposal by the Government of Poland for a Possible Joint-Venture Operation with the Enterprise – Report of the Secretary-General*, ISBA/24/C/12, 25 May 2018.

95 M. Remaoun, 'The International Seabed Authority and the Enterprise: how Africa is reinvigorating the principle of the common heritage of mankind', *Journal of Ocean Governance in Africa* 1, 2021, 1–37.

96 African Group, *Request for Consideration by the Council of the African Group's Proposal for the Operationalization of the Enterprise*, 6 July 2018. Available online <https://www.isa.org.jm/files/files/documents/alg-oboag-cntp.pdf> (accessed 18 August 2021).

97 Ibid.

98 ISA, *Decision of the Council of the International Seabed Authority Relating to the Special Representative of the Secretary-General of the International Seabed Authority for the Enterprise*, 1 March 2019, para. 3. Hereinafter 'ISA, *Decision of the Council of the International Seabed Authority*'.

99 ISA, *Report of the Chair of the Legal and Technical Commission on the work of the Commission at the first part of its twenty-sixth session*, ISBA/26/C/12, 9 March 2020, para. 41.

100 ISA, *Decision of the Council of the International Seabed Authority*, op. cit., note 98.

101 ISA, *Report of the Special Representative of the Secretary-General of the International Seabed Authority for the Enterprise*, ISBA/26/C/15, 13 May 2020. Hereinafter 'ISA, *Report of the Special Representative*'.

102 Section 2(1), Annex, 1994 Agreement.

103 ISA, *Final Report on the Periodic Review of the International Seabed Authority Pursuant to Article 154 of the United Nations Convention on the Law of the Sea*, ISBA/23/A/3, 8 February 2017, para. 21.

the LTC has not yet considered questions around establishing the Enterprise, despite this having been on its agenda since 2014,[104] presumably because of an unmanageable workload, which has been discussed elsewhere.[105]

The Enterprise is central to the operationalisation of the common heritage principle. It is designed to enable developing states and others to collectively and directly participate in the mining of minerals, without the significant risks of seeking active participation individually through becoming a sponsoring state.[106] The lack of political ambition at the ISA, with the exception of pressure from some developing states, is arguably depriving the Area regime of one of its most innovative, albeit also controversial, features.

The site-banking system

The second important measure to facilitate active participation by developing states in the Area regime was the so-called site-banking system or parallel system.[107] It was designed to ensure developing states can skip the costly process of locating a mining site with economic potential. Under the site-banking system, an applicant for an exploration contract with the ISA needs to submit relevant geological and biological data for an area that can sustain two separate mining operations, both in terms of size and estimated commercial value of the mineral resources. If successful, the applicant receives exclusive rights to explore and/or exploit one part of the application area, whereas the other part is reserved for mining operations by a developing state or the Enterprise.[108] This effectively lowers the upfront costs for developing states and the Enterprise.

Importantly, the Enterprise has privileged access to reserved areas, meaning reserved areas only become available to developing states if the Enterprise does not intend to develop them itself.[109] However, because of delays in becoming fully operational, the Enterprise has missed out on seven contracts that have already been granted for reserved areas. These are now under contract with mining corporations, often headquartered in the global north, that use individual developing states as their sponsoring states to obtain access to reserved areas.

As has been discussed elsewhere,[110] engaging in the Area regime as individual sponsoring states instead of collectively through the Enterprise increases the legal and financial risks for developing states. Specifically, sponsoring states may be held liable for environmental harm caused by their sponsored mining operator if they do not meet their due diligence obligations.[111] They potentially also face financial risks from foreign investor claims.[112] Despite these risks for sponsoring states, the site-banking system has to date been used only by individual developing states.

The site-banking system has been stifled through a regulatory change introduced by the ISA in 2010, which allows contractors exploring certain types of mineral deposits to offer the Enterprise

104 Ibid.; ISA, *Report of the Special Representative*, op. cit., note 101.

105 Jaeckel, op. cit., note 5, Ch. 8.3.

106 A. Jaeckel, 'Benefitting from the common heritage of humankind: from expectation to reality', *The International Journal of Marine and Coastal Law* 35, 2020, 1–22, p. 13.

107 Article 153, UNCLOS and articles 8, 9, Annex III, UNCLOS.

108 Articles 8, 9, Annex III, UNCLOS; sections 2(2), 2(5), 1(10), Annex, 1994 Agreement.

109 Article 9, Annex III, UNCLOS.

110 Jaeckel, op. cit., note 105, pp. 12–14.

111 ITLOS, *Responsibilities and Obligations of States*, op. cit., note 14.

112 A. Pecoraro, 'UNCLOS and investor claims for deep seabed mining in the Area: an investment law of the sea?', *ECILS Working Paper Series*, 2021.

an equity interest in its future mining operations instead of contributing a reserved area.[113] The change was introduced because some mineral deposits that were not yet known at the time of negotiating UNCLOS, are three-dimensional. As ISA documents summarise:

> [I]t would not be possible to determine two sites of equal estimated commercial value without substantial and costly exploration work. Consequently, it appeared to members of the Authority that it would be impracticable to implement a site-banking approach for polymetallic sulphides and cobalt-rich ferromanganese crusts in the same manner as for polymetallic nodules.[114]

This change resulted in significant consequences for the site-banking system. Of the 12 exploration contracts granted for sulphides and crusts, only one contributed a new reserved area to the pool.[115] This arguably reduces opportunities for developing states to actively participate in the Area regime, either as sponsoring states or collectively through the Enterprise. As a 2018 note by the ISA Secretariat highlights:

> Collectively, the reserved areas and the resources contained therein represent the core financial asset available to the Enterprise in the future and a key element in giving effect to the principle of the common heritage of mankind.[116]

It remains unclear how the equity interest option will be implemented and whether and how benefits will be generated for developing states.[117]

Benefit sharing

As alluded to in the introduction, central to the Area regime from its very inception was the notion that benefits derived from the Area would be shared equitably amongst all states, with special consideration being given to developing states.[118] However, the modalities of, and mechanisms for, benefit sharing remain contested,[119] as this section briefly discusses.

113 ISA, *Regulations on Prospecting and Exploration for Cobalt-rich Ferromanganese Crusts in the Area*, op. cit., note 66, regulations 16–19; ISA, *Regulations on Prospecting and Exploration for Polymetallic Sulphides in the Area*, op. cit., note 65, regulations 16–19; see also A. Jaeckel et al., 'Sharing benefits of the common heritage of mankind – is the deep seabed mining regime ready?', *Marine Policy* 70, 2016, 198–204.

114 ISA, *Issues related to the possible alignment of the Authority's regulations on prospecting and exploration concerning the offer of an equity interest in a joint venture arrangement*, ISBA/24/LTC/4, 6 February 2018, para. 10. Hereinafter 'ISA, *Issues related to the possible alignment of the Authority's regulations*'.

115 ISA, *Application for Approval of a Plan of Work for Exploration for Cobalt-Rich Ferromanganese Crusts by the Ministry of Natural Resources and Environment of the Russian Federation*, ISBA/19/LTC/12, 25 June 2013.

116 ISA, *Issues related to the possible alignment of the Authority's regulations*, op. cit., note 114, para. 13.

117 ISA, *Issues related to the possible alignment of the Authority's regulations*, op. cit., note 114; I. Feichtner, 'Sharing the riches of the sea: the redistributive and fiscal dimension of deep seabed exploitation', *European Journal of International Law* 30, 2019, 601–33.

118 Article 140, UNCLOS.

119 M. Bourrel et al., 'The common of heritage of mankind as a means to assess and advance equity in deep sea mining', *Marine Policy* 95, 2018, 311–16; Jaeckel et al., op. cit., note 110; A. Jaeckel et al., 'Conserving the common heritage of humankind – options for the deep-seabed mining regime', *Marine Policy* 78, 2017, 150–7.

UNCLOS specifically provides for the sharing of 'financial and other economic benefits' from activities in the Area.[120] This includes an equitable payment regime for profits generated from mining activities, which is discussed by Dingwall in detail in Chapter IV.2 of this book.[121] Here it suffices to say that the ISA's current proposal for sharing of revenues has been widely criticised[122] and discussed at several workshops, the summary of which has been lead-authored by an ISA contractor.[123] Discussions about alternative proposals are ongoing, including the question of how to design a payment regime that meets the ISA's mandate of acting on behalf of humankind[124] and reflects the full costs associated with seabed mining.[125]

UNCLOS also foresees benefits beyond direct economic ones, in particular relating to capacity building for developing states. As discussed elsewhere,[126] the types of benefits that are expected to be generated from the Area have changed over time. In the 1960s, seabed mining was thought to generate 'immeasurable wealth' and fund international development efforts,[127] a promise that appears preposterous today but ensured developing states would remain engaged in the UNCLOS negotiations.[128] As these expectations were adjusted, the framing of benefits shifted to supply security of critical minerals and lately to the contribution of seabed minerals to building a green economy.[129] The latter appears to be a form of corporate green washing[130] and frames seabed mining as

120 Article 140(2), UNCLOS.

121 J. Dingwall, 'The common heritage quandary: devising a global payment regime for exploitation activities in the deep seabed Area', in V. Tassin Campanella (ed), *Routledge handbook of seabed mining and the law of the sea*, op. cit., chapter IV.2.

122 See e.g. African Group, *Request for Consideration by the Council of the African Group's Proposal on the Economic Model/Payment Regime and Other Financial Matters in the Draft Exploitation Regulations under Review*, 9 July 2018. Available online <https://www.isa.org.jm/files/files/documents/nv.pdf> (accessed 18 August 2021). Hereinafter 'African Group, *Request for Consideration by the Council of the African Group's Proposal on the Economic Model/Payment Regime*'; Tonga, *Statement regarding agenda item 11: Draft Regulations for exploitation of mineral resources in the Area (Financial Model)*, 25 February 2019. Available online <https://www.isa.org.jm/files/files/documents/7-tg_financial_model.pdf> (accessed 18 August 2021); Deep Sea Conservation Coalition, *Statement regarding agenda item 11: Draft Regulations for exploitation of mineral resources in the Area (Financial Model)*, 25 February 2019. Available online <https://www.isa.org.jm/files/files/documents/17-dscc.pdf> (accessed 18 August 2021).

123 K. Van Nijen et al., 'The development of a payment regime for deep sea mining activities in the Area through stakeholder participation', *The International Journal of Marine and Coastal Law* 34, 2019, 1–31.

124 T. Thiele et al., *A Benefit Sharing Mechanism Appropriate for the Common Heritage of Mankind: Workshop Summary*, 2019. Available online <https://publications.iass-potsdam.de/rest/items/item_5009889_4/component/file_5009890/content> (accessed 18 August 2021); Feichtner, op. cit., note 117.

125 T. Thiele et al., *A Comprehensive Approach to the Payment Mechanism for Deep Seabed Mining,* IASS Policy Brief 1/2021, Institute for Advanced Sustainability Studies, 2021. Available online <https://publications.iass-potsdam.de/rest/items/item_6000737_2/component/file_6000738/content> (accessed 18 August 2021).

126 Jaeckel, op. cit., note 105.

127 UNGA, *Summary of Records for 1st to 9th Meetings* (Ad Hoc Committee to Study the Peaceful Uses of the Sea-Bed and the Ocean Floor Beyond the Limits of National Jurisdiction), UN Doc A/AC.135/SR.1-9, 10 May 1968, para. 69.

128 S. Ranganathan, 'Ocean floor grab: international law and the making of an extractive imaginary', *European Journal of International Law* 30(2), 2019, 573–600.

129 S. Christiansen et al., *Towards a Contemporary Vision for the Global Seafloor Implementing the Common Heritage of Mankind*, Heinrich-Böll-Stiftung, 2019. Available online <https://www.boell.de/en/2019/11/11/towards-contemporary-vision-global-seafloor-implementing-common-heritage-mankind> (accessed 18 August 2021), 60–62.

130 J. Childs, 'Greening the blue? Corporate strategies for legitimising deep sea mining', *Political Geography* 74, 2019, 102060; see also L. Casson et al., *In deep water*, Greenpeace Inc, 2019, p. 17; S. Teske et al., *Renewable Energy and Deep-Sea Mining: Supply, Demand and Scenarios*, Report prepared by ISF for J.M. Kaplan Fund, Oceans 5 and Synchronicity Earth, 2016.

a necessity rather than an opportunity for re-adjusting the global economic playing field, as was historically the case.[131] The debate remains dynamic with some car manufacturers and technology companies having recently rejected seabed mining until the environmental consequences can be adequately evaluated.[132]

Of course the Area is already generating benefits for humankind, including vital ecosystem services[133] and through marine science that increases knowledge about our life-support systems in the ocean and how to sustain them. Indeed, scientific knowledge of the deep oceans has improved dramatically in recent decades.[134] We now know that the 'deep ocean and seafloor are crucial to our lives through the services that they provide'[135] and that deep seabed mining could cause 'devastating, and potentially irreversible, impacts on marine life'.[136] In this regard, the current UN Decade of Ocean Science for Sustainable Development (2021–2030) offers an opportunity to scale up scientific research to better understand the role of deep ocean ecosystems and the effects that seabed mining might have on these.

Discussions around benefit sharing in the Area regime have started to consider not only benefits but also how the costs could be distributed equitably.[137] These costs include inter alia social costs,[138] environmental costs,[139] economic losses for land-based mineral producing economies including developing states,[140] and economic costs for sponsoring states from liability for environmental harm[141] and indeed from regulating seabed mining.[142] African states argue that seabed mining should 'only occur[] if it is demonstrably beneficial to mankind'.[143] They assert that:

> [A] proper reading of the UNCLOS and the Authority's mandate is for the Authority to develop Regulations that enable exploitation in the Area to occur only insofar as there would be (net) benefit to mankind as a whole. This must take into account all parameters set by the UNCLOS, including the effective protection of the marine environment, and

131 Christiansen et al., op. cit., note 129, 60–62.

132 D. Shukman, 'Companies back moratorium on deep sea mining', BBC News, 4 April 2021. Available online <https://www.bbc.com/news/science-environment-56607700> (accessed 18 August 2021).

133 J.T. Le et al., 'Incorporating ecosystem services into environmental management of deep-seabed mining', *Deep-Sea Research Part II: Topical Studies in Oceanography* 137, 2017, 486–503; A.R. Thurber et al., 'Ecosystem function and services provided by the deep sea', *Biogeosciences* 11, 2014, 3941–63; B.N. Orcutt et al., 'Impacts of deep-sea mining on microbial ecosystem services', *BioRxiv*, 2018, 463992.

134 R. Danovaro et al., 'Challenging the paradigms of deep-sea ecology', *Trends in Ecology & Evolution* 29, 2014, 465–75.

135 Thurber et al., op. cit., note 133.

136 O. Heffernan, 'Deep-sea dilemma', *Nature* 571, 2019, 465–68.

137 L.A. Levin et al., 'Challenges to the sustainability of deep-seabed mining', *Nature Sustainability* 3, 2020, 784–94; Feichtner, op. cit., note 117.

138 J.R. Wakefield and K. Myers, 'Social cost benefit analysis for deep sea minerals mining', *Marine Policy* 95, 2016, 346–55; Cardno, *An assessment of the costs and benefits of mining deep-sea minerals in the Pacific Island region*, SPC, 2016.

139 Jones et al., op. cit., note 50.

140 A. Lapteva et al., *Study of the potential impact of polymetallic nodules production from the area on the economies of developing land-based producers of those metals which are likely to be most seriously affected*, ISA, 2020. Available online <https://www.isa.org.jm/files/documents/impactstudy.pdf> (accessed 18 August 2021).

141 N. Craik et al., *Legal liability for environmental harm: synthesis and overview*, CIGI, Liability Issues for Deep Seabed Mining Series Paper No 1, 2018.

142 Levin et al., op. cit., note 137; Cardno, op. cit., note 138.

143 African Group, *Request for Consideration by the Council of the African Group's Proposal on the Economic Model/ Payment Regime*, op. cit., note 122.

ensuring optimum revenues for the Authority for equitable sharing, in accordance with the UNCLOS.[144]

This view is supported by scholars who argue that seabed mining in the Area should only be authorised if it delivers a net-positive benefit to humankind, which must include 'an assessment of the likely impacts of mining activities on the natural capital of the Area and on other potential uses of the deep sea'.[145]

As this discussion demonstrates, while UNCLOS requires the sharing of benefits associated with the Area regime, how this mandate will be implemented remains uncertain.

Compliance and enforcement

UNCLOS sets out unusually far-reaching compliance and enforcement powers for the ISA, although these are not yet realised in practice, as this section briefly discusses.

The ISA is mandated to 'exercise such control over activities in the Area as is necessary for the purpose of securing compliance' with UNCLOS, the Mining Code, and the contractors' approved plans of work.[146] Moreover, the ISA has 'the right to take at any time any measures provided for under [Part XI] to ensure compliance with its provisions and the exercise of the functions of control and regulation assigned to it thereunder or under any contract'.[147] These provisions essentially grant the ISA the power to determine for itself which measures it considers necessary to secure compliance.

One measure which is specifically provided for in UNCLOS is inspections of 'all installations in the Area used in connection with activities in the Area'.[148] While discussions about establishing an Inspectorate within the ISA have been ongoing, inspections are not yet used in practice. It remains unclear whether and how inspections will be carried out in the future and how an Inspectorate is to be positioned relative to the ISA Secretariat and Council to avoid conflicts of interests.[149]

As of August 2021, the only process used to monitor compliance of current exploration contractors is annual reporting by the contractors themselves about their activities[150] and 5-yearly reviews of the contractor's plans of work.[151] Self-evidently, these methods to monitor compliance are weak as they do not provide member states, or indeed humankind as a whole, with any independently collected information. What is more, annual reports and the contractors' plans of work remain con-

144 African Group, *Submission on the ISA Draft Strategic Plan 2019–2023*, 2018. Available online <https://www.isa.org.jm/files/documents/EN/SPlan/Subs/Algeria-obo-AG.pdf> (accessed 18 August 2021).

145 S. Christiansen et al., *The International Seabed Authority and the common heritage of mankind*, IASS Policy Brief 2/2018, Institute for Advanced Sustainability Studies, 2018. Available online <https://www.umweltbundesamt.de/sites/default/files/medien/2875/dokumente/chm_policy_brief.pdf> (accessed 18 August 2021).

146 Article 153(4), UNCLOS.

147 Article 153(5), ibid.

148 Article 153(5), UNCLOS.

149 ISA, *Information Relating to Compliance by Contractors with Plans of Work for Exploration*, ISBA/24/C/4 (ISA, *Information Relating to Compliance*), 16 January 2018.

150 See e.g. ISA, *Regulations on Prospecting and Exploration for Polymetallic Nodules in the Area*, op. cit., note 23, annex IV, section 10.

151 Section 4.4, Annex IV, UNCLOS; ISA, *Evaluation of Annual Reports of Contractors and Monitoring Compliance with Plans of Work for Exploration – Note by the Secretariat*, ISBA/24/LTC/3, 16 January 2018.

fidential, except for a brief summary of the former.[152] This lack of transparency makes it difficult for the public to have trust in the current compliance regime.

Non-compliance by ISA contractors can result in sanctions, such as termination or suspension of the contract or monetary penalties.[153] However, these sanctions can only be imposed if 'the contractor has been accorded a reasonable opportunity to exhaust the judicial remedies available to him under Part XI, section 5' of UNCLOS.[154] One exception is emergency orders as they allow the ISA Secretary General to temporarily suspend a contractor's operation if these 'have caused, are causing or pose a threat of serious harm to the marine environment'.[155] As yet, no enforcement actions have been taken by the ISA.[156]

Conclusion

The ISA is central to the Area regime, having the exclusive mandate to govern all minerals in the Area and determine the conditions for accessing them on behalf of humankind as a whole. As this chapter outlines, UNCLOS sets the parameters of the Area regime and grants the ISA broad powers to regulate, enforce, inspect, and oversee activities in the Area. Several mechanisms under the ISA's mandate are not yet fully operational, such as inspection of activities in the Area, the Enterprise, the payment mechanisms, and the broader benefit sharing regime. In light of these realities, the Area regime has been described as 'one of the least understood, and so far least operational, international regimes for the utilisation of some of the remotest and least accessible natural resources'.[157]

Most importantly, the ISA is tasked with acting on behalf of all of us in governing our common heritage of humankind. This concept provides the framework and interpretative lens for the ISA's role and mandate. A contested concept from its inception, the manner in which the common heritage of humankind concept finds expression in the Area regime has changed over time, including through the 1994 Agreement and more recent trends towards transparency in the work of international organisations. Alongside these changes, the knowledge base around the deep ocean and its mineral and biological resources has changed dramatically in recent decades.

With the ISA developing its first regulations for commercial-scale mineral exploitation, we are at a crucial moment in the evolution of the regime. Now is the time to determine how the common heritage concept will be operationalised over the coming decades if and when seabed mining in the Area becomes a reality. This involves balancing sometimes competing interests for revenue, advancement of developing states, environmental protection, transparency, industry profits, and the equitable sharing of the costs and benefits of seabed mining. How to give effect to the concept of the common heritage of humankind in light of these interests remains as contentious as ever.

152 See e.g. ISA, *Report of the Chair of the Legal and Technical Commission on the work of the Commission at the second part of its twenty-sixth session*, ISBA/26/C/12/Add.1, section B25, September 2020.

153 Article 18, Annex III, UNCLOS.

154 Ibid.

155 ISA, *Regulations on Prospecting and Exploration for Polymetallic Nodules in the Area*, op. cit., note 23, regulation 33.

156 ISA, *Information Relating to Compliance*, op. cit., note 149, para. 19.

157 D. French, 'From the depths: rich pickings of principles of sustainable development and general international law on the ocean floor — the Seabed Disputes Chamber's 2011 advisory opinion', *The International Journal of Marine and Coastal Law* 26, 2011, 525–68, pp. 526–7.

Acknowledgements

This chapter is current as of January 2022. Aline Jaeckel received funding from the Australian Research Council's DECRA scheme (grant number: DE190101081).

References

Articles, books, and reports

Ardron J.A., 'Transparency in the operations of the International Seabed Authority: An initial assessment', *Marine Policy* 95, 2018, 324–331.

——— et al., 'Incorporating transparency into the governance of deep-seabed mining in the Area beyond national jurisdiction', *Marine Policy* 89, 2018, 58–66.

Armas-Pfirter F.M., 'The international seabed authority and the protection of biodiversity', in A. de Paiva Toledo and V.J.M. Tassin (eds.), *Guide to the navigation of marine biodiversity beyond national jurisdiction*, Belo Horizonte: Editora D'Placido, 2017, 223–248.

Bourrel M. et al., 'The common of heritage of mankind as a means to assess and advance equity in deep sea mining', *Marine Policy* 95, 2018, 311–316.

Boyle A.E., 'Saving the world-implementation and enforcement of international environmental law through international institutions', *Journal of Environmental Law* 3(2), 1991, 229–245.

Brown E.D., *Sea-bed energy and minerals: The international legal regime, volume 2: Sea-bed mining*, Martinus Nijhoff Publishers, 2001, 113–116.

Casson L. et al., *In deep water*, Greenpeace Inc, 2019, 17.

Teske, S. et al., *Renewable energy and deep-sea mining: Supply, demand and scenarios*, Report prepared by ISF for J.M. Kaplan Fund, Oceans 5 and Synchronicity Earth, 2016.

Childs J., 'Greening the blue? corporate strategies for legitimising deep sea mining', *Political Geography* 74, 2019, 102060.

Christiansen S. et al., *The international seabed authority and the common heritage of mankind*, IASS Policy Brief 2/2018, Institute for Advanced Sustainability Studies, 2018. Available online <https://www.umweltbundesamt.de/sites/default/files/medien/2875/dokumente/chm_policy_brief.pdf> (accessed 18 August 2021).

——— *Towards a contemporary vision for the global seafloor implementing the common heritage of mankind*, Heinrich-Böll-Stiftung, 2019. Available online <https://www.boell.de/en/2019/11/11/towards-contemporary-vision-global-seafloor-implementing-common-heritage-mankind> (accessed 18 August 2021).

Churchill R. and Lowe A.V., *The law of the sea*, Manchester University Press ND, 1999.

Craik N. et al., *Legal liability for environmental harm: Synthesis and overview*, CIGI, Liability Issues for Deep Seabed Mining Series Paper No 1, 2018.

Danovaro R. et al., 'Challenging the paradigms of deep-sea ecology', *Trends in Ecology & Evolution* 29, 2014, 465–475.

Dingwall J., 'The common heritage quandary: Devising a global payment regime for exploitation activities in the deep seabed area', in V. Tassin Campanella (ed.), *Routledge handbook of seabed mining and the law of the sea*, London: Routledge, 2023, chapter IV.2.

Donaldson M. and Kingsbury B., 'The adoption of transparency policies in global governance institutions: Justifications, effects, and implications', *Annual Review of Law and Social Science* 9, 2013, 119–147.

Feichtner I., 'Sharing the riches of the sea: The redistributive and fiscal dimension of deep seabed exploitation', *European Journal of International Law* 30, 2019, 601–633.

Folkersen M.V. et al., 'Depths of uncertainty for deep-sea policy and legislation', *Global Environmental Change* 54, 2019, 1–5.

French D., 'From the depths: Rich pickings of principles of sustainable development and general international law on the ocean floor – The Seabed Disputes Chamber's 2011 advisory opinion', *The International Journal of Marine and Coastal Law* 26, 2011, 525–568.

Guilhon M. et al., 'Recognition of ecosystem-based management principles in key documents of the seabed mining regime: Implications and further recommendations', *ICES Journal of Marine Science* 78(3), 2021, 884–899.

Harrison J., *Making the law of the sea: A study in the development of international law*, Cambridge University Press.

Harrison J. and Pecoraro A., 'Dispute settlement and rights of participation in deep seabed mining disputes', in V. Tassin Campanella (ed.), *Routledge handbook of seabed mining and the law of the sea*, London: Routledge, 2023, chapter V.2.

Heffernan O., 'Deep-sea dilemma', *Nature* 571, 2019, 465–468.

Jaeckel A.L., 'An environmental management strategy for the international seabed authority? The legal basis', *The International Journal of Marine and Coastal Law* 30, 2015, 93–119.

——— 'Deep seabed mining and adaptive management: The procedural challenges for the international seabed authority', *Marine Policy* 70, 2016, 205–211.

——— et al., 'Sharing benefits of the common heritage of mankind - Is the deep seabed mining regime ready?', *Marine Policy* 70, 2016, 198–204.

——— et al., 'Conserving the common heritage of humankind – Options for the deep-seabed mining regime', *Marine Policy* 78, 2017, 150–157.

——— *The international seabed authority and the precautionary principle*, Brill Nijhoff, 2017.

——— 'Benefitting from the common heritage of humankind: from expectation to reality', *The International Journal of Marine and Coastal Law* 35, 2020, 1–22.

Jones D.O.B. et al., 'Mining deep-ocean mineral deposits: What are the ecological risks?', *Elements* 14, 2018, 325–330.

Komaki K. and Fluharty D., 'Options to improve transparency of environmental monitoring governance for polymetallic nodule mining in the Area', *Frontiers in Marine Science* 7, 2020, 247, 1–23.

Lapteva A. et al., *Study of the potential impact of polymetallic nodules production from the Area on the economies of developing land-based producers of those metals which are likely to be most seriously affected*, ISA, 2020. Available online <https://www.isa.org.jm/files/documents/impactstudy.pdf> (accessed 18 August 2021).

Le J.T. et al., 'Incorporating ecosystem services into environmental management of deep-seabed mining', *Deep-Sea Research Part II: Topical Studies in Oceanography* 137, 2017, 486–503.

Levin L.A. et al., 'Challenges to the sustainability of deep-seabed mining', *Nature Sustainability* 3, 2020, 784–794.

Lodge M.W., 'The deep seabed', in D. Rothwell et al. (eds.), *The Oxford handbook of the law of the sea*, Oxford University Press, 2015.

Midas Consortium, 'Managing impacts of deep sea resource exploitation: Research highlights', 2016. Available online <https://www.eu-midas.net/sites/default/files/downloads/MIDAS_research_highlights_low_res.pdf> (accessed 18 August 2021).

Nandan S.N. et al., *United Nations convention on the law of the sea, 1982: A commentary, volume VI*, Martinus Nijhoff Publishers, 2002.

——— et al., *The development of the regime for deep seabed mining*, Kluwer Law International, 2002.

Nelson Judge D., 'The international tribunal for the law of the sea', Presentation given at the Sensitization Seminar on the Work of the International Seabed Authority, 28–30 March 2011. Available online <www.isa.org.jm/files/documents/EN/Seminars/2011/ITLOS-DNelson.pdf> (accessed 18 August 2021).

Niner H.J. et al., 'Deep-sea mining with no net loss of biodiversity—An impossible aim', *Frontiers in Marine Science* 5, 2018, 53, 1–12.

Orcutt B.N. et al., 'Impacts of deep-sea mining on microbial ecosystem services', *BioRxiv*, 2018, 463992.

Oxman B.H., 'The 1994 agreement and the convention', *The American Journal of International Law* 88, 1994, 687–696.

Pecoraro A., 'UNCLOS and investor claims for deep seabed mining in the Area: An investment law of the sea?', *ECILS Working Paper Series*, 2021.

Preparatory Commission for the ISA and ITLOS, 8 March 1984, LOS/PCN/SCN.3/WP.1.

Ranganathan S., 'Ocean floor grab: International law and the making of an extractive imaginary', *European Journal of International Law* 30(2), 2019, 30, 573–600.

Remaoun M., 'The international seabed authority and the enterprise: How Africa is reinvigorating the principle of the common heritage of mankind', *Journal of Ocean Governance in Africa* 1, 2021, 1–37.

Schermers H.G. and Blokker N.M., *International institutional law*, 6th ed., Brill, 2018.

Tallberg J., 'Transparency', in J. Katz Cogan et al. (eds.), *The Oxford handbook of international organizations*, Oxford University Press, 2017, 1170–1192.

Treves T., 'Dispute settlement and seabed mining in the Area', in V. Tassin Campanella (ed.), *Routledge handbook of seabed mining and the law of the sea*, London: Routledge, 2023, chapter V.1.

Shukman D., 'Companies back moratorium on deep sea mining', *BBC News*, 4 April 2021. Available online <https://www.bbc.com/news/science-environment-56607700> (accessed 18 August 2021).

Thiele T. et al., *A benefit sharing mechanism appropriate for the common heritage of mankind: Workshop summary*, 2019. Available online <https://publications.iass-potsdam.de/rest/items/item_5009889_4/component/file_5009890/content> (accessed 18 August 2021).

——— et al., *A comprehensive approach to the payment mechanism for deep seabed mining*, IASS Policy Brief 1/2021, Institute for Advanced Sustainability Studies, 2021. Available online <https://publications.iass-potsdam.de/rest/items/item_6000737_2/component/file_6000738/content> (accessed 18 August 2021).

Thurber A.R. et al., 'Ecosystem function and services provided by the deep sea', *Biogeosciences* 11, 2014, 3941–3963.

UK Seabed Resources Ltd. Available online <https://www.lockheedmartin.com/en-gb/products/uk-seabed-resources/uk-seabed-resources-documents.html> (accessed 18 August 2021).

Van Nijen K. et al., 'The development of a payment regime for deep sea mining activities in the Area through stakeholder participation', *The International Journal of Marine and Coastal Law* 34, 2019, 1–31.

Wakefield J.R. and Myers K., 'Social cost benefit analysis for deep sea minerals mining', *Marine Policy* 95, 2016, 346–355.

Willaert K., 'Public participation in the context of deep sea mining: Luxury or legal obligation?' *Ocean and Coastal Management* 2020, 198.

Policy documents and regulatory instruments

ISA Documents

Egede, E., et al. *A Study on Issues Related to the Operationalization of the Enterprise*, ISA, 2019. Available online <https://www.isa.org.jm/node/19575> (accessed 18 August 2021).

ISA, *Application for Approval of a Plan of Work for Exploration for Cobalt-Rich Ferromanganese Crusts by the Ministry of Natural Resources and Environment of the Russian Federation*, 25 June 2013, ISBA/19/LTC/12.

——— *Considerations Relating to a Proposal by the Government of Poland for a Possible Joint-Venture Operation with the Enterprise - Report of the Secretary-General*, 25 May 2018, ISBA/24/C/12.

——— *Decision of the Council of the International Seabed Authority Relating to the Special Representative of the Secretary-General of the International Seabed Authority for the Enterprise*, 1 March 2019, ISBA/25/C/16.

——— *Draft Regulations on Exploitation of Mineral Resources in the Area*, 22 March 2019, ISBA/25/C/WP.1.

——— *Evaluation of Annual Reports of Contractors and Monitoring Compliance with Plans of Work for Exploration – Note by the Secretariat*, 16 January 2018, ISBA/24/LTC/3.

——— *Exploration Contracts*. Available online <https://www.isa.org.jm/exploration-contracts> (accessed 18 August 2021).

——— *Final Report on the Periodic Review of the International Seabed Authority Pursuant to Article 154 of the United Nations Convention on the Law of the Sea*, 8 February 2017, ISBA/23/A/3.

——— *Information Relating to Compliance by Contractors with Plans of Work for Exploration*, 16 January 2018, ISBA/24/C/4.

——— *Issues Related to the Possible Alignment of the Authority's Regulations on Prospecting and Exploration Concerning the Offer of an Equity Interest in a Joint Venture Arrangement*, 6 February 2018, ISBA/24/LTC/4.

——— *Legislative History of the Enterprise*, ISA, 2002. Available online <https://isa.org.jm/files/files/documents/enterprise-ae.pdf> (accessed 18 August 2021).

——— *Proposal for a Joint Venture Operation with the Enterprise*, 20 March 2013, ISBA/19/C/4.

——— *Recommendations for the Guidance of Contractors and Sponsoring States Relating to Training Programmes under Plans of Work for Exploration Issued by the Legal and Technical Commission,* 12 July 2013, ISBA/19/LTC/14.

——— *Regulations on Prospecting and Exploration for Cobalt-Rich Ferromanganese Crusts in the Area*, 22 October 2012, ISBA/18/A/11.

——— *Regulations on Prospecting and Exploration for Polymetallic Nodules in the Area*, ISBA/19/C/17, 22 July 2013.

——— *Regulations on Prospecting and Exploration for Polymetallic Sulphides in the Area*, 7 May 2010, ISBA/16/A/12/Rev.1.

——— *Report of the Chair of the Legal and Technical Commission on the Work of the Commission at the First Part of Its Twenty-Sixth Session*, 9 March 2020, ISBA/26/C/12.

——— *Report of the Chair of the Legal and Technical Commission on the Work of the Commission at the Second Part of Its Twenty-Sixth Session*, 25 September 2020, ISBA/26/C/12/Add.1.

——— *Report of the Secretary-General of the International Seabed Authority Under Article 166, Paragraph 4, of the United Nations Convention on the Law of the Sea*, 6 July 2020, ISBA/26/A/2.

——— *Report of the Special Representative of the Secretary-General of the International Seabed Authority for the Enterprise*, 13 May 2020, ISBA/26/C/15.

——— *Secretary-General's Informal Consultations on Outstanding Issues Relating to the Deep Seabed Mining Provisions of the United Nations Convention on the Law of the Sea: Collected Documents*, ISA, 2002, 79–84.

——— *The Council*. Available online <https://www.isa.org.jm/authority/council-members> (accessed 18 August 2021).

——— *The Mining Code: Recommendations*. Available online <https://www.isa.org.jm/mining-code/recommendations> (accessed 18 August 2021).

Statutes, cases and international documents

African Group, *Request for Consideration by the Council of the African Group's Proposal for the Operationalization of the Enterprise*, 6 July 2018. Available online <https://www.isa.org.jm/files/files/documents/alg-oboag-entp.pdf> (accessed 18 August 2021).

——— *Request for Consideration by the Council of the African Group's Proposal on the Economic Model/Payment Regime and Other Financial Matters in the Draft Exploitation Regulations Under Review*, 9 July 2018. Available online <https://www.isa.org.jm/files/files/documents/nv.pdf> (accessed 18 August 2021).

——— *Submission on the ISA Draft Strategic Plan 2019–2023*, 2018. Available online <https://www.isa.org.jm/files/documents/EN/SPlan/Subs/Algeria-obo-AG.pdf> (accessed 18 August 2021).

Agreement Relating to the Implementation of Part XI of the United Nations Convention on the Law of the Sea, 28 July 1994, 1836 UNTS 3.

Cardno, *An Assessment of the Costs and Benefits of Mining Deep-Sea Minerals in the Pacific Island Region*, SPC, 2016.

Deep Sea Conservation Coalition, *Statement Regarding Agenda Item 11: Draft Regulations for Exploitation of Mineral Resources in the Area (Financial Model)*, 25 February 2019. Available online <https://www.isa.org.jm/files/files/documents/17-dscc.pdf> (accessed 18 August 2021).

Final Act of the Third United Nations Conference on the Law of the Sea, Resolution II 'Governing Preparatory Investment In Pioneer Activities Relating To Polymetallic Nodules'.

Responsibilities and Obligations of States Sponsoring Persons and Entities with Respect to Activities in the Area, Advisory Opinion, ITLOS Reports 2011, case no 17.

Tonga, *Statement Regarding Agenda Item 11: Draft Regulations for Exploitation of Mineral Resources in the Area (Financial Model)*, 25 February 2019. Available online <https://www.isa.org.jm/files/files/documents/7-tg financial model.pdf> (accessed 18 August 2021).

UNGA, 1 November 1967, UN Doc A/C.1./PV.1516.

UNGA, *Summary of Records for 1st to 9th Meetings* (Ad Hoc Committee to Study the Peaceful Uses of the Sea-Bed and the Ocean Floor Beyond the Limits of National Jurisdiction), 10 May 1968, UN Doc A/AC.135/SR.1-9.

United Nations Convention on the Law of the Sea, 10 December 1982, 1833 UNTS 3.

IV.2
THE COMMON HERITAGE QUANDARY
Devising a global payment regime for exploitation activities in the deep seabed Area

Joanna Dingwall

Introduction

Presently, 'the most innovative legal regime ever designed by humankind for the equitable and sustainable use of natural resources is rapidly becoming a reality'.[1] This ambitious regime is the regulatory system for deep seabed mining beyond national jurisdiction (in the 'Area'). The regime is contained within the *United Nations Convention on the Law of the Sea* (UNCLOS or Convention),[2] as modified by the *Agreement on the Implementation of Part XI of UNCLOS* (1994 Agreement).[3] The Area, and its mineral resources, constitute the 'common heritage of mankind' (CHM).[4] Mining activities in the Area are to be carried out 'for the benefit of mankind as a whole' and financial and other economic benefits derived from mining activities in the Area are to be shared equitably, in a non-discriminatory manner, taking the needs of developing states into particular consideration.[5] The deep seabed and its resources are administered, on behalf of humanity, by the International Seabed Authority (ISA or Authority).[6]

The ISA is working to create a comprehensive Mining Code. A crucial, and controversial, aspect of this work will be for the ISA to develop an appropriate financial system for deep seabed mining in the Area (DSM). This financial system, which can be broadly styled as the 'payment regime', will include establishment of financial terms for exploitation contracts, determination of a method of revenue collection and creation of a means of benefit sharing and distribution. The payment regime encompasses all 'fiscal provisions on payments due to the Authority and

1 M. Lodge, Secretary-General of the International Seabed Authority, 'Opening remarks to ISA Council', 25 February 2019, p. 2, available online <https://isa.org.jm/files/files/documents/councilopen_0.pdf> (accessed 1 February 2022).

2 *United Nations Convention on the Law of the Sea*, 10 December 1982, 1833 UNTS 3.

3 *Agreement Relating to the Implementation of Part XI of the United Nations Convention on the Law of the Sea of 10 December 1982*, 28 July 1994, 1836 UNTS 3.

4 Article 136, UNCLOS.

5 Article 140, ibid.

6 Articles 136, 137, 156, ibid.

DOI: 10.4324/9780429426162-14

their distribution'.[7] Within this chapter, all of these financial aspects, including royalties, profit shares, contractor fees and administrative charges, will be referred to broadly as forming part of the intended 'payment regime' for exploitation activities in the Area.[8] This chapter will examine ISA progress towards achievement of a workable payment regime, while highlighting key challenges in realising this goal.

The following section will provide an overview of key features of the DSM regime. Thereafter, the main body of this chapter will examine progress towards achievement of a payment regime, taking account of the underlying Convention framework for financial aspects and ISA development of this through the Mining Code. This chapter will conclude with remarks on ISA progress towards the objective of attaining a suitable payment regime.

Key aspects of the United Nations Convention on the Law of the Sea deep sea mining regime

The Convention classifies the Area as constituting 'the sea-bed and ocean floor and subsoil thereof, beyond the limits of national jurisdiction'.[9] The regime's foundational principle is that '[t]he Area and its resources are the common heritage of mankind'.[10] Although UNCLOS affords a basic framework for DSM regulation, the ISA is charged with developing a comprehensive Mining Code.[11] The ISA holds significant powers to adopt rules, regulations and procedures required for the conduct of mining activities in the Area.[12] Thus far, the ISA has adopted three sets of regulations, addressing prospecting and exploration activities in respect of three categories of minerals (polymetallic nodules, polymetallic sulphides and cobalt-rich crusts[13]), plus environmental recommendations and other administrative or technical recommendations.

The ISA operates a contract-based system for mining activities.[14] To engage in exploration or exploitation, an actor must submit a plan of work to the ISA, which, if approved, forms a mining

7 I. Feichtner, 'Sharing the riches of the sea: The redistributive and fiscal dimension of deep seabed exploitation', *European Journal of International Law* 30, 2019, p. 602. See also K. Van Nijen et al., 'The development of a payment regime for deep sea mining activities in the Area through stakeholder participation', *International Journal of Marine and Coastal Law* 34, 2019, p. 5 (explaining '[a] financial regime for [DSM] has two components', the first being ISA collection of financial returns from contractors and the second being establishment of a mechanism for equitable distribution of benefits).

8 This chapter will not consider additional financial obligations that may accrue to ISA contractors at the domestic level, such as fees/tax liabilities imposed by sponsoring states (through domestic law and/or sponsorship agreements) or by any other states with links to contractors.

9 Article 1(1)(1) of UNCLOS (references to the deep seabed and the Area both refer to the 'Area' as defined here, and references to DSM relate to mining within the Area only).

10 Ibid., article 136. See N. Oral, 'The common heritage of mankind under international law: An overview', in V. Tassin Campanella (ed.), *Routledge handbook of seabed mining and the law of the sea*, London: Routledge, 2023, chapter I.2.

11 See ISA, 'Mining code', available online <www.isa.org.jm/mining-code> (accessed 1 February 2022).

12 Articles 140(2), 145, 160(2)(f), 162(2)(o), 165(2)(f) of UNCLOS, Article 17, Annex III; 1994 Agreement, annex, s. 1(1), (5)(f)–(g), (15).

13 ISA, Regulations on Prospecting and Exploration for Polymetallic Nodules in the Area (13 July 2000) ISBA/6/A/18, (updated 22 July 2013) ISBA/19/C/17 (amended by ISBA/19/A/12 (25 July 2013), ISBA/20/A/9 (24 July 2014)) (*Nodules Regulations*); ISA, Regulations on Prospecting and Exploration for Polymetallic Sulphides in the Area (7 May 2010) ISBA/16/A/12/Rev.1 (amended by ISBA/19/A/12 (25 July 2013) and ISBA/20/A/10 (24 July 2014)) (*Sulphides Regulations*); ISA, Regulations on Prospecting and Exploration for Cobalt-rich Ferromanganese Crusts in the Area (27 July 2012) ISBA/18/A/11 (amended by ISBA/19/A/12 (25 July 2013)) (*Cobalt Regulations*).

14 On this contract-based system's operation, see A. Jaeckel, 'The Area and the role of the International Seabed Authority', in V. Tassin Campanella (ed.), *Routledge handbook of seabed mining and the law of the sea*, op. cit., chapter IV.1.

contract with the ISA, conferring exclusive rights over a specific location in the deep seabed for exploration or exploitation purposes, in respect of a particular resource type, for a specified term.[15] Various participants are eligible to apply to conduct activities in the Area. These include States Parties to UNCLOS or their sponsored nationals, such as state entities or private corporate actors.[16] In addition, the ISA may ultimately play a direct role in mining activities, to be conducted by its intended mining arm, the Enterprise (once operational).[17]

Activities in the Area remain at the exploration stage. As of 1 February 2022, the ISA has entered 31 exploration contracts with a range of contractors, including states, state enterprises and several private commercial actors.[18] However, the move towards exploitation is gathering momentum. Amidst this increasing commercialisation of the Area, the following section will address the financial framework for DSM.

Devising a payment regime for deep sea mining

The ISA is working to establish a suitable payment regime. There are various strands to this endeavour, including determining financial terms for exploitation contracts (such as royalties, profit shares, contractor fees and administrative charges), establishing a method of revenue collection and securing a means of benefit sharing and distribution. Given the growing impetus towards exploitation, the ISA's work to develop a payment regime is attracting increasing attention and critique.[19] In order to provide interim assessment of ISA progress, this section will firstly identify the underlying Convention framework in respect of the regime's financial aspects, before considering ISA development of this through the Mining Code.

United Nations Convention on the Law of the Sea framework for benefit sharing in financial terms

Benefit sharing is one of the key premises of the CHM, and it includes sharing of financial benefits derived from DSM. The Convention, as modified by the 1994 Agreement, provides a broad framework for the financial regime while leaving the underlying details to be determined by future regulation.

Article 140 of UNCLOS contains the overarching principle that DSM activities are to be 'carried out for the benefit of mankind as a whole' taking the needs of developing states into 'particular consideration' (article 140 paragraph 1), with the key redistributive feature that the Authority is to provide for 'equitable sharing of financial and other economic benefits derived from activities in the Area through any appropriate mechanism, on a non-discriminatory basis' (article 140 paragraph 2). Such provision must be in accordance with the process in article 160 paragraph 2 (f)(i) of UNCLOS, requiring Assembly approval of relevant rules and procedures on equitable sharing of financial and other economic benefits on the basis of Council recommendations, taking particular

15 See Article 153(3) of UNCLOS, articles 3 and 16 of Annex III, UNCLOS; 1994 Agreement, annex, s. 1(9). The duration of exploration contracts is 15 years; exploitation contracts are likely to have 30-year terms.

16 Article 153(2)(b), UNCLOS.

17 Articles 153(2)(a), 158(2), 170, ibid.; 1994 Agreement, annex, s. 2.

18 ISA, 'Exploration contracts', available online <www.isa.org.jm/exploration-contracts> (accessed 1 February 2022).

19 See, e.g., T. Thiele, H. Damian and P. Singh, 'A comprehensive approach to the payment mechanism for deep seabed mining', IASS Policy Brief, 2021, available online <https://publications.iass-potsdam.de/rest/items/item_6000737_2/component/file_6000738/content> (accessed 1 February 2022).

account of developing state interests.[20] The Assembly is entrusted to decide upon 'equitable sharing of financial and other economic benefits',[21] thus in addition to its capacity to approve rules on equitable sharing, the Assembly is required to make 'the decision on the actual distribution'.[22]

Although the ISA is charged with devising a payment mechanism capable of sharing financial revenues, in fact, 'the provisions on financing of the ISA diminish the amount that will be available for redistribution'.[23] Article 173 paragraph 2 of UNCLOS provides that ISA administrative expenses are firstly to be satisfied out of ISA revenues, before redistribution may take place. As the move towards exploitation progresses, ISA costs are likely to be significant, given the extensive monitoring and compliance system required for effective implementation of the regime. Moreover, remaining revenues are to be used to compensate developing land-based producer states through an economic assistance fund,[24] and they may be used also to provide the Enterprise (once operational) with funds,[25] as well as being subject to distribution on an equitable basis.[26] Therefore, in practice, the pool of revenues available for ISA distribution will be curtailed by the ISA's financing arrangements.

In order to achieve equitable distribution, the Authority must firstly collect revenues from contractors. The Convention originally provided for financial terms of contracts in annex III, article 13 (a provision modified significantly by the 1994 Agreement).[27] In particular, article 13 paragraph 1 set out a series of objectives for the Authority when adopting rules concerning financial terms of mining contracts. These included the need 'to ensure optimal revenues' for the ISA from mining proceeds, while also making sure to 'attract investments and technology to the exploration and exploitation of the Area'.[28] Pre-modification, article 13 envisaged that the payment obligations would include an application fee for mining contracts, set at US$500,000 per application (article 13 paragraph 2); a fixed annual fee of US$1 million, intended to be payable by contractors every year from the date of entry into force of the contract (meaning that the ISA would have benefited from a revenue stream even before mining generated profits) (article 13 paragraph 3); and a detailed system for calculation of royalties or a combination of royalties and profit shares (article 13 paragraphs 4–10). This intended approach represented a hard-fought compromise between developing states (favouring upfront fees and royalty-only arrangements) and industrialised states (seeking to incentivise commercial investment by creating attractive financial terms).[29]

20 See also article 162(2)(o)(i), UNCLOS. See further 1994 Agreement, Annex, s. 9(7)(f), requiring Assembly/Council decisions on these rules to take into account recommendations by the Finance Committee. The Legal and Technical Commission also plays a key role in preparing these rules: UNCLOS, article 165(2)(f). Another aspect of the ISA's mandate regarding equitable sharing of financial benefits is to develop rules for payments/contributions under UNCLOS, article 82 regarding continental shelf exploitation beyond 200 nautical miles (Assembly/Council powers here are addressed in UNCLOS, articles 160(2)(f)(i), 162(2)(o)(i), respectively).

21 Article 160(2)(g), UNCLOS.

22 S. Vöneky and A. Höfelmeier, 'Article 140', in A. Proelss (ed.), *The United Nations Convention on the Law of the Sea: A commentary*, Munich: Beck Hart Nomos, 2017, p. 981.

23 Feichtner, op. cit., p. 619.

24 See articles 151(10), 173(2)(c), UNCLOS, read with 1994 Agreement, annex, s. 7.

25 Article 173(2)(b), UNCLOS.

26 Article 173(2)(a), ibid.

27 S. 8(2), Annex, 1994 Agreement.

28 Article 13(1)(a)-(b), Annex III, UNCLOS.

29 Feichtner, op. cit., p. 619. On this provision's difficult negotiating history, see G. Le Gurun, 'Annex III', in A. Proelss (ed.), *The United Nations Convention on the Law of the Sea: A commentary*, Munich: Beck Hart Nomos, 2017, p. 2206.

However, this compromise was rebalanced within the 1994 Agreement, in favour of more 'market-oriented' objectives.[30] The Convention's guiding financial objectives were augmented by the 1994 Agreement, providing an updated series of principles as the basis for establishing rules concerning contractual financial terms.[31] For example, the payment system 'should not be complicated and should not impose major administrative costs on the Authority or on a contractor', and it may feature 'a royalty system or a combination of a royalty and profit-sharing system'.[32] There should also be an element of flexibility built into it, so that it can be 'revised periodically in light of changing circumstances'.[33] The rates of payment should be comparable to those applicable in land-based mining.[34]

In addition to developing guiding principles in respect of financial terms of contracts, the 1994 Agreement also decimated the more detailed UNCLOS requirements for financial terms.[35] The 1994 Agreement retained the application fee for mining contracts, but set it at US$250,000 per mining phase.[36] It also postponed application of the annual fixed fee, rendering it payable only from 'the date of commencement of commercial production' and leaving the level of that fee to be established by the Council.[37] In a significant move, the 1994 Agreement 'abandons the formula for the determination of royalties and profit shares' previously contained within annex III, article 13,[38] leaving the payment mechanism to be further developed through the Mining Code on the basis of the 1994 Agreement's guiding principles, as already set out.[39] Accordingly, the specifics of the payment system were deferred by the 1994 Agreement and await solidification within the Mining Code, as the following section will address.

Regulatory development of the payment regime through the Mining Code

Overview of International Seabed Authority activities

In light of the increasing impetus towards exploitation, the ISA has been working to develop draft exploitation regulations. The ISA has released various iterations of draft regulations addressing the exploitation phase, developed in conjunction with stakeholder consultations, interactive workshops and other activities.[40] Presently, the ISA is striving to finalise the exploitation regime by July 2023.[41] This chapter will rely upon the most recent iteration of the draft exploitation regulations from March 2019 (and will refer to this draft as the 'DERs').[42]

30 1994 Agreement, preamble. For the argument that the 1994 Agreement shifted '[t]he focus of economic distributive justice consequences (…) from the equal distribution of earnings to the compensation of losses caused by activities in the Area' in light of the postponement of the operation of the Enterprise (originally intended to play a pivotal role in DSM and profit redistribution from the outset of the regime), see Vöneky and Höfelmeier, op. cit., p. 981.

31 S. 8(1), Annex, 1994 Agreement.

32 S. 8(1)(c), ibid.

33 S. 8(1)(e), ibid.

34 S. 8(1)(b), ibid. In practice, achieving comparability is proving 'difficult', as fiscal regimes of land-based mining vary; see Feichtner, op. cit., pp. 625–6.

35 See s. 8(2), Annex, 1994 Agreement, disapplying article 13(3)–(10), Annex III, UNCLOS.

36 Annex, s. 8(3), 1994 Agreement.

37 Ibid., s. 8(1)(d).

38 Feichtner, op. cit., p. 620.

39 See Annex, s. 8(1), 1994 Agreement. See also article 13(1), Annex III, UNCLOS.

40 See ISA, 'Mining code: Draft exploitation regulations', available online <www.isa.org.jm/mining-code/draft-exploitation-regulations> (accessed 1 February 2022).

41 ISA Council, 'Status of draft regulations on exploitation of mineral resources in the Area and a proposed roadmap for 2022 and 2023 – Report of Secretary-General', 23 August 2021, ISBA/26/C/44, paras 2, 12–13.

42 ISA LTC, 'Draft regulations on exploitation of mineral resources in the Area', 22 March 2019, ISBA/25/C/WP.1.

In developing the Mining Code, the ISA has conducted a number of consultations and other activities focusing specifically on aspects of the intended payment regime. For example, the ISA has issued a discussion paper on development and implementation of a payment mechanism[43] and held dedicated stakeholder surveys on the planned payment mechanism.[44] The ISA has also convened a series of workshops focusing on development of the payment regime.[45] In considering financial options, the ISA has sought advice from Massachusetts Institute of Technology (MIT), and MIT experts have been heavily involved in providing comparative studies of alternative financial models.[46] Moreover, the Council has established an open-ended working group (OEWG) to consider financial terms of mining contracts, and this group has met four times thus far, most recently in October 2020,[47] with preparations underway in February 2022 for the next meeting.[48]

Financial aspects of the exploration regulations

As regards payment obligations included within existing ISA regulations, the exploration regulations provide for an application fee (currently US$500,000).[49] Pursuant to an exploration contract, a contractor must pay an annual overhead charge (currently US$80,000).[50] However, given that existing contractors are conducting exploratory activities only and are not extracting minerals for commercial production, the exploration regulations do not provide for royalty payments or profit-sharing mechanisms.[51] Therefore, these pivotal aspects of the payment regime (i.e., revenue collection and distribution of profits) are deferred until the exploitation phase.

Financial aspects of the draft exploitation regulations

Payment obligations within the DERs remain a work in progress. Part VII of the DERs addresses financial terms of exploitation contracts, while Part VIII is dedicated to annual, administrative and

43 ISA, 'Discussion paper on development and implementation of a payment mechanism in the Area', March 2015, available online <www.isa.org.jm/files/documents/EN/WorkingPapers/DiscussionPaper-FinMech.pdf> (accessed 1 February 2022).

44 See ISA, '2015 payment mechanism survey', 2015, available online <www.isa.org.jm/survey/2015-payment-mechanism-survey> (accessed 1 February 2022); ISA, 'Comments on Refining Assumptions of the Financial Model', 6 April 2020, available online <https://isa.org.jm/files/files/documents/assumptions-tab_0.pdf> (accessed 1 February 2022).

45 For an overview of key workshop themes, see Van Nijen et al., op. cit.

46 See, e.g., MIT, 'Update: Report to the ISA on development of an economic model and system of payments for exploitation of polymetallic nodules in the Area based on stakeholder feedback', October 2020, available online <https://isa.org.jm/files/files/documents/Nodule%20Financial%20Payment%20System%20Report%20October%202020%20V3.pdf> (accessed 1 February 2022).

47 For OEWG documents and an overview of its work, see ISA, 'Mining code: Working groups', available online <https://isa.org.jm/mining-code/working-groups> (accessed 1 February 2022).

48 ISA Council, 'Statement by president of the council on work of the council during its resumed twenty-sixth session', 14 December 2021, ISBA/26/C/13/Add.1, p. 10.

49 Nodules Regulations, reg. 19; Sulphides and Cobalt Regulations, reg. 21 (cf. UNCLOS, Annex III, article 13(2) and s. 8(3), Annex, 1994 Agreement; on this fee's evolution, see Le Gurun, op. cit., p. 2208).

50 See section 10.5 of standard clauses to exploration contracts (fourth Annex of Nodules, Sulphides and Cobalt Regulations); see also ISA Council, 'Decision of Council of ISA Relating to Annual Overhead Charge Referred to in Section 10.5 of Standard Clauses for Exploration Contracts', 11 March 2021, ISBA/26/C/28.

51 Cf. article 13(3), Annex III, UNCLOS, providing for a fixed annual fee of US$1 million payable by contractors every year from date of entry into force of contract, which, as discussed, was disapplied by s. 8(2), Annex, 1994 Agreement (see also s. 8(1)(d), providing for a fixed annual fee of an amount to be determined, payable from 'the date of commencement of commercial production').

other applicable fees. Appendix II includes a schedule of these fees, while Appendix IV provides information concerning determination of royalty liabilities. Taking each of these elements in turn, Part VII, on financial terms of contracts, provides for equality of treatment: the Council must 'ensure equality of financial treatment and comparable financial obligations for Contractors' (reg. 62). Nevertheless, the Council may provide financial incentives to contractors in some scenarios (e.g., to attract contractors into entering joint ventures with the Enterprise (once operational), as per reg. 63).

The main focus of Part VII is on royalty payments. A contractor will be liable to make royalty payments upon commencement of commercial production (reg. 64). For these purposes, the definition of 'commercial production' becomes critical, as the threshold at which royalty liability begins to accrue. The current draft deems commercial production to have begun when a contractor 'engages in sustained large-scale recovery operations which yield a quantity of materials sufficient to indicate clearly that the principal purpose is large-scale production rather than production intended for information-gathering, analysis or the testing of equipment or plant'.[52] However, the draft acknowledges that '[a] clearer definition of commercial production will be needed'.[53] Defining the start date of commercial production will impact upon the revenues that accrue to the ISA, especially given the time-value of money (i.e., the basic financial principle that a sum of money received today is more valuable than an equal amount of money received in the future).

The remainder of Part VII addresses procedural details of the royalty returns system: methods of record-keeping, audit and inspection; anti-avoidance measures; and details of interest and penalties.[54] The DERs envisage a system for exploitation that may continue to evolve, including in relation to the payment mechanism. Part VII provides for periodic Council review of both the system of payment and rates of payments.[55] Moreover, the ISA intends that standards and guidelines are to play a key role in regulating exploitation, including in relation to financial aspects.[56]

The methodology and approach to determination of royalty liability are to be addressed within the DERs Appendix IV. This appendix will be at the heart of the payment mechanism, in determining the revenues that contractors must share with the Authority. However, for the time being, the methodology for calculation of royalties as set out in Appendix IV 'is indicative and presented for discussion only at this time'.[57] Presently, the Council is keeping all options on the table.[58] Developing this financial model is one of the key matters upon which the OEWG is engaged currently. In the first instance, the OEWG is focusing on determining a workable payment mechanism in respect of polymetallic nodules.[59]

52 DERs, Sch. (noting that this wording is taken from article 17(2)(g)), Annex III, UNCLOS.

53 DERs, Sch., fn. 1.

54 See, generally, DERs, regs 66–80.

55 Ibid., regs 81 and 82, respectively; see also reg. 107 (providing for a system of review of the regulations more generally).

56 Ibid., reg. 94 (adoption of standards relating to exploitation activities, to be 'legally binding' upon contractors (reg. 94(4)) and reg. 95 (issuance of guidelines of a technical or administrative nature). See also reg. 65(1) (guidelines concerning administration and management of royalty payments).

57 Appendix IV, ibid.

58 ISA Council, 'Statement by president of the council on work of the council during the first part of the twenty-sixth session', 26 March 2020, ISBA/26/C/13, para. 18 (agreeing that at this stage, 'no option for a payment system should be ruled out').

59 ISA Council, 'Report of the Chair on the outcome of the third meeting of the open-ended working group of the council in respect of development and negotiation of financial terms of contracts', 17 February 2020, ISBA/26/C/8, para. 14.

Extractive industries, such as mining, may be subject to various types of fiscal regimes. Commonly, these include elements such as unit-based royalties (based on volume or weight of ore removed), *ad valorem* or value-based royalties (typically based on market-value of resource components) or profit-based systems (based on profit share of mining activity), or some combination of these elements.[60] The OEWG has narrowed its focus to four potential financial systems, namely:

- A fixed rate *ad valorem* royalty mechanism (applying a flat rate over the entire period of production);
- A two-stage *ad valorem* royalty mechanism (applying a different rate for the second stage);
- A variable *ad valorem* royalty system (proposing a value-based fixed rate for the first stage and a variable rate for the second stage); and
- A combined *ad valorem* royalty and profit-based system (blending a fixed *ad valorem* rate with a profit-based approach).[61]

While the first three approaches are forms of value-based royalty systems, the fourth option proposes to include a profit-based element. These approaches accord with the 1994 Agreement's suggestion that a royalty system or a hybrid royalty/profit-based system should be considered for the payment mechanism.[62] In contrast, a purely profit-based approach would present 'a great risk, and could drastically undermine the objective of equitable benefit sharing, as creative accountancy could easily minimize the official profits of mining companies, resulting in less income for the Authority and, therefore, mankind as a whole'.[63]

Detailed economic analysis of these options is beyond the focus of this chapter.[64] However, an important consideration is that 'different systems bring with them varying amounts of potential income as well as risk'.[65] A mechanism premised on royalties may be lower risk, as it would afford the Authority with an income stream even if mining operations were unprofitable. Nevertheless, a royalties-only approach would render the Authority unable to benefit from profits in a buoyant

60 See overview of these approaches in MIT, 'Report to the ISA on development of an economic model and system of payments for exploitation of polymetallic nodules in the Area', 3 June 2019, pp. 11–12, available online <https://isa.org.jm/files/files/documents/paysysmodel-3jun.pdf> (accessed 1 February 2022).

61 ISBA/26/C/8, paras 2–3 (see also paras 5–10, for OEWG review of these options). For general introduction to these approaches, see MIT presentation at third OEWG meeting: MIT, 'ISA: Financial payment system working group meeting', Kingston, Jamaica, 13–14 February 2020, available online <https://isa.org.jm/files/files/documents/cost_workshop-ppt.pdf> (accessed 1 February 2022). See also MIT presentation following fourth OEWG meeting: MIT, 'Financial model updates polymetallic nodules', ISA Webinar, 26 October 2020, available online <https://isa.org.jm/files/files/documents/MIT_0.pdf> (accessed 1 February 2022) (focusing on three of the options: the two-stage *ad valorem* royalty mechanism; the variable *ad valorem* royalty system; and the combined *ad valorem* royalty/profit-based system, in light of stakeholder comments). In comparison, the payment system for continental shelf exploitation beyond 200 nautical miles is on an *ad valorem* royalty basis with a rate that increases over the project's lifetime: UNCLOS, article 82(2).

62 S. 8(1)(c), Annex,1994 Agreement.

63 K. Willaert, 'Effective protection of the marine environment and equitable benefit sharing in the Area: empty promises or feasible goals?', *Ocean Development and International Law* 51, 2020, p. 185.

64 For economic analysis, see, e.g., Y. Li et al., 'Analysis of the effect of payment mechanism on exploitation of polymetallic nodules in the Area', *Minerals* 11, 2021.

65 A. Jaeckel, J.A. Ardron and K.M. Gjerde, 'Sharing benefits of the common heritage of mankind – is the deep seabed mining regime ready?', *Marine Policy* 70, 2016, p. 200. For analysis of key considerations underpinning various financial systems, see Van Nijen et al., op. cit., p. 14ff; Thiele et al., op. cit., pp. 10–14.

metals market or in light of lower operating costs.[66] Therefore, there can be benefits to a hybrid system that incorporates a profit-share element. Moreover, some form of tiered approach to payment rates, such as incorporation of an initial 'light' *ad valorem* royalty rate that transitions to a 'full' *ad valorem* royalty rate, at the point at which the contractor begins to break-even, could play a role in incentivising first-movers in the industry, who face a significant cost and technological burden.[67]

As currently drafted, Appendix IV provides for an *ad valorem* royalty system, anticipating that a different value-based royalty rate will be applicable to each category of mineral extracted (nodules, sulphides or cobalt crusts), to be calculated on the basis of the value of metal components within the relevant mineral. In respect of each mineral type, commercial production is to be classed as taking place over two distinct periods (duration to be determined), with different rates applicable to each period. The relevant royalty rates have not yet been established. Notably, in evaluating different potential modelling approaches that may underlie the royalty system, MIT 'assumes a threshold value for the "commercial viability" of a mining operation where the internal rate of return (IRR) of that operation is in a range of 17–18%'.[68] Another factor is domestic state tax obligations, which are reflected in the modelling assumptions as a cost to the contractor,[69] and 'can have an influence on the choice of level of return to the ISA (for the CHM)'.[70]

In terms of contractor fees, which also form part of the Authority's fiscal arrangements, the DERs echo the approach of the exploration regulations, in requiring an application fee and an annual reporting fee.[71] Part VIII of the DERs addresses these fees (regs 84–88). Pursuant to Regulation 86, an applicant for an exploitation contract is to pay an application fee (level of fee to be determined, to be provided for in Appendix II). Regulation 84 provides for an annual reporting fee for contractors (level of fee to be established by Council decision 'from time to time', to be included in Appendix II). In addition, Regulation 85 provides for an annual fixed fee that the contractor will be liable to pay from the date of commencement of commercial production (this fee is to be established by the Council[72]). When considering the 'purpose, rationale and function' of this annual fixed fee, the ISA's Legal and Technical Commission has suggested that it should be viewed as 'part of a transition phase to bridge the period of funding prior to the receipt of royalties from commercial production'.[73] On this basis, Regulation 85 paragraph 4 provides that the annual fixed fee for any given year 'may be credited against any royalty or other amount payable under Part VII' of the DERs.

66 On considerations such as these, see Jaeckel et al., op. cit., p. 200; Feichtner, op. cit., pp. 626–7.

67 See Van Nijen et al., op. cit., pp. 21–4.

68 Chair of OEWG, 'Briefing note for the open-ended informal working group of the council on financial terms of contracts', 17 June 2019, para. 6, available online <https://isa.org.jm/files/files/documents/brief-payment-mechanism.pdf> (accessed 1 February 2022). On this assumption, see also MIT, 2020 Report, op. cit., para. 15; MIT, 2019 Report, op. cit., para. 7.

69 Chair of OEWG, op. cit., p. 4 (noting '[t]he MIT model assumes an effective rate of 25% in respect of State tax obligations, inclusive of any other fees payable'); see also MIT, 2019 Report, op. cit., para. 200; cf. MIT, 2020 Report, op. cit., para. 47 (for consideration of the impact of differing sponsoring state tax rates).

70 MIT, 2020 Report, op. cit., para. 47. Consideration of the implications of domestic taxes/fees upon ISA revenues is beyond this chapter's scope; for relevant analysis, see K. Willaert, 'On the legitimacy of national interests of sponsoring states: A deep sea mining conundrum', *International Journal of Marine and Coastal Law* 35, 2020.

71 For a breakdown of all payments, fees and penalties anticipated under the DERs, see Chair of OEWG, op. cit., Appendix IV.

72 DERs, reg. 85(1); the Council is to establish this fee in accordance with 1994 Agreement, Annex, s. 8(1)(d).

73 ISA LTC, 'Note on draft regulations on exploitation of mineral resources in the Area', 27 March 2019, ISBA/25/C/18, para. 33. For further analysis of the rationale behind this fee, see Van Nijen et al., op. cit., p. 13.

Also of relevance to the financial system, Part IV of the DERs provides for establishment of an environmental compensation fund (reg. 54), to assist in remediating environmental damage in the Area and to be used to promote and fund certain research and education and training programmes (reg. 55). This fund is to be financed partly through a percentage of contractor fees and penalties (reg. 56(a)-(b)). Also worthy of note is the requirement for contractors to lodge environmental performance guarantees with the Authority on or before commencement of commercial production (reg. 26). The amount of this guarantee is to be determined through guidelines and is intended to be commensurate with likely costs required for premature termination of mining activities, decommissioning arrangements and post-closure monitoring and management (reg. 26 paragraph 2). Moreover, contractors will be obliged to maintain insurance, which will also pose a cost to the contractor although it will not involve payment to the Authority (reg. 36). Costs such as these are also being factored into the financial modelling assumptions.[74]

Significantly, although the DERs contain draft provisions on financial terms of exploitation contracts, they do not address the benefit-sharing mechanism. The Authority has not yet developed a means for distributing revenues that it gathers from contractors in accordance with article 140 paragraph 2 of UNCLOS. As commentators have noted, '[t]his is a very difficult question and it raises complex questions of distributive justice',[75] together with considerations of inter-generational equity and environmental concerns.[76] At present, the Authority's consideration of the potential mechanism for equitable sharing of benefits is at an early stage, and 'few concrete developments or tangible progress can be reported so far'.[77] In a notable development, the ISA has released a detailed technical study examining the conceptual basis for equitable sharing and assessing alternative allocation formulae for direct distribution, together with evaluation of the potential to establish a Seabed Sustainability Fund 'to invest in people and in preserving and developing the Area sustainably so that it truly becomes a cherished heritage that maintains its inherent value for the generations to come'.[78] The Council has requested the Finance Committee to give further consideration to establishment of such a fund, and this will be discussed at the ISA during 2022 and 2023.[79]

Key challenges for International Seabed Authority development of the payment regime

As will be evident from the preceding overview, many aspects of the ISA's payment regime remain to be decided: not least the levels of applicable fees, the methodology for calculation of royalty

74 See overview in Chair of OEWG, op. cit., paras 17–21.

75 J. Harrison, 'Who benefits from the exploitation of non-living resources on the seabed? Operationalizing the benefit-sharing provisions in the UN Convention on the Law of the Sea', BeneLex Blog, July 2015, available online <https://benelexblog.wordpress.com/2015/07/01/who-benefits-from-the-exploitation-of-non-living-resources-on-the-seabed-operationalizing-the-benefit-sharing-provisions-in-the-un-convention-on-the-law-of-the-sea/> (accessed 1 February 2022).

76 M.W. Lodge, K. Segerson and D. Squires, 'Sharing and preserving the resources in the deep sea: Challenges for the International Seabed Authority', *International Journal of Marine and Coastal Law* 32, 2017, pp. 431–42.

77 K. Willaert, 'The financial aspects of deep sea mining: Common heritage of mankind or first-come-first-served?', *Journal of International Maritime Law* 25, 2019, p. 394.

78 ISA, 'Technical study no. 31: Equitable sharing of financial and other economic benefits from deep-seabed mining', 2021, p. 63, available online <http://ec2-100-26-58-69.compute-1.amazonaws.com/Documents/ISA-Technical-Study-31.pdf> (accessed 1 February 2022).

79 ISA, 'Equitable sharing of financial and other economic benefits from deep-sea mining', ISA Policy Brief, 01/2022, p. 7, available online <https://isa.org.jm/files/files/documents/policy_brief_benefit_sharing_01_2022.pdf> (accessed 1 February 2022).

payments and the ultimate profit-sharing mechanism by which the ISA may distribute revenues equitably. Considerable controversy endures concerning the development of these elements, given the differing ideological visions for DSM historically evident within the international community, with continuing tensions simmering between communitarian, egalitarian approaches and more individualistic, capitalist attitudes.[80] In establishing the payment mechanism, the Authority will need to tread a careful path towards balancing these competing ends.

Arguably, an overriding tension is between maximising the Authority's revenue share, on the one hand, and incentivising investment, on the other.[81] Feichtner notes that in determining the payment mechanism, 'the tension between the requirement to optimize proceeds for the Authority as formulated in UNCLOS, annex III, article 13:1 and the (perceived) need to attract investment and technology emerges as a main difficulty'.[82] To realise the CHM in financial terms, the regime must be capable of delivering a payment mechanism that can achieve meaningful benefit sharing in the longer term. This challenge is exacerbated if one takes inter-generational equity into account. As commentators note, DSM 'can be seen as the conversion of natural capital into financial capital', but discussion has been limited as to whether 'this financial capital is to be the exclusive preserve of current generations, or whether a portion of it should be set aside for future generations'.[83]

Nevertheless, contractors maintain that in order for the nascent deep seabed industry to become feasible in economic terms, there must be financial conditions that will attract investment, incentivise first-movers and foster an environment for a viable market for deep seabed minerals. For example, contractors argue that the 'returns required by investors in first-movers, which will necessarily take greater technical and economic risk, will be higher than those for followers'.[84] Accordingly, MIT has indicated that '[t]he right balance has to be found between how much money will remain with investors and how much money will be financing the common heritage for this to be an economically attractive endeavour for investors'.[85] On this basis, critics highlight that the profit expectation of commercial investors has become a 'guiding concern' for the design of the payment regime, at the expense of benefit sharing.[86] Some commentators contest this, arguing that 'the starting point' for the payment mechanism must be 'humankind's ownership of the mineral resources of the Area'.[87] This also raises concerns for benefit sharing, as revenues available for distribution in the CHM pool will be reduced depending on the underlying financial modelling assumptions

80 On this underlying tension, see M. Koskenniemi and M. Lehto, 'The privilege of universality: International law, economic ideology and seabed resources', *Nordic Journal of International Law* 65, 1996. See also analysis in J. Dingwall, *International law and corporate actors in deep seabed mining*, Oxford: Oxford University Press, 2021, Ch. 3.

81 See, e.g., ISA, 'Discussion paper', op. cit., p. 10.

82 Feichtner, op. cit., pp. 624–5.

83 Jaeckel et al., op. cit., p. 203.

84 Global Sea Mineral Resources NV, Nauru Ocean Resources Inc. and UK Seabed Resources Ltd, 'Industry position paper – ISA royalty regime', March 2020, p. 12, available online <https://isa.org.jm/files/files/documents/assumptions-tab_0.pdf> (accessed 1 February 2022).

85 IISD Reporting Services, 'Summary of the twenty-fourth annual session of the isa (second part): 16–26 July 2018', *Earth Negotiations Bulletin* 25:168, 29 July 2018, pp. 3–4, 17, available online <http://enb.iisd.org/download/pdf/enb25168e.pdf> (accessed 1 February 2022).

86 Feichtner, op. cit., p. 624; see also pp. 626–27 for critique of MIT reliance on IRR as the basis to determine 'how much of their revenue deep seabed miners have to share with the ISA', thereby rendering 'the monetary value of the CHM [as] a variable dependent on the profit expectations of investors'.

87 Thiele et al., op. cit., p. 10.

(including the threshold IRR considered necessary for investors to raise sufficient capital, projected domestic taxes and environmental costs).[88]

In this context, concerns are increasing, particularly amongst developing states (as vocalised by the ISA Council's African Group), that the potential economic models under consideration may not be sufficient to deliver 'fair compensation to mankind for the loss of resources to common ownership'.[89] There have also been vehement arguments that '[u]nless and until it can be proven that mining of the international seabed will provide global net benefit, and equitably support the world's poorest and most vulnerable populations, it should not be permitted to proceed'.[90] As a particular point of contention, the African Group has criticised the Authority's focus on IRR, questioning 'whether first-movers should be encouraged', on the grounds that '[l]and-based mining is capable of supplying the world with necessary minerals and if deep-sea mining is a more expensive and less efficient way of supplying metals it should not be subsidised to be competitive'.[91] A key concern in this regard is the potential negative impact of DSM on the economies of developing states that are land-based mineral producers.[92] In practice, these tensions are impacting negotiation of the payment regime, with certain blocs (including the African Group and the Latin American and Caribbean Group) expressing serious concerns about finalising the DERs by 2023, when 'critical questions persist regarding the mechanism for sharing equitably the benefits from seabed mining' and when the financial regime has not been agreed.[93]

A further complicating factor in determining benefit sharing in the DSM context is the need to take into account impacts on 'the natural capital of the seabed' when gauging economic costs and benefits of DSM; this aspect includes 'ecosystem services, such as climate regulation', the value of which is not readily quantifiable.[94] As Costanza describes, 'ecosystem services' are 'the ecological characteristics, functions, or processes that directly or indirectly contribute to sustainable human wellbeing', while 'natural capital' is formed of '[t]he ecosystems that provide the services'.[95] There is increasing awareness of the importance of taking natural capital into account as a key component when measuring global wealth.[96] However, providing an accurate valuation

88 See discussion in the preceding section. See also Feichtner, op. cit., p. 629 (noting that on the basis of the current approach, 'environmental safeguards directly reduce the share accruing to the ISA for redistribution').

89 Algeria, 'Statement on behalf of African Group to ISA Council – Agenda item 11: Financial model', 25 February 2019, p. 13, available online <https://isa.org.jm/files/files/documents/1-algeriaoboag_finmodel.pdf> (accessed 1 February 2022).

90 Deep Sea Conservation Coalition, 'Deep-sea mining: who stands to benefit?', June 2020, p. 4, available online <www.savethehighseas.org/wp-content/uploads/2020/07/DSCC FactSheet6 DSM_WhoBenefits_4pp_web.pdf> (accessed 1 February 2022).

91 Algeria, op. cit., p. 12.

92 Ibid., p. 13.

93 ISA Council, 'Submission of Members of Council of ISA from African Group in Relation to Request made by Nauru Pursuant to Section 1, Paragraph 15, of the 1994 Agreement', 13 July 2021, ISBA/26/C/40, paras 4, 7; ISA Council, 'Submission by Costa Rica in Relation to Request made by Nauru Pursuant to Section 1, Paragraph 15, of the 1994 Agreement', 13 October 2021, ISBA/26/C/47, para. 8.

94 A. Jaeckel, 'Benefitting from the common heritage of humankind: From expectation to reality', *International Journal of Marine and Coastal Law* 35, 2020, p. 667.

95 R. Costanza, 'Valuing natural capital and ecosystem services toward the goals of efficiency, fairness, and sustainability', *Ecosystem Service* 43, 2020, p. 1.

96 G.M. Lange, Q. Wodon and K. Carey (eds.), 'The changing wealth of nations 2018: Building a sustainable future', World Bank Group, 2018, available online <https://openknowledge.worldbank.org/handle/10986/29001> (accessed 1 February 2022); K.J. Arrow et al., 'Sustainability and the measurement of wealth', *Environment and Development Economics* 17, 2012.

of natural capital and ecosystem services poses considerable challenges. When measuring wealth, '[m]arket prices used to value natural capital typically do not reflect these ecosystem services or their value is not explicit, making it more difficult to manage natural capital to promote sustainable, long-term growth'.[97] Presently, commentators acknowledge that 'further progress is needed for the natural capital component of wealth to be comprehensively measured and its value properly attributed'.[98] These challenges are even more acute in relation to non-renewable forms of natural capital, such as mineral resources, which 'offer a one-time chance to finance development by investing resource rents'.[99]

Accordingly, to conduct an appropriate cost-benefit analysis of DSM 'would require not only an assessment of potential profits but also any costs it generates from impacts to ecosystem services'.[100] Some commentators argue for application of the principle of 'no net loss', whereby DSM should only be allowed to proceed 'if, taking all potential external costs into account, a net benefit can be clearly established'.[101] They also call for 'comprehensive assessment of natural capital and ecosystem services' when calculating financial benefits of DSM, including assessment of contractors' carbon footprints.[102] The difficulty of making accurate calculations is compounded when one takes into account the risks and uncertainties inherent within the nascent DSM industry. These include environmental risks,[103] together with various commercial risks that impact on the realisation of profit, such as fluctuating metal prices, technical feasibility and the rate of return for investors.

Given these competing concerns and challenges, significant work is necessary to develop the payment regime and ensure that it comports with CHM goals. Ultimately, a key element of the payment system may be the need for flexibility, to create a sustainable industry with room to adapt and enhance the Authority's revenue collection powers if and when the industry becomes established.[104] For example, commentators have cautioned that 'the ISA will need to balance the industry's need for some certainty and predictability regarding the "rules of the game" with the need to both promote and adapt to changes in technology (and other market conditions) over

97 Lange et al., op. cit., p. 5.

98 Ibid., p. 199; see, generally, pp. 199–207 on the challenges of quantifying ecosystem services and natural capital within wealth accounting. See also Costanza, op. cit., on the difficulties of valuing these elements, and the need to take into account 'the overarching goal of sustainable wellbeing of humans and rest of nature – i.e., the whole earth system' (p. 2), while noting that 'our ability to understand, quantify, and value the full range of [ecosystem services] and [natural capital] is still fairly limited' (p. 3). On measurement of natural capital asset prices in the context of wealth-based sustainability metrics, see E.P. Fenichel and Y. Hashida, 'Choices and the value of natural capital', *Oxford Review of Economic Policy* 35, 2019.

99 Lange et al., op. cit., p. 54; see also p. 61 (noting that 'transforming nonrenewable natural capital into other forms of wealth is a major development challenge').

100 Jaeckel, op. cit., p. 667.

101 Thiele et al., op. cit., p. 4.

102 Ibid., p. 6.

103 On the difficulties of quantifying and implementing environmental reparations in the DSM context, see C.R. Payne, 'State responsibility for deep seabed mining obligations', in V. Tassin Campanella (ed.), *Routledge handbook of seabed mining and the law of the sea*, op. cit., chapter II.2. See also generally M. Feria-Tinta and M. Kamga, 'Mining the bottom of the sea: Potential future disputes and the role of the International Tribunal for the Law of the Sea', in V. Tassin Campanella (ed.), *Routledge handbook of seabed mining and the law of the sea*, op. cit., chapter V.3.

104 For analysis of differing interpretations of 'sustainability' in the context of both blue economy and ecosystem approaches, see, e.g., World Wildlife Fund, 'Principles for a sustainable blue economy', 2018, available online <http://d2ouvy59p0dg6k.cloudfront.net/downloads/15_1471_blue_economy_6_pages_final.pdf> (accessed 1 February 2022).

time'.[105] Indeed, the ISA has warned that it will not be until much further in the future that the 'real economics of the industry unfolds' and becomes more apparent.[106]

Conclusion

As this chapter has addressed, one of the most fundamental challenges facing the Authority is to create a workable payment regime for exploitation activities. In order for such activities to commence, the financial terms would need to be attractive enough to entice investment within the Area and bring the fledgling DSM industry into fruition, while building a system capable of providing sufficient revenues to the Authority to implement its benefit-sharing objectives in the longer term. This is a challenging endeavour. Given the likely expense of the Authority's operating costs, as activities move towards exploitation with associated large-scale ISA monitoring and enforcement activities, the regime may be doing well to secure sufficient revenues for the ISA to finance itself. In the short to medium term, any significant redistribution of the financial benefits of DSM in terms of article 140 paragraph 2 of UNCLOS would appear to be extremely unlikely. In the longer term, by retaining flexibility within the payment regime for it to evolve in response to the changing industry conditions, the Authority's best hope may be to leave itself in an optimum position to tailor the payment mechanism, as the industry develops, to receive maximum returns. Within this context, the emerging payment regime must be scrutinised rigorously as it develops, in order to ensure that it can achieve a suitable balance consistent with CHM goals.

References

Agreement relating to the implementation of part XI of the United Nations convention on the law of the sea of 10 December 1982, 28 July 1994, 1836 UNTS 3.

Algeria, 'Statement on behalf of African Group to ISA Council – Agenda item 11: Financial model', 25 February 2019, available online <https://isa.org.jm/files/files/documents/1-algeriaoboag_finmodel.pdf> (accessed 1 February 2022).

Arrow K.J. et al., 'Sustainability and the measurement of wealth', *Environment and Development Economics* 17, 2012, 317–353.

Costanza R., 'Valuing natural capital and ecosystem services toward the goals of efficiency, fairness, and sustainability', *Ecosystem Service* 43, 2020, 1–7.

Deep Sea Conservation Coalition, 'Deep-sea mining: Who stands to benefit?', June 2020, available online <www.savethehighseas.org/wp-content/uploads/2020/07/DSCC_FactSheet6_DSM_WhoBenefits_4pp_web.pdf> (accessed 1 February 2022).

Dingwall J., *International law and corporate actors in deep seabed mining*, Oxford: OUP, 2021.

Feichtner I., 'Sharing the riches of the sea: The redistributive and fiscal dimension of deep seabed exploitation', *European Journal of International Law* 30, 2019, 601–633.

Fenichel E.P. and Hashida Y., 'Choices and the value of natural capital', *Oxford Review of Economic Policy* 35, 2019, 120–137.

Feria Tinta M. and Kamga M., 'Mining the bottom of the sea: Potential future disputes and the role of the international tribunal for the law of the sea', in V. Tassin Campanella (ed.), *Routledge handbook of seabed mining and the law of the sea*, London: Routledge, 2023, chapter V.3.

105 Lodge et al., op. cit., p. 457.

106 ISA, 'Discussion paper', op. cit., p. 9. Cf. Feichtner, op. cit., pp. 625–6 (arguing 'the notion of an "unfolding economy" is a myth' (p. 626) and the ISA's cautious, incremental approach to development of financial elements 'misses the opportunity that this law-making process offers for deconstructing notions of competitiveness, commercial viability and value' (p. 625)).

Global Sea Mineral Resources NV, Nauru Ocean Resources Inc. and UK Seabed Resources Ltd, 'Industry position paper – ISA royalty regime', March 2020, available online <https://isa.org.jm/files/files/documents/assumptions-tab_0.pdf> (accessed 1 February 2022).

Harrison J., 'Who benefits from the exploitation of non-living resources on the seabed? Operationalizing the benefit-sharing provisions in the UN Convention on the law of the sea', *BeneLex Blog*, July 2015, available online <https://benelexblog.wordpress.com/2015/07/01/who-benefits-from-the-exploitation-of-non-living-resources-on-the-seabed-operationalizing-the-benefit-sharing-provisions-in-the-un-convention-on-the-law-of-the-sea/> (accessed 1 February 2022).

IISD Reporting Services, 'Summary of the twenty-fourth annual session of the ISA (Second Part): 16–26 July 2018', *Earth Negotiations Bulletin* 25:168, 29 July 2018, available online <http://enb.iisd.org/download/pdf/enb25168e.pdf> (accessed 1 February 2022).

ISA, Regulations on Prospecting and Exploration for Polymetallic Nodules in the Area (13 July 2000) ISBA/6/A/18, (updated 22 July 2013) ISBA/19/C/17 (amended by ISBA/19/A/12 (25 July 2013) and ISBA/20/A/9 (24 July 2014)).

ISA, Regulations on Prospecting and Exploration for Polymetallic Sulphides in the Area (7 May 2010) ISBA/16/A/12/Rev.1 (amended by ISBA/19/A/12 (25 July 2013), ISBA/20/A/10 (24 July 2014)).

ISA, Regulations on Prospecting and Exploration for Cobalt-rich Ferromanganese Crusts in the Area (27 July 2012) ISBA/18/A/11 (amended by ISBA/19/A/12 (25 July 2013)).

ISA, '2015 payment mechanism survey', 2015, available online <www.isa.org.jm/survey/2015-payment-mechanism-survey> (accessed 1 February 2022).

ISA, 'Discussion paper on development and implementation of a payment mechanism in the Area', March 2015, available online <www.isa.org.jm/files/documents/EN/WorkingPapers/DiscussionPaper-FinMech.pdf> (accessed 1 February 2022).

ISA, 'Comments on refining assumptions of the financial model', 6 April 2020, available online <https://isa.org.jm/files/files/documents/assumptions-tab_0.pdf> (accessed 1 February 2022).

ISA, 'Technical study No. 31: Equitable sharing of financial and other economic benefits from deep-seabed mining', 2021, available online <http://ec2-100-26-58-69.compute-1.amazonaws.com/Documents/ISA-Technical-Study-31.pdf> (accessed 1 February 2022).

ISA, 'Equitable sharing of financial and other economic benefits from deep-sea mining', ISA Policy Brief, 01/2022, available online <https://isa.org.jm/files/files/documents/policy_brief_benefit_sharing_01_2022.pdf> (accessed 1 February 2022).

ISA, 'Exploration contracts', available online <www.isa.org.jm/exploration-contracts> (accessed 1 February 2022).

ISA, 'Mining code', available online <www.isa.org.jm/mining-code> (accessed 1 February 2022).

ISA, 'Mining code: Draft exploitation regulations', available online <www.isa.org.jm/mining-code/draft-exploitation-regulations> (accessed 1 February 2022).

ISA, 'Mining code: Working groups', available online <https://isa.org.jm/mining-code/working-groups> (accessed 1 February 2022).

ISA Chair of OEWG, 'Briefing note for the open-ended informal working group of the Council on Financial Terms of Contracts', 17 June 2019, available online <https://isa.org.jm/files/files/documents/brief-payment-mechanism.pdf> (accessed 1 February 2022).

ISA Council, 'Report of the chair on the outcome of the third meeting of the open-ended working group of the council in respect of development and negotiation of financial terms of contracts', 17 February 2020, ISBA/26/C/8.

ISA Council, 'Statement by President of the Council on work of the council during the first part of the twenty-sixth session', 26 March 2020, ISBA/26/C/13.

ISA Council, 'Decision of Council of ISA relating to annual overhead charge referred to in section 10.5 of standard clauses for exploration contracts', 11 March 2021, ISBA/26/C/28.

ISA Council, 'Submission of members of council of ISA from African Group in relation to request made by Nauru Pursuant to section 1, paragraph 15, of the 1994 agreement', 13 July 2021, ISBA/26/C/40.

ISA Council, 'Status of draft regulations on exploitation of mineral resources in the Area and a proposed roadmap for 2022 and 2023 – Report of secretary-general', 23 August 2021, ISBA/26/C/44.

ISA Council, 'Submission by Costa Rica in relation to request made by Nauru Pursuant to section 1, paragraph 15, of the 1994 agreement', 13 October 2021, ISBA/26/C/47.

ISA Council, 'Statement by President of the Council on work of the council during its resumed twenty-sixth session', 14 December 2021, ISBA/26/C/13/Add.1.

ISA LTC, 'Draft regulations on exploitation of mineral resources in the Area', 22 March 2019, ISBA/25/C/WP.1.

ISA LTC, 'Note on draft regulations on exploitation of mineral resources in the Area', 27 March 2019, ISBA/25/C/18.

Jaeckel A., 'Benefitting from the common heritage of humankind: From expectation to reality', *International Journal of Marine and Coastal Law* 35, 2020, 660–681.

Jaeckel A., 'The Area and the role of the international seabed authority', in V. Tassin Campanella (ed.), *Routledge handbook of seabed mining and the law of the sea*, London: Routledge, 2023, chapter IV.1.

Jaeckel A., Ardron J.A. and Gjerde K.M., 'Sharing benefits of the common heritage of mankind – Is the deep seabed mining regime ready?', *Marine Policy* 70, 2016, 198–204.

Koskenniemi M. and Lehto M., 'The privilege of universality: international law, economic ideology and seabed resources', *Nordic Journal of International Law* 65, 1996, 533–555.

Lange G.M., Wodon Q. and Carey K. (eds.) 'The changing wealth of nations 2018: Building a sustainable future', World Bank Group, 2018, available online <https://openknowledge.worldbank.org/handle/10986/29001> (accessed 1 February 2022).

Le Gurun G., 'Annex III', in A. Proelss (ed.), *The United Nations Convention on the Law of the Sea: A commentary*, Munich: Beck Hart Nomos, 2017.

Li Y. et al., 'Analysis of the effect of payment mechanism on exploitation of polymetallic nodules in the Area', *Minerals* 11, 2021, 1–22.

Lodge M., 'Opening remarks to ISA council', 25 February 2019, available online <https://isa.org.jm/files/files/documents/councilopen_0.pdf> (accessed 1 February 2022).

Lodge M.W., Segerson K. and Squires D., 'Sharing and preserving the resources in the deep sea: Challenges for the international seabed authority', *International Journal of Marine and Coastal Law* 32, 2017, 427–457.

MIT, 'Report to the ISA on development of an economic model and system of payments for exploitation of polymetallic nodules in the Area', 3 June 2019, available online <https://isa.org.jm/files/files/documents/paysysmodel-3jun.pdf> (accessed 1 February 2022).

MIT, 'ISA: Financial payment system working group meeting', Kingston, Jamaica, 13–14 February 2020, available online <https://isa.org.jm/files/files/documents/cost_workshop-ppt.pdf> (accessed 1 February 2022).

MIT, 'Update: Report to the ISA on development of an economic model and system of payments for exploitation of polymetallic nodules in the Area based on stakeholder feedback', October 2020, available online <https://isa.org.jm/files/files/documents/Nodule%20Financial%20Payment%20System%20Report%20October%202020%20V3.pdf> (accessed 1 February 2022).

MIT, 'Financial model updates polymetallic nodules', ISA Webinar, 26 October 2020, available online <https://isa.org.jm/files/files/documents/MIT_0.pdf> (accessed 1 February 2022).

Oral N., 'The common heritage of mankind under international law: An overview', in V. Tassin Campanella (ed.), *Routledge handbook of seabed mining and the law of the sea*, London: Routledge, 2023, chapter I.2.

Payne P., 'State responsibility for deep seabed mining obligations', in V. Tassin Campanella (ed.), *Routledge handbook of seabed mining and the law of the sea*, London: Routledge, 2023, chapter II.2.

Thiele T., Damian H. and Singh P., 'A comprehensive approach to the payment mechanism for deep seabed mining', IASS Policy Brief, 2021, available online <https://publications.iass-potsdam.de/rest/items/item_6000737_2/component/file_6000738/content> (accessed 1 February 2022).

United Nations convention on the law of the sea, 10 December 1982, 1833 UNTS 3.

Van Nijen K. et al., 'The development of a payment regime for deep sea mining activities in the Area through stakeholder participation', *International Journal of Marine and Coastal Law* 34, 2019, 1–31.

Vöneky S. and Höfelmeier A., 'Article 140', in A. Proelss (ed.), *The United Nations Convention on the Law of the Sea: A commentary*, Munich: Beck Hart Nomos, 2017.

Willaert K., 'The financial aspects of deep sea mining: Common heritage of mankind or first-come-first-served?', *Journal of International Maritime Law* 25, 2019, 387–395.

Willaert K., 'Effective protection of the marine environment and equitable benefit sharing in the Area: Empty promises or feasible goals?', *Ocean Development and International Law* 51, 2020, 175–192.

Willaert K., 'On the legitimacy of national interests of sponsoring states: A deep sea mining conundrum', *International Journal of Marine and Coastal Law* 35, 2020, 1–18.

World Wildlife Fund, 'Principles for a sustainable blue economy', 2018, available online <http://d2ouvy59p0dg6k.cloudfront.net/downloads/15_1471_blue_economy_6_pages_final.pdf> (accessed 1 February 2022).

IV.3

UPCOMING CHALLENGES FOR THE INTERNATIONAL SEABED AUTHORITY

Frida M. Armas Pfirter

Introduction

In this chapter we will analyze the future role of the International Seabed Authority (ISA) and the challenges that it faces, as the organization through which States Parties shall organize, carry out and control the activities in the Area on behalf of mankind as a whole, providing for the equitable sharing of financial and other economic benefits.[1]

To analyze the future role of ISA, it is important to go back to its origin in 1970, when United Nations General Assembly (UNGA) Resolution 2749 (XXV) declared that the area of the seabed and ocean floor and the subsoil thereof, beyond the limits of national jurisdiction, as well as its resources are the common heritage of mankind (CHM), the exploration and exploitation of which shall be carried out for the benefit of mankind as a whole.[2]

This Resolution established a third kind of legal regime other than the schemes of sovereignty, which applies to the territorial sea, and of freedom, which applies to the high seas.[3] The declaration of the seabed and ocean floor—the Area—as well as its resources as the common heritage of mankind implies that they are neither subject to the sovereign rights of the coastal State nor to the 'first-come, first-served' principle. The CHM principle was new to the law of the sea and the establishment of this regime called for an international mechanism to manage those resources for the benefit of humanity. Thus, the negotiations of the Third United Nations Conference on the Law of

1 Articles 137 (2), 140, 157, UNCLOS and Section 1, 1), Annex, 1994 Agreement.

2 United Nations General Assembly Resolution 2749 (XXV) of 17 December 1970, *Declaration of Principles Governing the Sea-Bed and the Ocean Floor, and the Subsoil Thereof, beyond the Limits of National Jurisdiction*. See N. Oral, 'The common heritage of mankind under international law: An overview', in V. Tassin Campanella (ed.), *Routledge handbook of seabed mining and the law of the sea*, Routledge, 2023, chapter I.2.

3 T. Scovazzi, 'The concept of common heritage of mankind and the resources of the seabed beyond the limits of national jurisdiction', *Los Recursos del Lecho y Subsuelo del Mar*, COPLA-CARI, Buenos Aires, (2006), pp. 140–141. See also: 'The "common heritage of mankind" principle and the equitable sharing of benefits', in A. Ascencio-Herrera and M.H. Nordquist (eds.), *The United Nations Convention on the Law of the Sea, Part XI Regime and the International Seabed Authority: A twenty-five year journey*, Brill, 2022, pp. 85–98.

DOI: 10.4324/9780429426162-15

the Sea resulted in an international organization that was unique in its functions and competences: the International Seabed Authority.[4]

That is why, as stated by the Secretary-General of the Authority, the very existence of the Authority has always been about 'the future', working to establish a regime that is enshrined in the Convention, but where everything remains to be done.[5]

The Authority is now at a key moment; all the activities developed in these years have furthered its capacities to successfully address the challenge that will allow it to transcend, implementing a mechanism for the exploitation of mineral resources in a way that benefits mankind as a whole, particularly the developing States.

The importance of the present time requires the Authority to be fully aware of the purpose for which it was created, and that it does not stop pursuing the dream that gave rise to it. The greatest challenge is to meet that objective in a manner that is adequate to the changes and developments taking place, but not accepting compromises that involve surrendering the governing principles.

So as to analyze the future challenges of the Authority, this chapter will consider the main aspects of the exploration phase and the next exploitation stage, taking into account the hazards to be avoided and what needs to be strengthened.

Organization and exploration stage

The consideration of the achievements made thus far gives us an optimistic outlook as, in a little over a quarter of a century since its creation, the ISA has exceeded the expectations, even with the restrictions implied by the cost-effectiveness principle both in terms of the establishment of organs and the frequency and duration of meetings.[6] Let us have a quick look at the instruments adopted, the contracts in force and the advances in the protection of the environment, considering in each one the underlying challenges.

Instruments

The Authority has adopted three sets of exploration regulations for the prospecting and exploration of polymetallic nodules (in 2000 and revised in 2013),[7] polymetallic sulphides (2010)[8] and cobalt-rich ferromanganese crusts (2012),[9] respectively.

These regulations are supplemented by Recommendations for the guidance of contractors and sponsoring States on different issues: the relinquishment of areas under exploration contracts for polymetallic sulphides or cobalt-rich ferromanganese crusts;[10] the reporting of actual and direct exploration expenditure;[11] the assessment of the possible environmental impacts arising from

4 UNCLOS, art. 157.

5 M.W. Lodge, Deep-sea Live Presentation, 18 February 2020. Available online <https://www.youtube.com/watch?v=QnPc59G8eqU> (accessed September 2022).

6 Section 1 (2), Annex, 1994 Agreement, 'In order to minimize costs to States Parties, all organs and subsidiary bodies to be established (…) shall be cost-effective. This principle shall also apply to the frequency, duration and scheduling of meetings'.

7 ISBA/19/A/9.

8 ISBA/16/A/12 Rev.1.

9 ISBA/18/A/11.

10 ISBA/25/LTC/8.

11 ISBA/21/LTC/11.

the exploration for marine minerals in the Area;[12] training programmes under plans of work for exploration;[13] and the content, format and structure of annual reports.[14] These Recommendations are issued by the Legal and Technical Commission (LTC) and periodically updated.

The documents adopted for the exploration phase are adequate, but once the Regulations for exploitation and the guidelines have been adopted, a revision shall be completed to verify the coordination of all instruments as they are all together part of the Mining Code.

Contracts for exploration

Since the adoption of the Regulations, the ISA has approved 31 contracts for exploration, with 22 contractors. Nineteen of these contracts are for polymetallic nodules and are located in the Clarion-Clipperton Fracture Zone (17), in the Central Indian Ocean Basin (1), and Western Pacific Ocean (1). There are seven contracts for exploration for polymetallic sulphides, in the South West Indian Ridge (1), Central Indian Ocean (3) and the Mid-Atlantic Ridge (3). The four contracts for exploration for cobalt-rich ferromanganese crusts are in the Western Pacific Ocean.[15]

The existence of these contracts allows the Authority, by means of the LTC, to supervise the work done by the contractors through an annual report on the activities carried out under the contract. The LTC considered them and presented its Report to the Council.[16] The Commission recognized the efforts made by the contractors to make progress in their work despite the constraints resulting from the coronavirus disease (Covid-19) pandemic.

The clear challenge regarding the contracts is the need for more transparency in terms of the content of the Reports and the handling of information so that, without breaching the confidentiality provided for in the rules, the Council can have a full picture of how contractual requirements are being met.

There have only been two renunciations or changes in relation to the contracts:

- Companhia de Pesquisa de Recursos Minerais S.A. (CPRM) has sent its renunciation to its rights in the exploration area contained in its contract for exploration for cobalt-rich ferromanganese crusts. At the same time, Brazil sent a notification terminating the sponsorship of CPRM.[17] This renunciation of the contract was not related to any difficulties with the system or a lack of interest; on the contrary, Brazil has made a partial submission of the outer limit of its continental shelf that includes the zone of the contract as continental shelf beyond 200 nautical miles, thus rendering the existing contract incompatible.[18]

12 ISBA/25/LTC/6/Rev.2 y Corr.2.

13 ISBA/21/LTC/14.

14 ISBA/21/LTC/15.

15 For more information, see the list of contracts on the website of ISA. Available online <https://isa.org.jm/exploration-contracts> (accessed September 2022). The contracts are for 15 years. Seven applications for the extension of the plan of work were approved in Session 21 cfr. ISBA/21/C/19. In the 26th Session, seven applications for five-year extensions were approved: one applicant (the Federal Institute for Geosciences and Natural Resources of the Federal Republic of Germany) sought an extension for the first time, while the other six contractors applied for extensions for a second time. After analyzing the data and information provided, the Commission recommended that the Council approve the seven applications (ISBA/26/C/31-17).

16 ISBA/26/C/12/Add.2

17 ISBA/27/C/28, paragraph 5 and ISBA/27/C/21/Add.1, paragraph 7.

18 E. Cavalcanti and M. Filho, *Remarks on Brazil's decision to terminate its sponsorship for its State company in contract with the International Seabed Authority*, in BILOS, Brazilian Institute for the Law of the Sea, November 16

- On 21 December 2021, the company Circular Metals Tuvalu Ltd. applied for the approval of a plan of work for the exploration for polymetallic nodules in the Clarion-Clipperton Zone sponsored by the Government of Tuvalu. The LTC started its consideration during the first part of the 27th session in March 2022. After that, the Government of Tuvalu notified the Authority of its 'decision to rescind Tuvalu's sponsorship of the seabed mining exploration application' and requested that 'no work plan for exploration of polymetallic nodules in the Clarion-Clipperton Zone should be approved as the Government of Tuvalu will no longer sponsor this work plan'. Consequently, Circular Metals Tuvalu Ltd. requested a postponement of its application 'until such time that Tuvalu can either suitably reaffirm its state sponsorship commitments or Circular Metal changes its nationality and sponsorship'.[19]

This is the first unilateral rescission of sponsorship, and it is significant for the future of the Authority both because environmental issues were mentioned and because it leads to consideration of the legal consequences that could come out of a decision to cancel sponsorship, even though, in this case, a contract with the Authority was not yet effective.[20]

The Authority faces a key issue that has to be considered, as there seems to be a growing tendency to demand that deep-sea mining activities stop, both at a national and international level. In the last sessions of the Authority, this tendency has been reflected in statements of some States and mainly non-governmental organizations (NGOs).[21]

Protection of the marine environment

The mandate to protect and preserve the marine environment and its living resources are expressly established throughout the Convention, starting with its Preamble.[22] And when the 1994 Agreement was adopted—12 years later—this objective was reaffirmed as it established that, between the entry into force of the United Nations Convention on the Law of the Sea (UNCLOS) and the approval of the first work plan for exploitation, the Authority has to concentrate on establishing and keeping under review rules, regulations and procedures incorporating applicable standards for the protection and preservation of the marine environment.[23]

Since the establishment of the Authority in 1994, environmental protection has remained one of its highest priorities.[24] This is reflected in the Regulations adopted, with their comprehensive regime

2020. Available online <http://www.ibdmar.org/2020/11/remarks-on-brazils-decision-to-terminate-its-sponsorship-for-its-state-company-in-contract-with-the-international-seabed-authority/> (accessed September 2022)

19 ISBA/27/C/16/Add.1, paragraphs 23–29.

20 See A. Pecoraro, *Disputes between deep seabed miners and their sponsoring state: The role of international law*, in Kluwer Arbitration Blog, July 6, 2022. Available online <http://arbitrationblog.kluwerarbitration.com/2022/07/06/disputes-between-deep-seabed-miners-and-their-sponsoring-state-the-role-of-international-law/> (accessed September 2022).

21 Deepsea conservation coalition, *Spain takes first step to ban deep-sea mining in its waters as global momentum for a stop to the industry grows*, 14 April 2022. Available online <https://www.savethehighseas.org/2022/04/14/spain-takes-first-step-to-ban-deep-sea-mining-in-its-waters-as-global-momentum-for-a-stop-to-the-industry-grows/> (accessed September 2022).

22 For a general study of the rights and obligations in the Area, see V. Tassin Campanella, Y. Cissé and D. Tladi, 'State rights and obligations of States on the continental shelf and the Area', in V. Tassin Campanella (ed.), *Routledge handbook of seabed mining and the law of the sea*, op. cit., chapter II.1.

23 Article 145, UNCLOS and section 1, paragraph 5 (g) and (k), Annex, 1994 Agreement.

24 Cf. ISA, *Protection of the seabed environment* (Brochure). Available online <https://www.isa.org.jm/sites/default/files/files /documents/eng4.pdf> (accessed September 2022). See also S. Nandan, M. Lodge, and S. Rosenne (eds.),

for monitoring and protecting the marine environment, in the environmental Recommendations, in the environmental management plan, and the marine scientific research coordinated and promoted by the Authority, whose main aim is to protect the environment.

The UNGA Resolutions on Oceans and the Law of the Sea reiterate every year the importance, pursuant to UNCLOS article 145, of the ongoing development by the ISA of rules, regulations and procedures to ensure the effective protection of the marine environment, the protection and conservation of the natural resources of the Area and the prevention of damage to its flora and fauna from the harmful effects that may arise from activities there. The Resolutions also recognize the importance of the responsibilities entrusted to the ISA by UNCLOS articles 143 and 145, which refer to marine scientific research and protection of the marine environment, respectively.[25]

It is undeniable that the Authority has made and is making an outstanding contribution to the development of the international environmental law as a way to implement the CHM principle.[26] The draft regulations on exploitation—in the current version—strengthen the environmental protection.

Exploitation phase

The Authority was created with the tools and capabilities to play the delicate role of protecting and preserving the common heritage of mankind while promoting the exploitation of the resources of the Area. In the exploration phase the foundations were laid and the ISA has to evolve into its unique mission: administer mineral resources for the benefit of humankind as a whole.

Draft exploitation regulations

As analyzed by Jaeckel,[27] the Council is currently considering draft regulations on exploitation of mineral resources in the Area. Even though the Authority began to develop these regulations in 2014 with a series of studies and workshops, the process was formally initiated in 2011, when the representative of Fiji requested the Council to begin the consideration of regulations for the exploitation of mineral resources of the Area.[28]

The draft exploitation regulations have been prepared by the LTC following a transparent process and a series of broad public consultations and have been under consideration by the Council since 2019. The Council decided to establish working groups as a way to make progress. The first one was established in July 2018, in relation to one of the most difficult issues: an open-ended

United Nations Convention on the Law of the Sea 1982 – A commentary, Martinus Nijhoff Publishers, 2002, pp. 192–196.

25 Among others: UNGA Resolution 2021 on Oceans and Law of the Sea, A/RES/76/62, paragraphs 64 and 69. See also F.M. Armas-Pfirter, 'The International Seabed Authority and the protection of biodiversity', in A. de Paiva Toledo and V.J.M. Tassin (eds.), *Guide to the navigation of marine biodiversity beyond national jurisdiction*, Belo Horizonte: Editora D'Placido, 2018, pp. 221–246.

26 See R. Wolfrum, 'The contribution of the regulations of the International Seabed Authority to the progressive development of international environmental law', *Peace and Order in the World's Ocean: Essays in Honor of Satya N. Nandan*, Brill, 2014, pp. 241–248.

27 A. Jaeckel, 'The Area and the role of the International Seabed Authority', in V. Tassin Campanella (ed.), *Routledge handbook of seabed mining and the law of the sea*, op. cit., chapter IV.1.

28 ISBA/17/C/22. For the complete list of the steps taken in the preparation of the draft regulations from 2011 to 2019 and the relevant documents see ISBA/26/C/44, Annexes I and II.

working group to discuss a payment mechanism and rates of payment for deep-sea mining.[29] In February 2020 three additional informal working groups were set: protection and preservation of the marine environment; inspection, compliance and enforcement; and institutional matters, respectively.

Given the delays caused by the impossibility to hold face-to-face meetings due to the pandemic, Nauru invoked a procedure provided for in the 1994 Agreement to exert pressure on the negotiations. With a letter dated 25 June 2021, the President of Nauru notified the Council of the intention of Nauru Ocean Resources Inc. to submit an application for the approval of a plan of work for exploitation in the Area.[30] This notification implies that the Council has two years after the request to complete the elaboration of the rules, regulations and procedures necessary to facilitate the approval of plans of work for exploitation in the Area.[31] To meet the deadline, the Secretary-General proposed a Road Map, which was approved in the 26th Session (2021)[32] with the warning that, if no substantial progress has been made by late 2022, the possibility to postpone the commencement of exploitation activities until after June 2023 will be considered as the legislation required is not yet available.

The request of Nauru has been received with reservations by several delegations as they consider that urgency should not be detrimental to the detailed analysis entailed by the adoption of such an important rule.[33]

The most important challenge now, in addition to achieving consensus on highly complex issues of the exploitation regulations, is that the momentum that Nauru and others tried to create is turning out to be, in some cases, counterproductive. Some delegations have requested, in various ways, a moratorium or postponement of the date of approval of the regulations, which is strongly supported by some NGOs.

Standards and guidelines for activities in the Area

The draft regulations on exploitation of mineral resources in the Area require certain standards and guidelines to support the implementation of the regulations.[34] The standards will be legally binding on contractors and the ISA, whereas the guidelines will be recommendatory.[35]

The Legal and Technical Commission is working on these standards and guidelines,[36] prioritizing the ones deemed necessary to be in place by the time of adoption of the draft regulations on exploitation. It is very important to take into account that the process for the development of these

29 This group is chaired by Mr. Olav Myklebust from Norway.

30 Nauru Ocean Resources Inc. is a Nauruan entity sponsored by Nauru. ISBA/26/C/38.

31 Section 1, paragraph 15 (b), of the Annex to the Agreement relating to the Implementation of Part XI of the United Nations Convention on the Law of the Sea of 10 December 1982. According to the Secretariat, the effective date of the request being 9 July 2021, the regulations should be adopted by 9 July 2023.

32 ISBA/26/C/CRP.2/Rev.1 and ISBA/26/C/44.

33 See ISBA/26/C/2: Comments on the draft regulations on the exploitation of mineral resources in the Area, by the Secretariat.

34 ISBA/25/C/WP.1.

35 See the mining code available online at <https://isa.org.jm/mining-code/standards-and-guidelines> (accessed September 2022).

36 See ibid. During the 25th session, the Council requested that the Legal and Technical Commission (LTC) undertake work on standards and guidelines as a matter of priority, noting the proposed process and schedule for the development of standards and guidelines contained in ISBA/25/C/19/Add.1, Annex and enclosures I and II.

standards and guidelines is provided for in an inclusive and transparent manner, including the circulation of the drafts for stakeholder consultations.[37] The drafts under analysis are:

- Draft guideline on the preparation and assessment of an application for the approval of a Plan of Work for exploitation
- Draft standard and guidelines on the development and application of environmental management systems
- Draft standard and guidelines on the form and calculation of an environmental performance guarantee
- Draft guidelines for the establishment of baseline environmental data
- Draft standard and guidelines for environmental impact assessments
- Draft guidelines for the preparation of an environmental impact statement
- Draft guidelines for the preparation of an environmental management and monitoring plan
- Draft guidelines on tools and techniques for hazard identification and risk assessment
- Draft standard and guidelines for the safe management and operation of mining vessels and installations
- Draft standard and guidelines for the preparation and implementation of emergency response and contingency plans.

The challenge that the LTC is successfully responding to is achieving a comprehensive regulation of exploitation, not only in terms of Regulations, but also of what is deemed necessary to be in place on a mandatory (standards) or a recommendatory basis (guidelines), with increasing transparency.

Financial terms of a contract and regulations on the equitable sharing of financial and other economic benefits

In UNCLOS, the States did more than merely uphold the concept of the CHM contained in Resolution 2749 (XXV). The Preamble of the Convention states that one of its goals is to develop the principle of CHM as a 'basic principle', stating that it cannot be amended in any future reform of the Convention, thus placing this principle above their own freedom to reform it.[38] Neither this principle nor the prohibition of amendment was modified in the 1994 Part XI Implementing Agreement (IA).[39] Accordingly, the States Parties and the ISA must ensure that the scope of this principle is not modified by the ISA's bodies or the activities of States.

There are several elements provided for in the Convention that the Authority must use to ensure that it manages resources for the benefit of mankind. Even though the protection of the marine environment is a key issue, the legal concept of CHM implies far more and includes, as a vital

37 As of July 2021, two stakeholder consultations have taken place: 20 August to 20 October 2020 and 8 April to 3 July 2021. For more information see online <https://www.isa.org.jm/news/stakeholder-consultations-draft-standards-and-guidelines-exploitation-mineral-resources-area> and <https://www.isa.org.jm/stakeholder-consultations-draft-standards-and-guidelines-support-implementation-draft-regulations> (both accessed September 2022).

38 Article 311 paragraph 6 of UNCLOS states: 'States Parties agree that there shall be no amendment to the basic principle relating to the common heritage of mankind set forth in article 136 and that they shall not be party to any agreement in derogation thereof'.

39 *Agreement relating to the Implementation of Part XI of the United Nations Convention on the Law of the Sea of 10 December 1982*, adopted 28 July 1994, 33 *ILM* 1309 (1994).

component, the equitable sharing of financial and other economic benefits derived from the activities in the Area.[40]

To ensure that the Authority is performing its tasks for the benefit of mankind it is essential to bear in mind two different but interlinked issues: the financial terms and payment mechanism of the contracts for deep sea mining and the equitable sharing of financial and other economic benefits derived from activities in the Area.[41]

The Financial Terms of the contracts have been under consideration since 2019 by an Open-ended Working Group.[42] On the second issue, the Finance Committee presented a Report, with a series of guiding questions for the consideration by the Council and the Assembly.[43] The consideration revolves around the direct distribution of monetary benefits and, as an alternative or adjunct method, the concept of a global seabed sustainability fund. The Council and the Assembly considered the Report of the Finance Committee and suggested that the Committee prepare a draft framework for financial regulations on the treatment of funds received from activities in the Area and a draft proposal for the establishment of a seabed sustainability fund.[44] The consideration of these two issues poses many challenges: how to use the money, how the monies are to be received, potential for reimbursing some of the monies received against budgetary contributions, administrative measures to ensure the money is used and accounted for appropriately, etc.[45]

Bearing in mind that the Authority represents various economic systems and ideological views, negotiations do not only boil down to finding a simple formula, which would be, per se, highly complex. It is important not to lose sight of the need to deal with the two issues simultaneously. Even though the financial terms of the contracts are needed for the approval of draft exploitation regulations, it would not be appropriate to establish the financial model and payment mechanism without taking account of their consequences for the benefit-sharing mechanism and vice versa.

Even though it is necessary not to lose sight of the fact that, for the regime to work, a profit margin for the investors must be ensured, it should not be ignored that the principle guiding the activities in the Area is the certainty that mineral resources are the common heritage of mankind. The challenge is to keep the concept of humankind's ownership as the key to resolving potential tensions or conflicting interpretations.[46]

Operationalization of the Enterprise

As analyzed in this book by Jaeckel,[47] the 1994 Agreement postponed the implementation of the Enterprise. The entire first stage of the Authority's activities took place without its existence. But, as the exploitation stage is approaching, it is important to operationalize the Enterprise by July 2023 so as to advance the mandate of UNCLOS and the provisions of the Council. This was repeatedly emphasized by some delegations, particularly the African Group, which stated that,

40 Article 160, paragraph 2 (f)(i) and article 162 (2)(o)(i), UNCLOS.

41 Section 9, paragraph 7 (d), Annex, 1994 Agreement.

42 J. Dingwall, 'The common heritage quandary: Devising a global payment regime for exploitation activities in the deep seabed area', in V. Tassin Campanella (ed.), *Routledge handbook of seabed mining and the law of the sea*, op. cit., chapter IV.2.

43 ISBA/26/A/24-ISBA/26/C/39, sect. VIII and Annex II.

44 ISBA/27/FC/2.

45 ISBA/27/A/8-ISBA/27/C/36, paragraphs 16–18.

46 The African Group has also repeatedly insisted that a prerequisite for any mining in the Area is a financial regime that properly compensates humanity for its resources and land-based miners for their losses.

47 Jaeckel, op. cit.

without the operationalization and autonomy of the Enterprise, including by the appointment of a Director-General and a governing board, some elements and mechanisms designed to operationalize the common heritage of humankind principle in the Area risked being eroded.[48]

A Special Representative of the Secretary-General for the Enterprise was appointed on a temporary basis in 2018 and his terms of reference are based on the decision of the Council.[49] He participates actively in the meetings of the Council and proposes amendments to the draft regulations, which emphasized but were not limited to the role that the Enterprise is expected to play in activities in the Area in keeping with the provisions of UNCLOS and the 1994 Agreement.[50]

The Council is considering the establishment of the position of Interim Director General within the Secretariat, following the step-by-step approach on the operationalization of the Enterprise.[51] As was stressed by the Special Representative and the Secretariat, this appointment would allow the Enterprise to begin its activities according to the Convention and the 1994 Agreement, and allow the Interim Director to contribute on the development of the regulations on exploitation, as well as represent the interest of the Enterprise in the Sessions of the Authority.[52]

Economic Planning Commission[53]

The constitution of the Economic Planning Commission was postponed by the 1994 Agreement and its functions transferred to the LTC until such time as the Council decides otherwise or until the approval of the first plan of work for exploitation.[54]

The Council considered a report about operationalization presented by the Secretariat. Whilst most delegations agreed on the need to ensure the operationalization of the Commission before the approval of the first plan of work for exploitation, others shared the view that further consideration would be required due to the financial implications on the budget of the Authority.[55]

Nothing has been decided so far and this remains a pending challenge, important for the future of the ISA. Should the Authority activate the organs whose operation was postponed by the 1994 Agreement, so that the system can develop as was originally provided for, or should it continue postponing their functioning on economic grounds?

Stakeholder consultations

As of August 2022, the ISA has 99 observers: 30 States that are not party to UNCLOS, 32 United Nations and other intergovernmental organizations, as well as 37 non-governmental organizations.

The Authority has always involved all stakeholders with workshops, consultations and capacity-building activities, and it is becoming increasingly common for the Authority to hold stakeholder consultations for substantive issues. Namely, in the process of drafting the exploitation regulations, the Secretariat increases its efforts to highlight the transparency of the whole process,

48 See online <https://isa.org.jm/files/files/documents/alg-oboag-entp.pdf> (accessed September 2022) and ISBA/26/C/40.

49 ISBA/25/C/36.

50 ISBA/26/C/15.

51 ISBA/27/C/34.

52 ISBA/27/C/21/Add.1, paragraphs 9–11.

53 ISBA/27/C/25.

54 Section 1, paragraph 4, Annex, 1994 Agreement.

55 ISBA/27/C/21/Add.1, paragraphs 31–33.

with a series of broad public consultations since the beginning.[56] In a logical feedback process, stakeholders are engaging and participating more and more frequently, with detailed and concrete contributions.[57]

The commitment of the ISA to a meaningful and informed engagement with all stakeholders in the work of the different organs and in the advancement of its mandate is reflected in the Strategic plan and the High-Level Action Plan.[58] In addition, the Secretariat developed a draft 'Communications and Stakeholder Engagement Strategy', and all the members of the Authority and all the other stakeholders were invited to submit their comments.[59]

Marine scientific research

Under article 143, paragraph 2, of the Convention, the Authority shall promote and encourage the conduct of marine scientific research in the Area and shall coordinate and disseminate the results of such research and analysis when available. The ISA may also carry out research in its own right. As part of its responsibilities, the Authority also has the duty to encourage appropriate programmes to be designed and implemented for the benefit of developing States and technologically less developed States, with a view to (a) strengthening their research capabilities, (b) training their personnel in the techniques and applications of research and (c) fostering the employment of their qualified personnel in research in the Area.[60]

Several initiatives are being undertaken by the Authority to effectively discharge its responsibilities, based on the mandate given to the Authority pursuant to the Convention and the Agreement. These initiatives are detailed in the strategic plan of the Authority for the period 2019–2023 as adopted by the Assembly in 2018.[61]

As regards the obligation of the contractors to develop training programmes for personnel from developing States and from the ISA, it is important to highlight that, up to now, there have been nearly 400 scientists benefiting from the training programmes. For them, being a part of surveys and working in the laboratories of contractors is the chance of a lifetime.

Conclusions

The increasing versatility and dynamism of the Authority has been demonstrated throughout its nearly 30 years of existence. The first stage of the most innovative legal regime for sustainable mining in the deep seabed ever has already been implemented. All the rules, regulations and procedures have been adopted by consensus and no unilateral claims of seabed resources have been presented since the entry into force of the Convention.

56 See a detail of the stakeholder consultations on the Draft Exploitation Regulations. Available online <https://isa.org.jm/mining-code/draft-exploitation-regulations>, <https://www.isa.org.jm/survey/stakeholder-survey-march-2014> and <https://www.isa.org.jm/survey/2015-payment-mechanism-survey> (accessed September 2022).

57 ISA, Submissions received with respect to the stakeholder consultations on Standards and Guidelines 2020–2021, available online <https://www.isa.org.jm/submissions-received-respect-stakeholder-consultations-standards-and-guidelines> (accessed September 2022).

58 See online <https://www.isa.org.jm/news/isa-opens-draft-communications-and-stakeholder-engagement-strategy-public-consultation> (accessed September 2022).

59 See online <https://isa.org.jm/files/files/documents/Draft_Comms_and_Stakeholder_Engagement_Strategy.pdf> (accessed September 2022).

60 UNCLOS, art. 143 (3).

61 ISBA/24/A/10, Annex.

Now the second and vital phase is coming. New horizons open as the beginning of the exploitation stage will require institutional improvements and changes, demanding more resources and capacity. At the same time, the income from exploration contracts will be allocated in the first place to cover the expenses of the Authority, which will result in more flexibility. It should be borne in mind that the ISA is not a separate entity from its Member States, and that is why it is so important to reach consensus and keep the consultation processes going.

To face the upcoming challenges, the Convention conferred the ISA with the necessary powers and functions.[62] These are not limited to Part XI and its Annexes, as the powers and functions of the ISA are set out throughout the text of the Convention.[63] Additionally, the ISA has 'incidental powers'—consistent with the Convention—necessary to exercise its powers and functions with respect to activities in the Area.[64] 'Incidental powers' are those unwritten powers necessary for an international organization to effectively implement such powers and functions as are expressly conferred upon it.[65] The Convention also allows the Assembly to make recommendations for encouraging the progressive development of international law and its codification.[66]

As stated by the current Secretary General of the Authority, without the Convention, its Part XI, which implements the principle of common heritage of mankind, and without the Authority, which acts on its behalf, the mineral resources of the deep seabed would be freely available for anyone, on a first-come, first-served basis with no global environmental standards or return for developing States.[67]

Instead, deep sea mineral exploration is currently one of the most tightly regulated activities in the oceans, as it can only be undertaken under a contract with the Authority and with the sponsorship of a State Party.

Nevertheless, several mechanisms provided in the Convention are not yet fully operational, such as the inspection of activities in the Area, the Enterprise, environmental impact assessment, due regard of the rights and interests of coastal States, among others. As mentioned in this book by Jaeckel,[68] because of the delays in becoming fully operational, potential contracts are missed.

In addition, the core of the system of CHM, that is, the payment mechanisms, the share of monetary and non-monetary benefits, the mechanism that will enable the full participation of developing States and the decision on how the benefits will be shared, are crucial pending issues.[69]

Taking into account that the circumstances for the exploitation of the deep seabed, with its unique ecosystems, are rather uncertain, it is an important task for the ISA to adopt a policy and regulatory framework for exploitation that, at the same time, ensures the effective protection of the marine environment. The future of the ISA depends largely on its flexibility to adapt, being able to keep pace with the progress in deep sea mining without giving up its mandate.

62 Article 157 (2), UNCLOS.

63 Arts. 82, 84.2, 143, 144, 160.2.j, 209, 256, 273, 274, 287.2, 288.3, 305, 308.3.5, 311.6, 314, 316.5, 319.1.a and b and 319.3, UNCLOS.

64 Art. 157 (2) in fine, UNCLOS.

65 See S.N. Nandan, M.W. Lodge and S. Rosenne (eds.), *The development of the regime for deep seabed mining* (Reprint of the Introduction to Volume VI of the University of Virginia Center for Oceans Law and Policy, Commentary on the 1982 Convention on the Law of the Sea), International Seabed Authority, Kingston, Jamaica, 2002, pp. 4–5.

66 Art. 160 (2) (j), UNCLOS.

67 M. Lodge, *The legal regime for the deep seabed under Part XI of the United Nations Convention on the Law of the Sea*, Video, Audiovisual Library of International Law, 11 December 2019. Available online <https://legal.un.org/avl/ls/Lodge_LS.html> (accessed September 2022).

68 See Jaeckel, op. cit.

69 See Dingwall, op. cit.

It is important to bear in mind that the Convention provides for an important mechanism to help the Authority in its responsibilities: the possibility to request the Seabed Disputes Chamber for an advisory opinion on legal questions arising within the scope of their activities. The ISA has already utilized this mechanism and essential concerns were clarified.[70]

References

Armas-Pfirter F.M., 'The "common heritage of mankind" principle and the equitable sharing of benefits', in Ascencio-Herrera and Nordquist (eds.), *The United Nations convention on the law of the sea, part XI regime and the international seabed authority: A twenty-five year journey*, Brill, 2022, pp. 85–98.

Armas-Pfirter F.M., 'The international seabed authority and the protection of biodiversity', in A. de Paiva Toledo and V.J.M. Tassin (eds.), *Guide to the navigation of marine biodiversity beyond national jurisdiction*, Belo Horizonte: Editora D'Placido, 2018, pp. 221–246.

Armas-Pfirter F.M., 'The seabed disputes chamber: Moving forward', in J. Norton Moore (ed.), *Legal order in the world's oceans: The UN convention on the law of the sea*, Brill Nijhoff, 2018, pp. 210–227.

Dingwall J., 'The common heritage quandary: Devising a global payment regime for exploitation activities in the deep seabed area', in V. Tassin Campanella (ed.), *Routledge handbook of seabed mining and the law of the sea*, London: Routledge, 2023, chapter IV.2.

Feria-Tinta M. and Kamga M., 'Mining the bottom of the sea: Potential future disputes and the role of the international tribunal for the law of the sea', in V. Tassin Campanella (ed.), *Routledge handbook of seabed mining and the law of the sea*, London: Routledge, 2023, chapter V.3.

International Seabed Authority, Kingston, Jamaica, *Protection of the seabed environment, brochure, March 2008.*

Jaeckel A., 'The Area and the role of the international seabed authority', in V. Tassin Campanella (ed.), *Routledge handbook of seabed mining and the law of the sea*, London: Routledge, 2023, chapter IV.1.

Nandan S.N., Lodge M.W. and Rosenne S. (eds.) *United Nations convention on the law of the sea 1982 – A commentary*, Martinus Nijhoff Publishers, 2002, 1016 pp.

Nandan S.N., Lodge M.W. and Rosenne S. (eds.) *The development of the regime for deep seabed mining* (Reprint of the Introduction to Volume VI of the University of Virginia Center for Oceans Law and Policy, Commentary on the 1982 Convention on the Law of the Sea) International Seabed Authority, Kingston, Jamaica, 2002.

Scovazzi T., 'The concept of common heritage of mankind and the resources of the seabed beyond the limits of national jurisdiction', in *Los Recursos del Lecho y Subsuelo del Mar*, Buenos Aires: COPLA-CARI, 2006, pp. 139–146.

Tuerk H., 'The international seabed area', in D. Attard, M. Fitzmaurice and N. Martinez (eds.), *The IMI manual on international maritime law – Volume I: The law of the sea*, Chapter 10, New York: Oxford University Press, 2014.

Wolfrum R., 'The contribution of the regulations of the international seabed authority to the progressive development of international environmental law', in *Peace and order in the world's ocean: Essays in honor of Satya N. Nandan*, London: Brill, 2014, pp. 241–248.

70 See M. Feria-Tinta and M. Kamga, 'Mining the bottom of the sea: Potential future disputes and the role of the International Tribunal for the Law of the Sea', in V. Tassin Campanella (ed.), *Routledge handbook of seabed mining and the law of the sea*, op. cit., chapter V.3. See also F. Armas-Pfirter, 'The seabed disputes chamber: Moving forward', in J. Norton Moore (ed.), *Legal order in the world's oceans: The UN Convention on the Law of the Sea*, Brill Nijhoff, 2018, pp. 210–227.

PART V

Dispute settlement

V.1

DISPUTE SETTLEMENT AND SEABED MINING IN THE AREA

Tullio Treves

Introduction

In the negotiations at the Third United Nations Conference on the Law of the Sea (1973–1982) that led to the adoption of the *United Nations Convention for the Law of the Sea* (UNCLOS) it was broadly agreed that the mechanism and regime concerning mining activities in the seabed and ocean floor beyond the limits of national jurisdiction (the 'Area') would need to be complemented by rules for the settlement of disputes.[1] Already in 1970, the Declaration on Principles Governing the Sea-Bed and the Ocean Floor, adopted by the UN General Assembly, had stated:

> The parties to any dispute relating to the activities in the Area and its resources shall resolve such disputes by the measures mentioned in article 33 of the Charter of the United Nations *and such procedures for settling disputes as may be agreed upon in the international regime to be established.*[2] (emphasis supplied)

The idea of a Seabed Tribunal as part of the new regime for deep seabed mining[3] under negotiation and with the International Organization to be established to administer it, the International Seabed Authority (ISA), was discussed in the First Committee of the Conference and incorporated firstly in the Informal Single Negotiating Text of 1975.[4] Article 24 (1) stated that among the 'principal organs' of the ISA there would be the 'Tribunal'. Articles 32 to 34 and 57 to 63 broached the structure of a nine-member Tribunal and its jurisdiction. A few months later, the document of the President of the Conference completing, as far as dispute-settlement was concerned, the Informal

1 The history of the negotiations, starting in the Seabed Committee in 1969, is set out in M.H. Nordquist, S. Rosenne, and L.B. Sohn (eds), *United Nations Convention on the Law of the Sea 1982: A commentary*, vol. 5, Nijhoff, 1989, pp. 332–37, pp. 399–403; and S. Nandan, S.W. Lodge, and S. Rosenne (eds), *United Nations Convention on the Law of the Sea 1982: A commentary*, vol. 6, Nijhoff, 2002, pp. 594–604.

2 Resolution 2749 (XXV) of 17 December 1970, para. 15.

3 Deep seabed mining is used in this article as a reference to activities conducted in the Area.

4 Revised single negotiating text, A/CONF.62/WP.8/Part I of 7 May 1975.

DOI: 10.4324/9780429426162-17

Single Negotiating Text,[5] was included in Annex IC of the Statute of an International Tribunal for the Law of the Sea, as part of a general system for the settlement of disputes concerning the interpretation and application of UNCLOS. The relationship of this International Tribunal with 'the Tribunal' mentioned in Part I was not clarified.

The proposals for a Tribunal made in the negotiations for deep seabed mining disputes and for an International Tribunal for the Law of the Sea (ITLOS) envisaged for other disputes concerning UNCLOS were merged later during the Conference. The merger was effected in the ICNT,[6] the first of the negotiating texts of the UN Law of the Sea Conference that set out all the parts of the future convention as an integrated whole. The 'Tribunal' for seabed mining disputes was replaced by the Seabed Disputes Chamber (SDC) which was no longer an organ of ISA but a Chamber of ITLOS with a particular status (it may be considered a tribunal within the Tribunal).[7] The SDC is the principal organ established by UNCLOS for the settlement of disputes concerning deep seabed mining.

The Seabed Disputes Chamber[8]

The composition of the Seabed Disputes Chamber, the selection of its members and their term of office

The SDC is 'composed of 11 members, selected by a majority of the elected members of the Tribunal from among them'.[9] The members of the SDC are not 'elected' but 'selected'. This has meant, in the practice of the Tribunal, that the composition of the SDC is the object of consultations conducted by the President of the Tribunal who then makes a proposal to the Tribunal which the Tribunal has in all cases approved by consensus. The composition of the SDC is renewed every three years as soon as possible after the composition of the Tribunal has been renewed through elections.[10]

In the composition of the SDC, 'the representation of the principal legal systems of the world and equitable geographical distribution must be assured'.[11] While the Assembly of the ISA 'may adopt recommendations of a general nature relating to such representation and distribution',[12] it has, up to now, refrained from doing so. The indications of the Statute as to the composition of the

5 Informal single negotiating text, A/CONF.62/WP.9 of 21 July 1975.

6 Informal Composite Negotiating Text, A/CONF.62/WP 10 of 15 July 1977.

7 M.H. Nordquist, S. Rosenne, and L.B. Sohn (eds), *United Nations Convention on the Law of the Sea 1982, A commentary*, vol. 5, Nijhoff, 1989, pp. 399–403.

8 UNCLOS deals with the SDC in Part XI, art. 159, para. (10, art. 162, para. 2 (u) and (v), art. 165 para. 2 I and (j) and sec. 5, arts 186–191, in Part XV, art. 287, para. 2, art. 288, para. 3, art. 290, para. 5, Annex VI (the Statute of the Tribunal), arts 35–40. The Rules of the Tribunal, adopted by ITLOS on 28 October 1997 (the Rules), contain provisions specifically concerning the SDC (arts 22–25, 105–123). Clarifications about the role of the SDC are set out in the SDC Advisory Opinion of 1 February 2011 *Responsibilities and obligations of States with respect to activities in the Area*, ITLOS, Reports, 2011, p. 4 ff, hereinafter 'Advisory Opinion of 2011'. The Resolution on the Internal Judicial Practice of the Tribunal, adopted on 31 October 1997 refers to the deliberations of ITLOS in its plenary composition. In its deliberations concerning Advisory Opinion of 2011 the SDC has applied it with the necessary adaptations required in particular by the fact that the Chamber has 11 and not 21 members. So, the Drafting Committee was of three and not of five (or more) members as in ITLOS.

9 Article 35, para. 1, Annex VI, UNCLOS.

10 Rules of the International Tribunal for the Law of the Sea ('Rules'), art. 23.

11 Article 35, para. 2, Annex VI, UNCLOS.

12 Ibid.

SDC are followed by a more or less automatic reflection of the same rule concerning the ITLOS as a whole and by an informally agreed formula for distributing the seats in the SDC between the judges of the SDC nationals of the five geographical groups at the UN General Assembly.[13]

The term of office of the members of the SDC ends on 30 September of the third year after the election.[14] Members may be (and often are) re-selected to serve a second consecutive term. Under article 35, paragraph 5 of Annex VI to UNCLOS, '[i]f proceedings are still pending at the end of any three-year term for which the Chamber has been selected, the Chamber shall complete the proceedings in its original composition'. This provision is similar but not identical to that of article 5 (3) of the same Annex stating that, although replaced, judges of the ITLOS 'shall finish any proceedings which they may have begun before the date of their replacement'. Article 17 of the Rules of the Tribunal clarifies this article specifying that the continuation of the participation in proceedings of the replaced judge shall be 'until the completion of any phase in respect of which the Tribunal has met in accordance with article 68' (initial deliberation after the closure of written proceeding). Although this is not provided for by a specific provision, this rule should be considered as applicable also to members of the SDC who have been replaced and continue to serve under article 35, paragraph 5 of Annex VI.

The President of the Seabed Disputes Chamber and the Registrar

The President of the SDC is elected by the SBC from among its members and for the term for which the SDC is selected.[15] The Rules concerning the presidency of ITLOS apply,[16] but, different from them, there is no provision for a Vice-President.

No provision regulates the relationship between the President of the SDC and the President of ITLOS. This marks the independent status granted to the SDC. In practice, especially when a case before the SDC is pending, contacts between the two Presidents are necessary in order to avoid overlapping meetings and more in general to keep the President of ITLOS informed in view of the fact that the judgments of SDC are 'considered as rendered by the Tribunal'.[17] Such contacts were in fact held during the proceedings for the Advisory Opinion of 2011.

The Registrar of ITLOS is the Registrar of the SDC. His Deputy and the staff of the Registry serve the SDC as they serve the ITLOS.

Ad hoc chambers

The SDC may constitute an ad hoc chamber of three of its members 'upon the request of any party to the dispute' to deal with disputes mentioned in article 187 (a) of UNCLOS (UNCLOS Annex VI, article 36, specifying that each party may appoint a member of the Chamber in case they do not agree on the composition proposed by the SDC). The possibility of resorting to an ad hoc chamber permits to submit unilaterally disputes between States Parties concerning the interpretation and application of Part XI of UNCLOS and connected annexes to a very small panel. It has never been resorted to. It may be criticized especially in light of the fact that submission of a case to an ad hoc Chamber of the Tribunal, normally composed of five members, on non-seabed mining issues

13 G. Eiriksson, *The International Tribunal for the Law of the Sea*, Martinus Nijhoff Publishers, 2000, p. 69.

14 Rules, art. 23.

15 Article 35 para. 4, Annex VI, UNCLOS; article 26 para. 1, Rules.

16 Article 26 para. 4, Rules.

17 Article 15 para. 5, Annex VI, UNCLOS.

requires the agreement of both parties.[18] The same disputes may, however, also be submitted to a special Chamber of the ITLOS but only if this is done by agreement of the parties.[19] No ad hoc chamber has been constituted so far.

The seabed disputes chamber and the International Seabed Authority

In its Advisory Opinion of 2011, the SDC describes its function and role in relation to the ISA as follows:

> The Chamber is a separate judicial body within the Tribunal entrusted, through its advisory and contentious jurisdiction, with the exclusive function of interpreting Part XI of the Convention and the relevant annexes and regulations that are the legal basis for the organization and management of activities in the Area.
>
> *(paragraph 25)*

Focusing on its advisory jurisdiction, the same Opinion specifies the role of the SDC as regards the ISA:

> The advisory jurisdiction is connected with the activities of the Assembly and the Council, the two principal organs of the Authority (…) In order to exercise its functions properly in accordance with the Convention, the Authority may require the assistance of an independent and impartial judicial body. This is the underlying reason for the advisory jurisdiction of the Chamber. *In the exercise of that jurisdiction, the Chamber is part of the system in which the Authority's organs operate, but its task within that system is to act as an independent and impartial body.*
>
> *(paragraph 26, emphasis supplied)*

Independence and impartiality for the benefit of the good functioning of the system are the key elements. The role of the SDC, both in its advisory and contentious jurisdiction, is further described as follows: 'The functions of the Chamber, set out in Part XI of the Convention, are relevant for the good governance of the Area' (paragraph 29).

The applicable law

The SDC must take its decisions, both in contentious and in advisory proceedings, on the basis of the law indicated by two provisions of UNCLOS: article 293, which, according to article 38 (1) of Annex VI, applies to ITLOS as well as to the SDC and the same article 38, specifically providing for the SDC. Under article 293, paragraph 1, the law to be applied is the UNCLOS and 'other rules of international law not incompatible' with it. UNCLOS Annex VI, article 38, specifies that in addition to what is provided in article 293, the SDC shall apply:

a) the rules, regulations and procedures of the Authority adopted in accordance with this Convention
b) the terms of contracts concerning activities in the Area in matters relating to those contracts.

18 Article 15 para. 2, ibid.
19 Article 188, para. 1 a), UNCLOS.

This extension of the applicable law beyond what is provided in article 293 of UNCLOS depends on the particular scope *ratione materiae* and *ratione personarum* of the SDC's jurisdiction.

The SDC has had an opportunity to apply Regulations adopted by the ISA in the Advisory Opinion of 2011. The Opinion also gives indications about the interpretation of such Regulations, as follows:

> The fact that these instruments are binding texts negotiated by States and adopted through a procedure similar to that used in multilateral conferences permits the Chamber to consider that the interpretation rules set out in the Vienna Convention may, by analogy, provide guidance as to their interpretation. In the specific case before the Chamber, the analogy is strengthened because of the close connection between these texts and the Convention.[20]

Contentious jurisdiction

Compulsory exclusive jurisdiction

The contentious jurisdiction of the SDC is compulsory. Once States become parties to UNCLOS they accept, and accept also for persons of their nationality or under their control, the right to institute proceedings and the obligation to submit to the SDC if another party triggers proceedings against them. The SDC contentious jurisdiction is thus compulsory. It is also exclusive because the disputes covered by the SDC's jurisdiction are excluded from the jurisdiction of ITLOS. Under article 287 paragraph 2 of UNCLOS:

> A declaration made under paragraph 1 [namely a declaration of preference for the adjudicating body entitled to exercise compulsory jurisdiction under UNCLOS] shall not affect or be affected by the obligation of a State Party to accept the jurisdiction of the Seabed Disputes Chamber of the International Tribunal for the Law of the Sea to the extent and in the manner provided for in Part XI, section 5.

UNCLOS article 288 paragraph 3 states that the SDC 'and any other chamber or arbitral tribunal referred to in Part XI, section 5, shall have jurisdiction in any matter which is submitted to it in accordance therewith', implying that other adjudicating bodies provided for in the UNCLOS do not enjoy such jurisdiction. The possible competence of an ad hoc Chamber of the ITLOS under article 188, paragraph 1 a), discussed above and of a commercial arbitration tribunal under UNCLOS Article 188, paragraph 1 b), c), d) discussed below, may be seen as the only exceptions to the exclusivity of the SDC's jurisdiction.

Article 187: jurisdiction **ratione personarum** *and* **ratione materiae**

UNCLOS article 187 defines the scope of the contentious jurisdiction of the SDC. It describes six categories of disputes covered by the SDC's jurisdiction. Such description indicates which entities

20 Advisory Opinion of 2011, para. 60. The Opinion further states in the same paragraph that: 'The ICJ seems to have adopted a similar approach when it states in its advisory opinion on *Accordance with International Law of the Unilateral Declaration of Independence in Respect of Kosovo*, that the rules on interpretation of the Vienna Convention "may provide guidance" as regards the interpretation of resolutions of the United Nations Security Council (ICJ, Advisory Opinion 22 July 2010, paragraph 94)'.

may be parties to each category of disputes and the object of the disputes included in each of these categories. Thus, article 187 defines the jurisdiction *ratione personarum* and *ratione materiae* of the SDC in contentious cases.

Juridiction ratione personarum – *the role of sponsoring States*

As far as jurisdiction *ratione personarum* is concerned, it must be noted that the parties to disputes before the SDC are of different kinds. As compared with other international courts and tribunals, it may be said that the SDC is the international adjudicating body before which the highest variety of entities may appear: States, the Authority, the Enterprise, State enterprises, and natural or juridical persons. Moreover, according to UNCLOS article 190, paragraph 1:

> If a natural or juridical person is a party to a dispute referred to in article 187, the sponsoring State shall be given notice thereof and shall have the right to participate in the proceedings by submitting written or oral statements. [21]

The notion and regime of the 'sponsoring State', first mentioned in UNCLOS article 153 paragraph 2 b) stating that in order to conduct activities in the Area a state enterprise and a natural or juridical person having the nationality of, or being effectively controlled by, a State party, must be sponsored by such States, are clarified in the Advisory Opinion of 2011. In particular, the Opinion specifies that:

> The connection between States Parties and domestic law entities required by the Convention is twofold, namely, that of nationality and that of effective control. (…) If another State or its nationals exercises effective control, the sponsorship of that State is also necessary.
>
> *(paragraph 77)*

and that:

> No provision of the Convention imposes an obligation on a State Party to sponsor an entity that holds its nationality or is controlled by it or by its nationals.
>
> *(paragraph 88)*

When a State has declared that it sponsors a contractor, article 139 of UNCLOS applies and so it is bound to adopt all the appropriate and necessary measures to secure effective compliance by the sponsored entity, as clarified by the Advisory Opinion of 2011.

Jurisdiction ratione materiae – *activities in the Area*

Regarding jurisdiction *ratione materiae*, the *chapeau* of article 187 makes it clear that the disputes over which the SDC has jurisdiction, whichever listed categories they belong to, must be 'disputes with respect to activities in the Area'.

21 Implementing UNCLOS article 190, articles 118 and 119 of the Rules provide for the modalities of participation of sponsoring States and for the consequences in case of non-participation. Article 120 of the Rules concerns the procedure when proceedings are brought before the SDC by notification of a special agreement.

A definition of 'activities in the Area' thus becomes essential to determine the jurisdiction *ratione materiae* of the SDC. While UNCLOS article 1, paragraph 3, defines 'activities in the Area' as 'all activities of exploration for, and exploitation of, the resources of the Area', and while 'resources of the Area' are defined in article 133 as 'mineral' resources, there is no definition of 'exploration and exploitation'. In its Advisory Opinion of 2011, the SDC examined a variety of provisions of UNCLOS including its annexes, and of the Regulations of the Authority, finding elements for a detailed description of 'exploration and exploitation' thus clarifying the meaning of 'activities in the Area'. According to the SDC these activities 'in the context of both exploration and exploitation, include[s], first of all, the recovery of minerals from the seabed and their lifting to the water surface' (paragraph 94). They moreover include 'drilling, dredging, excavation, disposal of waste, construction and operation or maintenance of installations, pipelines and other devices related to such activities' (paragraph 85) as well as 'coring, and excavation; disposal, dumping and discharge into the marine environment of sediment, wastes or other effluents' (paragraph 87). Moreover, under UNCLOS Annex III, article 17, paragraph 2 f), of the Convention, 'shipboard processing immediately above a mine site of minerals derived from that mine site' is to be considered as included in 'activities in the Area' (paragraph 88). The Advisory Opinion of 2011 further specifies that:

> Transportation to points on land from the part of the high seas superjacent to the part of the Area in which the contractor operates cannot be included in the notion of 'activities in the Area'.

However, 'transportation within that part of the high seas, when directly connected with extraction and lifting, should be included in activities in the Area' (paragraph 96).

Categories of disputes concerning activities in the Area: UNCLOS article 187

Article 187 sets out a list in six points, from (a) to (f), of the disputes concerning activities in the Area for which the contentious jurisdiction of the SDC is established. The list includes:

Firstly, article 187 (a) lists disputes between States Parties concerning the interpretation or application of Part XI of UNCLOS and Annexes III and IV relating thereto, which can be labelled normal international disputes.[22]

Secondly, article 187 (b) lists disputes that have clear similarities to those for which administrative judges are competent in certain States, and to some of those that may be submitted to the European Court of Justice. These are disputes concerning the relationship between States Parties and the Authority relating to alleged violations of Part XI, its annexes, and rules, regulations and procedures of the Authority, as well as 'acts of the Authority alleged to be in excess of jurisdiction or a misuse of power'.

Thirdly, article 187 (c) lists disputes we may call 'contractual'. These are disputes between parties – which may be the Authority, the Enterprise, natural or juridical persons and State enterprises – to a contract or plan of work concerning the interpretation of a contract or plan of work or acts or omissions of either party to a contract 'directed at the other party or directly affecting its legitimate interests'. Article 190, paragraph 2, aims at permitting a party to obtain that in these disputes, when one party is natural or juridical person, and the other a State, the dispute be conducted either by the

22 Article 187 (a), UNCLOS.

sponsoring State of the natural or juridical person against the other State, or by a juridical person of the nationality of the respondent State against the plaintiff natural or juridical person.[23] So a party may obtain that a dispute between a State and a natural or juridical person becomes either a State-to-State dispute or a dispute between private parties.

Fourthly, article 187 (d) mentions disputes of a 'pre-contractual' nature between the Authority and a prospective contractor (that must be sponsored by a State) for refusal to contract or legal issues arising in the contractual negotiations. The last two categories mentioned bear some analogy with disputes between States and private investors under the International Centre for Settlement of Investment Disputes (ICSID) and other conventions.

Fifthly, article 187 (e) includes disputes concerning the liability of the Authority, between the Authority 'and a State Party, a state enterprise or a natural or juridical person sponsored by a State Party'. The liability of the Authority must be within the terms of UNCLOS Annex III, article 22.[24]

Finally, article 187 (f) mentions 'any other disputes for which the jurisdiction of the Chamber is specifically provided in th[e] Convention'. The disputes which are sometimes considered to be comprised in this provision are those mentioned in article 185, paragraph 2, concerning the determination by the SDC that a State has 'grossly and persistently violated the provisions' of Part XI, and in sections 6 and 8 of the Annex to the Agreement relating to the Implementation of Part XI of the UNCLOS, of 28 July 1994. The latter provisions deal with disputes concerning the interpretation of the General Agreement on Tariffs and Trade and successor or superseding agreements when not all the parties to the dispute are parties to the agreement (section 6, paragraph f), ii)) and with disputes concerning the interpretation or application of rules and regulations relating to the financial terms of contracts (section 8, f)).

Disputes concerning activities in the Area not listed in article 187 and disputes included in the list of article 187 but not concerning activities in the Area

There may be disputes between States Parties concerning the interpretation or application of a provision of Part XI of UNCLOS, thus fulfilling a condition set out in article 187 (a), which do not concern 'activities in the Area' thus not fulfilling another condition set out in the same article.[25] An example could be a dispute concerning UNCLOS article 149, on archaeological and historical objects found in the Area, which is in Part XI but does not concern an 'activity in the Area' as defined in UNCLOS.

23 Article 190, para. 2 of UNCLOS is as follows: 'If an action is brought against a State Party by a natural or juridical person sponsored by another State Party in a dispute referred to in article 187, subparagraph (c), the respondent State may request the State sponsoring that person to appear in the proceedings on behalf of that person. Failing such appearance, the respondent State may arrange to be represented by a juridical person of its nationality'.

24 Article 22 of annex III of UNCLOS is as follows: 'The contractor shall have responsibility or liability for any damage arising out of wrongful acts in the conduct of its operations, account being taken of contributory acts or omissions by the Authority. Similarly, the Authority shall have responsibility or liability for any damage arising out of wrongful acts in the exercise of its powers and functions, including violations under article 168, paragraph 2, account being taken of contributory acts or omissions by the contractor. Liability in every case shall be for the actual amount of damage'. It seems noteworthy that article 187 (e) mentions disputes concerning the liability of the Authority referring to article 22 of annex III, while the latter provision refers also to the liability of the contractor. Jurisdiction on disputes for wrongful acts of a contractor – provided that they do not amount to violations of contracts which would be covered by article 187 (c) – seem not to be explicitly covered by the jurisdiction of the SDC.

25 T. Treves, 'Judicial action for the common heritage', in H. Hestermayer et al. (eds), *Law of the sea in dialogue*, Springer, 2010, p. 113.

There could also be disputes concerning 'activities in the Area' not covered by the categories listed in article 187. An example could be a dispute concerning overlapping claims of prospective contractors. In these cases, one of the requirements of jurisdiction of the SDC would be missing excluding the jurisdiction of the SDC.

These disputes should not, in my view, remain without a competent judge. In the first case mentioned, the jurisdiction of ITLOS would exist, as this would be a dispute between States Parties about the interpretation or application of an article of UNCLOS. The second case mentioned is more difficult and it is to be hoped that the ISA adopts a provision to deal with it. Lacking it, an effort would become necessary to adopt an extensive interpretation of article 187. An author has listed, as disputes that fall outside the SDC's jurisdiction, those concerning 'interference of activities in the Area with rights of third parties under High Seas; protection and preservation of the marine environment or marine scientific research' as well as disputes with a State non-party to UNCLOS.[26]

It may be debated whether disputes concerning non-compliance with the reasonable regard obligation set out in UNCLOS article 147, paragraphs 1 and 3 in case of interference between activities in the Area and the exercise of the freedom to lay cables or pipelines under UNCLOS article 87, paragraph 1 c), would be considered as concerning activities in the Area. If they would, they would fall under the jurisdiction of the SDC, while, if considered as concerning the interpretation or application of article 87, they would fall under the jurisdiction of the bodies competent under Part XV of UNCLOS.[27]

Exclusions of the contentious jurisdiction of the Seabed Disputes Chamber

Voluntary exclusions: special and ad hoc chambers, commercial arbitration

As mentioned above when discussing special chambers, as concerns disputes mentioned in article 187 (a), the jurisdiction of the SDC may be excluded, under article 188, paragraph 1 (a) when the parties by agreement submit one such dispute to a Special Chamber of ITLOS established according to UNCLOS Annex VI, articles 15 and 17, or one party submits it to a three-judge ad hoc chamber of the SDC.[28]

A further limitation to the jurisdiction of the SDC may concern disputes on the interpretation of contracts mentioned in article 187 (c) i). They may be submitted, at request of one party, to commercial arbitration. The commercial arbitral tribunal will, however, have no jurisdiction to adjudicate questions of interpretation of UNCLOS Part XI and relevant annexes. If such a question needs to be addressed, the arbitral tribunal shall suspend its proceedings and refer the question to the SDC for a ruling.[29] The decision of the arbitral tribunal shall follow the ruling of the SDC.[30] This mechanism was inspired by the 'preliminary rulings' under European Union (then European Community) law.

26 F.M. Armas-Pfirter, 'The seabed disputes chamber: Moving forward', in M.H. Nordquist, J.N. Moore, and R. Long (eds), *Legal order in the world's oceans, UN Convention on the Law of the Sea*, Brill Nijhoff, 2018, pp. 210–27, at p. 215.

27 T. Treves, '"Due regard" obligations under the 1982 UN Convention on the Law of the Sea: The lying of cables and activities in the Area', *The International Journal of Marine and Coastal Law* 24, 2019, 191–93.

28 Article 188, para. 1 b), UNCLOS.

29 Article 188, para. 2 a), ibid.

30 Article 188, para. 2 b), ibid.

Automatic exclusions: no exercise of discretion, no decision on the validity of rules and regulations

Under UNCLOS article 189, the SDC 'shall have no jurisdiction with regard to the exercise by the Authority of its discretionary powers' and 'in no case shall it substitute its discretion for that of the Authority'. Moreover, in exercising its jurisdiction pursuant to article 187, the SDC

> shall not pronounce itself on the question of whether any rules, regulations and procedures of the Authority are in conformity with th[e] Convention, nor declare invalid any such rules, regulations and procedures. Its jurisdiction in this regard shall be confined to deciding claims that the application of any rules, regulations and procedures of the Authority in individual cases would be in conflict with the contractual obligations of the parties to the dispute or their obligations under this Convention, claims concerning excess of jurisdiction or misuse of power, and to claims for damages to be paid or other remedy to be given to the party concerned for the failure of the other party to comply with its contractual obligations or its obligations under this Convention.

Provisional measures

Article 290, at paragraphs 1 and 5, specifies that the UNCLOS provisions concerning provisional measures are applicable to the SDC. So, a request for provisional measures may be submitted to the SDC 'to preserve the respective rights of the parties to the dispute or to prevent serious harm to the marine environment pending the final decision' (article 290, paragraph 1).

Thus, the possibility to utilize provisional measures to protect the marine environment, which is a characteristic of provisional measures under UNCLOS as compared to provisional measures under the ICJ Statute article 41, applies also as regards disputes concerning activities in the Area submitted to the SDC.

Enforcement

Article 39 of UNCLOS Annex VI contains a rare provision, comparable to article 54 of the ICSID Convention, concerning the enforcement of judgments of the SDC.[31] The provision is as follows:

> The decisions of the Chamber shall be enforceable in the territories of the States Parties in the same manner as judgments or orders of the highest court of the State Party in whose territory the enforcement is sought.

Compliance with this provision may require that States Parties to UNCLOS introduce modifications to their domestic law.

Advisory jurisdiction

General comments

The SDC is also endowed with advisory jurisdiction. The provisions of UNCLOS concerning such jurisdiction concern only the SDC, and not the ITLOS as a whole. Nevertheless, as is well

31 G. Cataldi, 'La mise en oeuvre des décisions des tribunaux internationaux dans l'ordre interne', in *Recueil des cours de l'académie de droit international de la haye*, t. 386, 2016, pp. 267–428, at pp. 368–71.

known, in its Advisory Opinion of 2 April 2015 on the *Request for Advisory Opinion submitted by the Sub-Regional Fisheries Commission*,[32] ITLOS made the controversial finding that the plenary Tribunal also has, in a few cases, an advisory jurisdiction. The basis of this finding was article 21 of UNCLOS Annex VI read together with a specific agreement providing for requests for advisory opinions to the ITLOS, and in light of article 138 of the Rules.

The Advisory Opinion of 2011 is, up to the time of writing, the only decision of the SDC, as no dispute has been submitted to it on the basis of its contentious jurisdiction. This Advisory Opinion attracted a lot of attention in the discussions within the ISA and in scholarly circles. It has also influenced in many regards the 2015 Advisory Opinion of the ITLOS. As already mentioned above, the Advisory Opinion of 2011 theorizes the role of the SDC as a part of the system to which the ISA belongs and whose task is to act as an independent and impartial body (paragraph 26). In concluding its general observations, the SDC further states that:

> The Chamber is mindful of the fact that by answering the questions it will assist the Council in the performance of its activities and contribute to the implementation of the Convention's regime.
>
> *(paragraph 30)*

The requests for an Advisory Opinion of the Seabed Disputes Chamber

Requests for advisory opinions may be submitted to the SDC by the ISA Assembly under article 159, paragraph 10, and by the ISA Council under article 191 of UNCLOS.

Under article 159, paragraph 10, an Advisory Opinion may be requested by the ISA Assembly upon request of one-quarter of its members 'on the conformity with this Convention [the UNCLOS] of a proposal before the Assembly on any matter'. The provision further states that the Assembly 'shall defer voting on the proposal pending receipt of the Advisory Opinion'. This provision envisages a direct involvement in the day-to-day work of the ISA Assembly. It seems to have been drafted on the basis of the assumptions that the Assembly is in session almost all the time, and that the SDC is able to respond to the request in a very short time. Both assumptions have proven unrealistic so it is understandable that there has been no attempt to utilize article 159, paragraph 10.

According to UNCLOS article 191:

> The Seabed Disputes Chamber shall give advisory opinions at the request of the Assembly or the Council on legal questions arising within the scope of their activities. Such opinions shall be given as a matter of urgency.

This was the provision invoked by the ISA Council in submitting the request for what was to be the Advisory Opinion of 2011. In interpreting the requirement of 'a request of...the Council', the SDC declared the request submitted to it valid because it was satisfied that it had been adopted by the Council by consensus 'in accordance with the internal rules of procedure of the Authority' (paragraph 35). In examining the requirement that the request must concern 'legal questions' the SDC observed that the questions submitted to it concerned 'the interpretation of provisions of the Convention and raise[d] issues of general international law' (paragraph 39). As regards the requirement that the legal question must arise within the scope of the activities of the requesting

32 ITLOS Reports 2015, 4.

organ, the SDC, after examining the provisions concerning the powers and functions of the ISA Council, concluded that 'the legal questions before it fall within the scope of the activities of the Council, since they relate to the exercise of its powers and functions, including its power to approve plans of work'(paragraph 44).

Are advisory opinions of the Seabed Disputes Chamber discretionary?

While article 65 of the ICJ Statute provides that the ICJ 'may give' advisory opinions, article 191 of UNCLOS states that the SDC 'shall give' such opinions. The Advisory Opinion of 2011 noted the difference and considered the argument according to which the SDC would have no discretion as to whether to entertain a request for an advisory opinion (paragraphs 47–48). It decided, however, that it was not 'necessary to pronounce on the consequences of that difference with respect to admissibility in the present case' (paragraph 49). In this context it is to be noted that article 138 of the Rules of the Tribunal, dealing with advisory opinions of ITLOS, uses the expression 'may give'. In its Advisory Opinion of 2 April 2015, ITLOS examined at length this provision without raising any doubt about it providing for a discretionary power.[33]

Procedure

Contentious cases

UNCLOS, including its Annex VI, does not contain provisions explicitly concerning procedure in cases before the SDC even though Annex VI's articles on default, right to intervene, requirements of judgments, and effect of decisions should be considered as applicable to the SDC. Provisions on procedure in the SDC are set out in articles 115 to 123 of the Rules. The basic rule is in article 115 according to which:

> Proceedings in contentious cases before the Seabed Disputes Chamber and its ad hoc chambers shall, subject to the provisions of the Convention, the Statute and these Rules relating specifically to the Seabed Disputes Chamber and its ad hoc chambers, be governed by the Rules applicable in contentious cases before the Tribunal.

Articles 117–121 of the Rules specifically concern disputes in contentious cases before the SDC. These provisions, however, do not apply, as specified in article 116, to disputes exclusively between States Parties and between States Parties and the Authority. These are the disputes envisaged in UNCLOS article 187 (a) and (b).

Thus, the procedure for contentious cases before ITLOS applies in full to the disputes between subjects of international law that fall under the SDC's jurisdiction. The proceedings are instituted either by notification of a special agreement or by written application.[34] The rules concerning ad hoc judges apply. The proceedings have a written and an oral phase and are concluded by a judgment. Intervention is also admitted.

Articles 117–119 concern disputes covered by article 187, (c) to (f), in which proceedings are instituted by means of an application. The requirements for the application are the usual ones, but

33 *Request for Advisory Opinion submitted by the Sub-Regional Fisheries Commission*, *ITLOS Reports 2015*, 4, at paras 70–79.

34 Article 24, Annex VI, UNCLOS.

data concerning the sponsoring State or States are to be included. The time limit for the respondent to lodge a defense is two months, in lieu of the six months indicated for the normal procedure before ITLOS.

Advisory proceedings

The procedure for advisory proceedings is set out in section H of the Rules.[35] The basic provision is in article 130 stating that the Chamber shall apply section H and 'be guided, to the extent to which it recognizes them to be applicable, by the provisions of the Statute and of these Rules applicable in contentious cases'.

Notice of the request for an advisory opinion shall be given to all States parties.[36] The SDC identifies the intergovernmental organizations 'which are likely to be able to furnish information on the question'.[37] According to article 133, paragraph 3, the SDC invites State Parties and the above-mentioned intergovernmental organization to submit a written statement within a prescribed – but modifiable – time limit. If the Chamber so decides, a second round of written pleadings may be held. The States and organizations that have submitted written statements may then participate in an oral hearing, if the SDC decides to hold it.[38] In the proceedings leading to the Advisory Opinion of 2011, two rounds of written pleadings and an oral hearing were held.

While not accepting requests by non-governmental organizations to participate as *amici curiae*, the SDC was sensitive to the need to give a voice to environmentally oriented organizations. Among the Intergovernmental Organizations invited there was the International Union for the Conservation of Nature (IUCN) which is a juridical person of Swiss law whose parties are numerous non-governmental organizations and more than 70 governments. Moreover, documents submitted by interested non-governmental organizations (Greenpeace International and World Wide Fund for Nature), although not made part of the case file, were posted on a separate section of the Tribunal's website.[39]

Experts

UNCLOS article 289 provides for the possibility, in cases involving technical or scientific matters, to have experts selected *ex officio* or at the request of the parties to sit with ITLOS without the right to vote. This article, under its terms, is not applicable to the SDC. Article 289 is clear in stating that it is applicable when the Tribunal is exercising its compulsory jurisdiction under section 2 of Part XV. Moreover, the article provides that the experts are to be chosen preferably from the lists mentioned in Annex VIII, article 2, which do not include experts in the scientific disciplines that may be involved in disputes before the SDC.

Nevertheless, it seems reasonable to suppose that if there were agreement between the parties and the Tribunal, experts of the kind mentioned in article 289 could be called to sit with the SDC. It must be noted that article 289 has never been applied by ITLOS. Therefore, it seems more likely

35 Articles 130–138, Rules.
36 Article 133, para. 1, ibid.
37 Article 133, para. 3, ibid.
38 Article 133, para. 4, ibid.
39 Advisory Opinion of 2011, paras 13–14. T. Treves, 'Non-governmental organizations before the international tribunal for the law of the sea: The advisory opinion of 1 February 2011', in *Le 90ème anniversaire de Boutros Boutros-Ghali, hommage du Curatorium à son président*, Hague Academy of International Law, 2012, pp. 255–62.

that the involvement of experts in proceedings before the SDC would be, as happened before ITLOS, through their inclusion in the ITLOS staff for the purposes of a case or in the parties' delegations.[40]

Conclusion

In more than a third of a century of existence the SDC has produced only one decision, namely the Advisory Opinion of 2011. Consequently, it is difficult and would be imprudent to make an assessment of its activity. Some observations may nonetheless be made.

First, it is not extraordinary that the SDC's jurisprudence is limited to one advisory opinion. Deep seabed mining has not yet started in earnest as the activities in the Area have been confined to the exploration stage. As regards the exploitation stage, which is the most likely to produce disputes, nothing has as yet happened on the ground, even though discussions within the International Seabed Authority concerning the adoption of a Regulation on Exploitation are well advanced.

Secondly, the Advisory Opinion of 2011 shows that the SDC is capable of giving a full meaning to its advisory jurisdiction by exercising a role in the system of the Authority answering with precision to the questions submitted to it by the Council and causing initiatives within the Council to comply with the suggestions contained in the Opinion.

Thirdly, the Advisory Opinion of 2011 shows that the SDC has played and might play again a role in interpreting UNCLOS in the context of general international law. It has made a contribution, in particular, to the development of international environmental law and of the law of State responsibility. Moreover, the 2011 Advisory Opinion has had an impact on the jurisprudence of ITLOS as a whole especially, but not limited to, on the full Tribunal's Advisory Opinion of 2015.

Fourthly, although no contentious cases have been submitted to the SDC, the provisions on the SDC's contentious jurisdiction are part and parcel of the UNCLOS seabed mining regime and have a role to play in the Authority's Regulations and contracts. The precise interpretation of the provisions concerning the different categories of disputes set out in UNCLOS article 187, and the role of chambers are among the key subjects yet to be developed in the case-law of the SDC. One may expect that once the first exploration activities in the deep seabed start, contentious cases may arise.

References

Akl J., 'The seabed disputes chamber of the international tribunal of the law of the sea', in P. Chandrasekhara Rao and R. Khan (eds.), *The international tribunal for the law of the sea: Law and practice*, The Hague: Kluwer, 2001, pp. 75–89.

Armas-Pfirter F.M., 'The seabed disputes chamber: Moving forward', in M.H. Nordquist, J.N. Moore and R. Long (eds.), *Legal order in the world's oceans: UN convention on the law of the sea*, Leiden: Nijhoff, 2018, pp. 210–227.

Burke C., 'Article 191. Advisory opinions', in A. Proelss (ed.), *United Nations convention on the law of the sea: A commentary*, Munich: Beck, 2017, pp. 1274–1276.

Cataldi C., 'La mise en oeuvre des décisions des tribunaux internationaux dans l'ordre interne', *Collected courses of the Hague Academy of International Law*, 386, 2016, pp. 267–428.

Chandrasekhara Rao P. and Gautier P., *The international tribunal for the law of the sea: Law practice and procedure*, Cheltenham: Edward Elgar, 2018.

40 T. Treves, 'Article 289 – experts', in A. Proelss (ed.), *United Nations Convention on the Law of the Sea: A commentary*, Beck, Hart, Nomos, 2018, p. 1863.

Eiriksson G., *The international tribunal for the law of the sea*, The Hague: Nijhoff, 2000.

Eiriksson G., 'Commentary to articles 115 to 123 of the rules of the tribunal', in P. Chandrasekhara Rao and P. Gautier (eds.), *The rules of the international tribunal for the law of the sea: A commentary*, Leiden: Nijhoff, 2006, pp. 331–345.

García García-Revillo M., *The contentious and advisory jurisdiction of the international tribunal for the law of the sea*, Leiden: Nijhoff, 2015.

Jesus J.L., 'Commentary to articles 130 to 138 of the rules of the tribunal', in P. Chandrasekhara Rao and P. Gautier (eds.), *The rules of the international tribunal for the law of the sea: A commentary*, Leiden: Nijhoff, 2006, pp. 373–394.

Nandan S., Lodge S.W. and Rosenne S. (eds.) *United Nations convention on the law of the sea 1982: A commentary*, vol. 6, Dordrecht: Nijhoff, 2002.

Nordquist M.H., Rosenne S. and Sohn L.B. (eds.) *United Nations convention on the law of the sea 1982: A commentary*, vol. 5, Dordrecht: Nijhoff, 1989.

Schatz V.J., 'Article 159. The assembly. Composition, procedure and voting', in A. Proelss (ed.), *United Nations convention on the law of the sea: A commentary*, Munich: Beck, 2017, pp. 1122–1132.

Seeberg-Elverfeldt N.-J., *The settlement of disputes in deep seabed mining*, Baden-Baden: Nomos, 1998.

Treves T., 'The jurisdiction of the international tribunal for the law of the sea', in P.P. Chandrasekhara Rao and R. Khan (eds.), *The international tribunal for the law of the sea: Law and practice*, The Hague: Kluwer, 2001, pp. 111–131.

Treves T., 'Judicial action for the common heritage', in H. Hestermeyer, N. Matz-Lück, A. Seibert-Fohr and S. Vöneky (eds.), *Law of the sea in dialogue*, Heidelberg: Springer, 2010, pp. 113–133.

Treves T., 'Non-governmental organizations before the international tribunal for the law of the sea: The advisory opinion of 1 February 2011', in *Le 90ème anniversaire de Boutros Boutros-Ghali, hommage du Curatorium à son Président*, Hague Academy of International Law, 2012, pp. 255–262.

Treves T., 'Article 289. Experts', in A. Proelss (ed.), *United Nations convention on the law of the sea: A commentary*, Munich: Beck, 2017, pp. 1863–1866.

Vrancken P.H.P., 'Annex VI. Section 4. Seabed disputes chamber', in A. Proelss (ed.), *United Nations convention on the law of the sea: A commentary*, Munich: Beck, 2017, pp. 2453–2463.

V.2

DISPUTE SETTLEMENT OPTIONS AND RIGHTS OF PARTICIPATION IN DEEP SEABED MINING DISPUTES

James Harrison and Alberto Pecoraro

Introduction

While the majority of contracts with the International Seabed Authority are held by states or state enterprises, private companies are increasingly investing in deep seabed mining in the Area, either directly or through public-private partnerships with states. The regime for deep seabed mining under Part XI of the *United Nations Convention on the Law of the Sea* (UNCLOS) was intentionally set up to accommodate such a divergence of actors. UNCLOS provides that activities in the Area may be carried out 'in association with the Authority by States parties or state enterprises or natural or juridical persons which possess the nationality of States Parties or are effectively controlled by them or their nationals'.[1] In practice, the arrangements underpinning deep seabed mining operations are increasingly complex. In many instances involving state enterprises or juridical persons, foreign investors stand behind deep seabed mining operators. A prominent example is UK Seabed Resources, which was sponsored by the UK and entered into a contract with the Authority while being a wholly owned subsidiary of Lockheed Martin, a US corporation. Nor is the involvement of foreign capital limited to the incorporation of subsidiaries in the state of sponsorship. Another relevant example is the joint venture between the Cook Islands Investment Corporation and the Belgian enterprise G-Tec Sea Mineral Resources NV to explore a contract area granted by the Authority to the former.

The diversity of actors involved in deep seabed mining has implications for the settlement of disputes concerning activities in the Area. The *sui generis* dispute settlement system in section 5 of Part XI expressly applies to several categories of dispute that might arise between the various actors involved in this activity. UNCLOS even establishes a dedicated body called the Seabed Disputes Chamber (SDC), which has been described as 'a tribunal within a tribunal',[2] as its 11 members are elected by judges of the International Tribunal for the Law of the Sea (ITLOS) from their own body, but 'it operates in practice as an autonomous international tribunal, with its own

1 *United Nations Convention on the Law of the Sea*, 10 December 1982, 1833 UNTS 396, article 153(2)(b).

2 H. Tuerk, 'The contribution of the International Tribunal for the Law of the Sea to international law', in E.J. Molenaar and A. Oude Elferink (eds), *The international legal regime of areas beyond national jurisdiction: Current and future developments*, Leiden: Martinus Nijhoff, 2010, p. 221.

DOI: 10.4324/9780429426162-18

president, its own rules of procedure and its own jurisdictional provisions'.[3] A characteristic feature of the SDC is its broader rules on standing and applicable law. The ITLOS Statute expressly provides that 'the Chamber shall be open to the States Parties, the Authority, and other entities referred to in Part XI, section 5'[4] and the SDC shall apply, in addition to other rules of international law applicable under article 293 of UNCLOS, 'the rules, regulations and procedures of the Authority (…) and the terms of contracts concerning activities in the Area'.[5] However, the SDC also operates alongside a number of other dispute settlement forums, some recognized by section 5 of Part XI and others operating independently.

To date, there have been few opportunities to test the operation of the Part XI dispute settlement system.[6] As a result, many important questions are unanswered, not least how these innovative provisions will be interpreted and applied in practice. The purpose of this chapter is to consider the types of contentious disputes that may arise in the context of deep seabed mining operations, the possible legal forums that are available to resolve such disputes, and the nature of the claims that may be made. In this respect, the chapter will analyze the scope of jurisdiction conferred on the SDC and other courts and tribunals seized under section 5 of Part XI. The chapter will also assess what other judicial forums may potentially be seized by actors involved in deep seabed mining operations. Finally, it will reflect upon the potential consequences arising from the diversity of forums available to settle deep seabed mining disputes.

Disputes concerning compliance with contractual undertakings of deep seabed mining operators

All deep seabed mining operations taking place in the Area are overseen by the Authority, which is unlike any other international organization in that it is not only a forum for the negotiation of rules relating to activities in areas beyond national jurisdiction, but it is also charged with applying those rules vis-à-vis states and non-state actors. The Authority is given powers to process and determine applications to carry out deep seabed mining, as well as to enforce the rules against authorized operators, be they states, state-owned enterprises or private companies.[7]

The main legal tool utilized by the Authority for this purpose is a contract between itself and the operator.[8] The contract is central to the regulatory regime in Part XI because it establishes a direct legal relationship between the Authority and each deep seabed mining operator. The content of the contract is to a large extent dictated by Part XI of UNCLOS and the related regulations adopted by the Authority, which include a set of standard clauses covering a range of issues, such as data collection, environmental protection and monitoring, labour standards, and health and safety.[9] These

3 J. Harrison, *Making the law of the sea*, Cambridge: Cambridge University Press, 2011, p. 147. See also in this book T. Treves, 'Dispute settlement and seabed mining in the Area', in V. Tassin Campanella (ed.), *Routledge handbook of seabed mining and the law of the sea*, London: Routledge, 2023, chapter V.1.

4 Article 37, Annex VI, UNCLOS.

5 Article 38, Annex VI, UNCLOS.

6 But see *Responsibilities and obligations of States sponsoring persons and entities with respect to activities in the Area*, Advisory Opinion, ITLOS Reports 2011.

7 Article 153(3)–(5), UNCLOS.

8 Article 153(3), UNCLOS. See also *Agreement relating to the implementation of Part XI of UNCLOS* (the 1994 Agreement), 16 November 1994, 1836 UNTS 3, Annex, section 2(4).

9 E.g. International Seabed Authority, Regulations on Prospecting and Exploration for Polymetallic Nodules in the Area (Nodules Regulations), Annex 4. There are some issues which are specific to each contract, such as the agreed plan of activities and the training program.

standard clauses are included in all exploration contracts entered into by the Authority, which furthermore requires that 'the contractor shall carry out exploration in accordance with the terms and conditions of this contract, the Regulations, Part XI of the Convention, the Agreement and other rules of international law not incompatible with the Convention'.[10] While they are not yet finalized, the exploitation regulations are likely to follow a similar pattern, giving the Authority significant influence in dictating the terms of any contract.

Given that the contract predominantly imposes obligations on the operator, an important category of disputes under the contract is likely to concern the performance of a deep seabed mining operator of its commitments under the contract and the associated plan of work.[11] Contractors are expected to report on their activities on a regular basis[12] and the Authority is empowered to monitor compliance, including through sending inspectors to the site of operations.[13] The Authority also has broad powers to 'enforce' the contract through the unilateral imposition of penalties against the operator based upon its own assessment of the operator's conduct.[14] Ultimately, the Authority may bring legal proceedings against the operator. While it is the Authority as a legal person which would be represented in proceedings, it is the Council which determines when to institute proceedings[15] and decisions would be subject to the complex voting formula contained in the 1994 Agreement.[16]

In the case of disputes concerning the implementation of the contract, the standard contractual terms simply refer back to section 5 of Part XI of UNCLOS, which makes clear that disputes 'concerning the interpretation or application of a relevant contract or plan of work' fall within the jurisdiction of the SDC.[17] Yet, this provision only confers jurisdiction on the SDC and it does not necessarily follow that a contractual dispute will always be submitted to the SDC. Of particular importance in this respect is article 188 paragraph 2 (a) of UNCLOS, which provides that 'disputes concerning the interpretation and application of a contract referred to in article 187, subparagraph (c)(i), shall be submitted, at the request of any party to the dispute, to binding commercial arbitration, unless the parties agree otherwise'. The language of this provision would appear to create a presumption that contractual disputes will be submitted to commercial arbitration, unless the parties agree to go to another forum, such as the SDC.

This provision clearly introduces significant flexibility to allow the parties to decide who will settle the dispute. Commercial arbitration will be conducted according to 'UNCITRAL Arbitration Rules or such other arbitration rules as may be prescribed in the rules, regulations and procedures of the Authority'.[18] The Authority has not yet agreed any alternative arbitration rules and UNCITRAL rules will apply until it does. At the time that UNCLOS was drafted, the relevant UNCITRAL Arbitration Rules were appended to UN General Assembly Resolution 31/98 of 15 December 1976. A more recent set of UNCITRAL rules was adopted in 2010,[19] although at least in terms of the

10 Section 13.1, Annex 4, ibid.

11 An operator may be able to justify a failure to perform its contractual obligations on the basis of force majeure which is defined in ibid., Annex 4, section 17.

12 Section 10, Annex 4, section 10, ibid.

13 Section 14, Annex 4, ibid.

14 Article 18(1)–(2), Annex III, UNCLOS.

15 Article 162(2)(u), ibid.

16 Section 3, para. 5, Annex, 1994 Agreement.

17 Article 187(c)(i), UNCLOS. It has been suggested that this provision does not cover disputes between the Authority and the Enterprise as the latter is 'an arm of the Authority'; A. Adede, 'The basic structure of the disputes settlement part of the law of the sea Convention', *Ocean Development and International Law* 11, 1982, 142.

18 Article 188(2)(c), UNCLOS.

19 See UNGA Resolution 65/22, 6 December 2010.

appointment of arbitrators, there is little difference between the two sets of rules – both rules refer to a default of three arbitrators, one appointed by each party to the arbitration and the presiding arbitrator to be agreed by the two appointed arbitrators, or failing such agreement, the appointing authority.[20]

There is, however, one major limitation to submitting contract disputes to commercial arbitration; UNCLOS makes clear that the competence of an arbitral tribunal is limited so that it 'shall have no jurisdiction to decide any question of interpretation of this Convention'.[21] Rather the arbitral tribunal must refer any question of treaty interpretation to the SDC for a ruling, either at the request of either party to the dispute or *proprio motu*.[22] Not only must an arbitral tribunal refer a question of interpretation of UNCLOS to the SDC, but any subsequent decision of the arbitral tribunal must be 'in conformity with the ruling of the [SDC]'.[23] The language used here suggests that arbitral tribunals must follow the decision of the SDC, otherwise any decision will be invalid due to being *ultra vires*.[24] The purpose of this reference procedure is to 'achieve unity of jurisprudence in respect of [Part XI]'.[25] At the same time, the exclusive competence of the SDC only applies to the interpretation of UNCLOS, not to other sources of applicable international law, such as the rules and regulations of the Authority.[26] Thus, only limited uniformity will be achieved by this procedure. Moreover, this reference procedure clearly has important implications for any arbitral proceedings and the benefits of commercial arbitration – namely the speed and flexibility for the parties – could to a large extent be outweighed if a reference to the SDC is made. In practice, there may be considerable uncertainty as to whether the reference procedure will be triggered, particularly as a reference may be made at any stage during the 'course of such arbitration'.[27] One way to remove such uncertainty is to submit the entire dispute to the SDC in the first place, but this will require the agreement of both parties.

Where a claim is brought against a natural or juridical person, the sponsoring state has a right to intervene in proceedings,[28] although the sponsoring state would not be able to initiate a claim under the contract directly, because it is not a party.[29] Of course, the sponsoring state may have other legal relations with an operator which may be the subject of dispute, as discussed below.

Disputes concerning the exercise of regulatory powers by the International Seabed Authority

Whereas the Authority is granted broad powers to regulate activities in the Area and it often has some discretion to determine how to apply its powers to individual situations, these powers are not unlimited. The main obligation imposed on the Authority by a contract is to respect the security

20 The 1976 UNCITRAL Arbitration Rules, rules 5 and 7; 2010 UNCITRAL Arbitration Rules, rules 7 and 9.

21 Article 188(2)(a), UNCLOS.

22 Article 188(2)(b), ibid.

23 Ibid.

24 The validity of an arbitral award would presumably have to be challenged in the national courts of the legal system under which the arbitral tribunal operated. Alternatively, one of the parties could resist the enforcement of the award based upon its alleged invalidity.

25 See M. Nordquist et al. (eds), *United Nations Convention on the Law of the Sea 1982: A commentary*, Volume VI, Leiden: Martinus Nijhoff, 2002, pp. 627–628.

26 Harrison (2011), op. cit., p. 148.

27 Article 188(b), UNCLOS.

28 Article 290(1), UNCLOS.

29 See I. Feichtner, 'Contractor liability for environmental damage resulting from deep seabed mining activities in the Area', *Marine Policy* 114, 2020, 7.

of tenure of the contractor and to 'ensure that no other entity operates in the exploration area for a different category of resources in a manner that might unreasonably interfere with the operations of the Contractor'.[30] In addition to this important contractual obligation on the Authority, further overarching limits on the exercise of its powers are found in UNCLOS, in the rules and regulations adopted by the Authority, and in the contracts themselves. Thus, the Authority must 'avoid discrimination in the exercise of its powers and functions'[31] and it must also 'uniformly apply rules, regulations, and procedures (...) for the exercise of its functions as set forth in Part XI'.[32] These limitations may constrain the manner in which the Authority exercises its powers of supervision over a contractor, including its powers of enforcement.[33] Indeed, more specific constraints apply to the enforcement powers of the Authority.

In relation to the application of monetary penalties by the Authority, UNCLOS imposes a much stricter limitation, by specifying that such penalties must be 'proportionate to the seriousness of the violation'.[34] In relation to the suspension or termination of a contract, article 18 paragraph 1 of Annex III provides:

> A contractor's rights under the contract may be suspended or terminated only in the following cases: (a) if in spite of warnings by the Authority, the contractor has conducted his activities in such a way as to result in serious, persistent and willful violations of the fundamental terms of the contract, Part XI and the rules, regulations and procedures of the Authority; or (b) if the contractor has failed to comply with a final binding decision of a dispute settlement body applicable to him.

These constraints are replicated in the standard terms of contracts.[35] These provisions would appear to be an exhaustive list,[36] meaning that the Authority cannot suspend or terminate a contract without complying with these conditions. This is consistent with the view of the Authority as an international organization with limited powers conferred by its constituent instrument.[37]

Many of these standards which purport to constrain the Authority's powers are open to interpretation. While there may be some discretion for the Authority to apply these terms to an individual situation,[38] the interpretation and application of these limitations is ultimately a question for a court or tribunal with jurisdiction over the relevant source of law. Indeed, UNCLOS is clear that penalties can only be enforced once 'the contractor has been accorded a reasonable opportunity to exhaust the judicial remedies available to him pursuant to Part XI, section 5'.[39]

30 The Authority also has an obligation to preserve the confidentiality of certain data submitted by contractors; see Nodules Regulations, Regulation 35.

31 Article 152(1), UNCLOS.

32 Article 17(1), Annex III, ibid.

33 For a discussion of these provisions, see J. Harrison, 'Checks and balances on the regulatory powers of the International Seabed Authority', in A. Ascencio-Herrera (ed.), *The United Nations Convention on the Law of the Sea, Part XI regime and the International Seabed Authority*, Leiden: Brill, forthcoming.

34 Article 18(2), Annex III, UNCLOS.

35 Section 21(1), Annex 4, Nodules Regulations.

36 Note that the standard clauses add a provision concerning insolvency and bankruptcy; ibid., Annex 4, section 21(1)(c). The Council may also suspend or terminate a contract if the contractor has been unable to perform its obligations by reason of force majeure which has persisted for a continuous period exceeding two years; ibid., section 21(2).

37 Article 157(2), UNCLOS.

38 See Harrison (forthcoming), op. cit.

39 Article 18(3), Annex III, UNCLOS. The standard clauses specify that the Authority shall give 60 days' notice of an intention to suspend or terminate the contract and the contractor may begin dispute settlement proceedings within this period; Nodules Regulations, Annex 4, section 21.3.

If a constraint derives from the terms of a contract, the dispute will fall within the jurisdiction of an arbitral tribunal or of the SDC as discussed in the previous section. When the dispute relates to limitations imposed directly by UNCLOS or by rules and regulations of the Authority, it will fall within the scope of article 188(c)(ii) which confers jurisdiction on the SDC concerning 'acts or omissions of a party to the contract relating to activities in the Area and directed to the other party or directly affecting its legitimate interests'. At the same time, the SDC's ability to exercise jurisdiction over this category of dispute must be understood in light of article 189, which provides that 'the [SDC] shall have no jurisdiction with regard to the exercise by the Authority of its discretionary powers in accordance with this Part; in no case shall it substitute its discretion for that of the Authority'.

An extreme interpretation of article 189 is that any decision that involves an exercise of discretion is protected from judicial proceedings.[40] Interpreting article 189 as a complete prohibition on the challenge of any discretionary powers would cover many, if not most, decisions of the Authority and it has been pointed out that such a conclusion would lead to a 'great gap in the dispute settlement mechanism' and 'from an applicant's perspective, this gap results in an ineffective remedial mechanism'.[41] An alternative interpretation of this provision simply reinforces the discretionary character of the Authority's regulatory power with a view to prohibiting challenges to any decisions which are made within the confines of the discretion that has been granted. Indeed, this interpretation would appear to be confirmed by the remainder of article 189, which says that 'jurisdiction in this regard shall be confined to deciding claims that the application of any rules, regulations and procedures of the Authority in individual cases would be in conflict with the contractual obligations of the parties to the dispute or their obligations under this Convention, claims concerning excess of jurisdiction or misuse of power'. Taken as a whole, it is therefore reasonable to interpret article 189 as confirming that it is possible to challenge the exercise of regulatory powers by the Authority, but any such challenge must be based upon an express limitation within the text of UNCLOS or the regulatory framework.[42] UNCLOS expressly forbids any challenge to the validity of the rules and regulations of the Authority, however, which is a matter within the preserve of the political organs of the Authority.[43]

Not only does section 5 of Part XI anticipate that deep seabed mining operators can bring claims against the Authority for breaching contractual provisions or abusing the limits of the power conferred upon it by UNCLOS and the associated regulations, but the jurisdiction of the SDC also cover disputes 'where it is alleged that the Authority has incurred liability as provided for in Annex III, article 22'.[44] This latter provision says that 'the Authority shall have responsibility or liability for any damage arising out of wrongful acts in the exercise of its powers and functions' and 'liability in every case shall be for the actual amount of the damage'.[45] It follows that a claim by a deep seabed mining operator may include a claim for financial compensation.

There is one further category of disputes concerning the regulatory powers of the Authority that is expressly foreseen by section 5 of Part XI of UNCLOS, namely 'disputes between the Authority

40 L. Sun, 'Dispute settlement relating to deep seabed mining: A participant's perspective', *Melbourne Journal of International Law* 18, 2017, 80.

41 Ibid.

42 See J. Dingwall, 'International investment protection in deep seabed mining beyond national jurisdiction', *Journal of World Investment and Trade* 19, 2018, 919.

43 Article 189, UNCLOS.

44 Article 187(c), ibid.

45 Article 22, Annex III, ibid.

and a prospective contractor (…) concerning the refusal of a contract or a legal issue arising in the negotiation of a contract'.[46] This provision underlines that the discretion of the Authority is limited, even before a contract is concluded. In this respect, UNCLOS lays down a strict procedure which must be followed by the Authority in approving contracts[47] and the conditions that must be met by an applicant are contained in UNCLOS and the associated Regulations. The dispute settlement procedure therefore allows an applicant to have recourse to the SDC to settle any disputes about the interpretation and application of these provisions,[48] albeit within the limits imposed by article 189, discussed above.

Disputes between operators and sponsoring states

Whereas the regulatory regime established by Part XI of UNCLOS is centered on the Authority as the trustee for the common heritage of mankind, states continue to have an essential regulatory role through the sponsorship of their nationals. State sponsorship is a *sine qua non* condition for obtaining a contract from the Authority. In this respect, article 153 paragraph 2 (b) of UNCLOS refers to natural or juridical persons which possess the nationality of states parties or are effectively controlled by them or their nationals 'when sponsored by such states'.[49] The importance of sponsorship is also underlined by the fact that its withdrawal may lead to the termination of the contract if the operator is unable to find an alternative sponsor within six months of the notice of withdrawal.[50]

Sponsoring states must ensure that exploration and exploitation activities in the Area are carried out in conformity with the legal framework derived from UNCLOS.[51] In its 2011 Advisory Opinion, the SDC made clear that 'the liability of the sponsoring State arises from its own failure to comply with its obligations under the Convention and related instruments' so that it does not bear residual liability for the actions of a sponsored entity.[52] However, sponsoring states have some discretion in designing the national legal regime applicable to sponsorship and they may even impose additional requirements on sponsored entities. For instance, UNCLOS explicitly recognizes the possibility for states to apply 'environmental or other laws and regulations more stringent than those in the rules, regulations and procedures of the Authority adopted pursuant to article 17, paragraph 2(f) [referring to the protection of the marine environment]'.[53]

The form of national requirements relating to deep seabed mining can vary from state to state. They can be expressed in primary legislation, licensing regimes, or contractual arrangements between the sponsoring state and deep seabed mining operators. So-called 'sponsorship agreements' embody the specific legal and economic bargain struck by the state and the operator. Such rules may also reflect other national interests, for example national gains from future mineral production in the Area, including 'employment; training; capacity building; technology transfer;

46 Article 187(d), ibid.

47 The original rules were modified by the Part XI Agreement, Annex, section 1.

48 See also section 3, para. 12, Annex, 1994 Agreement.

49 Article 153, UNCLOS.

50 See Regulation 29, Nodules Regulations.

51 Article 139, UNCLOS.

52 *Responsibilities and obligations of States sponsoring persons and entities with respect to activities in the Area*, op. cit., para. 204.

53 Article 21, Annex III, UNCLOS. See also article 209(2).

foreign investment; increased tax revenue; and national self-determination'.[54] In this context, the national laws of the Cook Islands, Fiji and Nauru specify that deep sea mining activities should be generally in the public interest of the state, taking into account the potential for capacity-building or local employment and long-term economic benefits.[55] With respect to the sharing of benefits or otherwise, UNCLOS and its related instruments do not articulate minimum standards for these arrangements[56] and so states have considerable leeway in determining their content.

Where sponsoring states do articulate specific requirements with which sponsored entities must comply, disputes may arise over their interpretation and application in practice. Such disputes could concern the compliance of a sponsored entity with the requirements. It is also possible that disputes may arise concerning the exercise of regulatory powers by the sponsoring state. Indeed, the authority of sponsoring states to regulate deep seabed mining operators under their jurisdiction is not unlimited and may be constrained in a number of ways. For example, it is likely that national administrative law imposes limits on the abuse of regulatory power. Constraints may also be expressly written into national deep seabed mining laws, as in the case of Kiribati's Seabed Minerals Act 2017, which obliges state authorities to

> not impose unnecessary, disproportionate, or duplicate regulatory burden on Sponsored Parties, nor impose requirements upon a Sponsored Party under this Act or Regulations to be made under this Act except insofar as these are consistent with existing requirements imposed by, the United Nations Convention on the Law of the Sea, the Rules of the Authority and other applicable standards of international law.[57]

This provision also alludes to the fact that there may be other sources of limitations imposed on sponsoring states stemming from international law.

A potential role for other rules of international law in this context is equally foreseen by article 138 of UNCLOS, which provides that:

> the general conduct of States in relation to the Area shall be in accordance with the provisions of this Part, the principles embodied in the Charter of the United Nations and other rules of international law in the interests of maintaining peace and security and promoting international cooperation and mutual understanding.[58]

The association of the term 'general' to the conduct of states and the lack of further limitations in this article suggests that it is susceptible to cover all state policies toward the sponsored corporate entity. The formulation 'other rules of international law' potentially includes the whole corpus of general international law, a result supported by the reasoning of courts and tribunals when

54 *Statement by the Republic of Nauru regarding the Questions Submitted to the Seabed Disputes Chamber for an Advisory Opinion on the Responsibilities and Obligations of States Sponsoring Entities with Respect to Activities in the International Seabed Area*, ITLOS Case No 17, 5 August 2010, para. 5.

55 K. Willaert, 'On the legitimacy of national interests of sponsoring states: A deep sea mining conundrum', *International Journal of Marine and Coastal Law* 36, 2020, 9.

56 A. Jaeckel et al., 'Sharing benefits of the common heritage of mankind – Is the deep seabed mining regime ready?', *Marine Policy* 70, 2016, 201.

57 See e.g. Republic of Kiribati Seabed Minerals Act 2017, section 93.

58 Article 138, UNCLOS.

interpreting similar *renvois* in other law of the sea cases.[59] Indeed, when ruling on the exercise of coastal state enforcement powers, tribunals have relied on other UNCLOS provisions similar to article 138 to conclude that:

> the exercise of enforcement powers by a (coastal) State in situations where the State derives these powers from provisions of the Convention is also governed by certain rules and principles of general international law, in particular the principle of reasonableness. This principle encompasses the principles of necessity and proportionality.[60]

Within the context of the Area, article 4 paragraph 4 of Annex III excludes the sponsoring state's liability for damage caused by its contractor, as long as that state has adopted laws and regulations and taken administrative measures which are 'within the framework of its legal system, reasonably appropriate for securing compliance by persons under its jurisdiction'.[61] According to the SDC 'reasonableness and non-arbitrariness must remain the hallmarks of any action taken by the sponsoring State'.[62] Article 4 paragraph 4 would then be the corollary of the wider standard of reasonableness that runs through UNCLOS. Some relevant criteria when applying this standard might be whether state policies were commensurate to a legitimate objective, whether state behavior contradicted previous representations, and whether adequate procedural guarantees were afforded to the private contractor.

Beyond the disciplines of UNCLOS, international investment law potentially imposes additional limitations on the exercise of regulatory powers by sponsoring states, at least when the sponsored activity involves an element of foreign investment. Relevant standards of protection for foreign investors can be found in a network of approximately 3,500 investment treaties with similar substantive protections, as well as the complementary customary international minimum standard of treatment, which has been described as prohibiting action that is:

> arbitrary, grossly unfair, unjust or idiosyncratic, is discriminatory and exposes the claimant to sectional or racial prejudice, or involves a lack of due process leading to an outcome which offends judicial propriety—as might be the case with a manifest failure of natural justice in judicial proceedings or a complete lack of transparency and candor in an administrative process. In applying this standard it is relevant that the treatment is in breach of representations made by the host State which were reasonably relied on by the claimant.[63]

Indeed, these sources are not mutually exclusive and both tribunals and commentators have attributed potential custom-generative effects to the thousands of existing investment treaties.[64] That being said, the applicability of international investment law is premised on the existence of a for-

59 *Chagos Marine Protected Area Arbitration (Republic of Mauritius v. the United Kingdom of Great Britain and Northern Ireland)*, Award, 18 March 2015, paras 503–516.

60 *Duzgit Integrity Arbitration (Malta v. São Tomé and Príncipe)*, Award, 5 September 2016, para. 209, referring to articles 49(3) and 293 of UNCLOS.

61 Article 4, Annex III, UNCLOS.

62 *Responsibilities and obligations of States sponsoring persons and entities with respect to activities in the Area*, op. cit., para. 230.

63 *Waste Management, Inc. v. United Mexican States*, ICSID Case No. ARB(AF)/00/3, Award, 30 April 2004, para. 98.

64 See e.g. *ADF Group v. United States*, ICSID No. ARB(AF)/00/1, Award, 9 January 2003, para. 173.

eign investment in the territory of a host state, which raises several questions about its application to deep seabed mining.

Firstly, activities in the Area must be carried out by enterprises or natural or juridical persons which possess the nationality of States Parties or are effectively controlled by them or their nationals.[65] At first blush, this may seem to exclude foreign investors, but international investment law recognizes that domestic companies may be treated as foreign investors because of 'foreign control'[66] or because 'incorporation in that State was required by it as a precondition for doing business there'.[67]

Secondly, the spatial application of international investment treaties is often predicated on investments 'in the territory' of a state,[68] which may seem to exclude investments that are primarily concerned with activities in areas beyond national jurisdiction. Nevertheless, arbitral jurisprudence has interpreted this territorial criterion loosely, either emphasizing the benefit that the state expects from that investment[69] or its regulatory control over that investment. As it was stated in *Bayview v. Mexico*:

> [a] salient characteristic [of an investment covered by the protection of chapter 11 of the North American Free Trade Agreement] will be that the investment is primarily regulated by the law of a State other than the State of the investor's nationality, and that this law is created and applied by that State which is not the State of the investor's nationality.[70]

Moreover, investment jurisprudence has emphasized the principle of 'economic unity' of an investment[71] under which arbitral tribunals have refused to subdivide the claimant's activities into services provided abroad and services provided in the host state. In *SGS v. the Philippines*, the tribunal held that pre-shipment inspection services performed in ports around the world but coordinated through a liaison office in the Philippines were sufficient to constitute an investment in the territory of the latter.[72] Other tribunals have verified that the operations performed by the claimant outside of the territory of the respondent state were part and parcel of a wider service ultimately performed inside that state.[73] This approach is premised upon the fact that there were certain assets constituting an investment in the host state so as to 'anchor' any operations performed outside.[74]

65 Article 153, UNCLOS.

66 *Convention on the Settlement of Investment Disputes between States and Nationals of other States*, 18 March 1965, 575 UNTS 159, article 25(2)(b).

67 International Law Commission, *Diplomatic Protection: text of the draft articles with commentaries*, UN Doc A/61/10, 2006, article 11.

68 In practice, many investment treaties include national zones of maritime jurisdiction within their territorial scope. See discussion in J. Harrison, 'International investment law and the regulation of the seabed', in C. Banet (ed.), *The law of the seabed: Access, uses and protection of seabed resources*, Leiden: Brill, 2020, pp. 485–488.

69 *Romak S.A. (Switzerland) v. Republic of Uzbekistan*, UNCITRAL, PCA Case No. AA280, Award, 26 November 2009, para. 237.

70 *Bayview Irrigation District et al. v. United Mexican States*, ICSID Case No. ARB(AF)/05/1, Award, 19 June 2007, para. 98.

71 See *Ambiente Ufficio SpA v. Argentina*, ICSID Case No ARB/08/9, Decision on Jurisdiction, 2 May 2013, para. 428.

72 *Société Générale de Surveillance SA v. Republic of the Philippines*, ICSID Case No ARB/02/6, Decision, 29 January 2004, paras 99–112.

73 *Deutsche Telekom AG v. India*, PCA Case No 2014-10, Interim Award, 13 December 2017, para. 151.

74 A. Pecoraro, 'Law of the sea and investment protection in deep seabed mining', *Melbourne Journal of International Law* 20, 2020, 550–560.

Whether or not this doctrine applies to activities in the Area may depend on the specific terms of the arrangement between the deep seabed mining operator and the sponsoring state.

The resulting question is how disputes between the sponsoring state and a sponsored entity may be settled. The answer obviously depends on the nature of the dispute and the source of law involved.

Some national statutes on deep seabed mining foresee specific dispute settlement mechanisms: while Tonga's legislation opts exclusively for the jurisdiction of national courts,[75] others select international arbitration in accordance with domestic arbitration laws. Similarly, licenses issued under the UK's deep seabed mining legislation also provide for recourse to arbitration.[76] The legislation of Tuvalu foresees International Centre for Settlement of Investment Disputes (ICSID) arbitration for disputes 'arising in connection with the administration of this Act',[77] which would seem to allow claims not only under the legislation itself but also under relevant standards, including international law.[78] In this respect, some insight may be derived from investment disputes based on national investment laws, where compromissory clauses premised on the existence of 'an investment dispute' were held to ground the tribunal's competence to hear both national and international legal claims.[79] Where a violation of substantive standards of international investment protection is alleged, investment treaty arbitration may provide an alternative forum for deep seabed mining operators to bring claims against sponsoring states, subject to the establishment of jurisdiction and satisfying any procedural prerequisites.[80]

The most difficult question is how disputes under a contract between the sponsoring state and the sponsored entity should be resolved. Such a contract may have its own specific provisions on dispute settlement, but there is also an important question of whether such contracts fall within the scope of section 5 of Part XI of UNCLOS. In other words, do such disputes fall within the jurisdiction of the SDC?

At the outset, it must be recognized that the relevant provision conferring jurisdiction on the SDC is drafted broadly. Thus article 187(c) refers to 'disputes between parties to a contract, being States Parties, the Authority, or the Enterprise, state enterprises and natural or juridical persons'. The precise scope of this provision is ambiguous and while it clearly includes contracts between the Authority and operators, as discussed above, it has also been argued that the wording in article 187(c) is sufficiently broad to include sponsorship agreements between states and contractors.[81]

This argument is buttressed by the explicit mention in article 190(2) of actions 'against a State Party by a natural or juridical person sponsored by another State Party in a dispute referred to in [article 187(c)]'. While article 190(2) does not expressly cover disputes between a sponsored entity

75 Tonga Seabed Minerals Act 2014, No. 10 of 2014, section 122.

76 Exploration Licence between the Secretary of State for Business Innovation and Skills and UK Seabed Resources LTD, 8 February 2013, clause 27.

77 Tuvalu Seabed Minerals Act 2014, No. 14 of 2014, section 126.

78 See also Republic of Kiribati Seabed Minerals Act 2017, section 130; Cook Islands Seabed Minerals Act 2019, section 160; Republic of Nauru International Seabed Minerals Act 2015, No. 26 of 2015, section 54.

79 *Stans Energy Corp. and Kutisay Mining LLC v. Kyrgyz Republic* (II), PCA Case No. 2015-32, paras 357, 360; *Interocean Oil Development Company and Interocean Oil Exploration Company v. Federal Republic of Nigeria*, ICSID Case No. ARB/13/20, Award, 6 October 2020, para. 160.

80 For a discussion of procedural requirements, see C. Schreuer, 'Travelling the BIT route: Of waiting periods, umbrella clauses and forks in the road', *The Journal of World Investment & Trade* 5, 2004, 231–256.

81 E.g. T. Davenport, *Responsibility and liability for damage arising out of activities in the Area: Potential claimants and possible Fora, Liability issues for deep seabed mining series*, 2019, Liability Issues for Deep Seabed Mining Series Paper No. 5, p. 11.

and its own sponsoring state, it would appear to support the conclusion that article 187(c) cannot be read as exclusively referring to disputes between the Authority and a contractor. Furthermore, the Authority's exploration and exploitation contracts only involve two parties – the contractor and the Authority – so article 190(2) cannot be read to refer to a dispute between two parties of the same exploration or exploitation contract.

However, other elements go against such a broad reading of article 187(c). The only context in which UNCLOS speaks of a contract is in relation to plans of work between the Authority and an operator.[82] When it comes to the relationship between sponsoring states and sponsored entities, the Part XI regime only calls for a certificate of sponsorship.[83] It would therefore seem that the drafters did not have in mind a contractual relationship between an operator and its sponsoring state.

The relevant *travaux préparatoires* also suggest that the negotiators did not envisage such contractual disputes being submitted to the dispute settlement system under section 5 of Part XI. Early drafts of the provision referred exclusively to 'disputes relating to the interpretation and application of (…) the terms and conditions of any contracts entered into by the Authority'.[84] During the course of negotiations, the scope of this provision was expanded so that it also expressly covered

> any dispute between States Parties to this Convention or between such State Party and a national of another State Party, or between nationals of different State Parties, or between a State Party and the Authority or the Enterprise concerning the conclusion of any contract, its interpretation or application or other activity in the Area which has arisen.[85]

This formulation and later drafts[86] confirm that a broader range of disputes fall within the jurisdiction of the SDC, but the discussions would appear to suggest that this change was motivated to allow consideration of 'disputes between contractors who had independent contracts with the Authority although they did not have a contract between themselves'.[87] In other words, this provision was still concerned with disputes about contracts entered into by an operator with the Authority, even if the scope of disputing parties was expanded. It is also this type of dispute between independent contractors which article 190 paragraph 2 would appear to be designed to address. The drafting history therefore suggests a more limited understanding of article 187(c). Nevertheless, the drafting history is not determinative of the issue[88] and it cannot be completely ruled out that the language of article 187(c) may be interpreted to cover this category of disputes.

Other disputes that may arise in the context of deep seabed mining

The previous sections have addressed the main disputes that may arise in the execution of deep seabed mining contracts under Part XI of UNCLOS, involving a range of actors, notably the

82 Article 153(3), UNCLOS.

83 Regulation 11, Nodules Regulations.

84 See Informal Single Negotiating Text/Part I (1975), article 33, reproduced in Nordquist et al., op. cit., p. 611.

85 Revised Single Negotiating Text (1976) Article 33(1)(b), reproduced in ibid., p. 613.

86 E.g. ICNT (1977) article 189: 'The Seabed Disputes Chamber of the Law of the Sea Tribunal shall also have jurisdiction with regard to … disputes brought by a State Party against a national of another State Party, or between nationals of different States Parties, regarding the interpretation or application of any contract between them, or in respect of their activities in the Area'; reproduced in ibid., p. 616.

87 See Report by the Chairman of the group of legal experts on the settlement of disputes relating to Part XI, contained in Document A/CONF.62/L.43, Appendix B.

88 *Vienna Convention on the Law of Treaties*, 23 May 1969, 1155 UNTS 331, article 32.

Authority, deep seabed mining operators and sponsoring states. This analysis does not cover all disputes that may arise in this context and before concluding, it is worthwhile mentioning a few broader categories of dispute that may arise in practice.

In particular, section 5 of Part XI makes clear that it does not foreclose the possibility of traditional state-to-state disputes arising over the interpretation and application of Part XI. The SDC is expressly conferred with jurisdiction to settle 'disputes between States Parties concerning the interpretation and application of this Part and the Annexes relating thereto'.[89] States are obliged to accept the jurisdiction of the SDC,[90] but during the negotiation of Part XI, there was extensive debate about whether the jurisdiction of the SDC should be exclusive, in order to 'ensure the unity of jurisprudence required for the [A]rea'[91] or whether states should have freedom to choose other dispute settlement options in line with 'customary practice'.[92] The latter view prevailed and states are accordingly given the option to unilaterally submit such disputes to either an ad hoc chamber of the SDC or, by agreement of both parties, to a special chamber of ITLOS.[93] Moreover, states may submit disputes to one of the forums selected by both parties to a dispute in declarations made under article 287 which covers 'the settlement of disputes concerning the interpretation or application of [the] Convention', including Part XI.[94] Where states have not made matching declarations, Annex VII arbitration is also an option.[95] In addition, states may have further flexibility to agree alternative methods given the explicit application of article 280 on freedom of choice 'to any dispute which pursuant to Part XI, section 5, is to be settled in accordance with procedure provided for in this Part'.[96] As a result of this flexibility, there are many different courts or tribunals which could end up interpreting Part XI, with potential implications for the integrity of the Part XI regime as a whole, as considered in the conclusion below.

Another broader category of dispute recognized under article 187 is disputes between a State Party and the Authority, which may cover general disputes about the exercise of powers by the Authority. For example, a particular coastal state may claim that the Authority has failed to give proper regard to the rights or interests of coastal states in accordance with article 142.[97]

Finally, there are other types of disputes which would appear to fall outside of the scope of section 5 of Part XI altogether.[98] One important exclusion is disputes concerning compliance by prospectors with their undertakings to the Authority that they will comply with UNCLOS and the regulations of the Authority.[99] A proposal to include this category of disputes was discussed during negotiations but rejected on the ground that 'prospectors had no contractual rights to be safeguarded'.[100] However, this would appear to be a lacuna in the dispute settlement system and 'as

89 Article 187(a), UNCLOS.

90 Confirmed by ibid., article 287(2).

91 See Report of the Chairman of the group of legal experts on the settlement of disputes relating to part XI of the informal composite negotiating text, A/CONF.62/C.1/L.25 and ADD.1 (1979) Annex III, Section 2(B).

92 Adede, op. cit., 142.

93 Article 188(1), UNCLOS.

94 See R. Churchill, 'Dispute settlement in the law of the sea – the context of the International Tribunal for the Law of the Sea and alternatives to it', in M.D. Evans (ed.), *Remedies in international law: The institutional dilemma*, Oxford: Hart, 1998, pp. 98–99.

95 Confirmed by article 290(5), UNCLOS.

96 Article 185, ibid.

97 Sun, op. cit., 14–15.

98 Ibid.

99 Nodules Regulations, Regulation 3(4)(d).

100 UN Document A/CONF.62/L.43 (1979) Appendix B, section 5.

there is no requirement for a prospector to have a sponsoring state, whether or not a claim could be successfully pursued through national courts would depend on the relevant law of the state in which a prospector was based'.[101]

Conclusion

The diversity of the actors carrying out activities in the Area complicates the settlement of disputes concerning deep seabed mining, as does the fact that the rules governing these activities come from several sources and change according to the identity of the parties. The SDC was created as the principal dispute settlement body for activities in the Area, but it operates alongside various other forums, some recognized by UNCLOS and others operating independently. National courts may also be competent, consistently with the important role which UNCLOS assigns to sponsoring states for the effective control over activities in the Area. Claims of operators against their sponsoring state could also potentially be brought before investment treaty tribunals, whose role was not foreseen in Part XI. Indeed, one dispute may trigger various dispute settlement mechanisms that apply different bodies of law, with potential increases in the time and costs associated with dispute settlement.

The plurality of dispute settlement forums also potentially poses challenges for the integrity of the Part XI regime, if the core instruments underpinning that regime are interpreted and applied by different judicial bodies. There are some safeguards built into section 5 of Part XI, such as the limitation on the power of commercial arbitral tribunals to interpret UNCLOS, but they only offer limited protection from a much broader threat. Of course, one cannot assume that fragmentation will occur simply because different bodies are involved in interpreting a single regime, but evidence from other areas of international law, as well as from some existing law of the sea jurisprudence,[102] demonstrates that the risk of incongruence cannot be completely dismissed. It will in large part be the responsibility of the actors involved in the dispute settlement system to ensure that this risk is avoided.

References

Adede A., 'The basic structure of the disputes settlement part of the law of the sea convention', *Ocean Development and International Law* 11, 1982, 125–148.

Churchill R., 'Dispute settlement in the law of the sea – The context of the international tribunal for the law of the sea and alternatives to it', in M.D. Evans (ed.), *Remedies in international law: The institutional dilemma*, Oxford: Hart, 1998, pp. 85–111.

Davenport T., *Responsibility and liability for damage arising out of activities in the Area: Potential claimants and possible Fora, liability issues for deep seabed mining series*, Liability Issues for Deep Seabed Mining Series Paper No 5, 2019. Online. Available: < https://www.cigionline.org/publications/responsibility-and-liability-damage-arising-out-activities-area-potential-claimants/> (accessed 10 September 2021).

Dingwall J., *International law and corporate actors in deep seabed mining*, Oxford: Oxford University Press, 2021.

101 J. Harrison, 'Resources of the international seabed Area', in E. Morgera and K. Kulovesk (eds), *Research handbook on international law and natural resources*, Cheltenham: Edward Elgar, 2016, p. 405.

102 Perhaps most famously the tension between the *Southern Bluefin Tuna Arbitration (New Zealand-Japan, Australia-Japan)*, Decision of 4 August 2000, UN Reports of International Arbitral Awards, vol. XXIII, 1–57, and the *South China Sea Arbitration (Republic of the Philippines v. the People's Republic of China)* Award on Jurisdiction and Admissibility concerning the interpretation of article 281 of UNCLOS.

Dingwall J., 'International investment protection in deep seabed mining beyond national jurisdiction', *Journal of World Investment and Trade* 19, 2018, 898–929.

Feichtner I., 'Contractor liability for environmental damage resulting from deep seabed mining activities in the Area', *Marine Policy* 114, 2020, article 103502.

Harrison J., *Making the law of the sea*, Cambridge: Cambridge University Press, 2011.

Harrison J., 'International investment law and the regulation of the seabed', in C. Banet (ed.), *The law of the seabed: Access, uses and protection of seabed resources*, Leiden: Brill, 2020, pp. 481–502.

Harrison J., 'Checks and balances on the regulatory powers of the international seabed authority', in A. Ascencio-Herrera (ed.), *The United Nations convention on the law of the sea, part XI regime and the international seabed authority*, Leiden: Brill, 2022, pp. 151-173.

Jaeckel A. et al., 'Sharing benefits of the common heritage of mankind – Is the deep seabed mining regime ready?', *Marine Policy* 70, 2016, 198–204.

Nordquist M. et al. (eds.) *United Nations convention on the law of the sea 1982: A commentary, volume VI*, Leiden: Martinus Nijhoff, 2002.

Pecoraro A., 'Law of the sea and investment protection in deep seabed mining', *Melbourne Journal of International Law* 20, 2019, 530–571.

Sun L., 'Dispute settlement relating to deep seabed mining: A participant's perspective', *Melbourne Journal of International Law* 18, 2017, 71–94.

Treves T., 'Dispute settlement and seabed mining in the Area', in V. Tassin Campanella (ed.), *Routledge handbook of seabed mining and the law of the sea*, London: Routledge, 2023, chapter V.1.

Tuerk H., 'The contribution of the international tribunal for the law of the sea to international law', in E.J. Molenaar and A. Oude Elferink (eds.), *The international legal regime of areas beyond national jurisdiction: Current and future developments*, Leiden: Martinus Nijhoff, 2010, pp. 217–230.

Willaert K., 'On the legitimacy of national interests of sponsoring states: A deep sea mining conundrum', *International Journal of Marine and Coastal Law* 36, 2020, 136–153.

V.3

MINING THE BOTTOM OF THE SEA

Potential future disputes and the role of the International Tribunal for the Law of the Sea

Monica Feria-Tinta and Maurice K. Kamga

Introduction

The seabed beyond national jurisdiction (the Area)[1] which as noted by scholars covers approximately half of the planet,[2] contains deposits of valuable minerals such as cobalt, manganese, copper, zinc, nickel and rare earth elements, particularly sought after by green technologies (including electric vehicles, wind turbines and solar cells) and tech-oriented industries such as the industry of smartphones.[3] The International Seabed Authority (ISA) has awarded 31 exploration contracts involving 22 contractors[4] so far. Exploration, however, may soon give way to exploitation. In June 2021, Nauru notified the ISA of the intention of Nauru Ocean Resources Inc (NORI), a subsidiary of a Canadian company called DeepGreen Mineral Corp., to apply for approval to begin mining in two years in the Clarion-Clipperton Zone in the North Pacific Ocean between Hawaii and Mexico.[5] As noted by Treves in Chapter V.1 of this book, it is precisely 'the exploitation stage which is the most likely to produce disputes'.[6] Faced with that reality, the topic of deep-sea mining is one of the areas which doubtlessly will feature in the International Tribunal for the Law of the Sea's (ITLOS) dispute settlement mechanisms and, possibly, be the subject of further advisory functions.

1 For a definition of 'the Area' see N. Oral, 'The common heritage of mankind under international law: An overview', in V. Tassin Campanella (ed.), *Routledge handbook of seabed mining and the law of the sea*, London: Routledge, 2023, chapter I.2. For more information about the various mineral resources, see also in this book W. Roest, M.R. Clark and H. Brekke, 'The scientific challenges of deep-sea mining', in V. Tassin Campanella (ed.), idem, chapter I.1.

2 J. Dingwall, 'Commercial mining activities in the deep seabed beyond national jurisdiction: The international legal framework', in C. Banet (ed.), *The law of the seabed*, Leiden: Brill Nijhoff, 2020, p. 137.

3 US Government Accountability Office (GAO), 'Science and tech spotlight: Deep-sea mining', 15 December 2021. Available online < https://www.gao.gov/products/gao-22-105507> (accessed 12 April 2022).

4 For the full list of exploration contractors, see the website of the International Seabed Authority. Available online <https://isa.org.jm/exploration-contracts> (accessed 1 June 2022).

5 H. Reid, 'Pacific Island of Nauru sets two year deadline for U.N. deep-sea mining rules', *Reuters*, 29 June 2021. Available online <https://www.reuters.com/business/environment/pacific-island-nauru-sets-two-year-deadline-deep-sea-mining-rules-2021-06-29/> (accessed 29 September 2021).

6 T. Treves, 'Dispute settlement and seabed mining in the Area', in V. Tassin Campanella (ed.), *Routledge handbook of seabed mining and the law of the sea*, op. cit., chapter V.1.

DOI: 10.4324/9780429426162-19

But the role of ITLOS in addressing deep-sea mining[7] may precede any exploitation stage.

The current tension between commercial interests for deep-sea exploitation (driven by the expanding world demand for raw materials) and environmental considerations is reflected in the recent demand for a moratorium on deep-sea mining in areas beyond national jurisdiction by the International Union for Conservation of Nature (IUCN)[8] (which emphasized the adoption of precautionary and ecosystem approaches, including the precautionary principle with regard to deep-sea mining), and in the different (sometimes contradictory) stances regional organs[9] and States are taking in relation to deep-sea and, more broadly, seabed mining.[10] The conflicting interests (between seabed exploitation or economic development considerations and environmental protection) have also reached national courts, albeit in relation to seabed mining within an exclusive economic zone (EEZ). In September 2021, New Zealand's Supreme Court denied seabed miners Trans Tasman Resources permission to mine the South Taranaki Bight based on a precautionary approach.[11]

For Gjerde, the current challenges regarding seabed mining in the Area arise from paradigms or assumptions about life in the deep sea – underlying part XI of UNCLOS – which have turned out to be incorrect: the assumption that life in the deep sea was dull, distant, of little interest, and that seabed mining therein could occur without much environmental disturbance; that the resources for exploration/exploitation were easily accessible, that the technology was right and that 'we just needed to develop some potato-harvesting-type machines to enable this new regime to go

7 By deep-sea mining we mean the process of retrieving mineral deposits from the deep sea, that is, the Area of the ocean below 200 meter depth, beyond national jurisdiction.

8 IUCN, WCC Motion 069, 'Protection of deep-ocean ecosystems and biodiversity through a moratorium on seabed mining', 29 September 2021. Available online < https://www.iucncongress2020.org/motion/069> (accessed 20 June 2022).

9 See for example the case of the European Union. While the European Commission's '2021 Strategic Foresight Report' (see in particular 4. Securing and diversifying supply of critical raw materials) takes a pro-seabed mining stance, the EU Biodiversity Strategy (see in particular 4.2.1. International Ocean Governance, of the European Commission, 'EU Biodiversity Strategy for 2030: Bringing nature back into our lives', COM (2020) 380 final, 20 May 2020) reflects a precautionary and ecosystem-based approach. For a discussion on this see *Sea at risk*, 'European Commission announces plans to step up deep-sea mining exploration on same day as IUCN adopts moratorium motion', 16 September 2021. Available online <https://seas-at-risk.org/general-news/european-commission-announces-plans-to-step-up-deep-sea-mining-exploration-on-same-day-as-iucn-adopts-moratorium-motion/> (accessed 1 June 2022). See also P.A. Singh, V. Tassin Campanella and F. Maes stating that 'the scope of [a] moratorium has fluctuated at the EU between the one proposed by the Commission under the EU Biodiversity Strategy, which is limited to the Area, and the one recently adopted by the Parliament, again covering both the continental shelf and the Area. Consequently, there seems to be inconsistencies within EU institutions on the position that should advocate on seabed mining on the continental shelf, although the position on the need for a moratorium on commercial-scale exploitation in the Area has always been clear'. P.A. Singh, V. Tassin Campanella and F. Maes, 'The European Union and seabed mining', in V. Tassin Campanella (ed.), *Routledge handbook of seabed mining and the law of the sea*, op. cit., chapter VI.1.4.

10 By way of example, for a discussion on the different positions State Parties to the EU are taking on this, see Singh, Tassin Campanella and Maes, ibid., p. 21.

11 *Trans-Tasman Resources Limited v Taranaki-Whanganui Conservation Board* [2021] NZSC 127 [30 September 2021]. Available online <https://www.courtsofnz.govt.nz/assets/cases/2021/2021-NZSC-127.pdf> (accessed 3 May 2022). For a discussion on the principles held in the case by the New Zealand's Supreme Court see R. Makgill, A. Jaeckel and K. MacMaster, 'Implementing the precautionary approach for seabed mining: A review of state practice', in V. Tassin Campanella (ed.), *Routledge handbook of seabed mining and the law of the sea*, op. cit., chapter I.3. For an earlier analysis of the New Zealand's Court of Appeal decision in the same case see R. Makgill, J.D. Gardner-Hopkins and N.R. Coates, 'Trans-Tasman Resources Limited v. Taranaki-Whanganui Conservation Board', *The International Journal of Marine and Coastal Law* 35 (4), 2020, 835–845.

forward'.[12] But at the same time, she suggests, in 1967, the drafters of UNCLOS launched a revolution in our approach to the law of the sea: a vision that all people could benefit from new-found resources of the deep sea (understood as the Area), where all nations and all peoples could come together through an international institution dedicated as a kind of trustee to operate on behalf of humankind as a whole; a regime dedicated to equity, encouraging and enabling participation by all States, and also a regime where you would be sharing any benefits of scientific discoveries as well as resource exploitation, all built on the premise that this legal regime would be able to ensure effective protection of the marine environment.[13] The critical gap was in what Gjerde calls a 'disconnection between science and law': the drafters of UNCLOS part XI were 'operating in the dark' for example, in ignorance of the significance of hydrothermal vents in the ocean, which were only discovered in 1977.[14] In other words, she suggests that the drafters of UNCLOS developed a whole regime based on the misapprehension that seabed mineral resources were easy to harvest and would not cause significant harm.[15]

This chapter explores what role if any the International Tribunal for the Law of the Sea (in particular the Seabed Disputes Chamber) may play in addressing the most urgent issues raised by deep-sea mining and clarification of the relevant legal notions under UNCLOS. It identifies some of the possible contentious issues and advisory requests that may arise in relation to deep-sea mining and the manner in which they may come under its jurisdiction: namely (1) ISA's possible request for an Advisory Opinion; (2) a possible contentious case against ISA before ITLOS; (3) the potential role of ITLOS in clarifying issues concerning the alignment between the deep-sea mining regime applicable to the Area with the regime governing seabed mining on the Continental Shelf, and other potential conflicts; and (4) substantive areas potentially giving rise to disputes, in particular, (i) the regulation of gas hydrates exploration/exploitation; (ii) sub-sea permafrost in the Arctic; (iii) deep-sea mining and climate change; and (iv) loss of biodiversity.

The International Seabed Authority's possible request for an Advisory Opinion

Section 1(15) of the Annex to the 1994 *Agreement Relating to the Implementation of part XI of the UN Convention on the Law of the Sea* (Annex to the 1994 Agreement) provides that the ISA 'shall elaborate and adopt [...] rules, regulations and procedures necessary to facilitate the approval of plans of work for exploration or exploitation' in the Area.[16] If a request is made by a State (as in the case of Nauru) it is provided that 'the Council shall, in accordance with article 162, paragraph 2(o), of the Convention,[17] complete the adoption of such rules, regulations and procedures within two years of the request' (section 1, paragraph 15 (b), of the Annex to the 1994 Agreement). The two-year period is to end by July 2023. Critically, Section 1, paragraph 15 (c) of the Annex to the

12 K.M Gjerde, *Current challenges regarding deep-sea mining and protection of ocean life beyond national boundaries*, Lauterpacht Centre for International Law, Public Lecture, 11 February 2022.

13 Ibid. For the evolution of rights and obligations of States on the continental shelf and the Area and related challenges, see V. Tassin Campanella, Y. Cissé and D. Tladi, 'State rights and obligations of States on the continental shelf and the Area', in V. Tassin Campanella (ed.), *Routledge handbook of seabed mining and the law of the sea*, op. cit., 2023, chapter II.1.

14 *National Geographic* (Resource Library), 'Deep sea hydrothermal vents'. Available online <https://www.nationalgeographic.org/media/deep-sea-hydrothermal-vents/> (accessed 20 June 2022).

15 Gjerde, op. cit.

16 Annex to the *Agreement relating to the Implementation of part XI of the United Nations Convention on the Law of the Sea of 10 December 1982*.

17 Article 162 (referring to powers and functions of the ISA Council) 2 (o), of UNCLOS.

1994 Agreement provides – in case the elaboration of the rules, regulations and procedures are not completed by the required term – the following:

> (c) If the Council has not completed the elaboration of the rules, regulations and procedures relating to exploitation within the prescribed time and an application for approval of a plan of work for exploitation is pending, it shall none the less consider and provisionally approve such plan of work based on the provisions of the Convention and any rules, regulations and procedures that the Council may have adopted provisionally, or on the basis of the norms, contained in the Convention and the terms and principles contained in this Annex as well as the principle of non-discrimination among contractors.

Now, under article 145 of UNCLOS, the ISA is also the entity responsible for adopting 'appropriate rules, regulations and procedures' for ensuring the effective protection of the marine environment from harmful effects in the Area. The only technical body within ISA which could provide environmental expertise at present is the Legal Technical Commission, which, commentators point out, is rather a small unit with 'little technical environmental expertise'.[18] Faced with these limitations but with the formidable task the ISA has before it, it may be possible for ISA to resort to the Seabed Disputes Chambers of ITLOS, for an Advisory Opinion on legal issues that would assist its task as a regulator (developing rules and procedures relating to deep-sea mining), while meeting its obligations of ensuring effective protection of the marine environment from harmful effects in the Area.[19] The request must contain a precise statement of the question to be submitted to the Chamber and must be signed by the Authority's duly qualified representative. The request also must specify the name of the person who is to represent the Authority during the advisory proceedings.

The word 'shall' contained in article 191 would appear to suggest that the Seabed Disputes Chamber is obliged to give the advisory opinion requested. However, the Chamber might be entitled to decline to reply to a request for an opinion if the request relates to a question which is not legal or if the question does not fall within the Authority's sphere of activity.[20]

A potential advisory opinion to be requested by the ISA could for example address 'the interpretation and application of section 1 paragraph 15' resolving the uncertainties surrounding the implications and consequences arising out of the invocation section 1(15) and guide the Council (the executive branch of the ISA) as it moves forward, as suggested by Singh.[21] But a potential

18 Gjerde, op. cit.

19 Article 191 of UNCLOS. The Council is the Executive organ of the ISA. For a discussion on the role of the Council see A. Jaeckel, 'The Area and the role of the International Seabed Authority', in V. Tassin Campanella (ed.), *Routledge handbook of seabed mining and the law of the sea*, op. cit., chapter IV.1. For further reading on the role of ISA and the UNCLOS Deep Seabed Mining Regime, see J. Dingwall, 'Commercial mining activities in the deep seabed beyond national jurisdiction: The international legal framework', in C. Banet (ed.), *The law of the seabed*, Leiden: Brill Nijhoff, 2020, p. 141.

20 By way of analogy see the basis in which the International Court of Justice has declined rendering an Opinion. See (the question is not a legal one), *Certain expenses of the United Nations (Article 17, paragraph 2, of the Charter)*, Advisory Opinion, ICJ Reports 1962, p. 155 or (the question does not fall within the sphere or competence of the requesting institution), *Legality of the Use by a State of Nuclear Weapons in Armed Conflict*, Advisory Opinion, ICJ Reports 1996 (I), p. 78, paragraph 25.

21 P. Singh, 'Can the invocation of the "two-year rule" at the International Seabed Authority be challenged?', *Deep-sea Mining Observer, Deep Sea-Mining News and Resources Blog*, 30 September 2021, Available online <https://

advisory opinion could also be addressed (i) to clarify notions such as the meaning of 'serious harm' (as differentiated from 'harmful effects')[22] in the context of deep-seabed mining (including what are the key factors or parameters to measure, to inform the decision about whether an impact constitutes serious harm or not);[23] (ii) what is required to meet the notion of 'effective protection' under UNCLOS; or (iii) what amounts to national 'effective control'[24] of an entity.

An ISA state member could also trigger the request for an Advisory Opinion by the ISA as was the case with Nauru in March 2010, when it requested the ISA Secretary-General to seek an advisory opinion from the ITLOS Seabed Disputes Chamber.[25]

A possible contentious case against the International Seabed Authority?

Potentially, State Parties to UNCLOS could also file a case against the ISA itself, for example, on the basis that it is failing in its obligations to ensure effective protection of the marine environment from harmful effects in the Area (by failing to regulate exploitation in accordance to UNCLOS) as required.[26] Article 187 of UNCLOS sets out the jurisdiction of the Seabed Disputes Chamber relating to 'disputes with respect to activities in the Area' including:

> (b) disputes between a State Party and the Authority concerning,
>
> (i) *acts or omissions of the Authority* or of a State Party alleged to be in violation of this Part of the Annexes relating thereto or of rules, regulations and procedures of the Authority adopted in accordance therewith; or

dsmobserver.com/2021/09/commentary-can-the-invocation-of-the-two-year-rule-at-the-international-seabed-authority-be-challenged/> (accessed 12 April 2022).

22 While article 145 of UNCLOS requires both States and the ISA to ensure 'effective protection' of the marine environment from 'harmful effects' which may arise from seabed mining activities, existing ISA regulations for seabed mineral exploration of manganese nodules, SMS and cobalt-rich crusts provide only a definition of 'serious harm' as aptly noted by L.A. Levin et al., 'Defining "serious harm" to the marine environment in the context of deep-seabed mining', *Marine Policy* 74, 2016, 245–259.

23 See for example L.A. Levin et al., arguing that defining 'serious harm' is critical to effective regulation of mining activities, including addressing the thresholds and indicators that can reflect 'significant adverse change'. Ibid.

24 For a discussion on the lack of clarity relating to how 'effective control' should be interpreted see K. Willaert and P. Singh, 'Deep sea mining partnerships with developing states: Favourable collaborations or opportunistic endeavours?', *The International Journal of Marine and Coastal Law* 36 (2), 2021, 199–217. See also A. Rojas and F. Philips, 'Effective control and deep seabed mining: Toward a definition', *Liability Issues for Deep Sebed Mining Series*, Paper No. 7, February 2019, arguing how the concept of effective control as used in UNCLOS 'has the potential to be defined as regulatory or economic control', p. 9.

25 *Responsibilities and Obligations of States Sponsoring Persons and Entities with Respect to Activities in the Area*, Advisory Opinion ('*Responsibilities and Obligations of Sponsoring States*'), 1 February 2011, ITLOS Reports 2011, p. 10.

26 At the time of the drafting of this chapter, the ISA was meeting at its council headquarters in Kingston, Jamaica, to develop regulations for deep-sea mining amidst growing concerns about alleged failings of transparency. Reportedly, 'Some states, including Germany, are also concerned that the ISA is developing its mining standards and guidelines behind closed doors, and that current knowledge of deep-sea ecosystems and the potential effects of mining on the marine environment are insufficient to allow it to go ahead'. See K. McVeigh, 'Sea regulator accused of deciding deep sea's future "behind closed doors"', *The Guardian*, 1 April 2022. Available online <https://www.theguardian.com/environment/2022/apr/01/worlds-seabed-regulator-accused-of-reckless-failings-over-deep-sea-mining> (accessed 1 April 2022).

(ii) acts of the Authority alleged to be in excess of jurisdiction or a misuse of power.[27] (emphasis added)

As noted by leading commentary, 'Per Art. 187 (b) (ii), a State Party may also make a complaint in circumstances when an act of the Authority was "in excess of jurisdiction or a misuse of power" '.[28]

The potential role of ITLOS in clarifying issues concerning the alignment between the deep-sea mining regime applicable to the Area with the regime governing seabed mining on the continental shelf, and other potential conflicts

There are also potential contentious issues that could arise from what Willaert has called 'the multitude of legal frameworks relevant to deep sea mining and their interactions'.[29] Bourrel et al. note for their part that the Common Heritage of Mankind principle

> has relevance in a number of ways for adjacent spaces, which are: the extended continental shelf of nations between 200 and 350 nautical miles; the seabed areas within national exclusive economic zones (EEZs); the water column above the Area; the living resources of the deep seabed, and in particular their marine genetic resources.[30]

A potential problematic issue in particular, as identified by Willaert, is for example, 'whether the deep sea mining regime applicable to the Area is well-aligned with the one governing the same activities on the continental shelf'.[31] He explains that activities similar to deep-sea mining are developing within areas under national jurisdiction (seabed mining), and argues that 'prominent mismatches between the two regimes might cause problems and concerns'.[32] One such problem is, as Willaert notes, the fact that exploration and exploitation operations on the continental shelf are governed by the national laws of coastal states which leads to various regulatory frameworks. He points out that it would be 'important that these domestic laws complement the efforts of the international community to protect deep sea ecosystems by including adequate environmental standards and conditions'.[33] He underlines, '[a]fter all, the various species living in and near the seabed or in the water column above do not take these legal boundaries into account and will not confine themselves to one or the other zone'.[34] Moreover, Willaert rightly points out that activities on the continental shelf of a coastal state 'may have a transboundary environmental impact'.[35] As a consequence he stresses that it would be very important that 'deep sea mining activities within national jurisdiction are adequately regulated and supervised, avoiding any legal gaps'.[36]

27 Article 187 b (i) and (ii), UNCLOS.

28 C. Burke, p. 1260 § 13, in A. Proelss (ed.), *United Nations Convention on the Law of the Sea, A commentary*, C.H. Beck, Hart, Nomos, 2017.

29 See K. Willaert, *Regulating deep sea mining: A myriad of legal frameworks*, Switzerland: Springer, 2021, p. 19.

30 M. Bourrel, T. Thiele and D. Currie, 'The common heritage of mankind as a means to assess and advance equity in deep sea mining', *Marine Policy*, July 2016, p. 6.

31 See K. Willaert, *Regulating deep sea mining: A myriad of legal frameworks*, op. cit., p. 19.

32 Ibid., p. 20.

33 Ibid.

34 Ibid.

35 Ibid.

36 Ibid.

To the extent that the meaning of 'effective control' (as noted earlier) in this context may not yet be sufficiently clear, it would appear that there is also a need for clarification of what the rules concerning transboundary harm would be. Further, the extended continental shelf regime, as aptly noted by Willaert, would raise additional questions regarding the way in which harmonization of the different regimes for seabed mining in the different areas should be achieved.[37]

To Verlaan it is '[UNCLOS'] own fragmented approach to the Area (defined as "the seabed and ocean floor, and subsoil thereof, beyond the limits of national jurisdiction")' which would 'not facilitate the task of ISA, because UNCLOS does not limit its marine environmental protection requirements to the Area'.[38] She argues that in the context of deep-sea mining, the scope of the ISA's marine environmental responsibilities in that sense, extends to 'the coastline', i.e. well beyond the Area and far into water within national jurisdiction, and must include 'prevention, reduction and control of interference with the ecological balance of the marine environment'.[39]

The above is further problematized if one is to consider non-State Parties to UNCLOS, raising the need for an assessment of 'the precise impact of non-ratification' on the deep-sea mining plans of said states.[40] As put by Willaert, this would involve determining the question, under international law, 'whether or not – and at what cost – non-states parties can exploit the abundant mineral resources on the ocean floor'.[41] He questions: 'Does non-ratification lead to free and unbridled access to the deep seabed, without any regard to the rules and conditions of the international regime, or does this preclude states from pursuing their deep sea mining ambitions?'[42]

ITLOS can potentially play a role in ensuring that the different legal frameworks relevant to deep-sea mining are harmonized.

Substantive areas potentially giving rise to disputes

In addition, the challenges regulating deep-sea mining include the interface with areas upon which very little was known in the past. Some of the areas that need to be considered in assessing deep-sea mining include (1) the regulation of gas hydrates; (2) the sub-sea permafrost in the Artic; and (3) the potential global impact of deep-sea mining on biodiversity loss and climate change. These all can potentially give rise to new types of disputes before ITLOS.

The regulation of gas hydrates exploration and exploitation

Gas hydrates are 'a crystalline solid formed of water and gas'.[43] Looking and acting much like ice, they contain huge amounts of methane.[44] They exist in huge quantities in marine sediments in a

37 Ibid., p. 26.

38 P. Verlaan, 'Environmental issues of deep-sea mining: A law of the sea perspective', in R. Sharma (ed.), *Environmental Issues of Deep-Sea Mining, Impacts, Consequences and Policy Perspective*, op. cit., p. 23, relying on article 145 of UNCLOS, 'which is the governing article applicable specifically to "activities in the Area"; other marine environmental protection requirements for these activities are found elsewhere [in UNCLOS], including Part XII, which is dedicated to marine environment'. Verlaan, ibid., p. 25, footnote 16.

39 Ibid., p. 25 citing UNCLOS, article 145(b).

40 See for example, the United States of America. K. Willaert, *Regulating deep sea mining: A myriad of legal frameworks*, op. cit., p. 26.

41 Ibid.

42 Ibid., p. 27.

43 United States Geological Survey ('USGS'), 'What are gas hydrates?' Official Website of the US Government. Available online <https://www.usgs.gov/faqs/what-are-gas-hydrates> (accessed 5 September 2021).

44 Ibid.

layer several hundred meters thick directly below the sea floor and in association with permafrost in the Arctic. Methane hydrate is believed to be 'the world's largest natural gas resource' and can be found in the shallow sediments of many deep ocean areas.[45] Scientific scholars note that enormous amounts of methane hydrate have been found beneath Arctic permafrost, beneath Antarctic ice and in sedimentary deposits along continental margins worldwide.[46] To the extent that deep-sea mining may tap into resources which would potentially release vast quantities of methane into the atmosphere, the question is what would the legal consequences be under UNCLOS? What would be the implications of this for the regulation of deep-sea mining? So far, the impacts of methane hydrate mining have not been examined under the prism of the UNCLOS by ITLOS. Admittedly, however, this new potential activity, the exploitation of gas hydrates, may give rise – as noted by former President of ITLOS Vladimir Golitsyn – to 'new types of disputes before the Tribunal in the years to come'.[47]

Scientists warn that 'hydrate mining could generate sub-marine landslides', and that 'dissociating the methane hydrates would destabilize the sea floor', and in the worst-case scenario that 'huge packages of sediments could slide downhill, triggering powerful tsunamis along coastal areas'.[48] Yan et al. suggest that the current legal framework is not adequately prepared to address transboundary harm triggered by the exploitation of offshore methane hydrates, in particular because 'the technology of such extraction is still at an experimental state, and potential risks remain uncertain – and even untraceable – for cross-jurisdictional claims'.[49] While Yan et al.'s focus is the Deep Seabed Mining Law of China, which the authors identify as a predominant nation exploring offshore methane hydrate extraction, their observations also consider UNCLOS.[50] What would 'the responsibility to ensure' by States, under article 139 paragraph 2 of UNCLOS entail in methane hydrate exploration? As noted by Vöneky and Höfelmeier, the scope of such a 'responsibility to ensure' is of an obligation of conduct or due diligence, not of result.[51] The obligation does not

45 H. M. King, 'Methane hydrate'; *Geoscience News and Information.* Available online <https://geology.com/articles/methane-hydrates/> (accessed 2 January 2022).

46 Ibid.

47 V. Golitsyn, 'The potential role of the Tribunal in light of its experience after 20 years' judicial activity' in *ITLOS at 20: Looking into the Future*, Symposium, 18 March 2017, pp. 5 and 6.

48 World Ocean Review, 'Methane hydrate', *WOR 3 Marine Resources – Opportunities and Risks 2014*. Available online <https://worldoceanreview.com/en/wor-3/methane-hydrate/mining-impacts/> (accessed 2 January 2022).

49 D. Yan et al., 'Governing the transboundary risks of offshore methane hydrate exploration in the seabed and ocean floor – an analysis on international provisions on chinese law', *Journal of World Energy Law and Business* 13, 2020, 185–203, p. 186.

50 While they refer to a number of relevant provisions of UNCLOS, they wrongly conclude that state responsibility for potential environmental harm caused by methane hydrate exploration is 'strict'. D. Yan, et al., 'Governing the transboundary risks of offshore methane hydrate exploration in the seabed and ocean floor – an analysis on international provisions on chinese law', *Journal of World Energy Law and Business* 13, 2020, 185–203, p. 191. It is pertinent to observe that article 139 of UNCLOS differentiates between responsibility and liability. In its 2011 Advisory Opinion, ITLOS held that under article 139 'the term "responsibility" refers to the primary obligation whereas the term "liability" refers to the secondary obligation, namely the consequences of a breach of the primary obligation'. *Responsibilities and Obligations of Sponsoring States*, para. 66. See also the discussion on article 139 in N. Bernaz and I. Pietropaoli, 'Developing a business and a human rights treaty: Lessons from the deep seabed mining regime under the United Nations Convention on the Law of the Sea', *Business and Human Rights Journal* 5 (2), pp. 214–215.

51 S. Vöneky and A. Höfelmeier, p. 972 §11, in A. Proelss (ed.), *United Nations Convention on the Law of the Sea, A commentary*, op. cit.

impose strict liability.[52] In international law – as they observe – the formulation has especially been used in connection with the general obligations of States to prevent transboundary harm stemming from activities conducted in their territory.[53] Yan et al. observe, in addition, that there is a need for outlining the scope of liability in the context of methane hydrate exploration, and the particular obligations coming from both sponsorship and application with a plan of exploration and exploitation.[54] The Seabed Disputes Chamber has already held that the precautionary approach is part of the due diligence obligation itself.[55] But what would that entail in the context of methane hydrate exploration or even exploitation?

A question is also raised on whether the 'Draft Articles on the Prevention of Transboundary Harm from Hazardous Activities' ('Draft Articles on the Prevention of Transboundary Harm')[56] and 'Principles on the Allocation of Loss in the Case of Transboundary Harm Arising Out of Hazardous Activities'[57] ('Principles on the Allocation of Loss' or 'The Principles') provide approaches and principles that could be useful to regulate methane hydrate exploration and exploitation.[58] For example, how is one to ensure the victim of transboundary damage in a case of methane hydrate exploration/exploitation access to prompt and adequate compensation? The commentary of Principle 1 of The Principles on the Allocation of Loss observes that hazardous activities coming within the scope of the draft principles are those not prohibited by international law and involving the 'risk of causing significant transboundary harm through their physical consequences'.[59] The Principles recognize that 'harm could occur despite implementation of the duties of prevention':

> Transboundary harm could occur for several other reasons not involving State responsibility. For instance, there could be a situation where the preventive measures were followed but actually proved inadequate, or where the particular risk that cause transboundary harm could not be identified at the time of initial authorization and hence appropriate preventive measures are not envisaged. In other words, transboundary harm could occur accidentally or it may take place in circumstances not originally anticipated. Further, harm could occur because of gradually accumulated adverse effects over a period of time.[60]

Indeed, for the purposes of the Principles it is assumed that duties of due diligence under the obligations of prevention have been fulfilled.[61] Yan et al. observe therefore that the Principles adopt a

52 Ibid.
53 Ibid.
54 Yan et al., op. cit., p. 191.
55 *Responsibilities and Obligations of Sponsoring States*, para. 130 *et seq.*
56 Draft articles on the Prevention of Transboundary Harm for Hazardous Activities with commentaries, 2001. Text adopted by the International Law Commission at its fifty-third session, in 2001, and submitted to the General Assembly as a part of the Commission's report covering the work of that session (A/56/10). Available online <https://legal.un.org/ilc/texts/instruments/english/commentaries/9_7_2001.pdf> (accessed 12 April 2022).
57 UN General Assembly Resolution 61/36 Annex, UN Doc A/Res/61/36, 18 December, 2006. See also Draft principles on the allocation of loss in the case of transboundary harm arising out hazardous activities, with commentaries, 2006, *Yearbook of the International Law Commission, 2006*, vol. II, Part Two.
58 Yan et al., op. cit., p. 199. See pp. 199–201 for an analysis of the approach of the Draft Articles on the Prevention of Transboundary Harm and its usefulness in the contest of methane hydrate extraction.
59 *Draft principles on the allocation of loss in the case of transboundary harm arising of hazardous activities, with commentaries*, 2006, Commentary (2) to Principle 1, p. 62.
60 Ibid., Commentary (7) to Principle 1, p. 63.
61 Ibid., Commentary (8) to Principle 1, p. 63.

strict-liability-'polluter pays' principle to ensure the victim of transboundary damage has access to prompt and adequate compensation.[62] Would this be important to consider in cases of harm arising from the extraction of methane hydrate, which fits the element of raising a 'risk of causing significant transboundary harm through their physical consequences'? Yan et al. see the benefits of following that approach. Applying strict liability, regardless of fault, could undoubtedly, suggest the same authors, pressure operators into being more careful when it comes to applying untested prospecting methods, therefore being beneficial for the environment, as well as in compliance with the general precautionary principles.[63] Note in that sense that the Principles would go further than article 22 of Annex III of UNCLOS where it is stated:

> The contractor shall have responsibility or liability for any damage *arising out of wrongful acts* in the conduct of its operations, account being taken of contributory acts or omissions by the Authority. Similarly, the Authority shall have responsibility or liability for any damage arising out of wrongful acts in the exercise of its powers and functions, including violations under article 168, paragraph 2, account being taken of contributory acts or omissions by the contractor. Liability in every case shall be for the actual amount of damage. (emphasis added)

Is there room for using such an approach reflected in the Principles within the interpretation of UNCLOS article 304?[64] More generally, there is also the question of what measures in the event of both national and international regulatory breaches by involved parties (the sponsoring States, the enterprises) should be put in place?[65] As posited by Yan et al.: Should monetary penalties be instituted? Should the ISA wield the authority to deliver such penalties?[66] The above questions can well be the subject of a further Advisory Opinion by the Seabed Disputes Chambers if prompted to do so.

Lastly, there are also warnings in scientific studies that 'an increased release of methane from the oceans could accelerate climate change'.[67] To date climate change has not yet come to the consideration of ITLOS. As Boyle noted, UNCLOS 'was negotiated at a time when climate change was not yet part of the international agenda'.[68] At the same time, he argues, UNCLOS was never meant to be a 'static or immutable legal regime'.[69] It would appear therefore, that the potential impacts of hydrate mining and correlative issues of climate change are matters likely to necessitate legal clarification under UNCLOS. Former President of ITLOS Vladimir Golitsyn would agree. In his opening Address to the Symposium *ITLOS at 20: Looking into the Future*, he observed: 'The

62 Yan et al., op. cit., p. 201.

63 Ibid.

64 Article 304 (Responsibility and liability for damage) of UNCLOS reads: 'The provisions of this Convention regarding responsibility and liability for damage are without prejudice to the application of existing rules and the development of further rules regarding responsibility and liability under international law'. As the commentary observes, this applies also to article 139. As Tams and Devaney note, 'The Convention's regime is not "self-contained" but can be complemented by external rules'. Tams and Devaney, in A. Proelss (ed.), *United Nations Convention on the Law of the Sea, A commentary*, op. cit., p. 1962, para. 1.

65 Yan et al., op. cit., p. 192.

66 Ibid.

67 World Ocean Review, 'Methane hydrate', op. cit.

68 A. Boyle, 'Protecting the marine environment from climate change', in E. Johansen et al. (eds), *The law of the sea and climate change*, Cambridge: Cambridge University Press, 2021, p. 83.

69 Ibid.

exploitation of gas hydrates has the potential to inflict significant harm on the marine environment and negatively affect the earth's climate' as there is 'the risk of methane escape into the atmosphere, which could further intensify the greenhouse effect'. [70]

Sub-sea permafrost in the Arctic

Sub-sea permafrost in the Arctic is 'generally relict terrestrial permafrost inundated after the last glaciation and now degrading under the overlying shelf sea'.[71] As with terrestrial permafrost, sub-sea permafrost 'is a substantial reservoir and/or a confining layer for gas and for gas hydrates'.[72] As explained by Portnov et al., 'permafrost and gas hydrates have been melting and releasing massive quantities of methane into the ocean and atmosphere'.[73] Chen et al. observe that Arctic sub-sea permafrost contains more organic carbon than the terrestrial counterpart and is undergoing fast degradation in response to climate warming.[74] In addition, scientists appear to have found evidence that the topology of the sea-floor might be changing, undergoing massive upheaval, in particular that the sub-sea permafrost would have thawed and collapsed.[75] It is suggested that this process could accelerate because the Arctic is now warming so quickly.[76]

The implications of these processes and the impact seabed mining could have in those processes constitute an additional area for consideration.

As noted by Golitsyn, the exploitation of gas hydrates contained in permafrost on land in the Arctic and which are primarily found in the continental slope of the ocean floor in the sea areas, is likely to take place in areas within the national jurisdiction of coastal States.[77] He observes as a consequence 'that the potential global impact raises the question of whether the regulation of the exploitation of gas hydrates [in such instances] should be solely a matter for the coastal State to regulate or whether it requires international regulation'.[78] He points out that as a result ITLOS 'may be faced with questions concerning the regulation of the exploitation of gas hydrates in future, for example in the context of compliance by coastal States concerned with general obligation of all State Parties to the Convention under article 192 'to protect and preserve the marine environment'.[79]

Deep-sea mining and climate change

Boyle suggests that as far as climate change mitigation strategies are concerned, UNCLOS, part XII (which he argues must be interpreted and applied with subsequent developments in interna-

70 Golitsyn, op. cit., p. 6.

71 Alfred-Wegener Institute Helmholtz-Zentrum Für Polar- und Meeresforschung, 'Submarine permafrost'. Available online <https://www.awi.de/en/science/geosciences/permafrost-research/research-focus/submarine-permafrost.html> (accessed 1 January 2022).

72 Ibid.

73 A. Portnov et al., 'Offshore permafrost decay and massive seabed methane escape in water depths', *Geophysical Research Letters*, Vol. 2013, 3962–3967, p. 3962.

74 M. Chen et al., 'Subsea permafrost as a potential major source of dissolved organic matter to the east siberian arctic shelf', *Science of the Total Environment* 777, 10 July 2021, 146100.

75 M. Simon, 'Underwater permafrost is a big, gassy wild card for the climate', *Wired*, 21 March 2022.

76 Ibid.

77 Golitsyn, op. cit., p. 6.

78 Ibid.

79 Ibid.

tional law and policy in mind) requires States to take the measures necessary to protect the marine environment from the harmful effects of anthropogenic climate change.[80] Prip likewise argues that while part XII does not refer to climate change-related impacts, 'this however does not imply that climate change induced harmful impacts cannot be considered'.[81]

Former ITLOS Judge Rüdiger Wolfrum would agree with that. In his view, the Convention is 'flexible enough to accommodate the issues which will confront us' including 'climate change'.[82]

Boyle notes that anthropogenic greenhouse gas emissions have already caused marine pollution as per scientific evidence.[83] This would amount, he posits, to an introduction of 'substances or energy' to the marine environment and a likelihood of the 'deleterious effect' required by article 1(1)(4) of UNCLOS.[84] From this perspective, the requirement of states to 'protect and preserve the marine environment' in article 192 would include preventing and combating climate change.[85] Prip suggests, further, that article 194 of UNCLOS which requires states to take all measures necessary to prevent pollution from any source, including from or through the atmosphere, should be interpreted to include prevention of greenhouse gas emissions.[86] This is an area which would certainly benefit from a legal pronouncement by ITLOS by way of an Advisory Opinion. Considering that 'nearly half a billion tonnes of carbon (the equivalent of more than 1.5 billion tonnes of carbon dioxide) are captured and stored by high seas ecosystems annually',[87] deep-sea mining effects on the climate is a matter that may well come under the jurisdiction of the Seabed Disputes Chamber. It is to be noted that while organizations such as Greenpeace International argue that deep-sea mining will disrupt the ocean's sequestration of carbon and make climate change worse,[88] companies wanting to exploit the deep sea, such as DeepGreen, deny this.[89]

There are also elsewhere arguments advanced to the effect that article 207 of UNCLOS requiring States to adopt laws and regulations to prevent, reduce and control pollution from land-based sources is relevant for greenhouse gas emissions and applicable to areas beyond national jurisdiction.[90]

It has been observed that since the adoption of UNCLOS in 1982, 'human activities in areas beyond national jurisdiction (ABNJ) have increased considerably, and climate change with its main stressors, ocean warming deoxygenation and ocean acidification, are expected to compound the impacts on high sea environment'.[91] Besides the main climate stressors, it has been noted,

80 A. Boyle, 'Protecting the marine environment from climate change', op. cit., p. 84.

81 C. Prip, 'Integrating climate change in the governance of areas beyond national jurisdiction', in E. Johansen et al. (eds), *The law of the sea and climate change*, op. cit., p 337.

82 Wolfrum intervention in *ITLOS at 20: Looking into the Future*, op. cit., p. 85.

83 A. Boyle, 'Protecting the Marine Environment from Climate Change', op. cit., p. 84.

84 Ibid.

85 Prip, op. cit.

86 Ibid.

87 Ibid.

88 See Greenpeace International, *In deep water: The emerging threat of deep sea mining*, Report, June 2019. Available online < https://oursharedseas.com/wp-content/uploads/2019/11/Greenpeace_In_Deep_Water-1.pdf> (accessed 17 May 2022), pp. 3 and 5.

89 DeepGreen, *DeepGreen responds to Greenpeace seabed mining report*, 31 July 2019. Available online https://www.maritime-executive.com/editorials/deepgreen-responds-to-greenpeace-seabed-mining-report (accessed 16 May 2022).

90 Prip, op. cit., p. 338.

91 Ibid., p. 337.

'there is evidence of large amounts of the strong greenhouse gas, methane, trapped in the seabed which may be released by human activities'.[92]

Loss of biodiversity

It is said that more than 80 percent of the ocean remains 'unmapped, unobserved and unexplored'.[93] As commentators observe, 'recent research has shown that the remote deep and open oceans host a major part of the world's biodiversity'.[94] Faced with this, the scientific community is calling for the facilitation of the adoption of precautionary and ecosystem approaches, including the precautionary principles with respect to deep-sea mining.[95] Rare earth elements in the deep sea, seen today as highly desirable commodities,[96] have a flip side, we are told: the potential loss of biodiversity and ecosystems as a consequence of deep-sea mining. A recent study by academics at Queen's University Belfast found that 'almost two-thirds of the hundreds of mollusc species that live in the deep sea are at risk of extinction'.[97]As noted above, the IUCN issued pronouncement 069 on protection of deep-ocean ecosystems and biodiversity through a moratorium on seabed mining.[98] This placed ensuring the effective protection of the marine environment from harmful effects of seabed mining activities in areas beyond national jurisdiction at the heart of the discussion on deep-sea mining.[99] The pronouncement emphasized 'the need to ensure sufficient scientific information on deep-sea biodiversity and ecosystems and an appropriate and transparent institutional structure prior to adopting [deep-sea mining] regulations'.[100] The pronouncement also recalled article 5 of the Convention on Biological Diversity and the commitments of States to the 2030 Agenda for Sustainable Development including sustainable development goals 12 and 14.[101] These references bring the topic of deep-sea mining within a larger context and raise the need to interpret UNCLOS (in particular deep-sea mining) in unity with other treaty regimes such as the Convention on Biological Diversity.[102] ITLOS can certainly play an important role as an interpreter of UNCLOS, including in its relation with the Convention on Biological Diversity. Such perspective would also need to integrate a harmonic relationship with new treaty regimes such as the Biodiversity Beyond National Jurisdiction (BBNJ) which will actually cover the seabed in the Area, albeit the BBNJ will contain its own mechanisms for settling disputes.[103]

92 Ibid.

93 Editorial, 'Our oceans'. *Newsroom*, 20 August 2020. https://rhinoreview.org/our-oceans-80-percent-unmapped-unobserved-and-unexplored-and-nearly-95-percent-unprotected/ (accessed 5 January 2022).

94 C. Prip, op. cit., p. 336.

95 IUCN World Conservation Congress, 069-Protection of deep-ocean ecosystems and biodiversity through a moratorium on seabed mining, op. cit.

96 Dingwall, op. cit., p. 158.

97 ITV, 'Almost two thirds of deep-sea species at risk of extinction', 10 December 2021.

98 IUCN World Conservation Congress, 069-Protection of deep-ocean ecosystems and biodiversity through a moratorium on seabed mining, op. cit.

99 Ibid.

100 Ibid.

101 Ibid.

102 For a discussion on conservation of biodiversity on the seabed, see F. Armas-Pfirter, 'The International Seabed Authority and the protection on biodiversity', in A. de Paiva and V. Tassin (eds), *Guide to the navigation of marine biodiversity beyond national jurisdiction*, D'Plácido Editora: Belo Horizonte, 2018, pp. 223–248.

103 On the discussions on said possible mechanisms see Y. Shi, 'Settlement of disputes in a BBNJ agreement: Opinions and analysis', *Marine Policy* 122, December 2020, 104156. For a discussion on – as referred by Gautier – 'the delicate questions of jurisdiction' raised by the 'juxtaposition of two different dispute resolution systems', see P.

Conclusion

Young's 1968 remark that 'uses of ocean space undreamed of in the past are in the making, and all the patterns that will eventually emerge cannot now be foreseen',[104] appears to have anticipated a world in which deep-sea mining would be potentially possible. To Gjerde, however, part XI of UNCLOS was built on several paradigms or assumptions about life in the deep sea that have turned out to be incorrect: 'It assumed that life in the deep-sea was dull, distant, of little interest to us, as human beings; that seabed mining could occur without much environmental disturbance; it assumed that these resources of the deep are easily accessible (…) and it assumed that the technology was right and we just needed to develop some potato-harvesting-type machines to enable this new regime to go forward'.[105]

In the quest to fill the gap of what Gjerde calls a disconnection between 'science and law', doubtlessly, ITLOS would play an increasing role. This chapter has explored what role if any ITLOS (in particular the Seabed Disputes Chamber) may play in addressing the most urgent issues raised by deep-sea mining and in the clarification of the relevant legal notions under UNCLOS. While, as noted by Treves, it is 'the exploitation stage which is the most likely to produce disputes'[106] this chapter posits that the role of ITLOS in addressing deep-sea mining issues may precede any exploitation stage. This chapter thus considers possible advisory opinions and contentious cases involving ISA as well as broader topics that could come to the jurisdiction of the Seabed Disputes Chamber. It also suggests that ITLOS could play an important role in harmonizing what Willaert has called 'the multitude of legal frameworks relevant to deep-sea mining and their interactions' ensuring cohesion of the law. ITLOS may also be key in providing legal clarity on various topics such as the regulation of gas hydrates, deep-sea mining and climate change by interpreting UNCLOS within the framework of broader international law. To some, urgent regulation of deep-sea mining may follow a bottom-up approach with examples such as New Zealand whose Supreme Court recently decided against a giant seabed mining proposal in the south Taranaki Bight.[107] However, the top-to-bottom approach appears equally needed in the current context in which Nauru has notified the ISA of the intention of Nauru Ocean Resources Inc (NORI), a subsidiary of a Canadian company called DeepGreen Mineral Corp., to apply for approval to begin mining in two years in the Clarion-Clipperton Zone in the North Pacific Ocean between Hawaii and Mexico.[108] But it is not only urgency, but also principle. Ensuring the unity of international law advocates for the importance of a top-to-bottom approach. What is certain is that the future docket of ITLOS will be dealing with increasing matters relating to the interpretation of UNCLOS in relation to deep-sea mining as this chapter proposes.

Gautier, 'Le règlement des différends' (Partie 3: 'Observations sur le règlement des différends relatifs au nouvel instrument sur la conservation et l'utilisation durable de la biodiversité marine des zones ne relevant pas de la juridiction nationale'), in A. de Paiva and V. Tassin (eds), op. cit., p. 690.

104 R. Young, 'The legal regime of the deep-sea floor', *American Journal of International Law* 62 (3), July 1968, 642–653.

105 Gjerde, op. cit.

106 Treves, op. cit.

107 *Trans-Tasman Resources Limited and Taranaki-Whanganui et al.*, SC 228/2022 [2021] NZSC 127. Available online <https://www.courtsofnz.govt.nz/assets/cases/2021/2021-NZSC-127.pdf> (accessed 1 February 2022).

108 'Pacific Island of Nauru sets two year deadline for U.N. deep-sea mining rules', op. cit.

References

Articles, books and chapters

Armas-Pfirter F., 'The international seabed authority and the protection on biodiversity', in A. de Paiva and V. Tassin (eds.), *Guide to the navigation of marine biodiversity beyond national jurisdiction*, D'Plácido Editora: Belo Horizonte, 2018, pp. 223–248.

Bernaz N. and Pietropaoli I., 'Developing a business and a human rights treaty: Lessons from the deep seabed mining regime under the United Nations Convention on the Law of the Sea', *Business and Human Rights Journal* 5(2), July 2020, 214–215.

Boyle A., 'Protecting the marine environment from climate change', in E. Johansen et al. (eds), *The law of the sea and climate change*, Cambridge: Cambridge University Press, 2021, pp. 81–103.

Chen M. et al., 'Subsea permafrost as a potential major source of dissolved organic matter to the East Siberian Arctic Shelf', *Science of the Total Environment* 777, 10 July 2021, 146100.

Dingwall J., 'Commercial mining activities in the deep seabed beyond national jurisdiction: The international legal framework', in C. Banet (ed.), *The law of the seabed*, Leiden, Boston: Brill Nijhoff, 2020, pp. 139–162.

Gautier P., 'Le Règlement des différends', in A. de Paiva and V. Tassin (eds.), *Guide to the navigation of marine biodiversity beyond national jurisdiction*, Belo Horizonte: D'Plácido Editora, 2018, pp. 665–693.

Golitsyn V., 'The potential role of the Tribunal in light of its experience after 20 years' judicial activity', in *ITLOS at 20: Looking into the Future*, Symposium, 18 March 2017, pp. 5–11.

Jaeckel A., 'The Area and the role of the international seabed authority', in V. Tassin Campanella (ed.), *Routledge handbook of seabed mining and the law of the sea*, London: Routledge, 2023, chapter IV.1.

Levin L.A. et al., 'Defining "serious harm" to the marine environment in the context of deep-seabed mining', *Marine Policy* 74, 2016, 245–259.

Makgill R., Gardner-Hopkins J.D. and Coates N.R., 'Trans-Tasman Resources Limited v. Taranaki-Whanganui conservation board', *The International Journal of Marine and Coastal Law* 35(4), 2020, 835–845.

Makgill R., Jaeckel A. and MacMaster K., 'Implementing the precautionary approach for seabed mining: A review of state practice', in V. Tassin Campanella (ed.), *Routledge handbook of seabed mining and the law of the sea*, London: Routledge, 2023, chapter I.3.

Oral N., 'The common heritage of mankind under international law: An overview', in V. Tassin Campanella (ed.), *Routledge handbook of seabed mining and the law of the sea*, London: Routledge, 2023, chapter I.2.

Portnov A. et al, 'Offshore permafrost decay and massive seabed methane escape in water depths', *Geophysical Research Letters* 40, 2013, 3962–3967.

Prip C., 'Integrating climate change in the governance of areas beyond national jurisdiction', in E. Johansen et al. (eds.), *The law of the sea and climate change*, Cambridge University Press, 2021, pp. 336–353.

Proelss A. (ed.) *United Nations convention on the law of the sea: A commentary*, München: C.H. Beck; Oxford: Hart; Baden-Baden: Nomos, 2017.

Rojas A. and Philips F., 'Effective control and deep seabed mining: Toward a definition', *Liability issues for Deep Sebed Mining Series*, Paper No. 7, February 2019.

Sharma R., 'Preface', in R. Sharma (ed.), *Environmental issues of deep-sea mining*, Switzerland: Springer, 2019, pp. xi–xii.

Shi Y., 'Settlement of disputes in a BBNJ agreement: Opinions and analysis', *Marine Policy* 122, December 2020, 104156.

Singh P, 'Can the invocation of the "two-year rule" at the International Seabed Authority be challenged?', *Deep-sea Mining Observer, Deep Sea-Mining News and Resources Blog*, 30 September 2021.

Singh P., Tassin Campanella V. and Maes F., 'The European Union and seabed mining', in V. Tassin Campanella (ed.), *Routledge handbook of seabed mining and the law of the sea*, London: Routledge, 2023, chapter VI.1.4.

Tassin Campanella V., Cissé Y. and Tladi D., 'State rights and obligations of States on the continental shelf and the Area', in V. Tassin Campanella (ed.), *Routledge handbook of seabed mining and the law of the sea*, London: Routledge, 2023, chapter II.1.

Treves T., 'Dispute settlement and seabed mining in the Area', in V. Tassin Campanella (ed.), *Routledge handbook of seabed mining and the law of the sea*, London: Routledge, 2023, chapter V.1.

Verlaan P., 'Environmental issues of deep-sea mining: A law of the sea perspective', in R. Sharma (eds.), *Environmental issues of deep-sea mining, impacts, consequences and policy perspective*, Switzerland: Springer, 2019, pp. 23–26.

Willaert K. and Singh P., 'Deep sea mining partnerships with developing states: Favourable collaborations or opportunistic endeavours?', *The International Journal of Marine and Coastal Law* 36(2), 2021, 199–217.

Willaert K., *Regulating deep sea mining: A myriad of legal frameworks*, Switzerland: Springer, 2021.

Yan D. et al., 'Governing the transboundary risks of offshore methane hydrate exploration in the seabed and ocean floor – An analysis on international provisions on Chinese law', *Journal of World Energy Law and Business* 13, 2020, 185–203.

Young R., 'The legal regime of the deep-sea floor', *American Journal of International Law* 62(3), July 1968, 642–653.

Judgments (international and national)

Certain Expenses of the United Nations (Article 17, Paragraph 2, of the Charter), Advisory Opinion, ICJ Reports 1962, p. 155.

Legality of the Use by a State of Nuclear Weapons in Armed Conflict, Advisory Opinion, ICJ Reports 1996 (I), p. 78.

Responsibilities and Obligations of States Sponsoring Persons and Entities with Respect to |Activities in the Area, Advisory Opinion (*'Responsibilities and Obligations of Sponsoring States'*), 1 February 2011, ITLOS Reports 2011, p. 10.

Trans-Tasman Resources Limited v Taranaki-Whanganui Conservation Board [2021] NZSC 127, 30 September 2021. Available online <https://www.courtsofnz.govt.nz/assets/cases/2021/2021-NZSC-127.pdf> (accessed 3 May 2022).

Treaties, governmental, UN, inter-governmental and regional organs documents and sources

Draft articles on the prevention of transboundary harm for hazardous activities with commentaries, 2001. Text adopted by the international law commission at its fifty-third session, in 2001, and submitted to the general assembly as a part of the commission's report covering the work of that session (A/56/10). Available online <https://legal.un.org/ilc/texts/instruments/english/commentaries/9_7_2001.pdf> (accessed 12 April 2022).

Draft principles on the allocation of loss in the case of transboundary harm arising out hazardous activities, with commentaries, 2006. Text adopted by the international law commission at its fifty-eighth session, in 2006, and submitted to the general assembly as a part of the commission's report covering the work of that session (A/61/10).

European Commission, EU biodiversity strategy for 2030: Bringing nature back into our lives, COM(2020) 380 final, 20 May 2020. Available online <https://eur-lex.europa.eu/legal-content/EN/TXT/?uri=CELEX:52020DC0380> (accessed 15 March 2022).

European Commission's 2021 strategic foresight report, (communication from the commission to the european parliament and the council, 2021 strategic foresight report the EU's capacity and freedom to act) COM/2021/750 final, 8 September 2021. Available online <https://eur-lex.europa.eu/legal-content/EN/ALL/?uri=COM%3A2021%3A750%3AFIN> (accessed 15 March 2022).

IUCN, WCC Motion 069, 'Protection of deep-ocean ecosystems and biodiversity through a moratorium on seabed mining', 29 September 2021, Available online <https://www.iucncongress2020.org/motion/069> (accessed 20 June 2022).

UN General Assembly Resolution 61/36 Annex, UN Doc A/Res/61/36 (18 December 2006).

United State Geological Survey ('USGS'), 'What are gas hydrates?' Official website of the US government. Available online <https://www.usgs.gov/faqs/what-are-gas-hydrates> (accessed 5 September 2021).

US Government Accountability Office (GAO), 'Science and tech spotlight: Deep-sea mining', 15 December 2021. Available online <https://www.gao.gov/products/gao-22-105507> (accessed 12 April 2022).

Public Lectures

Gjerde K.M., 'Current challenges regarding deep-sea mining and protection of ocean life beyond national boundaries', Lauterpacht Centre for International Law, Public Lecture, 11 February 2022.

Other Sources

Alfred-Wegener Institute Helmholtz-Zentrum Für Polar- und Meeresforschung, 'Submarine permafrost', Available online <https://www.awi.de/en/science/geosciences/permafrost-research/research-focus/submarine-permafrost.html> (accessed 1 January 2022).

DeepGreen, 'DeepGreen responds to greenpeace seabed mining', Report, 31 July 2019. Available online https://www.maritime-executive.com/editorials/deepgreen-responds-to-greenpeace-seabed-mining-report (accessed 16 May 2022).

Greenpeace International, *In Deep Water: The Emerging Threat of Deep Sea Mining*, Report, June 2019. Available online <https://oursharedseas.com/wp-content/uploads/2019/11/Greenpeace_In_Deep_Water-1.pdf> (accessed 17 May 2022).

ITV, 'Almost two thirds of deep-sea species at risk of extinction', 10 December 2021.

King H.M., 'Methane Hydrate', *Geoscience News and Information.* Available online <https://geology.com/articles/methane-hydrates/> (accessed 2 January 2022).

McVeigh K., 'Sea regulator accused of deciding deep sea's future "behind closed doors"', *The Guardian*, 1 April 2022.

National Geographic (Resource Library) 'Deep sea hydrothermal vents', Available online <https://www.nationalgeographic.org/media/deep-sea-hydrothermal-vents/> (accessed 20 June 2022).

Reid H., 'Pacific Island of Nauru sets two year deadline for U.N. deep-sea mining rules', *Reuters*, 29 June 2021. Available online <https://www.reuters.com/business/environment/pacific-island-nauru-sets-two-year-deadline-deep-sea-mining-rules-2021-06-29/> (accessed 29 September 2021).

Sea at risk, 'European Commission announces plans to step up deep-sea mining exploration on same day as IUCN adopts moratorium motion', 16 September 2021, Available online <https://seas-at-risk.org/general-news/european-commission-announces-plans-to-step-up-deep-sea-mining-exploration-on-same-day-as-iucn-adopts-moratorium-motion/> (accessed 1 June 2022).

Simon M., 'Underwater permafrost is a big, gassy wild card for the climate', *Wired*, 21 March 2022.

World Ocean Review, 'Methane Hydrate', *WOR 3 Marine Resources* – Opportunities and Risks | 2014. Available online <https://worldoceanreview.com/en/wor-3/methane-hydrate/mining-impacts/> (accessed 2 January 2022).

PART VI

Regional and national practice

The regional and national sections are intended to provide the reader with a critical assessment of seabed mining of minerals practice in the world. All regional and national sections are following a specific format provided by the editor to enable comparative reading. Some adjustments of this format have been made, when necessary, to highlight specificities.

While this part of the book intends to cover a wide and rich scope of practice, it is not intended to be exhaustive, nor representative of all State practice. It however aims at providing a wide view of States' positions, interests and challenges with regard to seabed mining of minerals, be these States supportive or not of the development of these seabed activities. By doing so, it also intends to become a key reference, and a starting point for complementary research on the matter.

Regions and States covered in this book have been selected based on the availability of a relevant national expert(s). A great number of States' practices are also included in the research chapters of this book. Readers are therefore invited to refer to these chapters to complement the information provided in the regional and national chapters.

DOI: 10.4324/9780429426162-20

VI.1

Regional practice

VI.1.1
AFRICA AND SEABED MINING

Edwin Egede

Introduction

Africa is an island continent surrounded by two major oceans, the Atlantic and Indian oceans, consisting of 55 states,[1] made up of 39 coastal states, including island states, and 16 landlocked states.[2] Africa was quite active in the development of the deep seabed mining regime that resulted in Part XI of the 1982 *United Nations Convention of the Law of the Sea* (UNCLOS) and the *Agreement relating to the implementation of part XI of UNCLOS* (the 1994 Agreement). The combined African coastal states continental shelf (CS) is vast, covering approximately 6.5 million square kilometres and rich in valuable resources such as hydrocarbons and minerals.[3] Africa is currently the largest regional grouping in the International Seabed Authority (ISA), the organisation responsible for organising and controlling mineral-related activities in the seabed and ocean floor and subsoil thereof, beyond the limits of national jurisdiction (the Area),[4] with 47 member states. Seabed mining in the Area is especially important for Africa because mining activities in this part of the sea may have an impact on the economies of African countries that produce minerals, which will eventually be exploited in the Area.[5] Furthermore, seabed mining activities in the Area near

1 Note that the Republic of South Sudan became the newest African state when it became independent on 9 July 2011 and has since become a member of both the African Union and the United Nations. Also, note the Saharawi Arab Democratic Republic, which became independent on 27 February 1976, though a member of the African Union, is not currently a member of the United Nations and there are still some issues on its recognition as a state, notably by Morocco. Morocco withdrew in 1984 from the Organization of African Unity because of its recognition of the Saharawi Arab Democratic Republic but has since been readmitted in 2017 to the African Union.

2 Sixteen African landlocked states, namely Botswana, Burkina Faso, Burundi, Central African Republic, Chad, Eswatini (formerly Swaziland), Ethiopia, Lesotho, Malawi, Mali, Niger, Rwanda, South Sudan, Uganda, Zambia, and Zimbabwe.

3 United Nations Economic Commission for Africa, *African Blue Economy Policy Handbook*, Addis Ababa: UNECA, 2016, p. 4.

4 See Article 1(1), UNCLOS.

5 See generally A. Lapteva et al., *Report to the International Seabed Authority: Study of the Potential Impact of Polymetallic Nodules Production from the Area on the Economies of Developing Land-based Products of Those Metals Which Are Likely to Be Most Seriously Affected*, Advance Unedited Version, English Only, 12 May 2020. Available online: <https://www.isa.org.jm/files/documents/impactstudy.pdf> (accessed 20 September 2021).

DOI: 10.4324/9780429426162-22

the African continent might have environmental effects for African coastal states. Besides, certain mineral resources may straddle the border between the Area and adjacent CS of African states, making them of direct interest to these countries.[6] Additionally, Africa is interested in seabed mining activities in the Area because of its potential to build up capacity in ocean science and technology. For instance, at the 2018 sustainable blue economy conference, jointly organised in Nairobi by Kenya, Canada, and Japan, the African Union (AU) requested, amongst other things, for '[h]elp [for] African countries in capacity building in exploitation of deep seas'.[7]

Geographical extent of the continental shelves and the Area

Under UNCLOS, the Area is defined in such a way that the outer limits of the CS of coastal states must be determined in order to clarify the geographical scope of the Area.[8] The AU in a decision urging its member states to make submissions to the United Nations Commission on the Limits of the Continental Shelf (CLCS) highlighted that there were 'major geopolitical and strategic stakes linked to the African continental shelf' and 'abundant mineral and biological resources, which constitute an important source of foreign currency earnings for the economic development of the continent'.[9] However, there are inconsistencies in African states' CS legislation on the CS's outer limit.[10] Indeed, some African states unequivocally declare the outer limit of their CS to be 200 nautical miles.[11] This is significant because some of these African states have made submissions to the CLCS.[12] Other states, despite being parties to UNCLOS, have retained the definition of their CS as 200 nautical mile depth or exploitability, as stated in Article 1 of the 1958 Geneva Convention on the CS.[13] It is hoped that these African states will take concrete steps to update their legislation to conform to UNCLOS.[14] Some have enacted legislation declaring that the CS's outer limits are

6 Article 142, UNCLOS.

7 The Nairobi statement of intent on advancing the global sustainable blue economy, p. 12. See also the summary of the commitments made during the sustainable blue economy conference 26–28 November 2018, Nairobi, Kenya, p. 14. Available online: <http://www.blueeconomyconference.go.ke/documents/> (accessed 20 September 2021). The Nairobi blue economy conference brought together over 18,000 participants from across the world and from diverse sectors.

8 Article 1(1) of UNCLOS states that the 'Area' is 'the sea-bed and ocean floor and subsoil thereof beyond the limits of national jurisdiction'.

9 Preamble 3, Decision on extension of the African continental shelf and climate change, Doc.EX.CL/391(XII), decisions and declarations of the 10th ordinary session of the Assembly of the AU, 31 January–2 February 2008.

10 See E. Egede, *Africa and the Deep Seabed Regime: Politics and International Law of the Common Heritage of Mankind*, Heidelberg: Springer, 2011, pp. 31–54.

11 See for example, article 17 of Cabo Verde's law No. 60/IV/92 of 21 December 1992; section 6(1) of Ghana's maritime zones (delimitation) law, 1986 and Section 11(1) of Sierra Leone's maritime zones (establishment) decree, 1996. See also in this book the practice of some African States with exploration blocks located in areas beyond national jurisdiction, C. Schofield and J. Mossop, 'The Article 82 Conundrum: Implementing Payment for the Exploitation of the Continental Shelf beyond 200 Nautical Miles', in V. Tassin Campanella (ed.), *Routledge Handbook of Seabed Mining and the Law of the Sea*, London: Routledge, 2023, chapter III.2.

12 For example, Ghana made submissions to the CLCS regarding its outer CS and the CLCS delivered its recommendation accepting the extended CS of Ghana in September 2014.

13 See for example, Egypt's presidential decision No. 1051 of 1958 concerning the continental shelf; section 2(k) of Sudan's territorial waters and continental shelf act 1970 and section 14(1) of Nigeria's petroleum act, cap.350, laws of the federation of Nigeria 1990.

14 Fortunately, Nigeria is already taking steps to update its legislation. See Section 14(1) and (2) of the Nigerian maritime zones (enactment) bill, 2020 (this bill is currently before the Nigerian national assembly and hopefully will be enacted soon).

the edge of the continental margin or 200 nautical miles where such outer edge does not extend to 200 nautical miles.[15] Others have simply declared their CS to be 'as defined in the Convention [UNCLOS], or as it may be defined by international convention from time to time'.[16] So far there have been 20 submissions from Africa regarding CS beyond 200 nautical miles that have been made to the CLCS. These submissions are at various stages, a few have had recommendations from the CLCS, some others are at various stages of the CLCS consideration processes, and a number of African states have only been able to submit their preliminary information indicative of the outer limits of CS beyond 200 nautical miles to the UN Secretary-General.[17] Although the AU has at various times urged its member states with CS beyond 200 nautical miles to make submissions to the CLCS in line with article 76 of UNCLOS, it has not really provided these states with practical assistance with their submissions.[18]

Governance of the seabed

In Africa, there are a variety of bodies with the competence to develop its seabed mining in the Area regulatory framework. As a result, Africa's seabed mining in the Area policy is fragmented. The main challenge is coordinating the various bodies' activities so that they can complement each other's efforts and avoid duplication of functions and roles. The following are key bodies that have so far played a role in the governance of the Area, as can be seen in the section on seabed mining in the Area regulation below.

African Union

The African Union, which succeeded the Organisation of African Unity (OAU), has played a key role in the development of key regulatory instruments on the African ocean (or blue economy), including seabed mining, such as the 2050 African integrated maritime (AIM) strategy, African charter on maritime security and safety and development in Africa (Lomé Charter) 2016, and the 2018 African blue economy strategy. The AU is a continental body made up of all African states with the goal of creating '[a]n integrated, prosperous, and peaceful Africa, driven by its own citizens and representing a dynamic force in the global arena'.[19] Although the African Union's constitutive Act does not specifically mention the law of the sea, it does state that the organisation's goals include promoting and defending African common positions on issues of concern to the continent and its peoples, as well as encouraging international cooperation and promoting

15 See for instance, article 4 of Mauritania's ordinance 88-120 of 31 August 1988 establishing the limits and the legal regime of the EEZ and the CS of Mauritania; Section 18 of Mauritius's maritime zone act No. 2 of 2005; Article 6 of Senegal's act No. 85-14 delimiting the continental shelf, 25 February 1985 and Section 11(1) and (2) of Seychelles' maritime zones act No. 2 of 1999, as amended by maritime zones (amendment) act No. 5 of 2009.

16 See Section 6(1) of Namibia's territorial sea and exclusive economic zone of Namibia, act No. 3 of 1990, 30 June 1990, as amended by territorial sea and exclusive economic zone of Namibia amendment act, 1991. See also section 8(1) of maritime zones act, No. 15 of 1994.

17 SPLOS/183 of 20 June 2008.

18 See for example paras 4, 5, and 6, decision on extension of the African continental shelf and climate change, Doc. EX.CL/391(XII), decisions and declarations of the 10th ordinary session of the Assembly of the AU, 31 January–2 February 2008.and para. 59 of the 2050 Africa's integrated maritime strategy adopted in 2014.

19 See African Union website. Available online: <https://au.int/en/overview > (accessed 20 September 2021).

sustainable development.[20] These goals have guided the AU's intervention in law of the sea issues at the global and regional levels.

The AU has several organs, as well as specialised agencies,[21] which have recently been involved in promoting the AU law of the sea agenda, including seabed mining in the Area.

Assembly

The AU's top policy and decision-making body, made up of the heads of state and government from all the member states, sets the AU's policies, decides its priorities, approves its yearly programme, and supervises its policies and decisions' execution. In its decision adopting the 2050 AIM strategy 2014 it reiterated 'the geostrategic importance of seas and oceans in the socio-economic development' and recognised 'that Africa's oceans and seas are essential to the sustainable development of the continent and that they occupy a critical position within the post-2015 development agenda and the formulation of the sustainable development goals (SDGs)'.[22] It then urged the Secretaries-general of the United Nations, the International Maritime Organization, the ISA, and the chairperson of the AU commission to support efforts to mobilise the resources required for the decision's implementation.[23] It also adopted a decision in 2016 requiring the AU commission (AUC) to adopt annexes to the Lomé Charter to include certain matters, including seabed mining in the Area which were not included in the original iteration of the charter.[24]

Regional Economic Communities

The Regional Economic Communities (RECs) are regional groupings of African states. All of them were formed prior to the AU's inception, have evolved independently, and have different roles and structures. The RECs serve as building blocks for regional economic integration between members of individual regions and they are eventually to lead to the creation of an African common market. The AU recognises eight RECs, including the economic community of West African states (ECOWAS). The ECOWAS consists of 15 member countries located in the Western region of Africa.[25] It was established in May 1975 through the treaty of Lagos, with a mandate of promoting economic integration in all fields of activity of the constituting countries.[26] In 2014 it adopted a maritime integrated strategy (MIS), which included seabed mining in the Area.

African Minerals Development Centre

The African Minerals Development Centre (AMDC) was set up in 2013 as an institutional framework to implement the African mining vision (AMV), which was adopted by African heads of state at the February 2009 AU summit after a meeting held the previous year by Ministers respon-

20 Article 3 of the African Union constitutive act.

21 See articles 5 (c) and 20, ibid.

22 Paras 1 and 7, Assembly decision on the adoption and implementation of the 2050 Africa's integrated maritime strategy (2050 AIM strategy), Doc. Assembly/AU/16(XXII) Add.1, Assembly/AU/Dec.496(XXII) of 2014.

23 Para. 17, ibid.

24 Assembly decision Ext/Assembly/AU/Dec.1 (VI) by the AU extraordinary summit, held on 15 October 2016.

25 The member states are Benin, Burkina Faso, Cape Verde, Cote d'Ivoire, The Gambia, Ghana, Guinea, Guinea Bissau, Liberia, Mali, Niger, Nigeria, Sierra Leone, Senegal, and Togo.

26 The initial treaty was signed in 1975 in Lagos, Nigeria. A revised treaty was adopted in 1993 in Cotonou, Benin Republic.

sible for mineral resources development.[27] One of the key aspects of the work of the AMDC is to leverage on Africa's blue economy and a vital aspect of the AMDC blue economy agenda is to develop and influence the formulation of emerging norms seabed mining in the Area, as well as to encourage African states to engage with seabed mining in the Area activities.[28] In 2016 the AMDC was granted observer status with the ISA, and it indicated that it aims to use this status to 'contribute to the establishment of a deep sea mining governance framework for Africa, and (...) the development of policies and regulatory frameworks for the deep sea mining sector'.[29]

The AU Border Programme

The African Union Border Programme (AUBP) was established in 2007 to assist in delimiting and demarcation of African boundaries, including the delimitation and delineation of maritime borders.[30] This author had in a previous write-up suggested that the AU through the AUBP could provide such assistance to African states, especially those that are least developed states, in delineating their outer CS.[31]

United Nations Economic Commission for Africa

The United Nations Economic Commission for Africa (UNECA), which was established in 1958 by the Economic and Social Council of the United Nations, is one of the United Nations' five regional commissions. Its mandate is to promote the economic and social development of its 54 member states, as well as to foster intra-regional integration and promote international cooperation for Africa's development. It was the first regional body in Africa to advocate for Africa to engage with seabed mining in the Area as an integral part of the African blue economy.[32]

Regulation of seabed mining activities.

The AU, unlike the European Union, is not a party to UNCLOS and the 1994 Agreement, and thus is not a member of the ISA. Nonetheless, 47 AU member states that are parties to UNCLOS and the 1994 Agreement are currently members of the ISA. The OAU, which preceded the AU, signed the final act of the Third United Nations Conference on the Law of the Sea. Under Article 156(3) of the UNCLOS, the OAU was entitled to participate in the ISA as an observer. Hence, the AU, as successor to the OAU, may apply to the ISA under Rule 82(1) (c) of the ISA Assembly rules of procedure to be recognised as an observer as the successor to the OAU.[33] It would be able to

27 See Statute of the AMDC.

28 UNECA/AMDC, *Harnessing Mineral Resources for Africa's Transformation: The AMDC Approach*, Addis Ababa: UNECA, 2017, pp. 9 and 15.

29 ISA Observers. Available online: <https://isa.org.jm/observers> (accessed 20 September 2021).

30 Declaration on the African Union border programme and its implementation modalities, Addis Ababa, BP/MIN/Decl. (II) of 7 June 2007.

31 E. Egede, 'Institutional Gaps in the 2050 Africa's Integrated Maritime Strategy', *Journal of Ocean Law and Governance in Africa* 1, 2016, 15–19.

32 See the *African Blue Economy Policy Handbook*, op. cit.

33 Para. 8(i) of Organization of African Unity, Fourth extraordinary session of the assembly of heads of state and government, 8–9 Sep. 1999, Sirte, Libya, declaration on the establishment of the African Union and article 33 of the AU constitutive act.

participate in the deliberations of the ISA Assembly and its subsidiary organs as an observer, but not in the decision-making.[34]

The seabed mining in the Area regulatory framework in Africa is underdeveloped, though there are currently regional initiatives underway to advance this framework. So far, no African state has enacted domestic legislation to regulate seabed mining in the Area. Unsurprisingly, there has been no significant investment in seabed mining in the Area to date. Africa is currently the only ISA regional grouping that has not sponsored a contractor to conduct exploration activities in the Area.

African Union and seabed mining in the Area

The AU adopted, in 2014, the 2050 AIM strategy to put forward an integrated and long-term approach to engaging with the continent's rivers, lakes, and oceans. Despite the obvious importance of the AIM strategy in promoting Africa's engagement with the blue economy, it made a critical omission by failing to engage with the Area and its resources, which are common heritage of mankind.[35] However, in 2015 the AU adopted Agenda 2063, a strategic framework for the socio-economic transformation of the continent over the next 50 years.[36] This long-term vision with seven aspirations that builds on and seeks to accelerate the implementation of continental initiatives for growth and sustainable development actually mentions seabed mining in the Area under Aspiration 1, titled '[a]prosperous Africa based on inclusive growth and sustainable development'. Under this aspiration the importance of the blue/ocean economy is underscored and it mentions seabed mining in the Area as one of the crucial blue growth areas, encouraging inter alia 'exploitation and beneficiation of deep sea mineral and other resources'.[37] Furthermore, Aspiration 7 mentions the importance of Africa having its 'rightful share of the global commons (land, oceans and space)', which of course include the Area.[38] In its first ten-year implementation plan of the Agenda 2063 the AU identified seabed mining as one of the important economic activities emanating from the African oceans and points to the '[c]ommission and complete prospection of seabed's for minerals and hydrocarbon potentials by 2023'.[39]

At an extraordinary summit held in Lomé, Togo, in 2016, the AU adopted the African Charter on Maritime Security, Safety and Development in Africa (the Lomé Charter), which sought to move the whole issue of engaging with the blue economy from a soft law approach to a more binding one.[40] When this Lomé Charter was adopted,[41] it was felt that certain Specialized Technical Committees (STCs) of the AU did not have the opportunity to be involved in the elaboration process, especially as regards the developmental aspects. As a result, the AU Assembly directed the AUC to take all necessary steps to convene the STCs of competence that did not participate in the

34 Article 82(2) and (3) of the ISA Assembly rules of procedure.

35 Articles 136 and 137 of UNCLOS. See the analysis of Egede, 'Institutional Gaps in the 2050 Africa's Integrated Maritime Strategy', op. cit. 19–26 on this.

36 See *Agenda 2063: The Africa We Want* (popular version), September 2015.

37 See Aspiration 1, para. 15, ibid.

38 Aspiration 7, ibid. See T. Brauninger and T. Konig, 'Making Rules for Governing Global Commons: The Case of Deep-Sea Mining', *Journal of Conflict Resolution* 44, 2000, 604–629.

39 AU *Agenda 2063: The Africa We Want* – first ten-year implementation plan 2014–2023, a shared strategic framework for inclusive growth and sustainable development, Addis Ababa: AU, 2015, pp. 8 and 61.

40 E. Egede, 'Africa's Lomé charter on maritime security: what are the next steps?' Available online: <http://www.safeseas.net/africas-lome-charter-on-maritime-security-what-are-the-next-steps/> (accessed 20 September 2021).

41 It was adopted by 35 African states and has so far been ratified by only two states, Republic of Benin and Togo. Under article 50(1) the charter would come into force 30 days after the deposit of the 15th ratification.

Charter's drafting, including STCs on trade, industry and minerals, transportation, infrastructures, energy and tourism, economic planning and integration, and any other relevant STCs, to prepare annexes to the Lomé Charter for consideration by the AU Assembly.[42]

In line with the Assembly's decision, the AUC convened an ad hoc expert group to develop the draft annexes, including aspects on seabed mining in the Area, which when adopted would form an integral part of the Lomé Charter.[43] These draft annexes, developed in 2017 and validated in a workshop bringing together stakeholders involved in marine affairs in Africa,[44] are presently being considered by the AU political processes.[45]

The AU's 2018 African blue economy strategy indicates that its purpose is 'to guide the development of an inclusive and sustainable blue economy that becomes a significant contributor to continental transformation and growth, through advancing knowledge' in various blue economy sectors, including 'the exploitation and beneficiation of deep sea mineral and other resources'.[46] It identifies seabed mining in the Area as one of the new frontiers of the blue economy with huge potential and pinpoints a gap in African expertise in this area.[47] It points out that deep sea mining (DSM), along with certain other sectors of the African blue economy, 'should be developed following a rigorous compensation scheme in place (avoid, reduce, compensate)', emphasising that African states should adhere to national, regional, and international standards and practices for the protection of the environment.[48] The strategy document opined that deep seabed mineral resources could be used to create a prosperous continent if this potential is harnessed by the setting of 'clear objectives with concrete milestones'.[49] It identified certain strategic objectives, such as the need to meet the growing demand for minerals and harness the potential of the seabed mining in the Area as an innovative industry through research and development. In doing this it advocated, amongst other things, the creation of the appropriate regulatory framework, the importance of engaging with seabed mining in the Area in a sustainable and environmentally friendly manner, as well as the need for capacity building and technology transfer.[50]

Further, the ECOWAS in its 2014 MIS under the heading 'Regulate mining and other exploitation of natural resources' touches briefly on seabed mining in the Area as part of its maritime strategy without elaborating in its priority actions how this would be developed. It states as follows:

The ocean and riverbeds are rich in oil and precious minerals that offer many competent authorities nationally and regionally. National governments must, under the guidance of the regional bodies, guide responsible extraction to the benefit of all their people. However, the extraction,

42 Assembly decision Ext/Assembly/AU/Dec.1 (VI) by the AU extraordinary summit, held on 15 October 2016.

43 Ibid. This author was privileged to be appointed as part of this group and was directly responsible for drafting the part of the Annexes relating to DSM.

44 Egede, 'Africa's Lomé charter on maritime security: what are the next steps?', op. cit.

45 See communique of the 858th meeting of the peace and security council (PSC), held on 16 July 2019, on the status of the implementation of the Lomé Charter, which restated the necessity of expediting 'the finalization of the draft Annexes, as integral part of the Lomé Charter, with a view to facilitating its rapid signature and ratification by Member States to allow the entry into force of this important instrument, as soon as possible'. Available online: <https://www.peaceau.org/uploads/eng-858th-psc-communique-maritime-security-lome.pdf> (accessed 20 September 2021).

46 Africa blue economy strategy 2018 at pp. xiv and 12. Available online: <https://au-ibar.org/strategy-documents> (accessed 20 September 2021).

47 Ibid. at p. 7.

48 Ibid. at pp. 14–15.

49 Ibid. at p. 21.

50 Ibid. at pp. 22, 27–28. See also Annex 4: Sustainable energy, mineral resources and innovative industries in the context of Africa blue economy strategy 2018, pp. 1–3, 10–14, 17, 18–19, 22, 27–30, 36–37.

exploration or deep sea mining of these raise concerns about potential environmental impacts. The protection of the marine environment is of utmost importance.[51]

While it is critical to emphasise the potential environmental impacts of seabed mining in the Area in the ECOWAS MIS, it is notable that it does not provide information also on the potential benefits of seabed mining in the Area, as the 2018 African blue economy strategy did, to provide a more balanced view on this.[52]

United Nations Economic Commission for Africa and seabed mining in the Area

The UNECA working with the AU AMDC has taken concrete steps towards supporting Africa's engagement with seabed mining in the Area activities.[53] In 2017, the UNECA and AMDC, along with the ISA and Uganda, a landlocked African state,[54] organised the Kampala workshop on 'Marine mineral resources of Africa's continental shelf and adjacent international seabed area – prospects for sustainable development of Africa's maritime domain in support of Africa's blue economy', which brought together over 60 participants from government mining ministries, international organisations, partner institutions, universities and other mining stakeholder groups. The aim of the workshop was to raise awareness among African states about the importance of Africa's involvement in sustainable seabed mining in the Area activities on Africa's CS and Area. It made several recommendations, including:

- encouraging governments of African ISA member states to participate actively in ISA activities and non-member African states to consider joining the ISA;
- advocating for the establishment of a collaborative body among African states to develop interest in seabed mining in the Area, using the Pacific countries as a model of cooperation;
- encouraging African states to form a collaborative body to sponsor contractors to conduct deep seabed exploration activities in reserved areas;
- improving the AIM strategy by developing a comprehensive and cohesive African position on seabed mining in the Area and the extension of the outer continental shelf; and
- advocating for a seabed mining in the Area policy framework that would serve as a foundation for the development of individual African states' seabed mining in the Area legal frameworks.[55]

Additionally, the UNECA organised in 2020 a workshop for the development of a strategic roadmap for the formulation of seabed mining in the Area regulations in the framework of Africa's blue

51 See para 74.

52 See L. Levin, D. Amon, and H. Lily, 'Challenges to the sustainability of deep-seabed mining', *Nature Sustainability* 3, 2020, 784–794.

53 The AMDC identified engaging with the African blue economy as one of its strategic objectives, specifically stating that it also 'works to developing international cooperation for activities in the international seabed areas'. See UNECA, *African Minerals Development Centre: Geological and Mineral Information Systems Harnessing Mineral Resources for Africa's Transformation*, Addis Ababa: UNECA, pp. 11 and 13.

54 The African Union commission, Grid Arendal (Norway), and the PEW Charitable Trust were also involved in the organisation of the workshop.

55 For more on this workshop and the recommendations, see generally ISA, *Marine Mineral Resources of Africa's Continental shelf and adjacent international seabed area: prospects for sustainable development of the African maritime domain in support of Africa's blue economy*, technical study No. 20, Kingston, Jamaica: ISA, 2017.

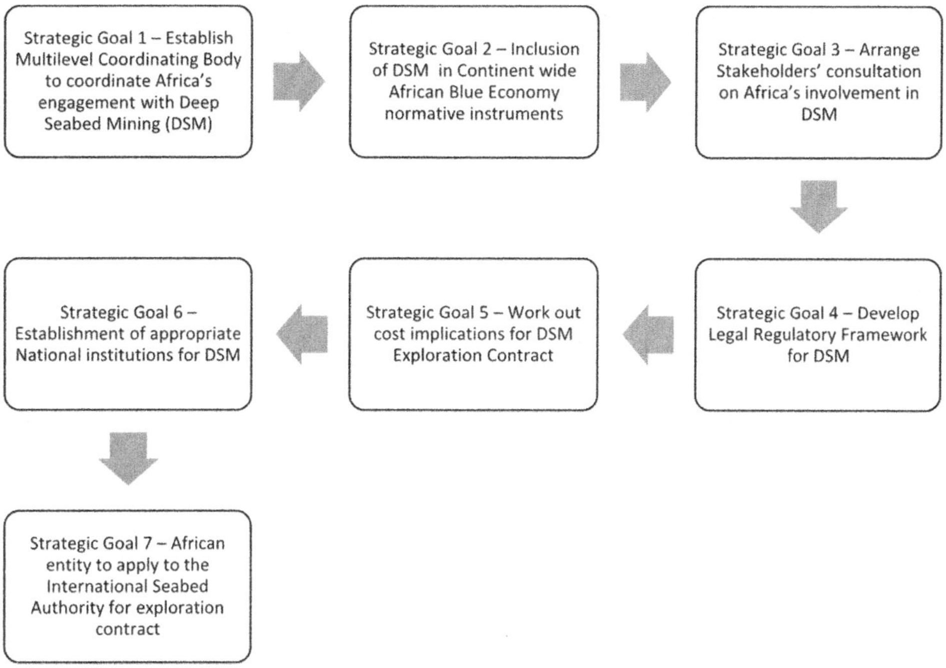

Figure VI.1.1 Seven Step Implementation of Strategic Roadmap

economy.[56] This workshop developed a strategic roadmap laying down seven steps that may be adopted for Africa's engagement with seabed mining in the Area (see Figure VI.1.1).[57]

The workshop also made several recommendations including: the need to work towards the realisation of technology transfer and capacity building; the establishment of centres of excellence for seabed mining in the Area; the review of continent-wide, REC, and national legal instruments on the blue economy to incorporate seabed mining in the Area; the encouragement of consortia between big African states and smaller ones to apply for seabed mining in the Area exploration contracts from the ISA;[58] and the conducting of stakeholder mapping on seabed mining in the Area. It also encouraged African states to continue lending support for the operationalisation of the Enterprise of the ISA;[59] UNECA to continue working with African states and the AUC towards the realisation of the seabed mining in the Area roadmap; and for UNECA/AMDC/AUC and other agencies to look for financial support for pilot projects to replicate and implement the seabed mining in the Area roadmap in the domestic setting of African states interested in seabed mining in the Area .[60]

56 This took place in Addis Ababa, Ethiopia, 28–29 January 2020.

57 UNECA, *Meeting report, strategic roadmap for the development of deep-sea mining regulations in the framework of Africa's blue economy*, Addis Ababa: UNECA, 2020.

58 Similar to the Interoceanmetal Joint Organization, a consortium that is an ISA contractor composed of the following states: Bulgaria, Cuba, the Czech Republic, Poland, the Russian Federation, and Slovakia.

59 See E. Egede, M. Pal, and E. Charles, *A study related to issues on the operationalization of the Enterprise: legal, technical and financial implications for the ISA and for states parties to the UNCLOS*, technical report 1/2019, Kingston, Jamaica, 2019.

60 UNECA, *Meeting report, strategic roadmap for the development of deep-sea mining regulations in the framework of Africa's blue economy*, op. cit.

International Seabed Authority African group and seabed mining in the Area

The ISA African group has made significant contributions towards developing the international regulatory framework of the Area, including the draft ISA exploitation code, training programmes, and operationalisation of the Enterprise.[61]

Conclusion

Africa played an active and important role in the negotiations of Area regime of UNCLOS. However, after the 1994 Agreement modified Part XI, there appeared to be a period of indifference on the part of Africa towards the regime. In recent years, a slew of instruments dealing with the African blue economy, including DSM, have been adopted. As a result, a coordination mechanism is required to synchronise the efforts of the various institutions adopting these instruments to achieve the goal of Africa's more active and coherent engagement with seabed mining in the Area. Furthermore, despite various efforts to encourage Africa's engagement with DSM, the region is still the only one that has not sponsored an entity to engage in DSM in the Area. Africa requires a clear action plan, possibly based on the UNECA strategic roadmap, to move the ideas of the various African blue economy instruments encouraging DSM engagement from paper to reality.

Acknowledgements

The author dedicates this chapter to his very good friend, Prince Emmanuel, for the invaluable contribution to this manuscript.

61 See for example: 'Training programmes for developing countries – submitted by the African group', ISBA/25/A/8 of 10 June 2019; 'Statement on behalf of the African group by Mr. Mehdi Remaoun, first secretary at the 25th Session of council of the international seabed authority – agenda item 11: financial model' of 25 February, 2019; 'African Group's submission to the international seabed authority: comments on the revised draft regulations on exploitation of mineral resources in the Area', September 2018; 'Statement by Algeria on behalf of the African group – request for consideration by the council of the African Group's proposal on the economic model/payment regime and other financial matters in the draft exploitation regulations under review' of 9 July 2018; 'Statement by Algeria on behalf of the African group – request for consideration by the council of the African Group's proposal for the operationalization of the Enterprise' of 6 July 2018.

VI.1.2
ANTARCTICA AND SEABED MINING

Leopoldo M. A. Godio

Introduction

The Antarctic continent has been subject to numerous international claims and unilateral/regional declarations from States that wish to assert their sovereignty therein. These controversies intensified during the 20th century with the start of the Cold War, which motivated the adoption of a basic framework to avoid the aggravation of the existing disputes.

Taking this into consideration, the International Council of Science (ISC) in 1955 discussed the status of this continent and decided to declare it as a special area of investigation signed by international cooperation. In particular, this meeting motivated the interest of governments in coordinating their presence in Antarctica and preceded the famous International Geophysical Year which paved the way to the *Antarctic Treaty* of 1959.

The Antarctic Treaty, adopted during the Cold War by a small number of signatory States,[1] establishes a consultation mechanism – implemented through the Antarctic Treaty Consultative Meetings (ATCM) – mainly focused on the exchange of information concerning matters of common interest over Antarctica.[2]

1 While Argentina, Australia, Chile, France, New Zealand, Norway and the United Kingdom have all territorial claims – sometimes overlapping – other States do not recognize any. In particular, the US and Russia maintain a 'basis of claim', not making nor acknowledging any entitlement. Consequently, all positions are explicitly protected by article IV, which preserves the status quo of the Area. It is on this basis of claims and their non-recognition that the system is erected. I. Brownlie, *Principles of Public International Law*, 6th Ed., Oxford: Oxford University Press, 2003, pp. 254–255.

2 From 1961 to 1994 the ATCM met once every two years, changing this pattern in 1994 to annual reunions. Every year, the original twelve Parties to the Treaty and those who demonstrated their interest in Antarctica (mainly by conducting substantial research activity), altogether called the 'Consultative Parties', meet 'for the purpose of exchanging information, consulting on matters of common interest pertaining to Antarctica, and formulating, considering and recommending measures in furtherance of the principles and objectives of the Treaty' (Art. IX). On this matter, a Latin American historical synthesis can be consulted: I.J. Cardone and P.G. Fontana, 'Latin-American contributions to the creation of the Antarctic regime', *The Polar Journal* 9(2), 2019, 300–323. The authors state that: 'if Antarctica is today a continent reserved to peaceful use and international cooperation in scientific research, along with natural and environmental conservation, it is thanks to the agreement reached by the twelve parties'. Ibid., p. 316.

DOI: 10.4324/9780429426162-23

In this line, article IV of the Antarctic Treaty constitutes the basis from which further development arises, up to the point of constituting a genuine System. This provision shelters all existing claims of sovereignty over Antarctica as they remain postponed until the future of this region is totally settled. Indeed, it also prevents an enlargement of the prevailing prerogatives and any other new entitlement that could arise from the Parties to the Treaty.

It is important to highlight the fact that without this directive we would not be in presence of this multilateral agreement, not only for the majorities required for adoption but also for the vote of confidence that it represented. In other words, the formula of article IV allowed the progress of the System without resolving or defining any territorial controversy, or even modifying the territorial status of the region.[3]

The following creation of the 1991 *Environmental Protocol to the Antarctic Treaty* established a moratorium concerning the execution of mining activities. Yet, for 50 years there is a general prohibition of mineral resource exploitation in the area. Nonetheless, this suspension contains an 'escape clause' that allows the Consultative Parties to disregard this Article once the term is reached and adopt a new mining regime.[4]

The purpose of the present chapter is to develop an objective analysis concerning the modern regulation applicable to mining activities in Antarctica. Indeed, the possible challenges concerning governance in this area, particularly regarding its interaction with the contemporary Law of the Sea, is one of the key aspects of our text.

Geographical extent of the exclusive economic zones and continental shelves

From time immemorial, several States sensed the existence of land surrounding the South Pole, but it was not until 1603 that expeditions began to explore this continent located beyond the 60 degrees South latitude.[5] On this particular matter, Argentina was the first State on the planet to establish a permanent observation base that is still on duty today.[6]

The Antarctic continent presents distinctive physical, geographic and meteorological conditions that make this zone unique and desirable. Indeed, it is a territory of 14,107,637 square kilometers, covered, almost at 99 percent, by a thick layer of ice and surrounded by ice formations, which raise the question whether ice can be subject to a territorial claim.[7]

Thus, during the austral winter, ice packs expand out to an area of 20 million square kilometers and retreat back to 4 million during summer. In effect, Antarctica becomes a pulsating continent, seasonally ringed by profound ice growth and decay. The contour of the Antarctic coastline is con-

3 A.S. Canio, 'Las competencias del Estado. Cuarta parte: el régimen jurídico de la Antártida', in R. Arredondo, *Curso de Derecho Internacional Público*, Buenos Aires: Ad-Hoc, 2020, pp. 222–223.

4 Protocol on Environmental Protection to the Antarctic Treaty, United Nations Treaty Series, Vol. 2941, article 7.

5 F. Villamizar Lamus, 'Antarctic Treaty and Antarctic Territory Protection Mechanisms', *Revista Chilena de Derecho* 40(2), 2013, 464–465.

6 On February 22, 1904, Argentina established the first permanent settlement in Antarctica called 'Base Antártica Orcadas'.

7 When drawing Antarctic baselines, it is convenient to distinguish ice shelves, fast ice, or pack ice since they can be used as diverse basepoints. Yet, none of the territorial claimants made any express reference to ice shelves in their Antarctic claims; therefore, this may indicate that petitioners see no need to treat ice shelves located on land any differently from the land itself. For further information, see H.D.T. Gutierrez Posse, *Guía para el Conocimiento de los Elementos del Derecho Internacional Público*, Buenos Aires: La Ley, 2008, p. 143; and S.B. Kaye and D.R. Rothwell, 'Southern Ocean Boundaries and Maritime Claims: Another Antarctic Challenge for the Law of the Sea', *Ocean Development and International Law* 33(3–4), 2002, 363–364.

stantly changing the determination of the traditional water baselines. Therefore, not only is there no 'low' water mark to use but also it is difficult to precisely ascertain any stable base points. This creates substantial uncertainty as regards the geographical extent of maritime zones.[8]

The continental shelf of Antarctica is wider than the column of water and extends further north of the 60 degrees south. Indeed, this is relevant to the Antarctic Treaty, since this body of law has no force beyond this latitude and no other international convention provides a uniform solution.[9] Thus, theoretically, there might be overlapping areas of extended continental shelf of the Antarctic continent with the territories of other States outside the Treaty Area, causing potential problems of maritime delimitation.[10]

Furthermore, potential areas of extended continental shelf raise substantial additional questions. While some derive from the physical setting and the logistical difficulties, others stem from the unique environment of the region. At present, few States possess the required data to determine whether a claim to an extended continental shelf can be substantiated. Particularly, Argentina presented a submission in 2009 including areas related to the Argentine Antarctic Territory – and approved by the Commission on the Limits of the Continental Shelf (CLCS) in 2017.[11] Nevertheless, every overlap with Antarctic areas was suspended by virtue of the Antarctic Treaty and safeguards of the international community.

One implication suggested by Joyner denotes that a contemporary claim to a 200-mile exclusive economic zone (EEZ) can overlap with previously designated areas of Antarctica. In depth, some could reasonably contend – in response to article IV of the Antarctic Treaty System (ATS) – that newly designated EEZ delimitations are neither 'new claims' nor 'enlargements' of previous ones, but merely a more precise definition of an existent claim or title.[12]

Finally, attention should be paid to the fact that non-claimant States perceive the status of zones offshore Antarctica from a different legal perspective. Their basic premise is that since no claim to sovereignty is recognized in fact or in law, States should not be present on the continent. Yet, the seven Claimant States may not be lawfully recognized, and Antarctica must remain a neutral zone.

Regulation of seabed activities

The Antarctic System constitutes a special regime that seeks to balance the controverted legal and geopolitical interests over Antarctica. The System is in permanent evolution since the signing of the Antarctic Treaty,[13] a convention that is the central nucleus of the entire subsequent legal framework.[14]

The Antarctic Treaty is the basis from which every other international/regional obligation arises. Twelve regular meetings produced a number of recommendations regarding the conservation of

8 Id.

9 It is useful to contrast that some other Conventions regulate Antarctica, for example the 1980 Convention on the Conservation of Antarctic Marine Living Resources, which applies to all Antarctic populations such as finfish, mollusks, crustaceans, and seabirds found south of the Antarctic Convergence. Furthermore, this can be applied to the continental shelf due to the existing biological integration of the living resources.

10 R.L. Harry, 'The Antarctic Regime and the Law of the Sea Convention: An Australian View', *Virginia Journal of International Law*, 21(4), 1981, 731–732.

11 CLCS, *Recommendations prepared by the Subcommission established for the consideration of the partial revised Submission made by Argentina*, Approved by the Commission, with amendments, on 17 March 2017.

12 We should not disregard the fact that the creation of a 200-mile EEZ is subsequent to the Antarctic Treaty: see C.C. Joyner, 'The Antarctic Treaty System and the Law of the Sea – Competing Regimes in the Southern Ocean', *International Journal of Marine and Coastal Law* 10(2), 1995, 310.

13 Entered into force on 23 June 1961.

14 R.E. Guyer, 'The Antarctic System', *Collected Courses of the Hague Academy of International Law* 139, 1973, 149 & ss.

the environment, living resources, telecommunications, transportation and tourism, among others. These encounters resulted in three multilateral agreements detailing conservation measures to protect Antarctic flora and fauna, seals and other marine life.[15]

In particular, the *1964 Agreed Measures for the Conservation of the Antarctic Flora and Fauna* contains an innovative set of environmental protection procedures. In a nutshell, it confines human intervention in the Antarctic ecosystem through the issuance of permits and the promulgation of specific regulation among the Parties. These were the first attempts under the Treaty to prioritize wildlife conservation and environmental protection due to the increase of human interest in exploration, science, fishing and mineral extraction.[16]

Subsequently, States negotiated and adopted the *1988 Wellington Convention*, which contained the express prohibition of mineral resource exploitation in the continent. This provision set a standard that was afterwards incorporated in the *1991 Protocol on Environmental Protection to the Antarctic Treaty* (PEPAT) in force nowadays. Indeed, the text of 1988 contained a clause of objective responsibility (*sine delicto*) for the damage occasioned to the Antarctic environment and the ecosystems associated. Thus, it included a regime devoted to the conservation of living resources, damages to third parties and their property, and the costs arising from environmental harms in view of to restoring the status quo ante.[17] Surprisingly, this multilateral convention did not enter into force as States failed to ratify it, and discussed a new treaty in 1991, which entered into force enlightening the criticisms to the Antarctic System.[18]

The creation of the PEPAT[19] witnessed the establishment of a Committee for Environmental Protection (CEP), oriented to control the environmental impact over Antarctica. This distinctive agency usually meets concurrently with the ATCM to address matters relating to ecological conservation and control management, and also to provide with further assistance. Nonetheless, besides these regular meetings, the Consultative Parties can also convene 'Special Antarctic Treaty Consultative Meetings' and 'Meetings of Experts' to address specific subjects. For instance, in 2017 a Special Meeting was held and matters like preservation of specific flora and fauna, ice harvesting, waste disposal and marine pollution were discussed.

At present, under this Protocol, there is a 50-year moratorium prohibiting all exploitative mining activities.[20] However, this suspension contains an express escape clause which allows the Consultative Parties (ATCPs) to wave this ban after the term occurs and establish, in exchange, a new mineral regime.[21] Consequently, it is mainly in the hands of the ATCPs to define the future of this system, protecting the integrity of Antarctica in view of preserving public welfare.

15 *Agreed Measures for the Conservation of Antarctic Fauna and Flora*, 2 June 1964; *Convention for the Conservation of Antarctic Seal*, 1 June 1972; *Convention for the Conservation of Antarctic Marine Living Resources*, 2 May 1980.

16 It is important to consider that the 1964 Agreed Measures were in force until 2011. For further information see A. Young, 'Antarctic Resource Jurisdiction and the Law of the Sea: A Question of Compromise', *Brooklyn Journal of International Law* 11(1), 1985, 52–59.

17 In detail, the Convention of 1988 includes a particular 'residual liability' from States due to sponsorship. J. Barboza, 'Responsabilidad internacional por actividades que afectan el medio ambiente en las regiones polares' in J.A. Consigli and A.E. Molinari, *Las regiones polares: estrategias, oportunidades y desafíos*, Buenos Aires: Consejo Argentino para las Relaciones Internacionales, 2010, pp. 95–96.

18 P. Sands et al., *Principles of International Environmental Law*, 3rd Ed., Cambridge: Cambridge University Press, 2012, pp. 153, 578, and 579.

19 Entered into force in January 14 1998.

20 Protocol on Environmental Protection to the Antarctic Treaty, United Nations Treaty Series, Vol. 2941, Article 7.

21 With respect to article 7, the prohibition on Antarctic mineral resource activities contained therein shall continue unless there is in force a binding legal regime on Antarctic mineral resource activities that includes an agreed means

Additionally, it designated Antarctica as a 'natural reserve, devoted to peace and science'[22] and set forth basic principles applicable to all human activities.[23] Most importantly, article VII prohibits all activities relating to Antarctic mineral resources, except for those of scientific research. Yet, until 2048 the Protocol can only be modified by unanimous agreement of all the Consultative Parties; however, the prohibition of mineral resource activities can only be removed if another binding legal regime enters into force.[24]

This document represents a landmark for environmental protection. Indeed, in accordance with article VII, the ATCP shall arrange individually or collectively continuous inspections in the area to reassure that all the prohibitions are being considered and respected. Conversely, article XV sets forth several directives to respond to environmental emergencies promptly, previous to the imposition of liability.[25]

Contemporarily, in 2005 the UN General Assembly adopted the 60/47 Resolution regarding the 'Question of Antarctica'. This recommendation updated and reinforced the rights and obligations of the Parties to the Antarctic Treaty. Therefore, the access of the international scientific community and specialized agencies of the United Nations should be open to enhance the conservation of this region and pursue future innovations in the region.[26]

In 2013 a crucial multi-year strategic working plan was developed by the ATCM oriented to help successive meetings focus on matters of critical priority and timeless importance, operate more efficiently, and schedule its agenda appropriately. In particular, different mechanisms for exploration, exploitation with scientific matters and management of mineral resources are periodically refined for a peaceful utilization of the Antarctic Continent.

Thus, a whole compound of harmonious and coordinated arrangements structures the activity in Antarctica and constitutes the overall configuration of the Antarctic Treaty System.[27] Indeed, the Antarctic Treaty, the Environmental Protocol, its Annexes and the regulations adopted within the framework of the ATCM, constitute a *corpus juris*, which allows a progressive elaboration of measures, resolutions and decisions to operate accordingly.[28]

Finally, this cluster of law is complemented by the United Nations Convention on the Law of the Sea (UNCLOS), which supplements the above-mentioned guidelines. Certainly, a more demanding reality requires a synergy of both systems to bring about comprehensive and expeditious responses to predicaments in Antarctica. What is more, a debate for an applicable regime to

for determining whether, and, if so, under which conditions, any such activities would be acceptable. This regime shall fully safeguard the interests of all States referred to in article IV of the Antarctic Treaty and apply the principles thereof. Therefore, if a modification or amendment to article 7 is proposed at a Review Conference referred to in paragraph 2 above, it shall include such a binding legal regime. If any such modification or amendment has not entered into force within 3 years of the date of its adoption, any Party may at any time thereafter notify to the Depositary of its withdrawal from this Protocol, and such withdrawal shall take effect 2 years after receipt of the notification by the Depositary. Ibid., article 25.

22 Protocol on Environmental Protection to the Antarctic Treaty, 2941 U.N.T.S. XX, entered into force January 14, 1998, Article 2.

23 For example: activities in the Antarctic Treaty area shall be planned and conducted on the basis of information sufficient to allow prior assessments and informed judgments about, their possible impacts on the Antarctic environment and dependent and associated ecosystems. Ibid., article 3.

24 Ibid., article 25.

25 Ibid., articles 15 and 16.

26 A/RES/60/47.

27 A.D. Abruza, 'El Tratado Antártico y su Sistema', *Boletín del Centro Naval* 863, 2013, 135–142.

28 A.S. Canio, loc. cit., note 3 supra, p. 219.

Antarctica's mineral resources began to be discussed – in general terms – in 1959.[29] In fact, part of the doctrine speculated on applying the concept of 'common heritage of mankind' as stated in Part XI of UNCLOS to this region.[30] However, these attempts vanished due to the complex negotiations of the Third United Nations Conference on the Law of the Sea, making the ATCMs the appropriate forum to define the future of the regime.[31]

Governance

Since the beginning of the 20th century, Argentina, the United Kingdom, New Zealand, France, Australia, Norway and Chile have made claims of sovereignty over different parts of the Antarctic continent. By the 1940s, other interested Nations, such as the United States, expressed their interest in agreeing to an Antarctic administration regarding different issues: (1) finding a solution to the treatment of Antarctica that could be generally accepted; (2) reaching an answer to disputes entailing the most affected States; and (3) facing the challenges that represent those States that do not participate in the discussions.

Later, during the Cold War, uncertainties concerning the status quo of Antarctica created a general concern to see the 'white continent' emerging as a new front of battle. Luckily, due to the increasing importance of international scientific cooperation, this possibility was gradually dispelled paving the way for an Antarctic dialogue that could allow further coordination.[32]

The 1959 Antarctic Treaty is not only a legal regime but also a geopolitical agreement. Based on article IV, its principles and decision-making system concerning mineral resources were examined vis-à-vis the Third Conference on the Law of the Sea, which instituted an objective regime. Particularly, it focused on a 'dual' dimension: firstly, the sovereignty asserted by the States Parties – which coexists with the position of other States, both Parties and Non-Parties who reserved its right of claim to the future – and secondly, the nature of a mineral regime, which would contain all the necessary elements and regulations to determine its correct functioning. In short, this is the approach that adequately meets the reality of the current Antarctic situation.

29 About this issue Orrego Vicuña states: 'When the subject of mineral resources was dealt with for the first time at the Sixth Consultative Meeting, discussions focused on a more elementary point, namely whether such a subject could be dealt with within the framework of the system or whether it should be entirely excluded. Although the problem was swiftly overcome since it was agreed in Recommendation VII-6 that it could properly be approached within the system, the division of opinion arose even more clearly in connection with the problem of a moratorium. The negotiations of the Seventh Consultative Meeting in 1972 devoted considerable time to the possibility, duration and conditions for such a moratorium, but without reaching agreement'. F. Orrego Vicuña, *Antarctic Mineral Exploitation. The Emerging Legal Framework*, Cambridge: Cambridge University Press, 1988, p. 51.

30 M.C.W. Pinto, 'The International Community and Antarctica', *University of Miami Law Review*, Vol. 33, 1978, pp. 475–487.

31 Orrego Vicuña affirms 'because of the fact that the Antarctic Treaty has not set up an international organization, at least in a formal sense, the fundamental competence to interpret the 1959 Treaty belongs to the parties to it and not to any specific organ or tribunal; however, as will be mentioned further below, the development of the Treaty framework has resulted in certain legal effects which are not altogether different from the case of an international organization, thus explaining the role of the Consultative Meetings in a certain institutional sense'. F. Orrego Vicuña, loc. cit., note 29 supra, p. 40.

32 F. Villamizar Lamus, Fernando, 'La prohibición de la explotación de minerales antárticos: derribando los mitos sobre su duración', *Revista Estudios Hemisféricos y Polares* 8-2, 2017, p. 39.

In this sense, not only access and exploitation to mineral resources are codified in the Antarctic Treaty, but also environmental standards to grant mining authorizations are regulated.[33] Thus, the operation of the International Seabed Authority, structured under UNCLOS, may create further pressures due both to the different models of cooperation between them and to the overlapping administration of mining activities in these particular geographical regions.[34]

In this line, we uncover different regulatory systems that could be applied to the same region both under the ATS and UNCLOS. In spite of possible similarities and potential scenarios where rules of the ISA could be applicable,[35] we should not imply an automatic application of principles of Part XI to areas regulated by the ATS. In short, this is the special system devoted to Antarctica and the principle of *lex specialis derogat legi generali* should not be disregarded.

The fact that the system of the ATS does not consider the principle of common heritage of mankind should not be used to justify an encroachment of these rules. In particular, while some standards set forth by the ISA could be applied by analogy to mineral extraction in Antarctica, a new body of law (possibly inspired in the latter) is expected to regulate all the particularities of such activities in this area.

There is no doubt regarding the intention of the international community to conduct mining activities in a peaceful manner. Nonetheless, not all of them appear to be compatible with article I of the Treaty; therefore, some shall not be undertaken with total freedom.[36] In this context, the drafting history of the Treaty reveals that mineral resource exploitation was excluded from the negotiations in order to safeguard an agreement on other matters of extreme priority such as territorial sovereignty. Thus, article I appears to be unrestricted due to the openness of its clauses, but we should interpret it in consonance with international practice and the other international conventions to justify limitations. In this line, the openness of some provisions presents a dilemma both with potential activities that could be carried out by State Parties, and also with the interpretation of the overall spirit intended to the Antarctic System.[37]

Essentially, the peaceful use and environmental protection concerning mineral resource exploitation is subject to the principles set forth in the *1991 Environmental Protocol to the Antarctic Treaty*. Yet, the foregoing does not ignore the current debates regarding the conservation and sustainable use of marine biological diversity in the areas beyond national jurisdiction (BBNJ).[38] In particular, this unveils a new challenge to the region as the prohibition of article 7 can be interpreted extensively to these matters.

In depth, despite the actual negotiation of regulation entailing BBNJ, this should never impinge on the mechanisms set forth in the Antarctic System. In this regard, a possible interaction between

33 For further information see article I of the 1959 Antarctic Treaty, articles 7 and 25 of the 1991 Protocol on Environmental Protection.

34 F. Orrego Vicuña, loc. cit., note 29 supra, p. 40.

35 Possible implementation of the ISA rules in the recognition of Status of the Antarctic System or when *renvoi* is needed for governance.

36 The Antarctic Treaty, 402 U.N.T.S. 71, entered into force June 23, 1961, Article I.

37 F. Orrego Vicuña, loc. cit., note 29 supra, pp. 43–44.

38 T. Heidar, 'Introduction' in A. de Paiva Toledo and V.J.M. Tassin (eds.), *Guide to the Navigation of Marine Biodiversity Beyond National Jurisdiction*, Belo Horizonte: Editora D'Plácido, 2018, pp. 41–57. Authors such as Leary affirm that the importance of these topics – in the context of the Antarctic System – constitutes an opportunity for designing a future institutional mechanism which respects the environmental protection set forth in the Madrid Protocol and its annexes. This jurist concludes that the Antarctic System could serve as a basis for future regulation of bioprospective activities in Antarctica. D.K. Leary, *International Law and the Genetic Resources of the Deep Sea*, Leiden: Martinus Nijhoff, 2007, pp. 69–74.

the two might be agreed among the State Parties or a subsequent agreement – inspired in the former – shall be reached maintaining the general standards of 1959.[39]

In consequence, it is necessary to reach consensus between the Consultative Parties concerning any activity developed therein. Moreover, States should consider article 25, paragraph 5 a) of the Madrid Protocol which states that any amendment concerning mineral resource exploitation would only be valid if a subsequent mandatory legal regime is agreed by the Parties.[40]

In this order of ideas, Tamburelli affirms that the prohibition of mineral resource exploitation is not conclusive.[41] Such prohibition only implies a moratorium of 50 years suspending the treatment of mineral resource exploitation among the Parties. Moreover, this moratorium can be called into question at any time if all the Parties unanimously agree to it. Therefore, the stability of the system can be easily overturned. Yet, the author notes that it does not seem unrealistic to interpret that some States have undertaken scientific research in Antarctica – and consequently acquired Consultative Party status – only in the conviction that a discussion concerning such topic will be opened within a few years.[42]

In relation to the extension of the continental shelf, many States have presented submissions before the CLCS with the view to secure their individual legal positions in accordance with article 76 of the Convention. In general, many of these proposals considered the special circumstances of Antarctica up to the 60th South parallel; nonetheless, the CLCS remained silent considering the rules set forth in the Antarctic System.[43] Yet, despite taking note of the positions of the parties on these matters, claims remain postponed until future negotiations.[44]

Moreover, Arpi notes the unique interplay between the Antarctic Treaty System and the Law of the Sea, addressing this phenomenon as a 'successful regime governing Antarctica […] partially overlapping and non-hierarchical'[45]. Moreover, this author asserts that this same synergy takes place concerning the establishment of the outer limits of the continental shelf and it is possible to consider it more as a 'competition' rather than a 'collaboration'. Yet, the Antarctic System always prevails in this area prioritizing its own decision-making forums, i.e., the ATCM.[46]

39 Negotiations concerning BBNJ took place during diverse conferences and forums of the UN, which crystallized in the General Assembly Resolution 59/24. From its reading, the intention to respect the special status and regulation of Antarctica is evident, since no mention to the region or the Antarctic System is made.

40 F. Villamizar Lamus, loc. cit., note 32 supra, p. 45. Doc.A/RES/59/24.

41 G. Tamburelli, 'Observations on the legal protection of the Arctic 69 and Antarctic environment and the international cooperation on the polar regions' in J.A. Consigli and A.E. Molinari, note 17 supra, pp. 83–84.

42 On this matter, we should include the agreed modalities to determine whether said activities could be accepted, their conditions and the safeguard of the interests of the States in accordance with the provisions of article IV of the Antarctic Treaty. Ibid., pp. 83–84.

43 See article IV of the Antarctic Treaty and CLCS/64. The issue of suspending territorial claims is referred to in submissions of Australia, New Zealand, France, Argentina, and Norway as well as in notes verbales by other Parties to the Antarctic Treaty.

44 Ibid. A special case is Australia, which claimed a portion of extended continental shelf based on three sub-Antarctic islands without territorial sovereignty dispute. About this, Liu affirms that despite the fact it has been approved by CLCS in the procedure, it is worth exploring what its legal effect is and whether it is contrary to the prohibition of any creation of any sovereign right in the Antarctic under the Antarctic Treaty. W. Liu, 'UNCLOS' Impact on and Implications for Antarctic Maritime Disputes', *China Oceans Law Review* 3, 2020, 70.

45 B. Arpi, 'Maps have meaning: why does a recent Argentine map have potential implications for Antarctic governance?', *Australian Journal of Maritime & Ocean Affairs* 13(2), 2021, 89.

46 Ibid., 90.

Conclusion

The Antarctic System constitutes a *sui generis* regime. Undeniably, its progress and evolution had a direct impact in the special practice of the law of the sea in Antarctica. Nonetheless, it is crucial to differentiate both systems in the international and regional governance of seas and oceans to avoid potential tensions, particularly in what refers to deep seabed mining and BBNJ.

The crucial point is to determine whether rights to mineral resources exist in the Antarctic region. While there are many views concerning this issue, no conclusive answer is adopted by the international community or the doctrine. Yet, we accept the existence of certain rights that are suspended for execution as the moratorium established by the Antarctic System does not affect the existence of a right.

The evolutive character of international law pays special attention to the continuous development of these rules. The Antarctic System is no exception to the duty of moderating and harmonizing different views, especially in such topics which demand a convergence of a unique regime applicable to Antarctica as a whole. In particular, challenges posed by the exploitation of mineral resources do not necessarily correspond to the original positions adopted by States Parties evidencing flexibility to unexpected scenarios. Therefore, a gradual openness is perceived in the international community as resources in the region are continuously increasing their value.

Finally, both the Antarctic System and the UNCLOS are oriented to international cooperation and the peaceful administration of common resources. Yet, while there might not exist hierarchy among these instruments, it is necessary to emphasize the special nature of the prior and its prevalence if a potential dispute arises among them.[47]

47 R.E. Guyer, loc. cit., note 14 supra, p. 224.

VI.1.3
THE ARCTIC AND SEABED MINING

Kristine Elfrida Dalaker and Hilde J. Woker

Introduction

Marine resources in the Arctic and the regulations that govern their exploration and exploitation have been largely affected, and limited to a great extent, by ice and darkness. These extreme conditions may explain why the regulation of and interest in deep sea mining (hereinafter 'DSM') activities in the Arctic is at an earlier stage than in other regions of the world.[1]

Although the search for hydrocarbon resources in the Arctic is longstanding, with the increasing global demand for mineral resources and the effects of climate change becoming more pronounced, the melting ice cover in the Arctic has given rise to a growing interest in determining the location and extent of mineral resources on the Arctic's seabed.

A common refrain from scientists operating in the Arctic is how little is known of the marine environment in this region that remains covered by ice and darkness for a significant part of the year. It is therefore no surprise that in these early stages of exploration of the Arctic's marine mineral resources, gaining scientific knowledge and understanding of these areas is the common underpinning of many initiatives that relate to DSM in the Arctic. An additional issue that requires consideration in the context of DSM activities in the Arctic region is that the geographical extent of the Area remains unclear and will depend on the resolution of various maritime boundaries and the establishment of final and binding limits on the basis of recommendations by the Commission on the Limits of the Continental Shelf (hereinafter CLCS), with much of the seabed in the Arctic claimed by coastal States. The status of the US as a non-State Party to the *United Nations Convention on the Law of the Sea* (hereinafter UNCLOS) also adds to the lack of clarity regarding Arctic entitlements, resulting in a region that is governed by customary international law, in addition to UNCLOS and other regional arrangements. These issues are discussed in more detail below, beginning with the geographical context of the Arctic and followed by a discussion of the particularities of Arctic governance and the various initiatives that are underway to determine

1 Due to the fact that jurisdictional boundaries in the Arctic have not yet been fully determined, for the purposes of this section, 'DSM' refers to the seabed mining of minerals in the Arctic, which includes areas within and/or beyond national jurisdiction.

 DOI: 10.4324/9780429426162-24

the extent of the mineral resources in the Arctic and to obtain a scientific understanding of the areas in which these resources are found.

Geographical extent of the exclusive economic zones and continental shelves

The fact that the regulation of DSM activities in the Arctic is at an early stage may be explained in part by the unique geographical scope of the region, as well as further contextual factors described in this section. The Arctic is the northernmost region of the Earth and includes the North Pole. Unlike the Antarctic (land surrounded by sea), the Arctic is sea surrounded by land. The Arctic also differs from Antarctica in that it is populated by permanent residents. The Arctic is home to 4 million people, 10 per cent of which are indigenous peoples.

Much of the marine Arctic is covered by ice, especially in the winter months. However, due to climate change the ice coverage in the Arctic is decreasing rapidly. The seabed of the Arctic is characterized by various seafloor highs, including the Gakkel Ridge, the Lomonosov Ridge, the Alpha Ridge, the Mendeleev Ridge and the Chukchi Plateau, in addition to the shelf areas that constitute the submerged prolongation of the Arctic land mass. It also comprises a number of basins, such as the Fram Basin, the Nansen Basin, the Canada Basin, the East Greenland Rift Basin and the West Greenland Rift Basin.

While there has always been a political interest in the Arctic, the melting of sea ice has created an increased interest in the resources of the Arctic, leading to narratives such as 'scramble for the Arctic'.[2] These narratives often reference the event in August 2007 in which the Russians planted their flag underneath the North Pole in the Lomonosov Ridge area, thus provoking protests from other Arctic coastal States. In fact, however, Arctic relations are characterized by cooperation, and many of the claims to resources in the Arctic are simply the implementation of the Arctic coastal States' rights pursuant to UNCLOS. There is also an increased interest in the Arctic from non-Arctic States (such as the EU, China, Japan, South Korea and Singapore) due to the possibility of newly available resources and shipping routes. There are three potentially viable shipping routes through the Arctic: the Northwest Passage, the Northern Sea Route and a transpolar route, although the latter is still inutile due to the presence of ice.

There are no universally accepted definitions of 'the Arctic', 'Arctic region', 'marine Arctic', 'Arctic Ocean', or 'Central Arctic Ocean'.[3] One of the main issues is whether the sea areas connecting the Arctic Ocean to the Atlantic and Pacific Oceans are part of the Arctic Ocean.[4] One could define the Arctic by reference to the Arctic Circle, which is found at roughly 66 degrees North.[5]

2 For a more representative view, see T.L. McDorman and C. Schofield, 'The Arctic Ocean Unscrambled: Competing Claims and Boundary Disputes', in K.N. Scott and D.L. VanderZwaag (eds.), *Research Handbook on Polar Law*, Cheltenham: Edward Elgar, 2020. See also T. Koivurova, 'Power Politics or Orderly Development?: Why Are States "Claiming" Large Areas of the Arctic Seabed?', in S. Silverburg (ed), *International Law: Contemporary Issues and Future Developments*, Boulder: Taylor & Francis, 2011.

3 E.J. Molenaar, 'The Arctic, the Arctic Council, and the Law of the Sea', in R.C. Beckman et al. (eds), *Governance of Arctic Shipping: Balancing Rights and Interests of Arctic States and User States*, Leiden: Brill Nijhoff, 2017, p. 26. 'Central Arctic Ocean' is understood in this section as the ocean areas north of the Arctic landmasses (excluding e.g., the Barents Sea) but not limited to the high seas of the Central Arctic Ocean.

4 A.G. Oude Elferink, E.J. Molenaar and D.R. Rothwell, 'The Regional Implementation of the Law of the Sea and the Polar Regions', in E. J. Molenaar, A.G. Oude Elferink and D.R. Rothwell (eds), *The Law of the Sea and the Polar Regions: Interactions between Global and Regional Regimes*, Leiden: Martinus Nijhoff, 2013, p. 9.

5 'What Is the Arctic? National Snow and Ice Data Center'. Available online <https://nsidc.org/cryosphere/arctic-meteorology/arctic.html> (accessed 24 March 2021).

Other definitions include the area north of the Arctic treeline, or the 10 degrees Celsius July isotherm.[6] The working groups of the Arctic Council define the Arctic differently, reflecting each of their interests.[7] For example, the Arctic Monitoring Assessment Program (hereinafter 'AMAP') defines the region incorporating elements of the Arctic Circle, political and vegetation boundaries, permafrost limits and major oceanographic features, whereas the Conservation of Arctic Flora and Fauna (hereinafter 'CAFF') Working Group largely follows the treeline.[8] The Polar Code generally defines Arctic waters with reference to the parallel of 60 degrees North, but in the Denmark Strait, the Norwegian Sea and the Barents Sea, the area is significantly limited to the north of that parallel.[9] On the other hand, the Agreement on Enhancing International Arctic Scientific Cooperation (hereinafter 'Scientific Cooperation Agreement') takes an expansive view of the Arctic region.[10] For the purposes of this section, 'the Arctic' and the 'marine Arctic' are used generally, but where specificity is required, such terms are defined by the context in which they are used.

Likewise, there are also different ways of defining the 'Arctic States' or 'Arctic coastal States'.[11] One usually distinguishes between the 'Arctic Five' – which comprises Norway, Denmark (in respect of Greenland), Canada, the United States and Russia – and the 'Arctic Eight', which additionally includes Iceland, Finland and Sweden. In this section, 'Arctic States' refers to the Arctic Eight, 'Arctic Ocean coastal States' refers to the Arctic Five and 'Arctic coastal States' refers to the Arctic Five in addition to Iceland.

All Arctic coastal States have declared maritime zones in accordance with UNCLOS. This includes the territorial sea, the exclusive economic zone (hereinafter 'EEZ') and the continental shelf.[12] Most of the marine Arctic is covered by the 200-nautical-mile entitlements of the Arctic coastal States. Due to climate change, the warming of the Arctic and sea level rise, these maritime zones (and the baselines from which they were measured) are vulnerable to change.[13] There are some overlapping entitlements, the majority of which have been delimited by maritime boundary agreements. Some boundaries are still (partially) unresolved,[14] such as the boundary between Canada and the United States in the Beaufort Sea and the overlapping continental shelf entitlements

6 Ibid.

7 GRID-Arendal. 'Boundaries of the Arctic Council Working Groups'. Available online <https://grid-arendal.herokuapp.com/resources/8387> (accessed 24 March 2021); K.N. Scott and D.L. VanderZwaag, 'Introduction to Polar Law', in K.N. Scott and D.L. VanderZwaag (eds), *Research Handbook on Polar Law*, Cheltenham: Edward Elgar, 2020, p. 5.

8 Scott and VanderZwaag, op. cit., p. 5.

9 See International Code for Ships Operating in Polar Waters (Polar Code) 2014, p. 9. The Polar Code was adopted through four IMO resolutions: International Code for Ships Operating in Polar Waters (Polar Code), Resolution MSC. 385(94) (21 November 2014, effective 1 January 2017); Amendments to the International Convention for the Safety of Life at Sea 1974, Resolution MSC. 386(94) (21 November 2014, effective 1 January 2017); International Code for Ships Operating in Polar Waters (Polar Code) Resolution MEPC. 265(68) (15 May 2015, effective 1 January 2017); Amendments to MARPOL Annexes I, II, IV and V, Resolution MEPC. 266(68) (15 May 2015, effective 1 January 2017).

10 Arctic Council, Agreement on Enhancing International Arctic Scientific Cooperation, Annex 1. Available online <https://oaarchive.arctic-council.org/handle/11374/1916> (accessed 24 March 2021).

11 Oude Elferink, Molenaar and Rothwell, op. cit., pp. 14–15.

12 Instead of claiming an EEZ around Jan Mayen and Svalbard, Norway has claimed a 200-nautical-mile exclusive fisheries zone around Jan Mayen and a 200-nautical-mile fisheries protection zone around Svalbard.

13 McDorman and Schofield, op. cit., p. 126; C. Schofield and B. Sas, 'Uncovered and Unstable Coasts: Climate Change and Territorial Sea Baselines in the Arctic', in S. Lalonde and T.L. McDorman (eds), *International Law and Politics of the Arctic Ocean: Essays in Honor of Donat Pharand*, Leiden: Brill Nijhoff, 2015.

14 See McDorman and Schofield, op. cit.

of Norway (Svalbard) and Denmark (Greenland), and there is a small gap in the continental shelf boundary between Canada and Denmark (Greenland) around Hans Island. Furthermore, the overlapping continental shelf claims to the Lomonosov Ridge area (Russia, Denmark and Canada), and in the Canada Basin/Alpha Ridge area (Canada, Russia and the US) will have to be resolved.

In addition, all Arctic coastal States have either already delineated the extent of their continental shelf entitlements beyond 200 nautical miles (hereinafter 'M') or are currently in the process of doing so.[15] Russia was the first Arctic coastal State to submit information to the CLCS in 2001 but received the recommendation to resubmit additional scientific data. Russia made its resubmission in 2015 and is currently awaiting recommendations from the CLCS. Its submission, encompassing 1,191,347 square kilometres in total,[16] includes a large portion of the Lomonosov Ridge (including the North Pole) and the Mendelev Rise. On 31 March 2021, Russia provided the CLCS with additional information in two addenda to its 2015 partial revised submission, which expands Russia's submission with an additional 705,000 square kilometres[17] to include the Gakkel Ridge as well as the Alpha Ridge.[18] According to its CLCS submissions, Russia's entitlement to a continental shelf now covers roughly 70 per cent of the seabed in the Central Arctic Ocean.[19] Norway submitted information with respect to areas in the Arctic Ocean, the Barents Sea and the Norwegian Sea to the CLCS in 2006 and received positive recommendations in 2009. Denmark's submission in respect of the continental shelf north of the Faroe Islands of 2009 received positive recommendations in 2014. Denmark also submitted information regarding the North-Eastern continental shelf of Greenland in 2013, and in December 2014, submitted information regarding the Northern Continental Shelf of Greenland, with proposed outer limits extending to the Russian 200-nautical-mile zone thus including the entire Lomonosov Ridge (and the North Pole) in its submission. For these latter two submissions, Denmark is still awaiting recommendations from the CLCS. Iceland submitted information concerning the Ægir Basin Area and the Western and Southern parts of the Reykjanes Ridge in 2009 and received recommendations from the CLCS in 2016. Iceland did not agree with the CLCS' final recommendations with respect to the Reykjanes Ridge, and submitted a revised partial submission on 31 March 2021. The revised submission is limited to the Reykjanes Ridge, as the Icelandic Government 'agrees with the recommendations provided for the Ægir Basin area'.[20] Canada submitted information regarding its continental shelf in the Arctic Ocean in 2019 – including part of the Lomonosov Ridge as well as the North Pole – and is still awaiting recommendations. The US – although not a party to UNCLOS – is

15 The executive summaries of the coastal States' submissions, as well as the summary of recommendations of the CLCS (if available) can be found at 'Submissions to the CLCS' <https://www.un.org/depts/los/clcs_new/commission_submissions.htm> (accessed 26 March 2021).

16 K. Hossain, 'Russia's Proposed Extended Continental Shelf in the Arctic Ocean: Science Setting the Stage for Law', *American Society of International Law (ASIL) Insights* 25, no. 8, 24 May 2021. Available online <https://www.asil.org/insights/volume/25/issue/8?fbclid=IwAR2ZMC28XZCunpSrse9UrlnSP5nRLlutWqV6l-kYvNMG2f3hq8xBDaEnVyg#_edn7> (accessed 1 July 2021).

17 Ibid.

18 CLCS.1.REV.2015.LOS.Add1. The addenda can be found at <https://www.un.org/Depts/los/clcs_new/submissions_files/submission_rus_rev1.htm> (accessed 22 April 2021).

19 M. Breum, 'Russia extends its claim to the Arctic Ocean seabed', *Arctic Today*, 4 April 2021. Available online <https://www.arctictoday.com/russia-extends-its-claim-to-the-arctic-ocean-seabed/?wallit_nosession=1> (accessed 1 July 2021).

20 'The Icelandic Continental Shelf – Revised Partial Submission' (Executive Summary), p. 5. Available online <https://www.un.org/depts/los/clcs_new/submissions_files/isl27_09/20210331IslRevEsSecure.pdf> (accessed 7 May 2021).

currently collecting data in accordance with article 76 of UNCLOS to establish the full extent of its continental shelf.[21]

Although most of the marine Arctic is subject to national jurisdiction of the Arctic coastal States, there are four pockets of high seas in the Arctic: the 'Banana Hole' in the Norwegian Sea, the 'Loophole' in the Barents Sea, the 'Donut Hole' in the central Bering Sea and the high seas of the Central Arctic Ocean. The Area in the Arctic, however, is undefined because not all outer limits of the continental shelf beyond 200 nautical miles (M) have been established yet. There is a very small pocket of the Area underneath the high seas pocket in the 'Banana Hole'. Until recently, it seemed likely that the Central Arctic Ocean would also have one small pocket of the Area (an area of some 157,000 km^2 in the Gakkel Ridge area).[22] However, according to Russia's recent addenda, Russia submits that the Gakkel Ridge area is part of its continental shelf beyond 200 M. Whether and to what extent the seabed in the Arctic will be subject to the regime of the Area will only become clear after all Arctic coastal States have established final and binding outer limits of their continental shelves on the basis of the recommendations of the CLCS.[23] This is unlikely to happen in the near future due to the heavy workload of the CLCS in processing coastal State submissions amongst other reasons.[24]

Governance of seabed mining activities

What makes Arctic regional governance unique from other regions of the world is a certain level of exceptionalism amongst the Arctic States with regard to the protection of the Arctic environment and the sustainable use of its resources. This was evidenced by the Ilulissat Declaration of May 2008 whereby the Arctic Ocean coastal States declared that they are in a unique position to address the potential impact on vulnerable ecosystems of '[c]limate change and the melting of ice, (…) the livelihoods of local inhabitants and indigenous communities, and the *potential exploitation of natural resources*'.[25] The Arctic Ocean coastal States also declared their commitment to the applicability of the law of the sea to the Arctic in the Declaration, confirming that there was no need for a new international legal regime for the Arctic Ocean.[26]

The Arctic suffers from many of the same shortcomings in ocean governance as other regions around the world, resulting in a patchwork of governance regimes consisting of binding and non-binding instruments that operate nationally, bilaterally, regionally, sectorally and/or globally. The

21 'U.S. Extended Continental Shelf Project' (United States Department of State). Available online <https://www.state.gov/u-s-extended-continental-shelf-project/> (accessed 24 March 2021). In a 1987 document attached to a memorandum, the US confirms its exercise of jurisdiction over its continental shelf had been and would continue to be 'in accordance with and to the full extent permitted by international law as reflected in Article 76'. United States, memorandum dated 17 November 1987 and attached document, 'United States Policy Governing the Continental Shelf of the United States of America', *Cumulative Digest of United States Practice in International Law, 1981–1988*, 1878–1879 and reprinted in J.R. and R.W. Smith, *United States Responses to Excessive Maritime Claims*, 3rd ed., Leiden: Martinus Nijhoff, 2012, pp. 187–188.

22 Molenaar, op. cit., pp. 26–27; L. Kullerud and O.R. Young, 'Adding a Gakkel Ridge Regime to the Evolving Arctic Ocean Governance Complex', *Marine Policy* 122, 2020, 104270, Map 2. In this context, Kullerud and Young had proposed a Gakkel Ridge Regime modelled after the Central Arctic Ocean Fisheries Agreement. See ibid.

23 Pursuant to UNCLOS Articles 1(1) and 76, defining the Area and the continental shelf respectively.

24 See also M.W. Lodge, 'The International Seabed Authority and the Arctic', in S. Wasum-Rainer, I. Winkelmann and K. Tiroch (eds), *Arctic Science, International Law and Climate Change: Legal Aspects of Marine Science in the Arctic Ocean*, Berlin: Springer, 2012, p. 179.

25 Ilulissat Declaration, 28 May 2008. Available online <https://cil.nus.edu.sg/wp-content/uploads/2017/07/2008-Ilulissat-Declaration.pdf> (accessed 24 March 2021) [emphasis added].

26 Ibid.

Arctic does not have a regional seas programme in place and does not enjoy the level of regulation that Antarctica does under the *Antarctic Treaty System*.[27] Rather, the Arctic is served by its main governance body: the Arctic Council. The Arctic States established the Arctic Council in 1996.[28] The Council is an intergovernmental forum that promotes cooperation, coordination and interaction amongst the Arctic States, Arctic indigenous communities and other Arctic inhabitants on common Arctic issues, with specific focus on issues of sustainable development and environmental protection in the Arctic.[29] Because the Arctic Council is not an international organization with legal personality, legal obligations fall upon the respective Arctic States individually.

The Arctic Council's work is carried out by eight Senior Arctic Officials (one from each Arctic State), six Permanent Participants (representing the indigenous peoples of the Arctic), six Working Groups[30] and 38 Observers (including 13 non-Arctic States and intergovernmental and nongovernmental organizations, including those that may relate to activities on the continental shelf and in the Area: the International Council for the Exploration of the Sea (hereinafter 'ICES'), the International Maritime Organization (hereinafter 'IMO'), and the OSPAR Commission (defined herein)).[31] The work of the Arctic Council is further supported by expert groups and task forces.[32]

The Arctic Council has facilitated the negotiation and adoption of three legally binding agreements: the Agreement on Cooperation on Aeronautical and Maritime Search and Rescue in the Arctic, the Agreement on Cooperation on Marine Oil Pollution Preparedness and Response in the Arctic and the Scientific Cooperation Agreement.[33] Other instruments, bodies and frameworks of relevance are discussed below.

Regulation of seabed mining activities

The discussion of the regulation of the continental shelf and the Area in the Arctic may be conducted at the international and regional levels. This section first discusses the international obligations that impact the regulation of the continental shelf and the Area in the Arctic. Given the early stage of exploration of the Arctic's marine mineral resources and the lack of regulation of DSM, this section then discusses regional and sectoral frameworks and initiatives that may impact future DSM activities.

International level

The international obligations impacting the regulation of the continental shelf and the Area in the Arctic stem from UNCLOS, the 1994 Agreement,[34] the Convention on Biological Diversity

27 For more information, see in this book L. Godio, 'Antarctica and Seabed Mining', in V. Tassin Campanella (ed), *Routledge Handbook of Seabed Mining and the Law of the Sea*, London: Routledge, 2023, chapter VI.1.2. See also E. Jiménez Pineda, 'South American Region and Seabed Mining', in V. Tassin Campanella (ed), idem, chapter VI.1.6.

28 Arctic Council, 'About the Arctic Council'. Available online <https://arctic-council.org/en/about/> (accessed 24 March 2021).

29 Ibid.

30 Arctic Council, 'Working Groups'. Available online <https://arctic-council.org/en/about/working-groups/> (accessed 24 March 2021).

31 Arctic Council, 'Arctic Council'. Available online <https://arctic-council.org/en/> (accessed 24 March 2021).

32 Ibid.

33 Arctic Council, 'Agreements'. Available online <https://arctic-council.org/index.php/en/our-work/agreements> (accessed 24 March 2021).

34 *Agreement relating to the implementation of Part XI of the United Nations Convention on the Law of the Sea of 10 December 1982*, 28 July 1994, 1836 UNTS 3.

(hereinafter CBD),[35] the Sustainable Development Goals, the Paris Agreement and customary international law. Furthermore, if and when a new implementing agreement on the protection and preservation of marine biodiversity in areas beyond national jurisdiction (hereinafter BBNJ) is finalized, this agreement would also impact the regulation of the continental shelf and the Area in the Arctic. Generally, these international obligations are not unique to the Arctic, and thus do not justify extensive discussion here. Notably, in addition to treaty law (UNCLOS, CBD, etc.), customary international law plays a prominent role in Arctic governance due to the absence of the US as a party to UNCLOS. Despite being the only Arctic State that is not a party to UNCLOS, the US has declared its acceptance of UNCLOS and its willingness to act in accordance with its provisions relating to 'traditional uses of the ocean – such as navigation and overflight'.[36]

Furthermore, there is one provision of UNCLOS that specifically applies to ice-covered areas: article 234. It is located within Part XII of UNCLOS on the protection and preservation of the marine environment and allows for more stringent environmental protection measures in ice-covered areas than otherwise allowed.[37] Although aspects of this provision remain unclear,[38] it is directly applicable to (some parts of) the marine Arctic. Although article 234 is predominantly concerned with activities in the EEZ, it could also impact DSM activities, as any vessel engaged in DSM within the limits of the EEZ would have to comply with the more stringent laws and regulations established by the coastal State pursuant to article 234.[39]

Regional level

In contrast to the international obligations outlined above, DSM activities are not regulated at the Arctic regional level, and no sustained efforts have been made to provide a regional framework.[40] Rather, regional and sectoral frameworks exist that relate to the regulation of activities on the continental shelf and the Area in the Arctic. One relevant example is the *Convention for the Protection of the Marine Environment of the North-East Atlantic* (hereinafter 'OSPAR'), which is a regional legal regime that regulates international cooperation on environmental protection in the North-East Atlantic.[41] Portions of OSPAR's geographical scope of application fall within the Arctic.[42] Therefore, any future exploration and exploitation of marine mineral

35 *Convention on Biological Diversity*, 5 June 1992, 1760 UNTS 79.

36 Statement on United States Ocean Policy (10 March 1983). Available at <https://www.reaganlibrary.gov/archives/speech/statement-united-states-oceans-policy> (accessed 24 March 2021). It remains unclear whether the US is prohibited from DSM activities in the Area given that it is not a party to UNCLOS but is a signatory to the 1994 Agreement. There is also a lack of clarity regarding whether certain provisions of UNCLOS that relate to DSM constitute customary international law.

37 UNCLOS, Art. 234.

38 See K. Bartenstein, 'The "Arctic Exception" in the Law of the Sea Convention: A Contribution to Safer Navigation in the Northwest Passage?', *Ocean Development & International Law*, 2011, vol. 42, 22; E. Franckx and L. Boone, 'Article 234', in A. Proelss (ed), *United Nations Convention on the Law of the Sea: A Commentary*, Munich: BECK, 2017.

39 On this point, see more generally the chapter in this book dedicated to rights and obligations of States, V. Tassin Campanella, Y. Cissé and D. Tladi, 'State Rights and Obligations of States on the Continental Shelf and the Area', in V. Tassin Campanella (ed), *Routledge Handbook of Seabed Mining and the Law of the Sea*, op. cit., II.1.

40 Unlike the MIN-Guide initiative in the EU and the Deep Sea Minerals Project that is aimed at Pacific Island States, no such regional initiatives exist in the Arctic.

41 *Convention for the Protection of the Marine Environment of the North-East Atlantic*, 22 September 1992, 23 LOSB 32.

42 Ibid., Art. 1(1).

resources in the Arctic will likely need to cooperate with the OSPAR Commission.[43] Similarly, any future exploration and exploitation need to be compatible with the Convention on Future Multilateral Cooperation in North-East Atlantic Fisheries and the Central Arctic Ocean Fisheries Agreement, and may need to consult with the Joint Norwegian-Russian Fisheries Commission as the geographic scope of these agreements and governing body may be impacted by DSM activities.[44]

The area in and around Svalbard is governed by the legal regime set out in the *Svalbard Treaty*. The Treaty was negotiated in the aftermath of World War I for the purpose of recognizing Norway's sovereignty over Svalbard (including Bear Island) subject to certain stipulations, including the non-discriminatory rights of the nationals of the High Contracting Parties to live, work and conduct business and commercial activities on the land territories of Svalbard (including mining operations).[45] The Svalbard Treaty may come into play if any of its High Contracting Parties should contemplate the exploration and exploitation of marine mineral resources that could arguably come within the geographic scope of application of the Treaty.[46] Norway has disputed the geographic scope of the Treaty, asserting its right to regulate the fishery resources within 200 M of Svalbard.[47] In addition, Norway maintains that the continental shelf around Svalbard is part of its mainland continental shelf.[48] Potential disputes could therefore arise under the Svalbard Treaty, especially given Norway's recent announcement that it will begin to issue licences for DSM activities within its areas of national jurisdiction, including on its continental shelf.[49]

In these early stages in the exploration of Arctic marine mineral resources, efforts have focused on gaining scientific knowledge and understanding of the extent of mineral resources on the continental shelf and in the Area of the Arctic, and the ecosystems in which these resources are found. Scientific knowledge of the Arctic's mineral resources and their surrounding marine ecosystems is being pursued through various fora of Arctic scientific cooperation, the first example of which is the Arctic Council. Firstly, the Arctic Council's Working Group on the Protection of the Marine Environment (hereinafter 'PAME') is working with the ICES and the North Pacific Marine Science Organization (hereinafter 'PICES') to produce an integrated ecosystem assessment of the Central Arctic Ocean. The terms of reference of the Joint ICES/PICES/PAME Working Group on

43 OSPAR included in its report (1999–2000) on the Implementation of the OSPAR Action Plan 1998–2003 that the exploration for solid minerals is an activity that would be assessed at a later date. Activities of OSPAR, June 1999–June 2000, Implementation of the OSPAR Action Plan 1998–2003 (update 1999), p. 35.

44 North-East Atlantic Fisheries Commission, 'Basic Texts'. Available online <https://www.neafc.org/basictexts> (accessed 24 March 2021). Central Arctic Ocean Fisheries Agreement. Available online <https://arctic-council.org/en/news/exploring-the-arctic-ocean-the-agreement-that-protects-an-unknown-ecosystem/> (accessed 24 March 2021). Joint Norwegian-Russian Fisheries Commission. Available online <https://www.jointfish.com/eng.html> (accessed 24 March 2021).

45 *Treaty between Norway, The United States of America, Denmark, France, Italy, Japan, the Netherlands, Great Britain and Ireland and the British Overseas Dominions and Sweden Concerning Spitsbergen*, 9 February 1920. After the Treaty came into force in 1925, the King of Norway proclaimed that the Treaty area be called Svalbard, rather than Spitsbergen.

46 Ibid.

47 Ø. Jensen, 'The Svalbard Treaty and Norwegian Sovereignty', *Arctic Review* 11, 2020, 82–107.

48 Ibid.

49 N. Adomaitis, 'Norway eyes sea change in deep dive for metals instead of oil', *Reuters*, 12 January 2021, accessed 24 March 2021. H. Carstens, 'Dyphavsmineraler på børs' *Geo365*, 24 March 2021. Available online <https://geo365-no.cdn.ampproject.org/c/s/geo365.no/dyphavsmineraler/dyphavsmineraler-pa-bors/amp/> (accessed 24 March 2021).

the Integrated Assessment of the Central Arctic Ocean (hereinafter 'WGICA') include the assessment of potential effects of recent, ongoing and future climatic and oceanographic changes on human activities, which include the exploitation of seabed minerals.[50] In line with its mandate, the Working Group's recent report highlights the threat that ocean mining may present if it expands into the Arctic.[51] More extensive reports on the potential exploitation of seabed minerals are expected to be issued by the WGICA in the coming years.

A second forum for Arctic scientific cooperation is facilitated by the Scientific Cooperation Agreement, which builds on Part XIII of UNCLOS and includes provisions to 'enhance cooperation in Scientific Activities in order to increase effectiveness and efficiency in the development of scientific knowledge about the Arctic'.[52] The scientific cooperation envisaged by the Agreement is evidenced by the work of the Arctic States and other stakeholders in their participation in the UN Decade of Ocean Science for Sustainable Development (2021–2030) (hereinafter 'Ocean Decade').[53] The Ocean Decade is an initiative organized under the auspices of the United Nations Educational, Scientific and Cultural Organization (hereinafter 'UNESCO') to provide for a common framework for the management of ocean science for the benefit of humanity.[54] The Intergovernmental Oceanographic Commission (hereinafter 'IOC') of UNESCO has enlisted the support of regional workshops in the development of an Implementation Plan for the Ocean Decade. Arctic stakeholders organized to support the IOC's initiative by developing the Ocean Decade Arctic Action Plan (hereinafter 'Action Plan').[55] One of the resulting transformative solutions proposed in the Action Plan includes, in part, mapping and increasing the knowledge of the deep seabed as a means of identifying the potential impacts of Arctic change on emerging maritime industries.[56]

Thirdly, another forum for scientific cooperation that may address future exploration and exploitation of mineral resources in the Arctic is the Arctic Science Ministerial process, which was first convened by the United States in 2016 under the auspices of the Arctic Council, with the aim of effecting greater Arctic science cooperation.[57] Two years later, Germany hosted the Second Arctic Science Ministerial.[58] The Third Arctic Science Ministerial was co-hosted by Japan and Iceland in 2021 in Japan.[59]

Lastly, the International Arctic Science Committee (hereinafter 'IASC') is a leading international science organization in the Arctic.[60] It was first founded by the Arctic States but has since

50 WGICA – ICES/PICES/PAME Working Group on Integrated Ecosystem Assessment (IEA) for the Central Arctic Ocean, 'WGICA Terms of Reference'. Available online <https://www.ices.dk/community/groups/Pages/WGICA.aspx> (accessed 24 March 2021).

51 ICES/PICES/PAME Working Group on Integrated Ecosystem Assessment (IEA) for the Central Arctic Ocean. Available online <https://doi.org/10.17895/ices.pub.7454> (accessed 24 March 2021).

52 Scientific Cooperation Agreement, op. cit., Art. 2.

53 United Nations Decade of Ocean Science for Sustainable Development. Available online <https://www.oceandecade.org/> (accessed 24 March 2021).

54 Ibid.

55 Ocean Decade Arctic Action Plan. Available online <https://www.oceandecade.dk/decade-actions/arctic-action-plan> (accessed 15 July 2021). The Ocean Decade Arctic Action Plan refers to the high level of support the Arctic States have given to policy, science and innovation, as evidenced in the Scientific Cooperation Agreement.

56 Ibid., pp. 27–28.

57 Arctic Science Ministerial, 'Conference Background'. Available online <https://www.arcticscienceministerial.org/en/conference-background-1741.html> (accessed 24 March 2021).

58 Ibid.

59 3rd Arctic Science Ministerial. Available online <https://asm3.org> (accessed 15 July 2021).

60 International Arctic Science Committee. Available online <https://iasc.info/> (accessed 24 March 2021).

widened its membership to 23 members.[61] The IASC's Marine Working Group would be a likely forum for scientific cooperation relating to DSM activities in the coming years.[62]

Although there is no formal coordination amongst the fora of cooperation described above, an aim of the Action Plan is to foster an inclusive approach that creates momentum within the community of stakeholders in the Arctic to 'deliver transformative ocean solutions for sustainable development in the Arctic'.[63] Therefore, maintaining momentum and strengthening this inclusive approach through the Third Arctic Ministerial and the IASC (among others) is seen as essential to meeting the overall aims of the Ocean Decade.[64] Thus, given that DSM activities are at in early stage of development in the Arctic, it is likely that the Action Plan will serve as the means through which the relevant fora of scientific cooperation will interact for the purpose of obtaining scientific knowledge and understanding of the Arctic deep seabed.

Conclusion

There is a relative lack of development of regulations for DSM activities in the Arctic. This is indicative of the significant challenges that are inherent in conducting such activities. The environmental vulnerability of the area, the extreme conditions of ice and darkness and the lack of infrastructure to support such activities are a few factors that may have hindered development.[65] Another important challenge to the development of DSM regulations is the lack of knowledge on the morphology and topography of the seabed of the Arctic. Initiatives such as the Seabed 2030 (initiative to map 100 per cent of the ocean floor by 2030),[66] together with the scientific cooperation initiatives described above, are intended to provide stakeholders with the requisite knowledge to inform their decision making on the regulation of the potential future exploitation of marine mineral resources in the Arctic. Regardless of the progress and success of these initiatives (among others), the regulation of future DSM activities in the Arctic will need to be based on science, made consistent with the work of the International Seabed Authority, developed in consultation with the Arctic Council and take into account the rights of the Arctic's indigenous peoples.

61 Ibid.

62 Ibid.

63 Action Plan, op. cit., p. 6.

64 Ibid.

65 See for example P. Rylandsholm, 'Environmental Challenges Related to Seabed Mining in the Arctic', 2016. Available online <https://www.arcticfrontiers.com/wp-content/uploads/downloads/2016/Arctic%20Frontiers%20Science/Presentations%2029%20January%202016/Part%20III%20Technology%20needs/04_Paal_Rylandsholm.pdf> (accessed 24 March 2021).

66 Nippon Foundation-GEBCO Seabed 2030 Project.

VI.1.4
THE EUROPEAN UNION AND SEABED MINING

Pradeep A. Singh, Virginie Tassin Campanella and Frank Maes

Introduction

The destruction suffered across Europe due to centuries of conquests and wars, particularly those that were inflicted during the Second World War, eventually gave birth to a strong desire to foster peace and mutual benefit across the borders of the European powers. The integration process that culminated in the formation of the European Union (EU) and its present form can be traced back to the creation of the European Coal and Steel Community (ECSC) by six countries (Belgium, France, West Germany, Italy, Luxembourg and The Netherlands) in 1951. Intended as an instrument to create a common market for two critical commodities, coal and steel, the concept evolved into the establishment of a broader common market to facilitate greater economic development through the setting up of the European Economic Community (EEC) in 1957. The EEC aimed to create an internal market without borders characterized by the free movement of people, goods, services and capital. To achieve this goal, common policies were established, in particular the common agricultural policy which, from 1970, included fisheries. Over the years, membership of the EEC grew along with the ambition to expand cooperation beyond economic or trade matters.

The Single European Act of 1986 marked a first transformation of the EEC towards a cooperation that was not exclusively economic. This aspiration was subsequently manifested through the 1991 Maastricht Treaty on the European Union. Thereafter followed a very clear acceleration of the enlargement of the EU, which imposed new revisions of the treaties (through the 1997 Treaty of Amsterdam and 2011 Treaty of Nice). The rejection of the European Constitution in 2005 finally encouraged the Member States (MS), after very long and difficult discussions, to accept the last major modification of the original treaties to date. By absorbing the EEC and integrating it into the EU, the subsequent 2009 Lisbon Treaty profoundly adapts the rules of the original treaties to allow better coordination of the MS, now at a total number of 27 (after the recent departure of the UK or 'Brexit').

Interests over the maritime dimension and the EU's competences over the seas were thus not obvious in the evolution and early construction of the EEC. Attention over maritime areas in the EU evolved over the years. Since the introduction of fisheries policies in 1970 (recently reformed in 2014), the EU has continued to introduce important regulations, directives and policies that have gone beyond economic interests and aimed at a stronger marine environmental or conserva-

DOI: 10.4324/9780429426162-25

tion focus. Growing interests in marine minerals among some MS adds an additional dimension to the economic potential of the marine space within and beyond the jurisdiction of the EU. While there seems to be a broad desire within the EU to secure marine minerals as a resource for future exploitation activities, an overarching conflict appears to be looming between the exploitation interests of certain MS and the wider interest of the EU in ensuring the protection of the marine environment. Consequently, and due to the relationship between the EU and its MS, seabed mining of mineral resources both in areas within the jurisdictions of its MS as well as beyond national jurisdiction (the Area) is presently a complex issue for the EU.

Geographical extent of the seabed within and beyond national jurisdiction

While normally covering the territorial sea and exclusive economic zone, this section will only consider the EU marine space comprising the continental shelf, both within and beyond 200 nautical miles of its 27 MS.[1] The resulting total seabed areas under jurisdiction of MS (including overseas territories)[2] extends to over 9 million square kilometres (km^2) in terms of the continental shelf, and nearly 6 million km^2 with respect to the extended continental shelf if such claims are accepted.

MS have been particularly active in the extension of the continental shelf. The extended continental shelf submission by France, Ireland, Spain and the United Kingdom in the area of the Celtic Sea and the Bay of Biscay was the first joint submission presented to the Commission on the Limits of the Continental Shelf in May 2006. Since then, other submissions have been made by Denmark, France, Ireland, Portugal, Spain and the UK.[3] In total, France has made eight submissions and joint submissions (due to its overseas territories), followed by Denmark with five submissions (due to Greenland). As of December 2021, Denmark, France, Ireland, Portugal and Spain still have a total of 12 pending submissions at the Commission on the Limits of the Continental Shelf (including, for France, joint submissions with other non-MS in the Indian and Pacific oceans).

In case of areas beyond national jurisdiction, several MS either hold or sponsor exploration contracts granted by the International Seabed Authority (ISA) for two resource types: polymetallic nodules in the Clarion-Clipperton Zone (Belgium, Bulgaria, Czech Republic, France, Germany, Poland and Slovakia) and polymetallic sulphides in the Mid-Atlantic Ridge and in the Central Indian Ocean Basin (Poland, France and Germany). No MS currently holds or sponsors exploration contracts for cobalt-rich ferromanganese crusts.

Governance framework of the European Union

The EU is a unique and unrivalled international organization. It has indeed granted citizenships to the nationals of its MS and its legislation can also directly apply to entities and citizens.[4] In

1 Including the marine space of the overseas territories of the MS.

2 To understand the application of EU Law in the various overseas territories of the MS, see D. Kochenov, 'The application of EU law in the EU's overseas regions, countries and territories after the entry into force of the Treaty of Lisbon', *Michigan State Journal of International Law* 20, 2012, 668–743.

3 The UK was still a MS of the EU at the time of its submission.

4 The inability of the traditional category of 'international organization' under international law to reflect the reality of the practices of the EU have encouraged some scholars to reconsider the terminology used to describe the EU. See e.g. J.P. Jacqué, 'La spécificité de l'Union', *Droit institutionnel de l'Union européenne*, Dalloz: Paris, 2012, p. 117: 'si l'on additionne l'ensemble des spécificités de l'Union, on réalise que l'on est en présence d'un phénomène qui ne répond plus à la notion traditionnelle d'organisation internationale, sauf à donner à cette notion une extension telle qu'elle puisse couvrir toutes les formes d'organisations sociales qui ne sont pas étatiques'.

the EU, the MS have transferred a degree of authority, and to a certain extent, sovereignty and decision-making powers[5] to three EU institutions: the Parliament, the European Council[6] and the Commission. MS are only directly represented in the European Council, while the Commission and the Parliament act autonomously vis-à-vis national country interests. Given the importance of these three institutions in EU governance, it is necessary to introduce them in order to better understand their roles and functions.

The members of the Parliament are directly elected by voters in the MS, and they mainly act according to transboundary lines of political parties in the EU. The Commission is the only institution empowered to initiate legislation, which needs to be further approved by the European Council and Parliament. In the adoption of legislative acts, a distinction is made between the ordinary legislative procedure (co-decision), which brings Parliament on an equal footing with the European Council, and the special legislative procedures, which apply only in specific cases where Parliament has only a consultative role. The ordinary legislative procedure has actually become the main legislative procedure on a wide range of areas limiting the powers of the MS since the Parliament does not represent the interests of the MS, but the interests of the EU based on party politics. This is particularly important for understanding the position of the Parliament and the Commission regarding seabed mining, which can be in contrast to the policy of MS, as reflected in the European Council.

Environmental protection (land and marine) is one of those areas for which legislation is adopted jointly. Since the *1997 Treaty of Amsterdam*, this topic has been high on the political agenda owing to the integration of sustainable development into the objectives of the EU (Art. 2 TUE). Its importance is further confirmed by Title XX of the *2007 Treaty on the Functioning of the European Union* (TFEU), dedicated to the environment, and more specifically by article 191 (1) stating that the EU policy on the environment shall, *inter alia*, pursue the preservation, protection and improvement of the quality of the environment, a prudent and rational utilization of natural resources, and promote measures at international level to deal with regional or worldwide environmental problems. The principle of precaution and the polluter pays principle is also at the heart of the TFEU[7] and thus has to be applied by the EU institutions, as well as by the MS. Finally, and especially within the context of seabed mining, it should be noted that the EU, in the elaboration of its environmental policy, shall take into account available scientific and technical data, environmental conditions in the various regions of the EU, the potential benefits and costs of action or lack of action, and the economic and social development of the EU as a whole, and the balanced development of its regions.[8] Although not included into the TFEU, the ecosystem approach also has a significant place in the EU marine legal framework.[9]

On top of these 'internal' EU competences based on the system of competence sharing with its MS, the EU also has 'external' competences as a party to international conventions, such as the *United Nations Convention on the Law of the Sea* (UNCLOS) and its three implementing agree-

5 Which can take the form of MS transferring exclusive competence to the EU or the EU having shared competence with MS.

6 The European Council is not to be confused with the Council of Europe, an international organization comprising 46 countries of Europe, set up to promote democracy and protect human rights and the rule of law in Europe.

7 Article 191 (2), TFEU.

8 Article 191 (3), ibid.

9 See for example, Directive 2008/56/EC (the EU Marine Strategy Framework Directive), Articles 3.4 and 3.5, Article 10 and Annexes I and IV, Regulation No 1380/2013 (the EU Common Fisheries Policy), Article 2.3, and Directive 2014/89/EU (the EU Marine Spatial Planning Directive), Article 5.

ments, all major multilateral environmental agreements and their protocols, such as the *Convention on Biological Diversity*, the *United Nations Framework Convention on Climate Change* and regional seas conventions covering the EU marine space.[10] As such, the EU has the same treaty obligations comparable to the other State Parties, including its own MS (the so-called mixed treaties). Consequently, rights and obligations covered by these conventions have become part of the EU competence and legislative power, next to the powers of the MS parties. This duality between internal and external competences often leads the EU, as a contracting party, to play an active role in the implementation of these conventions.[11] In this respect, the EU takes the lead to harmonize the national legislation of its MS by adopting EU legislation, such as regulations (binding act to be applied in its entirety and with direct effect in the national legislation) or most commonly through directives that need to be transposed into national legislation (binding act setting out a goal to achieve by the MS, but the MS remain free to decide how to do it).

Upon ratification of the UNCLOS, the EU has deposited a declaration of competences[12] stating its exclusive competence on matters relating to the conservation and management of fishing resources, and shared competence with its MS on matters relating to maritime transport, safety of shipping and prevention of pollution.[13] For the seabed beyond national jurisdiction of the MS, the EU has exclusive competence only on aspects relating to international trade arising out of seabed mining in the Area, by virtue of its commercial and customs policy. All other aspects related to the ISA regarding the management and protection of the Area and its resources are subject to a coordination mechanism between the EU and the MS.[14] Such coordination aims to improve the status of the EU as an international organization,[15] while accounting for the complex interaction dynamics between the national positions of each MS.

European Union regulatory framework applicable to seabed mining

Seabed mining on the continental shelf of Member States

Given the absence of specific EU legislation on the matter, seabed mining activities on the continental shelf (including the extended continental shelf) fall within the competence of the MS.[16] although, in case of environmental effects of those activities, the MS have to apply existing EU legislation to protect the marine environment and to conserve certain marine biological resources. Most of these legislations find their roots in international instruments which have been transposed into EU law. Particularly relevant for seabed mining are the conventions of the United Nations

10 Namely, the North East Atlantic Ocean, Mediterranean Sea and the Baltic Sea, which will be discussed below.

11 Even in some cases where the EU is not a party to the conventions, such as the IMO conventions: see N. Liu and F. Maes, 'The European Union and the International Maritime Organization: EU's external influence on the prevention of vessel-source pollution', *Journal of Maritime Law and Commerce*, 2010, 581–594.

12 UN Treaty Collection, UNCLOS – Declarations and Reservations: European Union. Available online <https://treaties.un.org/Pages/ViewDetailsIII.aspx?src=TREATY&mtdsg_no=XXI-6&chapter=21&Temp=mtdsg3&clang=_en> (accessed 22 December 2021).

13 Council Decision concerning the conclusion by the European Community of the United Nations Convention of 10 December 1982 on the Law of the Sea and the Agreement of 28 July 1994 relating to the implementation of Part XI thereof, 98/392/EC, 23 March 1998. See in particular Annex II.

14 Article 2, ibid.

15 The EU is an observer to the Council of the ISA, not a member. It has therefore no voting rights and therefore relies on MS to express and upheld its position within.

16 F. Arnesen, R. Greaves and A. Pozdnakova, 'European Union law and the seabed', in Catherine Banet (ed.), *The law of the seabed: access, users, and protection of the seabed*, Leiden: Brill Nijhoff, 2020, pp. 321–323.

Economic Commission for Europe, such as the *1991 Convention on Environmental Impact Assessment in a Transboundary Context* (Espoo Convention) and its 2003 Protocol on Strategic Environmental Assessment (Kiev Protocol),[17] and the *1998 Convention on Access to Information, Public Participation in Decision-making and Access to Justice in Environmental Matters* (Aarhus Convention).[18]

As clarified earlier, the environmental consequences and the measures to be taken in order to protect the marine environment from seabed mining are also based on EU legislation and are a shared competence.[19] The *Convention on Biological Diversity* is at the EU level partly implemented by the Birds Directive,[20] the Habitats Directive[21] and the Marine Strategy Framework Directive,[22] among others. The Habitats Directive aims to ensure biodiversity through the conservation of natural habitats[23] and species of wild fauna and flora of 'community interest' in the 'European territory of the MS to which the Treaty applies' (art. 2.1) by maintaining or restoring those habitats and species at a favourable conservation status (art. 2.2). The European Court of Justice confirmed that the Habitats Directive applies beyond the territorial waters of MS,[24] in so far as the MS or the EU exercise sovereign rights there, which was already existing state practice. It is therefore directly applicable on the continental shelf whereby the MS have sovereign rights according to art. 77 of UNCLOS. In particular, the Habitats Directive protects reefs and sea mammals as well as other habitats and species[25] that may be affected by seabed mining.[26] The Habitats and Birds Directives require MS to designate protected areas, respectively Special Areas of Conservation[27] and Special Protection Areas that form an ecological network called 'Natura 2000' under the Habitats Directive.[28] This network enables the natural habitat types and the spe-

17 1991 Convention on Environmental Impact Assessment in a Transboundary Context (Espoo Convention), 1989 U.N.T.S. 309; and 2003 Protocol on Strategic Environmental Assessment to the Convention on Environmental Impact Assessment in a Transboundary Context (Kiev Protocol), 2685 U.N.T.S. 140. The Kiev Protocol has been transposed into EU legislation by the 2001 Strategic Environmental Assessment Directive.

18 1998 Convention on Access to Information, Public Participation in Decision-Making and Access to Justice in Environmental Matters (Aarhus Convention), 2161 U.N.T.S. 447. The Aarhus Convention has been transposed into EU legislation by Directive 2003/4 on public access to information (first pillar) and Directive 2003/35 on public participation (second pillar).

19 Fisheries, the protection of fishing grounds and the conservation of marine biological resources of the sea under the EU fisheries policy is however an exclusive competence of the EU. See for example case Case 804/79, *Commission v United Kingdom* [1981] para. 18, ECLI:EU:C:1981:93.

20 Directive 79/409/EEC, amended in 2009 by Directive 2009/147/EC of the European Parliament and of the Council of 30 November 2009 on the conservation of wild birds.

21 Council Directive 92/43/EEC of 21 May 1992 on the conservation of natural habitats and of wild fauna and flora.

22 Directive 2008/56/EC of the European Parliament and of the Council of 17 June 2008 establishing a framework for Community action in the field of marine environmental policy.

23 Article 1.1 'Natural habitats means terrestrial or aquatic areas distinguished by geographic, abiotic and biotic features, whether entirely natural or semi-natural', Habitats Directive.

24 Case C-06/04, *Commission v United Kingdom* [2005], paras. 114 and 117, ECLI:EU:C:2005:626; see other EU case law in Arnesen, Greaves and Pozdnakova, op. cit., pp. 318 and 321.

25 Habitat Directive, Annex IV, where a strict protection regime must be applied across their entire natural range within the EU, both within and outside Natura 2000 sites.

26 ECORYS and MRAG, *Study to investigate state of knowledge of deep sea mining*, Final Report, Annex 2, 2014, p. 42. Available online <https://webgate.ec.europa.eu/maritimeforum/system/files/Annex%202%20Legal%20analysis_rev_1.pdf.> (accessed 21 March 2022). For EU habitats to be protected see European Commission, *Interpretation Manual of European Union Habitats*, April 2013.

27 Habitats Directive, Annex I and Annex II.

28 In the marine environment these are also called Marine Protected Areas (MPAs) in and beyond this particular EU context.

cies' habitats concerned to be maintained or, where appropriate, restored at a favourable conservation status in their natural range. To do so, MS need to avoid the deterioration of the special areas of conservation and the disturbance of their related species and may not adversely affect the integrity of the site. Proposed projects or plans concerning activities that are likely to have a significant effect on the site, whether in the site or outside, require an appropriate assessment. In case of a negative impact of seabed mining on the special areas of conservation, the activity can only be carried out for imperative reasons of overriding public interest and if compensation measures are taken to protect the overall coherence of the Natura 2000 networks.

To protect the marine biodiversity from the harmful effects of seabed mining in the EU (territorial sea, exclusive economic zone and continental shelf, including beyond 200 nm[29]), the 2008 Marine Strategy Framework Directive (MSF Directive)[30] is relevant. Its objective is to achieve a good environmental status (GES) of the EU marine waters by 2020,[31] with focus on the Baltic Sea, the North-East Atlantic Ocean, the Mediterranean Sea and the Black Sea. To achieve GES by 2020, each MS had to develop a strategy for its marine waters, which must be kept up-to-date and reviewed every six years. The strategy includes an initial assessment of the current environmental status of national marine waters, the establishment of environmental targets and associated indicators to achieve GES, the establishment of a monitoring programme for the assessment and the regular update of targets, and the development of a programme of measures designed to achieve or maintain GES, based on new criteria set out by the Commission in 2017 and indicative elements for the preparation of the marine strategies.[32] By doing so, the MSF Directive implements the obligation under UNCLOS to prevent, reduce and control pollution, including pollution of the seabed and subsoil, through the observation and measurement of risks or effects of pollution.[33] The new EU Biodiversity Strategy for 2030[34] further strengthens the protection of marine and seabed ecosystems and efforts to restore them to achieve GES.[35] To do so, it strives for the expansion of

29 See the interpretation of the geographical scope of the directive in the following document. EU Commission Staff Working Group, *Background document for the marine strategy framework directive on the determination of good environmental status and its links to assessments and the setting of environmental targets*, SWD (2020) 60 final and SWD (2020) 61 final, 25 June 2020.

30 Directive 2008/56/EC of the European Parliament and of the Council of 17 June 2008 establishing a framework for community action in the field of marine environmental policy (Marine Strategy Framework Directive). Moreover, as noted in the recent MSF Directive implementation report in 2020, 'analysing seabed integrity and analysing the entire food webs are novel approaches that are largely driven by the requirements of MSFD'. Report from the Commission to the European Parliament and the Council on the implementation of the MSF Directive, COM(2020) 259 final, 25 June 2020.

31 'Including the seabed and subsoil on the seaward side of the baseline from which the extent of territorial waters is measured extending to the outmost reach of the Area where a Member State has and/or exercises jurisdictional rights, in accordance with the UNCLOS'. MSF Directive, Article 3(1)(a).

32 It has been noted that 'in the case of seabed mining, where environmental impacts can only [be] estimated, owing to the many environmental and biodiversity unknowns, a precautionary approach, including the use of GES descriptors is essential in all commercial activities'. See ECORYS and MRAG, *Study to investigate state of knowledge of deep sea mining*, Interim Report, 2014, p. 128. Available online <https://webgate.ec.europa.eu/maritimeforum/sites/default/files/FGP96656%20DSM%20Interim%20report%20280314.pdf> (accessed 21 March 2022).

33 MSF Directive, preamble para. 17: 'The Community and its Member States are each parties to [UNCLOS and the 1994 Implementing Agreement]. The obligations of the Community and its Member States under those agreements should therefore be taken fully into account in this Directive'.

34 European Commission, *EU Biodiversity Strategy for 2030: Bringing nature back into our lives*, COM(2020) 380 final, 20 May 2020.

35 See the EU Nature Restoration Plan by 2030, commitment 13, 'The negative impact on sensitive species and habitats, including on the seabed through fishing and extraction activities, are substantially reduced to achieve good envi-

protected areas and the establishment of strictly protected areas for habitats and fish stocks recovery, and tackles practices that damage the seabed. Overall, the MSF Directive can be relevant to assess the effects of seabed mining towards the achievement of GES but does not appear to have the ambition nor the tools to restrict seabed mining as such.

The Environmental Impact Assessment (EIA) Directive[36] is one of the oldest EU environmental legislations. Together with the Strategic Environmental Assessment (SEA) Directive,[37] they apply, in a complementary way, to seabed mining activities on the continental shelf of MS. Indeed, the EIA Directive requires MS to assess significant environmental effects of public and private projects before permitting them, *ex-ante*, and initiate a process of public participation while the SEA Directive has the same objective, but limited to plans and programmes (for e.g. maritime spatial plans)[38] which are likely to have a significant effect on the environment in the MS.[39] The EIA Directive furthermore distinguishes between projects subject to a mandatory EIA (Annex I) and other projects (Annex II) which are subject to an EIA as determined by the MS according to specific selection criteria laid down in Annex III. Projects for which an EIA[40] indicates that significant effects might take place[41] mostly require adjustments from the original project in order to reduce or minimize those effects. In the case of seabed mining of mineral resources, only Annex II of the EIA Directive seems relevant owing to the category of 'extraction of minerals by marine or fluvial dredging'.[42]

It is evident that the SEA and EIA Directives complement each other. For instance, plans and programmes under the SEA Directive relate to EIA projects to be undertaken in the future and for which the plan or programme forms the legal basis. Likewise, other plans and programmes that are due to legislative, regulatory or administrative requirements can trigger the necessity to conduct a SEA. This is *inter alia* the case with management plans pursuant to Natura 2000 areas. Furthermore, if plans or programmes are not listed in the SEA Directive,[43] the MS anyhow has to carry out a screening procedure in order to understand if these plans or programmes do have

ronmental status'. Restoration efforts are to be undertaken through legally binding EU restoration targets, which, for some, are built on relevant legislations such as the Habitats and the MSF Directives. The legislative proposal setting binding nature restoration targets was due to be presented in December 2021 but was postponed until further notice.

36 Directive 85/337/EEC of the European Council 27 June 1985 on the assessment of the effects of certain public and private projects on the environment (revised via Directive 2014/52/EU of the European Parliament and of the Council of 16 April 2014 in amending Directive 2011/92/EU on the assessment of the effects of certain public and private projects on the environment).

37 Directive 2001/42/EC of the European Parliament and of the Council of 27 June 2001 on the assessment of the effects of certain plans and programmes on the environment.

38 Means plans and programmes including those co-financed by the EU, as well as any modification to them. See Article 2 (a), SEA Directive.

39 Recital 4, SEA Directive. For criteria determining the likely significance of effects, see Annex II therein.

40 The EIA shall describe and assess the direct and indirect effects of a project on: (a) population and human health; (b) biodiversity, with particular attention to species and habitats protected under Directive 92/43/EEC and Directive 2009/147/EC; (c) land, soil, water, air and climate; (d) material assets, cultural heritage and the landscape; (e) the interaction between the factors referred to in points (a) to (d). See Art. 3, EIA Directive. See also Annex IV of the same for references to noise, vibration and light, which are all relevant for seabed mining.

41 The likely significant effects of projects take into account the magnitude and spatial extent of the impact, its direct and transboundary nature, its intensity and complexity, its probability, expected onset, duration, frequency and reversibility, the cumulation of the impact with the impact of other existing and/or approved projects and the possibility of effectively reducing the impact. Annex III, EIA Directive.

42 Annex I only includes the case of the extraction of petroleum and natural gas, not the extraction of mineral resources. See Annex I (14), EIA Directive, ibid.

43 Article 3 (3), SEA Directive.

significant effects on the marine environment.[44] If they do, then the SEA Directive also applies.[45] In case seabed mining is part of a plan or programme or is considered by the MS as a plan or programme likely to have significant effects on the marine environment (which seems obvious in the case of seabed mining), the SEA Directive will thus apply and trigger the necessary consultation procedures with other MS (between relevant authorities, the public, neighbouring states whose environment is likely to be affected).[46]

Seabed mining in the Area

In addition to applicable regulatory framework under UNCLOS as well as subsequent rules, regulations and procedures developed by the ISA, MS carrying out or sponsoring persons and entities with respect to seabed mining activities in the Area are also subject to EU laws that may apply extra-territorially. The identification of the applicable legislation, however, reveals important uncertainties in the EU framework applicable on the seabed beyond national jurisdiction.

The Habitats Directive, for its part, appears to be rather straightforward. Since it is only applicable to areas within the jurisdiction of MS where they have sovereign rights,[47] it clearly excludes its implementation to the Area (and the High Seas). The MSF Directive on its side applies to the 'marine waters of MS', which includes the seabed and subsoil 'to the outmost reach of the area where a Member State has and/or jurisdictional rights, in accordance with UNCLOS'.[48] It thus applies to maritime zones within jurisdiction and, as mentioned by a working group of the EU Commission, to 'other types of jurisdictional designation'.[49] While the geographical coverage of the MSF Directive is firmly anchored in EU marine space, the application of the ecosystem approach together with concept of jurisdiction could allow the extension of the scope of application of this directive beyond the strict EU marine space. It should, however, be noted that jurisdictional issues are defined by each MS who decides where the MSF Directive applies. As a result, the question of implementation of the MSF Directive under the flag State jurisdiction could therefore be proposed by an MS undertaking exploration or future exploitation activities in the Area.

The EIA or SEA Directives offer interesting implementation mechanisms. They apply to public or private projects (EIA Directive), to plans and programmes (SEA Directive) which have significant effects on the marine environment, and they both integrate the notion of transboundary effect. While the scope of the EIA Directive does not explicitly exclude its application to projects in the Area, the reference to the notion of 'territory' and the expression 'significant effects on the environment in another Member States' in article 7, however, cast important doubts on its suitability for seabed mining in the Area. The same applies to the SEA Directive which uses the same expression in Recital 4 'significant effects on the environment in the Member States' while, however, restricting the transboundary consultation upon other MS (and thus not requiring transboundary

44 MS shall then take into account the criteria set out in Annex II. Art. 3 (4), ibid.

45 For more information on the scope and implementation of the SEA Directive, see European Commission, *Report from the Commission to the Council and the European Parliament under Art. 12 (3) of Directive 2001/42/EC on the assessment of the effects of certain plans and programmes on the environment*, COM(2017) 234 final, 15 May 2017.

46 ECORYS and MRAG, op. cit. at pp. 101–102.

47 See again, Case C-06/04, *Commission v United Kingdom* [2005], para. 114 and 117, ECLI:EU:C:2005:626; and other EU case law in Arnesen, Greaves and Pozdnakova, op. cit., pp. 318 and 321.

48 Article 3 (4) which refers to the definition of point (1) a) of Directive 2008/56/EC and coastal waters defined by point 7 of Article 2 of Directive 2000/60/EC and their seabed and subsoil.

49 SWD (2020) 60 final and SWD (2020) 61 final, op. cit.

consultation with non-MS countries, such as those conducting activities in the Area). The implementation of these two Directives in the Area, as they are, therefore appears very unlikely.

In view of the potential ratification by the EU, and subsequent entry into force, of the *Agreement under the United Nations Convention on the Law of the Sea on the conservation and sustainable use of marine biodiversity of areas beyond national jurisdiction* (the BBNJ Agreement), these directives might be amended.[50] Changes into EU law will anyhow be made to allow MS to comply with their future obligation to ensure the assessment of planned activities in areas beyond national jurisdiction. To this end, a mechanism of extra-territorial implementation through the flag State jurisdiction and control of MS could be introduced. With regard to thresholds and factors for the conduct of EIA and SEA, MS and the EU are allowed to maintain their own thresholds and standards, if these are equivalent or below the thresholds for EIA set under the BBNJ Agreement.[51]

To this end, the thresholds for EIA and SEA Directives, at present based on the 'significant effects on the marine environment', may be revised to integrate the wording adopted under the BBNJ Agreement's EIA screening phase, namely, 'more than a minor or transitory effect on the marine environment or the effects of the activity are unknown or poorly understood'.[52] The BBNJ Agreement's thresholds for the mandatory conduct of EIA based on 'substantial pollution of, or significant *and* harmful changes to the marine environment' may also be introduced. More specifically to the SEA Directive, changes could also be made to align the Directive with the BBNJ Agreement, namely, replacing the assessment of *reasonable* alternatives[53] with the broader requirement of the BBNJ Agreement, consisting of the assessment of alternatives (without the reasonable component).[54]

Finally, given the possibility that MS can jointly apply to conduct or choose to co-sponsor mining activities in the Area with non-MS, more clarity is needed as such arrangements may lead to potential conflict whereby MS would need to comply with EU Directives and other EU requirements, whereas non-MS (which may also potentially not be parties to the forthcoming BBNJ Agreement) might not feel the need to comply in the same way. Indeed, there is an existing precedent in the case of the Interoceanmetal Joint Organization (IOM), which holds an exploration contract with the ISA for polymetallic nodules, and is jointly co-sponsored by six countries, of which four are MS (Bulgaria, Czech Republic, Poland and Slovakia) and two are non-MS (Cuba and Russian Federation).

The European Union, its Member States and regional seas conventions

Some MS, and the EU in its own right, are parties to three regional seas conventions that those MS and the EU would have to comply with and implement accordingly. These conventions, which are also pertinent for seabed mining activities, are the *1992 Convention for the Protection of the Marine Environment of the North-East Atlantic* (OSPAR Convention); the *1995 Convention for the*

50 The obligation to conduct an EIA under the BBNJ Agreement allows for the State Party to conduct EIA in accordance with the BBNJ Agreement or according to the Party's national process. Art. 28, *Agreement under the United Nations Convention on the Law of the Sea on the conservation and sustainable use of marine biological diversity of areas beyond national jurisdiction*, June 2023. Hereinafter 'BBNJ Agreement'.

51 Article 29, para 4 b), BBNJ Agreement.

52 Article 30, para 1, see also para 2, ibid.

53 Article 5, SEA Directive.

54 Article 39, BBNJ Agreement, op. cit.

Protection of the Marine Environment and the Coastal Region of the Mediterranean (Barcelona Convention) and Protocols; and the *1992 Convention on the Protection of the Marine Environment of the Baltic Sea Area* (Helsinki Convention).

The OSPAR Convention

Eleven MS and the EU,[55] as well as Iceland, Norway, Switzerland and the UK, are parties to the OSPAR Convention.[56] The Convention covers the maritime area under national jurisdiction of the parties, but also extends to some parts that come under areas beyond national jurisdiction (ABNJ). One of the key obligations of the parties is the duty to apply the precautionary principle, but this duty is limited to substances and energy introduced in the marine environment that can, *inter alia*, harm living resources and marine ecosystems.[57] From a textual interpretation it seems that this precautionary principle does not cover all potential environmental impacts of seabed mining, which include *inter alia* suspended sediments, operational and discharge plumes, noise and vibrations.[58] Nevertheless, the parties can, individually or jointly, take more stringent measures with respect to the protection of the maritime area against the adverse effects of human activities.[59] They even have an obligation to 'take the necessary measures to protect the maritime area against the adverse effects of human activities so as to safeguard human health and to conserve marine ecosystems and, when practicable, restore marine areas which have been adversely affected'.[60]

The Convention is supplemented by five annexes. Despite its title, Annex III on the prevention and elimination of pollution from offshore sources does not apply in the case of seabed mining.[61] Only Annex V on the protection and conservation of the ecosystems, habitats, species and biological diversity of the OSPAR area is relevant for sea mining. In order to protect and conserve ecosystems and biological diversity of the OSPAR area,[62] marine protected areas (MPAs) have been designated in legally binding OSPAR decisions.[63] OSPAR MPAs are established with the aim to form an ecologically coherent network and to ensure their habitats and species are adequately protected against the adverse effects of human activities. Management measures that need to be taken in the MPAs are, however, adopted by recommendations which are not legally binding.[64] OSPAR

55 Belgium, Denmark, Finland, France, Germany, Ireland, Luxembourg, the Netherlands, Portugal, Spain and Sweden.

56 The *1992 Convention for the Protection of the Marine Environment of the North-East Atlantic* (OSPAR Convention), 2354 U.N.T.S. 67.

57 Article 2(2)(a), OSPAR Convention.

58 OSPAR, *Feeder Report to the 2023 QSR*, 2021, paragraph 6.7 mentions as potential impacts of the extraction of non-mineral resources linked to seabed mining: 'loss of substrate; changes to seabed integrity; operational suspended sediment and chemical plumes; re sedimentation from operational plume; discharge plume; increase in light; increase in noise levels and potential vibration; and release of sediment-bound or subsurface pore water toxic metals into the water column. Activities could also have impacts on other economic sectors, such as fisheries or the exploitation of biota for marine genetic resources. Understanding of the extent and nature of impacts is uncertain'.

59 Article 2(5), OSPAR Convention.

60 Article 2(1)(a), OSPAR Convention.

61 Annex III on offshore sources might at first sight seem relevant, but the Convention limits this Annex to offshore installations and offshore pipelines from which substances and energy reach the maritime area (article 1 (k) OSPAR Convention). While offshore installations and pipelines (article 1 (l) and (m) OSPAR Convention) are linked to offshore activities, article 1(j) of the OSPAR Convention limits its application to liquid and gaseous hydrocarbons, and is as such not relevant for seabed mining of solid minerals.

62 Article 2(a), Annex V, ibid.

63 Article 13(2), OSPAR Convention.

64 Article 13(5), OSPAR Convention.

MPAs are designated by the parties in areas under their jurisdiction, and in case of MS of the EU, these areas are mostly designated under the EU Birds and Habitats Directives.

More importantly, a restriction or prohibition on seabed mining activities does not automatically follow upon an OSPAR MPA designation. Consequently, unless it is explicitly provided otherwise, it is possible for seabed mining to occur in marine areas under national jurisdiction that have been designated as OSPAR MPAs (although this would seemingly be controversial and might be rebuked by other OSPAR parties). This is because for OSPAR MPAs under national jurisdiction, the coastal states concerned bear the responsibility to establish and implement management actions (programmes, measures, restrictions, EIA processes, among others), including with regard to seabed activities having an effect on the protection of the MPA.[65] Indeed, OSPAR provides a platform to coordinate the implementation of the MSF Directive.[66] As a result, the indicators of biological diversity and sea floor integrity[67] are applicable for the continental shelves of MS of the EU located in an MPA of OSPAR.[68]

OSPAR MPAs located in the High Seas and in the Area, collectively designated by the OSPAR parties, require cooperation with a competent international organization to take further management actions that have universal effects.[69] Cooperation with the ISA will in that case be obviously required to manage potential seabed mining activities. Although this cooperation is not explicitly mentioned in Annex V,[70] it follows from the legal status of the Area.[71] Indeed, the OSPAR Commission explicitly acknowledges the need to cooperate with the ISA in MPAs where seabed mining might have an effect on the protective measures to be taken.[72] A Memorandum of under-

65 OSPAR Recommendation 2003/3 on a Network of Marine Protected Areas adopted by OSPAR 2003 OSPAR 03/17/1, Annex 9, amended by OSPAR Recommendation 2010/2, OSPAR 10/23/1, Annex 7.

66 4.2. Strategy of the OSPAR Commission for the Protection of the Marine Environment of the North-East Atlantic 2030 (NEAC 2030): Agreement 2021-01, OSPAR 21/13/1, Annex 22.

67 A qualitative descriptor for GES for sea-floor integrity means that 'sea-floor integrity is at a level that ensures that the structure and functioning of the ecosystems are safeguarded and benthic ecosystems, in particular, are not adversely affected', Appendix 2 of Annex I of the MSF Directive.

68 See OSPAR, *Existing OSPAR measures in support of MSFD programmes of measures – 'OSPAR acquis'*, 2015.

69 OSPAR measures apply to OSPAR contracting parties only: 4.3 OSPAR's Regulatory Regime for establishing Marine Protected Areas (MPAs) in Areas Beyond National Jurisdiction (ABNJ) of the OSPAR Maritime Area, Summary Record-OSPAR 2009, OSPAR 09/22/1-E, Annex 6.

70 In contrast to fisheries, for which no programme or measure concerning the management of fisheries can be adopted under Annex V (Article 4(1), Annex V, ibid.), so cooperation with the EU (if under national jurisdiction of EU member states) and with relevant regional fisheries management organizations in ABNJ is necessary to take management actions. See e.g. Memorandum of understanding between the North East Atlantic Fisheries Commission (NEAFC) and the OSPAR Commission: Agreement 2008-4 and the NEAFC-OSPAR Collective arrangement between competent international organizations on cooperation and coordination regarding selected areas in areas beyond national jurisdiction in the North-East Atlantic: Agreement 2014-09.

71 Article 137 UNCLOS; see also article 145 UNCLOS on the protection of the marine environment in the Area.

72 See the OSPAR website <https://www.ospar.org/work-areas/bdc/species-habitats/implementation-of-species-and-habitat-recommendations> (accessed 21 April 2021); see also 3.2. b. (ii), OSPAR Recommendation 2003/3 on a Network of Marine Protected Areas; OSPAR Decision 2010/1 on the Establishment of the Milne Seamount Complex Marine Protected Area and OSPAR Recommendation 2010/12 on the Management of the Milne Seamount Complex Marine Protected Area, recognize in the preamble that 'a range of human activities occurring, or potentially occurring in the Milne Seamount Complex area are regulated in the frameworks of other competent authorities. These include, in particular [...] extraction of mineral resources (International Seabed Authority (ISA)'. The same reference to ISA can be found in OSPAR Decision 2021/01 on the Establishment of the North Atlantic Current and Evlanov Sea basin Marine Protected Area and OSPAR Recommendation 2021/01 on the Management of the North Atlantic Current and Evlanov Sea basin Marine Protected Area. Other decisions and recommendations focus mainly on the effects of high seas fisheries in OSPAR MPAs: Decisions and Recommendations regarding the Altair

standing was concluded in 2010 between the OSPAR Commission and the ISA[73] to strengthen cooperation and consultation between themselves, and to encourage marine scientific research in the sea areas of the North-East Atlantic beyond national jurisdiction. This Memorandum of understanding also supports the effectiveness of measures aimed at the conservation of biological diversity in those areas and the collection and exchange of environmental data. Notwithstanding the above, it must be stressed that as things currently stand, the ISA is under no strict obligation to respect or give effect to any MPA or other area-based conservation measures adopted in ABNJ by any other organization or treaty body (including OSPAR). As a result, it may consider and decide to approve exploration or future exploitation contracts in the Area that coincide or overlap with such measures.

It should also be noted that OSPAR MPAs located in the High Seas and the Area require OSPAR parties to manage human activities under their control in such a way as to achieve the conservation objectives of these MPAs. Such management measures include programmes and measures, such as awareness raising at national and international level, as well as sharing information about impacts of human activities and knowledge about the ecosystem and the biodiversity of MPAs. The OSPAR Code of conduct for responsible marine research in the deep seas and High Seas,[74] applicable to national research vessels and research institutions, also plays a key role in supporting and guiding the conduct of marine scientific research in MPAs, and helps ensure that plans for human activities, within or outside MPAs, are subjected to an EIA or an SEA if they have a potential conflict with the conservation objectives of the MPA. Last but not least, OSPAR also adopted a Guidance for good practice for communication with stakeholders on the establishment and management of marine protected areas,[75] recommending, in the planning of new activities and assessment of their potential impacts on the MPA, the use of best-available scientific advice and the involvement of relevant stakeholders in the planning process. To this end, OSPAR parties are expected to encourage third parties and international organizations to apply these programmes and measures.

Finally, it is important to highlight a recent development whereby a Task force for deep sea mining has been created under the Environmental Impacts of Human Activities Committee of OSPAR in 2019.[76] This Task force is led by the United Kingdom and supported by Belgium, Germany, Norway, Sweden and France.[77] Some exchanges have so far been made on the general positions of OSPAR parties relating to seabed mining, as well as on how they could meet their obligations under the OSPAR Convention. In 2021, Seas at Risk, an observer participant of the Task force, proposed a moratorium on seabed mining in the OSPAR Convention area. Although

Seamount, the Antialtair Seamount, the Josephine Seamount, Charlie-Gibbs South, Charlie-Gibbs North and the Mid-Atlantic Ridge north of the Azores High Seas.

73 Agreement 2010-9, OSPAR 10/23/0, Annex 12.

74 OSPAR Agreement 2008-1, OSPAR 08/24/1, Annex 6.

75 OSPAR Agreement 2008-2.

76 The term 'deep sea mining' in this context is used by OSPAR, and thus, it is unclear if the Task force will also cover seabed mining in shallow waters. The Task force covers the OSPAR Convention area and reports to EIHA. Unfortunately, the OSPAR website does not contain any direct web link to specifically highlight the work of the Task force. Nevertheless, details on the Task force and its work can be found in the minutes of the recent EIHA meetings. See especially documents relating to the meeting of March 2021 <https://www.ospar.org/meetings/archive/environmental-impact-of-human-activities-2021> and March 2022 <https://www.ospar.org/meetings/archive/environmental-impacts-of-human-activities-committee-1> (both accessed on 21 April 2022).

77 In addition to those OSPAR parties, several observers are also involved in the Task force. See document 'Annex 6 – NEAES Implementation Plan draft EIHA task templates', item 8, of the March 2021 EIHA meeting, op. cit.

this proposal was discussed, it did not receive any support from OSPAR parties.[78] Moving forward, the Task force is expected to continue working in 2022–2023 with the aim to produce a series of discussion papers relating to seabed mining on technical aspects, relevant OSPAR measures, and, if deemed appropriate based on discussions in 2023 on policy recommendations for OSPAR parties, including how OSPAR could further engage with the ISA.[79]

The Barcelona Convention

The Barcelona Convention[80] is an emblematic instrument which influenced the making of many other regional conventions due to the mechanism set up between the convention and its seven protocols.[81] It comprises 22 contracting parties[82] bordering the Mediterranean Sea, including the EU. Of direct interest to this section is the Offshore Protocol,[83] which aims to reduce and respond to the pollution resulting from the exploration and exploitation of the continental shelf, the seabed and its subsoil in the whole Mediterranean Sea.[84] Signed in 1994, it however only entered into force on 24 March 2011 and is today the second least ratified protocol of the Barcelona Convention with only eight ratifications.[85] Mainly focused on oil and gas activities to date,[86] the Offshore Protocol nevertheless embraces a broader scope as it covers all mineral resources whether solid, liquid or gaseous[87] and includes an exhaustive list of exploration and exploitation activities, relevant for seabed mining.

Its main feature is to establish a mechanism of prior authorization, subject to specific requirements,[88] assessing whether activities and related installations are following international

78 See document 'EIHA 2021 Summary Record', paragraphs 7.30–7.38, of the March 2021 EIHA meeting, op. cit.

79 See documents 'EIHA 2022 Summary Record', paragraphs 7.17–7.19, and 'Annex 5 – S7.05.03 revised task template', of the March 2022 EIHA meeting, op. cit.

80 The *1995 Convention for the Protection of the Mediterranean Sea Against Pollution* (Barcelona Convention), 1102 U.N.T.S. 27 (previously known as the 1976 Convention for the Protection of the Marine Environment and the Coastal Region of the Mediterranean).

81 The protocols are individually subject to a ratification mechanism.

82 Albania, Algeria, Bosnia and Herzegovina, Croatia, Cyprus, Egypt, France, Greece, Israel, Italy, Lebanon, Libya, Malta, Monaco, Montenegro, Morocco, Slovenia, Spain, Syrian Arab Republic, Tunisia, Turkey and the European Union.

83 *Protocol for the Protection of the Mediterranean Sea against Pollution Resulting from the Exploration and Exploitation of the Continental Shelf and the Seabed and Its Subsoil* (Madrid Offshore Protocol), 2010 U.N.T.S. 2742. This Protocol was complemented by a 2016 Action Plan aiming to integrate, among others, the Mediterranean strategy for sustainable management, as well as ten objectives and seven guiding principles. Of direct relevance for the relationship with EU Law, see article I.3 mentioning that the provisions of the Protocol 'shall be without prejudice to stricter provisions regulating the management of offshore activities contained in other existing or future national, regional or international instruments or programmes, when considering existing best practices for the development of standards for the Mediterranean region'.

84 This Protocol implements article 208 of UNCLOS and adopts a vertical and horizontal approach by covering the seabed, but also the waters. See article 2, para 1, Offshore Protocol, ibid.

85 Greece, France, Italy, Malta, Slovenia and Spain ratified the Convention but not the Offshore Protocol. Only Cyprus, Croatia and the European Union have ratified both.

86 Exploration activities cover scientific research, exploration, seismological activities, surveys of seabed and subsoil, sample taking and exploration drilling. Exploitation activities cover the establishment of an installation for the purpose of recovering resources and activities connected, development drilling, recovery, treatment and storage, transportation to shore by pipeline or body of ships, maintenance, repair and other ancillary operations. See Art. 1 d), Offshore Protocol.

87 Article 1 c), ibid.

88 Article 5, ibid.

standards and practice, and whether the operator has technical competence as well as financial capacity to carry out activities. The Offshore Protocol also strengthens the protection of Mediterranean specially protected areas[89] already given under the *1995 Specially Protected Area and Biological Diversity Protocol of the Barcelona Convention.*[90] These additional measures concern the granting of authorization and require (1) special restrictions or conditions such as the preparation or evaluation of environmental impact assessment, or the elaboration of special provisions for monitoring, removal of installations or prohibition of any discharge; and (2) intensifying exchange of information among stakeholders on matters affecting these Mediterranean specially protected areas.[91]

The transposition of the Offshore Protocol into EU law was done through the 2013 Directive on Safety of Offshore Oil and Gas Activities, although this remains incomplete. Indeed, this Directive only concerns oil and gas activities, while the scope of the Offshore Protocol covers exploration and exploitation activities of all mineral resources. Substantial amendments[92] to the Annexes of the Offshore Protocol were adopted in December 2021.[93] They mainly amend the list of prohibited disposal of harmful, noxious substances and materials,[94] the factors to be considered for the issue of permits[95] and environmental impact assessment.[96] The related guidelines for the conduct of environmental impact assessment have been also revised,[97] together with a broadening of the screening process to determine the obligation of an environmental impact assessment, and the deletion of the minimum thresholds in favour of a non-exhaustive list of activities. These amendments are supported by the EU,[98] which sees it as an opportunity to further affirm its ambition with regards to the protection of the marine environment. However, it remains to be seen if the EU will seize the opportunity of these amendments to fully implement the Offshore Protocol into EU law. Full implementation is indeed critical since Italy and Greece, which did not ratify the Offshore Protocol, might someday consider exploring and exploiting the polymetallic sulphides located on their continental shelves.[99] If this happens, the EU might find itself in an awkward situation where its legal responsibility (for failure to fully implement the Offshore Protocol and potential related damages) could be engaged under the Barcelona Convention.[100]

89 And any other areas established by a party. Article 21, ibid.

90 The MSPA Protocol was adopted in 1995 and entered in force in 1999. The European Union ratified it in 1995. This 1995 MSPA Protocol geographic scope covers the seabed and subsoil of the Mediterranean Sea. It comprises an obligation to take protection measures for the protection of MSPA including the regulation or prohibition of any activity involving the exploration or modification of the soil or the exploitation of the subsoil of the land part, the seabed and its subsoil. Article 6, c), 1995 Specially Protected Area and Biological Diversity Protocol.

91 Non-exhaustive list. See Article 21, Offshore Protocol.

92 Non exhaustive list. For the full list, see UNEP-MAP, *Amendments of the Annexes to the Mediterranean Offshore Protocol*, EP/MED WG.498/4, 12 May 2021.

93 Amendments to the Annexes to the Protocol for the Protection of the Mediterranean Sea against Pollution Resulting from Exploration and Exploitation of the Continental Shelf and the Seabed and its Subsoil, *Decision IG.25/7*, UNEP/MED IG. 25/27, December 2021.

94 Non-exhaustive list.

95 Annex III, C, 5), EP/MED WG.498/4, op. cit.

96 Annex IV, Article 1, ibid.

97 New definitions or modifications of 'baseline scenario', 'environmental assessment', 'offset', 'source', 'study area' are proposed, together with a deletion of the concept of 'restoration'.

98 European Commission, *Council Decision Proposal*, COM(2021) 668 Final, 26 October 2021.

99 For a map indicating the location of these resources, see the website of EMODnet of the European Union. Available online <https://webgate.ec.europa.eu/maritimeforum/en/node/4447> (accessed 24 April 2022).

100 Article 22 and Annex A, Barcelona Convention. See also article 8 of Annex A, clarifying the fact that the EU could appear as respondent in an arbitration case. Such scenario is, however, unlikely considering the political dimension that such proceeding entails.

The Helsinki Convention

The third and final regional agreement that applies to EU marine space is the *1992 Convention on the Protection of the Marine Environment of the Baltic Sea Area* (Helsinki Convention),[101] although some parts of the Baltic Sea area fall outside the jurisdiction of MS. The Helsinki Convention has ten contracting parties, including the EU and eight MS (Denmark, Estonia, Finland, Germany, Latvia, Lithuania, Poland and Sweden) as well as Russia, covering all coastal States of the Baltic Sea. Originally adopted in 1974, the Helsinki Convention was revised in 1992 to take into account geopolitical changes in the region (namely, the reunification of Germany and the fall of the USSR) as well as to address the pressing environmental challenges to the marine area that had emerged.[102] The Helsinki Convention entered into force on 17 January 2000, and currently comprises seven annexes. The governing body of the Helsinki Convention, the Baltic Marine Environment Commission (HELCOM), adopted the Baltic Sea Action Plan in 2007, which was recently revised in October 2021.[103] With respect to the EU specifically, the EU Strategy for the Baltic Sea Region was adopted in 2009,[104] alongside an Action Plan that was most recently revised in February 2021.[105] Moreover, following a HELCOM Ministerial Declaration in 2010, HELCOM also performs the role of coordinating the EU's MSF Directive to strive to harmonize national marine strategies of MS to achieve good environmental status in the Baltic Sea area.[106] In this respect, it has been observed that the Baltic Sea Action Plan and the MSF Directive have strong links to each other and are closely aligned.[107]

Compared to the other two regional agreements discussed earlier, HELCOM appears to be slightly lagging behind with respect to seabed mining coverage. While article 4, paragraph 1, stipulates that the Convention 'shall apply to the protection of the marine environment of the Baltic Sea Area which comprises the water-body and the seabed' and article 12 (on exploration and exploitation of the seabed and its subsoil) is broadly drafted with a focus on the protection of the marine environment,[108] the Convention's specific annex on offshore activities (Annex VI: prevention of pollution from offshore activities) explicitly specifies that it only targets the exploration and exploitation of offshore oil and gas.[109] Thus, in adopting such a specific definition for 'offshore activities', there is a clear gap in terms of regional regulation of seabed mining with respect to the

101 The *1992 Convention on the Protection of the Marine Environment of the Baltic Sea Area* (Helsinki Convention), 2009 U.N.T.S. 197, 13 ILM 546 (1974).

102 For a historical account of the Helsinki convention, see <https://helcom.fi/about-us/convention/> (accessed 20 February 2022).

103 Baltic Sea Action Plan, adopted 15 November 2007 and updated 20 October 2021. Available online <https://www.helcom.fi/wp-content/uploads/2019/08/BSAP_Final.pdf> and <https://helcom.fi/media/publications/Baltic-Sea-Action-Plan-2021-update.pdf> (accessed 20 February 2022).

104 Communication from the Commission to the European Parliament, the Council, the European Economic and Social Committee and the Committee of the Regions concerning the European Union Strategy for the Baltic Sea Region and Action Plan, COM(2009) 248 final, 10 June 2009.

105 Commission Staff Working Document, EU Strategy for the Baltic Sea Region Action Plan (COM(2009) 248 final), Revised Action Plan replacing the Action Plan of 17 March 2017, 15 February 2021.

106 HELCOM Ministerial Declaration on the implementation of the HELCOM Baltic Sea Action Plan, 20 May 2010, Moscow. Available online <https://helcom.fi/wp-content/uploads/2019/08/HELCOM-Moscow-Ministerial-Declaration-FINAL.pdf> (accessed 20 February 2022).

107 J. van Leeuwen, L. van Hoof and J. van Tatenhove, 'Institutional ambiguity in implementing the European Union Marine Strategy Framework Directive', *Marine Policy* 36(3), 2012, 636–643.

108 Helsinki Convention.

109 Annex VI, ibid.

Baltic Sea area (which the Helsinki Convention or its annexes have not covered to date). This gap is problematic, especially since it is known that there are significant numbers of mineral concretions on the continental shelf of Finland, for example, including ferromanganese deposits that have attracted mining interests.[110] In this respect, there has been a recent proposal to the Helsinki Commission to adopt a moratorium on seabed mining in the Baltic Sea area.[111]

Given the broad scope of the Convention text, as seen in article 4, paragraph 1 and article 12 (which do not limit its application to offshore oil and gas activities), it is entirely possible for Annex VI to be expanded to include seabed mining or for a new and dedicated annex on seabed mining to be developed in the future. Crucially, HELCOM parties have started to pay more attention to the topic of seabed mining in recent times. In the updated Baltic Sea Action Plan adopted by HELCOM in October 2021, the following is mentioned: 'in order to minimize the short and long-term impacts of seabed mining (excluding sand and gravel extraction), minerals should not be exploited before the effects of seabed mining on the marine environment, biodiversity and human activities have been sufficiently researched. The risks need to be understood and technologies and operational practices should be able to demonstrate that the environment is not seriously harmed by seabed mining activities, in line with the precautionary principle'.[112] As a consequence, it is entirely possible that HELCOM parties will build upon this political determination and continue to pay closer attention to future seabed mining activities in the Baltic Sea area and adopt appropriate binding measures and regulatory responses as necessary.

Further analysis and observations

Upon reflection on the original framework and subsequent evolution of the three regional seas conventions in response to seabed mining, especially in recent years, it seems clear that the theme is now an important agenda item under all three conventions. However, while some political will to address the topic has started to emerge, including through the adoption of specific measures, the regulatory responses remain largely deficient. For instance, from the perspective of regulatory instruments, while the Offshore Protocol under the Barcelona Convention is the only instrument across all three conventions that explicitly includes seabed mining in binding regulations, the fact remains that barely a third of the parties to the said Convention have ratified the Offshore Protocol. Moreover, the transposition of the Offshore Protocol into EU law remains incomplete as only elements relating to offshore oil and gas have been incorporated and not seabed mining. As a consequence, this may expose the legal responsibility of the EU, as a party to the Offshore Protocol, in case Italy or Greece someday choose to proceed with exploration and exploitation of seabed minerals on their respective continental shelves. In addition, apart from constant external pressure from advisory councils and non-governmental bodies to address seabed mining,[113] there

110 University of Helsinki, Sea floor mineral deposits are common in northern Baltic Sea, online edition, 2019. Available online <https://www.helsinki.fi/en/news/life-sciences/sea-floor-mineral-deposits-are-common-northern-baltic-sea> (accessed 22 December 2021).

111 Coalition Clean Baltic, 'Adoption of a moratorium on seabed mining in the Baltic Sea, including a moratorium on developing additional permissive regulations and exploitation and exploration contracts', Submission to HELCOM, 2019. Available online <https://portal.helcom.fi/workspaces/BSAP%20UP%20NEW%20ACTIONS-183/Shared%20Documents/Synopses%20-%20proposals%20received/Moratorium%20on%20seabed%20mining%20in%20the%20Baltic%20Sea.pdf> (accessed 22 December 2021).

112 HELCOM, Baltic Sea Action Plan as updated in 2021, op. cit., p. 40.

113 See for example, a recent statement from a large network of organizations delivered to the 2021 Conference of the Parties to the Barcelona Convention expressing concern about the environmental implications of deep-sea

seems to be at the moment little political will to actually engage directly with the topic under the Barcelona Convention, although this may change in the future.[114]

In contrast, while currently lagging behind in terms of not having extended its regulatory instruments to explicitly cover seabed mining, the OSPAR Commission and HELCOM seem to have embraced the need to take some concrete measures as well as political steps to address seabed mining. In the case of OSPAR, this can be seen (albeit to a limited extent) through measures that have been taken to designate MPAs, including those in ABNJ, as well as the recent establishment of the Task force on deep seabed mining to facilitate discussions and exchanges among its parties. However, in terms of political steps, HELCOM appears to have taken the lead by far, as reflected in its recently revised Baltic Sea Action Plan that specifically singles out seabed mining.

Moreover, it would seem to be quite apparent that the dynamics and composition of the various regional sea conventions carry an impact on the approach that has been taken to influence their future directions in the context of seabed mining. To this end, OSPAR makes an interesting case study for two reasons: one, the seabed resource potential within the Convention area is quite significant in relative comparison to the other two regimes, and two, the OSPAR Convention area extends, in some parts, into ABNJ. Furthermore, compared to the other two regimes and their respective compositions, some OSPAR parties have much more interest in seabed resources. These include several MS of the EU (Belgium,[115] France[116] and Germany[117]) as well as the UK[118] and Norway, although it must be stressed that with the exception of Norway, whose interests in seabed mining at the moment are primarily within its continental shelf, the interests of the other parties are

mining in the Mediterranean Sea <https://mio-ecsde.org/wp-content/uploads/2021/12/Statement-to-the-Ministers-at-COP22-of-the-Barcelona-Convention_3.pdf> (accessed 21 April 2022).

114 Especially if the EU decides to support the call for a moratorium of seabed mining activities within the Barcelona Convention to promote its 2030 Biodiversity Strategy. The authors however find that the EU position is still currently lacking political solidity to do so, especially with regards to seabed mining on continental shelves.

115 For more information on the position of Belgium towards seabed mining, see K. Willaert and F. Maes, 'Belgium and seabed mining', in V. Tassin Campanella (ed.), *Routledge handbook of seabed mining and the law of the sea*, London: Routledge, chapter VI.2.1.

116 Following a 2021 Revised Strategy for Deep Seabed applicable both *within* and *beyond* national jurisdiction, as well as a 2022 Military Deep Seabed Management Strategy, both with the intention to strengthen the State capacity of exploration while protecting industrial and military interests (Comité interministériel de la mer, *Dossier de presse*, March 2022 and Ministère des Armées, *Stratégie ministérielle de maîtrise des fonds marins*, February 2022), France is contemplating the suppression of the only moratorium of exploitation of mineral resources on the French continental shelf to access to sand resources (Outre Mer, Livre IV, Articles L. 611-1 and 2). In view of these developments, the French Senate conducted an information mission dedicated to the exploration, protection and exploitation of deep seabed areas, with a report recommending caution in moving forward with exploitation activities due to the lack of sufficient scientific information (French Senate, 'Abysses: la dernière frontière?', June 2022, available online <http://www.senat.fr/commission/missions/2021_fonds_marins.html> (accessed 19 August 2022)). Shortly after, at the 2022 UN Ocean Conference, the French President declared its ambition to stop 'high seas mining' and not allow ocean extractive activities to endanger key marine ecosystems. As a result, the French Parliament adopted in January 2023 an exploitation moratorium in the Area. The impact of this resolution on similar activities on the French continental shelf remains uncertain.

117 In November 2022, Germany called for a precautionary pause on seabed mining in the Area. For more information on the position of Germany towards seabed mining, see N. Matz-Lück, 'Germany and seabed mining', in V. Tassin Campanella (ed.), *Routledge handbook of seabed mining and the law of the sea*, op. cit., chapter VI.2.5.

118 For more information on the position of the United Kingdom towards seabed mining, see J. Harrison, 'The United Kingdom and seabed mining', in V. Tassin Campanella (ed.), *Routledge handbook of seabed mining and the law of the sea*, op. cit., chapter VI.2.14.

in seabed minerals located in areas outside OSPAR jurisdiction.[119] However, other OSPAR parties and MS of the EU seem more cautious about seabed mining within national jurisdiction despite having significant potential resources within their respective continental shelves. This is the case for Portugal,[120] but also for Spain, which recently in March 2022 issued a decree that effectively bans seabed mining on its continental shelf for the time being.[121]

In addition to the above, the BBNJ Agreement should also have a discernible impact on the cooperation and coherence between these various bodies and their respective arrangements (although such extent will vary, with OSPAR standing to be most affected), especially on the issues of standards, EIAs and area-based management tools (ABMTs).[122] These varying dynamics would likely complicate the decision-making processes at OSPAR and provide an indication that it may require more effort to take bold and ambitious steps to address seabed mining at OSPAR (in comparison to HELCOM, for example). It would therefore be very interesting to see how these regimes would evolve and respond to the theme of seabed mining, especially in the case of OSPAR. Finally, even though the positions on seabed mining that parties take in regional seas conventions are not necessarily the same as their respective positions at the ISA, the evolution of and developments that occur within the regional seas conventions could send impulses to and have implications on seabed mining in the Area, which will be discussed next.

The position of the European Union on seabed mining and recent developments in areas beyond national jurisdiction

Position of the European Union on seabed mining

Although the EU has not been very explicit on this matter, there appears to have been a discernible shift in terms of the position of the EU with respect to seabed mining in recent years. Between the early 2000s and early 2010s, the EU seemed to be supportive of these activities. This seemingly pro-mining inclination can be gleaned from, among others, the EU's interests in 'access to and affordability of mineral raw materials (that) are crucial for the sound functioning of the EU's economy' as expressed in 2008,[123] and promoting blue growth in the EU by 'assessing how European industry can become competitive in extracting minerals from the seafloor' as expressed in 2012,[124] as well as through the funding regulatory capacity-building projects such as the SPC-EU Deep

119 The situation of France in this respect is a unique one compared to the others (as Belgium, Germany and the UK's current seabed mineral interests are all located in the Area). French interests are primarily in seabed minerals outside of OSPAR jurisdiction, namely, minerals located on the continental shelves of French overseas territories, as well as in the Area.

120 See the national section of Portugal in this book. M. Neves and P. Madureira, 'Portugal and seabed mining', in V. Tassin Campanella (ed.), *Routledge handbook of seabed mining and the law of the sea*, op. cit., chapter VI.2.13.

121 Royal Decree 218/2022 on 29 March 2022 (modifying Royal Decree 79/2019 of 22 February 2019), entered into force on 13 April 2022, Preamble, h) endorsing the call of the EU parliament under the 2030 Biodiversity Strategy. The scope of this so-called prohibition is limited to the continental shelf of Spain according to article 6, paragraph 2, on the Law of the Protection of the Marine Environment, 41/2010 of 29 December 2010, as referred to in Royal Decree article 3, paragraph 3.

122 Indeed, there is a provision in the BBNJ Agreement related to high seas pockets; see article 21, para 4.

123 Communication from the Commission to the European Parliament and the Council, 'The raw materials initiative – meeting our critical needs for growth and jobs in Europe' (COM(2008) 699 final), 4 November 2008.

124 Communication from the Commission to the European Parliament, the Council, the European Economic and Social Committee and the Committee of the Regions, 'Blue Growth opportunities for marine and maritime sustainable growth' (COM(2012) 494 final), 13 September 2012.

Sea Minerals Project (initiated in 2011).[125] However, the mid-2010s exhibited a marked shift in the EU's positioning, whereby there has evidently been more circumspection and hesitance in subsequent outputs. This cautious attitude and support for the application of the precautionary principle can be observed via, among others, the 2014 ACP-EU Joint Parliamentary Resolution on Mining for Seabed Minerals,[126] the 2018 EU Parliament Resolution on international ocean governance calling for an international moratorium on commercial-scale seabed mining for the first time within the EU institutions,[127] the Commission's 2020 EU Biodiversity Strategy for 2030[128] and the related EU Biodiversity Strategy Parliament Resolution in June 2021,[129] as well as the recently revised EU International Ocean Governance Agenda in June 2022.[130]

The 2018 EU Parliament Resolution called on MS to stop sponsoring deep-sea mining exploration and exploitation licenses in the Area and not to issue permits for seabed mining on the continental shelf.[131] It also called on MS to support an international moratorium on commercial seabed mining exploitation licences until 'such time as the effects of (seabed mining) on the marine environment, biodiversity and human activities at sea have been studied and researched sufficiently and all possible risks are understood'.[132] Following this call, the scope of this moratorium has fluctuated at the EU between the one proposed by the Commission under the EU Biodiversity Strategy,[133] which is limited to the Area, and the one recently adopted by the Parliament, again covering both the continental shelf and the Area.[134] The recently revised EU International Ocean Governance agenda seems to also target both the continental shelf and the Area, although this is not explicitly specified.[135] While it does not mention the word 'moratorium', reference is made to the recent IUCN resolution adopted in September 2021 calling for one.[136] Moreover, the instrument

125 SPC-EU Deep Sea Minerals Project. More information available online <https://dsm.gsd.spc.int/> (accessed 24 December 2021). For more information on the position of the Pacific region towards seabed mining, see C. Diver€he Pacific Islands region and seabed mining', in V. Tassin Campanella (ed.), *Routledge handbook of seabed mining and the law of the sea*, op. cit., chapter VI.1.5.

126 ACP-EU Joint Parliamentary Assembly Resolution on mining for oil and minerals on the seabed in the context of sustainable development (ACP-EU/101.546/14/fin), 2 October 2014.

127 European Parliament Resolution on international ocean governance: an agenda for the future of our oceans in the context of the 2030 SDGs (2017/2055(INI)) (P8_TA(2018)0004), 16 January 2018.

128 European Commission, EU Biodiversity Strategy for 2030: Bringing nature back into our lives, COM(2020) 380 final, 20 May 2020.

129 European Parliament Resolution on the EU Biodiversity Strategy for 2030: Bringing nature back into our lives (2020/2273(INI)) (P9_TA(2021)0277), 9 June 2021.

130 Joint Communication to the European Parliament, the Council, the European Economic and Social Committee and the Committee Of The Regions, Setting the course for a sustainable blue planet – Joint Communication on the EU's International Ocean Governance agenda, JOIN(2022) 28 final, 24 June 2022.

131 Paragraph 40, (2017/2055(INI)) (P8_TA(2018)0004), op. cit.

132 Paragraph 42, ibid.

133 Section 4.2.1 at pp. 20–21, COM(2020) 380 final, op. cit.

134 As follows: 'calls on the Commission and the Member States to promote a moratorium, including at the International Seabed Authority, on deep-sea mining until such time as the effects of deep-sea mining on the marine environment, biodiversity and human activities at sea have been studied and researched sufficiently and deep sea mining can be managed to ensure no marine biodiversity loss nor degradation of marine ecosystems; emphasises the need for the Commission to cease funding for the development of deep-sea mining technology in line with a circular economy based on minimising, reusing and recycling minerals and metals'. Paragraph 184, (2020/2273(INI)) (P9_TA(2021)0277), op. cit.

135 See in the same way the EU Parliament Resolution, *Momentum for the ocean: strengthening ocean governance and biodiversity*, 2022/2836(RSP), 6 October 2022, paragraph 6.

136 JOIN(2022) 28 final, op. cit., at footnote 15 on p. 4. The said Motion 069 (protection of deep-ocean ecosystems and biodiversity through a moratorium on seabed mining) was passed at the IUCN World Conservation

does appear to adopt similar, if not stronger, terminology, including that the EU will 'continue to advocate for prohibiting deep-sea mining' until such time where existing scientific gaps are closed and it is possible to demonstrate that no harmful effects arise from mining.[137] This is a sharp contrast to the previous version of the International Ocean Governance agenda that was released in 2016,[138] which barely made any reference to seabed mining.[139] Consequently, there seems to be inconsistencies within EU institutions on the position that it should advocate on seabed mining on the continental shelf, although the position on the need for a moratorium on commercial-scale exploitation in the Area has always been clear. In this respect, however, it would seem that recent efforts are slowly and subtly seeking to streamline the EU's position pertaining to seabed mining on both the continental shelf and the Area.

Such shifting positions or changes in scope of coverage could probably be explained by tensions between the EU institutions with, on the one hand, (1) MS that are keen on exploring and possibly eventually exploiting the mineral resources of their own continental shelves and may also wish to take a similarly consistent position in the Area, as well as (2) those MS whose seabed mining interests lie exclusively in the Area, and (3) MS that do not currently possess any serious interests in seabed mining but would like to keep their options open for the future, or (4) those that may instead wish to limit their present involvement through the development and sale of mining equipment, technologies or vessels and other services to industry. On the other hand, potential friction and environmental concerns could also arise with (1) some MS with known abundant seabed mineral resources on their continental shelves, which have or are in the process of taking a more cautious approach to seabed mining within national jurisdiction, as well as (2) MS that do not have significant seabed mineral resource prospects on their continental shelves or current stakes in the Area, or (3) those MS that are landlocked or geographically disadvantaged and are concerned about the implications of seabed mining, that could actually harbor the desire to see a similarly cautious approach to seabed mining be replicated in the Area.

In any event, it can be surmised that while the need to ensure secure supply chains for critical metals still appears to be on the agenda of the EU,[140] especially in the light of ongoing geopolitical

Congress with overwhelming support and adopted as Resolution 122, which can be found on the IUCN website <https://portals.iucn.org/library/sites/library/files/resrecfiles/WCC_2020_RES_122_EN.pdf> (accessed 18 August 2022).

137 Ibid., pp. 4–5: 'On deep seabed mining, there is a broad consensus in the scientific community and among States that knowledge related to deep-sea environment and the impacts of mining are not comprehensive enough to enable evidence-based decision-making to allow for proceeding safely with exploitation. The EU will continue to advocate for prohibiting deep-sea mining until these scientific gaps are properly filled, that it can be demonstrated that no harmful effects arise from mining and, as required under the UNCLOS, the necessary provisions in the exploitation regulations for the effective protection of the marine environment are in place. The EU will continue to contribute to the negotiations of the exploitation regulations at the International Seabed Authority (ISA) to achieve a robust framework for marine environment protection, including standards and guidelines for threshold values and normative standards. In parallel, the EU is supporting research to improve knowledge on deep sea ecosystems and on monitoring and supervising technologies'.

138 Joint Communication to the European Parliament, the Council, the European Economic and Social Committee and the Committee of the Regions, International ocean governance: an agenda for the future of our oceans, JOIN(2016) 49 final, 10 November 2016.

139 That said, it is interesting to note that the instrument mentions on page 2 that: 'By 2018, the Commission will produce guidance on the exploration and exploitation of natural resources on the seabed in areas under national jurisdiction, to assist coastal Member States respect their duty under UNCLOS to protect and preserve the marine environment'.

140 COM(2008) 699 and COM(2012) 494 respectively, op. cit.

tensions, internal conflicts and war (and how these events could significantly affect the security of supply of critical metals to the EU),[141] the EU's current attitude towards seabed mining in the Area appears to be more cautious, supportive of a strong interpretation of the precautionary principle, and favouring the need to be satisfied that the effective protection of the marine environment can be assured before allowing commercial-scale mining to commence.

The role of the European Union at the International Seabed Authority

A 2021 proposal for an EU Council Decision[142] demonstrates that the EU is willing to develop a new and more effective way of contributing and exercising its internal and external[143] competences within the ISA. To do so, this proposal suggests adopting a common EU position for meetings of the ISA Council and Assembly. This position should be based on a two-tier approach and follow guiding principles and orientations, elaborated ahead by the European Council, which will then be implemented and adjusted for each meeting via non-papers prepared by the Commission and discussed by a 'Council Working Party'. The proposal comprises a strong focus on the protection of the marine environment, adherence to the precautionary principle and the ecosystem-based approach, and reliance on best available science. It also states that the EU 'should advocate that marine minerals in the international seabed area cannot be exploited before the effects of deep-sea mining on the marine environment, biodiversity and human activities have been sufficiently researched, the risks are understood and the technologies and operational practices are able to demonstrate no serious harm to the environment, in line with the precautionary approach'.[144] In reality, this could carry significant consequences, especially since a number of MS are on the ISA Council and could directly influence ISA rule-making and decision-making.[145] Preliminary exchanges seem to indicate that the proposal as it stands is not acceptable to some MS. Owing to the differing interests and positions of its MS with respect to seabed mining in the Area, it does not appear, at least in the near future, that the EU will be able to form and sustain a strong, united voice at the ISA.

Meanwhile, the EU is actively involved in the current work of the ISA. For instance, between 2020 and 2021, the EU submitted written comments in response to the calls for stakeholder input to ten sets of draft standards and guidelines for exploitation issued by the Legal and Technical Commission of the ISA.[146] The EU has also partnered with the ISA on the organization of environmental-related workshops in the past, for example, the Workshop on the Regional Environmental Management Plan (REMP) for the Area of the Northern Mid-Atlantic Ridge through the EU-funded Atlantic REMP Project. The EU has furthermore funded numerous multi-million research projects related to seabed mining, including co-funding the ISA's recently

141 See for example, K. Taylor, 'No green and digital transition without raw materials, EU warns', EURACTIV, 26 April 2022 <https://www.euractiv.com/section/circular-economy/news/no-green-and-digital-transition-without-raw-materials-eu-warns/> (accessed 1 June 2022).

142 Based on article 191 and article 218 (2), TFEU.

143 Article 3 (2), ibid.

144 Annex I to the Proposal for a Council decision on the position to be taken on behalf of the European Union at the meetings of the ISA Council and Assembly (COM(2021) 1), 5 January 2021.

145 The six MS in the 2022 composition of the Council are Czech Republic, France, Germany, Italy, the Netherlands and Poland.

146 See more information on the website of the ISA <https://www.isa.org.jm/submissions-received-respect-stakeholder-consultations-standards-and-guidelines> (accessed 22 December 2021).

launched Sustainable Seabed Knowledge Initiative (SSKI),[147] while some future projects have also been announced.[148]

Contribution of the European Union to the negotiations on biodiversity beyond national jurisdiction

The recently concluded negotiations on the BBNJ Agreement[149] allowed the EU an opportunity to voice its position for the standards of biological conservation and sustainable use to be applied to the Area. Considering the limitations faced by the EU within the ISA and the lack of clear EU regulations applicable for seabed mining in the Area, this opportunity was very much welcomed.

The EU took an active interest in this topic and was strongly engaged in the negotiations.[150] Since 2006, it made extensive contributions on ABMTs and EIA, particularly cumulative and transboundary ones.[151] Consistent with its internal regulations, the EU supported the strengthening of the ecosystem approach within the BBNJ Agreement. During the course of the negotiations, the EU made two significant proposals: (1) include, into the consultation mechanism of the BBNJ Agreement, the case of States with a continental shelf subjacent to a marine protected area placed in areas beyond national jurisdiction (promoting in this way the coherent management of deep seabed between areas *within* and *beyond* national jurisdiction);[152] and (2) under the topic of transboundary EIA, include the obligation according to which UNCLOS State Parties shall ensure that impacts in areas *within* national jurisdiction (so outside of the scope of the BBNJ Agreement, but under the scope of EU law for MS of the EU) will be taken into account when conducting EIA within the scope of the BBNJ Agreement.[153]

The BBNJ Agreement[154] includes both proposals with a stronger recognition of the ecosystem approach distilled throughout the EIA legal regime. The objectives of this regime expressly support the consideration of cumulative impacts and impacts in areas *within* national jurisdiction. While the term 'transboundary impact assessment' has been removed from the EIA legal regime,[155] the concept remains applicable. As a result, a State Party wishing to conduct a planned activity, under its jurisdiction or control *within* national jurisdiction, which may cause substantial pollution or significant and harmful changes to the marine environment in areas *beyond* national jurisdiction, is now under the obligation to ensure the conduct of an EIA in accordance with

147 See ISA website <https://www.isa.org.jm/sski> (accessed 18 August 2022): 'Launched at the 2022 UN Ocean Conference, SSKI will describe over one thousand new species from the regions of the Area that are currently being explored for mineral resources and may be targeted for future exploitation'.

148 For an overview, see Annex II of Seas at Risk, *At a crossroads: Europe's role in deep-sea mining*, 2021, pp. 25–26.

149 Intergovernmental conference on an international legally binding instrument under the United Nations Convention on the Law of the Sea on the conservation and sustainable use of marine biological diversity of areas beyond national jurisdiction. References made to this implementing agreement of UNCLOS are as 'BBNJ Agreement'.

150 See T. Heidar, 'Introduction', in A. de Paiva Toledo and V.J.M. Tassin (eds) *Guide to the navigation of marine biodiversity beyond national jurisdiction*, Belo Horizonte: Editora D'Placido, 2018, pp. 39–55.

151 Based on its own experience of cumulative and transboundary EIA within the EU marine space.

152 *Proposal submitted by delegations by 20 February 2020 for consideration at the fourth session*, A/CONF.232/2020/3, article 18 (European Union and its members), p. 168.

153 Ibid., article 26 (European Union and its members), p. 245.

154 General Assembly of the United Nations, *Agreement under the United Nations Convention on the Law of the Sea on the conservation and sustainable use of marine biological diversity of areas beyond national jurisdiction*, June 2023. Hereinafter 'BBNJ Agreement'.

155 It only remains in Annex I together with cumulative impacts. Annex I is however only applicable to the identification of areas according to Part III.

the BBNJ Agreement or its national process.[156] Other references to this *de facto* transboundary impact assessment are also included into the BBNJ Agreement's thresholds and factors to consider for EIA screening[157] and the process of the EIA (scoping, assessment and evaluation).[158] Finally, the consultation process applicable to EIAs in the BBNJ Agreement includes an obligation for States to 'give particular regard to comments concerning potential impacts in areas within national jurisdiction and provide written responses, as appropriate, specifically addressing such comments, including regarding any additional measures meant to address those potential impacts'.[159]

With regard to ABMTs, the ecosystem approach has been translated into a consultation mechanism with the coastal State in the case of establishment of any of these tools in the waters above the continental shelf.[160] This consultation will however only be triggered in cases where the ABMT 'would affect or could reasonably be expected to affect the superjacent waters above the seabed and subsoil' under which the coastal State exercises its sovereign rights. Considering the sensitivities regarding sovereign rights, it is very likely that this consultation process will be regularly triggered.

The ambition of the EU in the promotion of the ecosystem approach could, however, appear inconsistent at first sight. During the course of the negotiations, the EU indeed supported the view that the BBNJ Agreement should exclude instances where planned activities in areas beyond national jurisdiction are conducted where 'relevant legal instruments and frameworks, and relevant global, regional, sub-regional or sectoral bodies' have mandates for EIA.[161] This scenario, embodied in a more sophisticated way into the BBNJ Agreement,[162] can be seen to promote a multi-gear system and therefore create potential weaknesses in the implementation and cracks into its ambition. As concerns the EU, this can be reconciled by the fact that the EU is intending to develop its own standards and thresholds for projects, plans and programmes of seabed mining in the Area (through for example the EIA/SEA Directives), which will thus be applicable to its own MS, on the top of BBNJ and ISA obligations.

Conclusion

The genesis of the EU as it features today can be traced back to early efforts to foster peace among European countries that were once fierce rivals through economic cooperation, namely, through the creation of a common market for two commodities, coal and steel. While the original ambition to create a single market and customs union has significantly evolved over the years into an elaborate and expansive regime, it is interesting to observe that seabed mining returns the EU to the theme of commodities again, this time with respect to the potential of extracting marine minerals in the quest to retrieve valuable metals. Simultaneously, while the initial impetus was premised on economic interests, the EU has now grown and developed a strong focus on environmental and biodiversity protection and conservation, including over the ocean space. This is particularly visible with respect to implementation of numerous legislations covering marine areas under national

156 Obligation to conduct environmental impact assessment, article 28, paragraph 2, BBNJ Agreement.

157 Article 30, para 2, (e). Ibid.

158 Article 31, (b) and (c). Ibid.

159 Article 32, para 5. Ibid.

160 Article 19, para 6. Ibid.

161 Regardless of whether or not an EIA is required for the planned activity under the jurisdiction or control of a State Party. See comments of the EU on article 23, ibid., p. 224.

162 Article 29, para 4, BBNJ Agreement, op. cit.

jurisdiction of MS, including the continental shelf and extended continental shelf, which are subject to mining interests. However, the regulatory frameworks covering offshore activities remain incomplete as things currently stand, as these frameworks largely relate to oil and gas activities and are yet to be specifically extended to seabed mining of minerals for the most part. Beyond the national jurisdiction of MS, greater uncertainties also exist in relation to the application of the main EU directives that are relevant for mineral exploration and exploitation that are conducted or sponsored by MS in the Area. Consequently, it is clear that the theme of seabed mining demonstrates the uniqueness and complexity of governance at the EU level, with the EU possessing competences (whether exclusive or shared) on a wide range of matters over its MS on the one hand, as well as being a contracting party to numerous multilateral agreements in its own right and using this to implement its treaty obligations affecting its MS (and potentially interacting with their sovereignty and national interests) on the other hand.

In any case, the ambition of the EU for a healthy and productive ocean obviously extends well beyond EU marine space. The EU's International Ocean Governance Agenda, first adopted in 2016[163] and recently revised in 2022,[164] seeks to give effect to the UN Sustainable Development Goals (in particular, SDG 14) by supporting global efforts to ensure the effective protection of the environment and the conservation of biodiversity in all marine spaces, including in areas beyond national jurisdiction. This political agenda, alongside other international parallel developments (such as the post-2020 Global Biodiversity Framework under the 1992 Convention of Biological Diversity and the ongoing 2021–2030 UN Decade of Ocean Science for Sustainable Development), continues to guide the EU to protect the marine environment, promote sustainable uses of the seas and conserve marine biodiversity. Moreover, the EU's International Ocean Governance Agenda is not only designed to implement Agenda 2030 and international law as reflected in UNCLOS;[165] it is first and foremost an instrument of the new EU blue diplomacy developed to 'shape international ocean governance on the basis of (EU) experience'.[166] Applied to seabed mining of minerals, while the EU legal framework appears to be the most advanced in terms of regional regulations, the EU still has a long road to make before becoming a role model. That said, the efforts and steps taken by the EU, both internally and externally (including by contributing towards the work of the ISA and at the BBNJ negotiations), carry significant weight and are crucial in determining the fate of seabed mining, at the very least, insofar as they relate to the EU and bind the MS.

163 JOIN(2016) 49 final, op. cit.

164 JOIN(2022) 28 final, op. cit.

165 See sustainable development goal 14 c). General Assembly, *Transforming our world: the 2030 agenda for sustainable development*, A/RES/70/1, 25 September 2015.

166 'The EU is well placed to shape international ocean governance on the basis of its experience in developing sustainable approach to ocean management, notably through its environment policy (in particular its Marine Strategy Framework Directive), integrated maritime policy (in particular its Marine Spatial Planning Directive), reformed common fisheries policy, action against illegal, unregulated and unreported (IUU) fishing and its maritime transport policy': JOIN(216) 49 Final, op. cit., paragraph 1.2, p. 4. See also JOIN(2022) 28 final, op. cit., p. 4: 'The EU believes that leading by example can inspire progress and help create a shared vision for developing a sustainable approach to ocean management worldwide and recognises that true leadership starts at home'.

VI.1.5
THE PACIFIC ISLANDS REGION AND SEABED MINING

Cameron Diver

Introduction

The Pacific Islands region, also known as Oceania, is a vast oceanscape, generally accepted as covering the Micronesia, Melanesia and Polynesia sub-regions and, for the purposes of this chapter, includes the following 23 Pacific Island Countries and Territories: American Samoa, the Cook Islands, the Federated States of Micronesia, Fiji, French Polynesia, Guam, Kiribati, the Marshall Islands, Nauru, New Caledonia, New Zealand, Niue, the Northern Mariana Islands, Palau, Papua New Guinea, the Pitcairn Islands, Samoa, the Solomon Islands, Tokelau, Tonga, Tuvalu, Vanuatu and Wallis and Futuna. Whilst bordering the region and having significant interactions with its Pacific Island neighbours, Australia is conventionally excluded from the cultural and geographical definitions of Oceania.[1]

Regional cooperation and integration have been a feature of international relations in Oceania, in particular in the aftermath of World War II which saw the establishment of the region's first intergovernmental organisation, the South Pacific Commission (today known as the Pacific Community and by the acronym SPC) in 1947 by the then colonial powers Australia, France, the Netherlands, New Zealand, the United Kingdom and the United States of America. Since that time, many Pacific Islands gained independence[2] and, to meet the needs expressed by these States in their relations with each other and their partners, additional international organisations have emerged in the region, such as the Pacific Islands Forum (PIF) in 1971, the Forum Fisheries Agency (FFA) in 1979 and the Pacific Regional Environment Programme (SPREP) in 1993. In addition, as 'large ocean States',[3] all of the independent Pacific Island countries have ratified the *1982 United Nations Convention on the Law of the Sea* (UNCLOS).

1 F.J. West and S. Foster, 'Pacific Islands', *Encyclopedia Britannica*, 17 November 2020, Available online <https://www.britannica.com/place/Pacific-Islands> (accessed 26 August 2021).

2 Samoa gained independence on 1 January 1962, Nauru on 31 January 1968, Tonga on 4 June 1970, Fiji on 10 October 1970, Papua New Guinea on 16 September 1975, the Solomon Islands on 7 July 1978, Tuvalu on 1 October 1978, Kiribati on 12 July 1979, Vanuatu on 30 July 1980, the Marshall Islands on 21 October 1986, the Federated States of Micronesia on 3 November 1986, Palau on 1 October 1994.

3 This turn of phrase is often attributed to the former President of Palau, Tommy E. Remengesau Jr., who first used it to describe his country at the 2016 Congress of the International Union for the Conservation of Nature (IUCN). Since then and by extension it is now often used by other Small Island States with significant exclusive economic zones

DOI: 10.4324/9780429426162-26

The ocean is not only at the heart of the Pacific Islands' geography but also their shared ambition for sustainable development. Today, this vision is expressed through the 'Blue Pacific' as a vector for the countries of Oceania to harness the potential of their shared stewardship of the Pacific Ocean based on an explicit recognition of their shared ocean identity, ocean geography and ocean resources.[4] To deliver on the promise of the Blue Pacific, the leaders of PIF Member States have explicitly recognised the need 'to protect the health and resilience of the ocean and its resources'.[5] In this context, seabed mining of minerals is a divisive issue. The Pacific Ocean's considerable deposits of seabed minerals are viewed by some as a 'potential treasure trove',[6] a source of economic opportunity, employment and development. Others view seabed mining as a threat to sustainable development whose projected economic benefit[7] is offset by the lack of scientific knowledge on the effects it may have on the marine environment, deep sea and coastal ecosystems,[8] together with other economic activities (such as tourism) which make significant contributions to the gross domestic product (GDP) of Pacific Island nations. This situation has led to a number of regional initiatives to understand the impacts of seabed mining. In addition, Pacific Island countries, supported by regional and intergovernmental organisations, have produced a series of world-leading regional frameworks for such activities within areas under national jurisdiction in Oceania. However, there is currently no regional consensus on seabed mining and no formal, binding framework adopted by all Pacific Island countries to regulate exploration and exploitation of seabed minerals. This chapter aims to present those frameworks and the current challenges to crystallising a truly whole-of-region approach to seabed mining.

Geographical extent of the exclusive economic zones and continental shelves

The Pacific Islands region could easily be described as a 'Blue Continent': 23 countries and territories made up of 800,000 square kilometres of land[9] and around 30,569,000 square kilometres of exclusive economic zones (EEZs).[10] All Pacific Island countries are coastal States and, for the purposes of this chapter, the region's geographical extent includes areas under the national

to highlight the dichotomy between the size of their respective land mass and population and that of their exclusive economic zones.

4 Further information on what the 'Blue Pacific' is and on the development of the 2050 Strategy for the Blue Pacific Continent can be found via the following link. Available online <https://www.forumsec.org/2050strategy/> (accessed 18 January 2022).

5 Fifty-First Pacific Islands Forum, 6 August 2021, Forum Communiqué, paragraph 8.

6 R. Makgill and A.P. Linhares, 'Deep Seabed Mining: Key Obligations in the Emerging Regulation of Exploration and Development in the Pacific', in R. Warner and S. Kay (eds.), *Routledge Handbook of Maritime Regulation and Enforcement*, Taylor & Francis, 2016, p. 231.

7 As an illustration, a 2016 study commissioned by the Pacific Community estimated the net economic benefit from seabed mining could be: Papua New Guinea (seafloor-massive sulphides) USD 82.7 million; Cook Islands (manganese nodules) USD 467 million. See Cardno, *An Assessment of the Costs and Benefits of Mining Deep-Sea Minerals in the Pacific Island Region*, The Pacific Community (SPC), 2016, p. xvii.

8 'Fiji calls for sea-bed mining moratorium as Nautilus restructures', *Islands Business*, 14 August 2019. Available online <https://islandsbusiness.com/news-break/fiji-calls-for-sea-bed-mining-moratorium-as-nautilus-restructures/> (accessed 26 August 2021).

9 Of which New Zealand and Papua New Guinea make up around 90% of the total: See West and Foster, op. cit.

10 R.D. Gillet, 'B16. Pacific Islands Region', *FAO Fisheries Technical Paper 457, Review of the State of World Marine Fishery Resources*, 2005, p. 144. Available online <http://www.fao.org/3/y5852e/Y5852E16.pdf> (accessed 26 August 2021).

jurisdiction of the 23 Pacific Island countries and territories listed in the introduction, together with those expanses of high seas surrounding such areas and generally accepted to fall within the Western and Central Pacific Ocean.

While all Pacific Island countries have claimed an EEZ within the framework defined by UNCLOS there are 48 shared or overlapping maritime boundaries between countries in the region. Of these, 35 have been successfully negotiated and maritime boundary treaties concluded[11] and 13 remain to be agreed and signed.[12] Five Pacific Island countries have also yet to formally deposit their EEZ limits.[13] In addition, several Pacific Island countries are undertaking technical review and verification of their maritime boundary limits on the basis of new and improved data sets and new deposits to the United Nations and updates to domestic legislation may be forthcoming to reflect any amendments. It should also be noted that, at the 2021 Pacific Islands Forum, leaders of PIF Member States adopted a ground-breaking declaration on preserving maritime zones in the face of climate change-related sea-level rise.[14] This normative declaration provides a regional position on maintaining maritime zones established in accordance with UNCLOS and proclaims that 'the rights and entitlements that flow from them, shall continue to apply, without reduction, notwithstanding any physical changes connected to climate change-related sea-level rise'.[15]

As regards extended continental shelf (ECS) claims, in 2009 ten Pacific Island countries submitted preliminary claims concerning 17 areas to the United Nations Commission on the Limits of the Continental Shelf (CLCS). As of writing, only one submission from the region has received recommendations from the CLCS[16] leaving 16 ECS submissions at varying stages awaiting examination once full claims are lodged with the CLCS, including all required data.[17]

As a consequence, while a considerable amount of work has been accomplished to establish maritime boundaries and secure sovereignty and sovereign rights over such areas and their resources, there remains a degree of uncertainty today around the limits of areas under national jurisdiction in the Pacific Islands Region. This situation complicates matters as regards seabed mining and

11 However, of these signed treaties 11 have not yet entered into force or require confirmation that they have entered into force: Solomon Islands–Papua New Guinea; Federated States of Micronesia–Papua New Guinea; Tuvalu–France (Wallis and Futuna); Kiribati–Tuvalu; Kiribati–Nauru; Fiji–Tuvalu; Fiji–France (Wallis and Futuna); Marshall Islands–Kiribati; Marshall Islands–Kiribati–Nauru; Vanuatu–Solomon Islands.

12 The 13 remaining shared boundaries for which negotiations are yet to be concluded are: Tonga–Niue; Tonga–Samoa; Tonga–United States of America (American Samoa); Fiji–Solomon Islands; Vanuatu–France (New Caledonia); Samoa–United States of America (American Samoa); Palau–Philippines; Palau–Indonesia; Fiji–Tonga; Fiji–Vanuatu; Samoa–France (Wallis and Futuna); Samoa–New Zealand (Tokelau); Marshall Islands–United States of America (Wake Island).

13 Palau, Solomon Islands, Vanuatu, Tonga, Tokelau (New Zealand).

14 Declaration made on 6 August 2021 at the 51st Pacific Islands Forum by Australia, the Cook Islands, the Federated States of Micronesia, Fiji, French Polynesia, Kiribati, Nauru, New Caledonia, New Zealand, Niue, Palau, Papua New Guinea, the Republic of the Marshall Islands, Samoa, Solomon Islands, Tonga, Tuvalu and Vanuatu. Available online <https://www.forumsec.org/2021/08/11/declaration-on-preserving-maritime-zones-in-the-face-of-climate-change-related-sea-level-rise/> (accessed 30 August 2021).

15 Ibid.

16 The Ontong Java Plateau joint submission by the Federated States of Micronesia, Papua, New Guinea and the Solomon Islands for over 600,000 square kilometres of additional seabed. Recommendations from the CLCS in 2019.

17 The author would like to acknowledge the generous assistance of the Pacific Community's (SPC) Pacific Maritime Boundaries team which kindly provided much of the information contained in this paragraph, based on data from SPC's ongoing Pacific Maritime Boundaries Project.

Table VI.1.5.1 Pacific Island extended continental shelf claims

No.	*Pacific Island ECS Claims*	*Claimant Countries*
1	Ontong Java Plateau	FSM, Solomon Islands, PNG
2	Eauripik Rise	FSM, PNG, Tuvalu
3	Mussau Ridge	FSM, PNG
4	Charlotte Banks	Solomon Islands, Fiji
5	North Fiji Basin	Solomon Islands, Fiji, Vanuatu
6	Renell Ridge	Solomon Islands
7	South Fiji Basin – Lau Ridge-Northern	Fiji
8	Western Platform Area	Kiribati
9	Eastern Platform Area	Kiribati
10	Central Area	Kiribati
11	South Area	Kiribati
12	Manihiki Plateau	Cook Islands
13	Eastern Part of Kermadic Ridge	Tonga
14	Western Part of Lau-Colville Ridge	Tonga
15	South East Area	Palau
16	West Area	Palau
17	North Area	Palau

Note: FSM, Federated States of Micronesia; PNG, Papua New Guinea.
The author would like to acknowledge the generous assistance of the Pacific Community's (SPC) Pacific Maritime Boundaries team which kindly provided much of the information contained in this table;, based on data from SPC's ongoing Pacific Maritime Boundaries Project

potential requests for exploration or exploitation permits within and beyond areas under national jurisdiction, as, due to the number of maritime boundary treaties yet to enter into force or be concluded, together with the unresolved ECS claims, there are numerous zones with no absolute legal certainty as to the outer limits of EEZs or ECSs and areas of seabed which may be part of the Area.[18]

Governance and regulation of seabed mining activities

Pacific Island countries, supported by intergovernmental and regional organisations, have made considerable efforts at regional level to provide governance and regulatory frameworks for seabed mining activities. As early as 1999, Pacific Island countries had adopted, at regional level, a series of principles to guide the development of national offshore minerals policies. The 'Madang Guidelines'[19] contained 19 recommendations designed to assist Pacific Island governments develop effective national policy and legislative regimes to govern offshore mineral activities.

18 The Area is defined at article 1(1) of the United Nations Convention on the Law of the Sea as 'the seabed and ocean floor and subsoil thereof, beyond the limits of national jurisdiction'. For more information on the related impacts on the rights and obligations of States, see in this book V. Tassin Campanella, Y. Cissé and D. Tladi, 'State Rights and Obligations of States on the Continental Shelf and the Area', in V. Tassin Campanella (ed.), *Routledge Handbook of Seabed Mining and the Law of the Sea*, London: Routledge, 2023, chapter II.1. See also Ø. Jensen and B. Már Magnússon, 'The Extension of Sovereign Rights Beyond 200 Nautical Miles', in V. Tassin Campanella (ed.), idem, chapter III.1.

19 *The Madang Guidelines: Principles for the Development of National Offshore Mineral Policies*, SOPAC Miscellaneous Report 362, December 1999

The Guidelines also recognised, alongside the pioneering nature of any exploration and exploitation activities, the need to anticipate and appropriately manage environmental impacts, diverse stakeholder interests and, importantly for the Pacific region, the potential impact of such activities on fisheries. They also sought to address the often-complex relationship between government, industry and marine scientific research.

The Pacific-ACP States Regional Legislative and Regulatory Framework for Deep Sea Minerals Exploration and Exploitation[20] *– 2012*

Building on the Madang Guidelines and prepared under the Pacific Community (SPC)-European Union (EU) 10th European Development Fund (EDF10) Deep Sea Minerals Project,[21] the RLRF was, at the time of its launch at the 43rd Pacific Islands Forum in 2012, a world-first guide to policy and law development for seabed mining. The RLRF was welcomed by PIF Leaders who 'recommended that Forum Island Countries (FICs) consider using the Framework in formulating relevant national policy noting it highlights the need for a precautionary approach and addresses economic, social and environmental aspects to ensure sustainable resource use prevails'.[22]

The RLRF was designed to assist Pacific Island countries develop and enact national regulatory frameworks, taking into account their responsibility over areas under national jurisdiction together with duties as sponsoring States[23] for seabed mining activity in the Clarion Clipperton Zone.[24] Among other areas of focus, it covers the benefits of a regional approach (including a reminder of regional policy frameworks on the sustainable development, management and conservation of the ocean[25]), issues of legal rights to deep sea minerals, considerations relating to seabed mining policy at national level, and the international and regional legal obligations Pacific Island countries must take into account when deciding to open applications for seabed mining activities on its continental shelf.

As regards the latter, the RLRF underscores the obligations on States as regards seabed mining and its impacts under UNCLOS, the *1992 Convention on Biological Diversity* (CBD), international human rights instruments and general principles of international law in both areas under national jurisdiction and in the Area. It also includes consideration of the *1986 Convention for the*

20 Hereinafter 'RLRF'. Available online <https://dsm.gsd.spc.int/public/files/2014/RLRF2014.pdf> (accessed 31 August 2021).

21 See P. Singh, V. Tassin Campanella and F. Maes, 'The European Union and Seabed Mining', in V. Tassin Campanella (ed.), *Routledge Handbook of Seabed Mining and the Law of the Sea*, op. cit., chapter VI.1.4.

22 *Communiqué of the 43rd Pacific Islands Forum*, Rarotonga, Cook Islands, 28–30 August 2012, paragraph 5. Available online <http://www.forumsec.org/wp-content/uploads/2017/11/2012-Forum-Communique_-Rarotonga_-Cook-Islands-28-30-Aug.pdf> (accessed 31 August 2021).

23 As of writing, Nauru, Tonga, Kiribati and the Cook Islands have recognised seabed mining as an economic development opportunity and are sponsoring States in the Area.

24 The Clarion Clipperton Zone is located 100 nautical miles from the Line Islands EEZ of Kiribati and, at the time the RLRF was launched, the International Seabed Authority had approved 13 programmes of work in the CCZ of which three concerned 'Reserve Areas', which are reserved for developing countries to sponsor work programmes with private entities.

25 For example, the 'Pacific Islands Regional Ocean Policy and Framework for Integrated Strategic Action', 2002. Available online <https://www.forumsec.org/wp-content/uploads/2018/03/Pacific-Islands-Regional-Ocean-Policy-2002.pdf> (accessed 31 August 2021); and the 'Framework for a Pacific Oceanscape', 2010. Available online <https://www.forumsec.org/wp-content/uploads/2018/03/Framework-for-a-Pacific-Oceanscape-2010.pdf> (accessed 31 August 2021).

Protection of Natural Resources and the Environment of the South Pacific Region (the Noumea Convention) and its two protocols.[26] The Noumea Convention requires contracting Parties to prevent, reduce and control pollution in the Convention Area from any source and, in addition, to ensure sound environmental management and development of natural resources. Article 8 of the Convention provides specifically that 'Parties shall take all appropriate measures to prevent, reduce and control pollution in the Convention Area resulting directly or indirectly from exploration and exploitation of the seabed and its subsoil'.

The Pacific-ACP States Regional Environmental Management Framework for Deep Sea Minerals Exploration and Exploitation[27] *– 2016*

Four years after the Regional Legislative and Regulatory Framework for Deep Sea Minerals Exploration and Exploitation, SPC's Deep Sea Minerals Project published the REMF. This framework document contains an overview of deep sea mineral deposit environments and outlines potential environmental impacts of seabed mining projects, particularly within areas under national jurisdiction, together with management and mitigation strategies, including an environmental impact assessment report template. The REMF also highlights the need for decisions around seabed mining to be informed by science and society, as a means of ensuring effective environmental management practices and mechanisms. Like the RLRF, the REMF is designed as a guide to assist and inform the environmental components of seabed mining-related decision-making in Pacific Island countries.

The Pacific-ACP States Regional Financial Framework for Deep Sea Minerals Exploration and Exploitation[28] *– 2016*

2016 also saw the publication of the RFF, produced by SPC in collaboration with the Pacific Financial Technical Assistance Centre (PFTAC). The RFF provides an overview of key issues in the financial management of revenues and wealth associated with the potential development of deep sea minerals in the region. It contains, for information and use by Pacific Island countries, elements of a seabed mining fiscal management framework, design of a seabed mining revenue regime, recommendations on public financial management and the accompanying fiscal policy framework and guidance on seabed mining wealth management, including sovereign wealth funds.

The Pacific-ACP States Regional Scientific Research Guidelines for Deep Sea Minerals[29] *–2016*

The RSRG was the final set of seabed mining guidelines produced at regional level in 2016. Developed by SPC in collaboration with the National Institute of Water and Atmospheric Research (NIWA) of New Zealand, it expressly recognises that 'ocean policy and management is best imple-

26 Available online <https://www.sprep.org/convention-secretariat/noumea-convention> (accessed 31 August 2021).

27 Hereinafter 'REMF'. Available online <http://dsm.gsd.spc.int/images/public_files_2016/REMF2016.pdf> (accessed 31 August 2021).

28 Hereinafter 'RFF'. Available online <http://dsm.gsd.spc.int/images/public_files_2016/RFF2016.pdf> (accessed 31 August 2021)

29 Hereinafter 'RSRG'. Available online <https://dsm.gsd.spc.int/images/public_files_2016/RSRG2016.pdf> (accessed 31 August 2021).

mented when adequately informed by science'.[30] In addition, it underscores the pressing need for strong scientific research to inform decision-making on seabed mining. Recognising that many Pacific Island countries may not have the capacity to perform such research, the RSRG positions itself as a regional tool that provides key legal and science considerations that are essential to manage requests to conduct scientific research related to seabed mining within areas under national jurisdiction.

The RSRG focuses on the three deep sea mineral resources of greatest commercial interest in the region, namely manganese nodules, seafloor massive sulphides, and cobalt-rich crusts and contains scientific and regulatory guidelines for establishing national standards and regulations for marine scientific research, prospecting and exploration activities relating to seabed mining. It includes detailed information on current 'best practice' research techniques, covering aspects of survey design, sampling gear and the collection and processing of samples and data.

It should be noted that all the aforementioned Guidelines and Frameworks are non-binding. As such, whilst they inform decisions and policies on regulation of seabed mining activities, they cannot be considered constitutive of a legally binding regional governance mechanism for seabed mining. To fill that particular gap and further strengthen a region-wide approach, Pacific Island countries requested that SPC prepare a draft seabed mining treaty for consideration.

The Pacific Deep Sea Mining Agreement

Between 2015 and 2016, SPC (as the lead intergovernmental organisation on seabed mining issues in the Pacific region) consulted widely with Pacific Island countries and other stakeholders and developed a draft Regional Agreement for Cooperation among Pacific Island Countries and Territories to Support Responsible Deep Sea Mineral Management in the Pacific Region (the DSM Agreement).[31] The DSM Agreement was designed as a UNCLOS-compatible, binding international agreement to regulate cooperation between Parties, together with 'DSM activities'[32] and/or impacts within a defined 'DSM Zone'.[33]

While an exhaustive review of the DSM Agreement's provisions goes beyond the scope of this chapter, it is important to summarise some of its key provisions as an illustration of the Agreement's scope and intent to provide the Pacific region with a harmonised approach to the regulation of DSM activities:

Under article 4, paragraph 1, of the DSM Agreement, each Party agrees to take all appropriate measures, including where necessary the enactment and implementation of legislation, to ensure that any DSM activity licensed within national jurisdiction, and any installation it has authorised in connection with DSM activities, or any vessel used or intended to be used for DSM activities within the DSM Zone that is entitled to fly its flag, shall comply with the provisions of this Agreement.

30 Op. cit. RSRG at p. vi.

31 The DSM Agreement is not available for consultation online. The author is grateful to the Pacific Community for the access granted to the text of the Agreement and its explanatory notes.

32 DSM Activities are defined at article 1(5) of the DSM Agreement as 'all activities of prospecting for, exploration for, and exploitation of [deep-sea minerals] in the DSM zone'.

33 The DSM Zone is defined at article 1(8) of the DSM Agreement as 'all of the Contracting Parties' areas of national jurisdiction, including the exclusive economic zone and the continental shelf but excluding archipelagic waters and the territorial sea, taken together'.

Article 6, paragraph 1, requires Parties to coordinate and harmonise national seabed mining policies, laws and practice at the regional level, cooperate with each other (and with competent regional or international organisations) in areas such as marine scientific research, environmental management, monitoring, exchange and analysis of data, and generally to assist each other in fulfilling the obligations arising under this Agreement. In addition, Parties would also participate in, and comply with procedures for, the establishment and operation of a regional DSM database to be managed by the Pacific Community.

Pursuant to article 7, Parties must designate a national seabed mining authority, responsible for national seabed mining policy development and implementation, and identify which national agencies are responsible for issues such as mapping the seabed, delivering licences and environmental permits, collecting seabed mining taxes and royalties, managing public consultations and representing each Party at the International Seabed Authority (ISA).

The DSM Agreement's article 8 establishes a series of prohibited activities. In particular it prohibits DSM activities within national jurisdiction unless a licence has been delivered in accordance with applicable national rules and the terms of the Agreement. This is supplemented by a ban on activities that would unjustifiably or unnecessarily interfere with other legally protected uses of any part of the sea or the seabed, together with the obligation to strictly comply with part XI of UNCLOS for sponsorship and licensing of DSM activities in areas outside national jurisdiction.

Article 9 creates an obligation for each Party to have clear, accessible, detailed and, where possible, standardised national rules and processes for seabed mining licensing within national jurisdiction. The same article also encourages Parties to consider establishing a centralised regional authority for all seabed mining licensing on behalf of and under instruction from the Parties.

Other key provisions cover monitoring and enforcement mechanisms, community and indigenous rights, public participation, the exchange of information between Parties, comprehensive environmental management obligations, contingency planning, notification of serious incidents, mutual assistance, occupational health and safety, decommissioning, closure and site rehabilitation, sustainable management of revenue generated by DSM activities, cooperation in marine scientific research and a clear statement that the DSM Agreement shall not be construed as a derogation from the rights and obligations of Parties under any international agreement in force, including specifically UNCLOS and the Convention on Biological Diversity.

The DSM Agreement was therefore clearly designed to ensure a UNCLOS-compatible, harmonised, regional approach to the regulation and implementation of DSM activities in areas under national jurisdiction in the Pacific region. DSM activities outside of the defined DSM Zone would remain governed by the international regime for the Area.

Notwithstanding the considerable amount of work and consultation that took place to develop the DSM Agreement, it has not yet been adopted. The original intent was to submit the Agreement for consideration at the 48th Pacific Islands Forum in 2017 and, if approved, to then open it for signature. Timelines then slipped to 2019 when, following a regional seabed mining meeting held in Tonga in February 2019, Pacific Island countries decided to suspend the approval process pending finalisation and endorsement of the International Seabed Authority (ISA) draft regulations on exploitation of mineral resources in the Area.[34] This was to enable revisions to the DSM Agreement to ensure alignment and compatibility with those regulations.

34 International Seabed Authority Draft regulations on exploitation of mineral resources in the Area (ISBA/25/C/WP.1).

As such, apart from a considerable body of non-binding frameworks and guidelines, the Pacific Islands region does not yet have a region-wide, legally binding regulatory framework in place for seabed mining activities.

Conclusion

Since 2019, the decision made in Tonga to suspend finalising the DSM Agreement has not been revisited by Pacific Island countries. In fact, there has been what could be considered a splintering of interests with countries like Fiji, Papua New Guinea and Vanuatu calling for a moratorium on DSM in national waters until the conclusion of the United Nations Decade of Ocean Science for Sustainable Development in 2030[35] and strong opposition to any proposed ban from Pacific Island countries that would like to pursue seabed mining activities (in particular the Cook Islands,[36] Tonga, Nauru and Kiribati). This divide was further illustrated at the 7th Our Ocean Conference in Palau when, on 14 April 2022, a new political alliance was launched against seabed mining. The Pacific Parliamentarians' Alliance on Deep Sea Mining (PPADSM) includes members of parliament from the Autonomous Region of Bougainville, Fiji, French Polynesia, Guam, New Zealand, Palau, Papua New Guinea, the Solomon Islands, Tuvalu[37] and Vanuatu. Its members published the 'Our Ocean Call' which advocates, among other points, 'for an urgent need to suspend deep-sea mining activities in jurisdictions within the Pacific region, to allow for greater scientific understanding about potential impacts of deep-sea mining'.[38] At the regional intergovernmental level, one of the Pacific's regional organisations, the Pacific Regional Environment Programme (SPREP), placed the call for a moratorium on the agenda of its governing body meeting under the heading 'Deep Seabed Mining: a Pacific Environmental and Governance Challenge'. Through its working paper[39] and associated recommendations,[40] the SPREP Secretariat called for the Organisation to support the proposed ten-year moratorium on seabed mining in the Pacific Islands region. This

35 A moratorium was called for by the Prime Minister of Fiji at the 2019 Pacific Islands Forum, supported by the Prime Ministers of Papua New Guinea and Vanuatu, together with several civil society organisations. Interestingly, it appears that this call was sparked by the failure of Papua New Guinea's Solwara 1 DSM project which aimed to 'mine mineral-rich hydrothermal vents, formed by plumes of hot, acidic, mineral-rich water on the floor of the Bismarck Sea'. See B. Doherty, 'Collapse of PNG deep-sea mining venture sparks calls for moratorium', *The Guardian*, 16 September 2019. Available online <https://www.theguardian.com/world/2019/sep/16/collapse-of-png-deep-sea-mining-venture-sparks-calls-for-moratorium> (accessed 6 September 2021).

36 In March 2022, the Cook Islands approved seabed minerals exploration licences for three companies. See 'Seabed mineral exploration licences approved in the Cook Islands', *RNZ*, 14 March 2022. Available online <https://www.rnz.co.nz/international/pacific-news/463255/seabed-mineral-exploration-licences-approved-in-the-cook-islands> (accessed 19 April 2022).

37 On 14 April 2022, Tuvalu rescinded its sponsorship of Circular Metals Tuvalu Ltd. for seabed mining exploration in the Area. It is believed that this is the first example of a State unilaterally cancelling sponsorship for seabed mining activities in areas beyond national jurisdiction. See 'Tuvalu Cancels Its Sponsorship: The Role of International Law', *DSM Observer*, 2 May 2022. Available online <https://dsmobserver.com/2022/05/tuvalu-cancels-its-sponsorship-the-role-of-international-law/> (accessed 15 May 2022).

38 'High-level Regional Political Group on Deep Sea Mining Launched', *Scoop Independent News*, 14 April 2022. Available online <https://www.scoop.co.nz/stories/PO2204/S00079/high-level-regional-political-group-on-deep-sea-mining-launched.htm> (accessed 19 April 2022).

39 'Deep-Seabed Mining: A Pacific Environmental and Governance Challenge', 30SM/Officials/WP 8.4.3/Att.1. Available online <https://www.sprep.org/sites/default/files/30-SPREP-Meeting/Officials/Eng/WP_8.4.3_Att.1-DSM_position_paper.pdf> (accessed 6 September 2021).

40 Paragraph 14 of working paper 30SM/officials/WP.8.4.3 presents the SPREP Secretariat's proposed recommendations as follows: 'The Meeting is invited to:

proposal did not garner consensus during the discussions that took place from 7 to 9 September 2021. As the lead international organisation on seabed mining matters in the Pacific, SPC has taken a more neutral, science-based approach. It has consistently encouraged Pacific Island countries and partners to apply the precautionary approach and science-based decision-making in all deep seabed mineral activities in both national jurisdiction and the Area, to ensure that adverse impacts on the living resources of the ocean are avoided or minimised. The difference of viewpoints and the nuances between positions within the Pacific echoes that observed at international level, where conflicting narratives on the approach to seabed mining, its benefits and costs (particularly at environmental level) are a feature in ongoing discussions around the regulation of seabed mining and future seabed mining activities.[41]

The fact that many analyses of the technology needed for seabed mining activities, its potential environmental impacts and capacity to generate revenue are based on available data and best estimate, rather than real mining scenarios, has led many countries and investors to consider it as a high-risk venture with uncertain return on investment. However, alongside the threats highlighted by multiple studies, Pacific Island countries are continuously seeking to expand their small economic bases to boost economic growth and buttress their developing economies from external shocks such as natural disasters, the effects of climate change and the current and future impacts of the global Covid-19 pandemic. For some countries in the region, seabed mining (both within national jurisdiction and in the Area) is viewed as an opportunity for economic diversification. Increased marine scientific research and strong regulatory frameworks would contribute to acquiring the much-needed additional scientific data and information to enable Pacific Island countries to make informed decisions at national level on whether to authorise potential deep sea mineral exploration and exploitation activities, together with strengthening future regional frameworks and cooperation. In addition, as regards the Area, Pacific nations and other Small Island/ Large Ocean States have the opportunity to leverage their unique geography and work together to ensure that their specific circumstances are consistently raised and considered at the ISA Council and Assembly to secure reasonable benefits when seabed mining commences in the Area. What appears clear today is that worldwide demand for metals is growing exponentially[42] and there are limited ways to meet this growing demand, one of which is to extract seabed mineral resources. It seems probable that this situation will place pressure on Pacific Island countries, particularly as they seek to rebuild and recoup economic losses due to Covid-19. In this context, regional consultation, coordination and information sharing on seabed mining among all partners remain more relevant than ever to inform decision-making, minimise future risks and ensure an equitable, sustainable future for the countries of the Blue Pacific continent.

---

1) note the position paper prepared by the Secretariat on Deep Seabed Mining in maintaining the principles of the precautionary approach for PICTs;

2) support a 10-year moratorium on Deep Seabed Mining as part of implementation of the precautionary approach; and

3) endorse the Secretariat's recommendation for the Members to continue to apply the principles of the precautionary approach with regards to proposals for deep seabed mining activities.'

Available online <https://www.sprep.org/sites/default/files/30-SPREP-Meeting/Officials/Eng/WP_8.4.3-_Deep_Sea_Mining_DSM.pdf> (accessed 6 September 2021).

41 A. Hallgren and A. Hansson, 'Conflicting Narratives of Deep Sea Mining', *Sustainability* 13(9), 2021, 5261.

42 World Bank, *Mineral Production to Soar as Demand for Clean Energy Increases*, Press Release, Washington, 11 May 2020. Available online <https://www.worldbank.org/en/news/press-release/2020/05/11/mineral-production-to-soar-as-demand-for-clean-energy-increases> (accessed 6 September 2021).

VI.1.6

SOUTH AMERICAN REGION AND SEABED MINING

Eduardo Jiménez Pineda

Introduction

South America is a vast region of the American continent that has States in two different oceans: the Atlantic Ocean and the Pacific Ocean. On the one hand, the South American States riparian in the Atlantic Ocean (from south to north) are Argentina, Uruguay, Brazil, French Guyana (i.e., France on behalf of Guyana), Suriname, Guyana and Venezuela. On the other hand, South American Pacific States from south to north are Chile, Perú, Ecuador and Colombia.

This *bi-oceanic* character has a significant impact on the Law of the Sea approach of South American States and on their practice related to seabed mining. Contrary to other regions such as the European Union and Pacific Islands States,[1] South America does not have any regional framework governance structure with the result that there is limited cooperation among these States. Accordingly, there is a certain degree of inconsistency between the practice of the Atlantic countries and that of the South American Pacific States. In this sense, the active role on seabed mining of the Atlantic States clearly stands out when it is compared to the limited practice in this regard carried out by the Pacific ones.

South American States have had a remarkable interest in the oceans throughout history. As a result, some of these States have played an active role in the progressive development of the Law of the Sea, making a relevant contribution to it.[2] For instance, the claims of 'protection and control' rights in the sea adjacent to their coasts for 200 nautical miles made by States like Chile, Ecuador or Perú (in particular, through the *Declaración de Santiago*), following the Truman Proclamations, showed the innovative positions of these States concerning the Law of the Sea and contributed to the subsequent development of the exclusive economic zone and the continental shelf maritime areas.[3]

1 See P.A. Singh, V. Tassin Campanella, and F. Maes, 'The European Union and Seabed Mining', in V. Tassin Campanella (ed.), *Routledge Handbook of Seabed Mining and the Law of the Sea*, London: Routledge, 2023, chapter VI.1.4. See also C. Diver, 'The Pacific Islands Region and Seabed Mining', in V. Tassin Campanella (ed.), idem, chapter VI.1.5.

2 A. Aguilar Mawdsley, 'The Latin American Contribution to the Modern Law of the Sea', *Netherlands International Law Review* 39 (1), 1992, 63–88.

3 See D. Nelson, 'Exclusive Economic Zone', *Max Planck Encyclopedia of Public International Law*, Oxford Public International Law, 2008, para. 2; and P. Stoll, 'Continental Shelf', *Max Planck Encyclopedia of Public International Law*, Oxford Public International Law, 2008, para. 3.

 DOI: 10.4324/9780429426162-27

Nowadays, the region is still an important actor in the practice of the Law of the Sea due to the vast areas of oceans subjected to the sovereignty and sovereign rights of these States and to the invaluable natural resources existing in those maritime areas. In this regard, South America's current challenges can be deduced from the existence in Brazil of a contract between a company and the International Seabed Authority, from the quantity of submissions for the extension of the continental shelves (some of them very recent) and from the development of some national legislation about these maritime areas and their resources. Consequently, there is a huge geopolitical interest in the region, as can be seen from the *dispute* that could arise between Chile and Argentina concerning the delimitation of their maritime boundaries.[4] In a nutshell, this chapter will examine the geographical extent and governance framework of South America that are relevant to seabed mining.

Geographic extent of the exclusive economic zones and continental shelves

South American countries have been very active both in the development of the continental shelf and in the delimitation of their maritime boundaries. Firstly, some of these States developed in the past a practice with regard to the extension of their continental shelves subsequent to the adoption and entering into force of the 1958 Geneva Convention on the Continental Shelf.[5] Secondly, most of these States have delimited their maritime boundaries, some of them by means of an agreement reached between them, such as the 1981 *Treaty for the Maritime Delimitation between Brazil and France* (on behalf of French Guyana) and the 1972 *Agreement on the Maritime Boundary between Brazil and Uruguay*. Nonetheless, the majority of these maritime delimitations have been carried out by international courts and tribunals,[6] among others: (1) the Arbitration for the Delimitation between Guyana and Suriname;[7] (2) the delimitations of the maritime boundaries of Colombia;[8] (3) the delimitation by the International Court of Justice (ICJ) of the maritime boundary between Perú and Chile;[9] and (4) the arbitration for the delimitation of the maritime boundaries between Chile and Argentina.[10]

Atlantic perspective

Among the South American riparian States in the Atlantic Ocean, six of them (Argentina, Uruguay, Brazil,[11] France on behalf of French Guyana, Suriname and Guyana) have made, pursuant to arti-

4 See below pp. 8–9.

5 See J.G. Verner, 'Changes in the Law of the Sea: Latin American Contributions and Rationales', *Social and Economic Studies* 30 (2), 1981, 18–44; T. Alvarado Garaicoa, 'The Continental Shelf and the Extension of the Territorial Sea', *Miami Law Quarterly* 10 (4), 1956, 490–498; and F. Orrego Vicuña, 'Trends and Issues in the Law of the Sea as Applied in Latin America', *Ocean Development & International Law* 26, 1995, 93–103.

6 See P. Wojcikiewicz Almeida and J.M. Sorel (eds.), *Latin America and the International Court of Justice Contributions to International Law*, London: Routledge, 2018. In particular, Part V 'Material Contribution of Latin American Cases to the Development of International Law: Territorial and Maritime Disputes'.

7 *Award for the delimitation of the maritime boundary (Guyana v. Suriname)*, 17 September 2007, *Reports of International Arbitral Awards*, vol. XXX, p. 1.

8 For a detailed analysis of the position of Colombia towards seabed mining of minerals, see in this book E. Restrepo Uribe, 'Colombia and Seabed Mining', in V. Tassin Campanella (ed.), *Routledge Handbook of Seabed Mining and the Law of the Sea*, op. cit., chapter VI.2.3.

9 *Maritime Dispute (Peru v. Chile), Judgment, I.C.J. Reports 2014*, p. 3.

10 *Case concerning a dispute between Argentina and Chile concerning Beagle Channel (Argentina/Chile)*, 18 February 1977, *Reports of International Arbitral Awards*, vol. XXI, p. 53.

11 For a detailed analysis of Brazil, see in this book C. Costa de Oliveira and A. Flávia Barros-Platiau, 'Brazil and Seabed Mining', in V. Tassin Campanella (ed.), *Routledge Handbook of Seabed Mining and the Law of the Sea*, op. cit., chapter VI.2.2.

cle 76, paragraph 8, of the *United Nations Convention on the Law of the Sea* (UNCLOS) submissions to the Commission on the Limits of the Continental Shelf (CLCS).[12] Except for the submission made by Guyana for the reasons explained below, the other five States have extended their continental shelves in accordance with the recommendations made by the Commission to French Guyana (on 2 September 2009), to Suriname (on 30 March 2011), to Uruguay (on 19 August 2016), to Argentina (on 11 March 2016 and on 19 August 2016) and to Brazil (in respect of the Brazilian Southern Region on 8 March 2019).

It should be noted that Venezuela is not a State Party to the UNCLOS, and does not have an extended continental shelf due to two main reasons. The first one is the overlapping of the projections of its coasts within the 200 nautical miles with the projections of several neighbouring Caribbean States.

More importantly, there has been a historical territorial dispute between Venezuela and Guyana in existence since 1841, known as the Essequibo dispute, consisting of Venezuela's claim to sovereignty over this important territory currently under Guyana's sovereignty. There is still a pending case about this dispute submitted before the ICJ.[13] As a result, Venezuela made a communication in 2012 objecting to Guyana's submission – on the basis of the existence of this territorial dispute – blocking such submission under the terms of UNCLOS article 76, paragraph 10 and of the Annex 1 of the CLCS Rules of Procedure. Although Venezuela is not a State Party to the Convention, this communication has in fact precluded the CLCS from making its recommendations to Guyana.[14]

Since the maritime boundaries of the South American Atlantic States are established either by agreement or by a decision of an international tribunal, there are two problematic submissions for extended continental shelves on this side of the region, i.e., the already mentioned submission of Guyana and the submission made by Argentina.

Argentina made its submission to the CLCS on 21 April 2009, attracting comments from various States because of disagreements regarding the existence of maritime and/or land disputes on portions of the Argentinian extension submission: (1) United Kingdom of Great Britain and Northern Ireland (on 6 August 2009), (2) United States of America (on 19 August 2009), (3) Russian Federation (on 24 August 2009), (4) India (on 31 August 2009), (5) the Netherlands (on 30 September 2009) and (6) Japan (on 19 November 2009).[15]

The objection of the United Kingdom[16] was based on the dispute about the sovereignty 'over the Falkland Islands and over South Georgia and the South Sandwich Islands and the surrounding

12 These submissions can be consulted at the website of the Division for Ocean Affairs and the Law of the Sea (DOALOS): Brazil (CLCS.02.2004.LOS), France on behalf of French Guyana (CLCS.08.2007.LOS), Suriname (CLCS.15.2008.LOS), Uruguay (CLCS.21.2009.LOS), Guyana (CLCS.57.2011.LOS) and Argentina (CLCS.25.2009.LOS).

13 *Arbitral Award of 3 October 1899 (Guyana v. Venezuela), Judgment on Preliminary Objections, I.C.J. Reports 2020*, to be published.

14 Venezuela's Communication of 9 March 2012 with regard to the submission made by Guyana to the CLCS. In this communication, Venezuela stated that 'according to customary international law, and independently of not being party to the United Nations Convention on the Law of the Sea, it has right over the continental shelf extended beyond the outer limits of the continental shelf, belonging to the Atlantic region, rights that are regardless of its effective occupation and of any express declaration'. For a general analysis of the position of Guyana with regards to seabed mining of minerals, see B. Bojang and D. Streete, 'Guyana and Seabed Mining', in V. Tassin Campanella (ed.), *Routledge Handbook of Seabed Mining and the Law of the Sea*, op. cit., chapter VI.2.6.

15 These communications are available at the website of DOALOS.

16 For a detailed analysis of the position of the UK towards seabed mining, see in this book J. Harrison, 'The United Kingdom and Seabed Mining', in V. Tassin Campanella (ed.), *Routledge Handbook of Seabed Mining and the Law of the Sea*, op. cit., chapter VI.2.14.

maritime areas', that according to this State are under its sovereignty.[17] On the other hand, the Argentinian position regarding the Islas Malvinas, Georgias del Sur and Sandwich del Sur can be summarized as follows: 'The Argentine Republic has never recognized the illegitimate British occupation of the southern archipelagos, as the presence of the United Kingdom derives from the usurpation in 1833 of a part of the Argentine national territory, which was immediately protested and never consented by Argentina'.[18] Along with its recommendations, the Secretariat noted that 'a dispute exists' between both Governments 'concerning sovereignty over the Falkland Islands (Malvinas)'.[19] Interestingly, the submission of the United Kingdom in respect of the Falkland Islands on 11 May 2009 has been blocked by Argentina by means of its communication dated on 20 August 2009.[20]

On the contrary, the communications sent by the other five States were all in accordance with Article IV of the *Antarctic Treaty*. None of these States recognize any rights or claims in relation to territories located in the area covered by the Treaty. As pointed out by Godio, every overlap of the Argentinian submission with the Antarctic areas was suspended by virtue of the Antarctic Treaty and safeguards of the international community.[21]

As can be seen, Argentina has played an important role concerning the extension of its continental shelf. Despite the sovereignty disputes and the claims over areas that may fall under the Antarctic Treaty, Argentina has significantly and dynamically contributed to the development of the maritime areas where mining activities can be carried out under the jurisdiction of the State: the continental shelf and the extended continental shelf. However, the Argentinian example brings light to the lack of coordination and cooperation of these States at a regional level, leaving every State claiming its rights on their own, at most at a bilateral level.

Pacific perspective

South American Pacific States from north to south are Colombia, Ecuador, Perú and Chile. On this side of the region, the smaller number of States simplifies the territorial issues. In this sense, it must be welcomed that every maritime boundary between these four States is delimited, either by agreement (the boundaries between Colombia and Ecuador and between Ecuador and Perú, respectively[22]) or according to a judicial decision (the maritime delimitation between Ecuador and Chile by the ICJ Judgment of 2014).[23]

Even though there are no regional mechanisms in terms of governance of seabed mining, the international cooperation at a State level among these States must be highlighted. This cooperation is rooted in the contribution of some of these States to the very origin of the continental shelf (the previously mentioned *1952 Declaración de Santiago*) and could be gaining momentum consider-

17 CLCS.25.2009.LOS, note nº 84/09, p. 1.

18 Argentina's submission to the CLCS dated on 21 April 2009, op. cit., p. 8.

19 Summary of the recommendations of the CLCS approved on 11 March 2016, p. 1, note 2.

20 Along with its communication, Argentina stated that it 'categorically rejects the British submission and expressly requests that the Commission on the Limits of the Continental Shelf neither consider nor qualify it'.

21 See L. Godio, 'Antarctica and Seabed Mining', in V. Tassin Campanella (ed.), *Routledge Handbook of Seabed Mining and the Law of the Sea*, op. cit., chapter VI.1.2, p. 3.

22 See the following treaties: (1) *Convenio sobre delimitación de áreas marinas y submarinas y cooperación marítima entre las Repúblicas de Colombia y del Ecuador*, adopted in Quito on 23 August 1975; and (2) *Acuerdo por intercambio de Notas de contenido idéntico entre la República del Perú y la República del Ecuador sobre Límites Marítimos*, adopted on 2 May 2011.

23 *Maritime Dispute (Peru v. Chile), Judgment, I.C.J. Reports 2014*, op. cit.

ing the recent joint submission by Ecuador and Costa Rica as well as the Ecuadorian and Chilean submissions to the CLCS, as explained below. Among other reasons, because these submissions are recent, none of these States have delineated the outer limits of their extended continental shelves.

To start with, Colombia is not a State Party of the UNCLOS, but it is part of the Geneva Convention on the Continental Shelf.[24] Currently, Colombia is a party in two different disputes submitted by Nicaragua concerning the *Alleged violations of sovereign rights and maritime spaces in the Caribbean Sea*[25] and *the Question of the delimitation of the continental shelf between Nicaragua and Colombia beyond 200 nautical miles from the Nicaraguan Coast.*[26] This last case is particularly interesting to the subject of this chapter because of rights of a State (Colombia) as a non-UNCLOS State Party.

In its preliminary objections, Colombia upholds that UNCLOS article 76, paragraph 8, establishes a prerequisite that obliges Nicaragua to receive the CLCS' recommendations prior to the delimitation of the extended continental shelf, particularly in this context of frontal delimitation.[27] Regarding the Colombian rights in spite of its position as a non-State party to UNCLOS, Colombia states that Nicaragua must in any case comply with the obligations set out in article 76 and that Colombia has the right to be notified of the submission to the CLCS and to comment through communications on those submissions.[28]

The ICJ, on its judgment on preliminary objections, found that the request by Nicaragua was admissible.[29] As such, the future ICJ judgment on this dispute is well expected for its potential contribution to the legal certainty. In my view, it should clarify whether the CLCS' recommendations are or are not a prerequisite for the delimitation of the extended continental shelf in the geographical context of frontal delimitations.

For its part, Ecuador acceded to the UNCLOS on 24 September 2012. Recently, on 16 December 2020 Ecuador and Costa Rica jointly submitted information to the CLCS on the limits of the continental shelf beyond 200 nautical miles in the Panama Basin.[30] This submission, according to the Ecuadorian Ministry of Foreign Affairs, aims to achieve 'the geographical unity of the island territory with the continental territory throughout the seabed and the subsoil' – from the Ecuador mainland territory to the Galapagos' archipelago – in order to enhance sovereign rights over the

24 The 1958 Convention was ratified by Colombia on 8 June 1962. With regard to the no ratification by Colombia of UNCLOS and to the several maritime delimitations of these States, see E. Restrepo Uribe, 'Colombia case for seabed mining and UNCLOS', op. cit.

25 Case 155 (application instituting proceedings submitted by Nicaragua on 26 November 2013).

26 Case 154 (application instituting proceedings submitted by Nicaragua on 16 September 2013).

27 See *Preliminary objections of the Republic of Colombia*, vol. 1, 14 August 2014, pp. 164–165. According to Colombia, the delineation of the outer limits of the continental shelf is mandatory in the frontal delimitations in contrast with the lateral delimitations, where the international courts or tribunals do not need 'to determine the "outer limits" of the continental shelf and to await for the CLCS to make recommendations on the subject' (p. 165).

28 Ibid., p. 167. In the point 7.22 (p. 168), Colombia summarized this latest argument as follows: 'The role recognized for non-parties to UNCLOS in the work of the CLCS is further confirmation of the view that a non-Party can claim the inadmissibility of a request to the ICJ for delimitation of an area of continental shelf beyond 200 nautical miles when the procedure before the Commission has not reached its conclusion with the adoption of a recommendation concerning the coastal State's entitlement'.

29 *Question de la délimitation du plateau continental entre le Nicaragua et la Colombie au-delà de 200 milles marins de la côte nicaraguayenne (Nicaragua c. Colombie), exceptions préliminaires, arrêt, C.I.J. Recueil 2016*, para. 126, p. 140.

30 Joint submission made by Costa Rica and Ecuador, dated on 16 December 2020 (CLCS.86.2020.LOS).

existing resources.[31] Even more recently, on 1 March 2022, Ecuador again submitted information on the limits of the continental shelf beyond 200 nautical miles to the CLCS, on this occasion with regard to the Southern Region of the Carnegie Ridge.[32] In my opinion, this very recent submission corroborates the renewed interest of South American Pacific States on the continental shelf.

Finally, Chile, the South American State with the largest coastline in the Pacific Ocean and the tenth biggest exclusive economic zone (EEZ) in the world, has been part of UNCLOS since 25 August 1997. Five days after the Ecuadorian and Costa Rican joint submission, on 21 December 2020, Chile submitted information on the external limits of the continental shelf to the CLCS in respect of the Eastern Continental Shelf of Easter Island Province.[33] This island is located farther than 3,500 kilometres distance from the Chilean mainland, showing an ambitious aspiration of sovereign rights (*creeping jurisdiction*).[34] According to the Chilean *Dirección Nacional de Fronteras y Límites del Estado (DIFROL)*, the extension of the continental shelf in accordance with the information submitted to the CLCS would imply 'an area of 550.000 square kilometres where Chile exercise sovereign rights over the natural resources existing in the continental shelf'.[35] Moreover, on 28 February 2022, Chile submitted to the CLCS information on the limits of the continental shelf beyond 200 nautical miles in respect of the Western Continental Shelf of the Chilean Antarctic Territory.[36]

Interestingly, a new maritime *dispute* could be arising between Chile and Argentina – a Pacific and an Atlantic South American State – as a consequence of the update on 27 August 2021 of the Chilean *Carta Náutica nº 8*. This new version of the nautical chart includes an area of the continental shelf south of the Drake Passage and Cape Horn, that was previously considered as Argentina's continental shelf by the Argentinian *Ley Nacional* 27.557.[37] The Argentinian government reacted to the Chilean updated nautical chart stating that this change 'is against the Peace and Amity Treaty concluded between the two countries in 1984'[38] and that it is contrary to the *Ley Nacional* 27.557 that was adopted in accordance with the recommendations given by the CLCS.[39]

In my opinion, the emergence of this dispute may have been influenced by the elections recently held in both countries. Logically, the question of the exercise of the sovereign rights over the extended continental shelf, where the projections of both countries overlap, is a serious concern, particularly considering the history of the Argentina-Chile frontier cases.[40] Pursuant to the Peace

31 Ecuadorian Ministry of Foreign Affairs, press release dated on 16 December 2020.

32 Submission made by the Republic of Ecuador on 1 March 2022 (CLCS.90.2022.LOS). It is to be noted that this extension claim has not yet received any objection.

33 Partial submission made by Chile on 21 December 2020 (CLCS.87.2020.LOS). Ecuador and Chile held an exchange of experiences on the matter of the extended continental shelf in order to share scientific-technical knowledge with regard to the definition of the outer limits of the continental shelf within the framework of the *Memorandum of Understanding on Continental Shelf*, concluded on 6 June 2021.

34 Ibid.

35 DIFROL, press release dated on 21 December 2020.

36 Submission made by Chile on 28 February 2022 (CLCS.89.2022.LOS). In its submission, Chile requests to the Commission 'not to take any action for the time being with regard to the information in this submission that relates to the Western Continental Shelf appurtenant to the Chilean Antarctic Territory' (Notification, p. 2).

37 INFODEFENSA, 'El Gobierno de Chile rechaza el reclamo de Argentina por delimitación marítima austral', 30 August 2021.

38 L.A. de La Fayette, 'Beagle Channel Dispute', *Max Planck Encyclopedia of Public International Law*, Oxford Public International Law, 2009, in particular paras. 28 ss.

39 Argentinian Ministry of Foreign Affairs, press release nº 344/21, dated on 28 August 2021.

40 X. Hinrichs Oyarce, 'Argentina-Chile Frontier Cases', *Max Planck Encyclopedia of Public International Law*, Oxford Public International Law, 2019.

and Amity Treaty, disputes between these States should be settled by negotiations (article 4), by an international court or tribunal mutually agreed (article 4) or, in spite of such an agreement, through conciliation (article 5) or arbitration (article 6).[41] Therefore the negotiated settlement of this *in statu nascendi* dispute is desirable. Otherwise, it seems that Argentina has a stronger position in view of the delimitation of its extended continental shelf following the CLCS' recommendations.

The lack of regional governance framework and seabed mining national regulations

A predominant feature of the seabed mining practice in South America is the absolute lack of a regional governance framework. None of the several South American International Organizations – among others, MERCOSUR, UNASUR, SICA and ALADI[42] – have competence in terms of cooperation in Law of the Sea matters. Furthermore, there is no governance or regulatory framework at a regional level in contrast to other regions in the world, such as Europe, the Pacific Islands States or the South Asiatic States.[43]

In brief, the impact of the South American States on the progressive development of the Law of the Sea has been very creative, contributing through the practice to the crystallization of the EEZ and the CS or being an exemplary continent for the peaceful settlement of maritime disputes. However, when it comes to the cooperation at a regional level, there is not a common approach but instead mostly a miscellany of single practices that can be divided into the two oceanic projections of the continent: the Atlantic and Pacific *sides*.

Atlantic perspective

Some South American Atlantic States have been very active declaring significant marine protected areas (MPAs) where seabed mining activities cannot be carried out.[44] In this sense, Argentina has created several MPAs: the *Namuncurá – Banco Burdwood I* protected area (2013),[45] the *National System of Marine Protected Areas* (2014)[46] and the marine protected areas of *Namuncurá – Banco Burdwood II* and *Yaganes* (2018).[47] These three marine protected areas include both the EEZ and the CS within the 200 nautical miles. As a result, Argentina has around 10 per cent of its EEZ and CS covered by marine protected areas, which includes around 126,000 square kilometres.[48] Logically, the existence of these MPAs prevents any seabed mining developments to occur, although they foresee exploration activities as well as marine scientific research.[49]

41 F. Orrego Bauzá, 'Reflexiones sobre la controversia limítrofe entre Chile y Argentina', website of the Facultad de Derecho, Universidad de Chile, 21 October 2021.

42 MERCOSUR (Mercado Común del Sur); UNASUR (Unión de Naciones Suramericanas); SICA (Sistema de la Integración Centroamericana); and ALADI (Asociación Latinoamericana de Integración).

43 See Diver, op. cit., or T. Davenport, 'Southeast Asia and Seabed Mining', in V. Tassin Campanella (ed.), *Routledge Handbook of Seabed Mining and the Law of the Sea*, op. cit., chapter VI.1.7.

44 See A. Koschinsky et al., 'Deep-Sea Mining: Potential Environmental, Legal, Economic, and Societal Implications – An Interdisciplinary Research', *Integrated Environmental Assessment and Management* 14 (6), 2018, 1–20.

45 Ley nº 26.875, *Creación Área Marina Protegida Namuncurá – Banco Burdwood*, officially published 5 August 2013.

46 Ley nº 27.037, *Sistema Nacional de Áreas Marinas Protegidas*, officially published 16 December 2014.

47 Ley nº 27.490, *Créanse Áreas Marinas*, officially published 17 December 2018.

48 INICIATIVA PAMPA AZUL, 'Argentina cuenta con dos nuevas Áreas Marinas Protegidas', 2018.

49 See article 3 of Ley 26.875 and article 5 of Ley 27.037, op. cit.

On the contrary, this political will to establish marine protected areas contrasts with the out-of-date legislation about seabed mining in the continental shelf. As happens in most States in the world, most of these South American Atlantic States are not in the position to develop any activities of seabed mining on their continental shelves. As such, their regulations are not up to date. For example, Brazilian national regulations, as professors Oliveira and Barros-Platiau point out, have not yet been updated with regard to deep seabed mining both in the continental shelf and in the Area.[50] Similarly, Guyana's Mining Act (act nº 20 of 1989) does not foresee seabed mining activities.[51]

The lack of an updated regulatory framework of seabed mining activities in both the continental shelf and the Area is probably the reason why there is only one contract for the exploration of seabed resources in this region of South America. This contract for exploration of the cobalt-rich ferromanganese crusts was concluded between Companhia de Produção de Recursos Minerais (CPRM) and the International Seabed Authority (ISA) in the Rio Grande Rise and it is formally valid up to 2030.[52] The relevance of this contract at a regional level comes from the fact that, even though South America is also rich in polymetallic nodules and polymetallic sulfides, it is the sole contract for exploration currently in force.

Pacific perspective

On the Pacific side of the South American continent, the lack of cooperation at a regional level concerning seabed mining activities is again a prominent aspect. Moreover, the lack of provisions establishing the legal regime of mining activities in the continental shelf is a general feature among these four States, whether or not they are UNCLOS parties. For instance, the Chilean Mining Code only establishes in this regard the allowance of mining activities over the resources 'existing in the subsoil of the maritime waters subjected to the national jurisdiction'.[53]

Nevertheless, there is a significant exception in the lack of national regulations on seabed mining, i.e., the 2009 Mining Law of Ecuador.[54] This is a very interesting rule in the sense that it is the only mining law analysed that has a special regulation for the mining activities in the seabed. Particularly, chapter five of its IX title (special regimes) establishes in its article 146 that the 'exploitation of the mineral resources of any kind existing in the seabed is in charge of the National Institute of Geological Research, Mining, Metallurgical and of the Mining National Company, that will be able to conclude research agreements and service contracts'. Moreover, the General Rule to the Mining Law further develops the aforementioned law declaring in its article 18 (l) that the National Institute can 'execute the research and propose plans for the exploitation of the mineral resources of any kind existing in the seabed'.[55] Despite these advanced Ecuadorian regulations at the forefront of other South American States, its implementation and enforcement has been very

50 See Costa de Oliveira and Flávia Barros-Platiau, op. cit.

51 See Bojang and Streete, op. cit.

52 A.P. Silva, 'Brazil advances over the Area: The inclusion of the Rio Grande Rise within the Brazilian outer continental shelf and its consequences for other states and for the common heritage of mankind', *Marine Policy* 125, 2021, 1–10.

53 Article 30 of the Chilean Ley 18.248, *Código de Minería*, adopted on 26 September 1983, officially published 14 October 1983.

54 Ley 45, *Ley de Minería*, officially published 29 January 2009.

55 Decreto Ejecutivo 119, *Reglamento General a la Ley de Minería*, officially published 16 November 2009. Emphasis added.

limited.[56] In this sense, the activities and research projects of the National Institute have not yet dealt with seabed mining.

Conclusion

This chapter has reflected on the regional practice of South American States concerning seabed mining. As a first conclusion, South American States have played an active role throughout history in the progressive development of the Law of the Sea and in particular of the continental shelf, whose mineral resources are starting to be explored and could potentially be exploited.

A general interest of South American States – both Atlantic and Pacific – in the extension of their continental shelves can be highlighted. Moreover, the efforts made by these States for the delimitations of their maritime boundaries must be welcomed. However, the absolute lack of regional cooperation in this regard is remarkable, especially considering the proliferation of international organizations in South America.

The interest in extending the continental shelf or delimiting the maritime boundaries contrasts with the outdated instruments regulating seabed mining activities (with a few exceptions). This situation seems to show a shared trend between the Atlantic and the Pacific States of this region, namely the current lack of interest in seabed mining, both in the continental shelf and particularly in the Area. This conclusion may be explained by several factors: the high costs for these developing countries of the technology to explore and to exploit these mineral resources, the lack of regional frameworks of cooperation in this field or even the lack of interest in these resources due to the existence of land resources (cheaper and easier to exploit).

In this sense, probably as a consequence of the previously mentioned reasons, there is so far just one contract for exploration of mining resources of the Area in the Atlantic Ocean. Thus, South American Atlantic States are a bit more innovative on the matter of seabed mining activities than the Pacific ones.[57]

In any case, the adoption of updated mining codes by these States, that would establish the normative framework of seabed mining activities, could very likely help in overcoming the current uncertainties of these activities, particularly in terms of their environmental impact.[58] In other words, the updating of national legislations could potentially make a significant contribution by the sponsoring States for the development of seabed mining activities and could eventually increase the exploration and future exploitation of this minerals-rich region of the world.

56 For other examples of national legislations applicable to the exploitation of the seabed mineral resources, see S. Roux and C. Horsfield, 'Review of National Legislations Applicable to Seabed Mineral Resources Exploitation', in C. Banet (ed.), *The Law of the Seabed Access, Uses, and Protection of Seabed Resources*, Leiden: Brill, 2020, 287–314.

57 See Diver, op. cit.

58 X. Xu and G. Xue, 'Potential Contribution of Sponsoring State and Its National Legislation to the Deep Seabed Mining Regime', *Sustainability* 13 (9) 10784, 2021, 1–12.

VI.1.7
SOUTHEAST ASIA AND SEABED MINING

Tara Davenport

Introduction

Southeast Asia is a vast sub-region of Asia situated east of the Indian subcontinent, south of China and northwest of Australia. The core Southeast Asian states consist of Brunei, Cambodia, Indonesia, Malaysia, Myanmar, Laos, the Philippines, Singapore, Thailand and Vietnam. More recently, Timor-Leste and Papua New Guinea have also been described as 'Southeast Asian states,'[1] although they are also considered Pacific Island states. Southeast Asia is characterized by a rich diversity of languages, religion, political and legal systems as well as economic development attributable to a range of historical, geographical and political factors. Indeed, the territorial expanse of 'Southeast Asia' has only been resolved in the last three decades.[2] Territories in the region have been controlled by different empires followed by different colonial regimes and there has been no one unifying hegemonic power.[3] The idea of Southeast Asia as a distinct region only began to take shape after World War II when Southeast Asian states began the long march towards independence from their colonial masters.

Compared to the European Union (EU),[4] regional integration and co-operation in Southeast Asia has been incremental, shaped by an emphasis on sovereignty and non-interference as well as a preference for informal and flexible arrangements as opposed to legally binding agreements.[5] There are several regional co-operation frameworks between Southeast Asian states themselves and between Southeast Asian states and extra-regional actors. However, none of them have comprehensively *regulated* seabed mining either within or beyond national jurisdiction, and there cannot be said to be a regional approach to seabed mining. To this end, this chapter explores the

1 See discussion under 'ASEAN.'

2 The term 'Southeast Asia' was first applied in 1943 to a region that included parts of modern day South Asia (Sri Lanka and northeast India) and excluded the former Netherlands Indies and the Philippines: See C. Lin Sien (eds), *Southeast Asia Transformed: A Geography of Change*, Singapore: ISEAS, 2003, p. 1.

3 Ibid.

4 For more information, see in this book P. Singh, V. Tassin Campanella and F. Maes, 'The European Union and Seabed Mining,' in V. Tassin Campanella (ed), *Routledge Handbook of Seabed Mining and the Law of the Sea*, London: Routledge, 2023, chapter VI.1.4.

5 See discussion in this section under 'Governance.'

DOI: 10.4324/9780429426162-28

maritime geography of Southeast Asia, the interests of Southeast Asian states in seabed mining and the regional frameworks that are relevant to seabed mining. It then explains why seabed mining has not been comprehensively regulated from a regional perspective and outlines future challenges in developing a regional regulatory approach to seabed mining.

Geographical extent of the exclusive economic zones and continental shelves

The maritime character of Southeast Asia has been described as the first and primary unifying factor of Southeast Asia.[6] All Southeast Asian states are coastal states except for landlocked Laos, and two of these states (the Philippines and Indonesia) are the world's largest archipelagic states. Definitions of Southeast Asian waters have varied but for present purposes, this chapter adopts a broad definition of waters that are relevant to Southeast Asia from a governance perspective that coincides with scientific conceptions of the 'Indo-Pacific.' The Indo-Pacific has become popular in legal and policy literature and is said to cover the maritime space between the Indian and Pacific Oceans although it has been subject to 'variations in definitions depending on each actor and their own geographic positioning in the vast expanse.'[7] It includes maritime spaces that are within the national jurisdiction of Southeast Asian states (where at least one Southeast Asian state has a potential maritime claim, which is either uncontested or overlaps with the maritime claim of another Southeast Asian state or extra-regional states)[8] and maritime spaces in areas beyond national jurisdiction (ABNJ), on the basis that activities in ABNJ will inevitably impact areas within national jurisdiction.[9]

Maritime spaces under national jurisdiction

All Southeast Asian states, with the exception of Cambodia, have ratified the *1982 UN Convention on the Law of the Sea* (UNCLOS) and the *1994 Agreement relating to the implementation of Part XI of UNCLOS*.[10] Brunei, Cambodia, Indonesia, Malaysia, Myanmar, Papua New Guinea, the Philippines, Thailand, Timor-Leste and Vietnam have all claimed a 200 nautical mile (M) Exclusive Economic Zone (EEZ) and/or continental shelf.[11] Singapore (being

6 C. Lin Sien, op. cit., p. 5.

7 U. Das, 'What Is the Indo-Pacific?,' *The Diplomat*, 13 July 2019.

8 This includes the eastern part of the Andaman Sea, the South China Sea, the Gulf of Thailand, the Gulf of Tonkin, the Straits of Malacca and Singapore, the Celebes Sea, the Sulu Sea, the Arafura Sea, the Timor Sea, the Torres Strait and the Bismarck Sea.

9 E. Popova et al., 'Ecological Connectivity Between the Areas Beyond National Jurisdiction and Coastal Waters: Safeguarding Interests of Coastal Communities in Developing Countries,' *Marine Policy* 104 (2019) 90–102.

10 United Nations Treaty Collection (Chapter XXI).

11 Brunei (1982; Exclusive Economic Zone Proclamation, S4/1994; Royal Continental Shelf Proclamation 1954 No. S.41, 30 June 1954); Cambodia (Statement issued by the Spokesman of the Ministry of Foreign Affairs of 15 January 1978; Decree of the Council of State 13 July 1982); Indonesia (Act No. 5 of 1983 on the Indonesian Exclusive Economic Zone, 18 October 1983; Act No. 6 of 8 August 1996 regarding Indonesian Waters); Malaysia (Emergency (Essential Powers) Ordinance, No. 7, 1969; Exclusive Economic Zone Act No. 311; Continental Shelf Act 1966 – Act No. 57 of 28 July 1966, as amended by Act No. 83 of 1972); Myanmar (Myanmar Territorial Sea and Maritime Zones Law, 17 July 2017); Papua New Guinea (National Seas Act 1977, Act No. 7, 7 February 1977; Offshore Seas Proclamation 1978; Continental Shelf (Living Natural Resources) Act 1977, Act No. 5 of 7 February 1977 Amending the Continental Shelf (Living Natural Resources) Act 1974); Philippines (Presidential Decree No. 1599, 11 June 1978 establishing an EEZ; Presidential Proclamation No. 370, 20 March 1968); Thailand (Royal Proclamation establishing the EEZ of the Kingdom of Thailand, 23 February 1981); Timor-Leste (Maritime Borders

geographically disadvantaged due to its proximate location to Malaysia and Indonesia) has not enacted any legislation on maritime zones but has asserted that it can claim a 12 nautical miles (M) territorial sea and a 200 (M) EEZ in certain areas, the precise co-ordinates of which will be announced at an appropriate time.[12] Brunei, Indonesia, Myanmar, the Philippines, Malaysia and Vietnam (jointly), Vietnam, Malaysia and Papua New Guinea have either submitted preliminary information or made submissions on their extended continental shelf claims to the Commission on the Limits of the Continental Shelf (CLCS), not all of which have been subject to a final recommendation.[13]

Congested coastal geography in Southeast Asia has resulted in overlapping maritime claims, some of which have been subject to maritime boundary arrangements or provisional arrangements and some of which remain undelimited.[14] In particular, the South China Sea is the stage of complex disputes relating to sovereignty, maritime entitlement and maritime delimitation stemming from competing claims over offshore features found in the Spratly Islands, the Paracel Islands and Scarborough shoal. These disputes involve not only Southeast Asian states (Brunei, Malaysia, Philippines and Vietnam) but extra-regional actors such as China and Taiwan. While the 2016 Philippines / China Annex VII arbitration made findings on the maritime entitlement of offshore features in the Spratly Islands,[15] the continued existence of sovereignty, entitlement and delimitation disputes in the South China Sea, coupled with the absence of final CLCS recommendations on the majority of Southeast Asian CLCS claims, means that the extent of maritime areas under the national jurisdiction of Southeast Asian states has not been fully determined.

Areas beyond national jurisdiction

Despite uncertainty in the boundary between national jurisdiction and the Area, there are deep seabed areas in the Indian Ocean and Pacific Ocean which are clearly beyond the national jurisdiction of any Southeast Asian state (for example, the Clarion-Clipperton Fracture Zone in the Pacific Ocean and the Mid-Indian Range Basin in the Indian Ocean). There is also potentially a pocket of deep seabed in the South China Sea, although this is uncertain due to several factors. First, China has rejected the South China Sea Award, which only afforded high-tide features in the Spratly Islands a 12 (M) territorial sea, and asserts that it has an EEZ and continental shelf in the South China Sea coupled with historic rights outside these maritime zones.[16] Second, Malaysia's 2019 CLCS submission and future CLCS submissions by Vietnam and the Philippines encompass areas that would have been consid-

of the Territory of the Democratic Republic of Timor-Leste, Law No. 7/2002, 23 July 2002); Vietnam (2012 Law of the Sea Vietnam, 2 July 2012).

12 See exclusive economic zone: Text of Statement of the Ministry of Foreign Affairs on the Exclusive Economic Zone, 15 September 1980, Singapore Government Press Release 09-0/80/09/15; MFA Press Statement: International Court of Justice Awards Sovereignty of Pedra Branca to Singapore, 23 May 2008.

13 Commission on the Limits of the Continental Shelf (CLCS) website. The only CLCS claims which have been subject to a final recommendation are Indonesia's submission of 16 June 2008 for Northwest Sumatra Islands (CLCS/70, 11 May 2011, para. 9) and the Philippines' submission on 8 April 2009 in Benham Rise (CLCS/74, 12 April 2012, para. 35).

14 T. Davenport, 'Southeast Asian Approaches to Maritime Delimitation,' *Asian Journal of International Law* 4 (2), 2014, 309–357.

15 *South China Sea Arbitral Award under Annex VII of UNCLOS (Philippines/China)*, PCA Case No. 2013–19, 12 July 2016.

16 China's Notes Verbale to the CLCS dated 12 December 2019, 23 March 2020, 17 April 2020, 2 June 2020, 18 June 2020, 29 July 2020, 7 August 2020, 18 September 2020, 28 January 2021.

ered the Area.[17] Third, the maritime entitlement of the Paracel Islands (claimed by China, Taiwan and Vietnam) in the northern part of the South China Sea is not clear and again, any EEZ or continental shelf generated by the Paracel Islands could also encroach upon the Area.[18]

The interests of Southeast Asian states in seabed mining

Southeast Asia is reportedly rich in mineral resources and has potential for new discoveries. In 2018, minerals trade had an annual growth of 9 percent valued at USD249.8 billion and accounted for 8.9 percent of the trade of the ten member states of the Association of Southeast Asian Nations (ASEAN).[19] Minerals is predicted to emerge as one of the main growth drivers in Southeast Asian states' economies. [20]

While there is increasing data on terrestrial minerals in the region, seabed minerals data in maritime areas within the national jurisdiction of Southeast Asian states is sparse. Papua New Guinea is the only state that granted a license to Nautilus Minerals to mine sea-floor massive sulfides in its EEZ in the Bismarck Sea. The project was reportedly cancelled due to community resistance, funding issues and legal challenges,[21] and Papua New Guinea's Prime Minister has supported calls for a ten-year moratorium on seabed mining.[22] Apart from the Bismarck Sea, Chinese survey vessels have also reportedly found polymetallic nodules in the South China Sea, although the exact location is unclear.[23]

In the Area, licenses to explore mineral resources have been issued by the International Seabed Authority (ISA) to various states, state-owned enterprises and private companies in the Clarion-Clipperton Fracture Zone in the Pacific Ocean and the Mid-Indian Range Basin in the Indian Ocean. The Singapore-incorporated company, Ocean Minerals Singapore, is the only corporation sponsored by a Southeast Asian state (Singapore) to explore polymetallic nodules in the Clarion-Clipperton Zone.[24] Indonesia has had a seat in Group C of the ISA Council as a major net land-based exporter of minerals. Southeast Asian states such as Indonesia, Malaysia, Philippines, Singapore and Vietnam have had seats in Group E of the Council based on equitable geographical distribution.

Regional governance frameworks and the regulation of seabed mining

Seabed mining, whether in national jurisdiction or ABNJ is not extensively regulated on a regional level in Southeast Asia, particularly when compared to regional efforts underway in the EU[25]

17 Statement by Vietnam on its partial submission in respect of the North Area, Statement by the Chairman of the CLCS on the Progress of Work in the Commission, CLCS/64, 1 October 2009, para. 103; Partial submission of data and information on the outer limits of the continental shelf of the Republic of the Philippines, 8 April 2009, para. 3.4.

18 Vietnam has argued that the Paracel Islands are not entitled to any EEZ or continental shelf: See V. Ngoc Diep, 'Vietnam's Note Verbale on the South China Sea,' *Asia Maritime Transparency Initiative*, 5 May 2020.

19 ASEAN Secretariat, ASEAN Integration Report 2019, p. 107.

20 ASEAN Minerals Cooperation Plan 2016–2025 (AMCAP-III) Phase 1: 2016–2020, October 2016, para. 1.

21 B. Doherty, 'Collapse of PNG Deep-Sea Mining Venture Sparks Call for Moratorium', *The Guardian*, 15 September 2019.

22 B. Bainbridge, *PNG Pushing to Recover Millions from Deep Sea Mining Venture*, ABC, 26 August 2019.

23 'Chinese submersible discovers polymetallic nodules in South China Sea,' State Council, People's Republic of China, 6 May 2017.

24 ISA, Status of Contracts for Exploration, ISBA 26/C/4, 19 December 2019.

25 F. Arnesen, R. Greaves and A. Pozdnakova, 'European Union Law and the Seabed,' in C. Banet (ed), *The Law of the Seabed: Access, Uses and Protection of Seabed Resources*, Leiden: Brill Nijhoff, 2020, pp. 315–334. See as well Singh, Tassin Campanella and Maes, op. cit.

and the Pacific Islands.[26] There is no comprehensive regional regulatory approach although some regional frameworks have mentioned seabed mining in their documents. Four regional frameworks that have or could potentially regulate seabed mining are examined, all with varying degrees of formalization and institutionalization:[27] ASEAN, the Asia-Pacific Economic Co-operation (APEC), the Coordinating Body of the Seas of East Asia (COBSEA) and Partnerships in Environmental Management for the Seas of East Asia (PEMSEA).

ASEAN

ASEAN is the intergovernmental regional organization that is most relevant. It was established in 1967 in response to the 'petty nationalisms and jealousies' that characterized relations between the eight newly independent Southeast Asian states at that time.[28] Initially intended to 'institutionalize relations among the region's anti-communist states (Indonesia, Malaysia, the Philippines, Singapore and Thailand) and provide a forum to address anxieties about the actions of outside powers,'[29] ASEAN now includes Brunei, Vietnam, Laos, Myanmar and Cambodia. Timor-Leste and Papua New Guinea are observers at ASEAN and wish to join as full members.[30]

ASEAN has evolved from a loose and informal organization based on consultation and consensus to one that has attempted to concretize its legal and institutional decision-making procedures.[31] In 2007, ASEAN adopted the ASEAN Charter as the foundation for regional integration, aimed at giving ASEAN a legal personality, reforming ASEAN's institutional framework and entrenching a rules-based regime.[32] ASEAN follows a hierarchical structure with the ASEAN Summit, comprising heads of state, having 'ultimate control' of all major areas of governance in ASEAN and is the 'supreme policy-making body of ASEAN.'[33] The ASEAN Coordinating Council, consisting of the ASEAN Foreign Ministers, is the intermediary between the ASEAN Community Councils and other relevant bodies in implementing the agreements and decisions of the Summit.[34] The ASEAN Community Councils are divided into the three pillars of the ASEAN: the ASEAN Economic Community (AEC), ASEAN Political and Security Community (APSC) and the ASEAN Socio-

26 See Pacific-ACP States Regional Legislative and Regulatory Framework for Deep Sea Minerals Exploration and Exploitation, Prepared under the SPC-EU EDF1 Deep Sea Minerals Project, July 2012. Papua New Guinea and Timor-Leste are part of this regulatory framework. For more information on the Pacific region, see in this book C. Diver, 'Pacific Islands Region and Seabed Mining,' in V. Tassin Campanella (ed), *Routledge Handbook of Seabed Mining and the Law of the Sea*, op. cit., chapter VI 1.5.

27 For a detailed discussion of regional co-operation frameworks in Southeast Asia, see M. Oba, 'Further Development of Asian Regionalism: Institutional Hedging in an Uncertain Era,' *Journal of Contemporary East Asia Studies* 8 (2), 2019, 125–140; Centre for International Law (CIL), *Regional Cooperation for Protection of the Marine Environment in Southeast Asia: A Brief History*, 7 January 2019.

28 A. Acharya, *The Making of Southeast Asia: International Relations of a Region*, Singapore: ISEAS, 2012, 150.

29 Chia, op. cit. p. 1. ASEAN was formed through constitutive instruments such as the *1967 ASEAN Bangkok Declaration*, 8 August 1967 and the *1976 Treaty of Amity and Co-operation in Southeast Asia*, 24 February 1976.

30 ASEAN, *Chairman's Statement at the 36th ASEAN Summit*, 26 June 2020, para. 30; L. Hunt, 'Papua New Guinea Eyes ASEAN,' *The Diplomat*, 9 November 2011.

31 I. Deinla, *The Development of the Rule of Law in ASEAN: The State and Regional Integration*, Cambridge: Cambridge University Press, 2017, pp. 1–25.

32 Ibid.

33 Ibid., 141; ASEAN Charter 2007, article 7. For an overview of the organizational structure of ASEAN, see ASEAN website.

34 Article 8, ASEAN Charter 2007.

Cultural Community (ASSC).[35] The ASEAN Community Councils are supported by the ASEAN Sectoral Ministerial Bodies[36] who are in turn supported by committees and working groups that may involve private actors or experts.[37] There are several ASEAN-led organizations that support the work of ASEAN in different sectors, for example, the ASEAN Centre for Biodiversity, ASEAN Centre for Energy and the ASEAN Council on Petroleum.[38] There are also ASEAN-led cooperation mechanisms with external partners.[39]

While the ASEAN Charter was a step towards legalization and formalization as the basis of regional integration (as compared to its previous informality), ASEAN is different from other regional organizations. First, ASEAN is not a 'supranational international organization' like the EU which has a fundamental legal order with primacy over national legal orders and the authority to declare inconsistent legislation invalid.[40] ASEAN is firmly an 'intergovernmental organization' and any legal and policy development is determined by ASEAN Member States (AMS). Second, there are few institutional arrangements for accountability, nor legal institutions that can determine inconsistencies between national laws and ASEAN norms and there is no autonomous body that can perform enforcement functions.[41] Third, ASEAN lacks detailed procedural rules on decision-making. Decision-making is characterized by its practice of consultation and consensus, sometimes described as 'the ASEAN way.'[42] Where consensus cannot be achieved, the ASEAN Summit may decide how a specific decision can be made,[43] without prejudice to decision-making procedures contained in relevant ASEAN legal instruments,[44] as well as the discretion given to each ASEAN Community Council to prescribe its own rules of procedure.[45] Fourth, ASEAN has adopted a wide range of instruments, ranging from blueprints to workplans, but there is little guidance on how these instruments are concluded and their legal effect.[46] Many of these instruments fall largely in the category of 'soft law' but may still have normative value in that they guide the behavior of AMS and their officials, as well as the ASEAN bureaucracy.[47]

ASEAN (in contrast to the EU) is not a party to UNCLOS or any of the implementing agreements adopted under UNCLOS. Seabed mining has not been extensively addressed by ASEAN. However, two sectoral bodies potentially have mandates to address seabed mining: the ASEAN Economic Community (AEC) and the ASEAN Socio-Cultural Community (ASSC).

35 Ibid., article 9.
36 Ibid., article 10.
37 Deinla, op. cit. p. 137.
38 For a discussion on these organizations, see CIL, *A Brief History*, op. cit., 12–15.
39 ASEAN establishes bilateral relationships with external partners with different tiers of partnerships such as Dialogue Partners, Sectoral Dialogue Partner and Development Partner and co-operation ranges on a variety of issues under the three pillars. For a more detailed discussion, see ASEAN website.
40 Deinla, op. cit., p. 128.
41 Ibid.
42 Ibid., 1.
43 Articles 20 and 21, ASEAN Charter 2007.
44 Ibid., article 20 (3).
45 Ibid., article 21. For economic issues, ASEAN uses the ASEAN minus X formula which enables two or more AMS to move ahead on economic matters on the basis that the other members will follow at a later stage. ASEAN Minus X has been used on an ad-hoc basis on non-economic issues: See Ralf Emmers, 'ASEAN minus X: Should this formula be extended?,' RSIS Commentary, 24 October 2017.
46 See D. Aziz and R. Dehousse, 'The Instruments of Governance of ASEAN: An Inventory and Critical Analysis,' *ASEAN Integration Through Law Project*, ASEAN Governance, Management and External Legal Relations, CIL website.
47 Ibid.

The AEC has adopted several blueprints on economic cooperation. The most recent one, the AEC Blueprint 2025, recognizes the need to enhance trade and investment and strengthen cooperation and capacity for sustainable mineral development in the region.[48] The ASEAN Senior Officials Meeting (ASOMM) has adopted several co-operation action plans on minerals.[49] The latest action plan, the ASEAN Minerals Cooperation Action Plan (AMCP-III) for 2016 to 2025, set out its objective to 'further enhance ASEAN mineral sector dynamism with revitalized strategies and new initiatives towards boosting trade and investments, closer cooperation and strengthening capacity in sustainable mineral development for a more prosperous and integrated ASEAN.'[50] Strategic measures include facilitating and enhancing trade and investment in minerals; promoting environmentally and socially sustainable mineral development; strengthening institutional and human capacities in the ASEAN minerals sector; and maintaining an efficient and up-to-date ASEAN Minerals Database. The ASOMM is responsible for the implementation of AMCP-III and is assisted by ASEAN minerals working groups, namely, Working Groups on Trade and Investment in Minerals; Sustainable Minerals Development; Capacity Building in Minerals; and Minerals Information and Database; as well as the ASEAN Minerals Trust Fund, and the ASEAN Secretariat. There is no definition of 'mining' in any of the AMCPs, and there is nothing to indicate that the AMCPs are excluding or including seabed mining. However, the AMCP-III does state that 'to enhance sustainable mineral development, all AMS need to consider the environmental impacts of mining to people, biodiversity, forests and *water*' including ensuring that 'all mining activities in the ASEAN region are conducted sustainably, both during and after mining.'[51]

The ASSC would, in principle, have a mandate over seabed mining because of the impact of seabed mining on the marine environment. Environmental matters within ASEAN are overseen by the ASEAN Ministerial Meeting on the Environment. The ASEAN Senior Officials on the Environment (ASOEN) supervise seven subsidiary bodies and/or working groups that focus on strategic priorities which include Coastal and Marine Environment and Natural Resources and Biodiversity. The Fourth ASEAN State of the Environment Report acknowledged that 'shipping and sea-based activities, including oil spills, sludge disposal, ballast water changes and *mining* in coastal areas'[52] are threats to the marine environment. Other than that, ASEAN's current environmental focus on mining is limited to terrestrial mining and seabed mining has not been considered in detail. The most relevant Working Group would be the ASEAN Working Group on Coastal and Marine Environment and while it has a general mandate to ensure ASEAN's coastal and marine environment are sustainably managed, its focus has been on marine biodiversity conservation, oil spills, marine pollution mitigation, invasive alien species, marine debris and climate change.[53] Seabed mining has not come under its radar yet.

APEC

APEC has 21 member economies consisting of 8 Southeast Asian states (Brunei, Indonesia, Malaysia, Papua New Guinea, the Philippines, Singapore, Thailand and Vietnam) and 13 other

48 See ASEAN Economic Community Blueprint (AEC Blueprint) 2025, para. 62.

49 The ASEAN Senior Officials Meeting on Minerals (ASOMM) has adopted the ASEAN Minerals Cooperation Action Plan (AMCP-I) from 2005 to 2010, followed by AMCP-II from 2011 to 2015 and finally AMCP-III from 2016 to 2025.

50 AMCP-III, para. 14.

51 Ibid., para. 4 (emphasis added).

52 ASEAN Secretariat, Fourth State of the Environment Report, 2009, 49 (emphasis added).

53 ASEAN, ASEAN Co-operation on Coastal and Marine Environment, ASEAN website.

economies. It was established as an informal ministerial-level dialogue in 1989 and while some institutionalization has occurred, it remains a multilateral trade and economic dialogue forum. It eschews formal binding commitments but uses 'soft' outputs adopted at the ministerial level by consensus and implemented by working groups.[54]

APEC has a Senior Officials' Meeting Steering Committee on Economic and Technical Cooperation which has focused on terrestrial mining.[55] It also has a working group on Oceans and Fisheries.[56] The working group has not addressed seabed mining in a meaningful manner, although there was a 2002 APEC Report on current and emerging marine-related activities of APEC that mentions seabed mining as an example of an emerging activity relevant to APEC.[57]

COBSEA

COBSEA is a regional seas program adopted under the UN Environmental Programme (UNEP). It addresses the 'Seas of East Asia' which encompasses a series of large marine ecosystems in the East China Sea, the Yellow Sea, the South China Sea, the Sulu-Celebes Sea and the Indonesian Seas, and covers only areas under national jurisdiction. While other regional seas programs center around a binding treaty, COBSEA is an intergovernmental forum established by the 1981 East Asian Action Plan to deal with marine pollution in East Asian seas.[58] It brings together nine countries (Cambodia, China, Indonesia, Republic of Korea, Malaysia, the Philippines, Thailand, Singapore and Vietnam) to address different marine environmental issues, with current priorities focused on land-based pollution and marine plastics.[59] COBSEA has not explicitly addressed seabed mining.

PEMSEA

PEMSEA originated in the Global Environmental Facility (GEF) / UN Development Programme (UNDP) on prevention and management of marine pollution in the East Asian Seas with the International Maritime Organization as the executing body but has evolved into a self-sustaining regional co-ordination mechanism for the implementation of the Sustainable Development Strategy for the Seas of East Asia adopted by the GEF.[60] PEMSEA has 11 country partners consisting of Cambodia, China, Indonesia, Japan, Democratic People's Republic of Korea (DPRK), Laos, the Philippines, Republic of Korea, Singapore, Timor-Leste and Vietnam. PEMSEA is responsible for implementing the Sustainable Development Strategy for the Seas of East Asia including the UN Sustainable Development Goals and the Convention on Biological Diversity.[61]

54 S-Y. Peng, 'The Soft Law Approach to Regulatory Harmonization,' in J. Chaisse and T.-y. Lin, *International Economic Law and Governance: Essays in Honour of Mitsuo Matshushita*, Oxford: Oxford University Press, 2016, pp. 328, 340.

55 APEC Current Activities on Mining, APEC website.

56 APEC Ocean and Fisheries, ibid.

57 APEC Integrated Ocean Management Forum Two 'Think-Piece' on the Current and Emerging Marine-Related Activities of APEC, June 2002.

58 1981 Action Plan for the Protection and Development of the Marine and Coastal Areas of the East Asian Region, UNEP Regional Seas Reports and Studies No. 24, UNEP 1983.

59 COBSEA, Strategic Directions 2018–2022.

60 CIL, *A Brief History*, op. cit., 13.

61 PEMSEA's Sustainable Development Strategy for the Seas of East Asia: Implementation Plan 2018–2022.

PEMSEA, with its focus on the sustainable development of the blue economy, recognizes seabed mining as an industry relevant to East Asia. PEMSEA's 2003 Sustainable Development Strategy states that one of its objectives was to assess and manage the environmental risks of seabed mining[62] and its post-2020 Futures Report and Strategy also recognizes seabed mining as an industry that could add pressure to coastal and marine environments.[63]

Conclusion

Regional governance frameworks in Southeast Asia are not comprehensively tackling regulation of seabed mining. There are several possible reasons for this. First, there is a paucity of data on the existence of minerals in maritime areas within national jurisdiction and apart from the South China Sea and the Bismarck Sea, seabed mining does not appear to be contemplated. Second, the majority of Southeast Asian states are developing countries which may not have the financial and technological capabilities to search for, explore and exploit seabed minerals.[64] This may impede development of seabed mining within national jurisdiction but also in the Area, as ISA licenses are contingent on applicants having sufficient financial and technical capabilities.[65] Third, it is said that government officials, academics and citizens lack awareness on seabed mining, which means less opportunities for it to come up on the agendas of these regional bodies.[66] Fourth, the environmental priorities of existing regional frameworks are focused on threats such as climate change and marine plastics and the fact that seabed mining is not conducted on a large scale in areas within national jurisdiction means that it is not a priority.

Indeed, there are several factors that may pose challenges to the adoption of an effective regional strategy on seabed mining. First, Southeast Asian states and relevant co-operating extra-regional states have diverse national interests and concerns. Generating the political will to formulate common policies is not straightforward. In ASEAN, for example, AMS drive policy-making and consensus is generally needed in decision-making – not all AMS will have the same interests vis-à-vis seabed mining.

Second, regional frameworks in Southeast Asia utilize informal outputs that are couched in general terms to preserve maximum flexibility. Any regional instrument that purports to 'regulate' seabed mining will likely consist of flexible guidelines or implementation strategies. While these instruments have normative value in that they guide implementation by national policymakers, individual AMS will have different levels of implementation depending on their capabilities.

Third, and particularly in relation to ASEAN, while the marine environment is important, ASEAN's record on the protection of the marine environment 'remains largely to be developed.'[67] ASEAN itself has acknowledged that the slow progress in managing coastal and marine environments is due to, *inter alia*, 'a lack of irrefutable and clear information about the nature and extent

62 PEMSEA, *Sustainable Development Strategy for the Seas of East Asia: Regional Implementation of the World Summit on Sustainable Development Requirements for the Coasts and Oceans*, 2003.

63 PEMSEA, *Post-2020 Futures Report and Strategy*, 17.

64 A. Satrio Nugroho and I. Riswanti Putranti, 'International Seabed Regime in Southeast Asia: The Lack of ASEAN Member States' Role in Seabed Mining,' *Indonesian Perspective* 3 (1), 2018, 37–51.

65 Article 4, Annex III, UNCLOS.

66 Ibid.

67 K. Kheng Lian, N. Robinson and L. Lin-Heng, *ASEAN Environmental Legal Integration*, Cambridge: Cambridge University Press, 2016, p. 47.

of the problems affecting the coastal and marine environment; legal and institutional complexities; non-involvement of local communities, and weak multi-sectoral co-operation.'[68]

Fourth, the presence of sovereignty disputes and overlapping claims in areas which are purportedly under the jurisdiction of Southeast Asian states have historically stymied efforts to develop coherent regional policies on certain issues. Placing seabed mining on the agenda of regional frameworks risks highlighting regional tensions, particularly given China's dominance in seabed mining and its potential seabed mining activities in the South China Sea.[69]

Fifth, it is also not immediately clear which regional framework would be best suited to take the lead in developing regional policy on seabed mining. ASEAN may be the best place to start given the emphasis placed on ASEAN centrality, its inclusion of the core Southeast Asian states, its mandate over minerals and the environment, and its focus on sustainable development of resources. Singapore (which has an ISA license to explore the Area) and Malaysia and Indonesia (which have relatively developed offshore oil and gas industries and may need to look at seabed minerals given dwindling land resources)[70] could potentially drive the development of such regional policy. PEMSEA and COBSEA may also be suitable given their overt environmental mandates and their links to the UN, and PEMSEA may be more appropriate given that the issue is already on its agenda. The inclusion of extra-regional states in these frameworks could be a double-edged sword in that Japan, Korea and China have experience in seabed mining and could share their expertise but at the same time, their involvement could raise sensitive political issues relating to sovereignty disputes and overlapping maritime claims in Southeast Asian waters.

Notwithstanding these challenges, there are compelling reasons for regional frameworks to prepare for the possibility that seabed mining may occur within national jurisdictions in the future particularly as mineral supplies on land deplete. Further, these regional frameworks should also consider the implications of seabed mining taking place in ABNJ in the Indo-Pacific region, which will have an impact on Southeast Asian waters under national jurisdiction. Indeed, activities in ABNJ are receiving increasing attention from Southeast Asian states due to the ongoing negotiations of a new instrument on marine biodiversity in ABNJ and Southeast Asian states (such as Indonesia, the Philippines and Singapore) have been vocal about their positions on certain issues in the negotiations.[71] Undoubtedly, the time is ripe to think more deeply about whether seabed mining in the Indo-Pacific warrants a common, regional approach from states in Southeast Asia.

68 ASEAN Secretariat, Fourth State of Environment Report, op. cit., p. 49.

69 D. Long, 'Scramble for the Indo-Pacific Seabed,' *The Diplomat*, 16 November 2019.

70 Scholars from Malaysia and Indonesia, two of the largest Southeast Asian land producers of minerals, have argued that their governments should be considering seabed mining both within their own waters as well as in the Area given their dwindling land resources: See D. Puspitawati, 'Deep-Sea Mining Law in Indonesia: Challenges and Opportunities,' International Conference on Energy and Mining Law (ICEML 2018); N. Munirah Fuad et al., 'Mining the Deep Seabed: Is Malaysia Ready?,' *Asian Social Science* 13 (2), 2017, 107–115.

71 S. Nishanthi Gunasekara and Md Siaful Karim, 'The Role of ASEAN and Its Members in Promoting the Norm of Responsible Governance of Marine Biodiversity of Areas Beyond National Jurisdiction,' *Review of European and Comparative International Environmental Law* 30 (1), 2021, 128–137.

VI.2

National practice

VI.2.1
BELGIUM AND SEABED MINING

Klaas Willaert and Frank Maes

Introduction

Although the Belgian continental shelf is only relevant for sand and gravel mining, regulated by an elaborate legal framework, the role of Belgium within the context of seabed mining cannot be underestimated, as the Belgian company Global Sea Mineral Resources (GSR) plays a pivotal part in the development of seabed mining technology in the Clarion-Clipperton Zone.[1] Belgium adopted national legislation on seabed mining activities in the Area in 2013 and is closely involved in the development of seabed mining regulations by the International Seabed Authority (ISA).

Geographical extent of the exclusive economic zone, continental shelf and the Area

The Belgian exclusive economic zone (EEZ) and continental shelf geographically overlap and, starting beyond the territorial sea, cover 2,017 square kilometers (km^2) of the Belgian part of the North Sea (3,454 km^2), extending to approximately 47 nautical miles from the baseline.[2] On the Belgian continental shelf, which borders the continental shelves of France, the United Kingdom and the Netherlands, sand and gravel extraction is possible in dedicated zones. In practice, there is almost no gravel extraction, while sand extraction amounts to an annual volume of 3,000,000 to 4,000,000 m^3.[3] Belgian companies are worldwide leaders in dredging and beach nourishment,

1 Decision of the Council of the International Seabed Authority relating to a request for approval of a plan of work for exploration for polymetallic nodules submitted by G-TEC Sea Mineral Resources NV, 26 July 2012, *ISA Doc.* ISBA/18/C/28.

2 Article 2-3 Law of 22 April 1999 regarding the Belgian Exclusive Economic Zone in the North Sea, *BS* 10 July 1999, 26491 (hereinafter 'Law of 22 April 1999'); article 2 Law of 13 June 1969 regarding the exploration and exploitation of non-living resources of the territorial sea and the continental shelf, *BS* 8 October 1969, 9479; BMM, *Belgian Territorial Sea and Exclusive Economic Zone*. Available online <https://web.archive.org/web/20140416185045/http://www.mumm.ac.be/NL/Management/Atlas/map.php?TerritorialSeaEEZ> (accessed 9 December 2019).

3 FOD Economie, *Offshore sand and gravel extraction*. Available online <https://economie.fgov.be/nl/themas/ondernemingen/specifieke-sectoren/zand-en-grindwinning-op-de> (accessed 9 December 2019).

DOI: 10.4324/9780429426162-30

and due to this specific expertise, Belgium is also active in the Area. The contract area of GSR, a subsidiary of the Belgian DEME Group which is involved in seabed mining in the Area and is sponsored by Belgium, is located in the eastern-central part of the Clarion-Clipperton Zone in the Pacific Ocean and covers almost 76,728 km^2.[4]

Regulation of seabed mining activities

There is no seabed mining on the Belgian continental shelf due to the close proximity to the coast and the lack of depth, which reaches a maximum of 40 meters.[5] The general rules regarding exploration and exploitation activities on the Belgian continental shelf can be found in a Belgian law of 13 June 1969[6] and are further elaborated in royal decrees of 1 September 2004[7] and 21 October 2018.[8] Seabed mining activities in the Area are in turn governed by a separate legal framework, consisting of a Belgian law of 17 August 2013[9] and a royal decree of 4 October 2013.[10]

The Belgian legislation on the exploration and exploitation of minerals and other non-living resources located on the seabed or the subsoil of the Belgian continental shelf contains the conditions and procedures to grant concessions for sand and gravel extraction, giving effect to the exclusive sovereign rights granted by the *United Nations Convention on the Law of the Sea* (UNCLOS) to coastal states.[11] Concessions can only be issued in legally defined areas,[12] are awarded in the form of a ministerial decree,[13] are subject to a fee[14] and apply for a certain duration, which is usu-

4 Report and recommendations of the Legal and Technical Commission to the Council of the International Seabed Authority relating to an application for the approval of a plan of work for exploration for polymetallic nodules by G-TEC Sea Mineral Resources NV, 20 July 2012, *ISA Doc.* ISBA/18/C/19, 2; GSR, *How big is the area that GSR intends to harvest?* Available online <https://www.deme-group.com/gsr/frequently-asked-questions> (accessed 9 December 2019).

5 F. Maes, J. Schrijvers and A. Vanhulle (eds), *A Flood of Space. Towards a Spatial Structure Plan for the Sustainable Management of the North Sea*, Brussels: Belgian Science Policy, 2005, 32–33.

6 Law of 13 June 1969 regarding the exploration and exploitation of non-living resources of the territorial sea and the continental shelf, *BS* 8 October 1969, 9479 (hereinafter 'Law of 13 June 1969'), as amended by the Law of 22 April 1999.

7 Royal Decree of 1 September 2004 regarding the conditions and application procedure for concessions for exploration and exploitation of mineral and other non-living resources in the territorial sea and on the continental shelf, *BS* 7 October 2004, 70529 (hereinafter 'Royal Decree of 1 September 2004').

8 Royal Decree of 21 October 2018 regarding the rules concerning environmental impact assessment in pursuance of the Law of 13 June 1969 regarding the exploration and exploitation of non-living resources of the territorial sea and the continental shelf, *BS* 29 October 2018, 82314 (hereinafter 'Royal Decree of 21 October 2018').

9 Law of 17 August 2013 concerning the prospection, exploration and exploitation of the natural resources of the seabed and the subsoil beyond national jurisdiction, *BS* 16 September 2013, 65612 (hereinafter 'Law of 17 August 2013').

10 Royal Decree of 4 October 2013 concerning the prospection, exploration and exploitation of the natural resources of the seabed and the subsoil beyond national jurisdiction, *BS* 15 October 2013, 73061, as amended by Royal Decree of 10 January 2016, *BS* 22 January 2016, 4506 (hereinafter 'Royal Decree of 4 October 2013').

11 Article 77 UNCLOS.

12 These zones are indicated in marine spatial plans, of which the most recent one applies to the period 2020–2026 (article 15 Royal Decree of 22 May 2019 concerning the establishment of a marine spatial plan for the period 2020 until 2026 in the Belgian sea areas, *BS* 2 July 2019, 66980).

13 Article 15, paragraph 1 Royal Decree of 1 September 2004.

14 The fee that needs to be paid is calculated by multiplying the number of extracted cubic meters of gravel or sand with a specified factor, subject to an annual minimum, and is used to monitor the environmental effects of the exploitation activities (ibid., article 29).

ally 10 years and can be extended.[15] Each application for a concession is subject to an environmental impact assessment and a public consultation procedure.[16] A concession can only be awarded in the case of positive advice from the minister of environment, but the minister of economy takes the final decision.[17] After the granting of a concession, the exploitation is continuously monitored by black boxes on board of the vessels, providing data on position, volumes, duration, etc. Intolerable adverse effects on the marine environment can lead to total or partial cancellation or suspension of the concession.[18]

With regard to seabed mining in the Area, the relevant Belgian legislation implements the international rules of the UNCLOS, the *1994 Agreement relating to the implementation of Part XI of the UNCLOS* (1994 Agreement) and the ISA regulations by confirming the main principles regarding prospecting, exploration and exploitation.[19] Prior notification is required for prospecting,[20] while procedures and conditions for the granting of a certificate of sponsorship by the Belgian government are issued for exploration and exploitation activities by its nationals.[21] Comparable to the exploration and exploitation activities on the continental shelf, the decision-making process is characterized by strictly defined deadlines[22] and an inter-agency coordination mechanism is in place to assess applications: the minister of economy is charged with the final decision, but advice on environmental matters is provided by the ministry of environment.[23] An application file must contain information demonstrating the financial and technical ability of the applicant and a sound environmental impact study, but unlike its above-mentioned counterpart, the law does not provide for a public consultation procedure.[24] If the application is deemed complete and admissible, the minister of economy grants a non-transferable certificate of sponsorship, which is sent to the ISA by the ministry of foreign affairs.[25] The Belgian legislation contains an article which stresses the responsibility and liability of the contractor and requires them to take out appropriate insurance.[26] There are also provisions detailing the audit regime which is imposed on Belgian prospectors and contractors,[27] a clause determining the fees that need to be paid[28] and a section formulating sanctions in case of illegal actions.[29]

In 2019, the Belgian government concluded that certain aspects of the Belgian legislation on seabed mining activities in the Area could be improved and should be more aligned with the future exploitation regulations of the ISA. Among others, a more structured approach, a public consultation process and an elaborate monitoring regime would be introduced, initially by revising

15 Ibid., articles 16 and 20.

16 Article 3, paragraph 2 Law of 13 June 1969; ibid., article 10; article 12 Royal Decree of 21 October 2018.

17 Article 3, paragraph 3 Law of 13 June 1969; article 13-15 Royal Decree of 1 September 2004.

18 Article 3, paragraphs 2–3 Law of 13 June 1969.

19 Cf. article 3-9 Law of 17 August 2013; article 2 Royal Decree of 4 October 2013.

20 Article 6 Law of 17 August 2013.

21 Ibid., article 8; article 3-6 Royal Decree of 4 October 2013.

22 Article 4, article 5, article 6, paragraphs 2–3 and article 8, paragraphs 3–4 Royal Decree of 4 October 2013.

23 Ibid., articles 5–6.

24 Article 8, paragraph 2 Law of 17 August 2013; ibid., article 3, paragraph 2.

25 Article 6-7 Royal Decree of 4 October 2013.

26 Article 9 Law of 17 August 2013.

27 Apart from the submission of annual reports and other relevant information, the Belgian legislation also includes a general provision on remote monitoring during the exploitation phase, requiring the contractor to provide the necessary means of communication and digital connections (ibid., article 10; article 8 Royal Decree of 4 October 2013).

28 The Belgian government charges an application fee of €10,000 and an annual premium of €40,000 (article 11 Law of 17 August 2013).

29 Ibid., articles 12–15.

the implementing decision and eventually by amending the existing law. In 2020, this approach seemed to be altered, however, as the competent authorities expressed the ambition to accomplish a full-fledged reform of the law and royal decree at once.

Apart from domestic legislation, Belgium is also prominently involved in the development of ISA regulations, standards and guidelines. For example, within the context of the ISA draft exploitation regulations, Belgium advocated the introduction of independent expert reviews as a necessary step in the consideration of plans of work for exploitation to strengthen transparent and environmentally sound decision-making.[30] The legal and technical commission would choose three experts from a pre-compiled pool and their opinions would be taken into account when deciding to recommend the plan of work or not, without any legally binding power. However, support for the proposal was not unanimous: the ISA secretariat indicated in a discussion note that the proposed independent review process needs to provide actual added value and should not introduce additional complexities or costs to the process,[31] while several delegations in the council believed that the process should not necessarily be institutionalized, pointing out that there are existing possibilities to involve independent experts,[32] and expressed concerns about the effect of the proposed mechanism on the independent functioning of the legal and technical commission.[33] Nonetheless, Belgium's influence on the lawmaking processes at the ISA will only grow in the future, since it will serve as a member of the council for the period 2021–2024 in a rotation agreement with the Netherlands and Norway.[34]

Seabed activities and related decisions

On the Belgian continental shelf, several companies have been granted a concession for sand and gravel mining.[35] To extract polymetallic nodules from the Area, GSR submitted a request for approval of a plan of work to the secretary-general of the ISA on 31 May 2012.[36] Two certificates of sponsorship were issued, dated 8 May 2012 and 21 June 2012 respectively, and Belgium stated that it has a vested historical interest in the Clarion-Clipperton Zone through the work of Belgian professor Alphonse François Renard (1842–1903) and the past exploration efforts by the Belgian corporation *Union Minière* (now Umicore).[37] The legal and technical commission of the ISA considered the application by examining the submitted data and by evaluating the

30 ISA, *Strengthening the environmental scientific capacity of the International Seabed Authority*. Available online <https://www.isa.org.jm/document/statement-belgium-0> (accessed 5 February 2019).

31 Consideration of a mechanism and process for the independent review of environmental plans and performance assessments under the regulations on exploitation of mineral resources in the Area, 11 January 2019, *ISA Doc*. ISBA/25/C/10.

32 Cf. article 12, paragraph 4, b) Draft Regulations on Exploitation of Mineral Resources in the Area, 25 March 2019, *ISA Doc*. ISBA/25/C/WP.1.

33 'Summary of the Twenty-Fifth Annual Session of the Council of the International Seabed Authority (First Part): 25 February – 1 March 2019', *Earth Negotiations Bulletin* 25 (185), 2019.

34 ISA, *ISA Assembly elects new Council members for the period 2021–2024*. Available online <https://www.isa.org.jm/index.php/news/isa-assembly-elects-new-council-members-period-2021-2024> (accessed 9 March 2021).

35 Cf. article 49 Royal Decree of 1 September 2004.

36 Decision of the Council of the International Seabed Authority relating to a request for approval of a plan of work for exploration for polymetallic nodules submitted by G-TEC Sea Mineral Resources NV, 26 July 2012, *ISA Doc*. ISBA/18/C/28.

37 Indeed, the Area under application covered a part of the seabed where a license was formerly granted by the United States to Ocean Mining Associates (OMA), consisting of Tenneco, US Steel, Japan Mining Co. and *Union Minière* (Report and recommendations of the Legal and Technical Commission to the Council of the International Seabed

financial and technical qualifications of the applicant, and recommended approval of the plan of work to the council.[38] On 26 July 2018, the council followed the recommendation of the legal and technical commission and approved the plan of work for the exploration of polymetallic nodules submitted by GSR, resulting in a 15-year contract starting from 14 January 2013 to 13 January 2028.[39] Next to this, the reserved area initially contributed by GSR is being explored by a joint venture between the Cook Islands Investment Corporation and GSR, sponsored by the Cook Islands.[40]

The sponsorship by the Belgian government with regard to the seabed mining activities of GSR in the Area was not obtained in accordance with the current Belgian law, as this legislation was only enacted on 17 August 2013, but the implementing decision solved this problem through a transitional arrangement. The transitional provision specifies that applicants who have already signed a contract with the ISA should submit a request for a certificate of sponsorship within two months of the official publication of the royal decree.[41] Such a request was automatically deemed admissible and successful.

In 2020, a resolution advocating a moratorium on seabed mining was submitted and this led to a parliamentary hearing on 24 June 2020. Presentations by representatives of the competent national authorities, international experts and the secretary-general of the ISA were followed by a wide array of questions by the members of parliament. In January 2021, an adjusted resolution was adopted by the Belgian chamber of representatives, requesting the Belgian government to support fundamental scientific research and data collection with a view to enhance the knowledge regarding the deep sea and to further protect existing marine ecosystems, as well as to continue to observe the relevant environmental legislation and the precautionary principle when developing possible exploitation rules for seabed mining.[42]

Conclusion

As demonstrated, Belgium's role in seabed mining should not be neglected. Through sponsorship of exploration activities in the Area and its active involvement in the development of the ISA mining code, the country certainly plays its part. Belgium has a legal framework in place to govern sand and gravel extraction on its continental shelf and also adopted legislation to regulate seabed mining activities in the Area, both giving effect to the rules and principles of international law.[43] Mining activities on the Belgian continental shelf require a concession, while applications to the ISA for seabed mining activities in the Area necessitate a certificate of sponsorship. Both

Authority relating to an application for the approval of a plan of work for exploration for polymetallic nodules by G-TEC Sea Mineral Resources NV, 20 July 2012, *ISA Doc.* ISBA/18/C/19, 3).

38 Ibid.

39 Decision of the Council of the International Seabed Authority relating to a request for approval of a plan of work for exploration for polymetallic nodules submitted by G-TEC Sea Mineral Resources NV, 26 July 2012, *ISA Doc.* ISBA/18/C/28.

40 Application for approval of a plan of work for exploration for polymetallic nodules by the Cook Islands Investment Corporation, 8 November 2013, *ISA Doc.* ISBA/20/LTC/3, §12.

41 Article 9 Royal Decree of 4 October 2013.

42 De Kamer, *Resolution on deep sea mining (Doc 55 1687/003)*. Available online <https://www.dekamer.be/flwb/pdf/55/1687/55K1687003.pdf> (accessed 9 March 2021).

43 For European law applicable to Belgium, see in this book P. Singh, V. Tassin Campanella and F. Maes, 'The European Union and seabed mining', in V. Tassin Campanella (ed), *Routledge Handbook of Seabed Mining and the Law of the Sea*, London: Routledge, 2023, chapter VI.1.4.

procedures entail an inter-agency decision-making mechanism and an environmental impact study, although the issue of a certificate of sponsorship ultimately comes down to an admissibility test, without any review on the merits, and does not involve a public consultation process. The Belgian seabed mining legislation adheres closely to the international conventions and ISA regulations, but in order to prepare for the exploitation phase and enact several improvements, legislative reforms are underway.

VI.2.2
BRAZIL AND SEABED MINING

Carina Costa de Oliveira and Ana Flávia Barros-Platiau

Introduction

Land-based and offshore mining activities are so relevant for its economic development that Brazil has become a world-class producer of oil, natural gas and other minerals such as iron, ore, manganese and bauxite. The Brazilian pre-salt oil exploitation, which started in 2006, is an offshore oil reserve which accounted for 73 percent of Brazilian oil and gas in 2020. Regarding minerals, most of the offshore exploitation activities take place in the territorial sea, and are related to the extraction of sand, limestone, ilmenite, phosphates and coral limestone.[1] Most of the continental shelf is still unexplored but offers important perspectives for future exploitation. The geopolitical interests related to the South Atlantic also enlarged the Brazilian focus on seabed mining.[2] In this context, some geographical aspects of Brazil's marine reality will be presented below before explaining the applicable regulatory framework.

Geographical extent of the exclusive economic zone, continental shelf and the Area

Brazil has 3.5 million square kilometers of exclusive economic zone[3] and 7,367 km of coastline, comprising 17 federal states along the coast and 280 municipalities with more than 30 million inhabitants. The EEZ was named 'Blue Amazon' by the navy in 2004 and it is mentioned in the Ministry of defense's white book. Since the pre-salt is considered a strategic priority, the continental shelf extension was intended to protect the region from foreign drilling activities. On 17 May 2004, Brazil submitted a first request for the extension of its continental shelf to the Commission on the Limits of the Continental Shelf, and after that some revised submissions were

1 See on this issue: R.A Lima, *O licenciamento ambiental como instrumento para uma gestão integrada dos recursos minerais no espaço marinho brasileiro*, PhD thesis, University of Brasília Law Faculty, 2019.

2 For more information on the regional context, see in this book E. Jiménez Pineda, 'South American region and Seabed Mining' in V. Tassin Campanella (ed), *Routledge Handbook of Seabed Mining and the Law of the Sea*, London: Routledge, 2023, chapter VI.1.6.

3 Hereinafter 'EEZ'.

DOI: 10.4324/9780429426162-31

sent. In December 2018, Brazil presented its third partial revised submission which included the Rio Grande Rise. Resultantly, the area under Brazilian jurisdiction may be extended to 5.7 million square kilometers if the Brazilian submission is fully approved.

As for seabed mining in the Area, on 9 November 2015, Brazil, through the Companhia de Produção de Recursos Minerais (CPRM),[4] signed a contract with the International Seabed Authority[5] to explore cobalt-rich ferromanganese crusts in the Area. This was the first Brazilian contract signed to explore an Area of around 3 thousand square kilometers placed in the South Atlantic, the Rio Grande Rise, which is situated 1,200 km from the Brazilian coast. However, in January 2022, the Secretary-General informed members of ISA of a notification by CPRM renouncing without penalty the whole of its rights in the exploration area as defined by its contract for the exploration of cobalt-rich ferromanganese crusts and a notification from Brazil terminating its sponsorship of CPRM.[6] The reason why it happened is that the 2018 Brazilian submission to the Commission on the Limits of the Continental Shelf encompasses the area provided for in the contract.[7] CIRM's Resolution 17/2020 considered that a coastal State can exercise its rights within this extended continental shelf even before the recommendation of the Commission, based on the *United Nations Convention on the Law of the Sea* (UNCLOS), Article 77 paragraph 3, which accords 'the rights of the coastal State over the continental shelf do not depend on occupation, effective or notional, or any express proclamation'. Resolution 18/2020 reaffirmed this perspective pointing out that Brazil should terminate its sponsorship of CPRM.[8]

Regulation of seabed mining activities

The institutional framework

The Brazilian current practices regarding seabed mining have a sectorial approach instead of an integrated one. This implies that the sector is not treated in connection with other economic activities regulations and policies. The lack of integration is inherent to the Brazilian institutional framework to regulate oil and other minerals exploration and exploitation in areas within and beyond national jurisdiction.

The main federal institutions which regulate seabed mining in Brazil are the Ministry of defense, the mining and energy Ministry and the Ministry of environment. Regarding activities beyond national jurisdiction, the Ministry of foreign affairs (MRE) is also a relevant body for the negotiation of seabed mining rules. The Ministry of defense has the competence to support vessels for both drilling and production, for the maintenance of the vessel monitoring system and for the provision of logistical support for inspection activities. The mining and energy Ministry approves and controls the platforms. The Ministry of environment regulates environmental protection of the marine environment, having broad competence related to marine resources management and environmental impacts.

4 The CPRM is a Brazilian public company, connected to the Mining and Energy Ministry, responsible for the research in geology.

5 Hereinafter 'ISA'.

6 ISA, Council, *ISBA/27/C/28*, 18 May 2022, p. 2.

7 CIRM, Resolution no. 17, 15 September 2020. Available online <https://www.marinha.mil.br/secirm/sites/www.marinha.mil.br.secirm/files/documentos/atas/resolucao-17-2020.pdf> (accessed 5 June 2022).

8 CIRM, Resolution no. 18, 15 September 2020.

The Navy, via the Executive Secretariat for the Inter-ministerial Commission for Marine Resources,[9] coordinates the administrative body responsible for the policies for the marine environment created in 1974. This administrative body, called CIRM, is composed of a coordinator, who is a Navy commander, and 18 representatives from different federal administrative bodies. Some policies have been established since the Commission's creation through the National Policies for the Marine space. The first one was published in 1980 and the last one was published in 2005 (decree no. 5.377/2005). The objective of these policies is to guide the development of activities that are related to the use, the exploration and the exploitation of marine living, minerals and energetic resources at the territorial sea, the economic exclusive zone and the continental shelf, following national interests in a rational and sustainable way in order to achieve a social and economic development.[10] This broad policy is implemented by plans such as the national plan for the coast management established by the law no. 7.661/88 and regulated by the decree no. 5.300/2004. It is also implemented by different programs such as: the sectorial plan for the marine resources; the Antarctic program; the plan of mapping the Brazilian continental shelf; the program for marine literacy; and the national plan for coastal management. The most recent sectorial plan for the marine resources is the X Plan (decree 10.544/2020).

The specific regulatory agencies which are competent for the management of oil and mineral resources are the national agency for mining and the national oil agency. Both grant permits for the exploration and the exploitation of natural resources within the areas under national jurisdiction. They are directly connected to the mining and energy Ministry, the latter being also the competent authority to establish policies for the exploration and exploitation of areas beyond national jurisdiction. For instance, the Companhia de Produção de Recursos Minerais, which signed the exploration contract with ISA, is connected to this Ministry.

Even though the CIRM tried to integrate environmental considerations to the seabed mining policies, the articulation with economic priorities is always a challenge.[11] Politically speaking, the environmental Ministry is less powerful than the Ministry of defense and the mining and energy Ministry. Therefore, the protection of the environment, which should be a central part of the regulation of seabed mining, is not integrated to the national natural-resources allocation decision-making process. The mining and the oil regulatory agencies are responsible for decisions on the allocation of the resources and oftentimes the decision-making process does not consider marine environmental impacts. Consequently, the resource permit is usually granted based on the applicant's assertion that the exploitation of the resource will be profitable to the local, regional and national economy.

Marine pollution can be pointed out as an example. In cases of marine pollution caused by ships, for instance, the causes of the damage will be examined mainly through the spectrum of the specific shipping sector. In addition, the actions adopted to manage the pollution will also be isolated in a specific sector. Marine environmental management could be more efficient under a two-pronged integrated approach. Firstly, integrating the impacts on the environment at the core of the marine regulation would help achieve the goal of maintaining the marine ecosystem's integrity and resilience. Secondly, a permanent administrative body integrated to the management system of

9 Hereinafter 'SECIRM'.

10 Brazil, Decree no. 5.377/05, related to the National Politic for Sea Resources.

11 See on this issue: C.C. Oliveira, G.G.B.L Moraes and P.P. Andrade, 'The Limited Contribution of Environmental Law to the Sustainable Management of Marine Resources in Brazil: The Need for an Integrated Approach' in V. Mauerhofer, D. Rupo and L. Tarquinio (eds) *Sustainability and Law: General and Specific Aspects*, Cham, Switzerland: Springer, 2020, pp. 497–519.

the marine environment would simplify the control of activities with potential direct and indirect adverse effects.

In this sense, this sectoral approach conspicuously results in and aims at a stronger focus on the economic objectives than on the environmental and the social ones. This perspective can hinder the Brazilian compliance with the *United Nations Convention on the Law of the Sea*[12] obligations on the protection and the preservation of the marine environment.

The integration problem discussed in this first part will be complemented by the gaps in the seabed mining legal framework.

The seabed mining legal framework

The national existing regulation of seabed mining for minerals is outdated and contains many gaps. The oil and gas regulation is more recent and updated. These two legal frameworks will be analyzed for activities within and beyond national jurisdiction. For minerals, the main legal framework is the Mining Code which dates back to 1967 (decree no. 227). National mining regulation does not distinguish between land and sea drilling. Therefore, the peculiarities of the marine environment are not considered by this norm based on the fact that the focus is land-based mining.

Likewise, within the national mining rules there is no national specific provision on seabed mining in the Area. The CIRM defines the national general policies for the areas beyond national jurisdiction. Through the Ministry of foreign affairs and the navy, Brazil has been engaged in negotiating the Mining Code under the ISA. The country has been active in supporting the implementation of the common heritage of humankind principle as well as strengthening prevention and cooperation obligations. The international rules such as the UNCLOS and all the ISA norms are part of the international legal framework applicable to Brazil. Regarding the exploration and exploitation of mineral resources on the extended continental shelf, Brazil shall agree with the payment of royalties to the ISA, when it is implemented.[13]

As for the contract between CPRM and ISA in the Rio Grande Rise, it is formally valid up to 2030. However, in 2018 Brazil presented its third partial revised submission which included the Rio Grande Rise.[14] In this sense, the Secretary-General informed members of ISA of a notification by CPRM renouncing without penalty the whole of its rights in the contract.[15] Based on the Council's document on the status of contracts for exploration and related matters, CPRM 'has undertaken to fulfil all outstanding legal responsibilities under the contract and the precise nature of these responsibilities, and the timing of their implementation, remains under discussion between the secretariat, the contractor and the sponsoring State'.

One important issue regarding seabed mining is the obligation to conduct an Environmental Impact Assessment.[16] Brazil has been engaged in different negotiations which are connected

12 Hereinafter 'UNCLOS'.

13 Mining and Energy Ministry, *Report on the exploration and exploitation of oil and gas beyond 200 miles*, p. 15. Available online <http://antigo.mme.gov.br/documents/20182/0/RELAT_GT_200_mn_06fev20_v_assinado.pdf/5ac88d2f-f93f-8786-cd2d-a2221aab7739> (accessed 25 May 2021).

14 A.P. Silva, 'Brazil advances over the Area: The inclusion of the Rio Grande Rise within the Brazilian outer continental shelf and its consequences for other states and for the common heritage of mankind', *Marine Policy* 125, 2021, 104399.

15 ISA, Council, ISBA/27/C/28, 18 May 2022, p. 2. See also: IISD. ISA-25 Part 1#2. *Earth Negotiations Bulletin*, vol. 24, n. 181, 26 February 2019.

16 Hereinafter 'EIA'.

to the conservation and sustainable use of marine resources. One of these negotiations is the Intergovernmental Conference on an international legally binding instrument under the UNCLOS on the conservation and sustainable use of marine biological diversity of areas beyond national jurisdiction (BBNJ Agreement). Even if this negotiation deals mainly with marine biological diversity, some issues, such as EIA, are directly connected with the debates that have been carried out under the ISA mining code negotiations.

As for the legal framework to authorize the offshore exploration and the exploitation of natural resources, there is one legal regime for minerals and one for gas and oil. Regarding minerals, the administrative act which permits the exploitation is a norm from the Ministry of mining and energy based on the mining code. There is a granting act and, after that, a plan for the economic use. Thus, there is no contract signed by both parties (the federal state and the contractor). The national mining agency is responsible for managing these actions and plans.

In the case of oil and gas, the national agency for oil regulates the activities. This agency organizes the bidding and signature of the concession contract with the bid winner. The regime of production-sharing is applicable to the cases of pre-salt exploitation (statute no. 12.351, 2010). The contract is divided into two different phases: the first on the exploration and the second on the exploitation. The contractor must follow the environmental legislation and must ask for all the necessary permits to implement the contract. The payment of royalties is shared between the federal state, the states of the federation and the concerned municipalities. Until now, the agency promoted 16 bidding rounds for the exploration and exploitation of oil. In 2015, 266 blocks were offered, being 182 onshore and 84 offshore. However, there is a judicial process blocking it. The 17th and 18th rounds were already approved for 2020–2021. For these rounds, there is an issue related to the possibility of including some areas which go beyond 200 nautical miles, in other words, in the extended Brazilian continental shelf. A working group of civil servants sustained that this was technically possible.[17] In this sense, the 17th bidding round included 92 blocks, six of which are however partially or completely beyond the continental shelf.

For oil and gas, the legal framework is statute 9.478/1997. It provides for the national energy policy and regulates activities related to the oil monopoly as well as the conditions for authorization for the use of oil and gas. It also creates the national council on energy policy and the national oil agency. Exploration activities are under a state monopoly (article 4). Decree no. 2.455/1998 created the national oil agency. Lastly, the pre-salt area is regulated by a specific federal statute no. 12.351/2010.

Seabed activities and related decisions

Regarding UNCLOS and ISA obligations on the protection and the preservation of the marine environment, Brazil has a consistent legal framework to prevent and repair environmental damages. Some principles, such as the precautionary principle, have been used in courts and in administrative procedures in cases related to the exploration and exploitation of oil and minerals in Brazil. The precautionary principle is entrenched in some norms related to marine resources, but they usually refer to the coastal zone.[18] The use of the principle is not based on precise parameters,

17 Mining and energy Ministry. Available online <http://www.mme.gov.br/documents/20182/0/RELAT_GT_200_mn_06fev20_v_assinado.pdf/5ac88d2f-f93f-8786-cd2d-a2221aab7739> (accessed 21 March 2021).

18 For instance, Article 1 and Article 5, X, of decree n. 5.300/2004 and statute n. 7.661/1988. Both regulate the coastal zone. The decree 5.377/2005 approves the national policy for the marine resources also presents the principle under article 4.

and it is not yet possible to present a clear content as per the national case law. Nevertheless, there have been some contributions in terms of procedure, namely the reversal of the burden of proof.[19]

Regarding administrative procedures, one good example of the implementation of the precautionary principle is related to the exploration of oil in the *Foz do Amazonas* . The company Total E&P was granted a concession area at the amazonas river after a bidding procedure in 2013. In April 2018, the federal prosecutors issued a recommendation to the environmental administrative body and asked it to dismiss the environmental permit to the company, based on the precautionary principle.[20] The main argument was that the scientific evidence was not sufficient to decide whether there would not be an intolerable impact to the recently discovered coral reef in the region.

However, accidents such as oil spills are frequent in Brazil. In 2014, the oil agency reported a significant increase in the number of oil spill accidents.[21] These accidents bear testimony that there are still deep concerns regarding prevention and reparation of environmental damages related to oil exploration and exploitation. There are many institutional, material and procedural limits to the management of this type of disaster.[22]

In this context, there is a key legislative reform initiative underway which is specifically related to the ocean. The draft statute (PL 6969) was presented in 2013, but it has not yet been voted by congress representatives. It aims to reduce this fragmented institutional framework by proposing a general policy for the integrated management, the conservation and the sustainable use of the coastal and marine environment. It proposes to assemble and harmonize important objectives, definitions, principles and instruments applicable to the marine environment.

As aforementioned, the Brazilian legal framework is still patchy and inadequate. The mining code does not establish the difference between land-based and offshore mining activities. Moreover, there is no specific regulation for mining activities beyond national jurisdiction, which is an international obligation with which Brazil must comply. For instance, there are no specific national norms on the obligation to control the sponsored companies that have a contract with the ISA. The oil and gas regulation is more advanced, but it still has challenges to prevent and to repair damages.

Conclusion

Although Brazil has competitive offshore oil and gas exploration capacities, seabed mining activities are not economically viable yet. This is a reason why the national legislation is not evolving adequately. Brazil has implemented the general norms of the UNCLOS but has not yet updated the national legislation regarding seabed mining in the continental shelf and in the Area yet.

Because most of the rules currently applied to the Brazilian marine environment are based on the resources and not on the impact of the activities, the institutional design is fragmented and inadequate to tackle possible environmental impacts. One of the reasons that explains this scenario

19 See on this issue: C.C. Oliveira, G.G.B. Lima and F.R. Ferreira (eds), *A interpretação do princípio da precaução pelos tribunais: análise nacional, comparada e internacional*, São Paulo: Pontes Editores, 2019.

20 Brazil, Ministério Público Federal, *Recomendação nº 69/2018–MPF/PR/AP/GAPR4.*

21 Agência Nacional do Petróleo, *Relatório anual de segurança operacional das atividades de exploração e produção de petróleo e gás natural*, 2014, p. 57.

22 See on this issue: C.C. Oliveira, R.A. Lima and F. Salgueiro, 'Características do regime jurídico brasileiro de exploração dos recursos minerais marinhos: comparação da integração da variável ambiental nos setores de petróleo e de minério' in C.C. Oliveira et al., *A função do direito na gestão sustentável dos recursos minerais marinhos,* Rio de Janeiro: Editora Processo, 2021.

is that the decisions on environmental impacts and on the allocation of resources are sectorial, thus not integrated. The specific norms that regulate the marine environment usually provide for resource-based management, to the detriment of environmental concerns. Therefore, the 6969 draft statute is expected to provide for better integration between different sectors and activities, as well as contribute to the harmonization of procedural and substantial rules applicable to the marine environment.

VI.2.3
COLOMBIA AND SEABED MINING

Esteban Restrepo Uribe[1]

Introduction

Probably, the most sensible feature concerning Colombia's maritime domain is that the country is not an UNCLOS party. At the conclusion of the negotiations of the *United Nations Convention on the Law of the Sea* (UNCLOS), on 10 December 1982, Colombia signed the instrument, but, to date, has not ratified it.

The current practice of Colombia, therefore, poses interesting legal questions, especially regarding deep sea mining because of the possibility envisioned in its domestic mining regulations to engage in direct participation with the International Seabed Authority as a non-UNCLOS party.

In addition to that, the access and uses of the seabed and subsoil on its continental shelf are currently constrained by the expectations arising from the pending cases with Nicaragua before the International Court of Justice (ICJ), the conclusion of the boundary delimitation with Venezuela, suspended since 1992,[2] and a growing strong practice in establishing marine protected areas.

1 The opinions contained in this section are expressed in the personal capacity of the author and do not reflect the views of the institutions he is affiliated to.

2 Following the so-called 'Acta de San Pedro Alejandrino' of 1990, negotiations arrived at a dead point when Hugo Chaves came to power in Venezuela, and they have not restarted. Cfr. J. Londoño, *Colombia en el Laberinto del Caribe*, Bogotá: Ediciones Rosaristas, 2015, pp. 219–246. J. Londoño, *Episodios sobre la Fijación de las Fronteras Nacionales*, Bogotá: Ediciones Rosaristas, 2017, pp. 38–59. For an overview of the maritime question in the context of the bilateral relations, A. Zalamea, *Catálogo de Errores: la crisis colombo-venezolana*, Bogotá: Editorial Oveja Negra, 1987.

DOI: 10.4324/9780429426162-32

Colombia and the United Nations Convention on the Law of the Sea

On 29 April 1958, Colombia signed the Convention on the Territorial Sea and the Contiguous Zone, the Convention on the High Seas, the Convention on Fishing and Conservation of the Living Resources of the High Seas (CFCLR), the Convention on the Continental Shelf (CCS), and the Optional Protocol of Signature concerning the Compulsory Settlement of Disputes. Colombia ratified the CCS on 8 June 1962,[3] as well as the CFCLR on 3 January 1963.[4]

As referred above, despite having an active participation in the negotiations of UNCLOS, Colombia signed the *United Nations Convention on the Law of the Sea* but has not ratified it. Additionally, Colombia has not signed, nor ratified, the 1994 *Agreement relating to the Implementation of Part XI of the United Nations Convention on the Law of the Sea* of 10 December 1982[5], nor has it expressed its intention to do so.

The reasons for not ratifying UNCLOS are not clear. In 1984, the Government seemed determined to do so,[6] and one of the main reasons for that was the expectations and possibilities concerning the access to minerals of the ocean soil and subsoil. The issue was discussed and debated over the years in formal and informal fora and scenarios,[7] but since Nicaragua instituted proceedings against Colombia before the International Court of Justice in 2002, the question was put on hold and it was never made public why, when, or at what level it was decided not to ratify the Convention.

Geographical extent of the waters and continental shelf

Colombian maritime territory extends over 2,070,408 square kilometres (km^2). Of these, 55.15 per cent (1,141,748 km^2) covers the continental and insular areas,[8] and 44.85 per cent corresponds to maritime areas (589,560 km^2 in the Caribbean and 339,100 km^2 in the Pacific Ocean); all this with 4.171 kilometres (km) of coast, which spans over 2,582 kilometres (km) in the Caribbean and 1,589 km in the Pacific Ocean.[9]

3 Approved by Law No. 9 of 13 March 1961, ratified on 8 June 1962.

4 Approved by Law No. 119 of 24 November 1961, ratified on 3 January 1963.

5 United Nations, *Treaty Series*, vol. 1836, p. 3.

6 Ministerio de Relaciones Exteriores, *El Nuevo Derecho del Mar*, Imprenta Nacional: Colombia, 1983; Comisión Colombiana de Oceanografía & Dirección de Soberanía Territorial, *Análisis de la incidencia para Colombia al ratificar la Convención de las Naciones Unidas sobre el Derecho del Mar de 1982 (CONVEMAR), en lo relativo a las partes XII (Protección del Medio Marino), XIII (Investigación Científica Marina) y XIV (Desarrollo y Transmisión de Tecnología Marina)*, Ministerio de Relaciones Exteriores, 2000, enero.

7 G. Vega-Barbosa, S. Serebrenik-Beltrán, and M.C. Aponte-Martínez, 'Colombia y la Convención de Naciones Unidas sobre el Derecho del Mar: Análisis jurídico frente al dilema de la ratificación', *Revista chilena de derecho* 45-1, 2018, 105–130; J.J. Gori Leiva, 'El Derecho del Mar: Origen, aprobación y proyecciones de la nueva Convención', *Nueva Frontera*, 19 July 1982, pp. 31–32; 26 July 1982, pp. 25–28; 2 August 1982, pp. 28–30; 9 August 1982, pp. 25–29; G. Cavelier, *Política Internacional de Colombia: Tomo IV, 1957–1997*, Bogotá: Universidad Externado de Colombia, 1997; E. Gaviria Liévano, *La Desintegración del Archipiélago de San Andrés y el fallo de la Corte de La Haya*, Bogotá: TEMIS, 2014.

8 Related as 'submerged lands' in policy documents.

9 DIMAR, Colombia potencia bioceánica sostenible 2030, Documento CONPES 3090, 2019.

Delimitation

In the North, in the Caribbean, Colombia has borders with Panamá,[10] Costa Rica,[11] Nicaragua,[12] Honduras,[13] Jamaica,[14] Haiti,[15] and the Dominican Republic.[16] Colombia also shares joint development areas with the Dominican Republic and with Jamaica. This last one has a particular agreement for oil and gas.[17]

In their delimitation treaty of 1993, Jamaica and Colombia agreed to establish 'a zone of joint management, control, exploration and exploitation of the living and non-living resources'. The delimitation of the zone excludes two circular areas of 12 nautical miles surrounding the cays of the Seranilla Bank and the cays of Bajo Nuevo, 'pending the determination of the jurisdictional limits of each Party', in reference to two previous agreements on fishery resources from 1981 and 1984.[18] In 2008, Colombia and Jamaica signed a (simplified) *Agreement to Expand the Exploration of Hydrocarbon Resources in the Area.*

Concerning the cases instituted by Nicaragua against Colombia before the International Court of Justice on the delimitation of the extended continental shelf and on the violation of sovereign rights in the maritime areas adjudicated by the decision of 2012,[19] by Presidential Decree 1946 of 9 September 2013 – amended by Decree No. 1119 of 7 June 2014 – the Government established an 'integral contiguous zone' around the maritime spaces in the Archipelago of San Andrés, Providencia, and Santa Catalina. In August 2021, the Government announced the exclusion of the blocks located in the Caribbean Sea the Colombia basin ("Cuenca Colombia") from the fourth round of Permanent Process for the Allocation of Areas (PPAA), the 'Colombia Round 2021', for

10 *Treaty on the Delimitation of Marine and Submarine Areas and Related Matters between the Republic of Panama and the Republic of Colombia*, 20 November 1976 (entry into force: 30 November 1977).

11 *Treaty on Delimitation of Marine and Submarine Areas and Maritime Cooperation between the Republic of Colombia and the Republic of Costa Rica* (17 March 1977). In Colombia approved by Law 8 of 4 August 1978. The National Assembly of Costa Rica never approved it.

12 *Treaty Concerning Territorial Questions at Issue between Colombia and Nicaragua*, Managua, 24 March 1928. (in force 5 May 1930) Cfr. *Territorial and Maritime Dispute (Nicaragua v. Colombia), Preliminary Objections, Judgment, ICJ Reports 2007*, p. 832, para. 79.

13 *Maritime Delimitation Treaty between Colombia and Honduras*, 2 August 1986 (entry into force: 20 December 1999).

14 *Maritime Delimitation Treaty between Jamaica and the Republic of Colombia*, Kingston, 12 November 1993 (entry into force: 14 March 1994); *Bilateral (simplified) Agreement to Expand the Exploration of Hydrocarbon Resources in the Joint Regime Area (JRA) shared by Jamaica and Colombia*, 4 November 2008.

15 *Agreement on Delimitation of the Maritime Boundaries between the Republic of Colombia and the Republic of Haiti*, 17 February 1978 (entry into force: 16 February 1979).

16 *Agreement on Delimitation of Marine and Submarine Areas and Maritime Cooperation between the Republic of Colombia and the Dominican Republic*, 13 January 1978 (entry into force: 15 February 1979).

17 Located between the Jamaica coast and the Archipelago of San Andrés and Providencia. For more information on the regional context, see in this book E. Jiménez Pineda, 'South American region and seabed mining', in V. Tassin Campanella (ed.), *Routledge Handbook of Seabed Mining and the Law of the Sea*, London: Routledge, 2023, chapter VI.1.6.

18 J. Londoño, *Colombia en el Laberinto del Caribe*, Bogotá: Ediciones Rosaristas, 2015, pp. 291–296.

19 The related cases are: *Question of the Delimitation of the Continental Shelf between Nicaragua and Colombia beyond 200 Nautical Miles from the Nicaraguan Coast (Nicaragua v. Colombia), Preliminary Objections, Judgment, ICJ Reports 2016*, p. 100, Judgement, 13 July 2023 and *Alleged Violations of Sovereign Rights and Maritime Spaces in the Caribbean Sea (Nicaragua v. Colombia), Preliminary Objections, Judgment, ICJ Reports 2016*, p. 3. Judgement, ICJ Reports 2022, p.266. See V.J.M. Tassin, 'Territorial and Maritime Dispute (Nicaragua v. Colombia, 2001)', in P. Wojcikiewicz and J-M Sorel (eds), *Latin America and the International Court of Justice*, London: Routledge, 2017, pp. 225–236.

inshore and offshore exploration and production of oil and gas, to avoid any involvement with the cases.[20]

However, in the Judgment of the case concerning *the Alleged Violations of Sovereign Rights and Maritime Spaces in the Caribbean Sea (Nicaragua v. Colombia)*, delivered on April 21 2022, the International Court of Justice found, '(5) [By thirteen votes to two,] that the "integral contiguous zone" established by the Republic of Colombia by Presidential Decree 1946 of 9 September 2013, as amended by Decree 1119 of 17 June 2014, is not in conformity with customary international law, as set out in paragraphs 170 to 187'; and '(6) [By twelve votes to three,] that the Republic of Colombia must, by means of its own choosing, bring into conformity with customary international law the provisions of Presidential Decree 1946 of 9 September 2013, as amended by Decree 1119 of 17 June 2014, in so far as they relate to maritime areas declared by the Court in its 2012 Judgment to appertain to the Republic of Nicaragua'.

In the Pacific Ocean, Colombia has boundary agreements with Panama,[21] Ecuador,[22] and Costa Rica.[23] On 9 August 1979, it signed the Agreement for its incorporation into the 'South Pacific System', including the accession to the principles and fundamental principles of the Santiago Declaration of 1952, with Chile, Peru, and Ecuador, approved by Law No. 7 of 1980. According to its Preamble, 'none of the principles and fundamental norms referred to (the Declaration of Santiago) shall affect the sovereignty and jurisdiction of the States Parties on their respective continental shelf beyond 200 miles, in conformity with international law'.[24]

Marine protected areas

The expansion of maritime protected areas reflects a growing interest in the conservation and environmental protection over other considerations concerning the exploitation of the maritime resources. These areas include, in the Caribbean, the Seaflower Biosphere Reserve, established in 2000 under the umbrella of United Nations Educational Scientific and Cultural Organisation, which covers the insular and maritime territory of the Archipelago of San Andres, Providencia, and Santa Catalina (300,000 km^2); and in the Pacific, the Malpelo Flora and Fauna Sanctuary (27,000 km^2) and the Yuruparí – Malpelo National Integrated Management District (450,000 km^2).[25]

20 'Colombia tiene en la actualidad ocho contratos de costa afuera y offshore en vigencia', *La Republica,* 30 August 2021. Available online <https://www.larepublica.co/economia/colombia-tiene-actualmente-ocho-contratos-de-costa-afuera-y-offshore-en-vigencia-3224077 > (accessed on 22 December 2021).

21 *Treaty on the Delimitation of Marine and Submarine Areas and Related Matters between the Republic of Panama and the Republic of Colombia*, 20 November 1976 (entry into force: 30 November 1977).

22 *Tratado de Límites entre el Gobierno de la República de Colombia y el Gobierno de la República del Ecuador,* 15 July 1916 (in forcé on 26 January 1917); *Agreement Concerning Delimitation of Marine and Submarine Areas and Maritime Cooperation between the Republics of Colombia and Ecuador 23 August 1975* (entry into force on 22 December 1975); *Acuerdo para la Demarcación del Punto de Inicio de la Frontera Marítima en la Desembocadura del Río Mataje. Puerto de San Lorenzo*, Esmeraldas, Ecuador, 13 June 2012.

23 *Treaty on the Delimitation of Marine and Submarine Areas and Maritime Cooperation between the Republic of Colombia and the Republic of Costa Rica*, additional to the Treaty signed at San José on 17 March 1977, 6 April 1984 (entry into force: 20 February 2001).

24 Approved by Law 7 of 4 February1980, ratified on 12 March 1980.

25 Following COP 26 President Duque announced the establishment of new areas comprising 160,000 km^2 to comply with the initiative Global Ocean Alliance 30 by 30. Other institutional arrangements are the Environmental Coastal Units (UAC by their acronyms in Spanish), and the maritime component of the so-called '*línea negra*' (black lines), which refers to the ancestral lands of the indigenous communities of the Sierra Nevada de Santa Marta in the North coast – Arhuaco, Kogui, Wiwa and Kankuamo – as recognized by Decree No. 1500 of 2018 (art. 348).

Regulation of seabed mining activities

There is not a single comprehensive regime for the seabed and its resources. Like many countries,[26] the Political Constitution of 1990 (article 101) enlists the components of the Colombian territory, including the subsoil and the continental shelf, 'in accordance with international law or the laws of Colombia in the absence of international regulation'.

As mentioned above, Colombia signed and ratified the CCS convention of 1958 and in the course of the ICJ Territorial and Maritime dispute case with Nicaragua, Colombia recognized article 76, paragraph 1, of UNCLOS as customary international law. And in Law No. 10 of 4 August 1978, article 10, national sovereignty shall extend to the continental shelf for the purposes of exploring and exploiting its natural resources, without defining, nor regulating the continental shelf.

It should also be noted that although there are specific regulations for offshore gas and oil,[27] marine scientific research,[28] underwater cultural heritage,[29] and seabed mining, none of these legislations prevail, nor prevent the application of general environmental and maritime regulations in any given case.

A number of institutions are responsible for the formulation and execution of policies and regulations in the mining sector,[30] the Ministry of Mines, the National Mining Agency, the Geological Service Agency, and the Mining and Energy Planning Unit; at the environmental level, the National Authority for Environmental Licenses and the Regional Environmental Corporations; and for maritime activities, the National Maritime Authority (DIMAR).

In practice, inter-agency coordination is critical but difficult to achieve. The competence and powers of these institutions tend to overlap, affecting coordination and synergies between them.[31]

Mining activities are regulated by the Political Constitution and by the Mining Code adopted by Law No. 685 of 2001 (hereinafter the Code). Its Chapter XV, articles 137 through 151, upgraded the 'coastal and submarine mining' provided for in the previous Code, into 'seabed mining', which covers both mining on the continental shelf and in the Area.

Articles 6 and 143 of the Code reiterate the Constitutional principle (art. 332 of the Constitution) that mineral resources are the property of the State and, according to article 145 of the Code, their exploitation must be carried out through concession agreements with favourable concept from DIMAR. This requirement also applies to prospecting activities, with the correlative obligation of giving previous notice to DIMAR (arts. 39 and 40 of the Code).

As for mining and related activities in areas beyond Colombian maritime jurisdiction, the key provision is found in article 146 of the Code, according to which the participation of the State in the exploration and exploitation of minerals in the soil and subsoil on international waters, before the International Seabed Authority, shall be conducted through cooperation agreements with other States or through contracts of representation with private companies – whether national or foreign.

26 W. Arévalo Ramírez, 'Resistance to territorial and maritime delimitation judgments of the International Court of Justice and clashes with "territory clauses" in the Constitutions of Latin American states', *Leiden Journal of International Law* 35-1, March 2022, 185–208.

27 Decreto 1073 of 2015.

28 Decreto 644 of 1990 and 1 Decreto 070 of 2015.

29 Ley 1675 of 2013; Decreto 1698 of 2014; Decreto 1080 of 2015; Decreto 1530 of 2016; Decreto 1389 of 2017.

30 Decreto No. 1073 of 2015; Constitutional Court, Decision SU095/18, Case T-6.298.958, 11 October 2018, p. 4.

31 *Plan Nacional de Ordenamiento Minero (PNOM)*, Documento Anexo a Resolución UPME 0256, Bogotá, June 2014.

These provisions marked a departure from the previous Code of 1998 (Decree No. 2655 of 23 December 1998), under which only the Ministry of Mines and Energy and its entities could carry out submarine and coastal mining, including exploration and exploitation – directly or under agreement with other public entities or private companies. It reiterated general legal powers of DIMAR and required its previous favourable concept from DIMAR and the Ministry of Foreign Affairs (chapter XV, articles 118 through 122).

Articles 138 through 142 of the Code incorporate the UNCLOS definitions for the territorial sea, the contiguous zone, the continental shelf, and the exclusive economic zone. Interestingly enough, it does not include interior waters or the extended continental shelf, and instead of baselines, it refers to the 'external limits of territorial waters'.

The first hypothesis of article 146 referred to above, pertains to the direct participation of the State before the International Seabed Authority (ISA or the Authority). According to article 148, the application shall be filled by the State before the Authority, including the working plan, the compensations and economic burdens, and the management of benefits derived from the exploitation of the minerals, according to the pertinent international regulations or, in their absence, to the laws of the Republic of Colombia.

The second relates to participation through cooperation agreements with other States. Article 149 establishes that those agreements shall be negotiated and concluded on the basis of equity and good faith applicable in each case. For the conclusion and execution of each agreement, the National Mining Authority shall nominate a designated government agency.

The third has to do with the participation through delegation with private companies, whether foreign or national. According to article 150, the agreements of representation should establish that the delegation shall include the payments of fees and royalties, and to provide that the responsibility arisen from any breaches of contract, or from the damages to the environment against the Authority or against third parties, shall be assumed fully and with no limitation or restriction by the private company.

Article 151 of the Code contains a general provision applicable to cooperation or delegation agreements, requiring 'permanent and timely' transfer of technology, in favour of the State, covering a wide array of mechanisms for said transfer, including any form of scientific advancement, technical knowledge, manuals, designs, instructions, assistance, and any form of training.

Insofar as the Government of Colombia intends to keep the present status of the country as a non-UNCLOS party, it therefore poses complex questions on the possibilities for ISA to enter into agreements with non-UNCLOS parties, outside of the UNCLOS system, and conversely on whether non-UNCLOS parties could enter into agreement with ISA, while maintaining its non-UNCLOS status.

However, that seems not legally feasible. Two considerations can be advanced in that respect. In the first place, it is argued that, under the recognition of the Area as common heritage of mankind,[32] the provisions of articles 136, 137, 140, and 141 of UNCLOS among others, refer to 'all States', instead of 'Parties', as beneficiaries of the access to the Area and its resources.[33] Furthermore, the provisions requiring the Authority to grant non-discriminatory and equal access to the Area (art.

32 *Delimitation of Maritime Areas (St Pierre and Miquelon) (Canada and France) (1992) 31 ILM 1145*, 1172, para. 78; *Responsibilities and obligations of States with respect to activities in the Area, Advisory Opinion, 1 February 2011, ITLOS Reports 2011*, para. 226.

33 S. Vonеky and A. Hofelmeier, Articles 136 mn [18], 137 mn [14], 140 mn [6–12], 141 mn [9], in Proelss (ed.), *United Nations Convention on the Law of the Sea: a commentary*, 1st edition, Oxford: Hart and Baden-Baden: Nomos Verlagsgesellschaft, 2017, pp. 955, 973, 983–984.

152 of UNCLOS) to all States, as well as the obligations to refrain from claiming sovereignty or appropriating parts of the Area are of a customary nature and apply to non-UNCLOS Parties.[34]

In contrast, there seems to be no clear basis for seabed mining rights in the Area, under customary international law in general. According to Voneky and Hofelmeier, the practice of States and the *opinio juris* in this area are ambiguous.[35] It could moreover be argued that a parallel system based on customary international law would make ineffective the regime laid out by UNCLOS and the Agreement relating to the Implementation of Part XI of UNCLOS (1994 Agreement), where the ISA shall organize, carry out, and exercise control of the activities in the Area on behalf of mankind as a whole.

Similar arguments have been made concerning the requirement to assent to be bound to UNCLOS, when establishing the consent to the Agreement of 1994 contained in its article 4, paragraph 2 and the extent of the 1984 Provisional Understanding Regarding Deep Seabed Matters between the United States, Belgium, France, Germany, Italy, Japan, the Netherlands, and the United Kingdom, regarding deep seabed matters, and of the 1987 Agreement on the Resolution of Practical Problems between Belgium, Canada, Italy, Netherlands, and the Union of Soviet Socialist Republics.[36]

In the second place, as mentioned elsewhere in this work, activities in the Area shall be carried out in association with the ISA by States Parties, or by state enterprises or by nationals of States Parties or individuals that are effectively controlled by them or their nationals, when sponsored by such States (UNCLOS article 153, Annex III article 4 (a)).[37]

Additionally, a main contention for this case is whether, in the wording of article 18 of the Vienna Convention on the Law of Treaties of 1969, the agreements provided for in articles 146 to 150 of the Mining Code, outlined above, conform to the purpose and object of UNCLOS.[38] In that sense, a plausible approach could be to interpret said agreements as preliminary measures on the road to the ratification of UNCLOS.

Conclusion

To conclude, it can be argued that, despite the provisions of the Mining Code, policy and institutional arrangements for deep sea and seabed mining are still pending in Colombia. Official policy documents are silent on the matter[39] and there are a number of assignments awaiting, including strengthening inter-agency coordination, defining policy options for sponsorship, and the development of a precautionary approach for deep sea mining, among other things. And to that end, it is just possible that for the country, the time has come to rethink its relation to UNCLOS.

34 J. Siegfried, Article 152 mn [4], in Proelss (ed.), *UNCLOS*, 1st edition, Hart, 2017, pp. 1077–1078.

35 S. Voneky and A. Hofelmeier, in op. cit., pp. 963–964.

36 United Nations Treaty Collection Series Vol. 1409. I-23601; 26 I.L.M. 1502,1987. See S. Ranganathan, *Strategically Created Treaty Conflicts and the Politics of International Law*, Cambridge: Cambridge University Press, 2016, pp. 147–211.

37 *Responsibilities and obligations of States with respect to activities in the Area*, op. cit., par. 74–79.

38 Article 18 (a) of the *1969 Vienna Convention on the Law of Treaties*. See P. Gragl and M. Fitzmaurice, 'The Legal Character of Article 18 VCLT', *ICLQ* 68-3, 2019, 699–717.

39 Departamento Nacional de Planeación, *Colombia Potencia Bioceánica Sostenible 2030*, Documento CONPES 3090, Bogotá D.C., 31 March 2020; Vicepresidencia de la República-Comisión Colombiana del Océano-Armada de Colombia, *Intereses Marítimos Colombianos*, in Vicepresidencia de la República (ed.), Serie Publicaciones Especiales CCO, Bogotá D.C., 2021.

VI.2.4
CÔTE D'IVOIRE AND SEABED MINING

Yacouba Cissé

Introduction

On 26 March 1984, Côte d'Ivoire ratified the *United Nations Convention on the Law of the Sea* (UNCLOS or the Convention)[1] and adopted, subsequently, various legislations and regulations for its enforcement. The legal framework under which the mining activities are regulated is very dispersed and there is, so far, no specific domestic legislation dealing with the seabed mining of minerals. Concerning the mining activities in the continental shelf, Côte d'Ivoire has adopted laws and regulations in this regard, particularly on the issue relating to its continental shelf's outer limit and its delimitation. A lot remains to be done to put in place a regulatory framework adapted to seabed activities on the continental shelf and the Area.

Geographical context of the exclusive economic zone, continental shelf and the Area

The sedimentary basin of Côte d'Ivoire is formed by an onshore part of approximately 360 km in length and by an offshore area the length of which ranges between 80 and 120 km. The depth of the basin does not exceed 3,000 square meters. The worldwide ranking places Côte d'Ivoire at the 95th rank for the length of its continental shelf[2] and at the 76th rank for the length of its exclusive economic zone (EEZ). The length of its EEZ is actually ten times superior to that of its continental shelf.[3]

Côte d'Ivoire submitted on 8 May 2009 a demand to the United Nations Commission on the Limits of the Continental Shelf (CLCS) for the extension of its continental shelf,[4] which was

1 DOALOS, *Bulletin du droit de la mer* 41, 1999, p. 11.
2 This ranking should be revised now that Côte d'Ivoire can extend its continental shelf up to 350 M.
3 ADVANCE \d6 L. Lucchini and M. Voelckel, *Les États et la Mer, Le nationalisme maritime*, coll. Notes et études documentaires, Nos. 4451–4452, Paris, La documentation française, 1978, p. 70.
4 See *Côte d'Ivoire Executive Summary, submission for the extension of its Continental Shelf*, page 6, paragraph 6.1.

DOI: 10.4324/9780429426162-33

amended on 24 March 2016.[5] In its 2020 recommendation,[6] the CLCS agreed with the determination of fix points and 'recommends *also* that the delineation of the outer limits of the continental shelf be conducted (…) by straight lines not exceeding 60 nautical miles (M) in length, connecting fixed points, defined by coordinates of latitude and longitude'.[7] The marine area of Côte d'Ivoire could be estimated to 132,842 square kilometers (km^2) to which one must add 14,660 km^2 corresponding to the marine area gained after the recommendation of CLCS.

Regulation of seabed activities

When ratifying UNCLOS, Côte d'Ivoire became the tenth State having deposited its instruments of ratification at the General Secretariat of the United Nations (UN) and the fifth State[8] at African regional level. It also signed and ratified on 28 July 1995 the *Agreement relating to the implementation of Part XI of the Convention.*[9]

The Ivorian legislations implementing UNCLOS are perceived to be generally consistent with the provisions of that Convention. Let's however recall that the previous legislation of 1977 made no express reference to the concept of continental shelf. Côte d'Ivoire retained instead the notion of EEZ up to 200 M.[10] By legislating that way, one can interpret that Côte d'Ivoire's continental shelf under the 1977 legislation was included in the EEZ as a multipurpose maritime area under the Ivorian jurisdiction. This legislation was far from being innocent. During the negotiations of the UNCLOS, Côte d'Ivoire being aware of the narrowness of its continental shelf had indeed co-sponsored many draft articles on the EEZ.[11]

In fact, from a geological standpoint, the 1977 legislative drafting was designed to compensate the narrowness of its continental shelf, which, according to the previous geomorphologic studies could not go beyond 10 M. This legislation is today repealed following the entry into force of the UNCLOS and the adoption of a new maritime code and a mining code.

In addition to its domestic laws, Côte d'Ivoire is also a State Party to the regional legal instrument, the Abidjan Convention[12] and its Protocol on environmental norms and standards for offshore oil and gas exploration and exploitation activities,[13] dedicated to the regulation of offshore petroleum activities occurring in the Gulf of Guinea, running from Mauritania all the way down to South Africa.

The Abidjan Convention to which Côte d'Ivoire is a State Party is a Convention addressing a variety of marine issues including the protection of the marine and coastal environment against

5 CLCS, Amended submission submitted by the Republic of Côte d'Ivoire, 24 March 2016, p. 5.

6 CLCS, *Progress of work in the Commission on the Limits of the Continental Shelf*, CLCS/52/2, 25 March 2020, paras. 44–46.

7 CLCS 2016, ibid., p. 26.

8 DOALOS, *Bulletin du droit de la mer* 23, 1993.

9 Ibid., p. 12.

10 Cf., Law N° 77-926, article 3, para 1 on the EEZ. For more on the relationship between the EEZ and the continental shelf, see in this book V. Tassin Campanella, Y. Cissé and D. Tladi, 'State rights and obligations of States on the continental shelf and the Area', in V. Tassin Campanella (ed) *Routledge handbook of seabed mining and the law of the sea*, London: Routledge, 2023, chapter II.1.

11 Cf., United Nations, Third United Nations Conference on the Law of the Sea, Volume III, second commission, Caracas session, 1974, A/CONF.62/C.2/L.82, United Nations, New York, 1975, p. 278.

12 *Convention for Cooperation in the Protection and Development of the Marine and Coastal Environment of the Western, Central and Southern African Region*, signed in Abidjan in March 1981.

13 Its ratification is still pending at the time of writing of this article.

various sources of pollution. An additional Protocol to the Convention deals with the issue regarding the protection of the marine and coastal environment from the exploration and exploitation of the seabed mineral and mining resources. This legal regional instrument is of great value for Côte d'Ivoire in a sense that the country has no specific legislation dealing with marine protection against the offshore oil and gas exploration and exploitation. This regional legal instrument fills this lacuna and tends also to reinforce the legal framework dealing with the offshore mining activities occurring in Côte d'Ivoire's continental shelf up to 200 M and beyond.

The Maritime Code[14]

The Maritime Code is the main legal instrument dealing with commercial aspects of maritime transport law. However, some its chapters examine various domains pertaining to UNCLOS such as maritime limits, delimitation, and the legal regime and status of the maritime spaces. The Maritime Code defines Côte d'Ivoire's continental shelf as follows: 'The continental shelf includes, in conformity with UNCLOS, the deep sea and its subsoil up to the continental margin that is included in the exclusive economic zone'.[15] On its continental shelf, Côte d'Ivoire exercises its sovereign rights for the exploration and exploitation of its natural resources as stated by article 77 of UNCLOS.[16] These resources include all marine living and non-living resources such as mineral resources like offshore oil, gas, manganese, zinc, cobalt, gold, diamond, sand, and sponges. Côte d'Ivoire sovereign rights also include 'the exclusive right to construct any devices and installations and to make sure of their functioning and use'.[17] One can assume that the exercise of this right is only within Côte d'Ivoire's maritime limits and maritime boundaries. However, the definition provided by the Maritime Code seems to be a bit equivocal in a sense that it tends to combine Côte d'Ivoire's continental shelf with the EEZ limit up to 200 M. As a result, it does not take into account the notion of extended continental shelf of article 76 of UNCLOS. By limiting the continental margin to the limit of Côte d'Ivoire's EEZ, article 57 of the Maritime Code entertains a sort of ambiguity.

The Mining Code

The Mining Code provides a more accurate definition of the concept of continental shelf below and beyond 200 M. According to this code, minerals could be understood by 'all mineral substances, all mineral waters and all geothermal resources found in the soil and subsoil, the territorial waters, the exclusive economic zone and the continental shelf and its extension beyond 200 M up to the conventional limit internationally recognized by Côte d'Ivoire, are properties of the State of Côte d'Ivoire'.[18] It furthermore specifies activities which could be conducted under Côte d'Ivoire's jurisdiction and sovereignty by providing a list of specific offshore activities such as prospection, research, exploitation, detention, treatment, transport, transformation and trading.[19]

Regarding the Area, a decree for the application of the present Code, precisely the implementation of articles 3 and 4, would be necessary to cover all legal aspects of the seabed mining consistent with Part XI of the UNCLOS.

14 The Maritime Code: Law N° 2017-442 of 30 June 2017.
15 Ibid., chapter 3, article 57.
16 Op. cit., article 58.
17 Ibid., article 59.
18 The Mining Code: Law N° 2014-138 of 24 March 2014, article 3, *supra*, note 4.
19 Ibid., article 4.

The Petroleum Code

Certain provisions of the Petroleum Code were modified in 2012, notably the definition chapter.[20] The ordinance modifying this code seems to be quite similar to that contained in the Petroleum Code.

The new article 82 of the ordinance completes, to some extent, the Petroleum Code by stipulating that

> the exploitation and management of petroleum resources should be conducted in a transparency manner and taking into account the protection of the environment, as well as to preserving the interests of present and future generations. Any petroleum company, detaining a petroleum contract in the national territory should participate actively in applying the principles of transparency in the extractive industries in Cote d'Ivoire.

Chapter 2 of the Code deals with the ownership issue and provides that

> all deposits or natural concentration of hydrocarbons in the soil or sub-soil of the territory of the Republic of Côte d'Ivoire, its territorial sea, its exclusive economic zone and its continental shelf, discovered or not, are and remain the exclusive property of the State and over which the State exercises its sovereign rights.[21]

The running of petroleum activities and development, in land territory and in marine areas under Côte d'Ivoire jurisdiction are regulated by the Ivorian legislation.[22] Furthermore, no entities should undertake petroleum operations, including the owner of the surface, without prior authorization of the Côte d'Ivoire.[23] It is however up to the Côte d'Ivoire to directly undertake mining activities through its national petroleum and gas company acting on its behalf.[24] Finally, the Ivorian government can also authorize legal persons or entities, holding Ivorian nationality or foreign nationality, to perform petroleum activities through an oil contract with the State.[25]

For the enforcement of the law relating to the Petroleum Code, a decree has also been adopted. This decree is of importance because it introduces a depth criterion in the definition of the continental shelf which reads as follows: 'deep sea areas as the party of the exclusive economic zone and continental shelf situated at deep water distance equivalent or superior to 200 meters'.[26]

The Environment Code[27]

The Environment Code establishes a general framework for the protection of Côte d'Ivoire's global environment, including the marine and coastal environment. The 1996 Environment Code,

20 The Petroleum Code: Law N° 96-669 of August 1996, modified by the ordinance N° 2012-369 of 18 April 2012, article 1, chapter 1– article 1 (n) amended.

21 Id., article 4.

22 Id., article 3.

23 Id., article 3.

24 Id., article 5.

25 Id., article 6.

26 Decree N° 96-733 of 19 September on general modality of enforcement of law relating to the Petroleum Code.

27 The Environment Code: Law N° 96-766 of 3 October 1996.

which is about to be amended, describes Côte d'Ivoire's maritime zones or jurisdiction without however providing any reference to the resources at stakes.[28] This Code makes clear that the State is the owner of the oilfield and the natural concentration of hydrocarbons that exist in Côte d'Ivoire's land territory, including on its continental shelf.[29] The related decree[30] of implementation furthermore applies the polluter-pays principle to any company or individual involved in offshore mining activities in the continental shelf and in the Area. Pursuant to the Annex of this decree, this principle applies to sources of pollution relating to extractive industries, including the exploration and exploitation of offshore oil and natural gas.

The 2017 Coastal Law[31]

The coastal law promotes appropriate legal measures to maintain the physical, biological and chemical integrity of Côte d'Ivoire's shoreline[32] from marine pollution resulting from the discharge and the spill of offshore oil and gas explored and exploited from petroleum platforms at a distance more or less close to the coastline.

Attention should be paid to two articles of this 2017 Coastal Law. The first one is article 53 that stipulates: 'by derogation of the provisions of the mining Code, the extractions of materials are prohibited if there is a risk that compromise, directly or indirectly, the integrity of the beach (…) and the exploitation of marine cultures'. The second one is article 56 that poses the principle of precaution in these terms: 'are also submitted to an environmental assessment, all project for exploration or exploitation at sea, in deep-sea bed and in the subsoil'. These two articles pose the application of the precautionary principle before undertaking any mining activity in marine areas under Côte d'Ivoire's jurisdiction.

Contribution of Côte d'Ivoire to the United Nations Convention on the Law of the Sea

During the negotiations of the United Nations Convention on the Law of the Sea, Côte d'Ivoire was especially concerned with the topic of transfer of technologies, especially those related to the exploitation of the seabed mineral resources of the Area. Côte d'Ivoire was indeed willing to avoid the insertion of provisions which would lead to a 'mere' transfer of technology and was thus opposed to all provisions, related to the Area, that were unsatisfactory and contrary to its own interests and to ones of the Group of 77 led by China.

The country also led discussions on the need to protect the economy of the State producing mineral resources from land against the harmful consequences of the exploitation of the same resources from the Area. Indeed, at the time of the UNCLOS negotiations, Côte d'Ivoire was considered as a medium producer of minerals, particularly of manganese resources.[33] Côte d'Ivoire

28 Ibid, supra, note 6.

29 Id., article 36.

30 Decree N° 2012-1047 of 24 October 2012 establishing the modalities for the application of the polluter-pay principle as defined by the Law N° 96-766 of 3 October 1996 relating to the Code of the Environment.

31 The coastal Law N° 2017-378 of 2 June 2017 relating to the planning, the protection and integrated coastal zone management

32 Ibid., chapter 1, section 1, op. cit., note 5.

33 Cf., United Nations officials documents, Third United Nations Conference on the Law of the Sea, UN Officials Records, Vol. XIV, Resumed ninth session, Geneva, 1980, p. 145.

therefore proposed to distinguish between developing and developed States producers of minerals to establish a fair and equitable system of compensation. This proposal led to the agreement around articles 150 and 151 of the UNCLOS.

Perspectives

Côte d'Ivoire is facing present and future challenges in the development of its regulatory framework related to seabed mining. These challenges include addressing in the short or medium term, the following points: (1) building its proper technical and legal capacity in mining activities in the Area with the view to contributing significantly in decision-making regarding the 'Area', (2) creating and promoting a secure political environment and a functioning and efficient legal system designed to attract foreign investors, (3) taking measures for the protection of the marine and coastal environment, (4) reinforcing the cooperation at sea for a better understanding of mineral offshore development within its maritime jurisdiction and beyond and (5) dealing with maritime boundaries delimitation between coastal States.

In terms of legislative perspective, emphasis should be put on the adoption of a specific legislation, through a single Code, which will deal with issues related to the exploration and exploitation of resources of the continental shelf and the Area. The country should furthermore, through a decree or a legislation, define the geographical coordinates of latitude and longitude of its extended continental shelf, in accordance with the 2019 recommendations of the CLCS and give publicity to these limits according to article 84 of the UNCLOS.

A legislation on seabed activities on the continental shelf and in the Area should include provisions on the promotion and development of the marine scientific research to enable data collection as well as provisions aiming to attract foreign investors for the development of mineral resources within and beyond 200 M. The conditions under which Côte d'Ivoire provides its sponsoring to commercial entities registered under Ivorian law for the prospection and exploitation of polymetallic nodules of the Area is also a key topic to address. To this end, a competent national authority should be identified and vested with the power to regulate the access of the Area minerals and to monitor and manage the country's participation in mining activities in the Area. This legislation should, in addition, contain provisions relating to capacity-building on various aspects, including geological data acquisition, economic, financial, technical, environmental and legal aspects of seabed mining, as well as revenue sharing, and its equitable distribution as set out by article 82 of the UNCLOS.

The transfer of marine technologies and science should not be undermined in a sense that the know-how is key to promoting capacity-building and for a better understanding of the chain of mining development in the Area, as well as in the continental shelf. Côte d'Ivoire is already equipped with a Centre of Oceanographic Research that has contributed a lot to the teaching of oceanographic science. The lack of funding of the Centre is a major concern as marine research is not conducted to the extent it was in the past. The UNESCO Decade for the Ocean Science could be a good opportunity for Côte d'Ivoire to raise the necessity for an effective capacity-building in marine science and marine technology transfer that will enable the country to fully participate in seabed mining.

On an environmental point of view, a code on seabed mining should as well cover aspects such as the protection against pollution from seabed activities and other sources of pollution, and the protection of the marine biodiversity, including genetic resources and sedentary species.

Seabed activities and related decisions

The activities undertaken in Côte d'Ivoire's continental shelf up to 200 M concern the exploration and exploitation of both oil and gas resources. The other types of minerals (manganese, cobalt, diamond, zinc, gold, etc.) are not included in Côte d'Ivoire offshore mining strategy and policy. These minerals are exploited on land, not at sea for the time being.

Conclusion

Seabed mining is inextricably linked to maritime boundary delimitation. Côte d'Ivoire is dealing with continental shelf boundaries issues with Ghana and Liberia. The Ghana/Côte d'Ivoire case of the International Tribunal for the Law of the Sea (ITLOS)[34] is of particular interest since it dealt with petroleum deposits[35] straddling the maritime boundary.[36] These petroleum fields were developed by Tullow, an offshore foreign oil company whose ownership was contested by Côte d'Ivoire because of its location in the disputed area.[37] In this ITLOS case, both Côte d'Ivoire and Ghana insisted on the fundamental role played by offshore mineral resources in their respective economic development. As a result, the mining factor has been mainly argued by Côte d'Ivoire as a relevant circumstance to be taken into account in the delimitation process. For Côte d'Ivoire, considerations such as 'the exceptional presence of hydrocarbons in the contested marine area',[38] the 'location and distribution of hydrocarbons resources'[39] and the 'access to oil resources'[40] constitute relevant or special circumstances.

The maritime boundary delimitation between Côte d'Ivoire and Liberia is still outstanding. The settlement of this boundary will hopefully allow Côte d'Ivoire to benefit from an additional marine area and the extension of its continental shelf at the western side of the coast.

34 *Delimitation of the Maritime Boundary in the Atlantic Ocean (Ghana/Côte d'Ivoire)*, Judgment, ITLOS Reports 2017, p. 4. Case submitted under Annex IV of the Convention and establishing a special chamber for the settlement of the dispute.

35 The Jubilee field located in the sedimentary Tano Basin was indeed included in the disputed maritime area. Three hydrocarbons fields, called the 'ten blocks' (*Tweneboa-Enyera-Ntomme*), were discovered in this field.

36 Id., paras. 449, 451.

37 *Ghana/Côte d'Ivoire case, Counter-Memorial of Côte d'Ivoire*, p. 59.

38 Id., para. 406.

39 Id., paras. 437, 455.

40 Id., para. 438.

VI.2.5
GERMANY AND SEABED MINING

Nele Matz-Lück

Introduction

The German position on seabed mining is ambivalent and subject to change. On the one hand, the Federal Republic of Germany is engaged in exploration activities for deep-sea mineral resources in the Area with the aim to secure the supply of metals in a long-term perspective and has enacted national legislation as a basis for seabed mining.[1] On the other hand, it was announced in late 2022 that scientific knowledge on the environmental consequences is insufficient and has requested a 'precautionary pause' of exploitation on the international level until the effects upon the marine environment have been more thoroughly studied and understood.[2] Germany thus continues to demonstrate an active interest in marine scientific research on the effects and prospects of deep-sea mining. These interests are, in principle, supported by technological developments, which lead to improved opportunities for exploration and future exploitation. Germany shares its new political position with *inter alia* Spain and New Zealand and has received support from representatives of the German carmaker industry who stated that, for the time being, they would not buy metals retrieved from seabed mining.

The emphasis on sustainability and high environmental standards for seabed mining is remarkable from an economic point of view. The German economy is dependent upon imports of many raw materials, including metals such as manganese, copper, nickel and cobalt. The unpredictable fluctuation in commodity prices adds to the economic pressure to search for alternatives. The first prerequisite, however, is that seabed mining activities are economically feasible both from a general perspective as well as with regard to the German licence areas, in which an exploitation phase

1 Please note that the English titles of unilateral national acts, national acts of legislation and bilateral treaties are, with few exceptions, unofficial translations. For reference the full German title will be given in the relevant footnotes.

2 Opening statement by the German delegation at the ISA 27th session, 31 October 2022. Available online (in parts) <https://www.bmuv.de/en/pressrelease/marine-protection-germany-will-not-sponsor-deep-sea-mining-until-further-notice> (accessed 28 March 2023). See also speech by Federal Minister for the Environment, Nature Conservation, Nuclear Safety and Consumer Protection Steffi Lemke, at a CBD COP15 side event on 16 December 2022, available online <https://www.bmuv.de/rede/rede-von-steffi-lemke-the-deep-nature-of-the-sea-an-umbrella-partnership-for-the-protection-of-the-deep-sea> (accessed 28 March 2023).

 DOI: 10.4324/9780429426162-34

could follow the current exploration contracts. The second now seems to be that research points towards environmentally sustainable options. For geographical reasons the German continental shelf is too small and too shallow to allow for deep-sea mineral resource extraction and is, consequently, not a focus of German legislation or practice.

German economic interest and activities – as formulated before the call for the 'precautionary pause' – are supported by intensified European Union (EU) actions in this field.[3] Although since 2018 the EU Parliament has continuously called for a moratorium on commercial deep-sea mining until more research on the environmental effects, particularly on biological diversity, has been undertaken – thus being in line with the recent shift in the German position – seabed mining continues to be one element of the European 'blue growth strategy'. Although it is a comparably small sector, the EU Commission emphasizes its potential to generate growth and jobs for future generations, particularly with regard to European companies' experience in specialized ships and underwater handling technologies.[4] In addition to multilateral engagement, Germany has been actively seeking bilateral cooperation in this field as is demonstrated by the joint declaration of intent between France and Germany concerning cooperation in the field of seabed mining. The fate of such cooperation declarations in the light of the wish to postpone exploitation until environmental consequences have been more thoroughly studied, remains to be seen.

Geographical extent of exclusive economic zone, continental shelf and the Area

Based upon the provisions of the *United Nations Convention on the Law of the Sea* (UNCLOS) which concern the existence and breadth of maritime zones, the Federal Republic of Germany extended its territorial sea by unilateral proclamation on the extension of the German territorial sea to the maximum of 12 nautical miles (M) as of 1 January 1995.

On the same date the unilateral German proclamation of the establishment of an exclusive economic zone (EEZ) in the North Sea and the Baltic entered into force.[5] The German EEZ beyond the territorial sea covers an area of 32,991 square kilometres (km^2) (28,539 km^2 in the North Sea and 4,452 km^2 in the Baltic Sea). The German EEZ effectively consists of the water column above the continental shelf. While both maritime zones, the EEZ and the continental shelf, are regulated in distinct sections of the UNCLOS, they correspond in the case of Germany to an almost identical degree. Due to geographical reasons, the German continental shelf and EEZ in the North Sea and the Baltic Sea are relatively small and the zones had to be delimited with the opposite and lateral neighbouring States.

In the Area Germany currently holds one licence for the exploration of manganese nodules in the Clarion-Clipperton-Zone (CCZ) in the Equatorial North-eastern Pacific (since July 2006, extension granted until July 2026) and one licence for the exploration of polymetallic sulphides in the Indian Ocean (since May 2015). The German licence area in the CCZ encompasses a total of 75,000 km^2 and is divided into two regions. The smaller part of the German exploration area

3 See in this regard the regional section of this book dedicated to the European Union and seabed mining. P. Singh, V. Tassin Campanella and F. Maes, 'The European Union and Seabed Mining', in V. Tassin Campanella (ed), *Routledge handbook of seabed mining and the law of the sea*, London: Routledge, 2023, chapter VI.1.4.

4 EU, Communication from the Commission, *Blue Growth*, 13 September 2012, COM(2012)494 final, 10–11.

5 Proklamation der Bundesrepublik Deutschland über die Errichtung einer ausschließlichen Wirtschaftszone der Bundesrepublik Deutschland in der Nordsee und in der Ostsee, dated 25 November 1994, *Federal Law Gazette*, 1994, Part II, 3770.

measures 15,000 km^2 and is located in the central part of the CCZ. The other, significantly larger part is located in the eastern part of the manganese nodule belt and encompasses 60,000 km^2.

Regulation

Regulation of deep-sea mining activities on the continental shelf and the Area

Germany is a federal State. Legislative and administrative competence is divided between the federal level (*Bund*) and the State level (*Länder*). Mining activities on the continental shelf beyond 12 M as well as in the Area are regulated by federal statutes and governmental decrees.

Relevant German legislation

According to article 59 paragraph 2 of the German Constitution, the *Grundgesetz*, international treaties like the UNCLOS have to be incorporated into national law by federal statute. Such legal act expresses parliamentary consent and can be described as the national, i.e. internal, act of ratification. The German statute which incorporates the UNCLOS into German law entered into force on 15 June 1995.[6] This formal act of incorporation grants validity to the treaty as part of national German law but has to be distinguished from further implementing legislation. Since the majority of treaty norms are not self-executing, implementing national legislation is necessary to give effect to the treaty's regulations. Legal provisions, which give effect to or specify provisions of the UNCLOS or assign responsibilities for the implementation, can be found in different German legal statutes, depending upon the matter addressed by them and competence in the federal system.[7]

Traditionally, mining on Germany's continental shelf is regulated as part of the legal regime for mining on land. The continental shelf was first explicitly addressed by a governmental by-law to the Federal Mining Act, the Continental Shelf Mining Decree of 1989.[8] Meanwhile, it was replaced by the Decree on mining in the area of the territorial sea and continental shelf, of 2016.[9] This new governmental by-law addresses all offshore oil and gas activities and is particularly concerned with environmental protection, safety and labour standards, drilling, risk management and emergency preparedness. While the mining of loose sediments is mentioned in one article, offshore oil and gas activities are the by-law's focus. Other minerals, such as polymetallic nodules, have not been covered by the Decree for factual reasons, since such resources do not exist on the German continental shelf. More general regulations are established by the General Governmental Decree on all Mining Activities,[10] which concerns mining on land and offshore alike.

6 Gesetz zu dem Seerechtsübereinkommen der Vereinten Nationen vom 10. Dezember 1982, *Federal Law Gazette*, 1994, Part II, 1799.

7 One example that specifies Federal competence to regulate and implement international law with regard to maritime affairs is the Federal Maritime Responsibilities Act, i.e. Gesetz über die Aufgaben des Bundes auf dem Gebiet der Seeschifffahrt, *Federal Law Gazette*, 2002, Part I, 2976, last modified on 20 December 2022, *Federal Law Gazette*, 2022 Part I, 2752.

8 Bergverordnung für den Festlandsockel, *Federal Law Gazette*, 1989, Part I, 554 (no longer in force).

9 Bergverordnung für das Gebiet der Küstengewässer und des Festlandsockels (Offshore-Bergverordnung), *Federal Law Gazette*, 2016, Part I, 1866, last modified on 29 November 2018, *Federal Law Gazette*, 2018, Part I, 2034.

10 Bergverordnung für alle bergbaulichen Bereiche (Allgemeine Bergbauverordnung), *Federal Law Gazette*, 1995, Part I, 1466, last modified on 18 October 2017, *Federal Law Gazette*, 2017, Part I, 3584.

Mining in the Area was first provisionally regulated by the Act on Interim Regulation of Deep Seabed Mining[11] until Germany became a member of the UNCLOS and established a Seabed Mining Act.[12] This statute shall ensure compliance with Part XI of the UNCLOS, its Annex III and the Implementing Agreement[13] as well as the rules and regulations issued by the International Seabed Authority (ISA).[14] It is the relevant federal statute for all current and future activities in the Area, from prospecting and exploration to exploitation, under German sponsorship.

The Seabed Mining Act is the central piece of legislation to establish duties, responsibilities and liability. In accordance with article 5 prospectors and contractors are responsible for 1) compliance with all duties resulting from the UNCLOS, the Implementing Agreement, the Mining Code, all relevant German legislation and individual administrative decisions, 2) the safety of technical installations and 3) environmental protection in the Area. Additionally, prospectors and contractors have to designate individuals with particular qualifications that lead and supervise any activities and that can be held liable. The Act lists certain breaches of obligations that are sanctioned as misdemeanours with the result of a financial penalty. In grave cases that are qualified with regard to *inter alia* the endangerment of life or health of humans but also fauna and flora, criminal liability can lead to a fine or imprisonment of individuals.

While both the Seabed Mining Act and the Decree on Continental Shelf Mining have been modified and amended in the past, there are no apparent current legislative initiatives to change existing law or enact additional legislation. Rather, Germany has been actively engaged on the international level to develop and shape relevant regulations, e.g. the Mining Code of the ISA,[15] which in turn is implemented into national German law by reference in article 1 of the Seabed Mining Act.

Germany's position and contribution to the regulation of deep-sea mining activities in the Area

Based upon the dependency on commodity imports Germany has continuously expressed an interest in the extraction of metals from mineral resources of the deep seabed in the past. At the same time the need for environmental protection, sustainable mining practices and zero-waste use of manganese nodules are emphasized both nationally[16] and internationally.[17] They are the basis for the German political position to call for the 'precautionary pause' concerning potential exploitation activities. The Federal Government strongly advocates high environmental standards before the

11 Gesetz zur vorläufigen Regelung des Tiefseebergbaus, *Federal Law Gazette*, 1980, Part I, 1457. An unofficial English translation of the statute as the 'Act on Interim Regulation of Deep Seabed Mining' is published in *International Legal Materials*, 1981, 393.

12 Meeresbodenbergbaugesetz, *Federal Law Gazette*, 1995, Part I, 778, 782, last modified on 19 June 2020, *Federal Law Gazette*, 2020, Part I, 1328.

13 *Agreement relating to the implementation of Part XI of the United Nations Convention on the Law of the Sea of 10 December 1982*, provisionally applied by Germany by statute of 15 May 1995, *Federal Law Gazette*, 1995, Part II, 479; entry into force on 10 September 1996, *Federal Law Gazette*, 1996, Part II, 2511.

14 Art. 1, Seabed Mining Act

15 Germany took part in several textual proposals to update the Mining Code in 2022. Available at <https://www.isa.org.jm/proposals-submitted-after-july-2022-iwg-environment-part-3> (accessed 10 January 2023).

16 Federal Ministry for Economic Affairs and Energy, *Written response to the Brief Enquiry of several members of the Federal Parliament on the Federal Government's interest in deep seabed mining (Kleine Anfrage der Abgeordneten Steffi Lemke u.a. betr: 'Tiefseebergbauinteressen der Deutschen Bundesregierung')*, BT-Drucksache 19/14999, 1 et seq.

17 *Speech by the German Federal Minister of the Environment, Nature Conservation and Nuclear Safety at the Marine Regions Forum*, 2 October 2019. Available online <https://www.bmu.de/rede/rede-von-svenja-schulze-beim-marine-regions-forum/> (accessed 30 March 2021).

exploitation of deep-sea mineral resources begins and has expressed this view frequently via the German delegations to ISA Council and Legal and Technical Commission (LTC) meetings.[18] More recent statements show Germany's general concern for the marine environment[19] and more specifically an emphasis on the need to incorporate the precautionary approach into mining regulations,[20] the independent review of environmental plans and performance assessments,[21] transparency[22] and the need for normative environmental thresholds,[23] before requesting the 'precautionary pause' which is, in effect, a call for a moratorium on commercial seabed mining.

Seabed activities and related decisions

Authorization and State involvement

Currently, the Federal Government decides upon the application for exploration licences and any further activities. The contractor for exploration in both German licence areas is not a private entity but the Federal Institute for Geosciences and Natural Resources (*Bundesanstalt für Geowissenschaften und Rohstoffe*). This Institute is a technical-scientific government agency under the authority of the Federal Ministry for Economic Affairs and Energy.

The implementation of the Seabed Mining Act including the conditions for access are the responsibility of the *Landesamt für Bergbau, Energie und Geologie* (LBEG). This authority was established by the German State of Lower Saxony and is not a Federal authority as such. However, it is loaned to the Federation as far as the specific task of implementing the Seabed Mining Act is concerned. For all other matters it remains a regional agency.

When examining if an applicant meets the preconditions for approval the *Landesamt* has to cooperate with the Federal Maritime and Hydrographic Agency on matters of shipping and environmental protection. While not strictly bound by comments, the *Landesamt* has to take them into account in the decision-making process (article 4, paragraph 4, Seabed Mining Act), while the Federal Maritime and Hydrographic Agency shall submit its comments on environmental protection in consensus with the Federal Environment Agency.

Activities in the Area

Exploration

On behalf of the German Federal Government, the Federal Institute for Geosciences and Natural Resources conducts investigations into marine mineral resources for Germany's two licensed areas.

18 BT-Drucksache 19/14999, op. cit, 40.

19 ISA Assembly, Statement by the German delegation on the occasion of 25th anniversary commemorative session of the ISA Assembly, 25 July 2019. Available online <https://isa.org.jm/files/files/documents/germany_7.pdf> (accessed 30 March 2021).

20 ISA Council, Statement by the German delegation on document ISBA/25/C/8, 26 February 2019. Available online <https://www.isa.org.jm/files/files/documents/germany-c8.pdf> (accessed 30 March 2021).

21 ISA Council, Statement by the German delegation on document ISBA/25/C/10, 27 February 2019. Available online <https://isa.org.jm/files/files/documents/germany-c10.pdf> (accessed 30 March 2021).

22 ISA Council, Statement by the German delegation, 27 February 2019. Available online <https://isa.org.jm/files/files/documents/germany_4.pdf> (accessed 30 March 2021).

23 ISA Council, Normative environmental thresholds for deep-seabed mining, submitted by the delegation of Germany, ISBA/27/C/30, 10 June 2022. Available online <https://www.isa.org.jm/wp-content/uploads/2023/03/ISBA_27_C_30-2209138E.pdf> (accessed 28 March 2023).

In addition to conducting marine mineral exploration activities the Institute's Marine Resource Exploration sub-department undertakes further environmental studies. The Agency collaborates closely with the ISA and is a member of the Integrated Ocean Discovery Program (IODP).

The polymetallic nodules in the German licence area densely cover the ocean floor at water depths of 4,000 to 6,000 metres. They measure about 3 to 8 centimetres in diameter. The exploration contract had first been concluded for the common duration of 15 years. It was due to expire in July 2021 but was renewed for another five years until July 2026. At the time of the renewal technological and economic considerations had not yet allowed a transfer from exploration to an exploitation licence. At the same time, Germany maintained the interest in exclusive rights in the areas for exploration and potential future exploitation. The original considerations of the predecessor of today's German Federal Government, when Germany first applied for the exploration licence for manganese nodules in the CCZ in 2005, were still valid when the renewal was considered.[24] The current German policy to call for further studies on the environmental consequences does not contradict this. The request for time for further research is not a call for a permanent moratorium on seabed mining and does not imply that the German government will give up its exploration licences.

The licence area in the Indian Ocean for the exploration of polymetallic sulphides lies southwest of Madagascar. It amounts to 10,000 km^2, which are divided into 100 sulphide blocks, each of which is 10 × 10 km in size. The contract for the exploration of sulphides has been concluded for 15 years and could be transformed into a mining licence. The exploration licence aims at the identification of inactive polymetallic sulphide deposits. In addition to the exploration of ore deposits, the programme includes extensive and detailed baseline studies for the sustainable protection of the marine environment.

Contractors are selected in accordance with article 4 of the Seabed Mining Act. Any applicant for a contract needs the approval of the *Landesamt* and will be closely examined. An applicant will only be approved if the application and the plan of work meet all standards set by the UNCLOS, the Implementing Agreement and the rules and regulations issued by the ISA, and meet the criteria of reliability, sufficient funding and plausibility that the activities can be carried out on a commercial basis. So far, no private contractors have been engaged in exploration activities under German sponsorship and no exploitation contracts have been applied for due to the lack of regulations for exploitation in the Mining Code and the lack of economic feasibility to engage in commercial mining. In line with its new policy, the German government declared during the 2023 negotiations at the ISA that it would not sponsor any applications for commercial deep-sea mining of raw materials until further notice. At the same time Germany is urging other member states to follow suit and stop supporting applications for commercial exploitation.

Marine scientific research

Germany has been actively involved in different large transnational marine scientific research projects concerning the deep seabed and seabed mining in the past and present, e.g. JPIO Mining Impact I and II and MIDAS. In addition to that the Federal Government supplies funding for national research projects. The environmental effects, e.g. from ploughing and from sediment plumes, are the main concern of such research. Already in 1989 German scientists had started a disturbance experiment (DISCOL) in the Peruvian Basin to investigate the long-term conse-

24 BT-Drucksache 19/14999, op. cit., 22.

quences of deep-sea mining.[25] In 2021 and 2022 marine scientific research cruises led by German scientists in cooperation with DEME GSR, the contractor sponsored by Belgium for their exploration licence, tested a prototype of a nodule collector to study the consequences of the use of such technology.[26]

Conclusion

Germany diligently implements the UNCLOS, the 1994 Agreement and the rules and regulations by the ISA on deep seabed mining and obliges prospectors and contractors to comply with all relevant international and national regulations and decisions. On the international level, Germany has been campaigning for high environmental standards and a momentary pause of processes leading to exploitation as well as further improvements with regard to transparency and the effective functioning of the ISA. So far, the rules on access and supervision have not been put to the test with private applicants and contractors.

The political interest is of such a kind that Germany must be presumed to continue both the quest for and engagement in further marine scientific research on the environmental consequences, the relevant environmental standard-setting and for technological advancements. The underlying dilemma, however, if deep seabed mining can ever be reconciled with criteria of sustainability, particularly Sustainable Development Goal (SDG) 14, at all, will not be solved. Germany has been strongly advocating the SDG process and the national implementation of the 2030 Agenda. The change in policy to promote a 'precautionary pause' and the statement to not sponsor exploitation activities for the time being can be seen in this context.

25 See the DISCOL project. Available online <https://www.discol.de/de> (accessed 28 March 2023).

26 See the MiningImpact project. Available online <https://miningimpact.geomar.de/home> (accessed 28 March 2023).

VI.2.6
GUYANA AND SEABED MINING

Buba Bojang and Donnette Streete

Introduction

Efforts to create a marine economy plan have provided an opportunity to examine the existing maritime economy of Guyana. The aim is to determine the priorities and actions that can assist Guyana to grow its national economy in a way that includes good governance, protection and preservation of the marine environment and sustainable development of its maritime resources. The plan is to continue to strengthen existing sectors such as fisheries, transport and oil and gas, while setting the framework to tap into emerging areas which include marine biotechnology, renewable energy and seabed mining in areas under national jurisdiction. As the country continues to examine its options vis-à-vis its peculiar domestic circumstances, the exploitation and the utilization of the unexplored marine resources that are available for the social and economic benefit of the people of Guyana is the ultimate logical pursuit. One such unexplored marine extractive resources activity gaining increasing attention as an alternative, is deep-sea mining on the continental shelf of Guyana.

> Deep-sea mining is the process of retrieving mineral deposits from the deep sea – the area of the ocean below 200 m which covers about 65% of the Earth's surface.[1]

The world is becoming cognizant of the reality that the continuing reliance on coal and fossil fuel to meet energy demands is becoming unsustainable. Furthermore, there is obvious depletion of terrestrial deposits of metals such as copper, nickel, aluminum, manganese, zinc, lithium and cobalt, and the rising demand for these metals to produce technologically advanced applications and green technologies including wind turbines, solar panels and electric storage batteries.[2] So the principal drivers of this thrust towards deep-sea mining are a combination of technological advances in marine mining and processing, and an increase in the long-term demand for minerals, which is attributable to globalization and industrialization in the developing world.

1 IUCN, *Issues Brief*, July 2018. Available online <https://www.iucn.org/resources/issues-briefs/deep-sea-mining> (accessed 9 February 2022)

2 IUCN, op. cit.

DOI: 10.4324/9780429426162-35

Guyana gained significant international attention in 2015 as a new frontier in offshore oil exploration when Exxon announced a massive discovery of oil and gas reserves in its Stabroek Bloc, approximately 120 nautical miles (M) offshore. Since then, a total of twenty-two discoveries across the Stabroek block have been made, accounting for a resource estimate of more than eight billion barrels of oil equivalent. The flurry of activities offshore provides the opportunity to utilize existing interests and resources where applicable, to pursue deep-sea mining as another industry to develop. Though this industry is a logical next step for Guyana, the major challenge would be reconciling its 'green agenda' with its aim of realizing the sustainable development goals (SDGs) and meeting the needs of the Guyanese people utilizing the resources within its national jurisdiction.

That sustainable development conversation needs to begin immediately because the long-term effects of mineral extraction from the marine environment are known and the more prepared a state is to begin this venture, the better the result. The current discussions with respect to the oil and gas industry would provide impetus. The development of the marine economy of Guyana is dependent on the protection and preservation of the marine environment, which can only be achieved if all activities are coordinated and managed sustainably. Perhaps more importantly, a critical review of the legal and policy framework for the regulation of deep seabed mining activities on the continental shelf (CS) of Guyana would be required urgently, with a view to addressing any possible deficiencies in governance.

The fundamental question is whether Guyana is ready to explore deep-sea mining within its CS of potential resources other than oil and gas, such as nodules and crusts, as its next maritime extractive industry. This chapter seeks to evaluate the issue from a Guyanese perspective. It seeks to evaluate, in particular, the legal infrastructure currently in place in Guyana to accommodate deep-sea mining and identifies the particular environmental issues that should be taken into consideration.

Geographic extent of the exclusive economic zone, continental shelf and the Area

Guyana's ratification of the *United Nations Convention on the Law of the Sea* (UNCLOS) on 16 November 1993, was the sixtieth ratification that brought the Convention into force, twelve months later. Since one of the principal aims of UNCLOS is the definition of the limits of coastal and maritime boundaries, Guyana like other coastal States ratified the Convention in order to properly safeguard its rights and meet its international obligations in relation to the international law of the sea. Significantly, Guyana was able to rely on the provisions of the Convention to assert and protect its maritime entitlements when the maritime boundary with the Republic of Suriname was settled. Pursuant to articles 286 and 287 of the Convention and in accordance with Annex VII thereto, Guyana instituted proceedings against Suriname by notice of 24 February 2004. The arbitration proceedings concerned the delimitation of the Guyana/ Suriname maritime boundary and alleged breaches of international law by Suriname in the disputed maritime territory. In 2007, the Tribunal delimited the maritime boundary between the two States, securing for Guyana the portion of the territory in dispute in which she had already begun oil and gas exploration activities.[3]

In 2010, Guyana enacted the Maritime Zones Act (MZA)[4] to incorporate certain key provisions of UNCLOS into the Laws of Guyana. The MZA is therefore the main legislative framework

3 Reports of the International Arbitral Awards, *Award in the arbitration regarding the delimitation of the maritime boundary between Guyana and Suriname, Award of 17 September 2007.*

4 Laws of Guyana, Cap 63:01, Act No. 18 of 2010.

which regulates activities in Guyana's maritime spaces. It establishes, from the baseline, the limits of the territorial sea to a distance of 12 M, the contiguous zone to a distance of 24 M and the limits of the exclusive economic zone to a distance of 200 M. With regard to the continental shelf, the MZA provides that the continental shelf of Guyana comprises the seabed and the subsoil of the submarine areas to the outer edge of the continental margin or to a distance of 200 M, in accordance with article 76 of UNCLOS. The precise limits of the continental shelf are yet to be delimited as Guyana has made a submission to the Commission on the Limits of the Continental Shelf for an extension of an additional 150 M of its continental shelf. The submission was made in 2012 without prejudice to eventual maritime delimitation between Guyana and any neighboring State. In response to the submission of Guyana, the Government of the Bolivarian Republic of Guyana wrote to the Commission protesting the consideration of Guyana's submission on the ground that the continental shelf is formed by territory which is the subject of a territorial dispute between the two parties under the Geneva Agreement of 1966.[5] In its response, Guyana submitted to the Commission that there were no territorial disputes and no maritime boundary disputes or controversies which might affect the consideration of any portion of the outer limits of the submission. It was further indicated that the submission was made without prejudice to maritime boundary delimitation between Guyana and any other State. Taking these submissions into consideration, the Commission decided that, pursuant to article 5 of Annex II to the Convention and rule 42 of the Rules of Procedure, the submission would be addressed by a subcommission to be established in accordance with rule 51, paragraph 4 ter, of the Rules of Procedure, at a future session. The Commission also decided that it would revert to the consideration of the submission at the plenary level when the submission was next in line for consideration as queued in the order in which it was received.[6]

Apart from the maritime boundary delimitation with Suriname by arbitration in 2007, Guyana has no other delimited maritime boundary. The State has potential maritime boundaries with the Republic of Trinidad and Tobago, Barbados and the Bolivarian Republic of Venezuela, the latter being the subject of a dispute between the two States.

Regulation of seabed mining activities

The MZA articulates the rights of Guyana with respect to exploration and exploitation of resources of the submarine areas and the requirement of authorization of drilling for any purpose. It also enunciates the rights of Guyana and regulates the exploitation of resources under its jurisdiction in accordance with UNCLOS and general principles of international law, *inter alia*.

Section 21, paragraph 1, of the MZA outlines Guyana's rights in the continental shelf in accordance with the provisions of UNCLOS.

There is a clear established legal framework for the conduct of deep-sea mining in the continental shelf of Guyana which allows for key issues such as authorization and licensing, marine environment protection and conservation, and management of the activity to be carried out. In addition, there are other important pieces of legislation that would allow for a more robust frame-

5 Guyana has always maintained that the Geneva Agreement does not in fact recognize a territorial dispute between the two States but provides a mechanism for Venezuela to prove her claim of nullity of the 1899 Award which settled the land boundary between them. The judicial examination of the Award is currently the subject of a matter before the International Court of Justice.

6 Commission on the Limits of the Continental Shelf, *Progress of work in the Commission on the Limits of the Continental Shelf*, CLCS/74, 30 April 2012.

work to be applied in areas within national jurisdiction. However, neither the MZA nor any other piece of relevant legislation regulates activities in the Area.

In addition to the MZA, Guyana has in force the Mining Act of 1989 which regulates prospecting for and the mining of minerals, among others and matters or issues connected with the mining of minerals such as licensing and permits. The definition of minerals in the Act excludes water and petroleum. It provides that a mining 'claim' could include the seabed or other area beneath water and that both the exploration for, and exploitation of minerals other than oil and gas must be conducted by the holder of a license granted by the Commissioner of the Guyana Geology and Mines Commission. Although most of the provisions really address the mining of minerals on land and the legislation does not contemplate seabed mining, it does facilitate the enactment of regulations under the Act for a number of purposes including prospecting for and the mining of minerals at sea.[7] There is therefore a scope in the Act for the development of seabed mining regulations.

With respect to environmental issues, the Environmental Protection Act (EPA) 1996 is in place to provide for the management, conservation, protection and improvement of the environment, the prevention or control of pollution, the assessment of the impact of economic development on the environment, the sustainable use of natural resources and other related matters. The Act defines environment to include water, sea, seabed, marine and coastal areas with natural resources, clearly covering the continental shelf of Guyana. Since environmental concerns are key variables in determining the extraction of minerals from the seabed, this piece of legislation is critical. Section 11 provides that the developer of any project, which includes the extraction and conversion of minerals,[8] with the potential to significantly disrupt the environment, needs to apply for an environmental permit based on an environmental impact assessment (EIA) conducted by an independent entity, which is approved by the Environmental Protection Agency. Currently, the agency is working to update the EPA and its regulations to cater for the developments in the oil and gas industry and to update fees, fines and penalties in accordance with current economic realities. It is also contemplated that the legislative provisions would cater to any future activities. It is not clear whether there will be a specific reference to seabed mining.

In terms of legislative infrastructure, the Ministry of Foreign Affairs is responsible for administering the Maritime Zones Act, the Environmental Protection Agency for the Environmental Protection Act and the Guyana Geology and Mines Commission for the administration of the Mining Act.

Other considerations

There is no doubt that seabed mining could reap significant social and economic benefits for Guyana. However, these benefits should be weighed against the potential impact of seabed mining on the marine environment. In the first place, it would be critical for baseline data to be gathered for a determination of the state of the marine ecosystem prior to the conduct of any mining activity on the continental shelf. This initiative could be undertaken by the Government as a precondition to its further consideration of the activity, in which case it may be cost-prohibitive, or it could be done by proponents of the activity during the conduct of an EIA. Valuable information in relation to the biological and physical condition of the area could then be gleaned. The acquisition of this type of data is currently being done by the oil companies involved in exploration activities relating

7 Mining Act 1989, Section 135 (2) (a) and (b).

8 Environmental Protection Act 1998, schedule 4.

to the oil and gas sector as part of their EIA process, but it is not a process that is being driven by the government. The involvement of the government in data collection is however very important for overall marine spatial planning and the future uses of the continental shelf of Guyana.

Additionally, any scraping of the seabed for exploration or exploitation may cause disruption of habitats and ecosystems on the seabed. Unfortunately, because not enough is known about the ecosystem on the deep ocean floor, this disruption has the potential to wipe out entire species and related biodiversity. This lack of information may hinder the development of strategies to preserve these habitats and ecosystems. The application of precautionary principles concerning the protection and preservation of the marine environment should be given a high priority.

Seabed mining and in particular deep-sea mining can also affect the migratory pattern of marine species. Since migration is critical to the sustainability of species and their population, there must be some concern about the conservation of such population.[9] The fishing industry in Guyana is a significant driver of the economy, therefore, any potential disruption of these biological resources must be analyzed carefully.[10]

There is the need also to consider the potential pollution of the marine environment associated with deep-sea mining. Pollution can be caused by toxic chemicals released by equipment or vessels utilized in the mining process that could severely impact habitats.[11] Also, noise, light and vibration from equipment may affect specific types of biodiversity.

Seabed activities and related decisions

After the 2015 discoveries of massive hydrocarbon deposits in Guyana's offshore waters, the country began production in 2019. To date, these oil- and gas-related activities are the only form of deep-sea activities being conducted on Guyana's CS. No other investigation has been done based on global trends to ascertain whether any or what type of mineral deposits may be found in the CS.

The existing legal infrastructure has allowed for a multi-staged process to be concluded in order for such activities to be conducted. Section 8 of the Petroleum (Exploration and Production) Act[12] provides that anyone interested in the exploration or exploitation activity must apply for and be granted a license by the Minister responsible for the petroleum industry. Additionally, an interested party must also acquire an environmental permit from the Environmental Protection Agency after satisfying the criteria for granting of the permit or authorization. The preconditions for the granting of an environmental permit are fixed in the Environmental Protection (Authorisation) Regulations. Therefore, an interested party must interface with several agencies responsible for the implementation of each piece of legislation to conduct activities offshore Guyana, on the specific issues of licensing and permits, environmental impact assessments and the conduct of operations. Still, the discoveries and the journey towards crude oil production continue.

To date, Guyana has not authorized any activity related to deep-sea mining either in its continental shelf or in the Area. As a precursor, the State has taken the decision to actively participate in the discussions at the International Seabed Authority (ISA) in an attempt to understand the industry. Having not been an active participant during the period of consultation on the explora-

9 IUCN, op. cit.

10 Extractive Industries Transparency Initiative, Guyana. Website available online <https://www.gyeiti.org/fisheries#:~:text=In%202017%20the%20fisheries%20industry,2016%20and%207.70%25%20in%202017> (accessed 9 February 2022).

11 IUCN, op. cit.

12 Laws of Guyana, Cap 65:10, Act No.3 of 1986.

tion regulations and considering its developing interest in deep-sea mining, Guyana is actively considering the draft regulations and guidelines on exploitation. The particular interest is in the environmental policies included therein and the role of the sponsoring States and contractors. In this regard, the aim is to understand and be able to execute the difficult task of achieving a balance between advancing the industry locally within an effective legal framework for the exploitation of resources and the relevant environmental law considerations. With the development of its new Low Carbon Development Strategy 2030 (currently under public consultation), Guyana hopes to create a new-low-carbon economy by establishing incentives based on the value of the world's ecosystem services and promoting these as an essential component of a new model of global development based on the principle of sustainability. The policy will transcend all of the components of the local economy, including the oil and gas sector.

In *Thomas v. Environmental Protection Agency*, a Guyanese scientist Dr. Troy Thomas filed a case against the EPA of Guyana in the Supreme Court. Thomas alleged that the twenty-three-year permits that the EPA had issued to Esso Exploration (a subsidiary of Exxon) for oil exploration violated regulations under the Environmental Protection Act that limited such permit lengths to five years. The EPA had issued permits to Esso that ran through 2040 and 2043 and claimed in their defense that this was in keeping with the terms of the Production Sharing Agreement, signed between the company and the State. Thomas argued that issuing such a long permit in violation of law 'exposes Guyana and the rest of the world to serious, if not irreparable, harm and adverse consequences from climate change.' In a settlement of the matter, EPA agreed to reduce the term of the permits to five years, so that they would expire in 2022 and 2024, in keeping with the regulations under the Act.

Conclusion

Achieving the right balance between development and sustainability in the legal infrastructure for deep-sea mining vis-à-vis protection and preservation of the marine environment and sustainable development of marine resources is no easy feat for large-developed countries, much less a small developing country like Guyana. However, the small islands[13] and developing States (Guyana inclusive) are looking into the possibilities of deep-sea mining as a means to achieve economic development.[14] Is this needed in Guyana? Probably not in the short term, as the oil and gas industry advances, but preparations for the legal and technical infrastructure of the mining industry need to begin now, even as the country begins to take inventory of what potential for mineral deposits exists in areas within its national jurisdiction. This is because sustainable development requires that the needs of the current generation be met without compromising the ability of future generations to meet their needs. Therefore, achieving that right balance is a *condicio sine qua non*.

As a first step, Guyana must begin the process of reviewing and updating the current legal regime that it has in place to accommodate this emerging sector. Importantly, a harmonization of the institutional frameworks related to the application process, the licensing and permit processes, environmental management and monitoring processes and the liability and compensation pro-

13 For a detailed analysis of the context in the Pacific islands region, see in this book C. Diver, 'The Pacific Islands region and seabed mining,' in V. Tassin Campanella (ed), *Routledge handbook of seabed mining and the law of the sea*, London: Routledge, 2023, chapter VI.1.5.

14 For more information on the regional context, see in this book E. Jiménez Pineda, 'South American region and seabed mining,' in V. Tassin Campanella (ed), *Routledge handbook of seabed mining and the law of the sea*, op. cit., chapter VI.1.6.

cesses is necessary. Currently, all the relevant agencies work separately to fulfill their mandate, when an integrated approach would save time, money and cater to any blind spots particular agencies might miss. Such a system would require fluidity and flexibility for continuous adjustments to be made to give effect to the regime that best suits Guyana.

As a next step, the acquisition of baseline data is paramount before opening up the continental shelf to mining activities.[15] The operation of a benchmark from which to gauge the effects of mining activities is important in determining whether the potential effect of deep-sea mining is too costly for Guyana in terms of funding for data acquisition.

15 For challenges related to environmental data, see in this book W.R. Roest, M.R. Clark and H. Brekke, 'The scientific challenges of deep-sea mining,' in V. Tassin Campanella (ed), *Routledge handbook of seabed mining and the law of the sea*, op. cit., chapter I.1.

VI.2.7
ICELAND AND SEABED MINING

Bjarni Már Magnússon

Introduction

Seabed mining is not an issue within the government or in politics in Iceland. No legislation exists that regulates seabed mining explicitly, although there exists legislation relevant to the topic, mainly concerning the Icelandic state's ownership of resources on the seabed. The main developments currently that impact possible future seabed mining activities are proposed changes to the Icelandic constitution that are under consideration by the Icelandic parliament regarding the environment and natural resources.[1]

Geographical extent of the exclusive economic zone, continental shelf and the Area

Given Iceland's geographical location as an island in the middle of the North Atlantic, the maritime areas it controls are multiple times larger than its land territory. Iceland's maritime zones within 200 nautical miles (M) are approximately 758,000 square kilometres (km^2), whereas Icelandic territory is 102,775 km^2. Iceland and its neighbouring states have no outstanding delimitation disputes concerning maritime areas within 200 M. All such disputes have been settled with bilateral agreements.[2]

1 Frumvarp til stjórnarskipunarlaga um breytingu á stjórnarskrá lýðveldisins Íslands, nr. 33/1944, með síðari breytingum (forseti Íslands, ríkisstjórn, verkefni framkvæmdarvalds, umhverfisvernd, auðlindir náttúru Íslands og íslensk tunga), 2020–2021. Doc. 788 (case 466) [hereinafter Constitutional Bill]. Available online in Icelandic <https://www.althingi.is/altext/151/s/0787.html> (accessed 14 March 2021).

2 *Agreement between Iceland and Norway Concerning Fishery and Continental Shelf Questions*, 28 May 1980, 2124 UNTS 225; *Agreement between Norway and Iceland on the continental shelf between Iceland and Jan Mayen*, adopted 22 October 1981, 2124 UNTS 247; *Additional Protocol to the Agreement of 28 May 1980 between Norway and Iceland Concerning Fishery and Continental Shelf Questions and the Supplementary Agreement derived therefrom of 22 October 1981 on the Continental Shelf in the Area between Jan Mayen and Iceland*, 11 November 1997, 2127 UNTS 237; *Agreement between the Government of the Kingdom of Denmark along with the Local Government of Greenland on the one hand, and the Government of the Republic of Iceland on the other hand on the Delimitation of the Continental Shelf and the Fishery Zone in the Area between Greenland and Iceland*, 11 November 1997, 2074 UNTS 43; *Agreement between the Government of the Kingdom of Denmark, together with the Government of the Faroes, on the one hand, and the Government of Iceland, on the other hand, relating to the Maritime Delimitation in*

DOI: 10.4324/9780429426162-36

The continental shelf area to which Iceland believes it is entitled is more than 1,400,000 km^2 and consists of the Ægir Basin, the Reykjanes Ridge and the Hatton-Rockall area.[3] So far, the Commission on the Limits of the Continental Shelf has only fully accepted Iceland's arguments concerning its entitlement to the continental shelf in the Ægir Basin, east of Iceland.[4] Iceland has concluded two agreed minutes on the delimitation of the continental shelf beyond 200 M with neighbouring states.[5] Quadrilateral negotiations concerning the boundary delimitation of the Hatton-Rockall area have been ongoing between Iceland, Denmark (Faroe Islands), the UK and Ireland for almost four decades, without any solution.

Regulation of seabed mining activities

No Icelandic legislation exists that regulates seabed mining explicitly, and no Icelandic legislation addresses the Area. The main reason no legislation exists is that there has been no demand for legislation in the field from the industry or other actors.

Although no legislation exists that addresses seabed mining explicitly, a few acts are relevant in the context of the Icelandic exclusive economic zone (EEZ) and the continental shelf, mainly Act No. 41 of 1 June 1979 concerning the territorial sea, the contiguous zone, the economic zone and the continental shelf (Maritime Zones Act) and Act No. 73 of 18 May 1990 on the Ownership of the Icelandic State of resources on the seabed (Seabed Resources Act).[6] Both acts have been amended a few times.

Domestic acts concerning the seabed

Article 1 paragraph 1 of the Seabed Resources Act provides that the Icelandic state is the owner of all resources on or under the seabed beyond the 115 m net zone from the coast,[7] so far seawards

---

the area between the Faroe Islands and Iceland, 1 and 2 February 2007, bekendtgørelse No. 24, Danmarks Traktater (Lovtidende C) 16 March 2010.

3 Ministry for Foreign Affairs, 'Afhending greinargerðar Íslands til landgrunnsnefndar S.þ. um ytri mörk landgrunnsins utan 200 sjómílna'. Available at <https://www.stjornarradid.is/efst-a-baugi/frettir/stok-frett/2009/04/30/Afhending-greinargerdar-Islands-til-landgrunnsnefndar-S.th.-um-ytri-mork-landgrunnsins-utan-200-sjomilna/> (accessed 13 March 2021).

4 See Commission on the Limits of the Continental Shelf, 'Summary of Recommendations of the Commission on the Limits of the Continental Shelf in Regard to the Submission made by Iceland in the Ægis Basin Area and in the Western and Southern Parts of Reykjanes Ridge on 29 April 2009', 10 March 2016. Available online <https://www.un.org/Depts/los/clcs_new/submissions_files/isl27_09/2016_03_10_sc_isl.pdf> (accessed 15 March 2021).

5 *Agreed Minutes on the Delimitation of the Continental Shelf beyond 200 Nautical Miles between the Faroe Islands, Iceland and Norway in the Southern Part of the Banana Hole of the Northeast Atlantic* (adopted 20 September 2006). Available online <http://www.regjeringen.no/nn/dep/ud/dok/lover_regler/retningslinjer/2006/Agreed-Minutes.html?id=446839> accessed 15 March 2021; *Agreed Minutes on the Delimitation of the Continental Shelf beyond 200 Nautical Miles between Greenland and Iceland in the Irminger Sea* (adopted 16 January 2013). Available online <https://www.stjornarradid.is/media/utanrikisraduneyti-media/media/thjodrettarmal/agreed-minutes-og-vidaukar.pdf> (accessed 15 March 2021).

6 The official Icelandic versions of the acts are available online on the website of the Icelandic parliament: <http://www.althingi.is> (accessed 15 March 2021). An up-to-date English translation of the Maritime Zones Act is available online <https://www.government.is/library/04-Legislation/Act%20No%2041%201979%20as%20amended%20by%20Act%20No%2058%202017%20and%20Act%20No%2044%202018.pdf> (accessed 13 March 2021). No official English translation is available for the Seabed Resources Act. The translation of its provisions is the author's.

7 From 1281, the user rights of landowners of Icelandic land with a coastline have been defined within 115 m (or similar length) from the low watermark.

as the sovereign right of Iceland extends according to Icelandic laws, international treaties and bilateral treaties.[8] It has been pointed out by Icelandic scholars that it is questionable whether the term 'ownership' should be understood as the property of the Icelandic state or if it should be understood as the sovereign right of Iceland to legislate the utilisation and management of the seabed.[9] This issue will possibly be clarified with the proposed changes to the Icelandic constitutions discussed below.

The Maritime Zones Act and the Seabed Resources Act define seabed resources slightly differently. Whereas the Maritime Zones Act[10] sticks to the definition of the *United Nations Convention on the Law of the Sea* (UNCLOS)[11] in article 77 paragraph 1 and paragraph 4, the Seabed Resources Act excludes living creatures and defines, for the purposes of the act, natural resources as all of the seabed's living and non-living organisms.[12]

The Maritime Zones Act defines the maximum extent of the sovereign rights of Iceland and consequently the geographical scope of the Seabed Resources Act. The Maritime Zones Act incorporated important provisions of the 1977 Informal Composite Negotiating Text,[13] in which many of the main principles of UNCLOS were crystallised. The act's definition of the EEZ and the continental shelf aligns with articles 56–57, article 76 paragraph 1 and article 77 paragraphs 1 and 4 of UNCLOS.[14]

The continental shelf beyond 200 nautical miles

The geographical aspect of the Icelandic continental shelf beyond 200 M is a bit confusing. In Iceland's 2009 partial submission to the Commission on the Limits of the Continental Shelf (CLCS) with regard to the Ægir Basin area (northeast of Iceland) and in the western and southern parts of Reykjanes Ridge,[15] the Reykjanes Ridge is classified as a submarine elevation and not a submarine ridge, consequently justifying a continental shelf beyond 350 M.[16] A subcommission agreed with Iceland's arguments, whereas the full commission did not accept the recommendations of the subcommission.[17] It recommended only the use of points in the western part of Reykjanes Ridge up to 350 M from the baselines but refrained from recommending a limit for the southern

8 Interestingly, the provision makes an explicit distinction between international and bilateral treaties.

9 T. Örlygsson, K. Axelsson and V. S. Petersen, *Eignaréttur*, Reykjavik: Fons juris, 2020, p. 87.

10 Article 5 of the Maritime Zones Act.

11 10 December 1982, 1833 UNTS 396.

12 Article 1(2) of the Seabed Resources Act. Living creatures fall under *Act No. 79 of 26 May 1997* on *fishing* in Iceland's exclusive fishing zone, as amended.

13 Third United Nations Conference on the Law of the Sea, Official Records Vol. VII (Informal Composite Negotiation Text, Sixth Session) (15 July 1977) UN Doc. A/CONF. 62/WP.10, United Nations 1984. Available online <https://legal.un.org/diplomaticconferences/1973_los/docs/english/vol_8/a_conf62_wp10.pdf> (accessed 15 March 2021).

14 In addition, the Maritime Zones Act includes a general provision that incorporates article 192 of UNCLOS concerning the environment and two provisions that incorporate the core UNCLOS provisions on scientific research.

15 Republic of Iceland, 'The Icelandic Continental Shelf, Partial Submission to the Commission on the Limits of the Continental Shelf pursuant to article 76, paragraph 8 of the United Nations Convention on the Law of the Sea in respect of the Ægir Basin area and Reykjanes Ridge' (29 April 2009). Available online <https://www.un.org/Depts/los/clcs_new/submissions_files/isl27_09/isl2009executivesummary.pdf> (accessed 15 March 2021).

16 To exclude the possibility of states making enormous claims to the outer continental shelf, article 76(6) of LOSC provides that the outer limit of the continental shelf shall not exceed 350 M on submarine ridges. This does not apply to submarine elevations that are natural components of the continental margin. What complicates the situation is that paragraph 6 does not define what is meant by the term 'submarine ridges', or other provisions of LOSC.

17 Commission on the Limits of the Continental Shelf, op. cit.

part.[18] In short, the CLCS did not fully accept Iceland's arguments. Consequently, Iceland made a partial revised submission in 2021 in respect of the western, southern and south-eastern parts of the Reykjanes Ridge to support its previous arguments.[19]

Interestingly, Iceland's CLCS submissions, or any other public document or statement by the Icelandic government addressed internationally, in the context of its CLCS submission (of which this author is aware), does not refer directly or indirectly to regulation No. 196, 9 May 1985, concerning the delimitation of the continental shelf to the west, south and east,[20] which is still in force.[21] The regulation was promulgated in accordance with article 6 paragraph 2 of the Maritime Zones Act by the minister for foreign affairs, the same minister responsible for the CLCS submission. It was neither revoked before Iceland made a submission to the CLCS in 2009 nor in 2021, although it contradicts Iceland's argument that the Reykjanes Ridge is a submarine elevation. It notes the following:

> Segment FHG [Reykjanes Ridge] is defined by the 350 nautical mile distance limit from Iceland. The continental shelf boundary, if defined on the basis of the foot of the slope, extends beyond 350 nautical miles. But since in this area it lies on the Reykjanes submarine ridge, the boundary of the continental shelf is limited to 350 nautical mile distance from Iceland by article 76.[22]

No official explanation exists regarding this inconsistency. Many questions arise in this context. It is almost as if the Icelandic government is trying to pretend that the regulation does not exist. What is at least clear is that the outer limits of Iceland's continental shelf beyond 200 M on the Reykjanes Ridge are uncertain, which consequently means that the geographical scope of the Seabed Resources Act is not fixed.

License to exploit

No one is allowed to search for substances to exploit on or under the Icelandic seabed unless they have received a written licence from the National Energy Authority (Orkustofnun).[23] Without a written licence from the National Energy Authority, it is forbidden to remove or exploit substances from the seabed.[24] The National Energy Authority can decide or negotiate return for removal or

18 Ibid., pp. 22–23, paras. 72–80.

19 Republic of Iceland, 'The Icelandic Continental Shelf – Revised Partial Submission to the Commission on the Limits of the Continental Shelf pursuant to article 76, paragraph 8 of the United Nations Conventions on the Law of the Sea in respect of Reykjanes Ridge', 31 March 2021. Available online <https://www.un.org/Depts/los/clcs_new/submissions_files/isl27_09/20210331IslRevEsSecure.pdf> (accessed 21 June 2022).

20 The regulation was submitted to the Secretary General of the UN. Available online <https://www.un.org/Depts/los/LEGISLATIONANDTREATIES/PDFFILES/ISL_1985_Regulation> (accessed 15 March 2021). The official Icelandic version, which includes a map, can be found online at <https://www.reglugerd.is/reglugerdir/eftir-raduneytum/utanrikisraduneyti/nr/999> (accessed 21 June 2022). A recent publication about the Reykjanes Ridge makes no reference to the regulation at all: Helga Gudmundsdottir, 'The Case of Reykjanes Ridge', in T. Heidar (ed.) *New Knowledge and Changing Circumstances in the Law of the Sea*, Leiden: Brill, 2020, pp. 289–307.

21 On 19 June 1985, the UK delivered a protest note to Iceland regarding the regulation. So did the Irish Government on 20 June 1985. See Clive R. Symmons, 'The Rockall Dispute Deepens: An Analysis of Recent Danish and Icelandic Actions', *International & Comparative Law Quarterly* 35, 1986, 356–368.

22 Article 3 of Regulation No. 196 from 1985, op. cit.

23 Article 2 of the Natural Seabed Act.

24 Article 3(1), ibid.

exploitation it has authorised. The return shall generally be devoted to seabed and continental shelf research, as further decided by the minister of industries and innovation.[25] A licence to explore substances on or under the seabed shall be demarcated to a specific area and be temporary (max. thirty years), and it shall, for example, always state what measures the licence holder shall implement to avoid pollution and contamination of the environment.[26] When a licence is granted according to the act, the provisions of Act No. 106 from 2000 on environmental impact assessment shall be respected.[27] Before it is granted, the Environmental Agency and Institute of Natural History shall be consulted.[28] No one yet has applied for a licence to engage in seabed mining in the Icelandic EEZ or continental shelf.

In the beginning of the year 2021, the prime minister of Iceland introduced a bill to the parliament that contains provisions regarding the environment and natural resources. One provision in the proposed bill declares that all natural resources of Iceland, which are not privately owned, belong to the Icelandic people and that such resources shall be exploited in a sustainable manner for the benefit of the population.[29] Considerations concerning seabed mining had no influence on the drafting of the provision. At the time of this writing, it is unclear whether the bill has enough votes to pass.

The Icelandic government has no official position and has not contributed to the regulation of seabed mining activities in the Area.

Seabed activities and related decisions

The Icelandic government has not received any requests to issue a licence for activities related to seabed mining. In fact, no decisions have been made concerning seabed mining activities at all, probably because there is no pressure on the Icelandic government to do so. No cases concerning seabed mining have been brought before Icelandic courts, and academic literature in the Icelandic context is almost non-existent.

Conclusion

The legislation in place gives effect to UNCLOS, although the legislation is not sufficiently developed concerning seabed mining. The main conclusion is that seabed mining has not yet become an issue in Iceland, and no legislation exists that addresses seabed mining explicitly. Neither political nor commercial pressure exists that leads to governmental actions in the field. It is unlikely that anything remarkable will happen in this field in Iceland in the near future as the situation is currently.

25 Article 3(2), ibid.
26 Article 4(1), ibid.
27 Article 4(2), ibid.
28 Ibid.
29 Article 22 of the Constitutional Bill, op. cit.

VI.2.8
INDIA AND SEABED MINING

Ipshita Chaturvedi Sadhale

Introduction

Even before ratifying the *United Nations Convention on the Law of the Sea* (UNCLOS) in June 1995, India showed a serious interest in seabed mining of minerals and became the first pioneer investor to be registered for the development of a mine site in the international seabed area in the Indian Ocean, more specifically in the central Indian Ocean Basin (CIOB).[1] Since then, India has actively participated in the exploration of deep-sea minerals and signed two exploration contracts with the International Seabed Authority (ISA) for the exploration of polymetallic nodules[2] (2002–2017) and polymetallic sulphides[3] (2016–2031). India has exclusive rights to explore nodules in 75,000 square kilometres (km^2) of international waters until 2022. The estimated polymetallic nodule resource potential in the Area is 380 million tonnes, containing 4.7 million tonnes of nickel, 4.29 million tonnes of copper, 0.55 million tonnes of cobalt and 92.59 million tonnes of manganese.[4]

Very recently, the Indian government allocated a substantial budget towards a 'deep-ocean mission' discussed later in the article. This is to finance India's plan on exploring and identifying potential sites of multi-metal hydrothermal sulphides mineralisation along the Indian ocean mid-oceanic ridges in the Area.

1 India received the status of a 'pioneer investor' in 1987 and was initially allocated an area of 1,500,000 km^2 to develop technology to mine and extract metal from nodules.

2 India signed a contract with the ISA for a period of 15 years for carrying out various developmental works (survey and exploration, environmental impact assessment study, technology development in mining and metallurgy) in the retained area under a polymetallic nodules programme. This contract has been extended for another 5 years and currently ends in 2022.

3 Department of Science and Technology, *India signs contract for exploration of polymetallic sulphides with International Seabed Authority*, press release, 27 September 2016. Available online <https://dst.gov.in/pressrelease/india-signs-contract-exploration-polymetallic-sulphides-international-seabed-authority> (accessed 16 July 2021).

4 Ministry of Earth Sciences, *India's exclusive rights to explore polymetallic nodules from central Indian ocean seabed basin extended by five years*, press release, 21 August 2017. Available online <https://pib.gov.in/newsite/PrintRelease.aspx?relid=170138> (accessed 15 July 2021).

DOI: 10.4324/9780429426162-37

Geographical extent of the exclusive economic zone, continental shelf and the Area

India has a coastline of roughly 7,600 km and a continental shelf (CS) of 372,424 square kilometres (km^2).[5] India's exclusive economic zone (EEZ) spans 2,200,000 km^2 which is largely unexplored and unutilised, and is the focus of much discussion in India. The EEZ is equivalent to about 67 per cent of the land area of the country. To understand the geographical extent of India's continental shelf,[6] it is often useful to look at the Indian map upside down (south-up map orientation) to gauge how strong a maritime power India is.

In 2009, India made a partial submission to the United Nations Commission on the Limits of the Continental Shelf (CLCS) to extend its continental shelf (without prejudice to existing disputes) over 300,000 km^2 of seabed in the eastern part (shared with Myanmar and Sri Lanka) and the West (shared with Oman and Pakistan).[7] According to the Indian statement before the CLCS, despite there being bilateral agreements with most other States, certain maritime delimitations are still unclear. The submission has been contested by Myanmar, Bangladesh, Oman and Pakistan. No recommendations have been given on this so far.

When India became a pioneer investor in 1987, it was allocated a total area of 150,000 km^2 to carry out various developmental activities in the CIOB.[8] Following several surveys and upon fulfilment of obligations under the Third United Nations Conference on the Law of the Sea, by 2002, an area of 75,000 km^2 was identified and finalised for development.[9]

The Indian seabed mining site, which is the area of exploration of India's seabed mining technology in the Area, is about 1,450 nautical miles (M) from its port of operation in Goa and is among the most explored areas in India's oceanography programme. This Indian Ocean site was also the first deep-sea exploration programme in the country's attempt to explore mineral resources from the international seabed area.[10] Seabed mining activities in India are currently confined to the CIOB.

Regulation of seabed activities

Institutional framework

India does not have a consolidated oceans ministry at the federal level. There are also some challenges between the central and state governments with respect to various elements of oceans

5 Center for Coastal Zone Management and Coastal Shelter Belt, *Database on coastal states of India*, Available online <http://iomenvis.nic.in/index2.aspx?slid=758&sublinkid=119&langid=1&mid=1> (accessed 16 July 2021).

6 In 2014, the PCA awarded Bangladesh an area of 19,467 km^2 (almost 4/5th of the disputed maritime boundary) in a case of disputed maritime boundary between India and Bangladesh in the Bay of Bengal. While both parties voluntarily referred the dispute to the PCA, and have accepted its verdict, there remain some grey areas in the EEZ as an aftermath of the dispute.

7 Outer limits of the continental shelf beyond 200 M from the baselines: submissions to the commission: submissions by the Republic of India. Available online <https://www.un.org/depts/los/clcs_new/submissions_files/submission_ind_48_2009.htm> (accessed 15 July 2021).

8 India relinquished 50 per cent of the Area in accordance with UNCLOS obligations and was left with 75,000 km^2 by 2002.

9 Ministry of Earth Sciences, *India's exclusive rights to explore polymetallic nodules from central Indian ocean seabed basin extended by five years*, press release, 21 August 2017. Available online < https://pib.gov.in/newsite/PrintRelease.aspx?relid=170138> (accessed 31 March 2021).

10 B. Vijay Kumar, 'India and the common heritage concept in the international seabed area', *Current Science* 86, 2004, 783.

policy and law. However, for activities in the Area, the main institutional body is the Ministry of Earth Sciences (MoES).

The MoES deals with science and technology for exploration and exploitation of oceanic minerals. It is the umbrella ministry under which various institutions and organisations have been formed with distinct but interconnected mandates such as the National Institute of Ocean Technology (NIOT) and National Institute of Oceanography (NIO). NIOT is the body responsible for seabed mining technology and is engaged in the constant development of technologies for large-scale commercial mining operations, in particular for polymetallic nodules. It may be worthwhile to note that NIOT will be the biggest recipient of the deep ocean mission funds from the fiscal budget.

NIO works alongside NIOT and conducts Environmental Impact Assessments (EIAs) for development projects in marine areas. NIO was the main drafter of India's Environment Impact Statement (EIS) to the ISA.

When looking at the larger picture of regulating activities in the Indian CS and the Area, it is important to take stock of the other ministries that can influence laws that impact these oceanic activities. On the conservation side, issues like protection of marine biodiversity would fall under the auspices of the Ministry of Environment, Forests and Climate Change (MoEFCC). This ministry is responsible for conducting and forming environmental impact assessments, as well as regulations and rules related to marine biological diversity, including marine protected areas (through the Wildlife Institute of India).[11]

The Ministry of External Affairs (MEA) is in charge of participation and contribution in meetings, negotiations and discussions for ocean governance at the United Nations and other regional and bilateral conferences and discussions. They normally do this in conjunction with the Law Ministry.

Direct legislations

Mining in India is governed under the umbrella legislation of Mines and Minerals (development and regulation) Act that was adopted in 1957. This legislation set the tone for governing mining activities by authorising the central government to grant prospecting licences or mining leases within Indian territorial waters or the CS.[12] The Offshore Areas Mineral (development and regulation) Act came into effect in 2002 to exclusively govern the offshore mining sector in India and covered, in addition to territorial waters and the CS, mining in India's EEZ as well. The India Bureau of Mines[13] is the administering authority of these legislations. Section 20 of the Offshore Areas Act addresses any possible pollution occurring from oceanic mining and makes the operator of the mining activity liable for any marine pollution caused, while the Bureau of Mines is responsible for determining compensation and extent of marine pollution.

During the Third United Nations Conference on the Law of the Sea, India enacted the Territorial Waters, Continental Shelf, Exclusive Economic Zone and Other Maritime Zones Act of 1976 which prescribes the limits of the territorial waters, continental shelf, EEZ and other maritime

11 Started in 1982, the Wildlife Institute of India is an autonomous institution of the MoEFCC.

12 Section 13 (A) of the Mines and Minerals (development and regulation) Act, 1957.

13 The Bureau of Mines was established in 1948 and is run by another ministry – the Ministry of Mines, which is responsible for regulating onshore minerals.

zones of India and provides a legal framework for their control and regulation – more specifically on India's rights and jurisdiction over maritime zones and boundaries shared with other countries. The territorial waters law sets out the geographical extent of India's CS and the Area in accordance with the UNCLOS.

Other applicable legislations

The Constitution of India, which is the main source of law in India, also regulates deep-sea minerals. Art. 297 states that all lands, minerals and other things of value underlying the ocean within the territorial waters, or the continental shelf, or the exclusive economic zone, vests in the union and be held for the purposes of the union. Although the Constitution does not expressly mention the Area (as it cannot), it still remains the most powerful source of legislation in India which could potentially apply to seabed mining in the Area in so far as the technology is Indian.

Biodiversity laws of India through the Biodiversity Act, 2002 and relevant notifications apply to Indian biological resources and would apply to marine biodiversity within the Indian CS. Since marine biodiversity in the Area will not be an Indian resource, Indian laws would not apply.

Because mining activities in the Area will necessarily involve EIAs and strategies, it is important to also understand the legislative landscape of India's EIA law. The governing law for EIAs in India is the EIA Notification of 2006. In March 2020, the MoEFCC released a new draft EIA Notification[14] for public comments.[15] The Draft EIA 2020, once finalised, will supersede the 2006 EIA Notification.

It should be noted that both 2006 and 2020 notifications only apply to Indian territorial waters. However, the 2006 notification was restricted to impacts of terrestrial activities on India's territorial waters, whereas the new draft legislation extends EIAs to ocean-based activities as well. This includes all offshore structures, and the mining of rare earth/atomic minerals. While EIAs within the Indian EEZ are governed by the EIA notification, the NIO is made responsible for ocean-related EIAs, particularly in the Area. How the existing EIA law for oceanic activities prescribed by the MoEFCC and NIO's environment assessment of impacts of activities in the Area will interact with each other is currently unclear.

In the absence of an ocean ministry, there was an initiative by the government of India to form a 'national oceans council' that would act as a one-stop-shop for all ocean-related matters. Should this initiative be revived, seabed mining regulation in the Area could come under its ambit. In 2014, there were talks of drafting a new seabed mining law[16] that would pointedly regulate deep-sea mining in the Area. Since the deep ocean mission has received massive funds in the most recent budget (as discussed above), there might be a possibility that the seabed mining law gets drafted and, eventually, adopted.

14 The MoEFCC passed the draft EIA Notification, 2020 (Draft Notification) in exercise of the powers conferred upon it by Sections 3 paragraph 1, 3 paragraph 2(v) and 23 of the Environment Protection Act, 1986 read with Rule 5(3)(d) of the Environment (Protection) Rules, 1986.

15 The Draft EIA 2020 is contested and has received criticism by the public. Presently, the publication of the final notification has been stayed by the Karnataka high court till September 7, 2020.

16 A. Tiwari, 'Gujarat national law university to draft two key laws on deep-sea mining', *The Times of India*, 1 September 2018. Available online <https://timesofindia.indiatimes.com/home/environment/developmental-issues/gujarat-national-law-university-to-draft-two-key-laws-on-deep-sea-mining/articleshow/41381470.cms> (accessed 15 August 2021).

State position

India is an advocate of viewing the high seas as a common good and a 'common heritage of mankind'.[17] The surrender of 50 per cent of India's initially allotted area was not only in fulfilment of international obligations, but also was a matter of State position. India stands against 'discovery and occupation' in the Area and emphasises sharing profits for developing countries.[18] In the 25th annual session of the ISA, India emphasised that no preferential treatment should be given to any stakeholder during the operationalisation of the exploitation phase. India also considers geographical representation and decolonisation important aspects of seabed mining regulation. The suggestion (mostly by developed countries) that a separate roster of experts be made was questioned by India on the basis that there was no need to do so, considering the challenges associated with avoiding bias given the capacity limitations of developing countries.[19]

In a nutshell, technology and fair representation seem to be at the helm of the Indian position whereas environmental concerns are not emphasised enough.

Seabed mining activities and related decision

The 'deep ocean mission' was launched in India in 2018 to start the exploration of minerals in the CIOB from October 2019 and test deep-sea machines at 6,000 metres.[20] In July 2019, the NIOT partnered with the Russian Krylov state research centre to develop the machinery required to mine the seabed at 6,000 metres.[21] This project is specifically for mining potato-shaped polymetallic or manganese nodules.

Around USD 0.6 billion has been allocated to the deep-sea mission in the most recent budget of February 2021 to further India's initiatives in seabed mining.[22] The two main purposes of these funds are for deep ocean survey exploration, and projects for the conservation of deep-sea biodiversity.[23] The deep ocean mission is proposed to have six major components: (i) development of technologies for seabed mining, underwater vehicles and underwater robotics, (ii) development of ocean climate change advisory services, (iii) technological and conservational innovations of deep-sea biodiversity, (iv) deep ocean survey and exploration, (v) energy and freshwater from ocean and (vi) establishing an advanced marine biology station in Goa and foreign collaborations.[24]

17 Vijaykumar, op. cit.

18 Vijaykumar, op. cit., p. 788

19 Summary report of the 1st part of the 25th annual session of the ISA on 4–15 March 2019, *Earth Negotiations Bulletin*. Available online <https://enb.iisd.org/events/1st-part-25th-annual-session-international-seabed-authority-isa> (accessed 14 July 2021).

20 The manned expedition in a submersible vehicle (called Matsya 6000 currently) is being developed by the Indian space research organisation and the NIOT and is likely to be certified by Norway's DNV-GL.

21 U. Tejonmayam, 'India to test deep-sea mining machine at 6000 m by year-end', *The Times of India*, 8 August 2019. Available online <https://timesofindia.indiatimes.com/city/chennai/india-to-test-deep-sea-mining-machine-at-6000m-by-yr-end/articleshow/70578647.cms> (accessed 20 August 2021).

22 S. Chattopadhyay, 'India's deep-ocean mission putting money on the trenches', *The Financial Express*, 8 February 2021. Available online <https://www.financialexpress.com/lifestyle/science/indias-deep-ocean-mission-putting-money-in-the-trenches/2190061/> (accessed 30 August 2021).

23 Government of India, Budget 2021–2022. Available online <https://www.indiabudget.gov.in/doc/bh1.pdf> and <https://www.indiabudget.gov.in/doc/Budget_Speech.pdf> (accessed 16 July 2021).

24 The 332nd report of the department-related parliamentary standing committee on science and technology, environment, forests and climate change, Rajya sabha (parliament of India) March 2020. Available online <https://

While there is significant progress in developing technology for seabed exploration, there is neither information on the proposed research and development in conservation projects, nor any details on what these projects entail. Having said that, in line with the ISA's contract for exploration of nodules in January 2020, India submitted an environmental impact statement to the ISA for nodule collection trials in the CIOB. This was done as per ISA's Recommendations for the Guidance of Contracts[25] and Draft Regulations on Exploitation of Mineral Resources[26] in the Area. Till date, only two countries have submitted an environment impact statement (EIS) to the ISA, India being the second after Germany. India is one of the biggest contributors to the development of both seabed mining technology as well as EIS by being one of the first players in the sector. It is important to acknowledge that India submitted an EIS at a time when precedents are not available, neither by practice nor by any ISA template.

The EIS submitted[27] to the ISA entails, at the beginning, a description of the project, its activities, scope, structure as well as credentials of the project proponent followed by a description of the policy, legal and administrative context of the project. A dominant parameter of the EIS was scientific and technical information that is useful in evaluating the likely impacts of the proposed activity such as: description of the location and mineral resources and sediments present, description of the nodule collection and separation system, transport of the material to the surface and data on waves, wind and weather at the location. The technical information was followed by a description of the existing physicochemical and biological environment at the location. Then, the potential impacts that could occur due to the project were described based on available baseline, environmental variability and experimental data. Lastly, the assessment stated a plan for assessment of impact, monitoring, data-management and reporting.

Essentially, there are two main aspects of regulating deep-sea mining activities in India's CS and the Area. One is the exploration of the deep seabed which is dealt with by MoES and ministries dealing with science and technology. The other is regulating any environmental impacts the mining might have on the marine environment. While the contours of exploration governance have already been framed, apart from the EIS submitted by India, conservation plans do not appear to be developed cohesively. It will be interesting to see how the deep-sea mission will develop plans and projects to conserve marine biodiversity, particularly in the deep seabed. Once these plans are developed, provisions of the Indian biodiversity laws might also apply to any proposed mining activities. In the absence of a consolidated oceans ministry/council in India, linkages between the different ministries dealing with the two aspects of seabed mining regulation are unclear. This causes a fair amount of legislative and regulatory uncertainty, not only in seabed mining regulation but law implementation in India generally.

Conclusion

The main challenge in India in regulating seabed mining in India's EEZ and continental shelf is over-regulation and too many institutions involved with fragmented aspects of exploration and

rajyasabha.nic.in/rsnew/Committee_site/Committee_File/ReportFile/19/126/332_2020_12_17.pdf> (accessed 31 August 2021).

25 Recommendations for the guidance of contractors for the assessment of the possible environmental impacts arising from exploration for marine minerals in the Area, ISBA/25/LTC/6, 1 March 2013.

26 Draft Regulations on Exploitation of Mineral Resources in the Area, ISBA/24/LTC/WP.1, 30 April 2018.

27 The EIS follows the template at Annex IV of the Draft Regulations on Exploitation of Mineral Resources in the Area.

conservation activities, with no clarity on how the different laws and ministries will interact with each other. There is much to be desired on the conservation aspect in India's EEZ, continental shelf as well as the Area, and it must be developed effectively considering the headway made by Indian technology to mine the deep seabed. While Indian legislation currently governs the CS and EEZ, the legal and policy system has the capacity to quickly deploy laws on regulation of activities in the Area, as and when it is required.

VI.2.9
KOREA AND SEABED MINING

Hyun Jung Kim

Introduction

The Republic of Korea (ROK) has expressed its great interest in deep sea mining particularly since the *United Nations Convention on the Law of the Sea* (UNCLOS) was adopted. The ROK has established relevant domestic law and regulations, developed mining technologies and conducted exploration activities in its maritime zones and the Area. The country has also actively participated in activities of the International Seabed Authority. A recent legislative effort shows that the country has endeavoured to legislate an independent act on deep sea mining in the Area.

Geographical extent of exclusive economic zone, continental shelf and the Area

In 1970, the ROK divided the waters under its jurisdiction into seven mining areas.[1] After ratifying UNCLOS on 29 January 1996, the ROK proclaimed its 200 nautical mile (M) exclusive economic zone (EEZ) in accordance with the Convention.[2] The country also follows the definition of the continental shelf under article 76 paragraph 1 of UNCLOS.[3] The ROK has to date established eight mining areas with 12 sub-areas in its claimed continental shelf, which extend a total of approximately 303,683 square kilometres (km^2) according to the amended Submarine Mineral Resources Development Act[4] and its Enforcement Decree.[5]

1 Submarine Mineral Resources Development Act, Act No. 2184 (enforced on 1 January 1970; adopted on 1 January 1970); Enforcement Decree of the Submarine Mineral Resources Development Act, Presidential Decree No. 5020 (enforced on 30 May 1970; adopted on 30 May 2021).

2 Exclusive Economic Zone and Continental Shelf Act, Promulgation No. 14605 (enforced on 21 March 2017; partially amended), article 2(1).

3 Ibid., articles 2(1) and 2(2).

4 Submarine Mineral Resources Development Act, Act No. 14679 (enforced on 22 September 2017; originally adopted on 1 January 1970; last partially amended on 21 March 2017).

5 Enforcement Decree of the Submarine Mineral Resources Development Act, Presidential Decree No. 28212 (enforced on 26 July 2017; last partially amended on 26 July 2017); Korea National Oil Corporation, 'Business Information: Current Situation of Exploration in Domestic Continental Shelf' (as of 30 December 2020) (in Korean). Available online: <https://www.knoc.co.kr/sub03/sub03_1_2.jsp> (accessed 30 May 2021).

DOI: 10.4324/9780429426162-38

However, the country has maritime delimitation issues (EEZ and continental shelf) with its neighbouring states (China and Japan) because the waters surrounding the ROK (e.g., the Yellow Sea, the East Sea/Sea of Japan and the East China Sea) extend less than 400 M although all three states claim an EEZ of 200 M and a continental shelf extending more than 200 M.[6] The sole fixed delimitation line is the one established between the ROK and Japan by the *Agreement concerning the Establishment of Boundary in the Northern Part of the Continental Shelf adjacent to the Two Countries*.[7] The ROK has been negotiating maritime delimitation with China and Japan. Pending delimitation, the ROK concluded a provisional arrangement with Japan for joint development of the southern part of the overlapping continental shelf in 1974: the *Agreement between Japan and the Republic of Korea concerning Joint Development of the Southern Part of the Continental Shelf adjacent to the Two Countries*.[8] The joint development zone of 82,557 km^2 is situated in the ROK's mining area 7 and parts of its mining areas 4 and 5 under the Submarine Mineral Resources Development Act.[9] Furthermore, in December 2012 the ROK submitted information on the outer limits of the continental shelf beyond 200 M in the East China Sea to the Commission on the Limits of the Continental Shelf in accordance with article 76 paragraph 8 of UNCLOS. This partial submission comprises an undelimited area with Japan extending less than 400 M including the joint development zone. In its thirty-second session (2013), 'the Commission decided to defer further consideration of the submission and the notes verbales [received from Japan and the ROK] until such time as the submission was next in line for consideration, as queued in the order in which it was received' in 2013.[10]

Meanwhile, the ROK holds the right to explore non-living resources in the Area under three contracts with the ISA: the 2001 contract for the exploration for polymetallic nodules applicable to a 75,000 km^2 area in the Clarion-Clipperton Fracture Zone; the 2014 contract for polymetallic sulphides in a 10,000 km^2 area of the Central Indian Ridge; and the 2018 contract for cobalt-rich ferromanganese crusts in a 3,000 km^2 area in the east part of the Northern Mariana Islands in the Western Pacific Ocean.[11]

6 H.J. Kim, 'Governing Fishing Stocks in Northeast Asia's Disputed Waters: Preventing a "Tragedy of the Commons"?', *The International Journal of Marine and Coastal Law* 33(3), 2018, 495–496. For a detailed analysis of the Southeast Asia context towards seabed mining, see in this book T. Davenport, 'Southeast Asia and seabed mining' in V. Tassin Campanella (ed), *Routledge Handbook of Seabed Mining and the Law of the Sea*, London: Routledge, 2023, chapter VI.1.7.

7 *Agreement concerning the Establishment of Boundary in the Northern Part of the Continental Shelf adjacent to the Two Countries*, Republic of Korea and Japan, 30 January 1974 (in force 22 June 1978), 1225 UNTS 103 (1981), No. 19777.

8 *Agreement between Japan and the Republic of Korea concerning Joint Development of the Southern Part of the Continental Shelf adjacent to the Two Countries (with Agreed Minutes and Exchanges of Notes)*, Republic of Korea and Japan, 30 January 1974 (in force 22 June 1978), 1225 UNTS 113 (1981), No. 19778.

9 J.H. Choi et al., *A Research for the resuming the operation of the Korea-Japan Joint Development Agreement (in Korean)*, Busan: Korea Maritime Institute, 2019, p. 12; Korea National Oil Corporation, op. cit.

10 Commission on the Limits of the Continental Shelf, *Progress of Work in the Commission on the Limits of the Continental Shelf: Statement by the Chair*, Thirty-second session, CLCS/80,15 July–30 August 2013, para. 68.

11 Ministry of Oceans and Fisheries, *Korea, Creating the Future in an Unknown Space, the Deep Seabed – Conclusion of an Exploration Contract for Cobalt-rich Ferromanganese Crusts in the Western Pacific with the International Seabed Authority on the 27th (Tuesday)* (in Korean), Press release, 27 March 2018. Available online: <https://www.mof.go.kr/iframe/article/multi01/view.do?boardKey=10&articleKey=19379&searchCategory=&searchSelect=&searchValue=&searchDeptName=&searchStartDate=&searchEndDate=&currentPageNo=1> (accessed 30 May 2021).

Regulation of seabed activities

The ROK's Exclusive Economic Zone and Continental Shelf Act is legislated in accordance with UNCLOS. Indeed, according to this Act, the ROK has sovereign rights and jurisdiction in its EEZ identical to those under article 56 paragraph 1 of UNCLOS. It also exercises sovereign rights to explore and exploit mineral resources of the continental shelf as provided for in UNCLOS.[12]

Specific mining activities in the continental shelf are regulated by different domestic laws depending on the types of resources and location of mining activities.

First, the Mining Industry Act[13] provides for a basic framework for the ROK's mining industry that refers to the exploration for and exploitation of mineral resources (including petroleum) defined by its article 2 paragraph 1. This Act does not specify the location of the mining activities to be regulated; thus, mining activities in the ROK's land territory as well as in the seabed under its jurisdiction (EEZ and continental shelf) fall within the scope of this Act. The only exception is the development of petroleum in the seabed which is subject to the Submarine Mineral Resources Development Act.[14] According to the Mining Industry Act, mining rights consist of exploration and exploitation rights. It is mandatory to obtain permission for the establishment of respective mining rights from the Minister of Trade, Industry and Energy.[15] The Mining Industry Act also allows for the establishment of mining concessions, which are granted in accordance with a written contract for this purpose between an exploitation right holder and those who intend to hold a mining concession.[16] Such establishment is also subject to authorization from the same Minister.[17]

Second, the Submarine Mineral Resources Development Act[18] also applies to certain mining activities. Submarine mineral resources under this Act refer to petroleum, natural gas, etc. in the ROK's EEZ and continental shelves. Article 9 paragraph 4 of the Mining Industry Act provides that some provisions of the Submarine Mineral Resources Development Act apply *mutatis mutandis* to mining rights for petroleum. Therefore, the Submarine Mineral Resources Development Act is *lex specialis* of the Mining Industry Act for petroleum and natural gas in the ROK's EEZ and continental shelves.[19]

The ROK has currently established eight mining areas with 12 sub-areas extending a total of approximately 303,683 km^2 under the Submarine Mineral Resources Development Act and its Enforcement Decree. Only the ROK has submarine mining rights while submarine mining concessionaires may obtain permission from the Minister of Trade, Industry and Energy for establishment of concession rights (exploration right up to 10 years and exploitation right up to 30 years).[20] Concessionaires pay mining fees to the Minister when exploiting submarine minerals in concession areas.[21] An amendment to the Act in 2013 allowed the Minister to 'establish the submarine

12 Exclusive Economic Zone and Continental Shelf Act, op. cit., article 3.

13 Mining Industry Act, Promulgation No. 16127 (enforced on 1 April 2019; originally adopted in 1951; last partially amended on 31 December 2018).

14 Ibid., article 9(4).

15 Ibid., article 28(1).

16 Ibid., article 51(1).

17 Ibid., article 52.

18 Submarine Mineral Resources Development Act, Act No. 14679, op. cit.

19 H.Y. Yun, 'Critical Review of Domestic Laws and Regulations Related to Offshore Oil Activities' (in Korean), *Dankook Law Review* 42(2), 2018, 365.

20 Submarine Mineral Resources Development Act, Act No. 14679, op. cit., articles 4, 5 and 12.

21 Ibid., article 18(1).

mining concession right by dividing a submarine mining area into two or more areas'[22] to encourage concessionaires' participation. For the same purpose, the Minister may designate as promising mining areas submarine mining areas in which the exploitation of minerals of economic value is highly expected and publicly announce this.[23]

Meanwhile, according to the *1974 ROK–Japan Joint Development Agreement*, the two states agreed on joint exploration and exploitation of 'petroleum (including natural gas) resources and other underground minerals which are produced in association with such resources'.[24] To carry out the joint development, each state had to 'authorize one or more concessionaires with respect to each subzone' of the joint development zone defined in article 2 of the Agreement.[25] Authorized concessionaires 'enter into an operating agreement to carry out jointly exploration and exploitation of natural resources in the Joint Development Zone'.[26]

Finally, there is no specific domestic law applicable to seabed mining in the Area. According to article 6 paragraph 1 of the ROK's Constitution, treaties have the same effect as the ROK's law at a domestic level. Thus, the ROK has engaged in exploration in the Area in accordance with UNCLOS and the *Agreement relating to the Implementation of Part XI of the Convention*. There have been several attempts to legislate a seabed mining act in the Area since the early 1990s. The most recent effort was the ROK government's bill proposal presented in July 2018.[27] This bill—the Act on Management and Support of Seabed Activities etc.—was designed to establish a seabed mining management system for ROK nationals including private sector actors who intend to participate in activities in the Area in compliance with international law such as UNCLOS.[28] This bill was proposed in particular to ensure a sponsoring state's obligations under UNCLOS because the ROK's current legislation is not fully appropriate for regulating seabed activities.[29] Indeed, according to this bill, the ROK nationals who intend to engage in deep seabed activities in the Area shall obtain permission from the Minister of Oceans and Fisheries.[30] The bill also provides for the issuance of sponsorship to those who have obtained the Minister's permission.[31] The Minister may cancel the permission if the nationals concerned fail to meet requirements for permission.[32] However, this bill was abolished because the term of the twentieth (2016–20) National Assembly expired in May 2020. The ROK government has always been the contractor of all contracts with the ISA for exploration in the Area. Therefore, no substantial issue has arisen to date in the absence of a specific domestic law that applies to the mining activities in the Area. Nevertheless, in order to prepare for the private sector's possible participation in deep seabed min-

22 Ibid., article 3(3).
23 Ibid., article 3(4).
24 *Agreement between Japan and the Republic of Korea concerning Joint Development of the Southern Part of the Continental Shelf adjacent to the Two Countries (with Agreed Minutes and Exchanges of Notes)*, op. cit., article 1; see also its preamble.
25 Article 4(1), ibid.
26 Article 5(1), ibid.
27 National Assembly, Bill Information, (2014322) Bill for the Act on Management and Support of Seabed Activities etc. (proposed by the government) (in Korean). Available online: <http://likms.assembly.go.kr/bill/billDetail.do?billId=ARC_N1Q8Y0S7O1A0F1Q7Q0O6G5Q7X4N1G9> (accessed 30 May 2021).
28 Ibid., original text (in Korean), p. 1.
29 Y.H. Lee, 'Reviews on the Responsibilities and Obligations of States Sponsoring Persons and Entities with Respect to Activities in the Area' (in Korean), *Ocean and Polar Research* 33(4), 2011, 494–495.
30 National Assembly, op. cit., original text (in Korean), article 7, pp. 8–10.
31 Article 9, pp. 10–11, ibid.
32 Article 11, pp. 11–12, ibid.

ing activities, the government is expected to propose a new bill during the term of the twenty-first National Assembly.

According to the Marine Environment Management Act, mining activities in the continental shelf and the Area are subject to marine environmental impact assessment 'if the relevant business subject to licensing involves any of the following acts (including mining activities under the Mining Industry Act and the Submarine Mineral Resources Development Act) which is of at least the scale prescribed by Presidential Decree'.[33] The Minister of Oceans and Fisheries conducts this assessment upon request from a mining licence-granting agency (e.g. Ministry of Trade, Industry and Energy).[34]

Seabed activities and related decisions

In the 1970s after the enactment of the Submarine Mineral Resources Development Act, foreign oil companies started to engage in mining activities in the ROK's continental shelf; however, their exploration was not successful. The government explained that this was due to maritime delimitation issues with China and Japan and the companies' limited engagement.[35] The ROK has attempted to perform mining activities independently since the 1980s by establishing the Korea National Oil Corporation (KNOC) in 1979.[36] As of December 2020, KNOC conducted 47 exploratory drillings as well as 3D marine geophysical survey of 5,448 km^3.[37]

In contrast, there have been no joint exploration activities in the joint development zone under the *1974 ROK–Japan Agreement* since the early 1990s.[38] Although joint exploration was conducted such as seismic surveys and exploration wells during the period 1980–86, no concessionaires were authorized by either state until 2009.[39] KNOC was authorized by the ROK to engage in the exploration of subzone 1 of the joint development zone in 2009; however, the corporation could not conduct the exploration in the actual area in the absence of Japan's authorized concessionaire until the termination of its right in 2017.[40] In January 2020, KNOC again obtained authorization for exploration in the joint development zone.[41] No concessionaires have been authorized by Japan to date (as of April 2022). However, in mid-2020 the ROK and Japan have agreed to hold a meeting of the Republic of Korea–Japan Joint Commission, which has the mandate to deal with matters concerning the implementation of the 1974 Agreement.[42] Therefore, we await the outcome of the Commission's discussions.

33 Marine Environment Management Act, Promulgation No. 17007 (enforcement 1 January 2021; other laws and regulations amended on 18 February 2020), article 85.

34 Ibid.

35 Minister of Trade, Industry and Energy, 'Second Master Plan for Development of Submarine Mineral Resources' (in Korean), September 2014, p. 3. Available online: <https://www.korea.kr/archive/expDocView.do?docId=35540> (accessed 30 May 2021).

36 Ibid., p. 3.

37 Korea National Oil Corporation, op. cit.

38 H.J. Kim, 'What Did the Republic of Korea and Japan Mean by the Term "Joint Development" in Their 1974 Agreement?', *Marine Policy* 117, 2020, 2.

39 Ibid.

40 Ibid.

41 H.J. Kwon, 'Will the Dream of Mining Area 7' (in Korean), *JoongAng Ilbo*, 5 June 2020. Available online: <https://news.joins.com/article/23793906> (accessed 30 May 2021).

42 *Agreement between Japan and the Republic of Korea concerning Joint Development of the Southern Part of the Continental Shelf adjacent to the Two Countries (with Agreed Minutes and Exchanges of Notes)*, op. cit., Article 24(1); S.H. Hong, '"Mining Area 7" in the Continental Shelf, After That [Current Affairs Planning Change]' (in

Finally, the ROK holds three contracts for exploration in the Area with the ISA: exploration for polymetallic nodules (2001), seafloor polymetallic nodules (2014) and cobalt-rich ferromanganese crusts (2018). As shown by the fact that the ROK government (Ministry of Oceans and Fisheries: MOF) signed these contracts as a contractor, the ROK's mining activities in the Area are government-led. For example, in the early 1990s—before the entry into force of UNCLOS—the government decided to establish a plan for mining in the Area.[43] The ROK registered a mining area of 150,000 km^2 for polymetallic nodules in the Clarion-Clipperton Fracture Zone in 1994.[44] Afterwards, the government concluded a contract with the ISA in 2001 for the exploration for polymetallic nodules in a 75,000 km^2 area within this Zone.[45] The MOF selected the first mining area, which amounted to 20,000 km^2, in 2010.[46]

Besides contracts for exploration, the ROK government actively engaged in research on mining in the Area. Research activities have been conducted by the Korea Institute of Ocean Science and Technology (KIOST), a research institution with an independent corporation entity established under the Act on the Korea Institute of Ocean Science and Technology.[47] The MOF is its competent authority. As examples of its research activities, KIOST conducted pioneering surveys for polymetallic nodules with a 1,422-ton research vessel in the Clarion-Clipperton Fracture Zone in the early 1990s. These led the ROK to register the mining area. KIOST also manufactured a pilot mining robot—named Minero—for polymetallic nodules in 2007.[48]

Conclusion

The ROK has expressed its great interest in deep sea mining activities. The country is the third in the world to hold contracts to explore for three resources in the Area—polymetallic nodules, polymetallic sulphides and cobalt-rich ferromanganese crusts.[49] Since the entry into force of UNCLOS, the country has established and amended its domestic legislation in line with the Convention. However, there is no specific legislation applicable to mining in the Area despite several legislative attempts since the 1990s. Such legislation seems needed to fill possible legal lacunae at the domestic level and to ensure the ROK's better compliance with UNCLOS.

Korean), *KBS*, 7 August 2020. Available online: <https://news.kbs.co.kr/news/view.do?ncd=4511445&ref=A> (accessed 30 May 2021).

43 S.B. Chi and S. Hong, 'Development of Polymetallic Nodules in the NE Equatorial Pacific: Past, Present and Future' (in Korean), *Ocean and Polar Research* 36(4), 2014, 370.

44 Ibid.; Ministry of Oceans and Fisheries, Marine Development Division, *Current Status of the ROK's Development of Mineral Resources in the Area*, 22 February 2014, (in Korean). Available online: <https://www.mof.go.kr/article/view.do?articleKey=4740&boardKey=27&menuKey=322&currentPageNo=1> (accessed 30 May 2021).

45 International Seabed Authority, *The Republic of Korea and ISA Sign Exploration Contract*, 27 March 2018.

46 Ministry of Oceans and Fisheries, Marine Development Division, *Current Status of the ROK's Development of Mineral Resources in the Area*, (in Korean), op. cit., 22 February 2014.

47 *Act on the Korea Institute of Ocean Science and Technology*, Promulgation No. 16813 (enforced on 11 March 2020; last partially amended on 10 December 2019).

48 C-H. Lee et al., 'Study of Deepsea Mining Robot "MineRo" Using Table of Orthogonal Arrays Article information' (in Korean), *Journal of Ocean Engineering and Technology* 28(2), 2014, 152; Ministry of Oceans and Fisheries, Marine Development Division, *What Is a Mining Robot for Mineral Resources in the Area, Minero?*, 22 February 2014, (in Korean). Available online: <https://www.mof.go.kr/article/view.do?articleKey=4744&boardKey=27&menuKey=322&currentPageNo=1> (accessed 30 May 2021); Chi and Hong, op. cit., 370.

49 Ministry of Oceans and Fisheries, *Korea, Creating the Future in an Unknown Space, the Deep Seabed – Conclusion of an Exploration Contract for Cobalt-rich Ferromanganese Crusts in the Western Pacific with the International Seabed Authority on the 27th (Tuesday)* (in Korean), op. cit.

Acknowledgement

This article uses the translations of the ROK's domestic laws and regulations provided by the Korea Law Translation Center of the Korea Legislation Research Institute. Available online: <https://elaw.klri.re.kr/eng_service/main.do≥ (accessed on 30 May 2021) with modifications by the author where required. Other Non-English instruments are translated by the author.

VI.2.10
MAURITIUS AND SEABED MINING

Edwin Egede[1]

Introduction

Mauritius is an archipelagic small island developing State, composed of a group of islands, located in the Indian ocean and about 2000 kilometers off the coast of the African continent.[2] It became a party to both the *1982 United Nations Convention on the Law of the Sea* (UNCLOS) and the *1994 Agreement relating to the Implementation of Part XI of the UNCLOS* (the 1994 Agreement) on 4 November 1994. As an archipelagic State, Mauritius has taken a keen interest in the sea, including seabed mining within its national jurisdiction and deep seabed exploration beyond national boundaries, in order to support the development of its economy. It has enacted various laws to regulate seabed mining within its national jurisdiction and is currently working on legislation to regulate seabed mining beyond its national jurisdiction.

Geographical extent of the exclusive economic zone, continental shelf and the Area

The outer limits of Mauritius' exclusive economic zone (EEZ) and the continental shelf (CS), as well as its CS beyond 200 nautical miles (M) constitute part of the boundary of the deep seabed Area beyond national jurisdiction (the Area).[3] Mauritius has an EEZ of approximately 2.3 million square kilometers (km^2).[4] The 2005 Maritime Zones Act states that its EEZ 'is the area beyond and

1 The author dedicates this chapter to his very good friend, Prince Emmanuel, for the invaluable contribution to this manuscript.

2 See United States Department of State, Bureau of Oceans and International Environmental and Scientific Affairs, *Limits in the Seas*, No. 140, Mauritius: Archipelagic and other Maritime Claims and Boundaries, July 8, 2014, at p. 3. Available online <https://www.state.gov/wp-content/uploads/2019/11/LIS-140.pdf> (accessed 19 September 2021). Also see section 111 of its Constitution (as amended with effect from 1992) on what constitutes Mauritius.

3 Section 1, para. 1 of UNCLOS states the Area 'means the seabed and ocean floor and subsoil thereof, beyond the limits of national jurisdiction.'

4 See Sustainable Development Goals, Voluntary National Review Report of Mauritius 2019 (published by the Mauritius Ministry of Foreign Affairs, Regional Integration and International Trade) at p. 92. Available online <https://www.thecommonwealth.io/wp-content/uploads/2020/08/Mauritius_VNR_2019.pdf> (accessed 19 September 2021).

DOI: 10.4324/9780429426162-39

adjacent to the territorial sea of Mauritius that extends to the EEZ outer limit,'[5] and then defines the 'EEZ outer limit,' which the prime minister of the country may by regulations prescribe, as meaning 'a line of which every point is at a distance of 200 M from the nearest point of the baselines.'[6] Prior to the 2005 legislation the prime minister had adopted under the previous Maritime Zones Act 1977, the Maritime Zones (Exclusive Economic Zones) regulations on 27 December 1984, a subsidiary legislation. It set out the geographical coordinates to designate the EEZ of Mauritius in respect of the islands of Mauritius, Rodrigues, Cargados Carajos (St Brandon), Agalega and Tromelin, as well as the Chagos.[7] The regulations are still extant even though the 1977 Act was repealed by the 2005 legislation because of the latter's transitional and saving provisions.[8] The 2005 legislation defines the geographical extent of the CS as follows:

(1) The continental shelf of Mauritius comprises the seabed and subsoil of the submarine areas that extend beyond its territorial sea throughout the natural prolongation of its land territory – (a) subject to paragraph 2 of article 76 of UNCLOS, to the outer edge of the continental margin; or (b) where the outer edge of the continental margin does not extend up to that distance, a distance of 200 M from the baselines from which the breadth of the territorial sea is measured.
(2) Where, by virtue of paragraph 2 of article 76 of UNCLOS, the outer limits of the continental shelf require to be determined in accordance with paragraphs 4 to 6 of UNCLOS, the Prime Minister may make regulations to provide for the outer limit to be determined by any method specified in paragraph 4 of article 76 of UNCLOS.[9]

On 2 April 1980, Mauritius entered into a bilateral treaty with France delimiting between the EEZ between Mauritius and Reunion based on equidistance, which was considered an 'equitable system of delimitation.'[10] Also on 29 July 2008, it entered into a bilateral treaty with Seychelles delimiting between the EEZ of Mauritius (from the island of Agalega) and Seychelles (from the islands of Coëtivy, St Francois, Providence and Farquhar respectively) based on equidistance, which was considered an equitable solution as required by international law.[11]

On 1 December 2008 Mauritius and Seychelles made a joint submission to the United Nations Commission on the Limits of the Continental Shelf (CLCS) on the limits of their overlapping CS beyond 200 M in the region of the Mascarene plateau consisting of 396,000 km^2. The recommendations of the CLCS in regard to this submission was made on 30 March 2011.[12] After the CLCS recommendations, Mauritius entered into two treaties with Seychelles as regards the

5 Section 14, para. 1.
6 Section 14, paras 2 and 3.
7 Section 2.
8 Section 31, para. 1.
9 Section 18.
10 *Convention between the Government of the French Republic and the Government of Mauritius on the delimitation of the French and Mauritian economic zones between the islands of Reunion and Mauritius*, 2 April 1980.
11 Article 1 of the *Agreement between the Government of the Republic of Mauritius and the Government of the Republic of Seychelles on the delimitation of the exclusive economic zone between the Two States*, 29 July 2008. See Division for Ocean Affairs and the Law of the Sea Office of Legal Affairs (DOALOS), *Law of the Sea Bulletin*, 2009, no. 69, 106–108.
12 For the CLCS recommendations see summary of the recommendations of the CLCS in regard to the joint submission made by Mauritius and Seychelles concerning the Mascarene plateau region on 1 December 2008 – recommendations prepared by the Sub commission established for the consideration of the joint submission made by

Mascarene plateau region, namely the treaty concerning the joint exercise of sovereign rights over the continental shelf in the Mascarene plateau region between the Government of the Republic of Seychelles and the Government of the Republic of Mauritius and the treaty concerning the joint management of the continental shelf in the Mascarene Plateau region between the Government of the Republic of Seychelles and the Government of the Republic of Mauritius (both entered into force on 18 June 2012). Both treaties which clarify the outer limits of the extended CS, as recommended by the CLCS, have been deposited with both the United Nations Secretary-General and the International Seabed Authority (ISA) Secretary-General, as required by UNCLOS.[13]

After the recommendations of the CLCS regarding the joint submission with Seychelles in respect of the region of the Mascarene plateau, the Mauritius prime minister made the Maritime Zones Regulations 2012 (coordinates of outer limits of extended continental shelf in the Mascarene plateau region), as required by the 2005 Act.[14] This regulation confirms that the geodesic lines connecting the geographical coordinates of the points as set out in the Schedule, in line with the recommendations of the CLCS, shall be the outer limits of the extended continental shelf of Mauritius in the Mascarene plateau region.[15] Furthermore, Mauritius enacted in June 2012 the Maritime Zones (Amendment) Act,[16] which amended the 2005 Act, to reflect this joint management area (JMA) with Seychelles and to set out the precise delineating coordinates and the map of the JMA in the schedules of the 2012 legislation.[17]

Moreover, Mauritius on 6 May 2009 made a partial submission to the CLCS as regard the CS beyond 200 M in the region of Rodrigues island, which is currently being considered by the Commission.[18] It also had submitted in May 2009 to the CLCS a preliminary information concerning the CS beyond 200 M in the Chagos archipelago region and affirms that the Chagos archipelago has always been and remains an integral part of Mauritius' territory and is not a British Indian Ocean Territory (BIOT).[19] The recent International Court of Justice advisory opinion, entitled Legal Consequences of the Separation of the Chagos archipelago from Mauritius in 1965,[20] and United Nations General Assembly resolution 73/295 of 22 May 2019 would appear to confirm this. In view of the BIOT and the 2015 award of the arbitral tribunal it is therefore likely the UK would object to the CLCS considering any actual submission by Mauritius regarding the Chagos.[21]

Mauritius and Seychelles (adopted by the Sub commission on 25 March 2011 and adopted by the Commission on 30 March 2011).

13 See DOALOS *Law of the Sea Bulletin*, 2013, no. 79, 25–52. See article 84 of UNCLOS.

14 GN no. 96 of 2012 government gazette of Mauritius no. 50 of 17 May 2012. Available online <http://extwprlegs1.fao.org/docs/pdf/mat116864.pdf> (accessed 19 September 2021). This Regulation was deemed to have come into operation on the 13 of March 2012. See section 4.

15 Ibid., section 3.

16 Act no. 6 of 2012. See sections 3, 4 and 5.

17 See first and second schedules, ibid.

18 See CLCS/52/2 of 25 March 2020, paras. 73–76.

19 See preliminary information submitted by the Republic of Mauritius concerning the extended continental shelf in the Chagos archipelago region pursuant to the decision contained in SPLOS/183, Mus-pi-doc May 2009. Available online <https://www.un.org/depts/los/clcs_new/submissions_files/preliminary/mus_2009_preliminaryinfo.pdf> (accessed 19 September 2019).

20 *Legal consequences of the separation of the Chagos archipelago from Mauritius in 1965, Advisory Opinion, I.C.J. Reports 2019*, p. 95

21 For the 2015 award see *Chagos Marine Protected Area Arbitration (Mauritius v. United Kingdom), award of 18 March 2015*. Available online <https://pca-cpa.org/en/cases/11/> (accessed 19 September 2021). Also see DOALOS *Law of the Sea Bulletin*, 2008, no. 67, 13–38.

Moreover, there is the pending dispute between Mauritius and the Maldives before the International Tribunal for the Law of the Sea (ITLOS) on the delimitation of their EEZ and CS.[22]

Regulations of seabed mining activities

In 1970 Mauritius had enacted a territorial sea Act[23] describing its territorial sea, internal waters and baseline of its territorial sea,[24] as well as a continental shelf Act.[25] The latter Act had adopted verbatim the definition of CS in the 1958 Geneva Convention on the CS.[26] It subsequently enacted the Maritime Zones Act 1977,[27] which sought to encompass the various maritime zones of Mauritius in one legislation.[28] Eventually, it enacted the extant legislation, the Maritime Zones Act, 2005[29] which explicitly repealed the previous legislation.[30] It is important to note that the 2015 law provides that '[u]nless otherwise expressly provided, words and expressions defined in UNCLOS and used in this Act shall have the same meaning as in UNCLOS'[31] and '[n]otwithstanding any other enactment, UNCLOS shall have force of law in Mauritius.'[32]

The government bodies mainly responsible for seabed mining are the Department for Continental Shelf, Maritime Zones, Administration and Exploration (CSMZAE) and the Ministry of Blue Economy, Marine Resources, Fisheries and Shipping. The CSMZAE operates as a department in the Mauritius prime minister's office. Its main functions are to establish a legal and regulatory regime for the conduct of seabed mineral activities; to develop appropriate strategies and policies to ensure that seabed mineral activities are carried out in a sustainably manner, which safeguards the marine environment; to build up capacity in seabed mining and to regulate marine scientific research. It also is responsible for preparing the submissions to the CLCS for Mauritius outer CS.[33] The Ministry of Blue Economy, Marine Resources, Fisheries and Shipping also is 'focused on revitalizing the economy with mineral resources development.'[34] There is no clarity on how the competence on seabed mining activities is split between these two obviously impor-

22 *Dispute concerning delimitation of the maritime boundary between Mauritius and Maldives in the Indian ocean (Mauritius/Maldives), ITLOS, case No. 28* (pending at the time of writing this article). Available online <https://www.itlos.org/en/main/cases/list-of-cases/dispute-concerning-delimitation-of-the-maritime-boundary-between-mauritius-and-maldives-in-the-indian-ocean-mauritius/maldives/> (accessed 19 September 2022).

23 Act no. 4 of 1970.

24 See United States of America, Department of State, Bureau of Intelligence and Research, International Boundary Study, Series A, *Limits in the Seas*, No.41 straight baselines: Mauritius, 7 March 1972, pp. 2–7.

25 Act no. 5 of 1970.

26 See A. Blum, 'The Continental Shelf Convention and African Ratification,' *The Journal of Legal Pluralism and Unofficial Law* 4, 1972, 35–46 at 43.

27 Act no. 13 of 3 June 1977.

28 There is no explicit indication in this legislation that Acts nos. 4 and 5 of 1970 had been repealed. Although in section 14 it indicates that '[w]hen this Act is in conflict with any other enactment, this Act shall prevail.'

29 Act no. 2 of 2005. See DOALOS, *Law of the Sea Bulletin*, 2006, no. 62, 52–60.

30 In section 29 this legislation specifically repealed the previous Maritime Zones Act, the Continental Shelf Act no. 5 and the Territorial Sea Act no. 4.

31 Section 2, para. 2.

32 Section 3.

33 See CSMZAE presentation titled 'Importance of deep seabed exploration to support the development of a national blue economy – The case of Mauritius,' at *ISA Africa Deep Sea-bed Resources Project*, Third Workshop, 1–3 June 2021, Mauritius. Available online <https://www.isa.org.jm/event/workshop-promotion-sustainable-development-africas-deep-seabed-resources-support-africas-blue#presentations> (accessed 19 September 2021).

34 Mauritius Ministry of Blue Economy, Marine Resources, Fisheries and Shipping. Available online <https://blueeconomy.govmu.org/Pages/Blue-Economy.aspx> (accessed 19 September 2021).

tant bodies of government. Besides, as would be seen from the discourse below there is also the possibility of the involvement of other government ministers and bodies, such as the ministers responsible for mining of minerals, petroleum and the environment, in the whole process of seabed mining activities, which may further complicate matters as regards division of responsibilities.

Mauritius has sovereign rights to explore and exploit, conserve and manage the natural resources, including non-living, in the EEZ and CS under the 2005 legislation.[35] It is interesting to note this legislation does not explicitly engage with the obligation of Mauritius under article 82 of UNCLOS to make payments or contributions through the ISA for distribution to States Parties to the Convention on the basis of equitable sharing criteria in respect of its extended CS.[36] Another issue that may be of interest to the ISA is if there are resources that may straddle between areas within CS/EEZ of Mauritius and the Area as polymetallic nodules have been discovered to be distributed in the Mauritius CS/EEZ around Mascarene basin off Tromelin island.[37] On 29 April 2017, Mauritius adopted maritime zones (conduct of marine scientific research) regulation, under the 2015 legislation, which regulates the conduct of marine scientific research (MSR) within its national jurisdiction.[38] This regulation, which is largely consistent with UNCLOS,[39] defines MSR as 'any research or study, whether fundamental or applied, intended to increase knowledge about marine environment, including all its resources and living organisms and embraces all related scientific activity for the benefit of mankind and for peaceful purposes.'[40] This MSR can only be carried out with the approval of the relevant minister,[41] and shall not involve extraction of seabed minerals, unjustifiably interfere with other legitimate uses of the sea and shall be conducted in line with the precautionary principle and best environmental practices.[42] It is important to note that the regulation does not extend to MSR in the Area.

Under Mauritius' Minerals Act (MA) 1966, which covers a wide range of minerals,[43] the 'Government shall have the exclusive right to prospect for minerals in or under any land' and under regulations authorized by the President the relevant Minister with the responsibility for commerce and industry may 'authorise in writing any person to carry on prospecting operations in or under any land on behalf of the Government.'[44] This provision, however, focuses on minerals 'in or under any land'[45] and does cover seabed mining. There is also the Mauritius Petroleum Act (PA) 1970, which defines 'petroleum' as including 'any mineral oil or hydrocarbon, whether gaseous,

35 Sections 15, para. 1 and 19, para. 1.

36 See for instance, Section 5A of the New Zealand continental shelf Act, as amended by the continental shelf amendment Act no. 71 of 1996 and the Regulatory systems (economic development) amendment Act no. 62 of 2019, which provides that 'In specifying the rate of royalties for the purposes of subsection (2) or subsection (3), the Minister shall have regard to New Zealand's rights and obligations under article 82 of the Convention' and 'The Crown shall make all payments or contributions in kind required to be made to the Authority from time to time under the terms of article 82 of the Convention.'

37 See article 142 of UNCLOS and B.N. Nath and M.S. Prasad, 'Manganese nodules in the Exclusive Economic Zone of Mauritius,' *Marine Mining* 10, 1991, 303–335, and R. Sharma, 'First nodule to first mine-site: development of deep-sea mineral resources from the Indian Ocean,' *Current Science* 99, 2010, 750 at 757.

38 Section 2 of the 2017 regulation.

39 Part XIII, UNCLOS.

40 Section 2 of the 2017 regulation.

41 Sections 3 to 6.

42 Sections 5(n) and (p) and 7(ii).

43 Minerals include cobalt, copper, lithium, magnesium, manganese, molybdenum, nickel, titanium and zinc. See section 2.

44 Act no. 41 of 1966, op. cit., sections 3, 4 and 5.

45 Ibid.

liquid or solid, existing in its natural condition in strata, including crude oil, casinghead spirits, ozokerite, asphalt and natural gas.'[46] This definition of petroleum appears to indicate that this legislation is intended to cover only petroleum-based resources and not seabed minerals similar to those located in the Area. The PA 1970 stresses that the 'property in petroleum existing in Mauritius shall be deemed to be, and always to have been, vested in the State.'[47] It is important to note that under the Mauritius Constitution, 'Mauritius' includes not only the land territories and territorial sea, but also 'the continental shelf [CS] and such places or areas as may be designated by regulations made by the Prime Minister, rights over which are or may become exercisable by Mauritius.'[48] From this it would mean that mining of petroleum could extend to the CS. Furthermore, the Constitution is clear that nothing 'shall affect the making or operation of any law so far as it provides for the vesting in the State of the ownership of underground water or unextracted minerals.'[49] The relevant Minister responsible for petroleum mining may grant to an applicant with sufficient technical knowledge, experience and financial resources either a prospecting license or mining lease to either prospect or mine for petroleum.[50]

On the environmental side, Mauritius has a reasonably robust environmental legislation, the Environment Protection Act 2002, as amended in 2008.[51] Under the title 'environmental stewardship' this law declares that 'every person in Mauritius shall use his best endeavours to preserve and enhance the quality of life by caring responsibly for the natural environment of Mauritius.'[52] It set up an integrated coastal zone management committee to specifically deal with the protection of the environment in the coastal areas and maritime zones of Mauritius.[53] This legislation among other things requires environmental impact assessment (EIA) to carry out undertakings and addresses other environmental standards, including emergency measures and interventions, clean-ups and liability and recovery of expenses in the case of spills.[54] It states: 'Where a major threat to the environment is posed as a result of a spill or otherwise, the Prime Minister may in consultation with the Minister, declare an environmental emergency.'[55] However, it is notable that this legislation, unlike the MSR Regulations discussed above, does not refer to the precautionary approach (or principle), and it indicates 'national environmental standards,'[56] rather than specifying an obligation to apply best environmental practices. Mauritius has also set up a marine spatial planning (MSP) coordinating committee that has made significant progress in MSP in key maritime sectors, including the identification, selection, establishment and management of potential areas for new economic activities, such as specific areas for hydrocarbon and mineral resources.[57]

46 Act no. 6 of 1970, op. cit., section 2.
47 Ibid., section 3.
48 Mauritius Constitution 1968 with amendments through to 2016. See section 111, para. 1.
49 Ibid., section 8, para. 5.
50 Act no. 6 of 1970, sections 2, 4 and 6.
51 Act no. 19 of 2002 and Act no. 6 of 2008.
52 Section 2 of Act no. 19.
53 Ibid., section 50.
54 Ibid., Parts IV and V.
55 Ibid., section 34(1).
56 Ibid., sections 37–48.
57 R. Badal, CSMZAE, prime minister's office, *National training workshop on marine spatial planning*, 20 October 2020. Available online <https://www.mspglobal2030.org/wp-content/uploads/2020/11/MSProadmap_Presentation_Mauritius_20201020.pdf> (accessed 19 September 2021).

From the above, the various existing laws, which are not directly intended to regulate seabed mining, are limited to the seabed within Mauritius national jurisdiction and do not extend to the deep seabed Area beyond national jurisdiction.

Seabed activities and related decisions

Mauritius gives priority to the ocean economy,[58] and in 2013 it launched an ocean economy roadmap.[59] One of the new ocean clusters included in the roadmap was 'seabed exploration for hydrocarbon and minerals.'[60] A cabinet decision on 20 December 2013 procured the advisory services of the World Bank for the development of the legislative, regulatory and fiscal framework for a number of priority areas in the Mauritius ocean economy, including the hydrocarbon and the deep seabed mineral mining sector.[61] The cabinet decision indicated as follows:

> Besides hydrocarbon exploitation within the Mauritius Maritime Zone, there are unexplored opportunities for deep mineral mining in waters beyond our national jurisdiction under the framework of the UN Convention on the Law of the Sea (UNCLOS). Since mineral resources are administered by the International Seabed Authority, under a Common Heritage of Mankind approach, it is important for Mauritius to position itself to take advantage of the opportunity.[62]

Currently, there is no domestic legislation that directly deals with deep seabed mining, though there are indications that Seabed Mineral Bills are being finalized.[63] The intention is to enact two

58 See R. Cervigni and P.L. Scandizzo (eds.) *The Ocean Economy in Mauritius – Making It Happen, Making It Last*, Washington: World Bank Group, 2017. The Mauritius Ministry of Blue Economy, Marine Resources, Fisheries and Shipping defines the ocean economy as the 'proportion of the economy that relies on the ocean as an input to the production process' and the blue economy as 'the simultaneous promotion of economic growth, oceanic sustainability (sustaining ocean resources and ecosystem) and social inclusion.' Available online <https://blueconomy.govmu.org/Pages/Blue-Economy.aspx> (accessed 19 September 2021). On the other hand, the Mauritius 3-year Strategic Plan 2017/18–2019/20 'Rising to the Challenge of Our Ambitions' at p. 82 states: 'The ocean economy, also known as the blue economy, is defined as the sustainable use of the sea and its resources,' appearing to regard ocean economy and blue economy as synonymous. Available online <https://mauritiusassembly.govmu.org/Documents/Hansard/2017/appendix1.pdf#search=Seabed%20Mineral%20Bill> (accessed 19 September 2021).

59 See reference to Mauritius prime minister's office 2013, Ocean Economy: Road Map for Mauritius, in UNCTAD, *The Oceans Economy: Opportunities and Challenges for Small Island Developing States*, Geneva/New York: United Nations, 2014, p.6. https://unctad.org/system/files/official-document/ditcted2014d5_en.pdf (accessed 1 October 2023)

60 See A. Degnarain, 'The Ocean Economy: A Roadmap for Mauritius,' *Presentation at the SPC-EU Deep Sea Minerals Project, Regional Training Workshop on Deep Sea Minerals: Financial Aspects*, 13–16 May 2014, Cook Islands. Available online <http://dsm.gsd.spc.int/public/files/meetings/rartonga.may.2014/01_AshvinDegnarain_Mauritius_Presentation.pdf> (accessed 19 September 2021).

61 See para. 2 of the Decisions of Mauritius Cabinet held on 20 December 2013. Available online <https://pmo.govmu.org/CabinetDecision/2013/Cabdec20December2013.pdf#search=deep%20seabed%20mining> (accessed 19 September 2021).

62 Ibid.

63 See para. 5 of the Decisions of Mauritius Cabinet held on 21 August 2015. Available online <https://pmo.govmu.org/CabinetDecision/2015/Cabinet%20Decisions%20-21%20August%202015.pdf#search=Seabed%20Mineral%20Bill> (accessed 19 September 2021). See also Mauritius 'Government Programme 2020–2024: Towards an inclusive, high income and green Mauritius – Forging ahead together' which states: 'As part of its new industrial and trade policies, government will also focus on developing new economic pillars. Accordingly, it will come up with

separate laws on seabed mining activities – one managing seabed activities within the EEZ/CS and the other for the Area beyond national jurisdiction. The bills are also to address environmental impacts and safety aspects.[64] The primary objective of the Bill for 'the Area beyond national jurisdiction is to establish a legal framework for the sponsorship and the effective control of stakeholders involved in seabed mineral activities in the Area. The Bill shall comply with all relevant standards of ISA and obligations under UNCLOS.'[65]

Furthermore, in 2015, along with other Indian Ocean Rim Association (IORA) States, it adopted the Mauritius declaration on blue economy, which among other things, declared that IORA member states' priority sectors would include offshore hydrocarbons and seabed minerals, which should be 'developed in an environmentally sound manner for the socio-economic benefit of the population.'[66] By 2016 Mauritius had launched an international expression of interest (EOI) for seabed mining for sponsorship of application for the exploration of minerals in the Area. This EOI was closed on 18 January 2017. It is not clear if any progress has been made with this EOI.[67] However, it is intriguing that the country launched the EOI before relevant legislation regulating seabed mining had been enacted, though this is not unusual as there are States currently engaged in deep-sea mining activities without detailed domestic legal regimes in place.[68]

Conclusion

Mauritius has adopted a 2005 Maritime Zones Act and subsidiary legislation, which are largely consistent with UNCLOS, indicating the geographical extent of the maritime territories within its national jurisdiction.[69] It has also entered into bilateral treaties with Seychelles to delimit parts of its CS. Furthermore, it has made submissions to the CLCS for the delineation of its CS beyond 200 M, of which for one, the joint submission with Seychelles, the CLCS has delivered its recommendation. However, Mauritius has certain contested maritime boundaries with the UK as regards the Chagos archipelago, and France with respect to Tromelin and its overlapping EEZ/CS maritime

a unified regulatory framework, an offshore petroleum bill, a seabed mineral bill and set up a marine biotechnology hub, among others, to accelerate the development of the blue economy.' Available online <https://govmu.org/EN/newsgov/SitePages/2020/Government-Programme-2020-2024--Towards-an-inclusive,-high-income-and-green-Mauritius---Forging-ahead-together.aspx> (accessed 19 September 2021).

64 CSMZAE prime minister's office, 'Importance of deep seabed exploration to support the development of a national blue economy – The case of Mauritius,' *Africa's deep sea-bed resources project*, third workshop, Mauritius, 1–3 June 2021, pp. 56–66. Available online <https://www.isa.org.jm/files/ADSR-Mauritius-Workshop-Presentations-Day1-compressed.pdf> (accessed 19 September 2021).

65 Ibid. at p. 63.

66 Declaration of the Indian Ocean Rim Association on enhancing blue economy cooperation for sustainable development in the Indian ocean region (Mauritius declaration on blue economy), Mauritius, 2–3 September 2015, para. 2. See also para.7. Available online https://www.iora.int/media/8216/iora-mauritius-declaration-on-blue-economy.pdf (accessed 19 September 2021).

67 See Mauritius Economic Development Board, game changer industries. Available online <http://www.edbmauritius.com/opportunities/ocean-economy/game-changer-industries/> (accessed 19 September 2021).

68 See *Responsibilities and Obligations of States with respect to Activities in the Area, Advisory Opinion, 1 February 2011, ITLOS reports 2011*, p. 10, paras 223–224. For more on this advisory opinion, see in this book V. Tassin Campanella, Y. Cissé and D. Tladi, 'State rights and obligations of States on the continental shelf and the Area,' in V. Tassin Campanella (ed), *Routledge Handbook of Seabed Mining and the Law of the Sea*, London: Routledge, 2023, chapter II.1; see also C. Payne, 'State responsibility for deep seabed mining obligations,' in V. Tassin Campanella (ed), *Routledge Handbook of Seabed Mining and the Law of the Sea*, idem, chapter II.2.

69 For a regional African context, see in this book E. Egede, 'Africa and seabed mining,' in V. Tassin Campanella (ed), *Routledge Handbook of Seabed Mining and the Law of the Sea*, op. cit., chapter VI.1.1.

delimitation dispute with Maldives, which is pending before the ITLOS. These contested boundaries and outstanding submissions to the CLCS would have to be eventually resolved so that the progress towards determining the precise boundaries of the Area, which is the common heritage of mankind, may be achieved. Other existing legislation, such as the Minerals Act 1966, Petroleum Act 1970 and the Environment Protection Act 2002, as amended in 2008, are inadequate to cover seabed mining. Recognizing the limitations in its existing laws the Mauritius government is currently taking steps to enact two seabed mining bills, one to regulate seabed mining within national jurisdiction and the other for seabed mining in the Area.

VI.2.11

MOZAMBIQUE AND SEABED MINING

Estevão Stefane Mahanjane

Introduction

Mozambique is a sovereign coastal State, facing the Mozambique Channel, the Indian Ocean branch. Its experience in the seabed mining programmes of minerals is yet to come. The country has however a growing hydrocarbons business in ultra-deep waters above 2,000 metres associated with the exploration and production of large fossil reserves reported in the Rovuma Delta with approximately 200 trillion cubic feet of natural gas in place. Certainly, the country is proud of its mining programmes on land exploiting large reserves of coal, gold, graphite, Rubi, marble, tantalite, morganite, berilo, granite and gems. Activities of seabed mining of heavy minerals placer deposits are currently developed along the coastline (beaches), with the example of the Kenmare project reporting tons of reserves of ilmenite, rutile, monazite and zircon estimated for an exploitation project of more than 100 years.

These projects are being legislated by the Petroleum and Mining Laws updated on 18 August 2014 (Law No. 20/2014). Although Mozambique has ratified the *United Nations Convention on the Law of the Sea* (UNCLOS) and the *Agreement relating to the Implementation of Part XI of the United Nations Convention on the Law of the Sea* (1994 Agreement), it has not yet drafted specific legislation for seabed mining programmes of minerals on the continental shelf or for activities in the Area. The current mining law is a regulatory framework for mining activities in shallow water. With the creation of a new ministry in 2015 to address maritime affairs, more considerable dynamic and flexible actions have been innovated for the drafting of a timely legal framework package to enforce the State Authority at sea and maritime spatial planning.

Geographical extent of economic exclusive zone, continental shelf and the Area

The Mozambique Channel is shaped by the positions of Mozambique to the west and Madagascar to the east, portraying a narrow feature in the north, widening in the centre, and becoming diffuse in the south. The channel itself is about 1,600 kilometres long and 419 kilometres in average width at its narrowest point and reaches a depth of up to just over 6,000 metres, covering an extension of about 2,700 kilometres off the coast of Mozambique. The oceanographic features are dominated by a warm current, the Mozambique Current, flowing southwards in the channel, leading to the

DOI: 10.4324/9780429426162-40

Agulhas Current on the east coast of South Africa. Mozambique's hydrographic network has large rivers flowing into this channel, forming deltaic systems ranging from small to large systems that are part of the international literature, e.g., the Rovuma and Zambezi Deltas on the Mozambican side.

The definition of maritime limits results in an overlapping of exclusive economic zones (EEZ) with adjacent countries or countries with opposite sides from north to south, namely: Tanzania, Comoros, Juan da Nova Island, Madagascar, Islands Europe and Republic of South Africa.[1] In all these cases, there is a need to establish maritime boundaries which must be mutually agreed between the States involved, like the Agreement between Comoros, Mozambique and Tanzania signed on 5 December 2011.[2]

The definition of the legal continental shelf depicting a morphology of the submerged prolongation of the Mozambique's land territory (land mass) qualifies Mozambique to implement the provisions of article 76 of UNCLOS. It is located further south of the channel, in the region adjacent to the potential maritime boundaries between Mozambique and South Africa. In this maritime space, Mozambique has demonstrated its entitlement through the technical-scientific evidence to extend its continental shelf beyond 200 nautical miles (M). That exercise had ended on 7 July 2010[3] with the submission to the United Nations Commission on the Limits of the Continental Shelf (CLCS) of a proposal for the extension of its continental shelf, outlining an area equivalent to 1/5 of the total area of Mozambique's land territory. This outlined area is still subject to an examination by CLCS to issue recommendations to Mozambique for the delineation of the outer limits of the extended continental shelf, as established in paragraph 8 of article 76 of UNCLOS.

Regulation of seabed mining activities

The Republic of Mozambique has been a member of the United Nations since September 1975. It ratified the United Nations Convention on the Law of the Sea on 13 March 1997 by Resolution no. 21/96 of the Mozambique Parliament, entering into force on 12 April 1997.

The maritime spaces over which Mozambique claims national jurisdiction are defined in the following national legislation:[4]

- Decree-Law No. 47,771 of 27 June 1967 – delineation of straight baselines;
- Mozambique Council of Ministers Decree-Law No. 31/76 of 19 August 1976;
- Law No. 4/96 of 4 January 1996 – provisions proclaiming the delineation of straight baselines as well as maritime spaces under national jurisdiction. Such legislation claims jurisdiction over a territorial sea with a breadth of 12 M, a contiguous zone up to 24 M, an exclusive economic zone up to 200 M, and a continental shelf up to 200 M or to the outer edge of the continental margin, measured from the territorial sea baselines, respectively, taking into account the limits provided for in article 76 paragraphs 4 to 6 of the Convention.

1 For an analysis of the regional context, see in this book E. Egede, 'Africa and seabed mining' in V. Tassin Campanella (ed), *Routledge handbook of seabed mining and the law of the sea*, London: Routledge, 2023, chapter VI.1.1.

2 *Agreement on the delimitation of maritime borders between the Comoros, Mozambique and Tanzania*, Maputo 05 December 2011.

3 CLCS, *Submission of the Republic of Mozambique to the United Nations: Executive Summary*, 7 July 2010.

4 Both the Decree-Law No. 47,771 of 27 June 1967 and Mozambique's Council of Ministers Decree-Law No. 31/76 of 19 August 1976 contain provisions included in the Law No. 4/96 of 4 January 1996.

The Government of Mozambique created in 2015 the Minister of the Sea, Inland Waters and Fisheries (MIMAIP)[5] by Presidential Decree No. 01/2015 to exercise State Authority over the sea, inland waters and fisheries, thus among other attributions, promoting the use and exploitation of resources from the sea, inland waters and respective ecosystems.

In the exercise of its powers, MIMAIP proposed the Regulation of the Legal Regime for the Use of the National Maritime Space (RJUEM) approved by Decree No. 21/2017. It also revised the Law of the Sea No. 4/96 of 4 January 1996 which was then submitted to the Council of Ministers for endorsement and approved by the national Parliament in 2019 as new Law of the Sea No. 20/2019.

It is the role of MIMAIP to update the legal framework on maritime issues, in fact, in addition to updating existing legislation, it has also proposed to the government decrees to create marine research institutions and promote the blue economy goals. In this context, ProAzul[6] was created by Decree No. 91/2019 of 27 November 2019, to promote technical assistance to the Government of Mozambique for the development of the blue economy and the fulfilment of the sustainable development goals, especially sustainable development 14.[7]

As a key factor, the government launched in August 2019 the Maritime Spatial Planning Plan (POEM),[8] the implementation of which is still in progress. This Plan faces many challenges, which include respecting the principles of integrated management and sustainable development and overlapping EEZ claims between Mozambique and its neighbours. Among its goals, POEM aims to '[p]romote the sustainable, rational and efficient economic exploitation of the sea and marine resources' and [e]nsure the preservation, protection and recovery of natural values, biodiversity and coastal and marine ecosystems and the maintenance of the good environmental status of the marine environment'. It also aims to '[e]nsure legal security and transparency in the procedures for attributing titles for the private use of the maritime space, and allow the exercise of information and participation rights'.

In the midst of so many challenges, and in the drafting of the legal framework for the assessment of marine resources in Mozambique, there is a call for specific legislation for deep-sea mining activities on the continental shelf, in a coordination of institutions between State authorities at sea and mineral resources management.

Currently, the licensing authorities depend on the type of geological resources. The National Petroleum Institute (INP)[9] created by Decree No. 25/2004 of 20 August 2004, as a regulatory body, is responsible for administration and promotion of petroleum operations; and the National Institute of Mines (INAMI)[10] created by Law 20/2014, of 18 August 2014, as the regulatory authority for mining activity, is responsible for the guidelines for the participation of public and private organi-

5 For more information, see the website of MIMAIP. Available online < www.mimaip.gov.mz> (accessed 18 December 2021).

6 For more information, see the website of ProAzul. Available online <www.proazul.gov.mz> (accessed 18 December 2021).

7 United Nations, *Objective 14: conservation and sustainable use of oceans, seas and marine resources for sustainable development, Agenda 2030*, 2015.

8 For more information, see the website dedicated to the Marine Spatial Planning of Mozambique. Available online <www.poem.gov.mz> (accessed 18 December 2021).

9 For more information see the website of the National Petroleum Institute. Available online <www.inp.gov.mz> (accessed 18 December 2021).

10 For more information see the website of the National Institute of Mines. Available online <www.inami.gov.mz> (accessed 18 December 2021).

sations in the research, exploration, treatment, export and import of mining products and their derivatives.

Mozambican legislation for the mining and oil exploration and exploitation provides contracts for scientific research, exploration and production, and transport. Concession contracts are approved by the Central Government through the Council of Ministers, assigning rights to concessionaires within a stipulated time by law to carry out investigation, exploration, production and transport resources contributing to national economic development, considering social and environmental aspects. The entire process involves coordination between different actors, including government authorities, concessionaire companies, representatives of public institutions and civil society.

Seabed activities and related decisions

At present, seabed mining activities in national jurisdiction are carried out through the exploration and production of natural gas within the EEZ. Other activities are related to the exploitation of heavy minerals along the beach. Seabed mining occurs in shallow waters of less than 120 metres deep in placer deposits. Large mineral resources with significant reserves of heavy minerals (titanium minerals: ilmenite and rutile, as well as the zircon mineral) have sustained production at current rates for more than 100 years.

Reports since 2019 on the total proven and probable ore reserves are estimated at 1,584 million tons, grading 3.3 per cent of the total heavy mineral (THM). This represents 43 million tons of ilmenite, 2.9 million tons of zircon, 0.95 million tons of rutile and 0.17 million tons of monazite. The total ore resource (excluding reserves) under a combination of exploration licences and mining concessions is estimated at 6.4 billion tons, grading 2.9 per cent THM. This represents 150 million tons of ilmenite, 10 million tons of zircon and 3 million tons of rutile.

Worldwide oceans have proven accumulation of different types of mineralization that, among others, form large deposits in given geographic regions, e.g., phosphorite deposits, evaporite deposits, polymetallic sulphides, polymetallic nodules (cobalt and manganese), placer deposits, comprising heavy minerals, gold and diamonds, petroleum, natural gas and gas hydrates. Mozambican scientific research is however still lacking programmes in ascertaining the potential marine mineral resources on the continental shelf, in the EEZ and in the Area.

Departing from the global distribution of these resources and the literature, and on the basis of geological, oceanographic and climatic conditions, the Mozambique Channel seems to provide favourable geological and oceanographic conditions for the accumulation of billions of tons of polymetallic (manganese) nodules reserves, placer deposits and heavy minerals, as well as oil and natural gas.

Furthermore, data and information observed in preliminary studies through sampling made by marine expeditions carried out in the seventies (by the Lamont-Doherty Earth Observatory Laboratory, University of Columbia, United States of America), indicate the South of the Mozambique Channel including the region adjacent to the extended continental shelf of Mozambique, is rich in manganese nodules. Additional information has been collected there since then.[11] On average estimates, these resources portray very high degrees and may, in the future,

11 B.J. Murton, 'A global review of non-living resources on the extended continental shelf', *Revista Brasileiera de Geofisica* 18-3, 2000. Available online <https://doi.org/10.1590/S0102-261X2000000300007> (accessed 12 December 2021).

be favourable for manganese nodules and crust recovery. Finally, the density of nodules in the accumulation areas describes the highest average grades in tons per square kilometres, helping to estimate the reserves within the extended continental shelf area.[12] Real quantities still nevertheless require estimates.

Conclusion

Mozambique continues to face challenges in establishing mining legislation for offshore activities on the EEZ and continental shelf. Seabed mining activities in these areas of jurisdiction are expected to take place, including on the extended continental shelf through various programmes in the near future, programmes which will be placed under the blue economy development framework.

These national programmes may include scientific expeditions aimed to assess the reserves of manganese nodules, support maritime spatial planning within the national jurisdiction, hence, assisting the State in establishing a more precise legal framework for future exploitation projects.

12 For more information, see E.S. Mahanjane, *O Potencial geológico adormecido no Canal de Moçambique. Apresentação Oral (Virtual)*, 2a edição da Conferência Crescendo Azul. 19–21 November 2021 [https://crescendoazul.gov.mz/en/home/], and E.S. Mahanjane, *Recursos gológicos da plataforma continental, uma visão sobre o seu potencial em Moçambique*, Resumo apresentado no 2º Congresso nacional de Geologia de Moçambique. Maputo, 8–11 September 2014.

VI.2.12
NEW ZEALAND AND SEABED MINING

Robert Makgill† and Elizabeth Macpherson

Prior to publication of this chapter, Dr Robert Makgill sadly passed away. I would like to acknowledge the incredible contribution that Robert made to furthering our knowledge of international law, environmental law and the law of the sea throughout the world, and dedicate this chapter to his memory and legacy.

Introduction

A small island nation in the South Pacific, New Zealand has one of the largest exclusive economic zone (EEZ) and continental shelf areas in the world.[1] Known as 'Aotearoa' to the Indigenous Māori peoples, New Zealand is a former British colony and common law jurisdiction, founded upon the signing of *Te Tiriti o Waitangi* (*The Treaty of Waitangi*) in 1840. *Te Tiriti* and customary law recognise Māori peoples' rights to certain marine areas and resources. Legislation and policy have been enacted to partially codify public and customary rights to the coastline and territorial sea,[2] while Māori custom and practice remain extant under customary law.[3] Converse to the vastness of New Zealand's EEZ and continental shelf, there is very little available scientific information concerning environmental or ecosystem vulnerability to the potential impacts of sea-

1 R. Makgill, 'New Zealand', in R. Martella and B. Grosko (eds), *International Environmental Law: The Practitioner's Guide to the Laws of the Planet*, Chicago: American Bar Association, 2014, p. 909. According to the International Institute of Law of the Sea Studies (IILSS), New Zealand is ranked ninth in terms of size of EEZ at 4,420,565 km^2. International Institute for Law of the Sea Studies (IILSS), *Exclusive Economic Zone (EEZ) Map of the World*, 23 May 2021. Available online <http://iilss.net/exclusive-economic-zoneeez-map-of-the-world/> (accessed 8 December 2022).

2 R. Makgill, 'Feeling Left Out at Sea? Navigating No Ownership, Customary Rights and Resource Management', *Resource Management Theory & Practice*, 2012, 167–168.

3 *Trans-Tasman Resources v Taranaki-Whanganui Conservation Board* 2021 NZSC 127 (*TTR case*). See E. Macpherson, et al., 'Trans-Tasman Resources v Taranaki-Whanganui Conservation Board: A new 'high-water mark' for seabed mining', *New Zealand Journal of Environmental Law*, Forthcoming 2022; and A. Erueti, 'New Zealand/Aotearoa and the Rights of Māori to Natural Resources in Marine Areas', in S. Allen, N. Bankes and Ø. Ravna (eds), *The Rights of Indigenous Peoples in Marine Areas*, Oxford: Hart Publishing, 2019.

DOI: 10.4324/9780429426162-41

bed mining activities.[4] The past decade has witnessed increased commercial interest and industry pressure for seabed mining within New Zealand's EEZ and continental shelf. Applications for approval to undertake exploitation activities have been subject to high-profile legal challenges from environmental, fishing and Māori interest groups.

Geographical extent of the exclusive economic zone, continental shelf and the Area

New Zealand's coastline measures 18,000 km and its territorial waters encompass 16.3 million hectares.[5] The country's EEZ is estimated to be the ninth largest in the world, with an area of 4,420,565 square kilometres (km^2).[6] New Zealand claimed a 200 nautical mile (M) EEZ in 1971, in accordance with emerging principles of customary international law at the time. These principles were subsequently recognised and given clear expression under the *United Nations Convention on the Law of the Sea* (UNCLOS).[7] The submerged continental shelf of New Zealand's landmass[8] extends in some parts beyond 200 M,[9] including the area adjacent to Australia.[10] New Zealand has made claims for an extended continental shelf beyond 200 M in 2006[11] and 2012 (pending, together with Tuvalu and France).[12] In 2008 the Commission on the Limits of the Continental Shelf recognised that New Zealand established the outer limits of its continental shelf 'without prejudice to the outcome of future continental shelf delimitation negotiations in the South Fiji Basin, with Fiji and the Kingdom of Tonga, and possibly France (in respect of New Caledonia) in the area of the Three Kings Ridge'.[13] New Zealand does not claim an interest in the Area, nor has it attempted mining exploration in the Area. This is likely due to the size of its EEZ and continental shelf with offshore petroleum sites in production, and the identification of significant iron sand and phosphate nodule deposits.

4 R. Makgill and A.P. Linhares, 'Deep Seabed Mining – Key Obligations in the Emerging Regulation of Exploration and Development in the Pacific', in R. Warner and S. Kaye (eds), *Routledge Handbook of Maritime Regulation and Enforcement*, London: Routledge, 2016, pp. 231–232; and Reichelt-Brushett et al., 'Deep Seabed Mining and Communities: A Transdisciplinary Approach to Ecological Risk Assessment in the South Pacific', *Integrated Environmental Assessment and Management*, 2021, 1–10.

5 Makgill, 'New Zealand', op. cit.

6 IILSS, op. cit.

7 R. Makgill, J. Gardner-Hopkins, and N. Coates, 'Current Legal Developments: New Zealand', *The International Journal of Marine and Coastal Law* 35(4), 2020, 839 and 841; and Macpherson et al., op. cit.

8 The continental shelf is defined in s 2(1) of the Continental Shelf Act 1964 as that part of the New Zealand landmass that is submerged under the ocean.

9 GNS Science, 'NZ's Continental Shelf'. Available online <https://www.gns.cri.nz/Home/Learning/Science-Topics/Ocean-Floor/Undersea-New-Zealand/NZ-s-Continental-Shelf> (accessed 8 February 2022).

10 *Treaty between the Government of Australia and the Government of New Zealand establishing certain Exclusive Economic Zone and Continental Shelf Boundaries* 2441 UNTS 235,25 July 2004.

11 New Zealand Submission to the Commission on the Limits of the Continental Shelf pursuant to article 76 (8) of the United Nations Convention on the Law of the Sea: Executive Summary, CLCS / 52, 2006.

12 Joint Submission by Tuvalu, France and New Zealand (Tokelau) – in respect of the Area of the Robbie Ridge, CLCS / 80, 7 December 2012.

13 United Nations, Circular Communications from the Division for Ocean Affairs and the Law of the Sea Office of Legal Affairs, Mzn (Maritime Zone Notifications),18 December 2018; United Nations, Recommendations of the Commission on the Limits of the Continental Shelf in regard to the submission made by New Zealand on 19 April 2006, CLCS / 60, 22 August 2008.

Regulation of seabed activities

The New Zealand Government passed the Exclusive Economic Zone and Continental Shelf (Environmental Effects) Act 2012 (EEZ Act) in response to a regulatory vacuum for managing the environmental effects of minerals exploration and development in New Zealand's EEZ and continental shelf (for non-living resources including minerals, oil and gas).[14] Section 11 of the EEZ Act makes it clear that the EEZ Act is intended to continue or enable the implementation of New Zealand's obligations under various international conventions relating to the marine environment, including the UNCLOS and the *1992 Convention on Biological Diversity*.[15] The EEZ Act implements key principles under these international agreements, including protection of the marine environment from marine pollution and the precautionary approach.[16] It provides the regulatory measures required under UNCLOS for assessing the environmental effects of activities and development in the EEZ and continental shelf as part of marine consenting processes.

The guiding purposes of the EEZ Act are to 'promote the sustainable management' of the natural resources of the EEZ and continental shelf and 'protect the environment from pollution' by regulating or prohibiting the discharge of harmful substances and waste.[17] Sustainable management is defined as

> managing the use, development, and protection of natural resources in a way, or at a rate, that enables people to provide for their economic well-being while sustaining the potential of natural resources (excluding minerals) to meet the reasonably foreseeable needs of future generations; and safeguarding the life-supporting capacity of the environment; and avoiding, remedying, or mitigating any adverse effects of activities on the environment.[18]

The protection purpose establishes an environmental bottom line for pollution impacts under the EEZ Act.[19] Protection is a separate and additional consideration to whether the sustainable management goal is achieved.[20] The environmental bottom line requires that consent for a proposed discharge (i.e., pollution) must be refused where the environment cannot be protected from material harm. The Act's purposes are premised on an effects-based approach to managing activities, to enable integrated decision-making between the EEZ and the regulatory framework for terrestrial and territorial sea-based activities under the Resource Management Act 1991 (RMA).[21]

14 See *Greenpeace v Minister of Energy and Resources* 2012 NZHC 1422, which confirmed that there was no requirement for environmental effects assessment beyond the territorial sea.

15 EEZ Act, s 11. See Karen Scott, 'Does New Zealand Need an Oceans Policy in 2020?', *Ocean Yearbook*, 2020, 271-339.

16 R. Makgill, A. Jaeckel and K. MacMaster, 'The Precautionary Approach: Cautionary Progressions and Future Directions', in V. Tassin Campanella (ed.), *Routledge Handbook of Seabed Mining and the Law of the Sea*, London: Routledge, chapter I.3; see also Makgill, 'New Zealand', op. cit., and Makgill and Linhares, op. cit., p. 232. *Trans-Tasman Resources v Taranaki-Whanganui Conservation Board* 2021 NZSC 127 (*TTR Supreme Court*), per Young and France JJ, para. 100; *Trans-Tasman Resources Limited v The Taranaki-Whanganui Conservation Board & Ors* 2020 NZCA 86, 2020 21 ELRNZ 700, para. 3 (*TTR Court of Appeal*); and Macpherson et al., op. cit.

17 EEZ Act, s 10(1)(a) and (b).

18 Ibid., s 10(2).

19 *TTR Supreme Court*, op. cit., summary of result para. 3; per J. Glazebrook, paras. 239–250 and 267; per J. Williams, para. 294; and per CJ. Winkelmann, paras. 305 and 320. For a discussion, see Macpherson et al., op. cit.

20 *TTR Supreme Court*, op. cit., per J. Glazebrook, para. 245.

21 Makgill, Gardner-Hopkins and Coates, op. cit., 842–845.

The EEZ Act provides the Environmental Protection Authority (EPA)[22] with the powers and duties to administer the legislation, including considering applications for marine consents within the EEZ, monitoring, compliance and enforcement.[23] The EPA routinely delegates its decision-making powers to determine applications for marine consents to 'Decision-making Committees',[24] which have full decision-making powers under the EEZ Act.[25]

Although the purposes of the EEZ Act do not extend to social and cultural interests (which are assumed not to exist beyond the territorial sea),[26] the Act does include a specific Treaty of Waitangi provision in section 12, which recognises the Crown's obligations to Māori under *Te Tiriti*. The wording of the provision is specifically restricted to the role of the 'Māori Advisory Committee' to advise marine consent authorities, giving a 'Māori perspective',[27] a Māori right to comment on proposed regulations,[28] a requirement for consent authorities to take into account the effects of activities on Māori 'existing interests' (such as Indigenous customary rights and interests) and a requirement for the EPA to notify certain Māori groups of consent applications that may affect them. This provision is worded differently to comparable legislation applying to terrestrial land or the territorial sea, including the RMA, and includes procedural and substantive elements. The implications of the Treaty clause for marine consenting processes, in particular the need for decision-makers to take into account the effects of mining activities on existing interests held by Māori under state-based legislation and Māori law and custom, have just been elaborated by the Supreme Court, in the landmark decision discussed below.[29]

The EEZ Act sets out duties and restrictions on activities undertaken within the EEZ and continental shelf area. Pursuant to these rules, seabed mining (including taking or extraction of minerals from the sea or seabed)[30] can only occur in the EEZ and continental shelf where permitted by regulations or authorised by a marine consent.[31] Section 25 confirms that all persons carrying out activities in the EEZ have a general duty to avoid, remedy or mitigate adverse effects on the environment; and a duty to provide training and supervision to ensure compliance with the EEZ Act, regulations and any marine consents.

The EEZ Act establishes different rules and processes for activities classified as permitted, discretionary or prohibited under subordinate legislation (regulations).[32] Prescribed permitted activities,[33] which may be undertaken as of right, provided the operator complies with the regulatory conditions for that activity,[34] include marine scientific research, prospecting and exploration; certain marine structures; seismic surveys; and submarine cables. Discretionary activities require a marine consent to be obtained from the EPA before they can be undertaken,[35] and are generally

22 EEZ Act, s 14.
23 Makgill, Gardner-Hopkins and Coates, op. cit., 836.
24 Appointed under the Crown Entities Act 2004, s 16(a).
25 EEZ Act, ss 16(b) and 99(2). The EPA may also delegate its decision-making making power to a board of inquiry in the case of cross-boundary applications of national significance.
26 Makgill and Linhares, op. cit., p. 248.
27 EEZ Act, s 18. A statutory body established under Part 2 of the Environmental Protection Authority Act 2011 'to provide advice and assistance to the EPA on matters relating to policy, process, and decisions of the EPA', s 19.
28 EEZ Act, s 32.
29 *TTR Supreme Court*, op. cit. For a discussion, see Macpherson et al., op. cit.
30 EEZ Act, s 4, 'Interpretation', 'mining activity'.
31 Ibid., ss 20(1) and (2) or provided for as an existing activity or planned petroleum activity.
32 EEZ Act, s 29.
33 Permitted Activities Regulations 2013.
34 EEZ Act, s 35.
35 Ibid., s 36.

subject to notification and hearing requirements.[36] Public participation is generally encouraged, although exploration drilling for petroleum has been classified[37] as a non-notified discretionary activity,[38] meaning that consent applications for such activities do not need to be publicly notified. Prohibited activities may not be carried out under any circumstances, and marine consent for prohibited activities cannot be sought nor granted.[39]

All discretionary activities in the EEZ and the continental shelf must be authorised by a marine consent. Marine consent applications must fully describe the proposal and include an impact assessment,[40] the purpose of which is to provide information in such detail as corresponds to the scale and significance of effects that the proposed activity may have on the environment or existing interests, and to provide sufficient detail to enable the EPA and potentially affected persons to understand the nature of the activity and its effects on the environment.[41] Section 39 of the EEZ Act sets out the matters that an impact assessment must address, including a description of the activity, current state of the affected environment and potential effects of the activity on the environment and any existing interests (including cumulative effects). The impact assessment must also identify persons whose interests are likely to be affected by a proposed activity and outline any consultation that has been undertaken with them. The impact assessment must specify any methods or alternatives to avoid, remedy or mitigate any potential adverse effects on the environment.

The EPA has the power to commission an independent review of an impact assessment for a marine consent application or seek advice or information from the Māori Advisory Committee or any other person in relation to the application (including the applicant),[42] and has regularly done so in practice. In assessing an application for marine consent, the EPA must take into account a number of matters, including some concerned with the effect of the proposal on the environment and any existing interests, such as the importance of protecting 'the biological diversity and integrity of marine species, ecosystems, and processes' and 'rare and vulnerable ecosystems and the habitats of threatened species', but also non-environmental factors like 'the efficient use and development of natural resources' and 'the economic benefit to New Zealand of allowing the application'.[43] The requirement for the EPA to take into account 'existing interests' refers to third-party interests recognised or granted by law, including recognised rights of Māori peoples and the fishing industry (e.g., fishing rights or Māori customary title in the Territorial Sea).[44] The EPA is required to consider the potential for co-existence or exclusivity of the marine consent and existing interests.[45]

The EEZ Act sets out 'information principles', and requires the EPA to apply these when considering an application for a marine consent.[46] These information principles are intended to compel the decision-maker to 'make full use of its powers' to obtain the best available information

36 Ibid., ss 45(1), 46(1) and 50(b).

37 Non-Notified Activities Regulations 2014.

38 EEZ Act, s 29D(1).

39 Ibid., s 37(2).

40 Ibid., ss 38 and 39.

41 Ibid., ss 39(2)(a) and (b)

42 Ibid., s 44.

43 Ibid., s 59(2).

44 Ibid., s 4, 'Interpretation'. This may include statutory authorisations or permissions under common law or other legislation, including the Resource Management Act 1991, *Treaty of Waitangi Act 1975*, *Treaty of Waitangi (Fisheries Claims) Settlement Act 1992* or Marine and Coastal Area (Takutai Moana) Act 2011.

45 EEZ Act, s 60.

46 Ibid., s 61(1).

on which to base its decision.[47] The information principles are part of the overall precautionary approach under the EEZ Act, consistent with international law,[48] which requires the EPA to 'favour caution and environmental protection' where the information available is uncertain or inadequate.[49] If favouring caution and environmental protection means that an activity is likely to be refused consent, the EPA must first consider whether an adaptive management approach would allow the activity to be undertaken.[50] An adaptive management approach may be achieved via conditions attached to a marine consent, including requirements for staging, active and adaptive monitoring, review mechanisms or contingency planning.[51] Importantly, consistent with the EEZ Act's protection purpose, decision-makers are prohibited from applying an adaptive management approach to applications for marine discharge consents (i.e., pollution).[52] At the time of writing, seabed mining proponents have experienced great difficulty and cost attempting to obtain baseline information (on the receiving environment) necessary to support an adaptive management approach under the Act's information principles.[53]

Seabed activities and related decisions

As at 2021, no seabed mining applications have been granted approval under the EEZ Act. In New Zealand's emerging jurisprudence, key principles responsible for declining seabed mining proposals have included protection of the marine environment from pollution, the precautionary approach, adaptive management and existing Māori interests (including *tikanga* or law and custom).

OMV New Zealand Ltd, on the other hand, obtained approval for the drilling of development wells for petroleum production within the South Taranaki Bight EEZ in 2020.[54] The Decision-making Committee (DMC) found, in granting consent, that the overall effect of the development drilling programme was minor, effects would be temporary and the probability of an oil spill was low. The activities also had little to no effect on Māori economic interests, fishing activities or benthic communities as 'existing interests'. In these cases, the activities and their effects were reasonably well known and could be managed through consent conditions.

Seabed mining applications have been more controversial and met organised opposition by environmental, Māori and fishing interests concerned about the extraction and deposit of sediment on the surrounding marine environment.

47 'Best available information' is defined to mean the best information that, in the particular circumstances, is available without unreasonable cost, effort, or time, s 61(5) EEZ Act.

48 *Responsibilities and obligations of States with respect to activities in the Area, Advisory Opinion, 1 February 2011, ITLOS Reports 2011*, para. 131. See also C.J. Iorns Magallanes and G. Severinsen, 'Diving in the Deep End: Precaution and Seabed Mining in New Zealand's Exclusive Economic Zone', *New Zealand Journal of Public and International Law* 13(1), 2015, 201. On seabed mining rights and obligations, see also generally in this book V. Tassin Campanella, Y. Cissé and D. Tladi, 'State Rights and Obligations of States on the Continental Shelf and the Area', in V. Tassin Campanella (ed.), *Routledge Handbook of Seabed Mining and the Law of the Sea*, op. cit., chapter II.1 and C. Payne, 'State Responsibility for Deep Seabed Mining Obligations', in V. Tassin Campanella (ed.), *Routledge Handbook of Seabed Mining and the Law of the Sea*, idem, chapter II.2.

49 EEZ Act, s 61(2).

50 Ibid., s 61(3)

51 Ibid., s 64(2).

52 Ibid., s 61(4)(a)(ii).

53 Makgill, Jaeckel and MacMaster, op. cit.; Makgill and Linhares, op. cit., p. 232.

54 OMV Taranaki Limited: EEZ200011 Decision on Application for Marine Consent EEZ200011-1,8 May 2020, and Marine Discharge Consent EEZ200011-2,8 May 2020.

Chatham Rock Phosphate Limited, for example, sought approval to mine phosphorite nodules from the Chatham rise within an area of 10,192 km^2 (later reduced to 5,207 km^2) located more than 400 km east of Christchurch. In a February 2015 decision, the DMC refused the application for marine consent, with significant concerns around uncertainty of the environmental impacts, and the inadequacy of 'best available information'. Applying the 'information principles' under the EEZ Act, the DMC required Chatham Rock to provide substantial further information in relation to its proposed phosphate mining operation, including information on economic benefits to New Zealand, impacts on commercial fishing interests and various environmental species and processes, and commercial viability.[55] The DMC considered the effects of the mining activity on the benthic habitat across a significant area, and on stony coral habitats within the Mid Chatham Rise Benthic Protection Area, to be substantial, and found that an adaptive management approach could not manage adverse effects without considerable pre-mining research. Because Chatham Rock Phosphate had informed the DMC that this was not a viable option, such requirements could not be imposed without frustrating the consent. The Chatham Rise decision reinforced the need for adequate and certain information to establish a baseline for a precautionary approach, both about the nature of the receiving environment and the adverse effects of the project.[56]

Trans-Tasman Resources Ltd's (TTR) first and second application to mine iron sand within have South Taranaki Bight EEZ have been, by far, the most protracted. TTR, on its second application, was granted approval to excavate up to 50 million tonnes per year of seabed material containing iron sand for processing and exporting in 2017.[57] That decision was overturned by the High Court and subsequent appeals by TTR (with cross appeals by the respondents) went all the way to the Supreme Court, which released its decision in 2021.[58] The Supreme Court held that Part XII of UNCLOS, as set out in article 192, establishes a fundamental obligation on all State Parties to 'protect and preserve the marine environment'.[59] This includes obligations to take measures to prevent, reduce and control pollution of the marine environment (article 194). The Court found that the purpose of the Act was consistent with these obligations insofar as it requires protection of the environment from pollution which in turn establishes an environmental bottom line.

The Supreme Court held that a broad and generous construction of *Te Tiriti* clauses was required and that the Act provided a 'strong direction' that the effects of the proposed activity on existing interests (specifically on the fishing rights of Māori) are required to be accounted for in a manner that respects the Crown's obligation to give effect to the principles of *Te Tiriti* (including duties of partnership, good faith and active protection).[60] Aside from formal legal rights and interests, the Court confirmed that *tikanga* (Māori law and custom)-based customary rights and interests also constitute 'existing interests', and *tikanga* as law must be considered as 'other applicable law'.[61] The Court's decision therefore recognises a plurality of legal systems (international law,

55 R. Makgill and J. Gardiner-Hopkins, 'The Exclusive Economic Zone and Continental Shelf (Environmental Effects) Act 2012', in S. Blakeley (ed), *DSL Environmental Handbook*, Wellington: Brookers Ltd, Wellington, April 2016. In order to provide the information requested, Chatham Rock reduced the Area over which it ultimately sought consent to mine phosphate to half of that originally proposed: Chatham Rock Phosphate Limited, February 2015, EEZ000006.

56 Makgill and Linhares, op. cit., p. 251.

57 *Trans-Tasman Resources Ltd Marine Consents and Marine Discharge Consents Decision, Environmental Protection Authority, 3 August 2017.*

58 *TTR Supreme Court*, op. cit. For a discussion, see Macpherson et al., op. cit.

59 Ibid., para. 88.

60 Ibid., Summary of result para. 8.

61 EEZ Act, s 59(2)(1).

legislation, common law and Māori customary law) when it comes to satisfying state obligations to protect the marine environment alongside various rights and interests that different stakeholders exercise in relation to the marine environment.

Conclusion

The New Zealand Supreme Court's seabed mining judgment could herald 'a new high-water mark' for the consideration of seabed mining proposals, providing a 'strong statement on the kinds of measures States should implement in order to comply with their obligations towards seabed mining under international law' to protect the marine environment from pollution.[62] It suggests further possible paths towards environmental protection provided by obligations under both international conventions that New Zealand is a party to, and those environmental protections that are key components of *tikanga* Māori, recognised as law.

At the time of writing, the New Zealand Government is undertaking significant reform of the Resource Management Act 1991 (RMA), which may provide new opportunities for more integrated decision-making between the EEZ and the regulatory framework for terrestrial and territorial sea-based activities. The RMA reform project has been highly political, amidst competing societal and interest-group perspectives about the role and function of environmental regulation. In this context, it is important that New Zealand retains the effects-based, science-centric approach to decisions concerning acceptable levels of effect and risk in relation to seabed mining activities.

Acknowledgements

Our thanks to Jill Banwell and Karen Grant who helpfully provided research assistance for this chapter.

62 Macpherson et al., op. cit. See also Makgill et al., op. cit., at p. 837; C.J. Iorns Magallanes and G. Severinsen, op. cit. The authors note, to avoid confusion, for those wishing to review the various TTR decisions, that the EEZ Act was amended between the first and second application. This included new provisions for discharge consents and prohibition of an adaptive management approach for discharge consents. The EEZ Act was amended again following TTR's second application, the subject of Environment Court, High Court, Court of Appeal, and Supreme Court decisions (discussed below). That version of the EEZ Act, in force at the time of writing, essentially consolidated the marine and discharge consent provisions under one part of the Act (thereby repealing ss 87A to 87J).

VI.2.13
PORTUGAL AND SEABED MINING

Mariana Neves and Pedro Madureira

Introduction

Portugal has been a State Party of the *United Convention on the Law of the Sea* (UNCLOS) and the *1994 Agreement relating to the implementation of Part XI of the UNCLOS* (1994 Agreement) since 3 November 1997. It was a member of the executive body of the International Seabed Authority (ISA), the Council, between 2001 and 2008 when the regulations for prospecting and exploration for polymetallic sulphides and cobalt-rich ferromanganese crusts in the Area started to be considered. One of Portugal's main interests was to pursue the discussion on the regulations for polymetallic sulphides, following the launch of the first scientific research programmes on the hydrothermal vents within the Portuguese continental shelf (CS) in the last decade of the 20th century. In 2011, Portugal submitted its nomination of a candidate for election to the Legal and Technical Commission (LTC), an organ of the ISA's Council. The elected Portuguese member is currently serving for a second period of office.

In what concerns the marine natural resources, the main focus of Portugal has been on areas under national jurisdiction. Recently, on 6 May 2021, the National Ocean Strategy 2021–2030 was approved under the Resolution of the Council of Ministers (RCM) no. 68/2021 of 4 June 2021. It aims to enhance the contribution of the ocean to the national economy and it is based on the increase of the scientific knowledge and the protection of marine ecosystems and their functions, which are considered as crucial vectors for the sustainable development of Portugal.[1] The mapping and knowledge of the deep seabed as well as the development of technology and the promotion of surveys to assess the environmental, social and economic impacts of deep seabed mining have been set as two areas of priority intervention.[2] Two types of mineral metallic resources have been identified in the Portuguese CS – cobalt-rich ferromanganese crusts (west of the mainland, to the south of the Azores and northeast of Madeira archipelagos) and polymetallic sulphides (mainly present along the Mid-Atlantic Ridge). However, the potential of these occurrences to represent mineral deposits is yet to be determined both geologically and economically.

1 The roadmap to the implementation, monitoring and assessment of the National Ocean Strategy was established recently, under RCM no. 120/2021 of 1 September 2021.

2 Ibid., action nos. 96 and 105.

DOI: 10.4324/9780429426162-42

Geographical extent of the exclusive economic zone, continental shelf and the Area

According to UNCLOS, the Law no. 34/2006 of 28 July 2006 establishes the limits of the maritime areas under Portugal's sovereignty or jurisdiction as well as the powers of the State to be exercised in these areas and on the high seas.[3]

Portugal is an Atlantic coastal State with a large exclusive economic zone (EEZ) of around 1.7 million square kilometres (km^2) that results from the 200 nautical miles (M) measured from the baselines of the mainland, the Azores and Madeira archipelagos. Shortly after the UNCLOS ratification, Portugal created in 1998 the Interministerial Commission for the delineation of the outer limits of the Portuguese continental shelf. After the initial desktop study issued in 2003 and following the Commission's recommendations, the Task Group for the Extension of the Continental Shelf (EMEPC)[4] was established through RCM no. 9/2005 of 17 January 2005 with the main mission to prepare Portugal's submission in accordance with UNCLOS article 76. The EEZ and the CS geographically overlapped, until May 2009, when Portugal submitted a claim to the Commission on the Limits of the Continental Shelf (CLCS) regarding the continental shelf beyond 200 M. On August 2017 Portugal submitted an Addendum, which updated with new data and information the 2009 submission. From that date the CS beyond 200 M represents an addition of around 2.4 million km^2 of seabed and subsoil thereof to the Portuguese maritime space. The consideration of Portugal's submission started also in August 2017 and is still going on, at the sub-commission level. Although there are no agreed maritime boundaries with the two neighbouring States, Spain and Morocco, there are no unresolved land or maritime disputes with these countries in the sense referred to in Rule 46 and Annex I of the Rules of Procedure of the CLCS[5] and no objections have been made to the consideration of the Portuguese submission.

Regarding the Area, Portugal's main neighbour, it is relevant to say that the State is not conducting or sponsoring any seabed mining activities in the Area. However, a contract for exploration for polymetallic sulphides in the Area was granted to the Government of the Republic of Poland by the ISA in 2018 for an area located to the south of the natural prolongation of the Azores land territory, starting at the vicinity of the southern limit of the Portuguese continental shelf. Therefore, issues on the possible impacts on the marine environment in areas under national jurisdiction that may arise from transboundary effects of the activities conducted in areas beyond national jurisdiction (ABNJ) are of particular concern for Portugal.

Regulation of seabed activities[6]

Seabed mining on the continental shelf

The regulatory framework for seabed mining activities is set out firstly in the 1976 Portuguese Constitution. In accordance with lit. (a) and (c) of article 84, paragraph 1, both the seabed and

3 For the established baselines these were lastly set under the Decree-Law no. 495/85 of 29 November.

4 Portuguese acronym. Created as a temporary State entity, EMEPC has seen its term constantly extended by several acts. Presently, the EMEPC's mandate is established under the RCM no. 84-A/2016 of 28 December 2016, as amended by RCM no. 191/2019 of 11 November 2019. The main mission of the EMEPC is the collection and gathering of data and information to support Portugal's submission to the CLCS, as well as the interaction with it and the subcommission established to consider the Portuguese submission.

5 Commission on the Limits of the Continental Shelf, *Rules of Procedure of the Commission on the Limits of the Continental Shelf*, CLCS Doc. CLCS/40/Rev.1, 2008.

6 Please note that since there is no official translation to English, the authors have been translating the original text and titles of legal diplomas only for the purpose of the book.

mineral deposits are considered to be part of the public domain. Article 84, paragraph 2, further determines that the law shall define 'the regime, terms and conditions of use and limits'.

The maritime public domain is identified in Law no. 54/2005 of 15 November 2005, which establishes the legal regime for the ownership of water resources. Under its article 3 (d) 'the maritime depths contiguous to the (CS), including the whole (EEZ)' are part of the maritime public domain which, by its article 4, pertains exclusively to the State. In the autonomous regions of the Azores and Madeira, the jurisdiction over the maritime public domain is ensured by the respective competent regional services.[7] These autonomous regions have legislative autonomy in matters that are set in their political administrative statutes. However, according to the Constitution they are prevented to legislate about the definition and the regime governing the public domain, including the maritime public domain but have the power to participate in the definition of policies concerning territorial waters, the exclusive economic zone and the adjacent seabeds.[8]

The basis for the policy on marine spatial planning and management of the national maritime space was adopted under Law no. 17/2014 of 10 April 2014.[9] The long-term and uninterrupted private use of national maritime space may be granted by a concession contract for a maximum period of 50 years.[10] The granting of this right includes the obligation of effective use and the adoption of the necessary measures to obtain or maintain the good environmental status of the marine environment.[11] It does not grant its holder the right to use or exploit natural resources of the national maritime space.[12] If the exercise of an activity depends on the granting of a concession, licence or authorization these shall be obtained through the applicable legislation.[13]

In 2015, the Portuguese Parliament adopted Law no. 54/2015 of 22 June 2015, which established the general legal regime of disclosure and use of existing geological resources in the country, including those located in the national maritime space. The occurrences of hydrocarbons are out of the scope of this Law and are subject to a different legal regime.[14] Among the list of geological resources regulated under this diploma, there are the mineral deposits which are defined as mineral occurrences that due to their rarity, high specific value or importance in industrial processing of substances contained therein, have special economic interest.[15] The mineral deposits of the seabed and subsoil of the national maritime space are part of the State's public domain.[16] Therefore, the exploration and exploitation activities should follow a strategy based on the public interest which includes the promotion of the economic and social well-being of the population and the proper protection of the marine environment.

7 Article 28 (2).

8 Lit. (b) and (s) of article 227.

9 On this Law, recently amended by Law no. 1/2021 of 11 January, and subsequent developing legislation established under Decree-Law no. 38/2015 of 12 March, see V. Becker-Weinberg, 'Portugal's legal regime on marine spatial planning and management of the national maritime space', *Marine Policy* 61, 2015, 46–53.

10 Article 19.

11 Article 17 (4).

12 Article 18 (1).

13 Article 18 (2).

14 Article 1 (1) and (4). Decree-Law no. 109/94 of 26 April, in its amended version, establishes the legal framework for oil prospection, research and production activities. Worth mentioning is the recently published Law no. 98/2021 of 31 December 2021, that establishes the Portuguese Climate Basis Law. Under its article 45, the granting of new concessions for the exploration and exploitation of hydrocarbons is strictly prohibited in all national territory.

15 Lit. (a) of article 1 (2) and lit. (m) of article 2.

16 Article 5 (2).

The activities of disclosure and use of geological resources depend on the granting of the respective right of private use of the national maritime space[17] and also on the identification in the national maritime planning instruments (the situation plan[18] or allocation plan) where they are to be foreseen as potential activities.[19] The geological resources may be subject to four types of rights: preliminary assessment rights, prospecting rights, experimental exploration rights and exploration and exploitation rights.[20] Apart from granting of preliminary assessment rights, the attribution of other types of rights must be preceded by a consultation procedure with several entities with competence on various subjects.[21]

The procedure for attribution of exploration rights is initiated by the interested party when submitting an application to the Directorate General for Energy and Geology.[22] The exploitation rights are attributed to the holder of exploration rights over the concessioned area or by means of public tender with regard to available areas.[23] Contracts for prospecting can be granted for a maximum period of five years and the area allocated in the national maritime space cannot exceed 5,000 km^2.[24] Exploitation rights are granted for a period up to 90 years[25] and shall be compatible with the regulations concerning the environmental impact assessment.[26]

It is worth mentioning that this law shall be applied to the autonomous regions of the Azores and Madeira, with appropriate adaptations, through the competent regional bodies.[27] According to its article 65, paragraph 5, the contracts for granting rights of disclosure or use of geological resources located in the zones adjacent to the archipelagos, up to 200 M are to be concluded between the central administration, the competent regional body and the applicants.

Recently, the Portuguese Government adopted the Decree-Law no. 30/2021 of 7 May 2021,[28] that develops the general legal regime of disclosure and use of mineral deposits in the national territory established in Law no. 54/2015 of 22 June 2015. However, its article 3 paragraph 2 determines that the Decree-Law is not applicable to mineral deposits located in the national maritime space. These are to be subject to special legislation that has not been developed yet.[29]

17 Article 10 (2).

18 The current situation plan for the Mainland, Madeira archipelago and the extended continental shelf, has been adopted through RCM no. 203-A/2019 of 30 December 2019. Presently there are no potential identified areas for the exploration and exploitation of mineral resources. For more on this subject see the dedicated Geoportal https://www.psoem.pt/geoportal_psoem/ (accessed February 2022).

19 Article 40 (2) and 41 (4).

20 Article 13 (1).

21 Article 9.

22 Article 16 (1), 19 (1).

23 Article 26.

24 Lit. (a) and (b) of Article 20.

25 Article 27 (4).

26 Article 27 (2). The legal regime of environmental impact assessment is established in the EIA Directive 2011/92/EU as amended by the Directive 2014/52/EU. This regime has been transposed into national law by Decree-Law no. 151-B/2013 of 31 October in its amended version. According to it, all projects likely to have significant impacts on the environment must be subject to EIA prior to licensing or authorization. Although there is no specific mention to the activities of deep sea mining like exploration or exploitation, the national authorities will have to examine each project on a case-by-case basis. This regime applies to the activities conducted in the national maritime space and not in the Area. For more on EU law applicable to Portugal, see in this book P. Singh, V. Tassin Campanella and F. Maes, 'The European Union and seabed mining' in V. Tassin Campanella (ed), *Routledge handbook of seabed mining and the law of the sea*, London: Routledge, 2023, chapter VI.1.4.

27 Article 65.

28 This Decree-Law has already been amended by Law no. 10/2022 of 12 January 2022.

29 The Climate Basis Law (see footnote 14) has established under its article 46 (2) that the Government must proceed to the environmental regulation of mining activities in the maritime space, ensuring a strict protection of the marine environment.

Seabed mining in the Area

There is no legal framework for seabed mining activities in the Area for companies sponsored by Portugal.

As an ISA member, Portugal has been engaged in the consultations on the ISA draft standards and guidelines that have been developed by the LTC to support the implementation of the draft regulations on exploitation of mineral resources in the Area.[30] Substantial discussions on these regulations and the payment regime are taken at the ISA Council where Portugal currently does not have a seat.

In what concerns the effective protection of the marine environment from the harmful effects that may arise from exploration and future exploitation, Portugal has been particularly engaged with the ISA strategy towards the implementation of a Regional Environment Management Plan (REMP) for the North Atlantic. This goal was included in the Strategic Plan of the organization adopted by the Assembly in 2018 during its 24th Session.[31] In November 2019, the ISA, in collaboration with the Government of Portugal and the European Commission, convened a workshop held at the University of Évora, Portugal, to discuss the development of a REMP for the Area of the Northern Mid-Atlantic Ridge. The workshop provided an opportunity for experts from member States, as well as from the scientific community, and contractors to review available scientific information and consider environmental requirements for applying area-based management tools and addressing cumulative impacts from future exploitation activities at a regional scale.[32]

Seabed activities and related decisions

There are presently no concession contracts for prospecting, exploration or exploitation of marine mineral resources in the national maritime space. Despite the interest already shown in the past by mining companies, no titles of concession have been granted to seabed mining activities so far.

The most relevant example was the interest shown in 2008 and 2012 by the Canadian company Nautilus Minerals Inc. According to a public statement made in 2016 by the Regional Secretariat for the Sea, Science and Technology,[33] the company submitted, in 2008, a request for prospection and exploration of mineral resources in six areas in the CS adjacent to the Azores archipelago. That request had expired in light of the applicable legislation and existing regulations. Later in 2012, the Canadian company submitted five new requests[34] for prospection and exploration of mineral resources along the Mid-Atlantic Ridge, within the CS, near to some of the marine protected areas

30 International Seabed Authority, 'Submissions received with respect to the stakeholder consultations on standards and guidelines'. Available online <https://www.isa.org.jm/submissions-received respect-stakeholder-consultations -standards-and-guidelines> (accessed February 2022).

31 International Seabed Authority, *Decision of the Assembly of the International Seabed Authority relating to the strategic plan of the Authority for the period 2019–2023*, ISBA/24/A/10, 2018.

32 International Seabed Authority, *Report of the workshop on the regional environmental management plan for the Area of the northern mid-Atlantic Ridge*, 25–29 November 2019. Available online <https://isa.org.jm/files/files/documents/evora_workshop.pdf> (accessed February 2022).

33 Governo dos Açores, *Esclarecimento da Secretaria Regional do Mar, Ciência e Tecnologia*, 2016. Available online <http://www.azores.gov.pt/Gra/SRMCT-MAR/conteudos/noticias/2016/Setembro/Esclarecimento_da_Secretaria_Regional_do_Mar_Ciencia_e_Tecnologia.htm> (accessed in February 2022).

34 Application announcements (*Avisos*) 13357/2012, 13358/2012, 13359/2012, 13360/2012, Official Gazette, 2nd Series, no. 195 of 9 October; Application announcement (*Aviso*) 13446/2012, Official Gazette, 2nd Series, no. 196 of 10 October. Besides the publication of the application announcements and the public awareness that the requests were not granted, there is no official information on the reply given by the Portuguese Government.

that had been established in 2011. The Marine Park of the Azores, and its legal framework, was first established in the Regional Decree-Law no. 28/2011/A of 11 November 2011. It is the first and main instrument for conservation of marine protected areas (MPA) beyond the territorial sea. This legal framework was amended in 2016, by the Regional Decree-Law no. 13/2016/A of 19 July 2016, in order to include new protected areas such as those included in the Nautilus Minerals Inc. request. There are currently 15 MPAs beyond the territorial sea, in the EEZ and the CS adjacent to the Azores archipelago.[35] Within those areas, the extraction of mineral resources is a prohibited activity. Although the prospection activity isn't forbidden in the MPAs, it is limited and subject to a prior binding opinion of the regional body with competence on maritime affairs.

With regard to the Area, Portugal is not conducting nor sponsoring any activities. The reasons for it may be two-fold: the current focus on the extension procedure of the CS towards the adoption of recommendations from the CLCS and the lack of a technological/industrial cluster focused on the deep sea.

Conclusion

The Portuguese deep sea mining legal framework needs to be further developed in order to give full effect to the UNCLOS. Regarding seabed mining activities and mineral deposits in the national maritime space (including the CS), there is a specific legislation to be adopted and implemented. This will not be without its challenges taking into account several factors like the potential clash of competence between the national and regional governments, and, most importantly, the need for a full coordination and cooperation between the different competent bodies, the will of the civil society and its impact on decision-makers. With respect to seabed mining activities in the Area to be eventually conducted or sponsored by Portugal, the establishment of the relevant legal framework is not foreseen in the near future.

35 Some of these MPAs had been previously designated under the Convention for the Protection of the Marine Environment of the North-East Atlantic (OSPAR). Special reference should be made to four MPAs designated on the extended continental shelf adjacent to the Azores archipelago. Portugal submitted in 2006, under the OSPAR Convention, the first national MPA on the seabed of the extended continental shelf (Rainbow hydrothermal vent field). While its water column remains unprotected, three other areas to which Portugal established national MPAs on the seabed (Altair Seamount, Antialtair Seamount and Mid-Atlantic Ridge North of the Azores) had the international waters superjacent to them collectively classified by OSPAR. For more on this subject, see 'MPAs in areas beyond national jurisdiction', OSPAR. Available online <https://www.ospar.org/work-areas/bdc/marine-protected-areas/mpas-in-areas-beyond-national-jurisdiction> (accessed February 2022). See also M. Chantal Ribeiro, *A Protecção da Biodiversidade Marinha através de Áreas Protegidas nos Espaços Marítimos sob Soberania ou Jurisdição do Estado: Discussões e Soluções Jurídicas Contemporâneas. O Caso Português*, Coimbra Editora, 2013.

VI.2.14
THE UNITED KINGDOM AND SEABED MINING

James Harrison

Introduction

As an island nation, the United Kingdom (UK) has a long history as a leader in marine exploration and it has frequently been at the forefront of developments in the legal regime relating to marine resources. It was a UK-sponsored expedition led by Professor Wyville Thomson of the University of Edinburgh which first discovered polymetallic nodules on the deep seabed during its global voyage from 1872 to 1876. When commercial interest in the exploitation of seabed resources beyond the territorial sea began to surface in the mid-twentieth century, the UK once again led developments in this area.[1] However, the UK found itself unable to support the adoption of the 1982 *United Nations Convention on the Law of the Sea* (UNCLOS), in large part due to its opposition to the deep seabed mining regime in Part XI. Following agreement on modifications to Part XI in 1994, the UK became a party to UNCLOS and it has since developed its legal framework in order to implement its obligations relating to seabed mining with a view to remaining at the forefront of this field. Its focus in this respect has been on sponsoring activities in the Area, whereas its attitude towards areas within national jurisdiction has been more orientated towards marine environmental protection.

Geographical extent of the exclusive economic zone, continental shelf and the Area

The limits of the continental shelf in the UK are determined by Order in Council in accordance with the powers contained in the Continental Shelf Act 1964.[2] The continental shelf boundary largely coincides with the exclusive economic zone boundary but becoming a party to UNCLOS allowed the UK to make claims to an extended continental shelf in two main areas. In 2006, the

1 E.g. *Treaty between His Majesty in respect of the United Kingdom and the President of the United States of Venezuela relating to the submarine areas of the Gulf of Paria*, 22 September 1942, 205 LNTS 121.
2 See the Continental Shelf (Designation of Areas) Order 2013.

DOI: 10.4324/9780429426162-43

UK made a joint submission with France, Ireland and Spain in the area of the Celtic Sea and the Bay of Biscay to the south-west of the UK,[3] which was approved by the Commission on the Limits of the Continental Shelf in April 2009.[4] The UK has also made a submission in respect of the Hatton Rockall Area to the north-west of the UK, but it has not yet been considered by the Commission due to outstanding disputes with neighbouring states.[5]

The UK has also made claims to an extended continental shelf in relation to some of its overseas territories. In 2010, the Commission found that the UK was not entitled to an extended continental shelf around Ascension Island. The UK was critical of the recommendations of the Commission in this case, arguing that it was based upon a defective interpretation of UNCLOS.[6] The UK has also made a submission in respect of the Falkland Islands, South Georgia and the South Sandwich Islands, but due to a dispute over these territories, this submission has not yet been considered by the Commission.[7] The UK has not made a submission in relation to the Chagos Archipelago in the Indian Ocean given the sovereignty dispute with Mauritius over this territory. In 2019, following the Advisory Opinion of the International Court of Justice in which the Court held that the UK was in breach of its international obligations by failing to complete the decolonisation process in relation to the Chagos Archipelago,[8] Mauritius made its own submission to the Commission, to which the UK objected.[9] The UK maintains its claims to the territory, despite the January 2021 decision of a Special Chamber of the International Tribunal for the Law of the Sea confirming the right of Mauritius to delimit the maritime boundary with the Maldives, which include portions of the outer continental shelf abutting the Chagos Archipelago.[10] At the same time, the UK agreed in the so-called 1965 Lancaster House Undertaking that 'the benefits of any minerals or oil discovered in or near the Chagos Archipelago should revert to [Mauritius].'[11]

3 The UK was at that time part of the European Union. For more information on this, see in this book P. Singh, V. Tassin Campanella and F. Maes, 'The European Union and seabed mining,' in V. Tassin Campanella (ed.), *Routledge handbook of seabed mining and the law of the sea*, London: Routledge, 2023, chapter VI.1.4.

4 Statement by the Chairman of the Commission on the Limits of the Continental Shelf on the progress of the work of the Commission, Document CLCS/62, 20 April 2009, para. 14. Available online <https://documents-dds-ny.un.org/doc/UNDOC/GEN/N09/307/58/PDF/N0930758.pdf> (accessed 16 September 2021).

5 See C. Yiallourides, 'Continental shelf boundaries in the North Sea and the North Atlantic,' in G. Gordon et al. (eds), *Oil and gas law: Current practice and emerging trends: Vol. I*, Edinburgh: Edinburgh University Press, 2018, 3rd ed., pp. 229–237.

6 See communication from the United Kingdom to the Secretariat of the United Nations, 11 January 2011. Available online <https://www.un.org/depts/los/clcs_new/submissions_files/gbr08/gbr_nv_11jan2011.pdf> (accessed 16 September 2021).

7 See in this book E. Jiménez Pineda, 'South American region and seabed mining,' in V. Tassin Campanella (ed.), *Routledge handbook of seabed mining and the law of the sea*, op. cit., chapter VI.1.6.

8 *Legal Consequences of the Separation of the Chagos Archipelago from Mauritius in 1965, Advisory Opinion, I.C.J. Reports 2019*, p. 95. See also in this book E. Egede, 'Mauritius and seabed mining,' in V. Tassin Campanella (ed.), *Routledge handbook of seabed mining and the law of the sea*, op. cit., chapter VI.2.10.

9 See communication from the United Kingdom to the Secretariat of the United Nations, 28 June 2019. Available online <https://www.un.org/depts/los/clcs_new/submissions_files/mus1_82_2019/2019_06_28_GBR_NV_UN_001-OLA-2019-00636.pdf> (accessed 16 September 2021).

10 *Dispute concerning delimitation of the maritime boundary between Mauritius and Maldives in the Indian Ocean (Mauritius v. Maldives), Judgment*, 28 January 2021, ITLOS Case No. 28 (pending at the time of writing this article).

11 See *Chagos Marine Protected Area Arbitration (Mauritius v. United Kingdom)*, Award, 18 March 2015, PCA Case No. 2011-03, para. 77. The Tribunal held that the undertaking was binding by virtue of estoppel; ibid., para. 448.

Regulation of seabed mining activities

Seabed mining on the continental shelf

The management of the UK continental shelf is subject to a complex and multi-faceted legal framework. With the exception of coal[12] and petroleum,[13] the rights with respect to the natural resources of the continental shelf are vested in the Crown[14] and managed by the Crown Estate. It follows that the exploitation of these resources must be licensed by the Crown Estate[15] or by Crown Estate Scotland,[16] depending on their location. In addition, the UK Government and the devolved administrations also have a role to play in regulating such activities. Unlike the extensive legislative framework for the regulation of offshore oil and gas exploitation, the UK has no legislation dedicated to seabed mining on the UK continental shelf. Rather, this issue is addressed under the general marine licensing framework contained in the Marine and Coastal Access Act 2009, which requires a marine licence both for 'dredging' and more generally for the 'use [of] a vehicle, vessel, aircraft, marine structure or floating container to remove any substance or object from the sea bed within the UK marine licensing area.'[17] The precise licensing authority will depend upon the location of an activity, as marine licensing decisions in the Welsh and Scottish offshore zones are devolved to the relevant devolved administrations.[18] The licensing authority is required to have regard to the need to protect the environment, the need to protect human health and the need to prevent interference with legitimate uses of the sea when determining a licence application.[19] A developer may have to carry out a full environmental impact assessment and public consultation, if it is determined that the proposed activity is likely to have significant effects on the environment due to its size, nature or location.[20] If granted, licences can be subject to conditions[21] and 'a licensing authority may by notice vary, suspend or revoke a licence granted by it if it appears to the authority that there has been a breach of any of its provisions.'[22]

The powers to regulate seabed mining on the UK continental shelf are also constrained by relevant nature conservation legislation and in particular the existence of marine protected areas (MPAs). There are 72 offshore MPAs around the UK.[23] Of particular significance is the West of Scotland MPA, which offers protection to a range of seabed features and habitats, including seamounts, in a large area to the north-west of Scotland.[24] It is an offence to intentionally or recklessly destroy or damage any feature protected by an MPA[25] and regulatory authorities must not authorise any activity which is likely to have a significant risk of hindering the achievement of the conservation objectives of an MPA, unless the benefit to the public clearly outweighs the risk of damage to the environment and the person seeking authorisation undertakes measures of

12 Coal Industry Act 1994, s. 8.
13 Petroleum Act 1998, s. 2.
14 Continental Shelf Act 1964, s. 1(1).
15 Crown Estate Act 1961.
16 Scottish Crown Estate Act 2019.
17 Marine and Coastal Access Act 2009, ss. 65–66.
18 Ibid., s. 113. See also s. 76.
19 Ibid., s. 69.
20 See Marine Works (Environmental Impact Assessment) Regulations 2007.
21 Marine and Coastal Access Act 2009, s. 71.
22 Ibid., s. 72.
23 Available online <https://jncc.gov.uk/our-work/offshore-mpas/> (accessed 16 September 2021).
24 West of Scotland Marine Protected Area Order 2020.
25 Marine and Coastal Access Act 2009, s. 140(2)(d).

equivalent environmental benefit to the damage which the act will or is likely to have.[26] It has been recognised that 'there is the potential for the [West of Scotland MPA] to be of interest for deep-sea mining activities in the future – most notably for the mining of ferromanganese crusts that occur on the seamounts within the site,'[27] but the relevant conservation advice recognises that 'deep sea mining would be capable of damaging the protected features of the site were it to occur.'[28] These nature conservation provisions therefore potentially constrain the opportunities for seabed mining on the UK continental shelf.

The regulation of activities around the UK's overseas territories is carried out by the government of each territory. Many of the overseas territories have also established extensive MPAs in their offshore waters, which restrict seabed activities such as seabed mining. For example, mineral extraction is prohibited in the MPAs around South Georgia and the South Sandwich Islands[29] and the Pitcairn Islands,[30] and such a prohibition is also proposed for the Ascension Island MPA established in 2019.[31]

Seabed mining in the Area

The regulatory framework for seabed mining in the Area for companies sponsored by the UK is found in the Deep Sea Mining Act 1981, which was amended in 2014 in order to bring it into line with the requirements of Part XI of UNCLOS. The amended 1981 Act establishes a regime which allows the UK to license any UK national or body incorporated under the law of any part of the UK to carry out exploration or exploitation of mineral resources in the International Seabed Area.[32] Whilst the original 1981 Act only allowed the UK to license mining for polymetallic nodules, the 2014 amendments extend the scope of the licensing regime to mineral resources in general, which are defined, in line with article 133 of UNCLOS, as 'a solid, liquid or gaseous mineral resource.'[33] Subject to a fee, an exploration or exploitation licence may be granted by the Secretary of State, or by the Scottish Ministers in relation to Scottish nationals and companies. Ordinarily an exploration licence is granted for 10 years but may be extended for successive periods of five years.[34]

An important amendment introduced by the 2014 Act was to ensure that no exploration or exploitation licence could come into force before the date on which a contract granted by the Authority to the licensee had also come into force, thereby preventing the unilateral licensing of activities in the Area by the UK.[35] The Act also foresees that the terms of a licence will be directly connected to compliance with UNCLOS, any rules, regulations or procedures adopted by the Authority, and the provisions of the contract between the licensee and the Authority.[36] Yet, a licence may be subject

26 Ibid., s. 126.

27 Joint Nature Conservation Committee, *West of Scotland Deep-Sea Marine Reserve: Conservation Objectives and Management Advice*, March 2020, p. 19. Available online <https://data.jncc.gov.uk/data/37955242-d60b-4494-8e2c-94e93fb0de6f/west-of-scotland-conservation-objectives-management-advice.pdf> (accessed 16 September 2021).

28 Ibid.

29 Available online <https://www.gov.gs/environment/marine-protected-area/> (accessed 16 September 2021).

30 Pitcairn Islands Marine Protected Area Ordinance 2016, section 8.

31 Available online <https://www.ascension.gov.ac/map-marker/mpa-marine-protected-area> (accessed 16 September 2021).

32 Deep Sea Mining Act 1981, s. 1.

33 Ibid., s. 1(6).

34 Deep Sea Mining (Exploration Licences) Regulations 1984, regulation 4.

35 Deep Sea Mining Act 1981, s. 2(3). See also s. 3.

36 Ibid., s. 2(3A)(g)–(j).

to other conditions imposed by the Secretary of State or the Scottish Ministers. It is the establishment of such licence conditions which is the main regulatory tool available to the UK in order to control seabed mining by sponsored entities, particularly as licences may be revoked where any term or condition has not been complied with.[37] The legislation provides examples of the types of conditions that might be attached to a licence, including protecting the health, safety or welfare of persons employed in licensed or ancillary operations; the treatment of mineral resources once they have been mined; and the disposal of any waste generated from the processing of minerals or other operations. The licensing authority also has a broad power to unilaterally vary the conditions of licences where they are of the opinion that it is required in order to

> ensure the safety, health or welfare of persons engaged in any of the licensed operations or ancillary operations; protect any marine creatures, plants or other organisms or their habitat; [or] avoid a conflict with any obligation of the [UK] arising out of any international agreement in force for the [UK].[38]

This power provides a significant degree of flexibility to the regulatory regime under the revised 1981 Act, although these powers must be exercised in accordance with due process and they must respect the right to property under the European Convention on Human Rights.[39]

The legislation emphasises that the licensing authority shall 'have regard to the need to protect (as far as reasonably practicable) marine creatures, plants and other organisms and their habitat from any harmful effects which might result from any activities to be authorised by the licence,'[40] although a degree of discretion would appear to be afforded in deciding what levels of impact are acceptable.[41] During the passage of the 2014 amendments, there was some debate about whether this provision on marine environmental protection was sufficient, particularly in light of developments in international environmental law since 1981, such as the emergence of the precautionary approach.[42] Whilst amendments were resisted, assurances were given by government ministers that the highest possible environmental standards would be applied to operations licensed by the UK and it is possible that the UK could impose license conditions demanding compliance with stringent environmental standards in excess of standards applied by the Authority.[43] Moreover, it was underlined by the Government during the passage of the 2014 amendments that

> in carrying out their duties under section 5 [of the Act], Ministers would necessarily have to take into account the terms of the advisory opinion from [the Seabed Disputes Chamber of] the International Tribunal for the Law of the Sea given in 2011 [which] made it clear that,

37 Ibid., s. 6.

38 Ibid., s. 6(1).

39 See European Court of Human Rights, *Guide on Article 1 of Protocol 1 to the European Convention on Human Rights: Protection of Property,* Council of Europe, 2020. Available online <https://www.echr.coe.int/Documents/Guide_Art_1_Protocol_1_ENG.pdf> (accessed 16 September 2021).

40 Deep Sea Mining Act 1981, s. 5

41 Ibid., s. 5(2) makes clear that the Secretary of State to the Scottish Ministers may include conditions in a licence as they 'consider necessary or expedient to avoid or minimise any such harmful effects.'

42 See Consideration of the Bill, as amended in the Public Bill Committee, Hansard, House of Commons, 24 January 2014, vol. 574.

43 See e.g. Alistair Burt (Parliamentary Under-Secretary of State for Foreign and Commonwealth Affairs), Hansard, House of Commons, 6 September 2013, vol. 567; Lord Wallace of Saltaire, Hansard, House of Lords, 7 February 2014, vol. 752.

> in sponsoring applications to the (…) Authority, states have regard to their environmental obligations [and] that includes specifically the precautionary approach set out in the Rio Declaration.[44]

In this respect, conditions in the licences granted by the Secretary of State to date require the licensee to

> take all practicable measures, as far as reasonably possible using the best technology available to it, applying a precautionary approach and best environmental practices, to prevent pollution and any harmful effects to marine creatures, plants or other organisms and their habitats that might result from activities authorised under this licence, but not limited to any measures specified in the plan of work or the Licensee's contract with the Authority.[45]

This clause is subtly different to the equivalent provisions of the Exploration Regulations adopted by the Authority[46] and its broad terms could well lead to a dispute about whether sufficient action has been taken.

Licence holders are expected to report on their activities under the licence,[47] including information concerning the state of the marine environment and impacts of activities over time.[48] Under section 11, the Secretary of State or the Scottish Ministers may appoint inspectors to assist them in the implementation of the Act. The Act itself does not explain the powers to be exercised by inspectors, which must be set out in separate regulations[49] or by the licence conditions themselves.[50]

Should a dispute arise between the Secretary of State or the Scottish Ministers on the one hand and the licence holder on the other hand, it is anticipated that it will be referred to arbitration.[51] The 1981 Act also provides an enabling framework for the registration and enforcement of judicial decisions of the Seabed Disputes Chamber,[52] as well as arbitral awards rendered under article 188 paragraph 2 (a) of UNCLOS.[53]

Seabed activities and related decisions

At present, there is no mining on the UK continental shelf, although some aggregate dredging for sand and gravel is carried out in this zone, as well as extensive oil and gas operations.

In relation to the Area, the UK sponsors two contracts held by UK Seabed Resources Ltd for the exploration for polymetallic nodules in the Clarion-Clipperton Zone, the first running from

44 Ibid.

45 E.g. Exploration Licence between the Secretary of State for Business, Innovation and Skills and UK Seabed Resources Ltd (8 February 2013) clause 11(1) (on file with author).

46 Regulations on Prospecting and Exploration for Polymetallic Nodules in the Area and related matters, Decision ISBA/19/C/17, 22 July 2013, regulation 31(5).

47 Deep Sea Mining (Exploration Licences) Regulations 1984, Schedule, para. 13.

48 Ibid., Schedule, Annex 5, para. 2.

49 Deep Sea Mining Act 1981, Schedule 1, paras 6–11 and 17.

50 See Deep Sea Mining (Exploration Licences) Regulations 1984, Schedule, paras 15–16.

51 Ibid., Schedule, para. 24.

52 Deep Sea Mining Act 1981, s. 8A.

53 Ibid., s. 8C.

February 2013 to February 2028 and the second running from March 2016 to March 2031. This company is a wholly owned subsidiary of the US corporation Lockheed Martin.

Conclusion

The UK approach to regulating seabed mining both within and beyond national jurisdiction relies heavily upon a licensing regime, which leaves significant discretion to the licensing authority to determine the precise conditions under which an activity may proceed. There has been resistance to introducing any significant constraint on that discretion, although it has been emphasised that the UK will have to comply with its international obligations when exercising its powers under national law.

INDEX

Note: Page numbers in *italics* indicate figures, page numbers in **bold** indicate tables, and references following "n" refer to notes.

Ægir Basin 283, 387, 388n15
Aarhus Convention 294, 294n18
Abidjan Convention 366–7, 366n13
ABMTs *see* area-based management tools
ABNJ *see* areas beyond national jurisdiction
Acta de San Pedro Alejandrino 358n2
adaptive management *27*, 27–8; defined 62; EPA erred to manage pollution by 57–8; marine consent in 424; in *Newcastle v Upper Hunter Shire Council* 62; precautionary approach 72–3; prohibited in case of marine discharge consent 56; role in facilitating risk management 54; in *Sustain Our Sounds Inc v New Zealand King Salmon Company Ltd* 56; in *Telstra Corp Ltd* 62
adjacent 84, 138, 244, 268, 324, 406, 420, 429, 431, 435n35; coastal State 85, 109, 114; exclusive economic zones (EEZ) 415; extended continental shelf 417; International Seabed Area 127
advisory opinion 38, 108, 118, 121, 205, 219–22, 248, 250, 407, 434; of 2011 49, 51–3, 59, 210n8, 211–15, 219–22, 230, 246n50, 437; of 2015 219 20; of 2021 100n131; request for 220–1, 241–3; *see also* International Seabed Authority; Seabed Advisory Opinion; Seabed Disputes Chamber
Africa 261–70; African Minerals Development Centre (AMDC) 264–5; African Union Border Programme (AUBP) 265; Assembly 264; continental shelves and the Area 262–3; governance of the seabed 263–5; ISA African group 270; Regional Economic Communities (RECs) 264; seabed mining, regulation of activities 265–6; seabed mining in the Area 266–70; seven step implementation of strategic roadmap *269*; United Nations Economic Commission for Africa (UNECA) 265, 268–9
African Group 189, 270n61; on the Area 167; insisting on prerequisite for mining in the Area 201n46; seabed mining in the Area and 270
African integrated maritime (AIM) 263, 264, 266, 268
African Minerals Development Centre 264–5, 268, 268n53, 269
African mining vision 264
African Union 261n1, 262, 263–8
African Union Border Programme 265
agent 118n65; defined 118
ALADI 330
Alaska 131n12, 143
Alpha Ridge, Arctic 281, 283
AMAP *see* Arctic Monitoring Assessment Program
AMDC *see* African Minerals Development Centre
AMV *see* African mining vision
Antarctica 33, 271 9; 1980 Convention on the Conservation of Antarctic Marine Living Resources 273n9; common heritage of mankind (CHM) 41–3; continental shelves and 272–3; exclusive economic zones and 272–3; governance of seabed mining in 276–8; seabed activities, regulation of 273–6
Antarctic Treaty Consultative Meetings 271, 274, 275, 278; meeting of the Consultative Parties 271n2
Antarctic Treaty System 41, 41n55, 42, 271–8, 275n21, 275n23, 276n31, 285, 327
APEC *see* Asia-Pacific Economic Co-operation
Arctic Monitoring Assessment Program 282

Arctic Ocean 134, 138, 143, 280–9; Arctic Council 282, 285, 287–9; continental shelves and 281–4; exclusive economic zones and 281–4; regulation at international level 285–6; regulation at regional level 286–9; seabed mining activities, governance of 284–5; seabed mining regulation of activities 285–9; sub-sea permafrost in 249
the Area 103, 157–73, 178; in Belgium 346, 347; benefit sharing in 169–72; continental shelves and 262–3; contractors involved in the seabed mining 158–60, *159*; control of access to minerals in 164–5; core mandate of the International Seabed Authority 160–2; Côte d'Ivoire 365–6; defined 35, 98, 215; disputes regarding 215–17, 227–30; draft framework for financial regulations prepared by Finance Committee 201; EIAs involvement in 394; enforcement and compliance of 172–3; the Enterprise 166–8; entities sponsored by the States for mining 100; environmental impact assessments for 102; exploration and exploitation 6n26, 376–7; in Germany 373–4, 375–6; guidelines and standards for 199–200; in Guyana 380–1; in Iceland 386–7, 390; incidental powers of ISA for 204; in India 392; interest of Africa in seabed mining 262; ISA role in organizing and controlling 36, 70, 73, 99, 111, 158, 160–1, 163, 172, 179; jurisdiction *ratione materiae* 214–15; in Korea 398–9; marine scientific research in 203, 377–8; in Mauritius 405–8; in Mozambique 414–15; net proceeds, defined under article 133 36; in New Zealand 420; non-Party State involvement through States Parties 100; in Portugal 428, 431; principle for 36; regulation of deep seabed mining 163–4; responsibilities and obligations of States 38, 98–103; seabed mining in Africa 266–70; seabed mining in EU 297–8; seabed mining in UK 433–4, 436–8; site-banking system 168–9; standards and guidelines for activities in 199–200; States Parties not engaged in 101; trial of coastal state for violating 136; unilateral licensing in UK 436; US prohibited from DSM 286n36; vulnerability to resource overexploitation and environmental degradation 38
area-based management tools 307, 311, 312
areas beyond national jurisdiction 108, 110–11, 299, 300n70, 301, 335–6; area-based conservation measures 301; biological diversity, conservation and sustainable use of 39–40, 39n38; concern for reparations in 122; environmental impact assessment (EIA) and 97, 103; in European Union 39n37; increase in human activities in 250; loss of biodiversity 251; mishandling of revenues from seabed mining 107; OSPAR Convention in 306; preservation and protection of marine biodiversity in 286; principles of 98; seabed mining governance as public law 113; *see also* the Area; High Seas; freedom of the High Seas
Argentina 271n1, 272, 272n6, 324, 325, 326, 326n12, 327, 327n20; Argentine Antarctic Territory 273; claims of sovereignty 276; dispute with Chile 325, 329; MPAs created by 330
ARIO Articles on Responsibility of International Organizations
Articles on Responsibility of International Organizations 118, 118n67, 120
Articles on State Responsibility 108, 115, 116, 122
artificial islands 86, 88, 89, 90, 96, 110
ASEAN *see* Association of Southeast Asian Nations
Asia-Pacific Economic Co-operation 337, 339–40
ASR *see* Articles on State Responsibility
Association of Southeast Asian Nations 336, 337–9; ASEAN Centre for Biodiversity 338; ASEAN Centre for Energy 338; ASEAN Council on Petroleum 338; ASEAN Economic Community (AEC) 337, 338, 339; ASEAN Member States (AMS) 338, 338n45, 339, 341; ASEAN Minerals Cooperation Action Plan (AMCP-III) 339; ASEAN Ministerial Meeting on the Environment 339; ASEAN Political and Security Community (APSC) 337; ASEAN Senior Officials Meeting (ASOMM) 339, 339n49; ASEAN Senior Officials on the Environment (ASOEN) 339; ASEAN Socio-Cultural Community (ASSC) 337–8
ATCM *see* Antarctic Treaty Consultative Meetings
Atlantic Accord of 2005 149, 149n51
Atlantic Ocean 149, 324, 325, 332
ATS *see* Antarctic Treaty System
attribution: in EEZ 110; international law obligations 113–14; procedure for exploration rights 430
AU *see* African Union
AUBP *see* African Union Border Programme
Australia 146n32, 271n1, 276, 278n44, 314, 333; *Environment East Gippsland Inc. v VicForests* 61; Environment Protection and Biodiversity Conservation Act 1999 (EPBC Act) 60, 61; Great Barrier Reef Marine Park Act 1975 (GBMP Act) 60, 61; Minister for the Environment 60; *Newcastle v Upper Hunter Shire Council* 62; Northern Territory 60; precaution in seabed mining 60–2; *Telstra Corp Ltd v Hornsby Shire Council* 61, 62; Victorian Supreme Court 61

Baltic Sea 295, 304–6, 373
Barbados vs. Trinidad and Tobago Arbitration 88
Barcelona Convention 96, 298–9, 302–3, 305, 305n113, 306, 306n114
Barents Sea 282–4

baseline information 49, 57–8, 60, 69, 71, 73, 424
bathymetric maps 12, 15, 16, 17, 143n12
Bay du Nord Project 148, 148n47, 149
Bay of Bengal 94, 132–3, 392n6
Bay of Biscay 291, 434
Bayview v. Mexico 233
BBNJ Agreement 7n31, 39, 45, 85, 97, 103, 103n152, 251, 257, 298, 298n50, 307, 311–12, 355
Belgium 345–50, 364; continental shelf and 345–6; European Coal and Steel Community (ECSC) 290; exclusive economic zone and 345–6; polymetallic nodules 291; seabed activities and 348–9; seabed mining activities, regulation of 346–8
benefit sharing 36–7, 39, 142, 143, 169–72; common heritage of mankind (CHM) 180–2; European Union 39n37; in financial terms for UNCLOS 180–2; Moon Treaty 41; multilateral system 44
biodiversity 24, 97, 122, 383; composition of abyssal plains 20; conservation of 5; of deep-sea 395; loss of 72, 115, 245, 251; marine 122, 160, 286, 301, 342, 370, 393, 396, 416; regulations of India 394, 396; species-level, knowledge of 25
Biodiversity Act, 2002, India 394
BIOT *see* British Indian Ocean Territory
Bismarck Sea 336, 341
Black Sea 295
blue economy 86, 416; Africa 262, 263, 265–8, 268n53, 269, 270; Mauritius 412
Bordwin, H.J. 43
Borgese, E. M. 157
Brazil 146n32, 324, 325, 326n12, 351–7; continental shelf and 351–2; exclusive economic zone and 351–2; institutional framework 352–4; legal framework of seabed mining 354–5; seabed activities and 355–6; seabed mining activities, regulation of 352–5
breach 229, 435; of international law obligation 51, 107, 111–12, 114, 119, 380, 434; of liability 114–15; remedies 115–18; of State party obligations under UNCLOS 111
Brekke, H. 135
British Indian Ocean Territory 407
Brunei 148n43, 333, 334, 335, 337, 339
Bulgaria 298; polymetallic nodules 291

Cambodia 333, 334, 337, 340
Caminos, H. 151
Canada 43, 87, 146n32, 149, 262, 282, 283, 364; Article 82 148–50; *Castonguay Blasting v Ontario* 64; Federal Court of Canada 64; Fisheries Act 1985 63, 64; *Morton v Canada (2015)* 64, 68; *Morton v Canada (2019)* 64; Oceans Act 63; precaution in seabed mining 63–5; Supreme Court of Canada 64
Canada Basin, Arctic 281
capacity building 44, 135, 170, 202, 230–1, 262, 267, 269, 307, 370
carbonate compensation depth (CCD) 13
carbon dioxide storage 86, 90
Carver, R. 28
CBD *see* Convention on Biological Diversity
CCS *see* Convention on the Continental Shelf
CCZ *see* Clarion-Clipperton-Zone
Celtic Sea 291, 434
Census of Marine Life 11
Central Arctic Ocean Fisheries Agreement 287
central Indian Ocean Basin 196, 291, 391–2, 395, 396
Certain Activities case 116
CFCLR *see* Convention on Fishing and Conservation of the Living Resources of the High Seas
charts 92, 131, 136
Chatham Rock Phosphate Limited 425
Chen, M. 249
Chile 271n1, 276, 324, 327, 329, 361
China 148, 148n45, 281, 333, 335–6, 340, 342, 369, 399, 402; Deep Seabed Mining Law of 246
CHM *see* common heritage of mankind
Chukchi Plateau, Arctic 143, 281
CIOB *see* central Indian Ocean Basin
Circular Metals Tuvalu Ltd. 197
CJEU *see* Court of Justice of the European Union
Clarion-Clipperton-Zone 13, *13*, 23, 196, 197, 239, 318n24, 374, 335, 336, 399, 403; exploration licence for manganese nodules in 377; German licence area in 373; nodule fauna in 24
CLCS *see* Commission on the Limits of the Continental Shelf
climate change 86; deep-sea mining and 245, 249–51; effect of methane release on 248; hydrate mining and 248; increase of ice coverage in the Arctic 281; leading to warming of the Arctic and sea level rise 282
Coastal Law (2017) 369
COBSEA Coordinating Body of the Seas of East Asia
Colombia 147, 324, 328, 328n27, 358–64; continental shelf and 359–61; delimitation 360–1; geographical extent of the waters and 359–61; marine protected areas 361; seabed mining activities, regulation of 362–4; United Nations Convention on the Law of the Sea, and 359
Commission on the Limits of the Continental Shelf 83n10, 87, 90n64, 91, 91n71, 94, 94n89, 127, 137, 278n44, 308, 326; Africa, claims submitted by 262; Argentine Antarctic Territory 273; Brazil, claims submitted by 352; Brunei, claims submitted by 148n43; Celtic Sea and the Bay of Biscay, claims submitted by 291; coastal State on 91, 93, 132, 133; Colombia, claims submitted by 328; continental shelf claims

submitted to 335; contracts for exploration 196; Council Working Party 310; decision-making powers 292; delineation of the continental shelf 90; establish position of interim director 167; functions under UNCLOS 132, 326; Iceland, claims submitted by 388, 389; India, claims submitted by 392; International Law Commission 137n48; International Tribunal for the Law of the Sea, guidelines on 133; letter by Guyana to 381; Malaysia-Vietnam joint submission 148, 148n43; Mauritius and Seychelles 406n12, 407, 408; Member States and 308n134; New Zealand, claims submitted by 420; Pacific Island, claims submitted by 316; Portugal, claims submitted by 428, 428n4; processing of shelf submissions 138; role in broad margin states 136; Russia's revised submission 134, 283; Southeast Asia, claims submitted by 335; sovereign rights beyond 200 nautical miles 91, 131–3, 263, 329; state practice 134; UK, claims submitted by 434; Venezuela, claims submitted by 326n14

Committee for Environmental Protection (CEP), Antarctica 274

Committee for Mineral Reserves International Reporting Standards (CRIRSCO), Canada 16

Committee on Legal Issues of the Outer Limits of the Continental Shelf 137

commodities 1, 3n8, 251, 290, 312

common heritage of mankind 33–45, 143, 178–91, 194, 198, 200, 204; activities of the International Seabed Authority 182–91; application of 40–3; benefit sharing in finance 180–2; deep sea mining, payment regime for 180–2; payment mechanisms of 204; plant genetic resources 43–4; principle of 33–5, 194; Resolution 2749 (XXV) 200; United Nations Convention on the Law of the Sea deep sea mining 35–40, 179–80; World Heritage Convention 44–5

Comoros 415

Companhia de Produção de Recursos Minerais (CPRM), Brazil 196, 331, 352

compensation 117, 248, 267, 295, 363, 384; for environmental damage 116; environmental fund 187; noncompliance 117; restitution and 116; for the victims of pollution 118n62

Conservation of Arctic Flora and Fauna (CAFF) 282

Consultative Parties (ATCPs) 274, 275

continental shelf 5, 82, 85–95, 93n82; in Antarctica 272–3; and the Area 262–3; in Belgium 345–6; beyond 200 nautical miles 388–90; in Brazil 351–2; in Colombia 359–61; in Côte d'Ivoire 365–6; geographical extent, defined 406; in Germany 373–4; in Guyana 380–1; in Iceland 386–7; in India 392; in Korea 398–9; in Mauritius 405–8; in Mozambique 414–15; natural resources of 89–90; in New Zealand 420; in Pacific Islands 315–17; in Portugal 428–30; seabed mining in United Kingdom (UK) 433–6; single continental shelf 87; in South America 325–30; in Southeast Asia 334–6; sovereign rights and 130–3; *see also* extended continental shelf

Continental Shelf Act 1964, UK 433

Continental Shelf Convention 150–1

Continental Shelf Mining Decree of 1989 374

controlled source electromagnetic (CSEM) 16

Convention Concerning the Protection of the World Cultural and Natural Heritage *see* World Heritage Convention

Convention for the Protection of the Marine Environment of the North-East Atlantic 286, 287, 287n43, 300n72, 302, 307, 307n119, 432n35; Commission 285, 287, 301, 306; Convention 299–302, 299n61, 301, 301n76; MPAs 300, 301; OSPAR Action Plan 1998–2003 287n43

Convention on Biological Diversity 44, 58, 59, 285–6, 293, 294, 318, 421

Convention on Fishing and Conservation of the Living Resources of the High Seas 359

Convention on Future Multilateral Cooperation in North-East Atlantic Fisheries 287

Convention on the Continental Shelf 359, 362

Cook Islands 135, 231, 322n36

cooperation (obligation to cooperate) 38, 103

Coordinating Body of the Seas of East Asia 337, 340, 342

corporate responsibility 121

Costanza, R. 189

Costa Rica 116, 328, 329, 360, 361

Côte d'Ivoire 365–71; 2017 Coastal Law 369; the Area and 365–6; continental shelf and 365–6; Environment Code 368–9; exclusive economic zone and 365–6; legislative perspectives 370; Maritime Code 367; Mining Code 367; Petroleum Code 368; seabed activities, regulation of 366–70; United Nations Convention on the Law of the Sea 369–70

Court of Justice of the European Union 67

Crawford, J. 122

Crown Estate Scotland 435

crusts, as mineral resources of deep sea 14, 17–18

CS *see* continental shelf

CS Geneva Convention 2, 83–5, 85n34, 86n35, 128, 150, 408

Cuba 269n58, 298

customary international law 2, 107, 111, 135, 420; article 76 151, 152; article 82 150–2; of environmental protection 112; Principle 15 53; rights and obligations of States 98; Venezuela 326n14

customary rights 419, 422, 425
Czech Republic 269, 291, 298, 310

damages 85n31, 115; due to exploitation 4; environmental 4, 24, 52, 54, 61, 73, 115, 117, 118n62, 355, 356; to flora and fauna of the marine environment 70; transboundary 247, 248; from wrongful acts 216n24
Declaración de Santiago 324, 327
Decision-making Committee (DMC) 424, 425
decolonisation 34, 35, 84, 395, 434
DeepGreen Mineral Corp. 239, 252
Deep Seabed Mining Law of China 246
deep-sea habitats: biogeographic knowledge in *23*; biological investigations 12
deep sea minerals 12, 23, 373, 376; challenges in resource estimation 16; Constitution of India 394; exploitation and exploration 318–19; exploration regulations 204; regional scientific research guidelines for 319–20; scientific challenges related to 12, 18; terrestrial minerals and 5n19
deep sea mining 4, 11–29, 107–22, 178–9, 280, 280n1, 286n36, 301n76, 320; African blue economy 267; Agreement 320n33, 321, 322; benefit sharing in 180; biological communities of mineral resources 20–1; climate change and 249–51; closing scientific gaps 5n17; components of 18; cost-benefit analysis of 190; described 108n5, 280n1; disputes between operators and sponsoring states 230–5; disputes concerning contractual undertakings operators 225–7; disputes concerning exercise of regulatory powers by the ISA 227–30; environmental challenges of 20, 22–8; environmental impacts of 21–2; exploration challenges of 15–16; financial benefits of 191; forms of mineral resources present in 12–14; gas hydrates exploration and exploitation, regulation of 245–9; Germany, regulation of activities in 374–6; international law obligations, breach of 111–14; liability as consequences of breach in 114–15; limitation of scientific data and knowledge 23–5; moratorium of the World Wild Foundation in 2022 5n18; need of an ecosystem approach in 25–6, *26*; negative impact on economies of developing states 189; non-state actors and responsibility 118–22; opposition of exploitation activities in 5; payment regime for 180–2; regulation of 163–4, 179; regulation of activities in the Arctic 281; remedies as consequences of breach in 115–18; resource estimation, challenges of 16–18; technical challenges of 18–20; uncertainty associated with 26–8; United Nations Convention on the Law of the Sea 179–80; Zone 320n33
Deep Sea Mining Act 1981, UK 65, 436, 438
deepwater drilling 142, 143n9
defenses, international law obligations 114
delimitation 265, 328n27, 360–1; of continental shelf 328n28, 332; delineation of maritime borders and 265; maritime boundaries between Chile and Argentina 325; between the parties 93n82
delineation 86, 87n43, 90–5, 136, 137, 265, 328n27, 366, 412, 415, 428; delimitation of maritime borders and 265
Denmark 283, 291, 304, 387
Denmark Strait 282
Department for Continental Shelf, Maritime Zones, Administration and Exploration (CSMZAE), Mauritius 408, 408n33
DIFROL *see* Dirección Nacional de Fronteras y Límites del Estado
Dingwall, J. 100n133
Dirección Nacional de Fronteras y Límites del Estado 329
Directive on Safety of Offshore Oil and Gas Activities (2013) 303
Dominican Republic 360
Draft Norms on the Responsibilities of Transnational Corporations and Other Business Enterprises with regard to Human Rights 121n87
DSM *see* deep sea mining
due diligence 102; doctrine 53; obligation 38, 53, 70, 102, 113, 118, 158, 168, 247

East China Sea 340, 399
East Greenland Rift Basin, Arctic 281
East-Pacific Rise 14
economic community of West African states 264, 267, 268
ecosystem approach 12, 25–6, 240, 251, 292, 297, 311, 312
ecosystem services 189
ECOWAS *see* economic community of West African states
ECS *see* extended continental shelf
ECSC *see* European Coal and Steel Community
Ecuador 324, 327, 361
EEZ *see* exclusive economic zone
EEZ Act, New Zealand 55–9, 421, 422, 423, 424, 425, 426n62
Egypt 88n51, 262n13
EIA *see* environmental impact assessment
electric self-potential 16
emerging state practice 146–8
the Enterprise 36, 37, 157, 158, 161, 166–8; ISA operationalization of 201–2, 269
entities: commercial 370; forum shopping 103; non-State 100, 110, 111; private 6; public 363; responsibility of sponsored 121–2; sponsored by states 100, 112; State-owned and State-

controlled 113; States sponsoring persons and 38; transnational corporations 110
entitlement: Arctic 280; continental shelf beyond 200 nautical miles 93–4, 283; exclusive economic zone (EEZ) 129; maritime 336, 380; rights and 316
environmental baseline 23, 49, 73, 116
environmental impact assessment 38, 49, 52, 61, 65, 69, 97, 355, 382, 410; baseline information and 69, 71; BBNJ Agreement 97, 103, 298n50, 311–12; burden of proof 72; EIA Directive 296, 296n40, 297, 298, 430n26; India 394; Mauritius 410
environmental impacts: Adaptive management 27, *27*; of deep-sea mining 21–2, 299, 319, 323, 396; scientific certainty/uncertainties and 64, 73, 425
Environmental Protection Act (EPA), Guyana 382, 384 410
Environmental Protection Authority, New Zealand 57, 59, 422, 423, 424
Environment Code 368–9
Equatorial North-eastern Pacific 373
Equinor 148n47, 149
Espoo Convention 294, 294n17
Essequibo dispute 326
Estonia 304
EU *see* European Union
European Council 292, 292n6, 296n36, 310
European Economic Community (EEC) 290
European Parliament: Directive 2001/42/EC of 296n37; Directive 2004/35/CE 117n56; Directive 2008/56/EC of 294n22, 295n30; Directive 2009/147/EC 294n20; Directive 2014/52/EU 296n36
European Union 6, 66, 240n9, 265, 281, 290–313, 313n166, 324, 373; 1992 Convention on the Protection of the Marine Environment of the Baltic Sea Area (Helsinki Convention) 304–5; Barcelona Convention 302–3; contribution to negotiations on biodiversity beyond national jurisdiction 311–12; governance framework of 291–3; legal status of marine genetic resources 39n37; Member States of 298–307; OSPAR Convention 299–302; regional seas conventions of 298–307; role at the International Seabed Authority 310–11; seabed mining, regulatory framework applicable in 293–8; seabed mining in the Area 297–8; seabed mining on the continental shelf of Member States of 293–7; seabed within and beyond national jurisdiction 291, 307–12
European Union Environmental Liability Directive 117
exclusive economic zone 14, 108, 109, 129, 130, 146, 240; in Antarctica 272–3; in Arctic 281–4; in Belgium 345–6; in Brazil 351–2; continental shelf and 87–9; in Côte d'Ivoire 365–6; EEZ Act 55–9, 68, 421–5, 426n62; in Germany 373–4; in Guyana 380–1; in Iceland 386–7; in India 392; in Korea 398–9; in Mauritius 405–8; in Mozambique 414–15; in New Zealand 420; in Pacific Islands 315–17; in Portugal 428; in South America 325–30; in Southeast Asia 334–6; in United Kingdom (UK) 433–4
exclusive rights 84, 86–8, 90, 129, 168, 180, 367, 377, 391, 409
exploitation 302n86; deep sea minerals 319; financial aspects of regulations 183–7; gas hydrates 245–9; ISA draft regulations on 198–9; license for 389–90
exploration 302n86; challenges of deep-sea mining 15–16; deep sea minerals 319; extended continental shelf 146–8; financial aspects of regulations 183; gas hydrates 245–9; in Germany 376–8; ISA contracts for 196–7; organization stage and 195; stages of ISA 195–8
extended continental shelf 87, 90–4, 97, 109, 121, 244–5; in the Antarctic 273, 278n44; claims in the Pacific Islands 316, **317**; in Brazil 352, 354; in Colombia 360, 363; in Côte d'Ivoire 367, 370; and the European Union 291, 293, 313; of Mauritius 407; of Mozambique 417–18; of New Zealand 420; and payment (Article 82) 141–53; in Portugal 430, 432n35; in the South American region 326–30; in Southeast Asia 335; in the UK 433–4; *see also* BBNJ Agreement; Commission on the Limits of the Continental Shelf; common heritage of mankind; continental shelf; delineation; delimitation; High Seas; non-UNCLOS State parties; payment; sovereign rights; sovereignty; transboundary impact assessment
extension 91; BBNJ Agreement 97; beyond 200 nautical miles 91, 127–38; continental shelf 3, 278, 291, 325, 329, 332, 351, 365; of the protected area 85
Extension of the Continental Shelf (EMEPC), Portugal 428, 428n4
extractive industries 185, 368, 369

Falkland Islands (Malvinas) 326, 327
FAO *see* United Nations Food and Agricultural Organization
Federated States of Micronesia 135, 314, 314n2, 316n16
FFA *see* Forum Fisheries Agency
Fiji 198, 231, 314
Finland 282, 304, 305
fisheries 63, 83n12, 94, 97, 290, 299n58, 300n70, 416
Follow-up Programme 117
Forum Fisheries Agency 314
forum shopping 103

Fouquet, Y. 15
Fram Basin, Arctic 281
France 43, 271n1, 276, 291, 314, 324, 326n12, 345, 364; European Coal and Steel Community (ECSC) 290; Mauritius bilateral treaty with 406; polymetallic nodules 291
freedom of the High Seas 33, 34, 39, 83, 89, 98; artificial islands and other installations 89; fishing 110; marine scientific research 89, 90; navigation 34, 83, 89, 110; overflight 110; scientific research 41, 90; submarine cables and pipelines 83, 89
French Guyana 324–6
French Polynesia 314, 316n14, 322

Gakkel Ridge, Arctic 281, 283, 284
Galapagos Rift 14
gas hydrates 241, 245–9, 252, 417
GATT *see* General Agreement on Tariffs and Trade
GEBCO *see* General Bathymetric Chart of the World
General Agreement on Tariffs and Trade 216
General Bathymetric Chart of the World 143n12
Geneva Agreement of 1966 381, 381n5
Germany 43, 246n26, 304, 364, 372–8; the Area and 373–4; authorization and state involvement 376; continental shelf and 373–4; deep-sea mining activities, regulation of 374–6; exclusive economic zone and 373–4; exploration 376–8; legislation 374–5; polymetallic nodules 291; seabed activities and 376
Gjerde, K. M. 240, 241, 252
Global Sea Mineral Resources 19, 345, 346, 348, 349
good environmental status (GES) 295, 296
GRID-Arendal's Shelf Programme 135
Grotius, H. 34
GSR *see* Global Sea Mineral Resources
Guam 314, 322
Guyana 324, 325, 326, 326n12, 326n14, 379–85; the Area and 380–1; continental shelf and 380–1; exclusive economic zone and 380–1; Mining Act 331; seabed activities and 383–4; seabed mining activities, regulation of 381–2

Habitats Directive 294, 297, 300
Haiti 360
Hamburg, Germany 159
Hanqin Xue 122
Hans Island 283
Hawaii 239
Helsinki Convention 299, 304–5
High Seas 89, 97, 98, 109, 110
Höfelmeier, A. 246, 364
Honduras 360
HS *see* High Seas
hydrothermal sulphides, as mineral resources of deep sea 12–14, 90, 391
hydrothermal vents *13*, 14–15, 16, 322n35; polymetallic sulphides 23; seawater circulating in the ocean crust 13; sulphide deposits 18; ultramafic-hosted 12

IASC *see* International Arctic Science Committee
Iceland 299, 386–90; the Area and 386–7; continental shelf and 386–7; continental shelf beyond 200 nautical miles 388–90; domestic acts regarding the seabed 387–8; exclusive economic zone and 386–7; license for exploitation 389–90; seabed activities and 390; seabed mining activities, regulation of 387–90
ICJ *see* International Court of Justice
ICSID *see* International Centre for Settlement of Investment Disputes
IGO *see* inter-governmental organisation
ILA *see* International Law Association
ILC *see* International Law Commission
INAMI *see* National Institute of Mines
India 326, 391–7; the Area and 392; continental shelf and 392; direct legislations 393–4; exclusive economic zone and 392; institutional framework 392–3; legislations 394; seabed activities, regulation of 392–5; seabed mining activities and 395–6; state position in 395
India Bureau of Mines 393
Indian Ocean 336, 414
Indian Ocean Rim Association (IORA) States 412, 412n66
Indonesia 333, 334, 335, 336, 339
installations and structures 24–5, *26*, 85n31, 85n34, 86n35, 89n54–5, 96, 209, 299n61, 302–3, 320; artificial islands and 86, 88, 89, 89n54, 90, 96, 110; exclusive rights of the coastal States 86, 367; exploration and exploitation activities 302n86; of marine ecosystems 2; *renvoi* between article 80, to article 60 89; seabed mining regime *159*; three-dimension of sulphide deposit 16; *see also* offshore
Integrated Ocean Discovery Program 377
Intergovernmental Oceanographic Commission (IOC), India 288
International Arctic Science Committee 288–9
International Centre for Settlement of Investment Disputes 216, 218, 234
International Code for Ships Operating in Polar Waters 282, 282n9
International Council of Science 271
International Court of Justice 38, 84, 94n88, 116, 122, 129, 133, 135, 147, 150, 152, 218, 220, 325–8
International Law Association 143, 153
International Law Commission 82, 83n10, 83n12, 108, 128
International Maritime Organization 264
International Seabed Authority 13, 23, 28, 35, 87, 92, 111, 136, 141, 194–203, 331; activities

of 182–91; African group 270; challenges associated with payment regime 187–91; contentious case against 243–4; contracts and regulations on equitable sharing of financial and economic benefits 200–1; contracts for exploration 196–7; core mandate of 160–2; development of comprehensive deep sea mining code by 37; draft regulations on exploitation 49, 198–9; Economic Planning Commission 202; European Union (EU) role at 310–11; exploitation phases of 198–203; Exploration Regulations 49; exploration stages of 195–8; functions of 162; instruments 195–6; marine environment, protection of 197–8; marine scientific research in the Area 203; Mining Code 52, 69, 182–91; operationalization of the Enterprise 201–2; organization stages of 195–8; request for advisory opinion 241–3; stakeholder consultations 202–3; standards and guidelines for activities in the Area 199–200; structure of 36; *see also* advisory opinion
International Treaty on Plant Genetic Resources 44
International Tribunal for the Law the Sea 93, 93n82, 102, 108, 119, 159, 210–13, 217–22, 224–5, 236, 241–3, 244–5, 248–9, 251–2, 371, 408
International Undertaking on Plant Genetic Resources (International Undertaking) 43–4
International Union for the Conservation of Nature 38, 56, 221, 240, 251, 314n3
Interoceanmetal Joint Organization (IOM) 298
investment 90, 148n47, 191, 339; foreign investment 231–3; foreign treaties 121, 233–4, 237; incentivising 181, 188; international law 232–4; international protection 234; investment dispute 234; jurisprudence 233; return on 323
IOC-UNESCO *see* Intergovernmental Oceanographic Commission (IOC), India
IODP *see* Integrated Ocean Discovery Program
IORA *see* Indian Ocean Rim Association (IORA) States
Ireland 291, 326, 387, 434
ISA *see* International Seabed Authority
ISC International Council of Science
Islands Europe 415
Italy 290, 303, 305, 364
ITLOS *see* International Tribunal for the Law the Sea
IUCN *see* International Union for the Conservation of Nature

Jaeckel, A. 198, 201
Jamaica 158, 243n26, 360, 360n17
Jans, J. 66
Japan 43, 262, 281, 288, 326, 364, 399
Japan Oil, Gas and Metals National Corporation 19
Jarmache, E. 93n81
JOGMEC *see* Japan Oil, Gas and Metals National Corporation
Joint Norwegian-Russian Fisheries Commission 287
Juan da Nova Island 415

Kenya 87, 262
Kiev Protocol 294, 294n17
Kingston, Jamaica 158, 243n26
KIOST *see* Korea Institute of Ocean Science and Technology
Kiribati 135, 314; Seabed Minerals Act 2017 231
KNOC *see* Korea National Oil Corporation
Koh, T. 151
Korea 398–403; the Area and 398–9; continental shelf and 398–9; exclusive economic zone and 398–9; seabed activities, regulation of 400–3
Korea Institute of Ocean Science and Technology 403
Korea National Oil Corporation 402

Labrador 149
Lagos, treaty of 264, 264n26
Landesamt für Bergbau, Energie und Geologie 376
Laos 333, 334, 337, 340
Latin America 82, 189, 271n2
Latvia 304
Law of the Sea Conference 43, 210
LBEG Energie und Geologie, Landesamt für Bergbau
Legal and Technical Commission of ISA 51, 69, 119, 164–5, 167–8, 196–9, 199n36, 200, 202, 376, 427, 431
liability 246n50, 375, 377; arising out of wrongful acts 216n24, 229, 248; breach of 114–15; of companies engaged in seabed mining 114; compensation and 118n62; gap 118; methane hydrate exploration 247; royalty 184; of States 108, 110, 171, 230, 232
Lithuania 304
Lodge, M. 51
Lomé Charter 266–7, 267n45
Lomonosov Ridge, Arctic 281, 283
London, England 145n30
LTC *see* Legal and Technical Commission of ISA
Luxembourg 290

Madagascar 414, 415
Madrid Offshore Protocol 302n83, 303
Madrid Protocol 41, 42, 277n38, 278
Malaysia 148n43, 333–6, 339
manganese nodules 20, 85n31, 243n22, 320, 373–5, 377, 395, 417–18
Mare Liberum (Freedom of the Seas) (Grotius) 34
Marine and Coastal Access Act 2009, UK 435
Marine Park of the Azores 432

marine pollution 70, 250, 339, 340, 353, 369, 393, 421
marine protected area 85, 299, 301, 330, 435; in Colombia 361; in the Ross Sea 42; in UK 435
marine scientific research 6, 36, 90, 198, 203, 301, 320, 321, 323, 422; in the Area 203; on the continental shelf 89; Germany 377–8
Maritime Code 367
maritime integrated strategy 264, 267, 268
maritime spaces, national jurisdiction in Southeast Asia 334–5
Maritime Spatial Planning Plan (POEM), Mozambique 416
Maritime Zones (Amendment) Act, Mauritius 380–2, 388, 388n14, 407, 408, 412
Marshall Islands 314, 314n2
Mascarene Plateau, Indian Ocean 146n36, 406–7
Mauritius 405–13; the Area and 405–8; continental shelf and 405–8; exclusive economic zone in 405–8; marine spatial planning (MSP) 410; seabed activities and 411–12; seabed mining activities, regulations of 408–11
Mauritius' Minerals Act (MA) 1966 409
Mauritius Ministry of Blue Economy, Marine Resources, Fisheries and Shipping 411n58
Mauritius Petroleum Act (PA) 1970 409–10
Mauritius Seychelles Joint Management Area 92
McDorman, T. 149
Mediterranean Sea 88, 302–3
Melanesia 314
Mendeleev Ridge, Arctic 281
MERCOSUR 330
metals 3, 5n18, 6n28, 11, 186, 189, 299n58, 309, 312, 323, 372, 379
Mexico 14, 239, 252; phosphorite nodule 14
Micronesia 314
Mid-Atlantic Ridge 14, 431; polymetallic sulphides 291
Military Deep Seabed Management Strategy (2022) 306n116
Mining Act of 1989 382
Mining Code 51, 52, 69, 102, 103, 163, 172, 179, 180, 182–91, 331, 354, 362, 364, 367, 377
MiningImpact (European research project) 19
Mining Industry Act 400, 402
Mining Law of Ecuador (2009) 331
Minister of Oceans and Fisheries, Korea 401, 402
Minister of the Sea, Inland Waters and Fisheries (MIMAIP), Mozambique 416
Ministry of Earth Sciences (MoES), India 393, 396
Ministry of Environment, Forests and Climate Change (MoEFCC), India 393, 394, 394n14
Ministry of External Affairs (MEA), India 393
MIS *see* maritime integrated strategy
Molitor, M. 151
monitoring 145, 187, 422; environmental 20; metal markets 167; post-decision information gathering and 58; pre-commencement 57, 59; programmes 22, 25, 295
Moon 33, 40–1
Moon Treaty 40–2, 45
Morocco 261n1, 428
Mozambique 414–18; the Area and 414–15; continental shelf and 414–15; economic exclusive zone and 414–15; seabed mining activities 417–18; seabed mining activities, regulation of 415–17
Mozambique Channel 414, 417
MPA *see* marine protected area
MSF Directive 295, 295n30, 296, 297, 300 304
MSPA Protocol 303n90
multilateral system 43n70, 44
Myanmar 333, 334, 335

Nairobi 262n7
Namibia 14, 146n35, 263n16
Namuncurá – Banco Burdwood I 330
Namuncurá – Banco Burdwood II 330
Nansen Basin, Arctic 281
National Institute of Oceanography (NIO), India 393, 394
National Institute of Ocean Technology (NIOT), India 393, 395, 395n20
National Institute of Water and Atmospheric Research (NIWA), New Zealand 319
National Maritime Authority (DIMAR), Colombia 362–3
National Petroleum Institute (INP), Mozambique 416
natural prolongation 84, 94, 108, 130, 131, 406, 428
natural resources 83, 97, 109, 117, 173, 292, 329, 353, 362, 367; of continental shelf 89–90; exploitation of 36, 41, 42, 83, 84, 86, 87, 88, 89–90; Great Barrier Reef and its 60; Iceland 390; Moon and its 40; New Zealand 54; sustainable use of 61, 382
Nauru 231, 239, 314
Nauru Ocean Resources Inc (NORI) 199, 239, 252
Nautilus Minerals Inc. 431
negotiation (obligation to negotiate) 95
the Netherlands 314, 326, 345, 364; European Coal and Steel Community (ECSC) 290
New Caledonia 314
Newfoundland 149
New Zealand 43, 70, 150, 271n1, 276, 314, 419–26; the Area and 420; continental shelf and 420; Court of Appeal 58, 59; EEZ Act 55–9, 421, 422, 423, 424, 425, 426n62; environmental common law of 54; Environment Court 57, 59; exclusive economic zone and 420; High Court 57–8; information principles 423; phosphorite nodule 14; precaution in seabed mining 54–60; seabed activities, regulation of 421–4; seabed mining activities 424–6; Section 5A of continental shelf

Act 409n36; Supreme Court 56, 59, 240, 426; *Sustain Our Sounds Inc v New Zealand King Salmon Company Ltd* 56
NGOs *see* non-governmental organizations
Nicaragua 328, 360, 362
Nigeria 146n32, 262n14
1994 Agreement relating to the Implementation of Part XI of the UNCLOS 2, 37–9, 108, 110, 117, 119–20, 166, 180, 182, 182n30, 270, 347, 364, 414, 427; administrative system created for overseeing mining in the Area 112; in Nauru 199; preamble 182n30; UNCLOS and 111–17, 119, 158, 162
Niue 314
nodules, as mineral resources of deep sea 12–13, *13*, 17
non-governmental organizations 5, 28–9, 41, 197, 199, 202, 221, 305
non-state actors, deep seabed mining and 118–22
non-UNCLOS State parties 2, 7, 85n30, 91, 100, 101n135, 115, 119n69, 328, 358, 363, 364; *see also* Colombia, United States, Venezuela
Northern Mariana Islands 314, 399
North Pacific Marine Science Organization (PICES) 287
North Sea Continental Shelf case 129, 150
Norway 146n32, 149, 271n1, 276, 283, 299
Norwegian Sea 282, 284

OAU *see* Organisation of African Unity
obligations *see* right and obligations of States
offshore 380, 436; exploitation of methane hydrates 246, 246n50; foreign oil and gas companies 83, 342; guidelines for mining and drilling in New Zealand *27*; installations and pipelines 229n61; land-based mining 351, 356; legislations on structures 394; Offshore Protocol of the Barcelona Convention 96, 302, 302n85, 303–5; oil and gas exploitation 1, 18, 149–50, 153, 355, 361–2, 367, 369, 435; seabed minerals and hydrocarbons 412; *see also* installations and structures
Ocean Decade Arctic Action Plan (Action Plan) 288, 289
OEWG *see* open-ended working group
oil 3n8, 12, 382–3, 434, 438; 2013 Directive on Safety of Offshore Oil and Gas Activities 303; ACP-EU Joint Parliamentary Assembly Resolution 308n126; crude 410; discovery of oil fields at the Bay du Nord Project, Equinor 148n47; exclusive economic zone (EEZ) 144, 421; exploitation/exploitation/transportation of 89n54, 304, 355, 366, 371, 380, 382, 384, 417, 435; industry 153; institutional frameworks 352, 429n14; interests of the States 86; international companies 144, 371; monopoly 355; Offshore Protocol 302, 305; offshore 1, 18, 83, 149, 150, 153, 342, 351, 362, 367, 369, 374, 380; peak 1; pre-salt exploitation 351; presence at ocean and riverbeds 267; present in the Chukchi plateau 131n12; regulations for 6n26; regulatory agencies 353, 355; regulatory frameworks 313; right to explore and exploit 85n31; spills 339, 356, 424
OMV New Zealand Ltd 424
Open-Ended Ad Hoc Working Group 37
open-ended working group 183, 184–5
opposite 35, 92, 114, 128, 373, 415
Optional Protocol of Signature 358n2
Organisation of African Unity 263
OSPAR *see* Convention for the Protection of the Marine Environment of the North-East Atlantic
OSPAR Convention 298, 299–302, 299n58, 300n69, 300n72, 432n35
outer space, common heritage of mankind 40–1
Outer Space Treaty 40
Oxman, B. H. 42

Pacific Financial Technical Assistance Centre 319
Pacific Islands 314–23, 324; continental shelves and 315–17; deep sea minerals exploration and exploitation, regional environmental, legislative, regulatory and financial framework for 318–19; exclusive economic zones and 315–17; governance of seabed mining activities 317–22; Pacific Deep Sea Mining Agreement 320–2; regional scientific research guidelines for deep sea minerals 319–20; regulation of seabed mining activities 317–22
Pacific Islands Forum (PIF) 314, 315, 316, 318
Pacific Ocean 14, 134, 361; Arctic Ocean, and 134; areas beyond national jurisdiction 335; exclusive economic zone (EEZ) 329; polymetallic nodules 23; shared ocean identity 315
Pacific Regional Environment Programme 314
Palau 135, 314
PAME *see* Protection of the Marine Environment
Panamá 360
Papua New Guinea 135, 314, 333, 334, 335, 336, 339
Paracel Islands 335
Pardo, A. 34, 35, 157
Paris Agreement 3n8, 286
participation 57, 158, 321, 359, 362–3, 370, 393, 401, 416, 426; in deep seabed mining disputes 224–37; in the Ocean Decade 288; in proceedings 211; of sponsoring States 214n21; through enterprise and site-banking system 165–9
Partnerships in Environmental Management for the Seas of East Asia 337, 340–1, 342
payment 186; the Area 37, 109, 173, 178–91; Article 82 of UNCLOS 118, 141–53, 170, 173, 185n61, 409, 409n36; benefits to the Landlocked

States 109; coastal State obligation to sovereign rights 87; common heritage of mankind 37, 180–91, 204; distribution 87, 145, 178, 180, 183, 201, 370, 409; International Seabed Authority 37, 144–5, 173, 178–9, 184, 187–91, 409, 431; royalty 142, 152, 184, 185, 355, 363
PCA *see* Permanent Court of Arbitration
PCIJ *see* Permanent Court of International Justice
peace and security council (PSC) 267n45
PEMSEA *see* Partnerships in Environmental Management for the Seas of East Asia
Permanent Court of Arbitration 392n6
Permanent Court of International Justice 124
Permanent Process for the Allocation of Areas 360
Perú 324, 361
Petroleum Code 368
PFTAC *see* Pacific Financial Technical Assistance Centre
Philippines 148, 233, 333, 334, 335, 337, 339, 340, 342
pioneer investor *see* India
Pitcairn Islands 314
plant genetic resources 43–4, 45
Poland 298, 304, 428; polymetallic nodules 291
Polar Code *see* International Code for Ships Operating in Polar Waters
polymetallic nodules 1, 12–13, *13*, 15; Belgium 291; Clarion-Clipperton-Zone (CCZ) 438; Czech Republic 291; France 291; Germany 291; Pacific Ocean 23; Poland 291; Slovakia 291
polymetallic sulphide 20–1, 163, 179, 195, 196, 291, 303, 377, 391, 399, 427, 428
Polynesia 314
Portnov, A. 249
Portugal 291, 427–32; the Area and 428, 431; continental shelf and 428–30; exclusive economic zone and 428; Interministerial Commission 428; seabed activities, regulation of 428–31; seabed activities and 431–2
Portuguese Climate Basis Law 429n14
PPAA *see* Permanent Process for the Allocation of Areas
precautionary approach 4, 26–7, 240, 310, 376, 437, 438; adaptive management 56; under international environmental law 52; principle of New Zealand public law 54; science-based decision-making and 323; scientific uncertainty 52; for seabed mining 48–73
precaution in seabed mining 48–74; adaptive management 72–3; administrative context of 49–52; assessment of potential impacts 71; Australia 60–2; baseline information 71; burden of proof 72; Canada 63–5; described 68–70; in international law 52–4, 68; New Zealand 54–60; potential harm of 71–2; regulatory goal of 70–1; United Kingdom (UK) 65–8; *see also* deep seabed mining
production 22, 65, 87, 135, 142, 230, 352, 361, 383, 414, 417; "all" 144; of batteries 11; commercial 182–7; petroleum 424; support vessel 19
Protection of the Marine Environment 287
Protocol on Environmental Protection to the Antarctic Treaty (PEPAT) 272, 274, 277
publicity 92, 93, 370

Regional Economic Communities (RECs) 264
Regulation of the Legal Regime for the Use of the National Maritime Space 416
Regulations on Prospecting and Exploration for Cobalt-Rich Crusts 37
Regulations on Prospecting and Exploration for Polymetallic Nodules in the Area 37
Regulations on Prospecting and Exploration for Polymetallic Sulphides in the Area 37
remediation 115–17
Remengesau, T. E. Jr. 314n3
Renard, A. F. 348
reparation 115, 116, 122, 137, 356
Resource Management Act 1991 (RMA), New Zealand 55, 421, 426
responsibility: deep seabed mining and 118–22; international organization 118–21; of sponsored entities 121–2
restitution 115–17, 122
Reykjanes Ridge 283, 387, 388
right and obligations of States 81–103; during activities in the Area 98–103; continental shelf 82, 85–95; CS Geneva Convention 83–5; exclusive economic zone (EEZ) 87–9; International Law Commission 82; marine environment 95–8; United Nations Convention on the Law of the Sea 85–7
Rio Declaration 118n62; Principle 15 of 52, 58
RJUEM *see* Regulation of the Legal Regime for the Use of the National Maritime Space
Roach, J.A. 151
ROK–Japan Joint Development Agreement 401–2
Rovuma Delta 414
Royal Institute of International Affairs (Chatham House), UK 145n30
Russia 134, 146n32, 271n1, 282, 283, 298, 304, 326

Saharawi Arab Democratic Republic 261n1
Samoa 314
Schrijver, N. 34
SDC *see* Seabed Disputes Chamber
SDG *see* sustainable development goals
Seabed 2030 11, 289
seabed activities, regulation of: in Africa 265–6; in Antarctica 273–8; in Arctic 284–9; in the Area 266–70; in Belgium 346–8; in Brazil 352–5; in Colombia 362–4; contractors involved in 158–

60, *159*; economic pressure in 2; in European Union (EU) 293–8; in Germany 376; green technologies in 2; in Guyana 381–2, 383–4; in Iceland 387–90; in India 392–6; international law and 2, 52–4, 68; in Korea 400–3; in Mauritius 408–12; in Mozambique 415–18; in New Zealand 421–6; in Pacific Islands 317–22; in Portugal 428–32; in Southeast Asia 336; structure of *159*; in United Kingdom (UK) 435–9
Seabed Advisory Opinion 51–3, 59, 65, 68
Seabed Committee 87
Seabed Disputes Chamber 92n80, 108, 111, 115, 159, 209–22; ad hoc chambers 211–12, 217; advisory jurisdiction on 218–20; advisory opinions on 219–20; automatic exclusions 218; commercial arbitration 217; composition of members 210–11; compulsory exclusive jurisdiction 213; contentious cases 220–1; contentious jurisdiction 213–16; discretionary advisory opinions on 220; disputes concerning activities in the Area 215–17; enforcement 218; exclusions of the contentious jurisdiction of 217–18; experts opinion on 221–2; function and role as per ISA 212; ISA and 211–12; jurisdiction of 120, 136, 213–14, 217–18, 220, 229, 232, 234, 243, 250, 252; laws applicable in 212–13; no exercise of discretion 218; Part XI 38, 39, 242, 248; President and Registrar of 211; procedure for advisory proceedings 221; provisional measures 218; *ratione materiae*, jurisdiction 214–15; *ratione personarum*, jurisdiction 213–14; special chambers 217; term of office of the members of 211; validity of rules and regulations, no decision on 218; voluntary exclusions 217
Seabed Mining Act (Germany) 375
Seabed Resources Act (Iceland) 387
sediment: continental 13; dispersal of 24; marine 245; mining of loose 374; plumes 21, 57, 58, 70; resuspended 22; seafloor 20; shallow 246; substrates 14; superficial 15; thickness of 130, 132; water column 16, 22
semi-enclosed sea *see* Mediterranean Sea
SGS v. the Philippines 233
SICA 330
Singapore 281, 333, 336, 339
site-banking system 168–9
Slovakia 298
Smith, R.W. 151
Solomon Islands 135, 314
Solwara 1 project 19
Somalia 135
South Africa 14, 415
South America 324–32; Atlantic States 325–7, 330–1; continental shelves and 325–30; exclusive economic zones and 325–30; Pacific States 327–30, 331–2; regional governance framework, lack of 330–2; seabed mining national regulations, lack of 330–2
South China Sea 148, 335
Southeast Asia 333–42, 333n2; areas beyond national jurisdiction (ABNJ) 335–6; continental shelves and 334–6; exclusive economic zones and 334–6; interests states in seabed mining 336; maritime spaces under national jurisdiction 334–5; regional governance frameworks and 336–41; regulation of seabed mining and 336–41
South Fiji Basin 420
South Georgia 326
South Korea 281
South Pacific Commission 314
South Sandwich Islands 326
South West Indian Ridge 14, 196
sovereign rights 84, 87, 127–38; legal developments during 1945 and 1982 127–30; outer continental shelf, criteria for delineation 130–1; protection of territorial scope of the Area 135–7; role of the Commission on the Limits of the Continental Shelf (CLCS) 131–3; State practice 134–5
sovereignty 33–5, 38, 40, 45, 83n10, 122, 194, 272, 277, 342, 362, 364, 428, 434; decision-making powers and 292; Guyana 326; Law of the Sea 325; Norway 287; securing of 316; United Kingdom 326–7; Venezuela 326
Spain 291, 428
sponsored entities, responsibility of 121–2
sponsorship agreements 230
sponsor/sponsoring 100, 109–10, 112, 121, 214, 230–5, 291, 377; due diligence obligation 38, 160n25; liability of States for deep seabed mining 108; responsibilities and obligations of States 38; site-banking system 168
Spratly Islands 335
SPREP *see* Pacific Regional Environment Programme
Stockholm Declaration 118n62
St. Pierre Miquelon delimitation case 92–3
Strategic Environmental Assessment (SEA) Directive 296, 297
Suarez, J. L. 34–5
submarine areas 82, 108, 128, 381, 406
submarine cables and pipelines 83, 84, 89, 90, 110, 162, 217
Submarine Mineral Resources Development Act, Korea 399, 400
submission 91, 148; Argentina 327; Belgian legislation 347n27; coastal state 133; extended continental shelf 291, 325, 326, 335; Guyana 381; Iceland 389; Malaysia and Vietnam made joint 148n43; Mauritius 407; Portugal 428; Russia 283; United Kingdom 327, 434
Sudan 261n1, 262n13

sulphide deposits 14, 16, 18, 377
sulphide mineralisation 13–14
surface effects 22
Suriname 324, 325, 326n12
sustainability 4, 22, 28, 29, 63, 65, 162, 190n104, 201, 372, 378, 383, 384
Sustainable Blue Economy Finance Principles 4
sustainable development goals 264, 286, 313, 340, 380, 416; Sustainable Development Goal 12 251; Sustainable Development Goal 14 251, 313, 378, 416
Svalbard Treaty 287
Sweden 282, 301, 304
Switzerland 43, 299

Tanzania 415
technical challenges: of deep-sea mining 18–20; scientific and 14
technology (for transfer of technology) 2, 36, 44, 166, 230, 267, 269, 363, 369, 370
Te Tiriti o Waitangi (The Treaty of Waitangi) 1840 419, 422, 425
Thailand 333, 334, 339
Thomas, T. 384
Thomas v. Environmental Protection Agency 384
Thomson, W. 433
Three Kings Ridge 420
Timor-Leste 333, 334
Tokelau 314
Tonga 234, 314, 420
total heavy mineral (THM) 417
Trans-Atlantic Geotraverse (TAG) project 14
transboundary impact assessment 311–12
transnational corporation 107, 110, 121n87
Trans-Tasman Resources Ltd 56–9, 240, 425, 426n62
travaux preparatoires 235
Treaty of Paria (1942) 82
Treaty on the Functioning of the European Union (2007) (TFEU) 292
The Tribunal 94n89
Truman, H. 82
TTR *see* Trans-Tasman Resources Ltd
Tuvalu 135, 197, 234, 314

UK *see* United Kingdom
UK Seabed Resources Ltd 438
UN *see* United Nations
UNASUR 330
UNCITRAL *see* United Nations Commission on International Trade Law
UNCLOS *see* United Nations Convention on the Law of the Sea
UN Decade of Ocean Science for Sustainable Development (2021–2030) 171, 288, 289, 313, 322, 370
UNECA *see* United Nations Economic Commission for Africa
UN Environmental Programme (UNEP) 4, 340
UNESCO *see* United Nations Educational, Scientific and Cultural Organization
UNFCC *see* United Nations Framework Convention on Climate Change
UNGA *see* United Nations General Assembly
United Kingdom 43, 146n32, 234, 271n1, 276, 291, 299, 326, 327, 345, 364, 433–9; *BASF Agro BV and ECPA and ESA* 67; *Bova v Highland Council* 66; Brexit Trade and Cooperation Agreement 66; Court of Justice of the European Union (CJEU) 67; Deep Sea Mining Act 1981 (DSMA) 65; exclusive economic zone and 433–4; Inner Court of Scotland 66; Marine and Coastal Access Act 2010 (MCAA) 65; precaution in seabed mining 65–8; seabed activities and 435–9; seabed mining in the Area and 433–4, 436–8; seabed mining on continental shelf and 433–6; *Treaty of Paria* (1942) of Venezuela with 82
United Nations 128, 157, 262, 415
United Nations Commission on International Trade Law 226
United Nations Compensation Commission 117
United Nations Convention on the Law of the Sea 1, 2, 5, 7, 23, 33, 49, 50, 81, 85–7; administrative system created for overseeing mining in the Area 112; Article 1(1) of 250, 262n8; Article 3 of 132, 133; Article 4 of 132n16, 232; Article 5 (3) of 211; Article 13:1 of 188; Article 18(3) of 228n39; Article 21 of 219; Article 22 of 216n24, 248; Article 24 (1) of 209; Article 35 of 211; Article 38 of 212; Article 39 of 218; Article 42 of 136; Article 48 of 137; Article 56 of 89, 89n54–5, 130; Article 57 of 130; Article 60 of 86n38, 89, 96; Article 68 of 211; Article 76 of 127, 129–36, 150–2, 263, 284, 326, 328; Article 80 of 96; Article 82 of 95, 129, 141–53; Article 83 of 92, 95; Article 87 of 89n56; Article 115-123 of 115, 220; Article 117-121 of 220; Article 120 of 214n21; Article 130 of 221; Article 133 of 221; Article 136 of 35, 98; Article 137 of 35; Article 138 of 231, 232; Article 139 of 115, 214, 246n50; Article 140 of 180; Article 143 of 198, 203; Article 145 of 102, 198, 242, 243n22; Article 149 of 216; Article 153 of 214, 230; Article 156(3) of 265; Article 159 of 219; Article 168 of 248; Article 173 of 181; Article 187 of 120, 136, 213–18, 220, 226n17, 234, 235, 244; Article 188 of 217, 226, 229; Article 189 of 120, 218, 229; Article 190 of 214, 214n21, 215, 216, 216n23, 234; Article 191 of 219, 220, 242, 242n19; Article 192 of 102, 250; Article 194 of 58–9, 102; Article 206 of 94n91; Article 208 of 94n91; Article 209 of 101; Article 234 of 286;

Article 235 of 118; Article 279 of 92n80; Article 287 of 213; Article 288 of 213; Article 289 of 221; Article 290 of 218; Article 293 of 212–13, 225; Article 304 of 115, 248, 248n64; common heritage of mankind (CHM) 35–40; Part IV of 187; Part VI of 89; Part VIII of 186; Part VII of 98, 184; Part XI of 99, 99n120, 101, 108, 120, 158, 165, 178, 204, 210n8, 215, 216, 224, 225, 226, 229, 234, 236, 237, 240, 241; Part XII of 52, 53, 58, 70, 93, 96, 98, 101, 111, 286; Part XIII of 98, 288; Part XV of 92, 210n8; *See also* 1994 Agreement relating to the Implementation of Part XI of the UNCLOS; BBNJ Agreement
United Nations Economic Commission for Africa 265, 268–9, 270
United Nations Educational, Scientific and Cultural Organization 288, 361, 370
United Nations Food and Agricultural Organization 43
United Nations Framework Convention on Climate Change 293
United Nations General Assembly 34, 39, 42, 128, 138, 194, 198, 209, 211, 226, 275
United States 82, 117, 146n32, 149, 271n1, 282, 284n21, 314, 326, 364
Uruguay 324, 325, 326, 326n12
U.S. Extended Continental Shelf Project 284n21

Vanuatu 135, 314, 314n2, 322, 322n35
Vedder, H. 66
Venezuela 324, 326, 326n14; Treaty of Paria (1942) of United Kingdom with 82
Verlaan, P. 51, 245
Vicuña, O. 276n29, 276n31
Vienna Convention 53, 133
Vietnam 148, 148n43, 333, 334, 335, 336, 339
Voneky, S. 364
Vöneky, S. 246

Wallis and Futuna 314
water column 109, 115, 162, 244, 373, 432n35; active hydrothermal vents 16; biophysical characteristics of the seabed and 50; impacts 22; physical and chemical anomalies in 15; technological challenges 19
West Africa 135
Western Pacific Ocean 196, 399
West Germany 290
West Greenland Rift Basin, Arctic 281
WGICA Working Group on the Integrated Assessment of the Central Arctic Ocean
Willaert, K. 244, 245
Wolfrum, R. 137, 250
Working Group on the Integrated Assessment of the Central Arctic Ocean 287–8
World Heritage Convention 44–5

Yaganes 330
Young, R. 252

Made in the USA
Monee, IL
13 September 2026

62980169R00267